W9-BJD-969

Early Childhood Education Today

SEVENTH EDITION

Early Childhood Education Today

George S. Morrison

University of North Texas

Merrill,
an imprint of Prentice Hall
Upper Saddle River, New Jersey   *Columbus, Ohio*

Cover photo: © 1996 Arthur Tilley, FPG International
Editor: Ann Castel Davis
Developmental Editor: Linda Ashe Montgomery
Production Editor: Linda Hillis Bayma
Copy Editor: Robert L. Marcum
Photo Editor: Nancy Harre Ritz
Design Coordinator: Karrie M. Converse
Text Designer: Proof Positive/Farrowlyne Assoc., Inc. and Anne D. Flanagan
Color Insert Designer: Susan E. Frankenberry
Cover Designer: Brian Deep
Production Manager: Patricia A. Tonneman
Illustrations: Jane Lopez
Director of Marketing: Kevin Flanagan
Marketing Manager: Suzanne Stanton
Advertising/Marketing Coordinator: Julie Shough

This book was set in Korinna by The Clarinda Company and was printed and bound by R.R. Donnelley & Sons Company. The cover was printed by Phoenix Color Corp.

Printed in the United States of America

10 9 8 7 6 5 4 3 2 1

ISBN: 0-13-749979-5

Prentice-Hall International (UK) Limited, *London*
Prentice-Hall of Australia Pty. Limited, *Sydney*
Prentice-Hall of Canada, Inc., *Toronto*
Prentice-Hall Hispanoamericana, S. A., *Mexico*
Prentice-Hall of India Private Limited, *New Delhi*
Prentice-Hall of Japan, Inc., *Tokyo*
Simon & Schuster Asia Pte. Ltd., *Singapore*
Editora Prentice-Hall do Brasil, Ltda., *Rio de Janeiro*

Library of Congress Cataloging-in-Publication Data
Morrison, George S.
    Early childhood education today / George S. Morrison. — 7th ed.
        p.   cm.
    Includes bibliographical references and index.
    ISBN 0–13–749979–5
    1. Early childhood education—United States.
I. Title.
    LB1140.2.M67   1998
    372.21—dc21   97–19920
                                              CIP

Part-Opening Credits: Part 1, H. R. Clinton, *It Takes a Village* (New York: Simon and Schuster, 1996), p. 7; Part 2, J. Dewey, *Dewey on Education* (New York: Teachers College Press, 1959), p. 24; Part 3, I. Lilly, *Friedrich Froebel* (New York: Cambridge, 1967), p. 84; Part 4, S. Papert, *Mindstorms: Children, Computers, and Powerful Ideas* (New York: Basic Books, 1980), pp. 27–28; Part 5, H. Chang and L. Sakai, *Affirming Children's Roots: Cultural and Linguistic Diversity in Early Care and Education* (San Francisco: California Tomorrow, 1993), p. 9.

Photo Credits: American Montessori Society, p. 74; B. Anderson/Monkmeyer Press Photo Service, p. 78; Andy Brunk/Merrill, p. 258; Ben Chandler/Merrill, p. 68; Children's Hospital, p. 17; Arlene Collins/Monkmeyer Press Photo Service, p. 417; Corbis-Bettmann, pp. 61, 70; Scott Cunningham/Merrill, pp. 45, 100, 160, 214, 289, 319, 372, 430, 493, 496; Hermine Dreyfus/Monkmeyer Press Photo Service, p. 465; Diane Elmer, p. 186; IBM, p. 321; Indiana University Photographic Services, p. 65; Lloyd Lemerman/Merrill, p. 294; Anthony Magnacca/Merrill, pp. 9, 255, 270, 446, 483; Tina Manley, p. 34; Merrill, p. 196; George Morrison, p. 456; Ohio University Child Development Center, p. 80; Photo Edit, p. 50; Tom Pollak/Monkmeyer Press Photo Service, p. 475; Barbara Schwartz/Merrill, pp. 28, 40, 135, 232, 291, 311, 358, 509; Michael Siluk, p. 203; Anne Vega/Merrill, pp. 3, 42, 72, 95, 97, 103, 108, 123, 131, 137, 153, 156, 165, 171, 191, 200, 219, 221, 225, 239, 264, 269, 279, 295, 299, 353, 357, 427, 459, 468, 471, 506; Tom Watson/Merrill, pp. 337, 391, 394; Todd Yarrington/Merrill, pp. 38, 125, 228, 349, 369, 385, 507.

This book is affectionately dedicated to Betty Jane

About the Author

George S. Morrison, Ed.D., is professor of early childhood education and holder of the Velma E. Schmidt Endowed Chair in early childhood education at the University of North Texas. Professor Morrison's accomplishments include a Distinguished Academic Service Award from the Pennsylvania Department of Education, an Outstanding Alumni Award from the University of Pittsburgh School of Education, and the recipient of Outstanding Service and Teaching Awards from Florida International University.

Dr. Morrison is the author of many books on early childhood education, child development, curriculum, and teacher education. His professional affiliations include the National Association for the Education of Young Children (NAEYC), the Society for Research in Child Development (SRCD), the Association for Supervision and Curriculum Development (ASCD), the American Educational Research Association (AERA), and the Association of Teacher Educators (ATE).

Preface

Moving from one millennium to another promises to provide challenging but rewarding opportunities in the field of early childhood. As an early childhood professional you must be prepared to assist young children and their families in making the transition into the twenty-first century. I believe this seventh edition of *Early Childhood Education Today* will help prepare you and other professionals to rightfully, knowledgeably, confidently, and appropriately assume your roles of educating children, parents, and families to prepare them for the future.

GOALS AND COVERAGE

Early Childhood Education Today, Seventh Edition, provides a thorough introduction to the field of early childhood education. In a straightforward and engaging style, the book analyzes current issues and ideas and applies practical, developmentally appropriate strategies and models to early childhood programs. This edition has been extensively revised to reflect changes in society and the field of early childhood education. *Early Childhood Education Today,* Seventh Edition, is comprehensive in its overview of early childhood practices and has been reorganized into five parts:

Part One, "Early Childhood Education and Professional Development," begins with the chapter on professional development followed by current issues so readers can preview the foundation for learning about professional practice and current expectations in the field.

Part Two, "The Development of Early Childhood Programs," provides readers with a historical overview of the field of early childhood education. Chapters in Part Two include descriptions of Montessori and Piagetian-based programs, identifying how their influences on the field help educators recognize quality early childhood programs.

Part Three, "Developmentally Appropriate Programs and Practices," incorporates developmental knowledge of children from birth to age eight. Emphasis is placed on what constitutes developmentally appropriate practice for young children and strategies for appropriate discipline and behavioral guidance of young children, including the development of prosocial behaviors. All content and programmatic features reflect the latest thinking as outlined in the new NAEYC publication, *Developmentally Appropriate Practice in Early Childhood Programs,* Revised Edition. These practices are integrated and described in Part Three and appear in Appendix C for easy reference.

Part Four, "Developing Curricula to Meet the Special Needs of Young Children," addresses technology and its application to early childhood programs, multiculturalism and multiculturally appropriate practice, and developmentally appropriate practice for children with disabilities. Technology and ways professionals and children can benefit from technological literacy are foundationally discussed in Chapter 11, "Technology and Young Children: Education for the Information Age," and are integrated throughout the text. Helpful suggestions and World Wide Web addresses (URLs) put early childhood professionals electronically in touch with a world of early childhood information and research. The new multicultural Chapter 12, "Multiculturalism: Education for Living in a Diverse Society," encourages professionals to consider how society is changing and how they can provide for the needs of all children according to their race, culture, gender, socioeconomic status, and family background through culturally sensitive practices, programming, and environments. Chapter 13, "Children with Special Needs: Providing Appropriate Education for All," has been completely rewritten to reflect contemporary practices as specified in new legislation such as The Individuals with Disabilities Education Act (IDEA). Topics relating to inclusion and inclusive practices are thoroughly examined and discussed.

Part Five, "The Role of Families and the Federal Government in Developing Early Childhood Programs," covers critical areas of child care, families, and communities, discusses the role state and federal regulations play in supporting the education of families and young children, and explains how these regulations impact professional practice. Also identified is the support the government provides for early childhood educational programming. Chapter 16, "The Federal Government: Supporting Children's Success," has been extensively revised to reflect the new Head Start Performance Standards which guide how all Head Start programs must conduct their programs and deliver services.

NEW TO THE SEVENTH EDITION

In addition to the reorganization of the text and an extensive updating of the content, users of the sixth edition will find major new features in the seventh edition:

- Integrated video segments of current issues, "Video Viewpoints," help connect theory and practice. These segments bring to life important topics relating to young children and families and ask readers to respond to reflective questions which promote reflective discussions. A special table of contents identifies topics discussed and where they are located in the book.

- Four color inserts are included with this edition. The first insert, "Kidwatching: Developing Skills in Observation," identifies the professional skills and practices associated with observation of young children. Guidelines and checklists are provided to help early childhood professionals know how and why "kidwatching" is important for assessing children's growth and development and for assessing early childhood programs. The second color insert, "Observing Programs in Action: Nine Key Models," describes and illustrates nine outstanding programs. These profiles continue to reinforce the significant rule business and industry play in early childhood programming. The third insert, "Technology Programs in Action: Teaching and Learning with Computers," highlights two model programs and their use of computers to enhance learning during and after school. The fourth insert, "Including Children with Disabilities: Natural Settings Provide a Key," discusses the research that supports the inclusion of children with disabilities into regular classrooms and describes inclusive practices that can be implemented in the natural environment of child care centers, family daycare centers, preschools, kindergartens, primary grade classrooms, and playgrounds.

- A number of new cutting-edge "Programs in Action" are included in this new edition. These programs authentically portray what practitioners are doing today in real programs and classrooms.

- Important vignettes and personal philosophies by noted early childhood authorities (including James Comer of the Yale Child Development Center and Sarah Greene, executive director of Head Start) provide rich experiences and insight for professionals. These provocative, poignant descriptions are strategically placed throughout the text.

Like all previous editions, this seventh edition was written with a deep sense of pride for all who teach, care for, and parent young children. I heartily agree with Froebel, Montessori, and Dewey that the care and education of young children is a redemptive calling. I hope you also feel the pride and dedication that accompanies being a member of the profession.

ACKNOWLEDGMENTS

In the course of my teaching, service, and consulting, I meet and talk with many professionals who are deeply dedicated to doing their best for young children and their families. I am always touched, heartened, and encouraged by the openness, honesty, and unselfish sharing of ideas that characterize these professional colleagues. I take this opportunity to thank them publicly for helping me. Those who shared their time, talents, and ideas are Kay Albrecht, director, and Amanda Gorner, teacher, HeartsHome Early Learning Center, Houston, Texas; Susie Armstrong, Montessori School at Greenwood Plaza, Englewood, Colorado; Audubon Head Start, Owensboro, Kentucky; Jerold P. Bauch, director, The Betty Phillips Center for Parenthood Education, Peabody College, Nashville, Tennessee; Beverly Boals, professor, early childhood education, Arkansas State University; Joanna Bogin, director, Sunrise Children's Center, Amherst, New Hampshire; Laurie Brackett, The Stride Rite Corporation, Cambridge, Massachusetts; Bright Horizons, Cambridge, Massachusetts; Debbie Brown, professor, Eastern Kentucky University; Bernadette Caruso-Davis, University of Delaware; Yvonne Hatfield Clay, Longfellow School, Kansas City, Missouri; James Comer, Yale Child Study Center, New Haven, Connecticut; Mary Ann Coulson, past president, California Federation of Family Day Care Associations, Inc., and chair of the Federation of FDCA Education Project, Redwood City, California; Ruth Cripps, Shirley Crozier, and M. Shirley Wormsbecker, Alberta Children's Hospital, Calgary, Alberta, Canada; Roger Croteau, Children's Home Society, Miami, Florida; Diane Cushman, The St. Paul Companies, St. Paul, Minnesota; Mercedes Perez de Colon, director, National Family Resource Center for Avance; Betty De Pina, Parent/Child Center Coordinator and Sharon Franklin, lead teacher, Head Start Child and Family Services, Franklin, North Carolina; Susan Dittmer, executive director, Barnett Child Development Center, Jacksonville, Florida; Kathie Dobberteen, principal, La Mesa Dale

Elementary School, La Mesa, California; Fred Estrada, VISTA Magazine, Coral Gables, Florida; Betsy Evans, The Giving Tree School, Gill, Massachusetts; Antonio Fierro, kindergarten teacher, El Paso, Texas; Madeline Fried, The Thurgood Marshall Child Development Center, Herndon, Virginia; John H. Funk, kindergarten teacher, Salt Lake City, Utah; Lella Gandini, liaison to the United States for the Department of Early Education, Reggio Emilia; Ramón D. García-Barrios, director, Early Childhood Development Center, Texas A&M University–Corpus Christi; Gail Gonzalez, health care director, San Jose, California; Janet González-Mena, Napa Valley College, Suison, California; Sarah M. Greene, National Head Start Association, Alexandria, Virginia; Susan Haugland, Southeast Missouri State University; Paul E. Hochschwender, teacher, Ithan Elementary, Radnor, Pennsylvania; Chris Holicek, kindergarten teacher, Burleigh Elementary School, Brookfield, Wisconsin; Kathleen Holz, City and Country School, New York, New York; Kari Hull and Julie Morse, Lemon Avenue Elementary School, La Mesa, California; Ed Labinowicz, professor, Gresham, Oregon; Jean LaGrone, Westgate Elementary, Omaha, Nebraska; Beatriz Leyva-Cutler, The Bay Area Hispano Institute for Advancement, Berkeley, California; Antonia Lopez, The Foundation Center for Phenomenological Research, Sacramento, California; Barbara Lord, teacher, Lexington Park Elementary School, Lexington Park, Maryland; Beverly McGhee, headmistress, Alexander Montessori School, Miami, Florida; Richard A. Morris, Fel Pro Corporation, Skokie, Illinois; Lesley Mandel Morrow, professor and chair of the Department of Learning and Teaching, Rutgers University; Roger Myers, director, The Twenty-First Century School Program, Independence, Missouri; NationsBank Corporation, Charlotte, North Carolina; Judith A. Orion, consultant, The Montessori Institute, Denver, Colorado; Susan Palmer, Voyager Expanded Learning, Inc.; Carrie Peery, Hamilton Academic Achievement Academy, San Diego, California; Maxine Roberts, professor of education, Pittsburgh, Pennsylvania; Nancy Robinson, counselor, Grapevine Elementary, Grapevine, Texas; Margery Sher, The Thurgood Marshall Child Development Center, Herndon, Virginia; Linda Sholar, kindergarten teacher, Sangre Ridge Elementary School, Stillwater, Oklahoma; The Sick Child Care Center, San Jose, California; Edward J. Silver, Jr., teacher, Millington Elementary School, Millington, Maryland; Michelle Taylor, CDR, Lightfoot, Virginia; the teachers at Croissant Park Elementary School, Broward County, Florida; Sandy Tsurutome, director, Alexander D. Henderson University School, Florida Atlantic University, Boca Raton, Florida; Christi Turner, Velma E. Schmidt Teaching Associate, University of North Texas; U.S. Army Community and Family Support Center, Alexandria, Virginia; Mildred Vance, professor of education, Arkansas State University; David P. Weikart and Larry Scheinwart, High/Scope Educational Research Foundation, Ypsilanti, Michigan; Tamie Williams, The Tone School, Tacoma, Washington; and Marlene Zepeda, California State University, Los Angeles.

I would also like to thank the reviewers of the previous six editions as well as the following people who offered helpful comments on this edition: Audrey W. Beard, Albany State College; Ginny A. Buckner, Cuyahoga Community College, Russ Firlik, Sacred Heart University; Mary S. Link, Miami University (Oxford, Ohio); and Ruth Ann McCarbery, Ashland University at Elyria.

My editors at Merrill are the greatest I have ever had the pleasure of working with. I enjoy working with Ann Davis because of her vision for always wanting to make *Early Childhood Education Today* the best it can be in content, format, and design. The efforts of freelance copy editor Robert Marcum have been most appreciated. Robert challenged, questioned, and suggested in order to make *Early Childhood Education Today* readable and comprehensive. Linda Montgomery is an outstanding developmental editor with an extensive and rich knowledge of early childhood education. Linda brings a creative mind and can-do attitude to the developmental process. Linda Bayma is a patient, caring, and thorough production editor. I greatly appreciate her attention to details. She always smooths out all the bumps of the production process. Together, Ann, Robert, Linda, and Linda have made this seventh edition one of exceptional quality.

I want to particularly thank Paul Goertemiller who is a master of research, finding the most up-to-date information and designing charts or graphs. Naomi Armstrong provided the computer skills necessary to make electronic publishing possible. Betty Jane Morrison secured all the permissions and provided the loving support that is so important for all of life's activities.

Contents

Special Features

Early Childhood Education and Professional Development

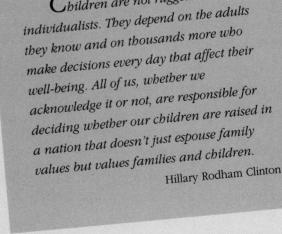

Children are not rugged individualists. They depend on the adults they know and on thousands more who make decisions every day that affect their well-being. All of us, whether we acknowledge it or not, are responsible for deciding whether our children are raised in a nation that doesn't just espouse family values but values families and children.

Hillary Rodham Clinton

1

C H A P T E R

1

What Does It
Mean to Be
a Professional?

Focus Questions

1. Who is an early childhood professional?

2. What is the knowledge base of the profession?

3. What qualities of early childhood professionals are worthy of emulation?

4. What is the terminology used by early childhood professionals?

5. What is the relationship among early childhood professionals' attitudes, character, and children's development?

6. What important themes and concepts contribute to becoming a good professional?

7. What are the essential attitudes, skills, and behaviors that will enable you to have a joyful, productive, and professional career?

8. How can developing a philosophy of early childhood education help you become a professional?

For all early childhood profession-als, the beginning of the twenty-first century promises to be an exciting and challenging time. As one millennium ends and another begins, early childhood education continues to be in the spotlight. The issues and oppor-tunities of the next quarter century will be exciting and challenging for all who work with young children and their families.

Today, the public is enthusiastic regarding the importance of children's early years in learning and development. Early childhood education's popularity and public and professional interest in children's early years will likely continue unabated.

WHO IS AN EARLY CHILDHOOD PROFESSIONAL?

The term *professional* is used often. But how would you explain it to someone who asked you, "Who is an early childhood professional?" What does *professional* mean?

Figure 1.1 outlines professional categories as identified by the National Association for the Education of Young Children (NAEYC). These categories reflect the association's efforts to continually enhance the concept of professionalism in early childhood education. As you identify the differences in these professional areas, reflect about their meaning for you and how you can start now to develop the necessary knowledge and skills for success at whatever level you select.

The Knowledge Base of the Profession

What knowledge do early childhood professionals need to possess? The early childhood profession identifies specific knowledge and abilities as the content of the profession: To work effectively with all young children—infants and toddlers, preschoolers, and primary school-age children (including those with special needs)—early childhood professionals must be able to do the following:

- Demonstrate a basic understanding of the early childhood profession and make a commitment to professionalism.

- Demonstrate a basic understanding of child development and apply this knowledge in practice.

- Observe and assess children's behavior for use in planning and individualizing teaching practices and curriculum.

- Establish and maintain an environment that ensures children's safety and their healthy development.

- Plan and implement a developmentally appropriate program that advances all areas of children's learning and development, including social, emotional, intellectual, and physical competence.

- Establish supportive relationships with children and implement developmentally appropriate techniques of guidance and group management.

- Establish positive and productive relationships with families.

- Support the uniqueness of each child, recognizing that children are best understood in the context of family, culture, and society.[1]

These items represent the core knowledge of the profession. Figure 1.2 shows how acquiring this core knowledge integrates with the ongoing process of becoming a professional. In this sense, the professional, at the moment of entry into the field, *at whatever level,* undertakes the responsibility to engage in increasing levels of preparation and knowledge acquisition.

THE PROCESS OF BECOMING A PROFESSIONAL

Acquiring core knowledge throughout one's professional life is embedded in the process of continuous professional development. When does a person step over the line, from being a nonprofessional to being a professional? When, if ever, does a person become a "finished" professional? These are not easy questions to answer. It makes the most sense to say that a person is always in the process of becoming a professional. The professional is never a "finished" product; one is always studying, learning, changing, and becoming more professional. The teachers of the year that you will read about in this chapter (see

Figure 1.1/*Definition of Early Childhood Professional Categories*

- **Early Childhood Professional Level VI**

  Successful completion of a Ph.D. or Ed.D. in a program conforming to NAEYC guidelines; OR
  Successful demonstration of the knowledge, performance, and dispositions expected as outcomes
  of a doctoral degree program conforming to NAEYC guidelines.

- **Early Childhood Professional Level V**

  Successful completion of a master's degree in a program that conforms to NAEYC guidelines; OR
  Successful demonstration of the knowledge, performance, and dispositions expected as outcomes
  of a master's degree program conforming to NAEYC guidelines.

- **Early Childhood Professional Level IV**

  Successful completion of a baccalaureate degree from a program conforming to NAEYC guidelines;
  OR
  State certificate meeting NAEYC/ATE certification guidelines; OR
  Successful completion of a baccalaureate degree in another field with more than 30 professional units
  in early childhood development/education including 300 hours of supervised teaching experience,
  including 150 hours each for two of the following three age groups: infants and toddlers, 3- to 5-
  year olds, or the primary grades; OR
  Successful demonstration of the knowledge, performance, and dispositions expected as outcomes
  of a baccalaureate degree program conforming to NAEYC guidelines.

- **Early Childhood Professional Level III**

  Successful completion of an associate degree from a program conforming to NAEYC guidelines; OR
  Successful completion of an associate degree in a related field, plus 30 units of professional studies in
  early childhood development/education including 300 hours of supervised teaching experience in an
  early childhood program; OR
  Successful demonstration of the knowledge, performance, and dispositions expected as outcomes of an
  associate degree program conforming to NAEYC guidelines.

- **Early Childhood Professional Level II**

  Successful completion of a one-year early childhood certificate program.
  Successful completion of the CDA Professional Preparation Program OR
  Completion of a systematic, comprehensive training program that prepares an individual to successfully
  acquire the CDA Credential through direct assessment.

- **Early Childhood Professional Level I**

  Individuals who are employed in an early childhood professional role working under supervision or with support
  (e.g., linkages with provider association or network or enrollment in supervised practicum) and participating
  in training designed to lead to the assessment of individual competencies or acquisition of a degree.

Source: "NAEYC Position Statement: A Conceptual Framework for Early Childhood Professional Development, 1994," *Young Children,* 49(3), p. 74.
Copyright © 1994 by the National Association for the Education of Young Children. Reprinted by permission.

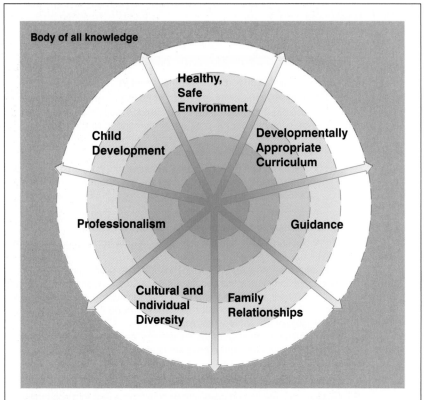

The dotted lines indicate stages of professional development achieved by the acquisition of recognized credentials that are based on professional standards of preparation. Moving from the innermost circle—the precredential level—individuals demonstrate knowledge required for the Child Development Associate (CDA) Credential and associate, baccalaureate, and advanced degrees. The arrows denote the continuum that extends from knowledge necessary for implementing effective practice to knowledge necessary for the generation and translation of knowledge; core knowledge is embedded within the larger body of all knowledge.

Source: From "Of Ladders and Lattices, Cores and Cones: Conceptualizing an Early Childhood Professional System," by Sue Bredekamp and Barbara Willer, 1992, *Young Children* 47(3), p. 49. Copyright © 1992 by the National Association for the Education of Young Children. Reprinted by permission.

Box 1.1) would not think of themselves as "completed" professionals. All would say that they have more to learn and more to do. Figure 1.3 shows this process of continuous professional development.

Becoming a professional means you will participate in training and education beyond the minimum needed for your present position. You will also want to consider your career objectives and the qualifications you might need for positions of increasing responsibility. The National Association for the Education of Young Children (NAEYC) has established the National Institute for Early Childhood Profes-

Figure 1.3/
*A Continuum
of Becoming
a Professional*

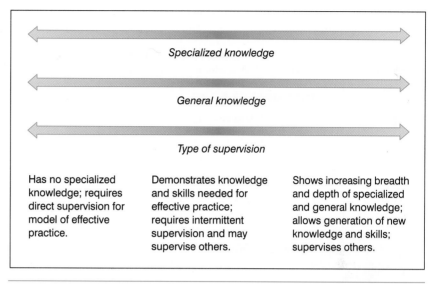

Specialized knowledge

General knowledge

Type of supervision

| Has no specialized knowledge; requires direct supervision for model of effective practice. | Demonstrates knowledge and skills needed for effective practice; requires intermittent supervision and may supervise others. | Shows increasing breadth and depth of specialized and general knowledge; allows generation of new knowledge and skills; supervises others. |

Source: From "A 'New' Paradigm of Early Childhood Professional Development," by Barbara Willer and Sue Bredekamp, *Young Children* 48(4), p. 65. Copyright © 1993 by the National Association for the Education of Young Children. Reprinted by permission.

sional Development, which conducts efforts to achieve an articulated, coordinated professional development system and helps make the early childhood profession even more professional. Another organization, the National Academy of Early Childhood Programs, specifies staff qualifications and training appropriate for positions in early childhood programs (Figure 1.4). Review these qualifications to determine how they apply to your career and life goals.

Qualities of Early Childhood Professionals

Currently, there is a great deal of discussion about quality in early childhood programs, which is directly related to the quality of the professionals in these programs. As you will discover throughout this book, merely discussing quality is not sufficient—professionals must involve themselves in activities that will promote quality in their lives and the lives of the children they teach and care for.

Anyone who has contemplated teaching has probably asked themselves, "Am I the kind of person suited for a career in early childhood education?" This question is difficult to answer honestly. In general, early childhood professionals should demonstrate the following qualities: love and respect for children, knowledge of children and their families, caring, compassion, courtesy, dedication, empathy, enthusiasm, friendliness, helpfulness, honesty, intelligence, kindness, motivation, patience, sensitivity, trust, understanding, and warmth. Home and early school experiences are critical for developing these qualities. So, if we want these qualities in our future professionals, we need to promote them now, in our teaching of young children. Toward that end, professionals might well concentrate on nurturing in themselves what is probably the most important of these characteristics: caring.

As a professional, you will work in classrooms, programs, and other settings in which

Figure 1.4/_Staff Qualifications and Development_

Staff role	Relevant Master's	Relevant Bachelor's	Relevant Associate's	CDA Credential	Some training	No training
DIRECTOR		Degree and 3 years experience				
MASTER TEACHER		Degree and 3 years experience				
TEACHER						
ASSISTANT TEACHER						
TEACHING ASSISTANT						

This figure does not include specialty roles such as educational coordinator, social services director, or other providers of special services. Individuals fulfilling these roles should possess the knowledge and qualifications required to fulfill their responsibilities effectively.

Source: National Academy of Early Childhood Programs, _Accreditation Criteria and Procedures of the National Academy of Early Childhood Programs,_ rev. ed. (Washington, D.C.: National Association for the Education of Young Children, 1991), p. 31. Reprinted by permission.

things do not always go smoothly, in which children do not always learn ably and well, in which children are not always clean and free from illness and hunger, in which children's and parents' backgrounds and ways of life are different from yours. If you truly care, being an early childhood professional is not easy. Caring means you will lose sleep trying

to find a way to help a child learn to read, that you will spend your own money to buy supplies, that you will spend long hours planning and gathering materials. Caring also means you will not leave your intelligence, enthusiasm, or talents at home but will bring them into the center, classroom, administration offices, boards of directors' meetings, or

Teaching is and should be a joyful experience for those who dedicate themselves to it. The profession demands and young children deserve the best from all who work with young children and their families. In what ways is teaching a joyful experience?

wherever you can make a difference in the lives of children and their families.

Terminology of Early Childhood Education

As an early childhood professional, you will want to have a command of the terminology used by the NAEYC and early childhood professionals (Tables 1.1, 1.2, and 1.3). The following paragraphs discuss these terms as used throughout this text.

We will use the term *professional* to refer to all who work with, care for, and teach children between birth and age eight. This desig-

nation is used for two reasons. First, it avoids the obvious confusion arising from such terms as *caregiver* and *teacher.* It is no longer easy or desirable to distinguish between someone who promotes care for and someone who teaches children. For example, the caregiving and educating roles are now blended so that a person who cares for infants is instructing them as well. However, in the preschool, kindergarten, and primary years, the term *teacher* is still and will continue to be used to designate professionals who teach children. Second, the early childhood profession is trying to upgrade the

Table 1.1/*Types of Early Childhood Programs*

Program	Purpose	Age
Early childhood program	Multipurpose	Birth to grade 3
Child care	Play/socialization; baby-sitting; physical care; provides parents opportunities to work; cognitive development; full-quality care	Birth to 6 years
High school child care programs	Provide child care for children of high school students, especially unwed parents; serve as an incentive for student/parents to finish high school and as a training program in child care and parenting skills	6 weeks to 5 years
Drop-off child care centers	Provide care for short periods of time while parents shop, exercise, or have appointments	Infancy through the primary grades
After-school care	Provides care for children after school hours	Children of school age; generally K to 6
Family day care	Provides care for a group of children in a home setting; generally custodial in nature	Variable
Employer child care	Different settings for meeting child care	Variable; usually as early as 6 weeks to the beginning of school
Corporate child care	Same as employer child care	Same as employer child care
Proprietary care	Provides care and/or education to children; designed to make a profit	6 weeks to entrance into first grade
Nursery school (public or private)	Play/socialization; cognitive development	2 to 4 years
Preschool (public or privare)	Play/socialization; cognitive development	2½ to 5 years
Parent cooperative preschool	Play/socialization; preparation for kindergarten and first grade; baby-sitting; cognitive development	2 to 5 years
Baby-sitting cooperatives (co-op)	Provide parents with reliable baby-sitting; parents sit for others' children in return for reciprocal services	All ages
Prekindergarten	Play/socialization; cognitive development; preparation for kindergarten	3½ to 5 years
Junior kindergarten	Prekindergarten program	Primarily 4-year-olds
Senior kindergarten	Basically the same as regular kindergarten	Same as kindergarten
Kindergarten	Preparation for first grade; developmentally appropriate activities for 4½- to 6-year-olds; increasingly viewed as the grade before the first grade and as a regular part of the public school program	4 to 6 years

Table 1.1/*Continued*

Program	Purpose	Age
Pre-first grade	Preparation for first grade; often for students who "failed" or did not do well in kindergarten	5 to 6 years
Interim first grade	Provides children with an additional year of kindergarten and readiness activities prior to and as preparation for first grade	5 to 6 years
Transitional or transition classes	Classes specifically designed to provide for children of the same developmental age	Variable
Developmental kindergarten	Same as regular kindergarten; often enrolls children who have completed one or more years in an early childhood special education program	5 to 6 years
Transitional kindergarten	Extended learning of kindergarten preparation for first grade	Variable
Preprimary	Preparation for first grade	5 to 6 years
Primary	Teaches skills associated with grades 1, 2, and 3	6 to 8 years
Toy lending libraries	Provide parents and children with games, toys, and other materials that can be used for learning purposes; housed in libraries, vans, or early childhood centers	Birth through primary years
Lekotek	Resource center for families who have children with special needs; sometimes referred to as a *toy* or *play library* (*lekotek* is a Scandinavian word that means play library)	Birth through primary years
Infants stimulation programs (also called parent/infant stimulation and mommy and me programs)	Programs for enhancing sensory and cognitive development of infants and young toddlers through exercise and play; activities include general sensory stimulation for children and educational information and advice for parents	3 months to 2 years
Multiage grades or groups	Groups or classes of children of various ages; generally spanning 2 to 3 years per group	Variable
Dual-age classroom	An organizational plan in which children from two grade levels are grouped together; another term for multiage grouping and for maintaining reasonable student-teacher ratios	Variable
Learning families	Another name for multiage grouping. However, the emphasis is on practices that create a family atmosphere and encourage living and learning as a family. The term was commonly used in open education programs. Its revival signifies the reemergence of progressive and child-centered approaches	Variable

continued

Table 1.1/_Continued_

Program	Purpose	Age
Junior first grade	Preparation for first grade	5 to 6 years
Split class	Teaches basic academic and social skills of grades involved	Variable, but usually primary
Head Start	Play/socialization; academic learning; comprehensive social and health services; prepares children for kindergarten and first grade	2 to 6 years
Follow Through	Extended Head Start services to grades 1, 2, and 3	6 to 8 years
Private schools	Provide care and/or education	Usually preschool through high school
Department of Children, Youth, and Families	A multipurpose agency of many state and county governments; usually provides such services as administration of state and federal monies, child care licensing, and protective services.	All
Health and Human Services	Same as Dept. of Children, Youth, and Families	All
Health and Social Services	Same as Dept. of Children, Youth, and Families	All
Home Start	Provides Head Start service in the home setting	Birth to 6 or 7 years
Laboratory school	Provides demonstration programs for preservice teachers; conducts research	Variable; birth through senior high
Child and Family Resource Program	Delivers Head Start services to families	Birth to 8 years
Montessori school (preschool and grade school)	Provides programs that use the philosophy, procedures, and materials developed by Maria Montessori (see chapter 3)	1 to 8 years
Open education	Child-centered learning in an environment characterized by freedom and learning through activities based on children's interests	2 to 8 years
British primary school	Implements the practices and procedures of open education	2 to 8 years
Magnet school	Specializes in subjects and curriculum designed to attract students; usually has a theme (e.g., performing arts); designed to give parents choices and to integrate schools	5 to 18 years

Table 1.2/*Names for Children*

Name	Description	Age
Baby	Generic term referring to a child from birth through the first 2 years of life	Birth to 2 years
Neonate	Child during the first month of life, from Latin words *neo* (new) and *natus* (born); usually used by nurses, pediatric specialists, and people working in the area of child development	Birth to 1 month
Infants	Children from birth to the beginning of independent walking (about 12 months of age)	Birth to 1 year
Toddlers	Children from the beginning of independent walking to about age 3; the term *toddler* is derived from the lunging, tottering, precarious balanced movement of children as they learn to walk.	13 months to 3 years
Preschoolers	Children between toddler age and age of entrance into kindergarten or first grade; because kindergarten is becoming more widespread, it is customary to refer to 4-year-olds as preschoolers.	3 to 5 years
Child/children	Generic term for individuals from birth through the elementary grades	Birth to 8 years
The very young	Used to identify and specify children from birth through preschool	Birth to 5 years

image and role of all those who work with young children. Referring to everyone as professionals helps achieve this goal.

Early childhood refers to the period from birth to age eight, a standard and accepted definition used by NAEYC.[2] (At the same time, professionals recognize that prenatal development is also important.) The term frequently refers to children who have not yet reached school age, and the public often uses it to refer to children in any type of preschool.

Early childhood programs provide "services for children from birth through age eight in part-day and full-day group programs in centers, homes, and institutions; kindergartens and primary schools; and recreational programs."[3]

Early childhood education consists of the services provided in early childhood settings.

It is common for professionals in this field to use the terms *early childhood* and *early childhood education* synonymously.

Other terms frequently used when discussing the education of young children are *nursery school* and *preschool*. *Nursery school* is a program for the education of two-, three-, and four-year-old children. Many nursery schools are half-day programs, usually designed for children whose mothers do not work outside the home, although many children who have two working parents do attend. The purpose of nursery school is to provide for active learning in a play setting. In some instances the kindergarten curriculum has been pushed down into the nursery school, replacing with a formal teacher-centered setting the child-centered program in an informal play setting that characterizes a good nursery school. *Preschool* generally

Table **1.3**/*Professionals Who Care For and Educate Young Children*

Title	Description
Early childhood professional	This is the preferred title for anyone who works with young children in any capacity. This designation reflects the growing belief of the early childhood profession that people who work with children at any level are professionals and as such are worthy of the respect, remuneration, and responsibilities that go with being a professional.
Early childhood educator	Works with young children and has committed to self-development by participating in specialized training and programs to extend professional knowledge and competence
Early childhood teacher	Responsible for planning and conducting a developmentally and educationally appropriate program for a group or classroom of children; supervises an assistant teacher or aide; usually has a bachelor's degree in early childhood, elementary education, or child development
Early childhood assistant teacher	Assists the teacher in conducting a developmentally and educationally appropriate program for a group or classroom; frequently acts as a coteacher but may lack education or training to be classified as a teacher (many people who have teacher qualifications serve as an assistant teacher because they enjoy the program or because the position of teacher is not available); usually has a high school diploma or associate degree and is involved in professional development
Early childhood associate teacher	Plans and implements activities with children; has an associate degree and/or the CDA credential; may also be responsible for care and education of a group of children
Aide	Assists the teacher and teacher assistant when requested; usually considered an entry-level position
Director	Develops and implements a center or school program; supervises all staff; may teach a group of children
Home visitor	Conducts a home-based child development/education program; works with children, families, and staff members
Child development associate	Has completed a CDA assessment and received the CDA credential*
Caregiver	Provides care, education, and protection for the very young in or outside the home; includes parents, relatives, child care workers, and early childhood teachers
Parent	Provides the child with basic care, direction, support, protection, and guidance
Volunteer	Contributes time, services, and talents to support staff. Usually are parents, retired persons, grandparents, and university/college/high school students

*CDA National Credentialing Program, *Child Development Associate Assessment System and Competency Standards* (Washington, D.C.: CDA National Credentialing Program, 1985), p. 551.

means any educational program for children prior to their entrance into kindergarten.

Preschool programs for three- and four-year-old children are rapidly becoming a part of the public school system, particularly those designed to serve low-income children and their families. For example, the Dade County, Florida, public schools operate more than 150 preschool programs for three- and four-year-old children.

When a public school or other agency operates one program for five-year-olds and another for four-year-olds, the term *kindergarten* is applied to the former and *nursery school* or *preschool* to the latter. Public school kindergarten is now almost universal for five-year-old children (see Chap. 8), so it can no longer be thought of as "preschool." Kindergarten is now part of the elementary grades K through 6, and the designation is almost universally used.

The term *prekindergarten* is growing in use and refers to programs for four-year-olds attending a program prior to kindergarten. Another term, *transitional kindergarten,* designates a program for children who are not ready for kindergarten and who can benefit from another year of the program. The term *transitional* also refers to grade school programs that provide additional opportunities for children to master skills associated with a particular grade. Transitional programs do not usually appear beyond the second and third grades.

Junior first grade or *pre-first grade* are transitional programs between kindergarten and first grade designed to help five-year-olds get ready to enter first grade. Not all children are equally "ready" to benefit from typical first grade because of their range of mental ages and experiential backgrounds, and children frequently benefit from such special programs. The goal of many early childhood professionals is to have all children learning at levels appropriate for them.

Preprimary refers to programs for children prior to their entering first grade; *primary* means first, second, and third grades. In some school districts primary grade children are taught in classes that include two grade levels. In these split or nongraded classes, first and second graders and second and third graders are taught in a single class. Split classes are seldom composed of upper-elementary children. Reasons for split classes are increasing or decreasing school enrollments, influences of child-centered practices, and teacher contracts that limit class size.

A *parent cooperative* preschool is a school formed and controlled by parents for their children. Programs of this type are generally operated democratically, with the parents hiring the staff. Often, some of the parents are hired to direct or staff the program. Being part of a cooperative means parents have some responsibility for assisting in the program.

The term *child care* encompasses many programs and services for preschool children. *Day care* is a term used for child care that most people engaged in the care of young children recognize as outmoded. *Child care* is more accurate and descriptive because it focuses on children themselves. The primary purpose of child care programs is to care for young children who are not in school and for schoolage children before and after school hours. Programs may have a total quality orientation or an educational orientation, and some may offer primarily baby-sitting or custodial care. Many programs have a sliding-fee schedule based on parents' ability to pay. Quality child care programs are increasingly characterized by comprehensive services that address children's total physical, social, emotional, creative, and intellectual needs. Today, parents, the public, and the profession understand that child care means providing physical care and educational programs for the whole child.

A large number of *family day care* programs provide child care services in the homes of caregivers. This alternative to center-based programs usually accommodates a maximum of four or five children in a *family day care home*. Formerly custodial in nature, there is a growing trend for caregivers to provide a full range of services in their homes.

Church-related or *church-sponsored* preschool and elementary programs are quite common and are becoming more popular. These programs usually have a cognitive, basic skills emphasis within a context of religious doctrine and discipline. These programs, which often charge tuition, are popular because of their emphasis on the basic skills and a no-nonsense approach to learning and teaching.

Head Start is a federally sponsored program for children from low-income families. Established by the Economic Opportunity Act of 1964, Head Start is intended to help children and their families overcome the effects of poverty. *Follow Through* extends Head Start programs to children in grades 1 through 3 and works with school personnel rather than apart from the schools.

Public and private agencies, including colleges, universities, hospitals, and corporations, operate many kinds of *demonstration programs*. Many colleges and universities with schools of education have a *laboratory school* used primarily for research in teaching methods, demonstration of exemplary programs and activities, and teacher training. Many of these schools also develop materials and programs for children with physical and learning disabilities.

As the name implies, a *toy library* makes toys and other learning materials available to children, parents, child care providers, and teachers. Toy libraries may be housed in libraries, shopping malls, churches, preschools, and mobile vans. Many toy libraries are supported by user fees and parent and community volunteers.

PREPARING FOR A CAREER IN EARLY CHILDHOOD EDUCATION

A career as an early childhood professional can be greatly rewarding. We discuss here what you can do to make your career happy and productive for yourself, and for the children and families you work with.

Start now to develop a philosophy of education and teaching. Base your philosophy on what you believe about children and the learning process, how you think children should be taught, and on your present values. Your philosophy of teaching will be your guide for classroom practice. Many teachers fill the school day and children's lives with unrelated activities, without considering whether these activities match their teaching objectives. So much of teaching is based on no philosophy at all. In fact, your philosophy may be the only guide to help you teach for, as surprising as it may seem, many schools operate without a written philosophy. Basing your teaching on a philosophy will help you fill children's school days with activities to help them learn and develop to their fullest potential.

As you develop your philosophy during preservice training, discuss it with friends, professors, and in-service teachers, and be willing to revise it as you gain new knowledge and insights. Developing a philosophy will not automatically make you a good teacher, but it will provide a foundation on which to build a good teaching career. (An added benefit of developing a philosophy is that it will help you respond professionally during job interviews.) See the following section for a fuller discussion of this topic.

Examine your willingness to dedicate yourself to teaching. Acquaint yourself thoroughly with what teaching involves. Visit many different kinds of schools. Is the school atmosphere one in which you want to spend the rest of your life? Talk with several teachers to learn what is involved in teaching. Ask yourself, "Am I willing to work hard? Am I willing to give more time to teaching than a teaching contract may specify? Are teachers the kind of people with whom I want to work? Do I have the physical energy for teaching? Do I have the enthusiasm necessary for good teaching?"

Honestly analyze your attitudes and feelings toward children. Do you really want to work with young children, or would you be

Honestly analyze your feelings and attitudes toward working with young children. Not everyone has the skills or temperament required for effective teaching of young children. Volunteer activities provide an excellent opportunity to expand your vision of working with young children, learn new skills, and match your abilities to the ages of children you can work with best. What volunteer experiences can you engage in as a preparation for teaching?

happier in another field? During your interactions with children, constantly test your attitudes toward them and their families. If you decide that working with children is not for you because of how you feel about them, then by all means do not teach.

Honestly believe that all children are capable of learning. Some parents lament that those who work with young children act as though their children cannot learn because of their culture or socioeconomic background. All children have the right to be taught by a professional who believes they are capable of learning to the fullest capacity.

As you enter the teaching profession, you will find other ways to make your career more productive and rewarding. We consider some of these ways here.

Be willing to improve your skills and increase your knowledge. Many professionals choose to do this by returning to school, which is usually encouraged by state requirements for permanent or continuing certification. Many teachers fulfill the requirements through a master's degree. A trend in teacher certification is to allow accumulation of a specified number of "points," gained through college credits, in-service programs, attendance at professional meetings and conferences, and other professional involvements. These points then count toward certification and take the place of college courses.

Reading is one method of self-improvement; a less obvious method is to force change by periodically teaching at different grade levels. By changing grade and age levels, teachers gain new insights into and perspectives on children and teaching. Whatever method you choose for self-improvement, you should recognize the need for constant retraining. While some school districts and early childhood programs do provide opportunities for retraining, most of the responsibility will be yours.

Be willing to try new things. Learning about and trying new methods is an important dimension of professionalism. As a new and developing professional you will want to consider and explore the possibilities for you and your children to get involved in and try new things.

Be enthusiastic for teaching and in your teaching. Time and again the one attribute that seems to separate the good teacher from the mediocre is enthusiasm. Trying to be enthusiastic will help a great deal on your professional journey.

Adjust to the ever-emerging new careers of teaching and society. All careers are molded by the needs of society and the resources available. Some professionals and some early childhood programs waste potential and miss opportunities because of unwillingness to adjust to changing circumstances and conditions.

Explore the possibilities for educational service in fields other than the public school. Do not limit your career choices and alternatives because of your limited conception of the professional's role. Some believe teacher education prepares one only for a teaching role. On the contrary; other opportunities for service are available in religious organizations; federal, state, and local agencies; private educational enterprises; hospitals; libraries; and in social work. Do not feel pressured to choose a major during your first year or two in college. Take a variety of electives that will help you in career choices, and talk to vocational counselors. Do not make up your mind too quickly about teaching a certain grade level or age range. Many teachers find out, much to their surprise, that the grade level they *thought* was best for them was not. Remain flexible about what grade or subject to teach.

Seize every educational opportunity to enhance your training program and career. Through wise course selection, you can strengthen your weaknesses and explore new alternatives. For example, if your program of studies requires a certain number of social

science credits, use them to explore areas such as sociology and anthropology, which have fascinating relationships to education. Electives that practicing teachers sometimes wish they had taken in college are keyboarding, first aid, audiovisual aids and media, behavior modification/management, special education, creative writing, and arts and crafts. And of course, as a teacher, you can never have too strong a background in child development.

Seek every opportunity for experiences with all kinds of children in all kinds of settings. Individuals often limit themselves to experiences in one setting (e.g., the public schools) and ignore church schools, child care programs, private and nonprofit agencies (e.g., March of Dimes, Easter Seal Society, etc.), and babysitting as venues to broaden and expand their knowledge of children. These experiences may often be work related and can be quite rewarding: You will not only broaden your knowledge, but such work may also help you determine the ages and kinds of children you want to work with and the settings you are comfortable in. These positions may pay little or nothing, but be willing to volunteer your services. Volunteer positions have a way of leading to paid positions. Many career possibilities and opportunities can become available this way.

Maintain an open-door policy. Welcome into your classroom parents, colleagues, college students, and all who want to know what schools and centers are doing. Being an early childhood professional need not be a lonely endeavor.

Go where the opportunities are. Sometimes people lock themselves into a particular geographic area or age range of children. Some locations may have an oversupply of professionals; other areas, especially urban centers, have a chronic shortage of professionals. Cities usually offer challenging and rewarding opportunities. There will always be a job if you are willing to go where the jobs are.

Developing a Philosophy of Education

A philosophy of education is a set of beliefs about how children develop and learn and what and how they should be taught. Your philosophy of education is based on your philosophy of life. What you believe about yourself, about others, and about life infuses and determines your philosophy of education. Knowing what others believe is important and useful for it can help you clarify what you believe; but when it is all said and done, *you* have to decide what you believe. What you believe moment by moment, day by day, influences what you will teach and how you will teach it.

A philosophy of life and education is more than an opinion. A personal philosophy is based on core values and beliefs. Core values of life relate to your beliefs about the nature of life, the purpose of life, your role and calling in life, and your relationship and responsibilities to others. Core beliefs and values about education and teaching include what you believe about the nature of children, the purpose of education, how people learn, the role of teachers, and what is worth knowing.

Your philosophy of education will guide and direct your daily teaching. Your beliefs about how children learn best will determine whether you individualize instruction or try to teach the same thing in the same way to everyone. Your philosophy will determine whether you help children do things for themselves or whether you do things for them. The following paragraphs describe ways to go about developing your philosophy.

Read widely in textbooks, journals, and other professional literature to get ideas and points of view. A word of caution: When people refer to philosophies of education, they often think only of historic influences. This is only part of the information available for writing a philosophy. Make sure you explore contemporary ideas as well, for these will also have a strong influence on you as a professional.

As you read through and study this text, make notes and reflect about your developing philosophy of education. The following headings will help you get started:

- I believe the purposes of education are . . .

- I believe that children learn best when they are taught under certain conditions and in certain ways. Some of these are . . .

- The curriculum of any classroom should include certain "basics" that contribute to children's social, emotional, intellectual, and physical development. These basics are . . .

- Children learn best in an environment that promotes learning. Features of a good learning environment are . . .

- All children have certain needs that must be met if they are to grow and learn at their best. Some of these basic needs are . . .

- I would meet these needs by . . .

- A teacher should have certain qualities and behave in certain ways. Qualities I think important for teaching are . . .

Once you have determined your philosophy of education, write it down, and have other people read it. This helps you clarify your ideas and redefine your thoughts, because your philosophy should be understandable to others (they do not necessarily have to agree with you).

Talk with successful teachers and other educators. The accounts of the Teachers of the Year (Box 1.1) and Voices from the Field (see Chap. 4) are evidence that a philosophy can help a person become an above-average

BOX 1.1 Teachers of the Year

JEAN LAGRONE, 1996 NEBRASKA TEACHER OF THE YEAR—SECOND GRADE

The beauty of the teaching profession is that wisdom comes with experience, which then magnifies both the pleasure and power of instruction. After twenty years of classroom experience, I am more integrated than ever with teaching. There is no profession more fulfilling and exciting. Each teaching assignment presents a new opportunity to examine learning theory, curriculum, discipline, motivation, and assessment. The complexity exhilarates me: creating a good learning environment, developing appropriate individualized instruction, maintaining discipline, helping children grow in their social skills, and holding myself accountable for their educational success.

Through teaching, I am continually acquiring a deeper understanding of the ebb and flow of the learning process. During undergraduate training, my methods classes were taught "hands-on" in a local elementary school. I learned to develop self-paced programs for each child. After graduation, I taught in the same school district, where my pupils were inner-city, at-risk students in both second and third grades.

In 1982, my husband and I moved to the small, mountain community of High Rolls, New Mexico. I was a dorm parent at New Mexico School for the Visually Handicapped and curriculum director for the Mescalero Apache bilingual program, and taught for seven years in a country school that served forty-five students, grades K–6. In 1985, I earned my master's degree in curriculum development, specializing in teaching writing to elementary students.

Teaching in a country school, I learned an immeasurable amount about curriculum scope and sequence and how children master concepts as they mature. By teaching the same subject at all grade levels, I learned that skills evolve incrementally over time as they are retaught and practiced with increasing sophistication. Observing the same children year after year taught me how children approach academic challenges at different ages.

I next taught kindergarten in a rural, bilingual school near the United States–Mexico border. Many of my students were not well prepared for school; some had never even held a pencil or crayon! These students, many of whom spoke no English, taught me that hands-on activities are powerful modes for "discovery learning" and give children who speak different languages the chance to learn together.

After two years, I was selected to direct an innovative, computer-based reading and writing program. I conducted the lab for first grade classes, and developed an adapted program for those students learning in Spanish. I found that frequent writing sessions increased the effectiveness of reading instruction, and the students are empowered when they view themselves as authors and researchers. To continue students' growth in writing, I wrote and implemented a K–6 writing curriculum and supervised the second and third grade teachers as they initiated the program.

I am currently teaching second grade at Westgate Elementary in Omaha, Nebraska, where I am active in the district's new teacher mentoring program. I have helped develop K–12 math and science guidelines for the district's outcome-based education plan, worked on training manuals for the early childhood program, and served on language arts, math, and science committees.

Our district has recently adopted a new discovery-based science program. It has been my responsibility to train the teachers. As a lead teacher in the Nebraska Math and Science Initiative, I regularly facilitate teacher workshops that nurture teachers' commitment to math and science instruction that fosters students' love of learning. Our ultimate goal is for all students, regardless of race or gender, to see math and science as integral and positive parts of their world.

The Mr. Wizard Foundation selected me to be featured on the program, *Teacher to Teacher with Mr. Wizard,* shown on Nickelodeon. A camera crew filmed as I taught science in the classroom and conducted teacher training for math and science programs. The eight segments featuring my classroom are part of a fifty-program series designed to train teachers in teaching discovery-based science. I also agreed to be part of a group of teachers from *Teacher to Teacher* to lead training sessions for schools across the United States. I am proud to be actively involved in the change from textbook-driven, isolated content to discovery-based integrated learning. I want to share with other teachers my love and enthusiasm for teaching and to instill in students my excitement for learning.

As the 1996 Nebraska Teacher of the Year, I conducted workshops and spoke to various groups, using as the core of my message my enthusiasm for effective and exciting programs and my respect for the teaching profession. I recognize that today's students will shape tomorrow's world. Educating these students is a tremendous responsibility, a challenge that thousands of caring, involved teachers meet daily.

My greatest contribution to teaching is the excitement, knowledge, and expertise I bring to the classroom. I respect each student's ability to grasp sophisticated ideas, and promote concept development by planning lessons and activities that build on previous discoveries, encouraging learners to make multiple mental connections. Students create meaning by interacting with materials, their classroom, and their teacher. Managing a classroom in a manner that builds teamwork and a sense of citizenship and community is important to me. I treat children with respect and show them how to treat each other respectfully. Working together to make the classroom a good place to exhibit honesty, respect, and responsibility, students develop a sense of their own importance and of the value of their peers.

Teaching is the best job in the world! It is not easy, and can't be done in eight hours, then left at the office. An outstanding teacher must be able to juggle many responsibilities and do many jobs well. Teaching demands great dedication, and good teachers find motivation and rewards in their classrooms every day. A well-run classroom is an assembly of people united by the love of learning. It is a joyous place where self-discipline and a sense of wonder about the world flourish together.

EDWARD J. SILVER, JR., 1996 MARYLAND TEACHER OF THE YEAR—THIRD GRADE

The overriding belief that governs my teaching is that all children can learn and naturally want to learn. Children desire to explore and make sense of the world around them. My responsibility as a teacher is to develop a learning environment that fosters this inclination. This involves five components.

1. *Learning must be meaningful.* School must be an engaging, motivating place that builds on children's natural curiosity. In my classroom I try to embed learning in meaningful, motivational activities. Instead of simply teaching a unit on the moon, the students enter an astronaut training program to prepare for a simulated mission. Students learn about erosion by studying how to improve a school playground with the goal of advising the principal about their findings. Students plan class parties, which requires them to make a budget, to create invitations, and to write out instructions for activities. Learning in a meaningful context nourishes students' natural curiosity.

2. *Learning must be "hands on."* Children learn best when manipulating their world. Activities that I employ are based on children exploring the world using concrete items. In science, I try to use experiments daily, while in math we use manipulatives to solidify students' understanding of concepts.

3. *Learning must build connections.* Children learn best when they see how all learning is interrelated. In my teaching, I build units around unified themes. If students understand that what they are learning is not isolated information but part of the fabric that they encounter in all subject areas, it allows them to learn with greater depth and thus acquire better understanding. This also involves writing and communication. When children are given time to write about their learning, they reflect on it and connect new understanding to existing knowledge.

4. *Learning must be collaborative.* Working cooperatively is both a means and an end. Children who discuss with others what they are learning are more actively involved in that learning and are more organized in their thinking. Children also need to learn how to work as a team to accomplish their goals. In my classroom, children work in groups in all subject areas. The learning experience involves discussion, group projects, and peer tutoring.

5. *Learning must be safe.* Learning is inherently risky because it involves questioning present understanding. If children are to move away from the commonplace, they need to be in a warm, accepting environment that fosters risk taking. I try to build such a community. My class becomes a family where we do not tolerate "putdowns," and where we emphasize kindness and encouragement.

Let me transport you to a day in my third grade class at Millington Elementary School.

The morning's energy level is high. Almost immediately there is a buzz of excitement as students check their science experiments from the day before. Other children are curled up in the reading corner with copies of a new book about the earth, still others finish their work publishing a class book of poetry. After a period of time, I give a signal and all the students gather on the rug for the day's orientation. As a class we are studying geology. Our theme, entitled "KOGEASI" (Kids On a Geological Exploration And Scientific Investigation), is built around a secret mission to be the first people to travel to the center of the earth. As a class we begin our study day with a theme song, a secret handshake, and a raucous salute (ROCK!). Enthusiastic about the mission, students brief the class on their learning projects. One group is finding information to chart the layers of the earth. Another group is designing the vehicle for the voyage. A third group is researching plate tectonics and designing a model of continental shift. Findings and problems are listed on chart paper taped to the wall. While the students report, my role is that of class facilitator.

Students then engage in a series of teacher-directed and student-initiated learning opportunities. Math is taught in a problem-solving format

where skills are applied to solve the effects of ground cover on erosion. Students record measurements, graph and interpret data, and write about their findings. In reading, children read nonfiction books on the earth and learn to distinguish main ideas from supporting details. Social studies finds students in different parts of the room studying topographical maps. Throughout the day, students may write in a reflection journal about what they are learning, and often use technology (calculators and computers) as a tool to maximize their learning.

As the day ends, the class meets again on the rug to summarize the day's learnings and to help plan the next day's goals. My students are enthusiastic about learning and are becoming convinced that learning is an important and meaningful part of a full life.

JOHN H. FUNK, 1996 UTAH TEACHER OF THE YEAR—KINDERGARTEN

As a kindergarten teacher, I have decided that how I begin my students' schooling career may determine the success of the rest of their education. My goals include providing a measure of stability in a perhaps unstable life, a safe, secure, and loving environment for each student, and an opportunity for a great start to the educational process. I make my room and my lesson plans as interesting and exciting as possible.

Kindergarten is the introduction to public education. Kindergarten teachers need to begin by teaching students about their surroundings and about how all of the academic skills they are learning will help them have a complete and happy life and better understand their world. The attitude toward school that kindergarten students develop can remain with them throughout their school career.

Students should be in school every day. Teachers are the catalysts to make school a place where children want to be. We are on a year-round school schedule, attending for nine weeks followed by a three-week break. To help students develop a positive attitude about school, I make every effort to have that same attitude. Our classroom motto is, "I Like School." Whenever we are going on break, we don't say, "Hurrah, we get a vacation!" Instead, we always say, "Oh dear! We have to take a break from school. We would rather keep going every day. This is where we want to be." Not only do the children look forward to returning to school, but so do I! We are excited to go to school each day. I have had a number of students call me at home to ask if we could come back to school. The rewards I have felt as a teacher center around my students' attitudes about wanting to be at school with me. How can you not feel fantastic when you have fifty best friends?

An effective teacher doesn't cease to care about students just because the school day is over. Teachers should be constant positive examples of caring. For me, personally caring and loving each child has yielded amazing results. I am much more conscientious about the contents of my lesson plans and more concerned about each child's success. Working with kindergarten students and studying the latest research has made me concerned about attending to the developmental stages of five-year-olds. As we approach academic skills we must remember their individual stages of development. Teachers shouldn't reflect the attitude, "Today we are learning addition. Put everything else away." Research tells us that young children learn best when *all* subjects are integrated together. We must begin teaching the "whole child."

Education can compete with other forms of excitement and entertainment in the world. Young students naturally become interested about and want to learn something new. My efforts are channeled to helping them achieve that harmony and love of learning, beginning their early school experience in a tactile and visual way. "Let's find everything in the world that is red. How does red feel? Taste? Smell? Sound? Look?"

My answers to critics of education is this: We must begin to teach our young children as *children* instead of as mini-adults. Giving our children hands-on, developmental experiences will help to build a strong foundation for their further education. Too many students are advancing through their school years with shaky and unsure foundations. Children who feel like failures at five will surely be failures at fifteen. My hope is that educators will teach as *children* so that when they become adults they will *be* adults.

teacher. Talking with others exposes you to their points of view and stimulates your thinking.

Finally, evaluate your philosophy against this checklist:

- Does my philosophy accurately relate my beliefs about teaching? Have I been honest with myself?

- Is it understandable to me and others?

- Does it provide practical guidance for teaching?

- Are my ideas consistent with each other?

- Does what I believe make good sense?

- Have I been comprehensive, stating my beliefs about (1) how children learn, (2) what children should be taught, (3) how children should be taught, (4) the conditions under which children learn best, and (5) the qualities of a good teacher?

A Good Teacher: A Lesson from History

It is worthwhile to look at the history of early childhood education for ideas about good teachers. In fact, we need look no further than Froebel, father of the kindergarten:

I understand it thus. She [the mother] says, "I bring my child—take care of it, as I would do"; or "Do with my child what is right to do"; or "Do it better than I am able to do it." A silent agreement is made between the parents and you, the teacher; the child is passed from hand to hand, from heart to heart. What else can you do but be a mother to the little one, for the hour, morning or day when you have the sacred charge of a young soul? In hope and trust the child is brought to you, and you have to show yourself worthy of the confidence which is placed in your skill, your experience and your knowledge.[4]

Ethical Standards for the Profession

A professional is an ethical person. The profession of early childhood education has a set of ethical standards to guide our thinking and behavior. As an early childhood educator, you will want to be a good teacher as judged by the profession. NAEYC has developed both a Statement of Commitment and a Code of Ethical Conduct (see Appendix A). Following is the Statement of Commitment:

As an individual who works with young children, I commit myself to furthering the values of early childhood education as they are reflected in the NAEYC Code of Ethical Conduct. To the best of my ability I will:

- *Ensure that programs for young children are based on current knowledge of child development and early childhood education.*
- *Respect and support families in their task of nurturing children.*
- *Respect colleagues in early childhood education and support them in maintaining the NAEYC Code of Ethical Conduct.*
- *Serve as an advocate for children, their families and their teachers in community and society.*
- *Maintain high standards of professional conduct.*
- *Recognize how personal values, opinions, and biases can affect professional judgment.*
- *Be open to new ideas and be willing to learn from the suggestions of others.*
- *Continue to learn, grow, and contribute as a professional.*
- *Honor the ideals and principles of the NAEYC Code of Ethical Conduct.*[5]

WHAT DOES THE FUTURE HOLD FOR THE EARLY CHILDHOOD PROFESSIONAL?

In preparing to undertake the professional challenges of the next century, many have attempted to forecast what life then will be like. As a result, essential features of the future have become evident that will influence and determine the nature of the professional's necessary core knowledge, skills, and behaviors:

- The population of the United States will become even more diverse than it is today. Diversity training must be an essential part of the training of early childhood professionals, enabling them to work with children, parents, and families from all cultural and socioeconomic backgrounds.
- More services to children will be delivered in and through the family system. This means that early childhood professionals will need to know adult growth and development and how to meet adult needs.
- Early childhood programs will begin to serve different types of children in different ways. This is particularly true as a continuing impact of PL 94–142 and PL 99–457. There are more young children with disabilities, birth to age five, in programs designed to meet their and their families' needs. This situation means new programs will be developed, and teachers will be trained or retrained to provide appropriate services. The fields of early childhood education and early childhood special education are fast becoming one. As full inclusion reaches more programs, professionals have to be trained in both areas to appropriately meet the needs of all children and their families.
- Public sector spending for educating young children and their families will increase. Early childhood education will continue to be a source of great interest and the focus of the public's attention. This means that early childhood professionals will have to assume their rightful role in helping allocate resources and ensure that they are wisely used.
- Business and industry will play larger roles than at present in the education of young children and their families, and in supporting services that achieve this goal. Early childhood professionals must be prepared to

work cooperatively and collaboratively as professionals with this sector of society. Indeed, these linkages provide a challenging opportunity to expand and enrich early childhood programs.

• Technology will play an even greater role than presently in learning at all levels. Part of professional development involves developing technological literacy in oneself and a willingness to foster technological literacy in children.

• Society in the twenty-first century will be much different than it was even a decade ago. As a result, the role of the early childhood professional will continue to change and evolve. You will read throughout this book about these changes. Not only must professionals reconceptualize their own roles, they must also rethink their responsibilities to children and their families.

This reconceptualization is critical for the professional in the twenty-first century. For example, early childhood professionals seldom think of themselves as part of one of the most effective crime prevention programs, but it is so. In one case, the High/Scope Perry Preschool Study found that children born in poverty who participated in a high-quality, active-learning preschool program at ages three and four have fewer criminal arrests than adults who received no preschool program as children.[6]

• We will see a stronger movement toward the professionalization of teaching, already evident from our previous discussion of professionalism. This professionalization is part of the national effort to improve education. The public recognizes, albeit belatedly, that real and lasting changes in education will occur when teachers are trained and treated as professionals. The emphasis on professionalism will require teachers to assume more responsibility for their own behavior and for their professional development.

• As an early childhood educator, you must be prepared to take your place in a world in which learning is valued and respected. You should also be prepared to devote your career to continually learning new skills and gaining new knowledge.

• <u>Learning will be considered a lifelong process</u>. All early childhood professionals will be expected to engage in a process of continuous learning, growth, and development across their life span. We will see an intensification of training as professionalism demands higher levels of competence. Early childhood teachers and child care workers will probably have to take additional training through the Child Development Association (CDA), in-service training, or college-related courses. Early childhood professionals will be challenged and often required to demonstrate professionalism through courses, workshops, and certificate programs.

• Professional roles will expand. A higher degree of professionalism will bring greater responsibility and decision making. The role of early childhood professionals will continue to be reconceptualized. Teachers will be trained to work with parents, design curriculum materials, plan programs for paraprofessionals, and work cooperatively with community agencies, including business and industry.

Many schools currently operate a system of differentiated staffing and employ teachers and aides with differing role functions, levels of responsibility, training, and salary. Also, as the currently popular school-based management movement grows, more teachers will be involved in decisions about how schools operate and how and what children will learn.

Differentiated staffing will be accompanied by differentiated teaching. There will be closer attention to different learning styles. Greater attention to learning styles will also involve greater use of concrete learning materials, self-selected activities, and students as tutors.

• Professionals and community agencies will develop more collaborative, cooperative relationships. Teaching is an integral part of the broader range of human services and helping professions. The sharp lines that have traditionally separated social work, the health professions, and education are gradually blurring. Unfortunately, members of these professions are often reluctant to admit that other professionals can provide meaningful services that complement their own. There is also a trend toward resolving social problems through interdisciplinary programs, to which each profession contributes its particular expertise.

Involvement in the early childhood profession can be a joyful experience for those who dedicate themselves to it. The profession demands, and young children deserve, the best of teachers and caregivers. Becoming a good professional requires a lot of hard work and dedication. All who call themselves "professional" must accept the challenges and responsibilities that are part of the title.

ACTIVITIES FOR FURTHER ENRICHMENT

1. Recall your own teachers. List which of their characteristics you would imitate and which you would try to avoid as a teacher.

2. You are in charge of the professional development of a child care center for the coming year. Identify ten topics for in-service training that you think would be appropriate for all professionals in the center.

3. Write several paragraphs about the importance of professional training in the field of early childhood education.

4. Reflect on your years in the primary grades. What experiences do you consider most meaningful? Why? Would these experiences be valid learning experiences for children today? How and why?

5. Interview five early childhood professionals to determine what they think constitutes

professionalism and how professions can be more involved in increasing professionalism.

6. Talk with other professionals about careers that relate to children and parents. How did they come to their jobs? Is there evidence that they planned for these careers? Do you think you would enjoy an alternative career in education? Why?

7. Put your philosophy of education in writing, and share it with your classmates. Have them critique it for comprehensiveness, clarity, and meaning. How do you feel about the changes they suggested?

8. List the reasons you have decided to become an early childhood professional. Share and compare the list with your classmates. What conclusions can you draw from the lists?

9. Read the accounts of Teachers of the Year. Write a report about what impressed you most about their accounts, what outstanding qualities these teachers demonstrate, and why they were able to become Teachers of the Year.

10. List ten characteristics and qualities you think are essential for an early childhood professional. Compare your list with one of your classmates. How are they similar and different?

READINGS FOR FURTHER ENRICHMENT

Borich, G. *Becoming a Teacher* (Bristol, PA: Falmer Press, 1995).

Using an interralated series of conversion dialogues between practicing teachers, school principals, and a journalist, the author presents a story of how schools and teachers can become more effective.

Darling-Hammond, L., Wise, A., & Klein, S. *A Licence to Teach: Building a Profession for the 21st Century* (Boulder, CO: Westview Press, 1995).

The authors explore the need for reform in both teacher preparation and licensure. They contend that a meaningful license to teach is the key to creating successful schools in the next century. Internships, various forms of performance measures, and performance-oriented licensing receive in-depth treatment.

Johnson, J., & McCracken, J. (eds.). *The Early Childhood Career Lattice: Perspectives on Professional Development* (Washington, D.C.: National Association for the Education of Young Children, 1994).

Introduces thirty-nine key leaders representing many facets of the diverse early childhood field, who offer their perspectives on achieving an articulated professional development system, reflected in the early childhood career lattice.

Jones, E. (ed.). *Growing Teachers: Partnerships in Staff Development* (Washington, D.C.: National Association for the Development of Young Children, 1993).

Individuals from many different settings—and the sensitive mentors who helped facilitate their growth—tell of their satisfying personal journeys toward more effective teaching.

Walling, D. (ed.). *Teachers as Leaders* (Bloomington, IN: Phi Delta Kappa Educational Foundation, 1994).

The twenty essays in this book provide diverse perspectives on the professional development of teachers.

NOTES

1. Barbara Willer and Sue Bredekamp, "A 'New' Paradigm of Early Childhood Professional Development," *Young Children,* 47(3) 1993, p. 64.
2. National Academy of Early Childhood Programs, *Accreditation Criteria and Procedures* (Washington, D.C.: National Association for the Education of Young Children, 1984), p. x.
3. National Association for the Education of Young Children, *Early Childhood Teacher Education Guidelines* (Washington, D.C.: Author, 1982), p. xii.
4. Friedrich Froebel, *Moether's Songs, Games, and Stories* (New York: Arno, 1976), p. xxxiii.
5. *Code of Ethical Conduct and Statement of Commitment* by S. Feeney and K. Kipnis, 1992, Washington, D.C.: The National Association for the Education of Young Children. Copyright © 1992 by NAEYC. Reprinted by permission.
6. Lawrence J. Schweinhart, H. V. Barnes, and David P. Weikart, *Significant Benefits: The High/Scope Perry Preschool Study through Age 27* (Ypsilanti, MI: High/Scope, 1993), p. xv.

Early Childhood Education Today

Focus Questions

1. What contemporary influences have created interest in early childhood education?

2. How does public policy influence early childhood education?

3. What are our views of children and how do these views influence the education of young children?

4. What are social, political, economic, and educational issues that influence childrearing and teaching?

Many contemporary social issues affect decisions that families and early childhood professionals are making about the education and care of young children. Problems of child abuse, the numbers of children who live in poverty, infant mortality, and society's inability to meet the needs of all children are perennial sources of controversy and concern to which people continue to seek solutions. The emergence of new ideas and issues relating to the education and care of young children and the quest to provide educationally and developmentally appropriate programs keep the field of early childhood education in a state of disequilibrium. Early childhood professionals are constantly challenged to determine what is best for young children and their families given the needs and challenges of society today.

CONTEMPORARY ISSUES AFFECTING EARLY CHILDHOOD EDUCATION

Women's Movement

The women's movement has had a tremendous and long-lasting influence on infants, young children, and early childhood education. A major reason for the interest in infants and infant care is that many women want quality out-of-home care for their infants. True equality for women depends partly on relieving them of the constant care of children. As women have more choices about how best to conduct their lives and the lives of their children, demand increases for more, and more comprehensive, child care. The women's movement has helped enlighten parents regarding their rights as parents, including helping them learn how to advocate on behalf of themselves and their children for better health services, child care, programs for earlier education and parenting, and family-friendly work environments.

Working Parents

More and more families find that both parents must work to make ends meet. An increasing percentage of mothers with children under six are currently employed (62 percent in 1995), which creates a greater need for early childhood programs (Figure 2.1). This demand brings a beneficial recognition to early childhood programs and encourages early childhood professionals to meet parents' needs. Unfortunately, the urgent need for child care has encouraged some ill-prepared people to establish programs who do not necessarily have children's or parents' best interests in mind.

Demand is high enough that good programs have not yet had a chance to drive inferior ones from the child care marketplace. For their part, some parents are not able or willing to evaluate programs and select the best ones for their children, which also encourages poor-quality programs to stay in operation.

Rising Incomes

Ironically, while the need for two incomes generates interest in early childhood, rising incomes are also a factor. Many parents with middle-level incomes are willing to invest money in early education for their children. They look for nursery schools and preschool programs they feel will give their children a good start in life. Montessori schools and franchised operations have benefited in the process. In the last several years, the Montessori system especially has experienced a tremendous boom, in the number of both individuals seeking Montessori teacher training and preschool enrollments (see Chap. 4). Some parents of three- and four-year-olds spend almost as much in tuition to send their children to good preschools as parents of eighteen-year-olds do to send their children to state-supported universities.

Single Parents

The number of one-parent families, male and female, continues to increase. Certain ethnic groups are disproportionately represented in single-parent families. Figure 2.2 illustrates these trends. These increases are attributable to several factors. First, pregnancy rates are higher among lower socioeconomic groups. Second, teenage pregnancy rates in poor white, Hispanic, and African American populations are sometimes higher due to lower education levels, economic constraints, and fewer opportunities for individuals. In addition, a complex interplay of personal issues,

Figure 2.1/*Percentage of Mothers in the Labor Force*

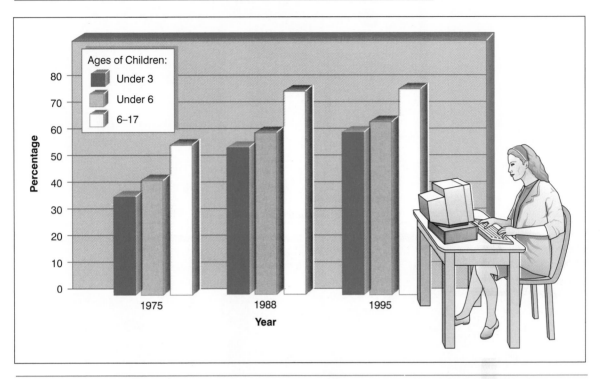

Source: U.S. Bureau of Labor Statistics, 1996.

such as family, religious, and cultural conflicts affect teenage pregnancy rates. In 1995, 37 percent of families were headed by females and 5 percent were headed by males.

People become single parents for a number of reasons: Half of all marriages end in divorce; some people choose single parenthood; and some, such as many teenagers, become parents by default. In addition, liberalized adoption procedures, artificial insemination, surrogate childbearing, and general public support for single parents make this lifestyle an attractive option for some people. The reality is that more women are having babies without marrying (Figure 2.3).

No matter how people become single parents, the extent of single parenthood has tremendous implications for early childhood professionals. In response to growing single parenthood, early childhood programs are developing curricula to help children and their parents deal with the stress of family breakups. Professionals are called on to help children adjust to the guilt they often feel and to their changed family pattern and lifestyle. In addition to needing assistance with child care, single parents frequently seek help in childrearing, especially in regard to discipline. Early childhood professionals are often asked to conduct seminars to help parents gain these skills. Additionally, the increasing number of children living in single-parent families challenges early childhood professionals to find ways to help children grow up within this context.

Figure 2.2/ *Percentage of Families with Children*

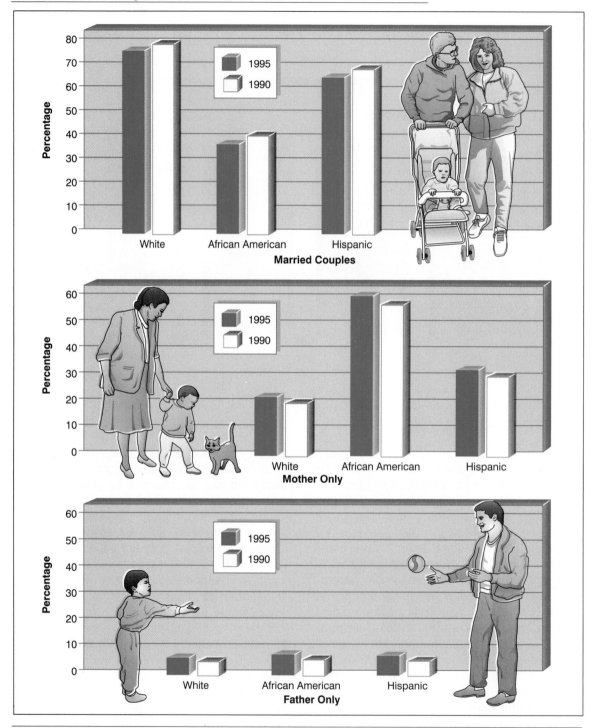

Source: Bureau of the Census, Current Population Reports, Series P20-483, "Household and Family Characteristics," 1995.

Figure 2.3/ *Percentage of Never-Married Women Age Fifteen to Forty-Four Who Have Children (1994)*

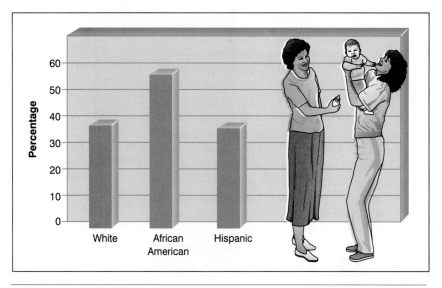

Source: U.S. Bureau of the Census. *Table 1, Marital status of persons 15 years and over, by age, sex, and race, 1994.*

VIDEO VIEWPOINT

CHILDREN GROWING UP WITHOUT FATHERS

Living in homes without fathers is a reality that affects the lives of growing numbers of children in the United States. In 25 percent of American households mothers are raising 40 million children alone. These are children that may never see or have contact with their biological fathers.

Reflective Discussion Questions: Why are we as a society so concerned about the absence of fathers in children's formative years? From your own background and experiences, what are some consequences for children being reared in homes without fathers? What does research show are some outcomes for children who are reared in homes without fathers? Why is having two parents in the home important for children? What are some critical behaviors that fathers role model for their children? In what ways do fathers make a critical difference in the lives of children? Why is it important for mothers and fathers to tell their children "I love you"?

Reflective Decision Making: What can you as an early childhood professional do to make a difference in the lives of the children and their mothers living in homes without fathers? Make a list of community based services that would be of help to families without fathers? How could you as an early childhood professional link children and their mothers to community based services?

As recently as the 1980s, early professionals were not as concerned about how to assist and support unwed parents and children from single-parent families, but today they recognize that these parents want and need their help. How well early childhood professionals meet the needs of single parents can make a difference in how successful single parents are in their new roles.

Fathers

A continuing change in early childhood today is that fathers have rediscovered the joys of parenting and working with young children. Men are. playing an active role in providing basic care, love, and nurturance to their children. The definition of fatherhood has changed; a father is no longer stereotypically unemotional, detached from everyday responsibilities of child care, authoritarian, and a disciplinarian. Fathers no longer isolate themselves from childrearing only because they are male. Men are more concerned about their role of fatherhood and their participation in family events before, during, and after the birth of their children. Fathers want to be involved in the whole process of childrearing. Because so many men feel unprepared for fatherhood, agencies such as hospitals and community colleges are providing courses and seminars to introduce fathers to the joys, rewards, and responsibilities of fathering.

Fathers no longer quietly acquiesce to giving up custody of their children in a divorce. Men are becoming single parents through adoption and surrogate childbearing. (Figure 2.2 shows the percentage of single families headed by fathers.) Fathers' rights groups have tremendous implications for the family court system and traditional interpretations of family law. Fathers are also receiving some of the employment benefits that have traditionally gone only to women, such as paternity leaves, flexible work schedules, and sick leave for family illness.

Teenage Parents: Children Having Children

Teenage pregnancies continue to be a problem. Each year one out of ten, or 1.1 million,

Teenage pregnancies continue to be a problem for a number of reasons. The financial costs of teenage child bearing are high, including costs to young mothers and their children. Teenage parents are less likely to complete their education and are more likely to have limited career and economic opportunities. How might early childhood programs help teenage parents meet their needs and the needs of their children?

teenagers become pregnant. The following facts about teenage pregnancy dramatically demonstrate its extent and effects:[1]

- In 1994, for women aged fifteen through nineteen, there were 62.1 births per 1,000, up from 59.9 in 1990. (Note that this is the *birth* rate, not the *pregnancy* rate. Many states do not report the number of teenagers who have had abortions, so there is really no way of determining the pregnancy rate for the nation as a whole.)

- For states that do report pregnancy rates, Georgia had the highest, with 110.6 per 1,000 teenage women.

- Mississippi has the highest birth rate for teenagers, with 81 births per 1,000.

Concerned legislators, public policy developers, and national leaders view teenage pregnancy as symptomatic of the problems of society in general. They worry about the demand for public health and welfare services, envision a drain on taxpayer dollars, and decry the loss of future potential because of school dropouts. From an early childhood point of view, teenage pregnancies create greater demand for infant and toddler child care and programs to help teenagers learn how to be good parents. The staff of an early childhood program must often provide nurturance for both children and parents, because the parents themselves may not be emotionally mature. Emotional maturity is necessary for parents to engage in a giving relationship with children. Early childhood professionals must nurture and help teenage parents who lack parenting characteristics of any kind.

On the other end of the continuum, some parents have sufficient disposable income and are willing to spend it on enriching their and their children's lives. Parents enroll themselves and their infants and toddlers in self-improvement programs promoted as physi-

cally and cognitively stimulating. Courses designed for expectant parents, new parents, and grandparents are now a standard part of the curriculum of many community colleges and schools. During one semester at a local community college, for example, parents could select from these courses: Parent/Infant Enrichment, Play Activities with the Preschool Child, Discipline Strategies That Work, Movement and Play Activities, Creative Learning—Storytelling/Drama, Toilet Learning, Choosing a Preschool for Your Child, Building Your Child's Self-Esteem, and Developmental Screening for Infants. Many of the courses required registration of both parents and their young children!

Stimulation/enrichment programs help popularize the importance of the very early years. Infant–parent stimulation programs catch the fancy of young parents who want "the best" for their children and are willing to spend time, effort, and money to see that they get it. This allows early childhood professionals to address the importance of the early years. It also creates a climate of acceptance for very early education and an arena in which early childhood professionals are heard. Infant stimulation programs stimulate more than infants. Parent groups discuss how to help children get along with others, how to cope with the loss of childhood, how to reduce stress in children's lives, how to nurture in the nineties, ways to accommodate diverse lifestyles, how to extend more rights to children, and how to parent in an electronic era, in which children seemingly see and know all.

Changing Families

The concept of "family" is in a continual state of change, as a result of the social issues discussed here and for many other reasons. The definition of what a family is varies as society changes. Consider the following ways families have changed in the twentieth century:

1. *Structure.* Families now include arrangements other than the traditional nuclear family:
   - single-parent families, headed by mothers or fathers
   - stepfamilies, including individuals related either by marriage or adoption
   - heterosexual, gay, or lesbian significant others living together as families
   - extended families, which may include grandparents, uncles, aunts, other relatives, and individuals not related by kinship

2. *Roles.* As families change, so do the roles that parents and other family members perform. For example:
   - More parents work and have less time for their children and family affairs.
   - Working parents must combine roles of both parents and employees. The many hats that parents wear increase as families change.

3. *Responsibilities.* As families change, many parents are not able to provide or cannot afford to pay for adequate and necessary care for their children. Some parents find that buffering their children from social ills such as drugs, violence, and delinquency is more than they can handle. Also, some parents are consumed by problems of their own and have little time or attention for their children.

As families continue to change, early childhood professionals must continue to develop creative ways to provide services to children and families.

Families and Early Childhood

How to best meet children's needs and how to best meet these needs in culturally appropriate ways are always primary goals of early childhood education. Early childhood professionals agree that a good way to meet the needs of children is through their families, whatever that family unit may be (Figure 2.4). Providing for children's needs through and within the family system makes sense for a number of reasons. First, this system has the primary responsibility for meeting many children's needs. So, helping families function means that everyone stands to benefit. Helping people in a family unit—mother, father, grandparents, and others—be better parents helps them and their children.

Second, family problems and issues must often be addressed first for children to be helped effectively. For example, helping parents gain access to adequate, affordable health care means that the whole family, including children, will be healthier.

Third, early childhood professionals can do many things concurrently with children and their families that will benefit both. Literacy is a good example. Early childhood professionals are taking a family approach to helping children, their parents, and other family members learn how to read, write, speak, and listen. Teaching parents to read helps them understand the importance of supporting and promoting their children in the learning and teaching process.

Fourth, addressing the needs of children and their families as a whole, known as a *holistic* approach to education and the delivery of services, enables early childhood professionals and others to address a range of social concerns simultaneously. Literacy, health care and education, abuse prevention, AIDS education, and parenting programs are examples of this family-centered approach. Professionals will expand and refine this approach throughout the coming years.

Figure 2.4/*Two Models Illustrating a New Paradigm for Providing Early Childhood Services*

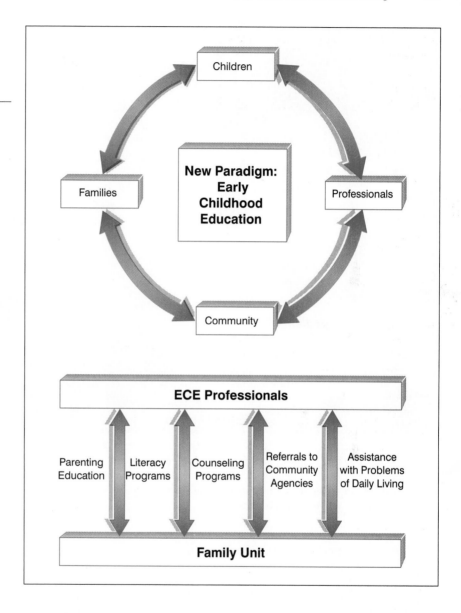

PARADIGM SHIFTS IN EARLY CHILDHOOD EDUCATION

Because of the changing needs of society and therefore of families, the field of early childhood education is in constant flux. It can truly be said about early childhood education that

change, often dramatic change, is predictable. The changes in early childhood education that occurred since 1980 have resulted in identifiable paradigm shifts. (A *paradigm* is a model for how things occur or happen.) Following are some of the critically important paradigm shifts occurring in early childhood education today:

Children's development begins in the family system. The family system, with the help and support of early childhood programs, provides for children's basic needs. It makes sense for early childhood professionals to work with and through the family system in the delivery of their services. How can you, as an early childhood professional, work in and through children's families to support their development?

- *Family-centered programs.* Early childhood professionals are now working within the family system to provide the most meaningful education and services to children and their families.

- *Two-generation programs.* It is common now for early childhood professionals to work with children and their parents, and in many cases grandparents, to develop such skills as literacy and parenting. Three-generational programs are becoming more commonplace.

- *Collaborative efforts with other agencies.* Increasing numbers of early childhood professionals are working cooperatively and collaboratively with professionals from other agencies to combine resources and to integrate their work.

- *An ecological/holistic approach.* Early childhood professionals now realize that they have to deliver a range of services to children and their families in family and community settings. Professionals recognize now more than ever that they must provide for children's physical, social, and emotional needs as well as for their cognitive needs.

- *Child-centered programs.* Increasingly, what early childhood professionals do in their programs focuses on the needs of children and their families rather than their own needs or those of their agencies. In addition, child-centered programs emphasize that actively involving children in learning is the preferred method of education and is the process by which children learn best. Today, the teaching/learning process centers on having children involved as active participants in their own learning and cognitive development as opposed to passive recipients of knowledge through teacher-directed learning, worksheets, and the like. Active learning is in; passivity is out.

Social changes that cause paradigm shifts in the field of early childhood education also form the basis for public policy pronouncements and initiatives. For example, today we hear a lot about the debate between those who believe the family is the most important unit in children's care, education, and development and those who believe that it "takes a village"—the community—to adequately rear and provide for children. Which approach is best, and how to implement each, is at the heart of public policy formulations.

Public Policy and Early Childhood Education

At no time in U.S. history has there been so much interest and involvement by early childhood professionals in the development of public policy. Public policies relating to early childhood education affect and influence the lives of children, parents, families,

and professionals working in the field. They are implemented through official statements, pronouncements, and legislation. Public policies determine what ages children can enter school, what immunizations are required before children enter any program, how child care programs should operate, and how to provide appropriate care and education for children with special needs.

Many social issues have tremendous public policy implications for young children, families, and early childhood professionals. For example, societal violence leads to proposals for how to protect children from violence, how to provide violence-free homes and educational environments, how to teach children to get along nonviolently with others, and how to reduce violence on television. How to reduce the amount of violence presented on television in turn leads to discussions and proposals for ways to limit children's television viewing (proposals include "pulling the plug" on television; use of the V-chip, which will enable parents to block out programs with violent content; boycotting companies whose advertisements support programs with violent content; and proposals to limit violence shown during primetime viewing hours). Early childhood professionals play important roles in these and other public policy debates and formulations. Throughout this text, you will find many other instances in which public policy outlines specific kinds of programs for children and families and the circumstances and funding under which they are to be delivered.

As early childhood professionals become increasingly involved in advocacy activities, they and their professional organizations issue position statements designed to influence public policy prior to its enactment and implementation. Child advocacy agencies draft position papers on topics ranging from developmentally appropriate practices for young children to the pros and cons of developing

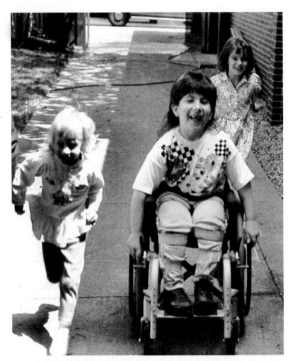

Early childhood professionals serve as strong advocates for children with special needs. Many gains by children and their families result from professionals and professional organizations playing important advocacy roles. In what ways can you be an advocate for young children and families?

public school programs for four-year-olds. NAEYC, for example, is a strong advocate for developmentally appropriate practices in early childhood programs. Agencies such as the Children's Defense Fund influence national and state legislation for programs to help children and families. This political reality is beneficial to all—children, parents, families, and early childhood professionals—for it helps ensure that policymakers will consider children's and families' best interests when making decisions that affect them.

Evidence of Public Interest in Early Childhood Daily newspapers provide ample evidence of the nation's interest in young children. Figure 2.5 shows a few recent newspaper headlines that have called attention to young children, their parents, families, and agencies that serve them.

Mass media magazines such as *Working Mother* and *Parenting,* which include child-rearing information, help quench the insatiable desire of parents and the public for information about child care and rearing. Many agencies such as hospitals and health clinics also provide parent-oriented publications.

Figure 2.5/*Early Childhood in the News*

"Early Learning Crucial for Children" (*Chicago Tribune,* May 9, 1996)

"Officials Wary of Early-School Price Tag" (*Boston Globe,* January 5, 1996)

"Kindergarten Cutback Plan Angers Parents—Fight Move to Half-Day Classes" (*Dallas Morning News,* March 3, 1996)

"Politics and People: A Much Needed Rally for Children" (*Wall Street Journal,* May 30, 1996)

"Concerned Parents Push Character Movement" (*Los Angeles Times,* May 28, 1996)

"Is Your Child Safe?" (*Chicago Tribune,* March 9, 1996)

""First Lady's Wish is to Help Women, Children Overcome" (*Chicago Tribune,* February 19, 1997)

"Hoping for Best on Child Care" (*Boston Globe,* February 8, 1997)

"Volunteer Tutors: Can They Teach Johnny to Read" (*Christian Science Monitor,* February 5, 1997)

Politics and Early Childhood Education

The more early childhood is in the news, the more it generates public interest and attention; this is part of the political context of early childhood education. And, whatever else can be said about education, one point holds true: education is political. Politicians and politics exert a powerful influence in determining what gets taught, how it is taught, to whom it is taught, and by whom. Early childhood education is no exception.

An important political and educational event occurred in 1989 when President George Bush and the governors of all fifty states met at the University of Virginia to set national education goals. One result of this meeting was the release in 1991 of *America 2000: An Education Strategy,* which outlined six educational goals or national standards. These, and two additional goals, were passed as part of the Goals 2000: Educate America Act in 1994. The eight goals are shown in Figure 2.6.

These goals have generated a great deal of debate, particularly concerning what they mean and how best to achieve them. Goals 1, 2, 6, 7, and 8 have had and will continue to have particular implications for early childhood education. Goal 1 obviously affects children's readiness for school. Goal 2 is pertinent because the early childhood years are seen as the place to prevent school dropout. Many public school programs for three- and four-year-old children are funded specifically as beginning efforts to keep children in school at a later age. Goal 6 has encouraged many intergenerational literacy and family literacy programs in which children, their parents, and other family members are taught to read. Goal 7 supports the drug prevention programs implemented in early childhood programs, again on the premise that early prevention is much more effective than later treatment. And, goal 8 makes implicit as part of national policy the importance of home–school partnerships. Implementation of goal 8 is treated in detail in Chapter 15.

Figure 2.6/*Goals 2000*

The Goals 2000: Educate America Act includes these eight goals to be achieved by 2000:

1. All children in America will start school ready to learn.
2. The high school graduation rate will increase to at least 90 percent.
3. All students will leave grades four, eight, and twelve having demonstrated competency over challenging subject matter . . . , and [all students will be] prepared for responsible citizenship, further learning, and productive employment.
4. The nation's teaching force will have access to programs for the continued improvement of their professionals skills.
5. The United States students will be first in the world in mathematics and science achievement.
6. Every adult American will be literate.
7. Every school in America will be free of drugs and violence and will offer a disciplined environment conducive to learning.
8. Every school and home will engage in partnerships that will increase parental involvement and participation in promoting the social, emotional, and academic growth of children.

Source: U.S. Department of Education, 1994.

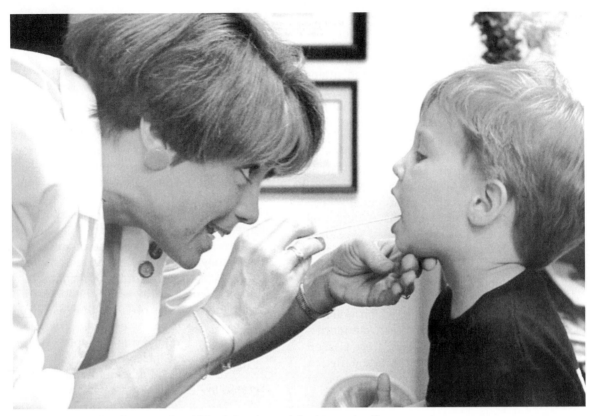

Readiness is now viewed as promoting children's learning and development in all areas. Readiness includes health and physical growth, such as being well rested, fed, and properly immunized. If children are physically, socially, and emotionally healthy, they are more motivated to learn. How does children's health status affect their readiness for learning?

Readiness   Goal 1, known as "the readiness goal," has generated particular interest in early childhood education among politicians and early childhood professionals in determining precisely what readiness means. This examination has resulted in a reconceptualization of readiness.

Previously, *readiness* was generally viewed as the process of children getting ready for school. In this sense, readiness has been viewed in relation to school and the ability to read and write. This conception has traditionally placed on children responsibility for "getting ready." It also implies that if a child is not ready, as judged by a test or some other criteria, then the child should not enter kindergarten, first grade, or other program. This practice often leads to keeping children out of school for a year while they "get ready" or failing them or holding them back in kindergarten or preschool.

The early childhood profession would like to get away from the use of the term *readiness*. Instead, professionals would like to hold their discussions wihin and direct their actions around the context of "children's learning and development." The National Education Goals Panel, the group charged with assessing the nation's progress toward achieving U.S. education goals by the year 2000, has identified five "critical dimensions" as constituting children's early learning and development.

- *Physical well-being and motor development*—health and physical growth, ranging from being rested, fed properly, immunized, and healthy to being able to run, jump, use crayons, and work puzzles

- *Social and emotional development*—the sense of personal well-being that allows a child to participate fully and constructively in classroom activities

- *Approaches toward learning*—the curiosity, creativity, motivation, independence, cooperativeness, interest, and persistence that enable children from all cultures to maximize their learning

- *Language usage*—talking, listening, scribbling, and composing that enable children to communicate effectively and express thoughts, feelings, and experiences

- *Cognition and general knowledge*—familiarity with basic information, including patterns, relationships, and cause and effect, needed to solve problems in everyday life

These dimensions bring more meaning to the concept and process of readiness. They enable early childhood professionals to focus on specific skills, behaviors, and attitudes that will enable children to be successful in school and in life.

State Involvement in Early Childhood Programs

Beginning about 1980, the federal government began cutting many program budgets and this cutting, and in some cases elimina-tion of programs, continues in the 1990s. Federal monies had a stimulating effect on early childhood programs in the 1960s and 1970s, but these cuts have had a dampening effect. Private agencies and state governments had to take over support of some programs, and others had to close, so that some families and children had to cope with reduced services or no services at all.

All the fifty states are taking a lead in developing programs for young children, stimulated by these budgetary changes. As federal dollars shift to other programs, states are responding by initiating programs of their own, funded from both federal allocations and other sources, including lottery monies and increased taxes on commodities and consumer goods such as cigarettes.

In addition, instead of giving monies directly to specific programs, many federal dollars are consolidated into what are known as *block grants*—sums of money given to states to provide services according to broad general guidelines. In essence, the states, not the federal government, control how the money is spent and the nature of the programs funded. As targeted federal support for early education becomes subject to different methods of funding, it may well be that states will finance replacement, alternative, and substitute programs. This involvement will grow and strengthen as the states make greater commitments to child care and early education programs, especially for children from low-income families. For example, the majority of states have appropriated monies for prekindergarten programs to serve at-risk four-year-old children.

This trend will accelerate. With direct funding comes control. When agencies contribute funding for programs, they also help determine the direction the programs will take, the policies that govern them, and which children and families they will serve. Federal support for early childhood and related programs

Figure 2.7/*Percentage of Families with Children Living in Poverty*

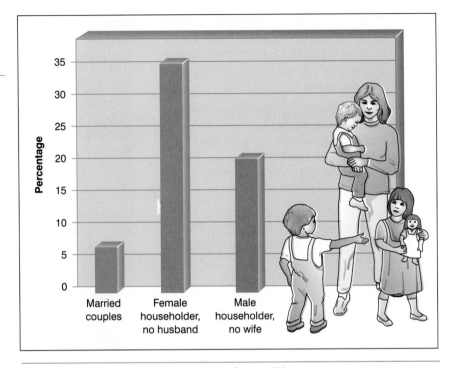

Source: U.S. Department of Commerce, Bureau of the Census, 1995.

will likely continue to be scarce, with the exception of Head Start. Increased support from private agencies, contributions, and volunteerism constitute legitimate alternatives to federal funds.

Not everyone, however, agrees that declining federal support for early childhood and other programs is a good idea. Critics of the declining federal presence in early childhood programs maintain that the results are harmful for women, children, and families. They specifically cite increases in the number of women and children living in poverty and a higher infant mortality rate. Figure 2.7 shows the percentage of families living in poverty. Note particularly that experienced in single-female-headed families.

Advocacy Reduced funding for early childhood programs requires early childhood pro-

fessionals to be strong advocates on behalf of children and their families. Early professionals should be in the vanguard of efforts to influence public policy and develop public awareness about providing for children in the early years. Programs that commit to and depend on federal monies must recognize their vulnerability to shifts in political attitudes and to swings, both up and down, in federal support. Agencies that provide money can also take it away. Strong advocacy is part of the solution to this dilemma.

The Public Schools and Early Education

Traditionally, the majority of preschool programs were operated by private agencies or agencies supported wholly or in part by federal funds to help the poor, the unemployed, working parents, and disadvantaged chil-

Kidwatching
Developing Skills in Observation

There is only one basis for observation: the children must be free to express themselves and thus reveal those needs and attitudes which would otherwise remain hidden or repressed in an environment that did not permit them to act spontaneously. An observer obviously needs something to observe, and if he must be trained in order to be able to see and recognize objective truth, he must also have at his disposal children placed in such an environment that they can manifest their natural traits.

(Maria Montessori,
The Discovery of the Child
[New York: Ballantine Books, 1980], p. 46)

What Is Observation?

Professionals recognize that children are more than what is measured by any particular test. Observation is an "authentic" means of learning about children and what they know and are able to do, especially as it occurs in more *naturalistic settings* such as classrooms, child care centers, playgrounds, and homes. Observation is the intentional, systematic looking at the behavior of a child or children in a particular setting, program, or situation. Observation is sometimes referred to as "kidwatching," and is an excellent way to find out about children's behaviors and learning.

Purposes of Observation

Observation is designed to gather information on which to base decisions, make recommendations, develop curriculum, plan activities and learning strategies, and to assess children's growth, development, and learning. For example, sometimes when professionals and parents look at children, they do not really see or concern themselves with what children are doing or why children are engaged in a particular behavior or activity as long as children are safe and orderly. However, children's behaviors provide insight into children and their behaviors. The significance and importance of critical behaviors go undetected if observation is done casually and is limited to "unsystematic looking." The purposes of observation then include:

- *To determine the cognitive, linguistic, social, emotional, and physical development of children.* A developmental checklist (see Figure A) is one way professionals can systematically observe and chart the development of children.
- *To identify children's interests and learning styles.* Today, teachers are very interested in developing learning activities, materials, and classroom centers based on children's interests, preferences, and learning styles.

Figure A/*Emergent Literacy Behaviors Checklist*
Use the following checklist to assess and date the student's progress as an emergent reader and writer.

Name: Age:	Observed	Not Observed
demonstrates visual acuity		
demonstrates hearing acuity		
Print Concepts		
recognizes left-to-right sequencing		
recognizes top, down directionality		
asks what print says		
connects meaning between two objects, pictures		
models reading out loud		
models adult silent reading (newspapers, books, etc.)		
recognizes that print has different meanings (informational, entertainment, etc.)		
Comprehension Behaviors		
follows oral directions		
draws correct pictures from oral directions		
recognizes story sequence in pictures		
interprets pictures		
sees links in story ideas		
links personal experiences with text (story, title)		
logically reasons story plot/conclusions		
sees patterns in similar stories		
Writing Behaviors		
makes meaningful scribbles (attempts to make letter-like shapes)		
draws recursive scribbles (rows of cursive-like writing)		
makes strings of "letters"		
uses one or more consonants to represent words		
uses inventive spellings		

- **To plan.** The professional practice of teaching requires planning on a daily, ongoing basis. Observation provides useful, authentic, and solid information enabling teachers to intentionally plan for activities rather than to make decisions on little or no information.
- **To meet the needs of individual children.** Meeting the needs of individual children is an important part of teaching and learning. Observation provides information about the individual needs of children. For example, a child may be advanced cognitively but be overly aggressive and lack the social skills necessary to play cooperatively and interact with others. Through observation, a teacher can gather information to develop a plan for helping the child learn how to play with others.
- **To determine progress.** Systematic observation, over time, provides a rich, valuable, and informative source of information about how individual children and groups of children are learning and progressing in their learning and behavior.
- **To provide information to parents.** Professionals report to and conference with parents on an ongoing basis. Observational information adds to other information teachers have, such as test results and child work samples, and provides a fuller and more complete picture of individual children.
- **Self-insight.** Observational information can help professionals learn more about themselves and what to do to help children.

Advantages of Intentional, Systematic Observation

There are a number of advantages to gathering data through observation:

- One advantage to systematic, purposeful observation is that it enables professionals to collect information about children they might not otherwise gather through other sources. A great deal of the consequences, causes, and reactions to children's behavior can only be assessed through observation. Observation enables you to gather data that cannot be assessed by formal, standardized tests, questioning, or parent and child interviews.
- Observation is ideally suited to learning more about children in play settings. Observation affords you the opportunity to note a child's social behavior in a play group and discern how cooperatively he or she interacts with peers. Observing a child at play gives professionals a wealth of information about developmental levels, social skills, and what the child is or is not learning in play settings.
- Observation allows you to learn a lot about children's prosocial behavior and peer interactions. It can help you plan for appropriate and inclusive activities to promote the social growth of young children. Additionally, your observations can serve as the basis for developing multicultural activities to benefit all children.
- Observation of children's abilities provides a basis for the assessment of what they are able to do developmentally. Many learning skills are developed sequentially, such as the refinement of large motor skills before small motor skills. Through observation, professionals can determine whether children's abilities are within a normal range of growth and development.
- Observation is useful to assess children's performance over time. Documentation of daily, weekly, and monthly observations of children's behaviors and learning provides a database for the cumulative evaluation of each child's achievement and development.
- Observation helps you provide concrete information for use in reporting to and conferencing with parents. Increasingly, reports to parents about children involve professionals' observations and children's work samples so parents and educators can collaborate to determine how to help children develop cognitively, socially, emotionally, and physically.

In summary, intentional observation is a useful, informative, and powerful means for informing and guiding teaching and helping ensure the learning of all children.

Steps for Conducting Observations

The steps involved in the process of systematic, purposeful observation are shown in Figure B.

STEP 1: Plan for Observation

Planning is an important part of the observation process. Everything you do regarding observation should be planned for in advance of the observation. A good guide to follow in planning is to ask the questions who, what, where, when, and how.

Setting goals for observation is an important part of the planning process. Goals allow you to reflect on *why* you want to observe and thus direct your efforts to *what* you will observe. Stating a goal focuses your attention on the purpose of your observation. Goals, for example, that direct your attention to the effectiveness of your efforts in providing an inclusive classroom, program, and efforts to fully include an exceptional child into the classroom might read like this:

Goal #1: To determine what modifications might be necessary in the classroom to facilitate access to all parts of the classroom for Dana in her wheelchair.

Goal #2: To assess the development of prosocial behavioral characteristics other children display to Dana while interacting in the classroom.

STEP 2: Conduct the Observation

While conducting your observation, it is imperative that you be objective, specific, and as thorough as possible. For example, during your observation of Dana and her peers you notice that there is not enough room for Dana to manipulate her wheelchair past the easel and shelf where the crayons are kept. None of her peers noticed that Dana could not reach the crayons and helped her get them. Dana had to ask one of the children to get the crayons for her.

STEP 3: Interpret the Data

All observations can and should result in some kind of interpretation. Interpretation serves several important functions. First, it puts your observations into perspective, that is, in relation to what you already know and do not know of events and behaviors of your children. Second, interpretation helps you make sense of what you have observed and enables you to use your professional knowledge to interpret what you have seen. Third, interpretation has the potential to make you grow as a professional and learn to anticipate representative behavior indicative of normal growth and development under given conditions and what might not be representative of appropriate growth, development, and learning for each child. Fourth, interpretation forms the foundation for the implementation, necessary adaptations, or modifications in a program or curriculum. In this observation, you can note that Dana's only exceptionality is that she is physically disabled. Her growth in other areas is normal, and she displays excellent social skills in that she is accepted by others, knows when to ask for help, and is able to ask for help. When Dana asks for help, she receives it.

STEP 4: Implement the Data

The implementation phase means that you commit to do something with the results of the "findings" of your observation. For example, although Dana's behavior in your observation was appro-

Figure B/*Four Steps for Effective Observation*

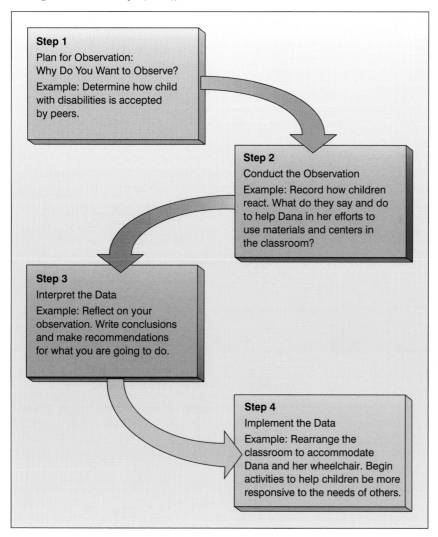

Step 1

Plan for Observation:
Why Do You Want to Observe?

Example: Determine how child with disabilities is accepted by peers.

Step 2

Conduct the Observation

Example: Record how children react. What do they say and do to help Dana in her efforts to use materials and centers in the classroom?

Step 3

Interpret the Data

Example: Reflect on your observation. Write conclusions and make recommendations for what you are going to do.

Step 4

Implement the Data

Example: Rearrange the classroom to accommodate Dana and her wheelchair. Begin activities to help children be more responsive to the needs of others.

priate, many of the children can benefit from activities designed to help them recognize and respond to the needs of others. The physical environment of the classroom as well needs some modification in the rearrangement of mov-able furniture to make it more accessible for Dana. Also, implementation means you report to parents or others. Implementing, that is, doing something with the results of your observations, is the most important part of the process.

Observation In Action

Welcome to Ms. Liz's classroom. Will is the child you will be observing. He is the energetic young boy dressed in overalls and a yellow shirt. You are encouraged to learn as much as you can about Will, his peers, his teacher (Ms. Liz), and the classroom. Before you focus on individual photographs, observe the classroom in general. Reflect on the following questions:

- What general statements would you make regarding classroom arrangement, organization, materials, and equipment? Based on your observation, what recommendations would you make if this were your classroom? Would you arrange your classroom differently?
- Based on your observation of the children's involvement with materials and their peers, what can you say about their development, social competence, and play behavior? How do the children and Ms. Liz get along?
- Do the children in the classroom feel comfortable taking risks, working together, and expressing emotions?
- Do you think Ms. Liz operates a child-centered classroom? How does your observation support your answer?
- Do you think the children spend more time participating in hands-on experiences or teacher-related experiences?
- Can Ms. Liz's classroom be characterized as an active learning environment? How and why?
- What can you infer regarding gender equity and how boys and girls are treated in Ms. Liz's classroom?

- List five things children learn from large motor activities. How does outdoor play support children's learning?

Literacy development is important in early childhood programs. In P–1, what is Ms. Liz doing to support the children's literacy development? What can you infer from the children's behavior regarding their literacy development? Note in P–2 how Ms. Liz supports Will's autonomy and "what he can do for himself." Based on your observation in P–3, what are five things Will knows about reading? What do you notice about the behavior of Will's peers? What does their behavior indicate to you?

P–1

P–2

P–3

Personal Reflection: Focus once again on P–2. Do you agree with Ms. Liz allowing Will to take the picture book from her? Would you have allowed Will to read the book to the other children? What can Ms. Liz do to involve the other children in Will's retelling of the story?

P–4

In P–4, you see Will and his friend Ryan building a tall tower. What can you tell about Will's willingness to engage in cooperative play with other children? What can you infer from Will's behavior and facial expression about the activity? Observe how the top of the red tower is falling on the child behind Will.

Personal Reflection: Would you allow Will and his peers to build their tower as high as they are building it? Why or why not?

P–5

In P–5, observe how Will responds to the accident of the falling tower. What does Will's behavior tell you? What can you tell about Ms. Liz's behavior? What can you say about the behavior of Ryan (the child in the background behind Ms. Liz)?

Personal Reflection: As a classroom teacher, how would you handle a situation in which a child was not seriously injured?

P–6

Personal Reflection: According to Parten, how would you categorize Will and Megan's play behavior in P–6? Based on your observation, what are some things that Will and Megan are learning? Are the materials appropriate for them to use?

P–7

Observe Will's determination and physical effort in P–7. What are some things you can learn through observation in the outdoors? What developmental skills is Will enhancing through his outdoor play?

Personal Reflection: What are some outdoor activities that you would include in your early childhood program? How would you provide for Will's safety and the safety of all children in outdoor play? What are some inferences you can make about outdoor safety?

P–8

During the parent-teacher conference depicted in P–8, observe Will's facial expression and body language. What do they tell you? Does Will's mother seem supportive of him?

Personal Reflection: Will is participating in the conference between Will's mother and Ms. Liz. Do you think he should or should not be involved in the parent-teacher conference? Why or why not? Do you think Ms. Liz and Will's mother value Will's participation? What are the pros and cons of Will participating in the conference?

Merrill/Prentice Hall thanks Director Vicki Yun, Ms. Liz, Will Sims, and the children of LaPetite Academy of Dublin, Ohio, for allowing us to take photographs. Photos by Anthony Magnacca.

Using an Observational Guide

Observation is a valuable tool for all professionals and should help inform them and guide your teaching of young children. A sample observation form you can use is shown in Figure C. You can also check other sources to develop more specific observation guides you could use as checklists to track developmental behaviors with individual children.

Figure C/*A Sample Observation Guide*

Name: (Your Name) _____

Date: _____

Time: _____

Location: _____

Classroom or Setting: _____

Purpose of Observing: _____

Prediction or Expectations of Findings: _____

Significant Events During Observation:

Reflective Analysis of Significant Events: (This reflection should include what you have learned.)

List at least three ways you can use or apply what you observed to your future teaching.

dren. But times have changed. All parents exert great pressure on public school officials and state legislatures to sponsor and fund additional preschool and early childhood programs. Increasingly, preschools provide a full range of services for children and families with an emphasis on providing for the whole child.

Another trend is to conduct preschool programs in the public schools. Currently, California, Florida, New York, North Carolina, and Texas support preschools, and nationwide, about 500,000 preschool children are enrolled in public school programs. As preschool programs admit more three- and four-year-olds nationwide, opportunities for teachers of young children will grow.

The spread of preschools reflects changing family patterns, especially the rise in single-parent families and families with two adult wage earners. Demand for preschools also relates to their use in early childhood intervention programs and to the popular belief that three- and four-year-old children are ready, willing, and able to learn.

Parents lobby for public support of early childhood education for a number of reasons. First, because working parents cannot find quality child care for their children, they believe the public schools hold the solution to child care needs. Second, the persistent belief that children are a nation's greatest wealth makes it seem sensible to provide services to avoid future school and learning problems. Third, many people believe that early public schooling, especially for children from low-income families, is necessary if the United States is to promote equal opportunity for all. They argue that low-income children begin school already far behind their more fortunate middle-class counterparts, and that the best way to keep them from falling hopelessly behind is for them to begin school earlier. Fourth, some parents cannot afford quality child care. They believe preschools, furnished

at the public's expense, are a reasonable, cost-efficient way to meet child care needs. A fifth reason for the demand for public school involvement relates to the "competent child." Parents want academic programs for their children at an earlier age and look, naturally, to the public schools to provide programs that will help their children succeed in life. Sixth, today's parents are the best educated in U.S. history. These well-educated parents are causing a boom in preschool programs that emphasize earlier and more comprehensive education for young children.

The alignment of the public schools with early childhood programs is becoming increasingly popular. Several arguments favor such an alignment. First, some professionals think it is not wise to train nonteachers for

Early public schooling is a reality for growing numbers of the nation's children. Research clearly shows that the early years are important years for learning. It makes sense then to provide preschool and early intervention services for young children. What evidence can you see that children are beginning the schooling process at earlier ages?

preschool positions when trained professionals are available. Second, some professionals think it makes sense to put the responsibility for educating and caring for the nation's children under the sponsorship of one agency—the public schools. For their part, public school teachers and the unions that represent them are anxious to bring early childhood programs within the structure of the public school system. Third, many public schools have already moved into the area of child care and preschool programs for three- and four-year-old children.

There is by no means consensus that universal public schooling or even anything approaching it should be available for very young children. Critics of the effort to place preschool programs in the public schools give three reasons for their stance. First, they cite the failure of public education to do a good job of teaching young children for whom they currently provide programs. They ask, "How can public schools handle an expanded role if they have not done a good job with what they are already supposed to do?" Second, some critics say that public school teachers are not trained in the specific skills needed in Head Start, child care, and other preschool programs. A third, more convincing argument relates to money: Having the public schools assume the responsibility of preschool programs would probably cost several billion dollars.

Nonetheless, it seems inevitable that the presence of the public schools in early childhood education will continue to expand. Given the fact that so many public schools offer programs for three- and four-year-olds, can programs for infants and toddlers be far behind?

Business Involvement in Early Childhood Programs

Many corporations and businesses are finding that early childhood education is a good investment. Corporations are increasingly dissatisfied with the products of the nation's schools. They have to spend millions of dollars teaching their employees such basic skills as reading and writing. Corporate executives think it makes more sense to invest in literacy in the early rather than in the later years. In this sense, corporations see their investments in children and families as social investments; that is, investing in children and families pays dividends to all. This social investment approach to early childhood and other programs is also based in part on economics. A dollar invested in quality child care, drug prevention programs, literacy programs, and health programs (e.g., immunizations) will save money later through drug-free, literate, healthy adults. (One formula that corporate executives and politicians often use is that $1 invested in the early childhood years saves $7 in the adolescent and adult years.)

Consequently, companies such as American Telephone & Telegraph and Johnson & Johnson are spending considerable amounts of money on early childhood programs. The Stride Rite Corporation in particular has a reputation as a leader in providing programs for children and families. Stride Rite was the first company to provide on-site child care for its employees (see Figure 3.1, the Time Line, in Chap. 3) and the first to offer intergenerational care for children and the elderly in the same facility. Additionally, many corporations such as Barnett Bank and Glaxo Wellcome provide on-site child care services. A description of these programs and Stride Rite's appears in the second color insert, "Observing Progams in Action."

Increasingly, the private and governmental sectors are asking businesses to help them assist underserved populations. For example, the federal government is seeking business aid in paying for a new pregnancy handbook designed to help reduce the infant mortality rate. The eighty-two-page *Health*

New Beginnings

A Community Collaboration

New Beginnings is a collaborative effort involving San Diego, San Diego County, San Diego City Schools, the San Diego Housing Commission, and the San Diego Community College District. These five public agencies, along with the University of California–San Diego and the Children's Hospital and Health Center, are engaged in a long-term effort of institutional change as well as providing school-linked direct services to children and families.

The New Beginnings concept of interagency collaboration began in 1988 in a series of conversations among executives from the major public agencies serving children and families in San Diego County. The executives agreed that children and families in poverty in their communities had urgent needs and that their agencies provided services to many of the same children and families. They were concerned that none of the agencies were able to focus effectively on preventing negative outcomes for children. From these initial conversations grew a commitment to refocus and restructure public services so that they would be more effective and accessible to families.

Identifying Family Needs

A feasibility study conducted in 1990 focused on the needs of families and children at Hamilton Elementary School, which serves nearly 1,300 children in grades K through 5 in a densely populated, ethnically diverse, low-income neighborhood of East San Diego. One aspect of the feasibility study placed a social worker from the Department of Social Services on the school site to work with families and children. Other components included interviews with families in their homes, meetings with families at the school, and analyses of how clients are served by multiple agencies. The information gathered was used to develop findings, conclusions, and a plan for implementation. A major conclusion of the study was that most of the constraints limiting integrated services are issues of policy or practice, not insurmountable legal obstacles.

New Beginnings is not a project or program to be taken as a package and implemented. Rather, it is a set of basic principles:

- Services and activities for families need to be focused on prevention.
- Services need to be for families as a whole, not fragmented by the presenting "problem" or a single "client."
- Services need to be responsive to the needs of families, not the convenience of agencies and their staff.
- Agencies need to reallocate and realign resources that already exist before looking for infusions of new money.
- Implementation of the collaborative process and the basic principles needs to be adapted to the needs of each community.

A Multiservice Center

The first application of these concepts is at a demonstration site located on the campus of Hamilton Academic Achievement Academy. This is a multiservice center designed to provide accessible, nonfragmented access to families in the school's attendance area. Services provided at the center, opened in September 1991, include information and referral, parenting and adult education classes, workshops, counseling, case management, family advocacy, and service planning. The center also provides basic health care, including immunizations, Child Health and Disability Prevention (CHDP) exams, and minor treatment, as well as mental health services for children. The staff at the center includes a coordinator, an administrative assistant, a secretary/receptionist, and three full-time and three part-time family service advocates. Coming from existing partner agencies to work in new roles, staff members form an interdisciplinary service team to help meet the many needs of families and children. Other members of the extended team remain in their home agencies but provide services specifically targeted to families in the Hamilton attendance area.

Contributed by Carrie Peery, principal, Hamilton Academic Achievement Academy—the site of New Beginnings, Integrated Services for Children and Families, San Diego, CA.

Diary provides information on prenatal care and health care for children during the first two years of life. The $6.00 publication is also seen as a means of empowering parents and actively involving them in their health and that of their children. Federal officials will use the money from businesses to distribute free copies of the *Health Diary* in fifteen cities participating in Healthy Start, a federal program begun in 1991 to improve prenatal care.

In short, early childhood education and young children have captured the attention of the nation. They compete with budget deficits, nuclear arms treaties, and summit meetings for primetime media attention. Consequently, early childhood professionals must learn more about how to care for, educate, and rear children so they can advise parents, legislators, and those who formulate public policy when looked to for guidance in determining what is best for the nation's children.

The Ecology of Early Childhood

Public policy initiatives and legislation are implemented in programs such as child care centers, public schools, and community agencies, and within families and homes. It is therefore important for us to consider these environments. *Ecology* is the study of how people interact with their environments and the consequences (good and bad) of these interactions. Early childhood professionals are very much interested in how children interact with their environments and how an environment affects them.

Early childhood ecological considerations apply to three levels. The first level is an examination of environments, how they are structured and arranged to promote children's maximum growth. For example, early childhood professionals are sensitive to the influence the child care environment has on health, safety, and physical and intellectual develop-

ment. Sensitive professionals seek ways to structure environments so they are less stressful, more healthful, less dangerous, and more accommodating to children's developmental needs. Likewise, they arrange environments to welcome and support parents. For example, many early childhood programs provide parent rooms and lounges and furnish them with couches, comfortable chairs, parenting pamphlets, magazines, and other material that supports children's literacy development.

At the second level, early childhood professionals focus on how environments interact with each other. Professionals and parents are both part of children's environments, and how they interact affects children. For example, the extent to which a child's home and family supports her literacy development greatly influences how well she learns to speak, write, and read. An unfavorable ecological setting, one without printed materials—books, magazines, and newspapers—and that does not encourage language development, negatively influences a child's literacy development. Early childhood professionals who are attuned to the importance of the interaction between educational settings and homes will initiate programs of parent involvement and family support.

Political and social environments represent a third, more abstract level of interaction. For example, in Florida, kindergarten is compulsory for all children five years of age as of September 1. What effects does such political policy have on young children? Some people worry that children who are five by September 1 are "too old" when they enter kindergarten. Others are concerned about the cost and trauma parents undergo to find quality child care because their children were born a day or month too late. Others see an advantage to the September 1 age limit in that children are older when they come to school and therefore are more "ready" to learn. Early childhood professionals try to influence political processes so they are most beneficial to and supportive of children's and families' growth and development.

Ecological considerations interest early childhood and child development researchers in another way. They want to know how children's natural environments—their homes, families, child care centers, peer groups, and communities—influence their behavior. Say, for example, that a researcher is interested in knowing more about the factors that affect young children's toy selection. She designs a laboratory experiment, gathers data, and arrives at certain conclusions. But these laboratory conclusions may not explain how children choose toys in their homes. Members of the early childhood profession, parents, social workers, legislators, and others are beginning to care about such ecological relationships. Such considerations will undoubtedly play an even more important role in early childhood as the years go by. Crucial to such discussions are the views people have of young children, and how those views affect their attitudes and opinions.

How Do Views of Children Make Lasting Influences?

How people view children determines how they teach and rear them and how society responds to their needs. As you read here about how people and society view children, try to clarify and change, when appropriate, what you believe. Also, identify social, environmental, and political factors that tend to support each particular view. Sometimes, of course, views overlap, so it is possible to synthesize ideas from several perspectives into a particular personal view.

Miniature Adults Childhood has not always been considered a distinct period of life. During medieval times, the notion of childhood did not exist; little distinction was made between children and adults. The con-

cept of children as miniature adults was logical for the time and conditions of medieval Europe. Economic conditions did not allow for a long childhood dependency. The only characteristics that separated children from adults were size and age. Children were expected to act as adults in every way, and they did so.

In many respects the twentieth century is no different, because children are still viewed and treated as adults. Concern is growing that childhood as we knew or remember it is disappearing. Children are viewed as pseudoadults; they even dress like adults, in designer clothes and expensive athletic shoes. Some believe that childhood is not only endangered but already gone. Others fear that, even when allowed a childhood, children are hurried and forced to grow up too fast too soon.

Childhood and children are endangered in another way. In many countries of Latin America, Africa, and Asia, children are, of necessity, expected to be economically productive. They are members of the adult working world at age four, five, or six. The United Nations Educational, Scientific and Cultural Organization (UNESCO) estimates that 100 million children around the world work and live in city streets. In many countries children are involved in war as active participants and casualties. In the United States, as in many urban areas, children participate in gang-related and other activities as though they were adults. Almost daily, newspapers show these children dead or wounded and waiting for help.

In the United States, where child labor laws protect children from the world of adult work and exploitation, some people advocate allowing children to enter the workplace at earlier ages and for lower wages. In some rural settings, young children still have economic value. Approximately one million migrant children annually pick crops and help their parents earn a livelihood (see Chap. 10). At

Although children have been and still are viewed as miniature adults, early childhood professionals should not treat them as such. What are some educational consequences of treating children as miniature adults?

the other end of the spectrum, child actors and models engage in highly profitable, and what some call glamorous, careers.

Encouraging children to act like adults and hurrying them toward adulthood causes conflicts between capabilities and expectations, particularly when early childhood professionals demand adultlike behavior from children and set unrealistic expectations. Problems associated with learning, behavior, and social skills can occur when children are constantly presented with tasks and ac-

tivities that are developmentally inappropriate for them.

The Competent Child   The 1960s ushered in a renewal of interest in very young children and how they learn. Many research studies (see Chap. 3) have focused on the importance of the early years and challenged professionals and parents to reconsider the role early learning plays in lifelong learning. As a result of this renewed interest, parents placed great intellectual importance on early learning. This change in parental attitudes resulted in what David Elkind calls the "concept of the competent infant." He believes that this image of competency is promoted and reinforced by such social conditions as divorce, increasing numbers of single parents, and two-career families. Elkind explains as follows:

The concept of the competent infant is clearly more in keeping with these contemporary family styles. . . . A competent infant can cope with the separation from parents at an early age. He or she is able to adjust with minimal difficulty to babysitters, day care centers, full-day nursery schools and so on. If some parents feel residual pangs of guilt about leaving their young offspring in out-of-home care, they can place their youngster in a high-pressure academic program. If the child were not in such a program, the parents tell themselves, he or she would fall behind peers and would not be able to compete academically when it is time to enter kindergarten. From this perspective, high-pressure academic programs are for the young child's "own good."[2]

Many parents embrace the concept of the competent child as compatible with what they want to achieve in their own lives. Upwardly mobile, career-oriented parents want children who can achieve at an early age. Parents want to begin early to assure success and advancement for their competent children. The view of the competent child is alive and well in the United States. Indeed, some parents believe that their children possess the competence and resiliency to deal with the problems associated with growing up as well as divorce, poverty, and lack of health care.

The Child as Sinful

Based primarily on the religious belief in original sin, the view of the child as sinful was widely accepted in the fourteenth through eighteenth centuries, and particularly in colonial North America during the Puritan era of the sixteenth and seventeenth centuries. Misbehavior was a sign of this inherent sin. Those who sought to correct misbehavior emphasized forcing children to behave and using corporal punishment whenever "necessary." Misbehavior was taken as proof of the devil's influence, and "beating the devil out" of the child was an acceptable solution.

This view of inherent sinfulness persists, manifested in the belief that children need to be controlled through rigid supervision and insistence on unquestioning obedience to and respect for adults. Educational institutions are perceived as places in which children can be taught "right" behavior. The number of private and parochial or religious schools that emphasize respect, obedience, and correct behavior is growing because of parents' hopes of rearing children who are less susceptible to the temptations of crime, drugs, and declining moral values. Also, many Christian religious conservatives advocate a "biblical" approach to childrearing, encouraging parents to raise their children to obey them. Disobedience is viewed as sinful, and obedience is promoted, in part, through strict discipline.

Blank Tablets

The English philosopher John Locke (1632–1704) believed that children were born into the world as *tabula rasa,* or blank tablets. After extensive observations, Locke concluded, "There is not the least appearance of any settled ideas at all in them; especially of ideas answering the terms which make up those universal propositions that are esteemed innate principles."[3] Locke believed that children's experiences, through sensory impressions, determined what they learned and consequently what they became. The blank tablet view presupposes no innate genetic code or inborn traits; that is, children are born with no predisposition toward any behavior except what is characteristic of human beings. The sum of what a child becomes depends on the nature and quality of experience; in other words, environment is the primary determinant.

The blank tablet view has several implications for teaching and childrearing. If children are seen as empty vessels to be filled, the teacher's job is to fill them—to present knowledge without regard to needs, interests, or readiness for learning. What is important is that children learn what is taught. Children become what adults make of them.

This view deemphasizes individual differences and assumes that as children are exposed to the same environmental influences, they will tend to behave and even think the same. This concept is the basis for many educational beliefs and practices in socialist countries. Children begin schooling early, often at six weeks of age, and are taught a standard curriculum that promotes a common political consciousness. They are expected to behave in ways that are consistent with and appropriate to how a citizen of the state should behave.

Growing Plants   A perennially popular view of children envisages them as growing plants with the educator or parent acting as gardener. Classrooms and homes are greenhouses in which children grow and mature in harmony with their natural growth patterns. A consequence of growth and maturing is that children *unfold*, much as a flower blooms under the proper conditions. In other words, what children become results from natural growth and a nurturing environment. Two key ingredients of this natural unfolding are play and readiness. The content and process of learning are included in play, and materials and activities are designed to promote play.

Children become ready for learning through motivation and play. This concept prompts teaching subjects or skills when children reach the point at which they can benefit from appropriate instruction. Lack of readiness to learn indicates that the child has not sufficiently matured; the natural process of unfolding has not occurred.

Belief in this concept is evident in certain social and educational policies, such as proposals to raise the age requirements for entry into kindergartens and first grade so that children have more time to mature and get ready for school (as discussed previously). Many people also believe each child's maturation occurs in accordance with an innate timetable, that there is a "best time" for learning specific tasks. They feel it is important to allow time for children's inner tendencies to develop and that teachers and parents should not "force" learning. This maturation process is as important, if not more so, than children's experiences. Many contemporary programs operate on the unfolding concept, whether or not it is explicitly stated.

Evidence for the widespread view of children as growing plants is poignantly illustrated by one father's reflections on the results and implications of his son's kindergarten screening test. This father was struck by the fact that his son had performed adequately, but not perfectly, and wondered what relevance the kindergarten screening test actually had to his son's future school performance.

We then went upstairs to water some late seedlings that go into our garden for fall. Radicchio . . . broccoli, lettuce and cauliflower. Noah ran his finger over the sprouts and giggled. They tickled. There they were, uncounted dozens of sprouts, all green, all about the same height.

And it came to me.

As I nurture and fertilize and pull the weeds that will want to clog this boy's growing-up years, he, too, will come to fruition. I'll have some control over that—some, not total, I realize. He may turn out to be the finest of the group, the biggest broccoli, the finest head of radicchio. He may command respect, praise and a high price in the marketplace of life.[4]

Property   The view that children are property has persisted throughout history. Its foundation is that children are the property of their parents or institutions. This view is justified in part by the idea that, as creators of children, parents have a right to them and their labors. Children are, in a real sense, the property of their parents. Parents have broad authority and jurisdiction over their children. Interestingly, few laws interfere with the right of parents to control their children's lives, although this situation is changing somewhat as children are given more rights and the rights they have are protected.

Laws (although difficult to enforce) protect children from physical and emotional abuse. Where there are compulsory attendance laws, parents must send their children to school. Generally, however, parents have a free hand in dealing with their children. Legislatures and courts are reluctant to interfere in what is considered a sacrosanct parent–child relationship. Parents are generally free to exercise full authority over their children. Within certain broad limits, most parents feel their children are theirs to do with as they please. Parents who embrace this view see themselves as their children's decision makers and may place their own best interests above those of their children.

Investments in the Future   Closely associated with the notion of children as property is the view that children represent future wealth or potential for parents and a nation. Since medieval times, people have viewed childrearing as an investment in the future. Many parents assume (not always consciously) that, when they are no longer able to work or must retire, their children will provide for them. Consequently, having children becomes a means to an end. Seeing that children are clothed and fed ensures their future economic contribution to their parents.

This view of children as investments, particularly in their parents' future, is being dramatically played out in contemporary society. More middle-age adults are becoming "parents" to their own aging and ill parents. This

group, known as the "sandwich generation," also is taking care of their grandchildren, because their own children have surrendered responsibility for childrearing as a result of divorce, death, abandonment, or other circumstances. Many of these middle-age parents who thought they were investing in their future through their children may not have any investment at all.

Over the last several decades, some social policy in the United States has been based partly on the view that children are future investments for society in general. Many programs are built on the underlying assumption that preventing problems in childhood leads to more productive adulthood. An extension of this attitude is that preventing a problem is less expensive than curing one. Some local educational programs thus emphasize identifying the problems of children and their families early in order to take preventive rather than remedial action. As professionals, we also know that besides being more expensive, remediation is not as effective as prevention.

Particularly during the 1960s, many federal programs were based on the idea of conserving one of the country's greatest resources—its children. Head Start, Follow Through, and child welfare programs are products of this view, which has resulted in a "human capital" or "investment" rationale for child care and other services.

The public believes a primary goal of education is to develop children who will be productive and help protect the nation against foreign competition. Therefore, the early education of young children in "good" programs is seen as one way to strengthen the United States economically. Thus, the country's best defense against outside economic forces is a well-educated, economically productive population. From this perspective, then, investing in children is seen as an investment in the country. Also, the view that children are our greatest wealth implies that we cannot and should not waste this potential.

Some believe, however, that this perspective of children as an investment in the future fails to consider children's intrinsic human worth. Trying to make a nation stronger through its children tends to emphasize national priorities over individuals. Also, solving a nation's "problems" is not and should not be viewed primarily as a "children's" problem.

Children as Persons with Rights A contemporary legal and humanistic view recognizes children as individuals with rights of their own. While children are often still treated as economic commodities and individuals who need protection, their rights are beginning to be defined, promoted, and defended. Since children are not organized into political groups, others must act as their advocates. Courts and social service agencies are becoming particular defenders.

In 1989, the United Nations (UN) Convention on the Rights of the Child was adopted by 159 member states of the UN General Assembly. The convention, in reality a human treaty, went into effect on 2 September 1990, after ratification by more than twenty nations. It has the status of a legally binding treaty for all nations who sign it.

The convention contains fifty-four articles, and the highlights are printed in Appendix B. The articles convey a very strong view of the child as a family member and individual. You will note that the convention combines political, civil, economic, and cultural rights. In this sense, the convention acknowledges that health and economic well-being are also essential to political freedoms and rights. In addition, by extending rights to individual children, the convention challenges the view of children as property.

The National Education Association (NEA), the nation's largest teachers' professional organization, adopted the following *Bill of Rights for Children* as presented to the NEA Representative Assembly on 4 July 1991:

We, the People of the United States, in order to achieve a more perfect society, fulfill our moral obligations, further our founding ideals and preserve the continued blessings of liberty, do hereby proclaim this Bill of Rights for Children.

I. *No child in a land of abundance shall be wanting for plentiful and nutritional food.*
II. *A society as advanced in medical knowledge and abilities as ours shall not deny medical attention to any child in need.*
III. *Whereas security is an essential requirement for a child's healthy development, the basic security of a place to live shall be guaranteed to every child.*
IV. *To ensure the potential of the individual and nation, every child at school shall have the right to a quality education.*
V. *The government, whose primary role is to protect and defend at all levels, shall assure that children are safeguarded from abuse, violence, and discrimination.*[5]

Although children of the world and nation are gaining more rights, societal attitudes toward children's rights are often still ambivalent. Some children's rights supporters believe children need advocates to act on their behalf. They maintain children are politically disenfranchised, economically disadvantaged, the personal property of their parents, vulnerable to abuse and exploitation because of their lack of experience, and have passive legal status. On the other hand, many people, including some parents, feel they should be allowed to raise their children as they think best, free of interference from children's rights advocates.

Rights are being extended to children in ways that would not have been thought possible even ten years ago. Particularly in the area of fetal rights, parents are encountering conflicts between their rights and the lives of their unborn children. Many states require places that sell liquor to post a sign reading, "Warning:

Drinking alcoholic beverages during pregnancy can cause birth defects." Major controversies are arising between the right of the unborn and the rights of pregnant women. Such questions as, "What rights of the pregnant woman supersede those of her unborn child?" and "Does the government or other agency have the right to intervene in a woman's life on behalf of her unborn child?" are not easy to answer. Controversy continues between those groups that advocate for the rights of the unborn fetus and groups that advocate for a mother's rights, including privacy, emotional and physical integrity, and self-determination. Viewpoints as to whose rights take precedence—the fetus's or the mother's—are becoming increasingly polarized.

The debate regarding children's rights will continue as the rights of children become further defined and clarified through the judicial system. The rights of all children will be examined, and more special interest groups will join the trend to gain even more rights for children.

A review of the ways we view children leads to some intriguing questions. In this generation, are parents and professionals as child centered as they should be? Are early childhood professionals interested in helping children receive the best so they can realize their best? What we know we should do and what we do are often two different things. Public and social policies often supersede our interest in children. Wars, national defense, and economics sometimes take precedence over questions of what is best for children.

The Return of Child-Centered Education

As early childhood professionals and the public increasingly view children as persons with rights, educators are implementing more child-centered approaches. The field of early childhood education has always been to a greater or lesser degree child centered, and

today it is decidedly more so. This rediscovery and reemphasis on child-centered education is occurring for a number of reasons. First, society in general is much more interested in the whole child and efforts to address *all* of children's needs, not just their academic needs. As a result, there is much more concern for encouraging children to be healthy and lead healthy lifestyles. Consequently, interest in children's immunizations and seeing that all children are fully immunized by age two has received a lot of attention. Programs to help children be free of drugs are common in early childhood and primary programs. Concern for the welfare of children in all areas of their growth and development is evident.

Evidence for the rebirth of child-centered approaches to early childhood education is also seen in such pedagogical practices as cooperative learning (see Chap. 9), having children make choices about what they will learn and how, and the use of activities and strategies to promote children's thinking. Other child-centered approaches very much in evidence are programs designed to promote children's self-esteem; multiage grouping; having professionals stay with or teach the same group of children for more than one year; transition programs that help children move easily from program to program, grade to grade, and agency to agency; and concern for children's health, safety, and nutrition.

ACTIVITIES FOR FURTHER ENRICHMENT

1. Review early childhood literature and daily newspapers to identify statements of public policy and issues relating to public policy. What are the issues involved in each? In what ways do you agree or disagree with these policies?

2. Interview parents who have children under age eight to determine how they view their

children: miniature adults, the competent child, the child as sinful, blank tablets, growing plants, property, investments in the future, or as persons with rights. How do they think their view(s) influences their child-rearing patterns?

3. Contact agencies that provide services to single parents, teenage parents, and families in need. How do these programs influence early childhood education programs in your local community?

4. Interview single parents and determine what effects and influences single parenting has on children. In what ways is single parenting stressful to parents and children? How can early childhood programs support and help single parents?

5. The emphasis on early education has prompted some critics and experts to charge that parents and early childhood professionals are making children grow up too soon, too fast. Interview parents and preschool teachers to determine their views on this topic. Do you agree or disagree with the data you gather?

6. Find out what problems early childhood professionals in local preschools and child care centers face as a result of divorce, abuse, and other types of stress in children's lives. How do they help with these problems?

7. Investigate the types of preschool programs available in your community. Who may attend them? How are they financed? What percentage of the children who attend have mothers working outside the home?

8. Over a period of several weeks or a month, collect articles from newspapers and magazines relating to infants, toddlers, and preschoolers, and categorize them by topic (child abuse, nutrition, etc.). What topics were given the most coverage? Why? What topics or trends are emerging in early education, according to this media coverage? Do you agree with everything you read? Can you find instances in which information

or advice may be inaccurate, inappropriate, or contradictory?

9. Visit attorneys, legal aid societies, juvenile courts, and other agencies. List the legal rights children already have. Do you think children have some rights they should not have? Which ones? Why?

10. List factors that support the argument that childhood is disappearing or has disappeared. Then make a list to support the opposite viewpoint—that childhood is not disappearing.

11. Visit corporations and businesses in your area, and determine what they are doing to support education and family programs.

12. List at least five social, political, and economic conditions of modern society, and explain how these conditions influence how people view, treat, and care for the very young.

13. List at least five significant contributions you believe good early childhood education programs can make in the lives of young children.

READINGS FOR FURTHER ENRICHMENT

Chenoweth, K. (ed.). *Creating Schools for All Our Students: What 12 Schools Have to Say* (Reston, VA: Council for Exceptional Children, 1995).

A report of the findings of a team of educators and parents brought together at the Working Forum on Inclusive Schools, a pioneering effort of ten major national educational organizations.

Davis, B. *How to Involve Parents in Multicultural School* (Alexandria, VA: ASCD, 1995).

Includes clear examples and emphasizes "giving good customer service" to help you break new ground creating successful parent involvement programs. As schools become more culturally and ethnically diverse, you can use the book's practical suggestions for enlisting the support and assistance of parents who may not speak the language or understand the customs you take for granted.

McLaughlin, M. W., Merita Irby, and J. Langman. *Urban Sanctuaries: Neighborhood Organizations in the Lives and Futures of Inner-City Youth* (San Francisco: Jossey-Bass, 1994).

Examines the importance of "safe havens," community-based organizations that put the needs of youth first, in the lives of inner-city youth. The authors explain how these "sanctuaries" have succeeded in weaning youth away from gangs. These successful community agencies resemble families, in which individuals are valued and rules of membership are clear.

Morton-Young, T. *After-School and Parent Education Programs for At-Risk Youth and Their Families: A Guide to Organizing and Operating a Community-Based Center for Basic Educational Skills Reinforcement, Homework Assistance, Cultural Enrichment, and Parent Involvement Focus* (Springfield, IL: Charles C Thomas, 1995).

A practical and useful guide for teachers and others as they consider ways to extend their involvement with families and their community.

NOTES

1. "Teen Pregnancy Rates Increase for Fifth Year," *Miami Herald,* 3 Oct. 1993; Annie E. Casey Foundation, *Kids Count Data Book* (1995).
2. David Elkind, "Formal Education and Early Education: An Essential Difference," *Phi Delta Kappan* 67 (1986), p. 634.
3. John Locke, *An Essay Concerning Human Understanding* (New York: Dover, 1959), pp. 92–93.
4. Paul Wilkes, "The First Test of Childhood," *Newsweek* 114 (1989), p. 8.
5. National Education Association, *Bill of Rights for Children* (Washington, D.C.: Author, 1991).

The Development of Early Childhood Programs

PART TWO

The teacher is not in the school to impose certain ideas or to form certain habits in the child, but is there as a member of the community to select the influences which shall affect the child and to assist him in properly responding to these influences.

John Dewey

59

C H A P T E R

3

The Past — Prologue to the Present

Focus Questions

1. Why is it important to know the ideas and theories of great educators?

2. What are the basic beliefs of Luther, Comenius, Locke, Rousseau, Pestalozzi, Owen, Froebel, Montessori, Dewey, Piaget, Vygotsky, Maslow, Erikson, and Gardner?

3. How have the beliefs and ideas of great educators influenced early childhood programs?

4. What are the basic concepts that are essential to high-quality early childhood programs and education?

5. Why is it important to have an appreciation for the professional accomplishments and contributions of great educators to the field of early childhood education?

6. What events have significantly influenced the field of early childhood education?

7. How have people, agencies, and legislation influenced early childhood education?

There are at least five reasons to know about the ideas and theories of great educators who have influenced the field of early childhood education. By reading of the hopes, ideas, and accomplishments of people our profession judges famous, we realize that today's ideas build on the past.

WHY IS THE PAST IMPORTANT?

Rebirth of Ideas

Old ideas and theories have a way of being reborn. Good ideas and practices persist over time and tend to be recycled through educational thought and practices in ten- to twenty-year periods. For example, many practices popular in the 1970s, such as family grouping, child-centered education, and active learning, are now popular again as the twenty-first century approaches.

Old ideas and practices seldom get recycled exactly in their previous form. They are changed and modified as necessary for contemporary society and situations. Knowing about these former ideas and practices helps us recognize them when they do come around again. Most important, this knowledge enables you to be an active participant in the recycling process of applying good practices of previous years to contemporary practice. We can more fully appreciate this recycling if we understand the roots of the early education profession.

Build the Dream

Many ideas of famous educators are still dreams, despite the advances we attribute to modern education. In this regard, we are the inheritors of a long line of thinkers as far back as Socrates and Plato. We should acknowledge this inheritance and use it as a base to build meaningful teaching careers and lives for children and their families. We have an obligation to continue to build the dream.

Implement Current Practice

Ideas expressed by early educators help us better understand how to implement current teaching strategies, whatever they may be. For instance, Rousseau, Froebel, and Montessori all believed children should be taught with dignity and respect. This attitude toward children is essential to an understanding of good educational practice and contributes to good teaching and quality programs.

Empower Professionals

Theories about how young children grow, develop, and learn decisively shape educational and childrearing practices. Some parents and teachers may not realize, however, what assumptions form the foundations of their daily practices. Studying beliefs of the great educators helps parents and early childhood educators clarify what they do and gives them insight into their actions. In this sense, knowing about theories liberates the uninformed from ignorance and empowers professionals and parents. As a consequence, they are able to implement developmentally appropriate practices with confidence.

Inspire Professionals

Exploring, analyzing, and discovering the roots of early childhood education helps *inspire* professionals. Recurring rediscovery forces people to contrast current practices with what others have advocated. Examining sources of beliefs helps clarify modern practice, and reading and studying others' ideas make us rethink our own beliefs and positions. In this regard, the history of the great educators and their beliefs can keep us current. When we pause long enough to listen to what they have to say, we frequently find a new insight or idea that motivates us to continue our quest to be the best we can be.

HISTORICAL INFLUENCES ON EARLY CHILDHOOD EDUCATION

Martin Luther

While the primary impact of the Protestant Reformation was religious, other far-reaching effects were secular. Two of these were universal education and literacy, both topics very much in the forefront of educational practice today.

In Europe, the sixteenth century was a time of great social, religious, and economic upheaval, partly because of the Renaissance and partly because of the Reformation. Great emphasis was placed on formal schooling to teach children how to read, the impetus for which is generally attributed to Martin Luther (1483–1546) and the Reformation he spurred.

The question of what to teach is an issue in any educational endeavor. Does society create schools and then decide what to teach, or do the needs of society determine what schools it will establish to meet desired goals? This is a question early childhood professionals wrestle with today. In the case of European education of that time, Luther emphasized the necessity of establishing schools to teach children to read. Simply stated, Luther replaced the authority of the hierarchy of the Catholic Church with the authority of the Bible. Believing that individuals were free to work out their own salvation through the Scriptures meant that people had to learn to read the Bible in their native tongue.

This concept marked the real beginning of teaching and learning in people's native language, or *vernacular,* as opposed to Latin, the official language of the Catholic Church. Before the Reformation, only the wealthy or those preparing for a religious vocation learned to read or write Latin. Luther translated the Bible into German. Other translations followed, finally making the Bible available to people in their own language. In this way, the Protestant Reformation encouraged and supported popular universal education.

Luther believed the family was the most important institution in the education of children. To this end, he encouraged parents to provide religious instruction and vocational education in the home. Throughout his life Luther remained a champion of education, writing letters and treatises and preaching sermons on the subject. His best-known letter on education is the *Letter to the Mayors and Aldermen of All the Cities of Germany in Behalf of Christian Schools,* written in 1524. In this letter, Luther argues for public support of education:

> *Therefore it will be the duty of the mayors and council to exercise the greatest care over the young. For since the happiness, honor, and life of the city are committed to their hands, they would be held recreant before God and the world, if they did not, day and night, with all their power, seek its welfare and improvement. Now the welfare of a city does not consist alone in great treasures, firm walls, beautiful houses, and munitions of war; indeed, where all these are found, and reckless fools come into power, the city sustains the greatest injury. But the highest welfare, safety, and power of a city consists in able, learned, wise, upright, cultivated citizens, who can secure, preserve, and utilize every treasure and advantage.[1]*

Out of the Reformation evolved other religious denominations, all interested in preserving the Christian faith and keeping their followers within the fold of their church. Most of the major denominations, such as Calvinism and Lutheranism, established their own schools to provide literacy and religious knowledge. Education and schooling have long been considered not only socializing forces but also means of religious and moral instruction. Many religious groups have always had rather extensive school programs, for this is one way to help ensure that children born into a faith will continue in it. Religious schools are a means of defending and perpetuating faith as well as a place in which converts can learn about and become strong in a particular faith.

Today, many churches and synagogues operate early childhood programs. A growing number of parents want early childhood programs that support their values, beliefs, and culture. They look for and find such programs operated by religious organizations. Furthermore, religious preschools tend to provide programs that emphasize cognitive and social learning through play. Parents see such programs as a satisfactory alternative to what they consider to be the pushing and hurrying of some academically based preschool programs.

John Amos Comenius

John Amos Comenius (1592–1670) was born in Moravia, a former province of the Czech Republic, and became a Moravian minister. He spent his life serving as a bishop, teaching school, and writing textbooks. Of his many writings, those that have received the most attention are *The Great Didactic* and the *Orbis Pictus (The World in Pictures)*, considered the first picture book for children.

Just as Luther's religious beliefs formed the basis for his educational ideas, so too with Comenius. In fact, throughout this discussion of the influence of great men and women on educational thought and practice, you will see a parallel interest in religion and education. It has always been obvious to religious individuals that what they believe gives shape, form, and substance to what they teach, and that, to a large degree, what is taught determines the extent to which religious beliefs are maintained and extended.

Comenius believed that humans are born in the image of God. Therefore, each individual has an obligation and duty to be educated to the fullest extent of one's abilities so as to fulfill this godlike image. Since so much depends on education, then, as far as Comenius was concerned, it should begin in the early years.

It is the nature of everything that comes into being, that while tender it is easily bent and formed, but that, when it has grown hard, it is not easy to alter. Wax, when soft, can be easily fashioned and shaped; when hard it cracks readily. A young plant can be planted, transplanted, pruned, and bent this way or that. When it has become a tree these processes are impossible.[2]

Comenius believed that education should follow the order of nature. Following this order implies a timetable for growth and learning, and early childhood professionals must observe this pattern to avoid forcing learning before children are ready. This belief is reflected in Montessori's concept of sensitive periods (see Chap. 4), Piaget's stages of development (see Chap. 5), and the developmentally appropriate practices of today. Comenius also thought that learning is best achieved when the senses are involved and that sensory education forms the basis for all learning.

Comenius said that the golden rule of teaching should be to place everything before the senses; for example, that children should not be taught the names of objects apart from the objects themselves or pictures of the objects. *Orbis Pictus* helped children learn the names of things and concepts, as they appeared during Comenius's time, through pictures and words. Comenius's emphasis on the concrete and the sensory is a pedagogical principle early childhood professionals still try to grasp fully and implement. Many contemporary programs stress sensory learning, and several early childhood materials promote learning through the senses.

A broad view of Comenius's total concept of education is evident by examining some of his principles of teaching:

Following in the footsteps of nature we find that the process of education will be easy

    i. *If it begins early, before the mind is corrupted.*

    ii. *If the mind be duly prepared to receive it.*

(104)

LI.

Piſcatio.

Fiſhing.

The Fiſher-man 1.
catcheth fiſh,
   either on the ſhoar,
with an Hook, 2.
which hangeth by a line
from the angling-rod,
and on which
the bait ſticketh;
   or with a
Cleek-Net, 3.
which hanging
on a Pole, 4.
is put into the water;
   or in a Boat, 5.
with a Trammel-Net 6.
   or with a Weel, 7.
which is laid in
the water by Night.

(105)

Piſcator 1.
captat piſces,
   ſive, in littore,
Hamo, 2.
qui ab *arundine*
filo pendet,
& cui inhæret
Eſca ;
   ſive
Fundâ, 3.
quæ pendens
Perticâ, 4.
aquæ immittitur ;
   ſive, in *Cymba*, 5.
Reti, 6.
   ſive *Naſſa*, 7.
quæ per Noctem
demergitur.

Orbis Pictus was the first picture book for children. This illustration demonstrates Comenius's emphasis on using sensory education as a means for teaching. What are some ways that early childhood professionals use children's senses to help them learn?

iii. If it proceeds from the general to the particular.
iv. And from what is easy to what is more difficult.
v. If the pupil be not overburdened by too many subjects.
vi. And if progress be slow in every case.
vii. If the intellect be forced to nothing to which its natural bent does not incline it, in accordance with its age and with the right method.
viii. If everything be taught through the medium of the senses.
ix. And if the use of everything taught be continually kept in view.
x. If everything be taught according to one and the same method.

These, I say, are the principles to be adopted if education is to be easy and pleasant.[3]

A noticeable trend in education today is to make learning, as Comenius suggested, simpler and more pleasant. Comenius's two most significant contributions to today's education are books with illustrations and the emphasis on sensory training found in many early childhood programs: We take the former for granted and naturally assume that the latter is a necessary basis for learning.

John Locke

John Locke (1632–1704) popularized the *tabula rasa*, or *blank tablet*, view of children.

The extent of Locke's influence on modern early childhood education and practice is probably unappreciated by many who daily implement practices based on his theories. More precisely, Locke developed the theory of and laid the foundation for *environmentalism*—the belief that the environment, not innate characteristics, determines what children will become.

Locke, born in Somerset, England, was a physician, philosopher, and social scientist. His ideas about education were first applied when his cousin and her husband asked him for childrearing advice. His letters to them were published in 1693 as *Some Thoughts Concerning Education*. Many of his philosophical ideas directly relating to education are also found in *An Essay Concerning Human Understanding*. Locke's assumption in regard to human learning and nature was that there are no innate ideas. This belief gave rise to his theory of the mind as a blank tablet or "white paper." As Locke explains,

Let us suppose the mind to be, as we say, white paper void of all characters, without ideas. How comes it to be furnished? Whence comes it by that vast store which the busy and boundless fancy of man has painted on it with an almost endless variety? Whence has it all the materials of reason and knowledge? To this I answer, in one word, from experience; in that all our knowledge is founded, and from that it ultimately derives itself.[4]

For Locke, then, environment forms the mind. The implications of this belief are clearly reflected in modern educational practice. The notion of the primacy of environmental influences is particularly evident in programs that encourage and promote early education as a means of overcoming or compensating for a poor or disadvantaged environment. Based partly on the idea that all children are born with the same general capacity for mental development and learning, these programs also assume that differences in learning, achievement, and behavior are attributable to environmental factors such as home and family conditions, socioeconomic context, early education, and experiences. Programs of early schooling, especially the current move for public schooling for three- and four-year-olds, work on the premise that "disadvantaged" children fail to have the experiences of their "more advantaged" counterparts. In fact, it is not uncommon to provide public funding for early schooling for those who are considered disadvantaged and to design such programs especially for them.

Because Locke believed that experiences determine the nature of the individual, sensory training became a prominent feature in the application of his theory to education. He and others who followed him believed that the best way to make children receptive to experiences was to train their senses. In this regard, Locke exerted considerable influence on others, particularly Maria Montessori, who developed her system of early education based on sensory training.

Jean-Jacques Rousseau

Jean-Jacques Rousseau (1712–1778) is best remembered by educators for his book *Émile*, in which he raises a hypothetical child from birth to adolescence. Rousseau's theories were radical for his time. The opening lines of *Émile* set the tone not only for Rousseau's educational views but many of his political ideas as well: "God makes all things good; man meddles with them and they become evil."[5]

Rousseau advocated a return to nature and an approach to educating children called *naturalism*. To Rousseau, naturalism meant abandoning society's artificiality and pretentiousness. A naturalistic education permits growth without undue interference or restrictions. Indeed, Rousseau wanted Émile to admire and emulate Daniel Defoe's Robinson Crusoe as an example of a resourceful person living close to and in harmony with nature. Rousseau would probably argue against such modern practices as dress codes, compulsory attendance, minimum basic skills, frequent and standardized testing, and ability grouping, on the grounds that they are "unnatural."

There is some current tendency in American education to emphasize naturalism by replacing practices such as regimentation, compulsory assignments, and school-imposed regulations with less structured processes. Indeed, contemporary practices stress naturalism whether or not practitioners are always aware of it. For example, family grouping seeks to create a more natural familylike atmosphere in schools and classrooms, literacy programs emphasize literature from the natural environment (e.g., using menus to show children how reading is important in their everyday lives), and conflict resolution programs teach children how to get along with others.

According to Rousseau, natural education promotes and encourages qualities such as happiness, spontaneity, and the inquisitiveness associated with childhood. In his method, parents and teachers allow children to develop according to their natural abilities, do not interfere with development by forcing education, and tend not to overprotect them from the corrupting influences of society. Rousseau felt that Émile's education occurred through three sources: nature, people, and things. He elaborates:

All that we lack at birth and need when grown up is given us by education. This education comes to us from nature, from men, or from things. The internal development of our faculties and organs is the education of nature. . . . It is not enough merely to keep children alive. They should learn to bear the blows of fortune; to meet either wealth or poverty, to live if need be

in the frosts of Iceland or on the sweltering rock of Malta.[6]

Rousseau believed, however, that although parents and others have control over education that comes from social and sensory experiences, they have no control over natural growth. In essence, this is the idea of *unfolding,* in which the nature of children—what they are to be—unfolds as a result of maturation according to their innate timetables. We should observe the child's growth and provide experiences at appropriate times. Some educators interpret this as a *laissez-faire* or "let alone" approach to parenting and education.

Educational historians point to Rousseau as dividing the historic and modern periods of education. Rousseau established a way of thinking about the young child that is reflected in innovators of educational practice such as Pestalozzi and Froebel. His concept of natural unfolding echoes Comenius and appears in current programs that stress promoting children's readiness as a factor in learning. Piaget's developmental stages also reinforce Rousseau's thinking about the importance of natural development. Educational practices that provide an environment in which children can become autonomous and self-regulating have a basis in his philosophy. The common element in all the approaches that advocate educating in a free, natural environment is the view of children as essentially good and capable of great achievement. It is the responsibility of early childhood professionals and parents to apply appropriate educational strategies at the right time, enabling all children to reach their full potential.

Perhaps the most famous contemporary example of the laissez-faire approach to childrearing and education is found in A. S. Neill's book *Summerhill,* which was also the name of his famous school. Neill presents a

Rousseau maintained that a natural education encourages qualities such as happiness, spontaneity, and inquisitiveness. What should parents and teachers do to provide experiences where children can respond to innate timetables for learning?

strong case for freedom and self-regulation. He and his wife wanted "to make the school fit the child—instead of making the child fit the school." Therefore,

We set out to make a school in which we should allow children freedom to be themselves. In order to do this, we had to renounce all discipline, all direction, all suggestion, all moral training, all religious instruction. We have been called brave, but it did not require courage. All it required was what we had—a complete belief in the child as a good, not an evil, being. For almost forty years, this belief in the goodness of the child has never wavered; it rather has become a final faith.[7]

Johann Heinrich Pestalozzi

Johann Heinrich Pestalozzi (1746–1827) was greatly influenced by Rousseau and his *Émile*. In fact, Pestalozzi was so impressed by Rousseau's back-to-nature concepts that he purchased a farm he hoped would become a center for new and experimental methods in agriculture. While engaged in farming, Pestalozzi became more and more interested in education and, in 1774, started a school at his farm called Neuhof. There Pestalozzi developed his ideas of the integration of home life, vocational education, and education for reading and writing. Because the cost of trying his ideas was much greater than the tuition he was able to collect, this educational enterprise went bankrupt.

Pestalozzi spent the next twenty years writing about his educational ideas and practices. From such writings as *Leonard and Gertrude,* which was read as a romantic novel rather than for its educational ideas, Pestalozzi became well known as a writer and educator. He spent his later years developing and perfecting his ideas at various schools throughout Europe.

Rousseau's influence is most apparent in Pestalozzi's belief that education should follow the child's nature. His dedication to this concept is demonstrated by his rearing his only son, Jean-Jacques, using *Émile* as a guide. His methods were based on harmonizing nature and educational practices:

And what is this method? It is a method which simply follows the path of Nature, or, in other words, which leads the child slowly, and by his own efforts, from sense-impressions to abstract ideas. Another advantage of this method is that it does not unduly exalt the master, inasmuch as he never appears as a superior being, but, like kindly Nature, lives and works with the children, his equals, seeming rather to learn with them than to teach them with authority.[8]

Unfortunately, Pestalozzi did not have much success rearing his son according to Rousseau's tenets, as evidenced by Jean-Jacques's inability to read and write by age twelve. This may be due to either his physical condition (he was thought to be epileptic) or Pestalozzi's inability to translate Rousseau's abstract ideas into practice. Pestalozzi was able, however, to refine his own pedagogical ideas as a result of the process.

Probably the most important lesson from Pestalozzi's experience is that in the process of education, early childhood professionals cannot rely solely on children's own initiative and expect them to learn all they need

to know. Although some children do teach themselves to read, parents and others have created the climate and conditions for that beginning reading process. To expect that children will be or can be responsible for learning basic skills and appropriate social behaviors by themselves is simply asking too much.

Pestalozzi believed all education is based on sensory impressions and that through the proper sensory experiences, children can achieve their natural potential. This belief led to "object lessons." As the name implies, Pestalozzi thought the best way to learn many concepts was through *manipulatives,* such as counting, measuring, feeling, and touching. Pestalozzi believed the best teachers were those who taught children, not subjects. He also believed in multiage grouping. Pestalozzi anticipated by about 175 years the many family-centered programs of today that help parents teach their young children in the home. He believed mothers could best teach their children and wrote two books, *How Gertrude Teaches Her Children* and *Book for Mothers,* detailing procedures to do this. He felt that "the time is drawing near when methods of teaching will be so simplified that each mother will be able not only to teach her children without help, but continue her own education at the same time."[9]

Robert Owen

It is often the case that people who affect the course of educational thought and practice are visionaries in political and social affairs as well. Robert Owen (1771–1858) is no exception. Owen's influences on education resulted from his entrepreneurial activities associated with New Lanark, Scotland, a model mill town he managed. Owen was an *environmentalist;* that is, he believed that the environment in which children are reared is the main factor contributing to their beliefs, behavior, and achievement. Consequently, he maintained that society and persons acting in the best interests of society can shape children's individual characters. He also was a *Utopian,* believing that by controlling the circumstances and consequent outcomes of childrearing, it was possible to build a new and perhaps more perfect society. Such a deterministic view of childrearing and education pushes free will to the background and makes environmental conditions the dominant force in directing and determining human behavior. As Owen explained it:

Any character, from the best to the worst, from the most ignorant to the most enlightened may be given to any community, even to the world at large, by the application of proper means; which means are to a great extent at the command and under the control of those who have influence in the affairs of men.[10]

Owen believed that good traits were instilled at an early age and that children's behavior was influenced primarily by the environment. Thus, in Owen, we see influences of both Locke's blank tablet and Rousseau's idea of innate goodness.

To implement his beliefs, Owen opened an infant school in 1816 at New Lanark, designed to provide care for about a hundred children aged eighteen months to ten years while their parents worked in his cotton mills. This led to the opening of the first infant school in London in 1818. Part of Owen's motivation for opening the infant schools was to get the children away from their uneducated parents. Indeed, to provide education for his workers and transform them into "rational beings," Owen opened a night school for them, as well.

Robert Owen believed that infant schools were an ideal way to provide for the needs of young children while their families worked. Today we are still trying to provide for quality infant care for working parents. What are some issues facing early childhood professionals as they try to provide quality programs for young children?

While we tend to think that early education for children from low-income families began with Head Start in 1965, Owen's infant school came over a hundred years before! Owen also had Utopian ideas regarding communal living and practice. In 1824, he purchased the village of New Harmony, Indiana, for a grand experiment in communal living. Part of the community included a center for a hundred infants. The New Harmony experiment failed, but Owen's legacy lived on in the infant schools of England. These eventually developed into kindergartens, influenced by European educators.

Owen's efforts and accomplishments have several noteworthy aspects. First, his infant school preceded Froebel's kindergarten by about a quarter of a century. Second, Owen's ideas and practices influenced educators as to the importance of early education and the relationship between education and societal improvements, an idea much in vogue in current educational practice. In addition, early childhood professionals and other professionals today, not unlike in Owen's time, seek through education to reform society and provide a better world for all humankind.

Friedrich Wilhelm Froebel

Friedrich Wilhelm Froebel (1782–1852) devoted his life to developing a system for educating young children. While his contemporary, Pestalozzi, with whom he studied and worked, advocated a system for teaching, Froebel developed a curriculum and educational methodology. In the process, Froebel earned the distinction, the "father of the kindergarten." As a result of his close relationship with Pestalozzi and of reading the works of Rousseau, Froebel decided to open a school and put his ideas into practice.

Froebel's primary contributions to educational thought and practice are in the areas of learning, curriculum, methodology, and teacher training. His concept of children and how they learn is based, in part, on the idea of unfolding, held by Comenius and Pestalozzi before him. The educator's role, whether parent or teacher, is to observe this natural unfolding and provide activities that will enable children to learn what they are ready to learn when they are ready to learn. The teacher's role is to help children develop their inherent qualities for learning. In this sense, the teacher is a designer of experiences and activities. This notion of teacher as facilitator was reinforced later by both Montessori and Piaget, both undoubtedly influenced by Froebel, who believed as follows:

Therefore, education in instruction and training, originally and in its first principles, should necessarily be passive, following (only guarding and protecting), not prescriptive, categorical, interfering.

Indeed, in its very essence, education should have these characteristics; for the undisturbed operation of the Divine Unity is necessarily good—cannot be otherwise than good. This necessity implies that the young human being—as it were, still in process of creation—would seek, although still unconsciously, as a product of nature, yet decidedly and surely, that which is in itself best; and, moreover, in a form wholly adapted to his condition, as well as to his disposition, his powers, and means.[11]

Consistent with his idea of unfolding, comparable to the process of a flower blooming from a bud, Froebel compared the child to a seed that is planted, germinates, brings forth a new shoot, and grows from a young, tender plant to a mature fruit-producing one. He likened the role of educator to that of gardener. In his *kindergarten,* or "garden of children," he envisioned children being educated in close harmony with their own nature and the nature of the universe. Children unfold their uniqueness in play, and it is in the area of unfolding and learning through play that

Froebel makes one of his greatest contributions to the early childhood curriculum.

Play is the purest, most spiritual activity of man at this stage, and, at the same time, typical of human life as a whole—of the inner hidden natural life in man and all things. It gives, therefore, joy, freedom, contentment, inner and outer rest, peace with the world. It holds the sources of all that is good. A child that plays thoroughly, with self-active determination, persevering until physical fatigue forbids, will surely be a thorough, determined man, capable of self-sacrifice for the promotion of the welfare of himself and others. Is not the most beautiful expression of child-life at this time a playing child?—a child wholly absorbed in his play? —a child that has fallen asleep while so absorbed?

As already indicated, play at this time is not trivial, it is highly serious and of deep significance. Cultivate and foster it, O mother; protect and guard it, O father! To the calm, keen vision of one who truly knows human nature, the spontaneous play of the child discloses the future inner life of the man.

The plays of childhood are the germinal leaves of all later life; for the whole man is developed and shown in these, in his tenderest dispositions, in his innermost tendencies. [12]

All the great educators believed play to be the basis for learning and thus incorporated play into their curriculum. When planning programs and activities, early childhood professionals should provide many opportunities for children to participate in play. What would you say to parents who asked you about the importance of play in their child's growth and development?

Froebel knew from experience, however, that unstructured play represented a potential danger and that it was quite likely, as Pestalozzi learned with his son Jean-Jacques, that a child left to his own devices may not learn much. Without guidance and direction and a prepared environment in which to learn, there was a real possibility that little or the wrong kind of learning would occur.

According to Froebel, the teacher is responsible for guidance and direction so children can become creative, contributing members of society. To achieve this end, Froebel developed a systematic, planned curriculum for the education of young children. Its bases were "gifts," "occupations," songs he composed, and educational games. *Gifts* were objects for children to handle and use in accordance with teachers' instructions, so they could learn shape, size, color, and concepts involved in counting, measuring, contrasting, and comparison. The first gift was a set of six balls of yarn, each a different color, with six lengths of yarn the same colors as the balls. Part of the purpose of this gift was to teach color recognition.

Froebel felt that the ball (meaning any spherical object) played an important role in education; consequently, he placed a great deal of emphasis on its use. He also believed the ball was a perfect symbol for humankind's unity with the divine, a concept he felt was important but is difficult for us to understand. Froebel said of the ball, "Even the word *ball,* in our significant language, is full of expression and meaning, pointing out that the ball is, as it were, an image of the all; but the ball itself has such an extraordinary charm, such a constant attraction for early childhood, as well as for later youth, that it is beyond comparison the first as well as the most important plaything of childhood especially."[13]

The second gift consisted of a cube, a cylinder, and a sphere. *Occupations* were materials designed for developing various skills, primarily psychomotor, through activities such as sewing with a sewing board, drawing pictures by following the dots, modeling with clay, cutting, stringing beads, weaving, drawing, pasting, and folding paper. Many of the games or plays Froebel developed were based on his gifts.

Froebel is called the "father of the kindergarten" because he devoted his life to developing both a program for young children and a system of training for kindergarten teachers. Many of the concepts and activities of the gifts and occupations are similar to activities that many kindergarten and other early childhood programs provide.

Froebel's recognition of the importance of learning through play is reinforced by contemporary early childhood professionals who plan and structure their programs around play activities. Other features of Froebel's kindergarten that remain are the play circle, where children sit in a circle for learning, and singing songs to reinforce concepts taught with "gifts" and "occupations." Froebel was the first educator to develop a planned, systematic program for educating young children. He also was the first to encourage young, unmarried women to become teachers, a break with tradition that caused Froebel no small amount of criticism and was one reason his methods encountered opposition.

Common Beliefs of Great Educators

All the educators discussed in this section held certain basic premises in common. First, they believed strongly in the important role of the family in educating children and laying the foundation for all future learning. Second, they believed in the importance of educating children early in life. Consequently, they advocated schooling either in the home or in a school setting. Third, they felt parents needed training and help to be good parents and their children's first teachers. They recognized that for education to begin early in life, it was imperative that parents have materials and training to do a good job (as we will discuss in Chap. 15). Educators and politicians are rediscovering how important parents are in the educational process. Parent involvement is being encouraged in public schools and other agencies, and we are learning what great educators have known all along: that parents are their children's first, and perhaps best, teachers.

Modern Influences

Maria Montessori

Maria Montessori (1870–1952) devoted her life to developing a system for educating young children. Her system has influenced virtually all subsequent early childhood programs. A precocious young woman who thought of undertaking either mathematics or engineering as a career, she instead chose medicine. Despite the obstacles to entering a field traditionally closed to women, she became the first woman in Italy to earn a medical degree. Following this achievement, she was appointed assistant instructor in the psychiatric clinic of the University of Rome. At that time, it was customary not to distinguish between children with mental retardation and those who were mentally ill, and her work brought her into contact with mentally retarded children who had been committed to insane asylums. Although Montessori's first intention was to study children's diseases, she soon became interested in educational solutions for problems such as deafness, paralysis, and "idiocy."

At that time she said, "I differed from my colleagues in that I instinctively felt that mental deficiency was more of an educational than medical problem."[14] Montessori became interested in the work of Edouard Seguin, a pioneer in the development of an educational system for children with mental retardation, and of Jean Itard, who developed an educational system for individuals who were both deaf and mute. Montessori credits Itard and Seguin with inspiring her to continue her studies with mentally retarded children. She wrote of her initial efforts at educating children:

I succeeded in teaching a number of the idiots from the asylums both to read and to write so well that I was able to present them at a public school for an examination together with normal children. And they passed the examination successfully.[15]

Montessori believed that the physical and social environments have a significant influence on learning. In a Montessori approach, the classroom is viewed as an ecological system where students, teachers, and the organization of the classroom all interact to optimize teaching and learning.

This was a remarkable achievement, which aroused interest in both Montessori and in her methods. Montessori, however, was already considering something else:

While everyone else was admiring the progress made by my defective charges, I was trying to discover the reasons which could have reduced the healthy, happy pupils of the ordinary schools to such a low state that in the intelligence test they were on the level with my own unfortunate pupils.[16]

While continuing to study and prepare herself for the task of educating children, Montessori came upon the opportunity to perfect her methods and implement them with nondisabled schoolage children quite by chance. In 1906 she was invited by the director general of the Roman Association for Good Building to organize schools for young children of families who occupied the tenement houses constructed by the association. In the first school, named the Casa dei Bambini, or Children's House, she tested her ideas and gained insights into children and teaching that led to the perfection of her system.

Montessori was profoundly religious, and a religious undertone is reflected throughout her work. She often quoted from the Bible to support her points. For example, at the dedication ceremonies of the first Children's House, she read from Isaiah 60:1-5 and ended by saying, "Perhaps, this Children's House can become a new Jerusalem, which, if it is spread out among the abandoned people of the world, can bring a new light to education."[17] Her religious dedication to the fundamental sacredness and uniqueness of every child and subsequent grounding of educational processes in a religious conviction undoubtedly account for some of her remarkable achievements as a person and educator. Thus, her system functions well for those who are willing to dedicate themselves to teaching as if it were a religious vocation.

We discuss Montessori's system in detail in Chapter 4.

John Dewey

John Dewey (1859–1952) represents a truly American influence on U.S. education. Through his positions as professor of philosophy at the University of Chicago and Columbia University, his extensive writing, and the educational practices of his many followers, Dewey did more than any other person to redirect the course of education in the United States.

Dewey's theory of schooling, usually called *progressivism,* emphasizes children and their interests rather than subject matter. From this child-centered emphasis comes the terms *child-centered curriculum* and *child-centered school.* The progressive education philosophy also maintains that schools should be concerned with preparing children for the realities of today rather than some vague future time. As expressed by Dewey in *My Pedagogical Creed,* "education, therefore, is a process of living and not a preparation for future living."[18] Thus, out of daily life should come the activities in which children learn about life and the skills necessary for living.

What is included in Dewey's concept of children's interests? "Not some one thing," he explained; "it is a name for the fact that a course of action, an occupation, or pursuit absorbs the powers of an individual in a thorough-going way."[19] In a classroom based on Dewey's ideas, children are involved with physical activities, utilization of things, intellectual pursuits, and social interaction. Physical activities include running, jumping, and active involvement with materials. In this phase the child begins the process of education and develops other interest areas that form the basis for doing and learning. The growing child learns to use tools and materials to construct things. Dewey felt that an ideal expression for this interest was daily living activities or occupations such as cooking and carpentry.

To promote an interest in the intellectual—solving problems, discovering new things, and figuring out how things work—children are given opportunities for inquiry and discovery. Dewey also believed that *social interest,* referring to interactions with people, was encouraged in a democratically run classroom.

While Dewey believed the curriculum should be built on the interests of children, he also felt it was the teacher's responsibility to plan for and capitalize on opportunities to integrate or weave traditional subject matter through and around the fabric of these interests. Dewey describes a school based on his ideas:

All of the schools . . . as compared with traditional schools [exhibit] a common emphasis upon respect for individuality and for increased freedom; a common disposition to build upon the nature and experience of the boys and girls that come to them, instead of imposing from without external subject-matter standards. They all display a certain atmosphere of informality, because experience has proved that formalization is hostile to genuine mental activity and to sincere emotional expression and growth. Emphasis upon activity as distinct from passivity is one of the common factors.[20]

Teachers who integrate subjects, use thematic units, and encourage problem-solving activities and critical thinking are philosophically indebted to Dewey.

There has been much misinterpretation and criticism of the progressive movement and of Dewey's ideas, especially by those who favor a traditional approach that emphasizes the basic subjects and skills. Actually, Dewey was not opposed to teaching basic skills or topics. He did believe, however, that traditional educational strategies *imposed* knowledge on children, whereas their interests should be a springboard for involvement with skills and subject matter.

The accumulation and acquisition of information for purposes of reproduction in recitation and examination is made too much of. "Knowledge," in the sense of information, means the working capital, the indispensable resources of further inquiry; of finding out, or learning, more things. Frequently it is treated as an end itself, and then the goal becomes to heap it up and display it when called for. This static, cold-storage ideal of knowledge is inimical to educative development. It not only lets occasions for thinking go unused, but it swamps thinking. No one could construct a house on ground cluttered with miscellaneous junk. Pupils who have stored their "minds" with all kinds of material which they have never put to intellectual uses are sure to be hampered when they try to think. They have no practice in selecting what is appropriate, and no criterion to go by; everything is on the same dead static level.[21]

Dewey not only influenced educational thought and practice in the United States but also exerted a strong influence on the educational thought and practice of other countries who embrace his concept of incorporating work and education. The idea of "socially useful education" is still evident in contemporary China, Russia, and some Eastern European countries.

Jean Piaget

Jean Piaget (1896–1980) studied in Paris, where he worked with Theodore Simon at the Alfred Binet laboratory, standardizing tests of reasoning for use with children. (Binet and Simon developed a scale for measuring intelligence.) This experience provided the foundation for Piaget's clinical method of interviewing, used in studying children's intellectual development. As Piaget recalls, "Thus I engaged my subjects in conversations patterned after psychiatric questioning, with the aim of discovering something about the reasoning process underlying their right, but especially their

PROGRAM IN ACTION

THE CITY & COUNTRY SCHOOL TODAY

The City & Country School, founded by Caroline Pratt in 1914, is an example of a progressive school that continues to educate children using the curriculum structure that was set forth over eighty years ago: "giving children experiences and materials that will fit their stage of development and have inherent in them unlimited opportunities for learning." Pratt, a teacher, sought to provide a school environment that suited the way children learn best—by doing.

Basic, Open-Ended Materials

The younger groups (ages two through seven) use basic, open-ended materials to reconstruct what they are learning about the world and organize their information and thinking in meaningful ways. Materials such as blocks, clay, water, paint, and wood are chosen because of their simplicity, flexibility, and the challenging possibilities that they offer. The blocks, developed by Pratt, are the mainspring of the curriculum today as they were in the early days of the school. It is City & Country School's belief that an early childhood curriculum based on open-ended materials fosters independence, motivation, and interest, all essential components of learning.

The Jobs Program

The Lower School curriculum provides a firm foundation for the more formal academic skills that children must master in later years. The Jobs Program was developed to play the central role in groups aged eight through thirteen. Each group has a specific job to perform related to the school's functioning as an integrated community. These jobs provide both a natural impetus for perfecting skills in reading, writing, spelling, and mathematics and a relevant framework for the exploration of social studies and the arts.

Beyond their work with blocks and jobs, children at City & Country are given opportunities to experience art, music, dramatics, foreign languages, science, computer, and woodworking, often integrated with their classroom work.

Located in the Greenwich Village district of New York City on 13th Street, the school currently has an enrollment of 240 students between the ages of two and thirteen. It continues to exemplify child-centered education.

Contributed by Kathleen Holz, principal of the City & Country School.

wrong, answers."[22] The emphasis on this method helps explain why some developers of a Piaget-based early childhood curriculum encourage the teacher's use of questioning procedures to promote thinking.

Following his work with children in Paris, which established the direction of his life work, Piaget became associated with the Institute J. J. Rousseau in Geneva and began studying intellectual development. Piaget's own three children played a major role in his studies, and many of his consequent insights about children's intellectual development are based on his observations and work with them. Using his own children in his studies caused some to criticize his findings. His theory, however, is based on not only his research but also literally hundreds of other studies involving thousands of children. Piaget came to these conclusions about early childhood education:

- Children play an active role in their own cognitive development.

- Mental and physical activity are important for children's cognitive development.

- Experiences constitute the raw materials children use to develop mental structures.

- Children develop cognitively through interaction with and adaptation to the environment.

- Development is a continuous process.

- Development results from maturation and the *transactions* or interactions between children and the physical and social environments.

Piaget also popularized the age/stage approach to cognitive development and influenced others to apply the theory to other processes such as moral, language, and social development. He encouraged and inspired many psychologists and educators to develop educational curricula and programs utilizing his ideas and promoted interest in

Piaget was interested in learning how children think and view the world. He concluded that children's thinking is not "wrong" but is qualitatively different from adult thought. What two examples can you give for how children's thinking differs from adult thinking?

the study of young children's cognitive development that has in turn contributed to the interest in infant development and education. We discuss Piagetian education in detail in Chapter 5.

Lev Vygotsky

Lev Vygotsky (1896–1934), a contemporary of Piaget, increasingly inspires the practices of early childhood professionals. Vygotsky's theory of development is particularly useful in describing children's mental, language, and social development. His theory also has many implications for how children's play promotes language and social development.

Vygotsky believed that children's mental, language, and social development is supported and enhanced by others through social interaction. This view is opposite from the Piagetian perspective in which children are much more solitary developers of their own intelligence and language. For Vygotsky, development is supported by social interaction and "learning awakens a variety of developmental processes that are able to operate only when the child is interacting with people in his environment and in collaboration with his peers. Once these processes are internalized, they become part of the child's independent developmental achievement."[23] Further, Vygotsky believed that beginning at birth, children seek out adults for social interaction, and development occurs through these interactions.

For early childhood professionals, one of Vygotsky's most important concepts is the *zone of proximal development,* which Vygotsky defines as

that area of development into which a child can be led in the course of interaction with a more competent partner, either adult or peer. [It] is not some clear-cut space that exists independently of the process of joint activity itself. Rather, it is the difference between what the child can accom-

plish independently and what he or she can achieve in conjunction with another, more competent person. The zone is thus created in the course of social interaction.[24]

From Vygotsky's point of view,

Learning is not development; however, properly organized learning results in mental development and sets in motion a variety of developmental processes that would be impossible apart from learning. Thus, learning is a necessary part and universal aspect of the process of developing culturally organized, specifically human, psychological functions.[25]

For Vygotsky, learning is directly related to the course of child development.

Intersubjectivity is a second Vygotsky concept. Intersubjectivity is based on the idea that "individuals come to a task, problem, or conversation with their own subjective ways of making sense of it. If they then discuss their differing viewpoints, shared understanding may be attained. . . . In other words, in the course of communication participants may arrive at some mutually agreed-upon, or intersubjective, understanding."[26] Communication or dialogue between teacher and child literally becomes a means for helping children "scaffold," that is, develop new concepts and think their way to higher-level concepts.

This intersubjectivity is similar to Piaget's theory that disequilibrium sets the stage for assimilation and accommodation, and, consequently, new schemes develop (see Chap. 5). Furthermore, Vygotsky believed that as a result of teacher-child collaboration, the child uses concepts learned in the collaborative process to solve problems when the teacher is not present. As Vygotsky said, the child "continues to act in collaboration even though the teacher is not standing near him. . . . This help—this aspect of collaboration— is invisibly present. It is continued in what looks from the outside like the child's independent solution of the problem."[27] According to Vygotsky, social interactions and collaboration are essential ingredients in the processes of learning and development.

Many current practices such as cooperative learning, joint problem solving, coaching, collaboration, mentoring, and other forms of assisted learning are consistent with Vygotsky's theory of development.

Abraham Maslow

Abraham Maslow (1890–1970) developed a theory of motivation based on the satisfaction of needs. Maslow identified self-actualization or self-fulfillment as the highest need but maintained that self-actualization cannot be achieved until certain basic needs are met. These basic needs include life essentials, such as food, safety, and security, belongingness and love, achievement and prestige, and aesthetic needs. We discuss Maslow's hierarchy of needs in greater detail in Chapter 6.

Erik Erikson

Erik H. Erikson (1902–1994) developed an influential theory of psychosocial development. Cognitive development occurs hand in hand with social development; you cannot separate the two. This is why Erikson's theory is so important. According to Erikson, children's personalities and social skills grow and develop within the context of society and in response to society's demands, expectations, values, and social institutions, such as families, schools, and other programs, such as child care centers. Adults, especially parents and teachers, are principal components of these environments and therefore play a powerful role in helping or hindering children in their personality and cognitive development. For example, school-age children must deal with demands to learn new skills or risk a sense of incompetence—a crisis of "industry versus inferiority." We discuss Erikson's theory in more detail in Chapter 6.

Howard Gardner

Howard Gardner (1943–) is codirector of Harvard Project Zero and directs research on such themes as children's appreciation of figurative language, children's play and narrative abilities, the development of musical competence, and children's facility with media and technology, including television and computers.

Gardner personifies how the past, present, and future of children's education integrate with each other. As a contemporary theorist, he is changing our ideas about children's intellectual development and of how to promote their cognitive development. Gardner challenges early childhood professionals—indeed, all professionals—with his theory of *multiple intelligences.*

According to Gardner's theory of multiple intelligences, children demonstrate intelligence across a range of seven intelligences. Why is Gardner's theory so popular? How would you apply his theory in early childhood programs to accommodate giftedness in certain identified areas of intelligence?

According to Piaget, mature biological thinking, or intelligence, consists of mainly logical/mathematical activities, such as classification, seriation, numeration, time, and spatial relations. This view of intelligence as a single set of mental skills, measurable by an intelligence test, is the way it is generally conceived by educators and the public. Gardner, on the other hand, believes differently:

a human intellectual competence must entail a set of skills of problem solving—enabling the individual to resolve genuine problems or difficulties *that he or she encounters and, when appropriate, to create an effective product—and must also entail the potential for* finding or creating problems: *thereby laying the groundwork for the acquisition of new knowledge.*[28]

Based on this view, Gardner identifies seven intelligences: linguistic, musical, logical-mathematical, spatial, bodily-kinesthetic, interpersonal, and intrapersonal. This view of intelligence and its components has and will undoubtedly continue to influence educational thought and practice. (See Chap. 9 for a Program in Action feature, "They Won't See Boundaries," describing a program based on Gardner's seven intelligences.)

FROM LUTHER TO VYGOTSKY: BASIC CONCEPTS ESSENTIAL TO GOOD EDUCATIONAL PRACTICES

As They Relate to Children

- Everyone needs to learn how to read and write.

- Children learn best when they use all their senses.

- All children are capable of being educated.

- All children should be educated to the fullest extent of their abilities.

- Education should begin early in life.

- Children should not be forced to learn but should be appropriately taught what they are ready to learn and should be prepared for the next stage of learning.

- Learning activities should be interesting and meaningful.

- Social interactions with teachers and peers are a necessary part of development.

As They Relate to Teachers

- Teachers must show love and respect for all children.

- Teachers should be dedicated to the teaching profession.

- Good teaching is based on a theory, a philosophy, goals, and objectives.

- Children's learning is enhanced through the use of concrete materials.

- Teaching should move from the concrete to the abstract.

- Observation is a key means for determining children's needs.

- Teaching should be a planned, systematic process.

- Teaching should be child centered rather than adult or subject centered.

- Teaching should be based on children's interests.

- Teachers should collaborate with children as a means of promoting development.

As They Relate to Parents

- The family is an important institution in children's education and development.

- Parents are their children's primary educators.

PROGRAM IN ACTION

WHY ISN'T EVERYONE JUST LIKE ME?

I remember well my own first grade experience. I was six years old in 1966 and entered school for the first time in a small rural school in Tennessee. The school's approach was a traditional one. My teacher, Mrs. Staton, led us through daily exercises in counting, adding, subtracting, copying letters, and reading. Although I'll never forget the hours spent at my table solving problems with the aid of a large box of buttons, it was the daily reading lesson that most appealed to me. It was during this reading time that I knew I could experience success, gain the approval of my peers, and please the awesome Mrs. Staton. During the reading lesson, each of the thirty students in the classroom took his or her own copy of the *Tip* book and opened it to the same page. We then began to read aloud, one at a time, until every student had received a turn. I anxiously awaited my turn by counting the people at my table and the lines on the page to see which line would be mine to read. Then when my turn arrived, I read my line, and knew that reading words had to be one of the most magnificent activities in which a person could engage.

However, not every student in the classroom shared my enthusiasm for reading. Sammy, for instance, hated the daily reading time. Sammy could climb the trees behind the school faster than any other person in school, and he knew the names of most creatures that were captured from the stream near our recess area. His confidence seemed to disappear, though, when he sat in class and waited his turn to read. I remember how he sat rigidly in his chair and gripped his *Tip* book as he stumbled over the words, hoping that his reading turn would soon end. Many years later as I finished my first year of teaching first grade, I thought of Sammy and his resemblance to many students in my own classroom who seemed even as six-year-olds to already hate school because they rarely felt successful in its setting. Much to my dismay, many of my students disliked reading and struggled to demonstrate their knowledge in any written form. Often I wondered, "Why?"

I wondered about similar things through the years. Why was it so easy for my father and my husband to reason problems logically, while I worked to answer questions by talking or acting them out? Why are my own sons, who have been raised in the same home, by the same parents, so different in strengths and weaknesses? Why do many of my coworkers seem to be such linear thinkers, while others find it easy to think cyclically or dimensionally? The answers to these questions became apparent to me a few years ago as I participated in a professional training seminar. It provided the missing link in what I believed about how students learn; my teaching style was transformed.

Accounting for Differences

To encourage statewide educational changes mandated by the Kentucky Educational Reform Act (KERA), Kentucky's Department of Education and the Kentucky Arts Council cosponsored a yearlong training series that equipped teachers with ways to implement Howard Gardner's theory of multiple intelligences. This theory confirmed what I already believed concerning the diverse intelligences of all people, and implementation strategies presented in the training gave me the foundation upon which I made daring changes in the organization of my primary classroom.

Gardner's theory currently credits all people with possessing, although not having developed to dominance, seven different intelligences. The two intelligences which our culture has valued most in the past (as was obvious in the description of my own first grade classroom) are the verbal/linguistic intelligence and the logical/mathematical intelligence. People dominant in the verbal/linguistic intelligence may enjoy reading, writing, or speaking, while those dominant in the logical/mathematical intelligence may solve mathematical problems quickly, accurately, and logically. Although in the past many schools have steered their curriculum toward these two intelligences, recent trends, especially in Kentucky, have pushed educators to place emphasis on the development of the other five intelligences, to assist students in nurturing their "whole" potential. As a result, classroom strategies have begun to provide ways for students to "show what they know" using their other five intelligences. Those intelligences are: bodily/kinesthetic (dominant in physical or hands-on activities), musical/rhythmic (adept in hearing, playing, performing music), visual/spatial (skillful in drawing or reading maps, charts, etc.), interpersonal (comfortable working in groups), and intrapersonal (comfortable working alone).

Planning for Learner Differences

After closely examining my teaching strategies, it became apparent that my classroom practices leaned heavily toward my own dominant intelligences, and provided few opportunities for my students to grow by using the intelligences where I myself was weak. This prompted me to study closely the works of David Lazear in his book, *Seven Ways of Knowing.* In this book, Mr. Lazear provided a "multiple intelligences toolbox," which enabled me to quickly glance at my weekly lesson plans and verify that my unit lessons contained strategies that encouraged the growth of all seven intelligences. It became my goal for each lesson presented in my classroom to provide activities addressing at least four of the seven intelligences. In this way, students were more likely to experience instruction that accommodated at least one of their dominant intelligences.

Even as six- and seven-year-olds, my primary students spent time exploring their own personalities and strengths. I encouraged these students to use their dominant intelligences to help develop their weaker ones. When students presented projects, they tried to address different intelligences to assist their audience (peers and parents) in learning from the presentation. Part of the project evaluation included an assessment of the number and quality of intelligences used.

The next bold step in my transformation into a multiple intelligence teacher came with the initiation of learning centers in my primary classroom. It was my initial desire to set up one learning center for each intelligence; however, when I began the process of rearranging my furniture and materials, it became apparent that many materials overlapped from one intelligence to another. Because of this, I ended up organizing my classroom into twelve learning centers and an area for large-group instruction that required students to cluster around the teacher on the floor.

Setting up the centers was indeed a bold step, for two reasons. First of all, I had never used centers in my classroom and had previously only experienced success with most students by using teaching strategies I had employed for years. Second, all the tables in my room had to be placed in the centers, which left no other place for students to work independently or in small groups. This required students to develop responsibility by not letting center materials distract them from the lesson at hand, unless these materials could assist with the lesson.

Tasks in each center focused on current topics from our unit of study by utilizing the intelligences around which each center was based. For instance, while studying a unit on "Families," students might spend time in the Research Center finding locations on a map and writing facts about a state in which a family member lives. In the Reading Center, students would have opportunities to read numerous books about families. In the Math Center, students would make a graph of the different hair colors for the family members of the group.

Benefits

The use of these multiple intelligence centers was beneficial in several ways. The types of tasks completed in the centers fit logically into the Kentucky Early Learning Profile (KELP), a portfolio assessment tool developed by the Kentucky Primary Assessment Committee as a statewide model. In addition, while students completed tasks in the centers, I had the opportunity

continued

to write anecdotal notes in their KELP records. I often obtained valuable information about students' dominant intelligences by observing which centers they chose when allowed free time to return to a center. Interestingly, students often returned to centers and completed the same tasks simply because the task fit their dominant intelligences and consequently made them feel successful.

As part of the KELP ongoing assessment, I conducted several "interviews" with each student in my classroom throughout the school year. For absolutely 100 percent of the students questioned, "center time" was ranked as one of their two favorite activities of the day. (The other highly ranked activities were lunch, recess, and P.E.) One of my special memories of "center time" was the day I noticed two six-year-old girls sitting in the Conference Center where students normally sit to give me a signal that they need to talk with me about something. When I approached the girls and asked if they needed a conference with me, one of the girls replied, "No. We're having our own conference." As I eavesdropped on their conversation, I found that these young ladies really were conducting an interview modeled after the teacher/student interviews used in the KELP. That became one of many incidents in which the students led the focus of the center activities, and the teacher was the greatest learner of all.

Contributed by Debbie Brown, assistant professor, Model Laboratory School, Eastern Kentucky University, Richmond, KY.

- Parents must guide and direct young children's learning.

- Parents should be involved in any educational program designed for their children.

- Everyone should have knowledge of and training for childrearing.

HOW HAS THE RECENT PAST INFLUENCED EARLY CHILDHOOD EDUCATION?

To fully understand the current basis for the public's interest in early childhood education and young children, we need to look back a half-century to three significant events: (1) the general acceptance of claims that the public schools were not successfully teaching reading and related skills; (2) the boycott of city buses by blacks in Montgomery, Alabama, on 1 December 1955; and (3) the launching of the satellite *Sputnik I* by the Soviet Union on 4 October 1957.

These events changed early childhood education in two important ways. First, in and of themselves, they influenced specific policies, programs, and legislation affecting young children and their families. Second, they affected people's attitudes toward and ways of thinking about what is best for young children.

How the United States educates its children and how well the schools fulfill their appointed tasks are always topics of national discussion and debate. Hardly a day passes that the schools are not criticized in some way. Schooling and public criticism go hand in hand. Before the 1960s, reading was taught by the whole sightword approach. Students learned to recognize discrete whole words through basal readers, such as the Dick and Jane series ("Oh, oh look! See Spot run!"). This approach was used successfully to teach many of your grandparents how to read. During the 1950s, a host of articles and books detailed "why children cannot read," followed in 1955 by the publication of Rudolf Flesch's *Why Johnny Can't Read.* Flesch criticized schools for the way reading was taught.

Critics and parents began to question the methodology and results of the teaching of reading and other basic skills. Parents demanded schools and programs that would teach these skills. Many parents felt that traditional play-oriented preschools and public school programs that emphasized socialization were not preparing their children for attending college or earning a living. Programs that stressed cognitive learning became popular with parents who wanted to give their children both an early start and a good foundation in learning.

Flesch's criticism of reading methods laid the groundwork for introducing the phonetic approach to reading, a system based on having children learn that letters represent sounds. As children learn such skills as initial consonant sounds, blends, digraphs (a pair of letters representing a specific speech sound), silent consonants, and medial and final consonants, they can "sound out" the majority of words they encounter. This phonetic method, which was and is championed by Jeanne Chall, replaced the sightword method.

As you might expect, given the inevitable swing of the education pendulum, during the 1980s and early 1990s the phonetic approach encountered criticism and challenges in the name of whole language and emerging literacy (see Chaps. 8 and 9). It is fair to say that the early childhood profession enthusiastically embraced whole language as the method of choice and justified its use on the basis of "developmentally appropriate practice." Today, there is a growing resurgence of support for phonics instruction based on reports of the number of young children who do not read well.

The Montgomery bus boycott set in motion a series of court cases and demonstrations for civil rights and human dignity. The fight for civil liberties spread quickly to the school arena. As a result, the rights of children and parents to public education were clarified and extended. Many of the new federal and state regulations and laws that affect children with disabilities, the disadvantaged, and abused children are essentially civil rights legislation, rather than being purely educational legislation.

Included in this legislation, and undoubtedly the two most important for early childhood, are Public Law 94–142, the Education for All Handicapped Children Act, and PL 99–457, the Education of the Handicapped Act Amendments, both of which extend rights to educational and social services to special needs children and their parents and families. Both laws, with their tremendous educational implications, also broaden and extend civil rights. Consequently, children have been granted rights to a free, appropriate, individualized education, as well as humane treatment (see Chap. 13 for an expanded discussion).

Spurred by the Soviet Union's launching of *Sputniks I* and *II* in 1957, the U.S. government in 1958 passed the National Defense Education Act to meet national needs, particularly in the sciences. What made it possible for the Soviets to launch *Sputnik?* Examination of the Soviet educational system led to the conclusion that it provided educational opportunities at an earlier age than did the U.S. public schools. Some educators began to wonder if we too should not teach children at a younger age; a surge of interest in early education resulted.

Research

At the same time that Soviet space achievements brought a reappraisal of our educational system, research studies were also influencing our ideas about how children learn, how to teach them, and what they should learn. These studies led to a major shift in basic educational premises concerning what children can achieve. Research by B. S. Bloom and J. M. Hunt enabled early childhood professionals to arrive at the following conclusions:

1. The period of most rapid intellectual growth occurs before age eight. The extent to which children will become intelligent, based on those things by which we measure intelligence and school achievement, is determined long before many children enter school. The notion of promoting cognitive development implies that children benefit from home environments that are conducive to learning and early school-like experiences, especially for children from environments that place them at risk of not developing their full potential.

2. It is increasingly evident that children are not born with fixed intelligences. This outdated concept fails to do justice to people's tremendous capacity for learning and change. In addition, evidence supports developmental intelligence. The extent to which individual intelligence develops depends on many variables, such as experiences, child-rearing practices, economic factors, nutrition, and the quality of prenatal and postnatal environments. Inherited genetic characteristics set a broad framework within which intelligence will develop. Heredity sets the limits, while environment determines the extent to which individuals achieve these limits.

3. Children reared in homes that are not intellectually stimulating may also lag intellectually behind their counterparts reared in more advantaged environments. Implications concerning the home environment are obvious. Experience shows that children who lack an environment that promotes learning

opportunities may be at risk throughout life. On the other hand, homes that offer intellectual stimulation tend to produce children who do well in school.

Poverty

During the 1960s, the United States "rediscovered" the poor and recognized that not everyone enjoyed affluence. In 1964, Congress enacted the Economic Opportunity Act (EOA). The EOA was designed to wage a war on poverty on several fronts. Head Start, created by the EOA, attempted to break intergenerational cycles of poverty by providing education and social opportunities for preschool children of families living in poverty (see Chap. 16).

Head Start played as big a role, if not the biggest, as any other single force in interesting the nation in educating young children. Although programs for children had been sponsored by the federal government during the Great Depression and World War II, these were primarily designed to free mothers for jobs in defense plants. Head Start marked the first time that children and their families were the intended beneficiaries of the services.

The Open Education Movement

We can trace the foundations of open education to Pestalozzi, Froebel, Montessori, and Dewey, although they did not use the same terminology. Montessori might be called the first modern open educator, because she allowed children to enjoy freedom within a prepared environment. She also encouraged individualized instruction, and most important, insisted on respect for children.

Interest in open education in the United States began in the 1960s when many educators and critics called attention to the ways schools were stifling student initiative, freedom, and self-direction. Schools were compared to prisons; critics described students sitting apathetically in straight rows, passively listening to robotlike teachers, with little or no real learning taking place. In short, classrooms and learning were assumed to be devoid of enthusiasm, joy, and self-direction. Educators and schools were challenged to involve students in learning and to abolish policies and procedures that were detrimental to students' physical and mental health. In essence, schools were challenged to become happy places of learning.

Concurrently, school reformers in the United States discovered the British Primary School, a comprehensive education program characterized by respect for children, responsiveness to children's needs, and learning through interests.

Open education is an attempt to restructure preschool and primary classrooms into settings that support individuality, promote independence, encourage freedom, and demonstrate respect for children. In this context, open education is a logical extension of many of the ideas of Montessori, Dewey, and Piaget. It encourages children to become involved in their own learning, and teachers allow children to make choices about how and what they learn. Teachers can conduct an open program regardless of the physical, social, or financial setting of the school or community.

Open education is an environment in which children are free from authoritarian adults and arbitrary rules. Contrary to popular misconception, children are not free to do everything they choose. Within broad guidelines, however (ideally established by teachers, students, and administrators), children are free to move about the room, carry on conversations, and engage in learning activities based on their interests.

Open education is child-centered learning. Adults do not do all the talking, decision making, organizing, and planning when it is children who need to develop these skills.

Open education seeks to return the emphasis to the child, where it rightfully belongs.

Open education teachers respect students and believe children are capable of assuming responsibility for their own learning. Teachers consider themselves primarily teachers of *children,* not of subject matter, and feel confident with all students in all subject areas. They are keen observers, for many of the decisions regarding instruction and activities depend on thorough knowledge of what the children have accomplished. Adjectives that describe the open teacher's role include *learner, guide, facilitator, catalyst,* and *director.*

The Rebirth of Open Education Ideas

A familiar maxim in the worlds of fashion, design, and education says, "If it's good, it will be back in ten or fifteen years." Many open education ideas have been reborn and embodied in contemporary practices. The following are examples:

- Developmentally appropriate curricula and practices designed to meet children's developmental needs (see Chap. 6)

- Whole language, emergent literacy, and other practices designed to integrate processes of reading, writing, and speaking (see Chaps. 8 and 9)

- Renewed interest in child-centered versus teacher- and subject-centered teaching and learning

- Multiage and family grouping. Interestingly, many early educators have always attempted to make their programs resemble a family. This same tendency is evident today in classrooms in which children are grouped as "families," consisting of different ages, responsibilities are shared, and children arrive at decisions after discussion among "family" members. Grouping children into families provides not only structure but an identity and security in which to learn.

- Programs that involve children in active learning and choices (see, for example, the High/Scope curriculum, Chap. 5)

- The project approach

- Cooperative learning (see Chap. 9)

- Family-centered programs. The emphasis on parent involvement underscores the historic importance of the family as a context in which to conduct education.

RECURRING THEMES

Certain processes are common to good teaching regardless of time or place. Respecting children, attending to individual differences, and getting children interested and involved in their learning are the framework of quality educational programs. Reading about and examining the experiences of great educators help keep this vision before us. Box 3.1 provides a chronology of the major events in the history of early childhood education.

BOX 3.1 Time Line: The History of Early Childhood Education

The following material summarizes key events cumulatively affecting early childhood education as we know it today.

1524   Martin Luther argued for public support of education for all children in his *Letter to the Mayors and Aldermen of All the Cities of Germany in Behalf of Christian Schools.*

1628   John Amos Comenius's *The Great Didactic* proclaimed the value of education for all children according to the laws of nature.

1762   Jean-Jacques Rousseau wrote *Émile,* explaining that education should take into account the child's natural growth and interests.

1780   Robert Raikes initiated the Sunday School movement in England to teach Bible study and religion to children.

1801   Johann Pestalozzi wrote *How Gertrude Teaches Her Children,* emphasizing home education and learning by discovery.

1816   Robert Owen set up a nursery school in Great Britain at the New Lanark Cotton Mills, believing that early education could counteract bad influences of the home.

1817   Thomas Gallaudet founded the first residential school for the deaf in Hartford, Connecticut.

1824   The American Sunday School Union was started with the purpose of initiating Sunday schools around the United States.

1836   William McGuffey began publishing the *Eclectic Reader* for elementary school children; his writing had a strong impact on moral and literary attitudes in the nineteenth century.

1837   Friedrich Froebel, known as the "father of the kindergarten," established the first kindergarten in Blankenburgh, Germany.

1837   Horace Mann began his job as secretary of the Massachusetts State Board of Education; he is often called the "father of the common schools" because of the role he played in helping set up the elementary school system in the United States.

1837   Edouard Seguin, influenced by Jean Itard, started the first school for the feebleminded in France.

1856   Mrs. Carl Schurz established the first kindergarten in the United States in Watertown, Wisconsin; the school was founded for children of German immigrants, and the program was conducted in German.

1860   Elizabeth Peabody opened a private kindergarten in Boston, Massachusetts, for English-speaking children.

1869 The first special education class for the deaf was founded in Boston

1871 The first public kindergarten in North America was started in Ontario, Canada.

1873 Susan Blow opened the first public school kindergarten in the United States in St. Louis, Missouri, as a cooperative effort with William Harris, superintendent of schools.

1876 A model kindergarten was shown at the Philadelphia Centennial Exposition.

1880 First teacher-training program for teachers of kindergarten began in Oshkosh Normal School, Philadelphia.

1884 The American Association of Elementary, Kindergarten, and Nursery School Educators was founded to serve in a consulting capacity for other educators.

1892 The International Kindergarten Union (IKU) was founded.

1896 John Dewey started the Laboratory School at the University of Chicago, basing his program on child-centered learning with an emphasis on life experiences.

1905 Sigmund Freud wrote *Three Essays of the Theory of Sexuality,* emphasizing the value of a healthy emotional environment during childhood.

1907 Maria Montessori started her first preschool in Rome called Children's House; her now-famous teaching method was based on the theory that children learn best by themselves in a properly prepared environment.

1909 The first White House Conference on Children was convened by Theodore Roosevelt.

1911 Arnold Gesell, well known for his research on the importance of the preschool years, began child development study at Yale University.

1911 Margaret and Rachel McMillan founded an open-air nursery school in Great Britain, in which the class met outdoors and emphasis was on healthy living.

1912 Arnold and Beatrice Gesell wrote *The Normal Child and Primary Education.*

1915 Eva McLin started the first U.S. Montessori nursery school in New York City.

1915 The Child Education Foundation of New York City founded a nursery school using Montessori's principles.

1918 The first public nursery schools were started in Great Britain.

1919 Harriet Johnson started the Nursery School of the Bureau of Educational Experiments, later to become the Bank Street College of Education.

1921 Patty Smith Hill started a progressive, laboratory nursery school at Columbia Teachers College.

1921 A. S. Neill founded Summerhill, an experimental school based on the ideas of Rousseau and Dewey.

1922 With Edna Noble White as its first director, the Merrill-Palmer Institute Nursery School opened in Detroit, with the purpose of preparing women in proper child care; at this time, the Institute was known as the Merrill-Palmer School of Motherhood and Home Training.

1922 Abigail Eliot, influenced by the open-air school in Great Britain and basing her program on personal hygiene and proper behavior, started the Ruggles Street Nursery School in Boston.

1924 *Childhood Education,* the first professional journal in early childhood education, was published by the IKU.

1926 The National Committee on Nursery Schools was initiated by Patty Smith Hill at Columbia Teachers College; now called the National Association for the Education of Young Children, it provides guidance and consultant services for educators.

1926 The National Association of Nursery Education (NANE) was founded.

1930 The IKU changed its name to the Association for Childhood Education.

1933 The Work Projects Administration (WPA) provided money to start nursery schools so that unemployed teachers would have jobs.

1935 First toy lending library, Toy Loan, was founded in Los Angeles.

1940 The Lanham Act provided funds for child care during World War II, mainly for day care centers for children whose mothers worked in the war effort.

1943 Kaiser Child Care Centers opened in Portland, Oregon, to provide twenty-four-hour child care for children of mothers working in war-related industries.

1944 The journal *Young Children* was first published by the NANE.

1946 Dr. Benjamin Spock wrote the *Common Sense Book of Baby and Child Care.*

1950 Erik Erikson published his writings on the "eight ages or stages" of personality growth and development and identified growth and development and identified "tasks" for each stage of development; the information, known as "Personality in the Making," formed the basis for the 1950 White House Conference on Children and Youth.

1952 Jean Piaget's *The Origins of Intelligence in Children* was published in English translation.

1955 Rudolf Flesch's *Why Johnny Can't Read* criticized the schools for their methodology in teaching reading and other basic skills.

1957 The Soviet Union launched *Sputnik,* sparking renewed interest in other educational systems and marking the beginning of the "rediscovery" of early childhood education.

1958 The National Defense Education Act was passed to provide federal funds for improving education in the sciences, mathematics, and foreign languages.

1960 Katharine Whiteside Taylor founded the American Council of Parent Cooperatives for those interested in exchanging ideas in preschool education; it later became the Parent Cooperative Preschools International.

1960 The Day Care and Child Development Council of America was formed to publicize the need for quality services for children.

1964 At its Miami Beach conference, the NANE became the National Association for the Education of Young Children (NAEYC).

1964 The Economic Opportunity Act of 1964 was passed as the beginning of the war on poverty and was the foundation for Head Start.

1965 The Elementary and Secondary Education Act was passed to provide federal money for programs for educationally deprived children.

1965 The Head Start Program began with federal money allocated for preschool education; the early programs were known as child development centers.

1966 The Bureau of Education for the Handicapped was established.

1967 The Follow Through Program was initiated to extend the Head Start Program into the primary grades.

1968 B. F. Skinner wrote *The Technology of Teaching,* which outlines a programmed approach to learning.

1968 The federal government established the Handicapped Children's Early Education Program to fund model preschool programs for children with disabilities.

1970 The White House Conference on Children and Youth was held.

1971 The Stride Rite Corporation in Boston was the first to start a corporate-supported child care program.

1972 The National Home Start Program began for the purpose of involving parents in their children's education.

1975 Public Law 94–142, the Education for All Handicapped Children Act, was passed mandating a free and appropriate education for all children with disabilities and extending many rights to parents of such children.

1979 The International Year of the Child was sponsored by the United Nations and designated by Executive Order.

1980 The first American lekotek (toy-lending library) opened its doors in Evanston, Illinois.

1980 The White House Conference on Families was held.

1981 The Head Start Act of 1981 (Omnibus Budget Reconciliation Act of 1981, Public Law 97–35) was passed to extend Head Start and provide for effective delivery of comprehensive services to economically disadvantaged children and their families.

1981 The Education Consolidation and Improvement Act (ECIA) was passed, consolidating many federal support programs for education.

1981 Secretary of Education Terrell Bell announced the establishment of the National Commission on Excellence in Education.

1982 The Mississippi legislature established mandatory statewide public kindergarten.

1983 An Arkansas commission chaired by Hillary Clinton calls for mandatory kindergarten and lower pupil-teacher ratios in the early grades.

1984 The High/Scope Educational Foundation released a study that it said documented the value of high-quality preschool programs for poor children. This study will be cited repeatedly in coming years by those favoring expansion of Head Start and other early-years programs.

1985 Head Start celebrated its twentieth anniversary with a Joint Resolution of the Senate House "reaffirming congressional support."

1986 The U. S. secretary of education proclaimed this the Year of the Elementary School, saying, "Let's do all we can this year to remind this nation that the time our children spend in elementary school is crucial to everything they will do for the rest of their lives."

1986 Public Law 99-457 (the Education of the Handicapped Act Amendments) established a national policy on early intervention that recognizes its benefits, provides assistance to states to build systems of service delivery, and recognizes the unique role of families in the development of their children with disabilities.

1987 Congress created the National Commission to Prevent Infant Mortality.

1988 Vermont announced plans to assess student performance on the basis of work portfolios as well as text scores.

1989 The United Nations Convention on the Rights of the Child was adopted by the UN General Assembly.

1990 The United Nations Convention on the Rights of the Child went into effect following its signing by twenty nations.

1990 Head Start celebrated its twenty-fifth anniversary.

1991 Education Alternatives, Inc., a for-profit firm, opened South Pointe Elementary School in Miami, Florida, the first public school in the nation to be run by a private company.

1991 The Carnegie Foundation issued "Ready to Learn," a plan to ensure children's readiness for school.

1994 The United Nations declared 1994 the Year of the Indigenous Child.

All great educators have believed in the basic goodness of children, that is, that children by nature tend to behave in socially acceptable ways. They believed it was the role of the teacher to provide the environment for this goodness to manifest itself. Young children learn to behave in certain ways according to how they are treated, the role models they have to emulate, and the environments in which they have to grow. Children do not emerge from the womb with a propensity toward badness but tend to grow and behave as they are treated and taught.

A central point that Luther, Comenius, Pestalozzi, Froebel, Montessori, and Dewey sought to make about our work as educators, regardless of context—parent or early childhood professional—is that we must do it well and act as though we really care about those for whom we have been called to serve.

ACTIVITIES FOR FURTHER ENRICHMENT

1. Compare classrooms you attended as a child to early education classrooms you are now visiting. What are the major similarities and differences? How do you explain the differences?

2. Do you think most teachers are aware of the historic influences on their teaching? Why is it important for teachers to be aware of these influences?

3. Many teachers of young children are more Froebelian in their approach to teaching than they realize. Can you find evidence to support this statement?

4. Some critics of education feel that schools have assumed (or have been given) too much responsibility for teaching too many things. Do you think certain subjects or services could be taught or provided through

another institution or agency? If so, which ones? Why?

5. Reflect on your experiences in elementary school. What experiences were most meaningful? Why? What teachers do you remember best? Why?

6. Interview the parents of children who attend a parochial school. Find out why they send their children to these schools. Do you agree or disagree with their reasons?

7. Reexamine Comenius's ten basic principles of teaching. Are they applicable today? Which do you agree with most and least?

8. Is it really necessary for children to learn through their senses? Why?

9. To what extent do religious beliefs determine educational practice? Give specific examples from your own experiences and observations to support your answer.

10. Why does society in general and education in particular not always follow the best educational practices advocated by many great educators?

11. Have you observed instances in which children were left to their own whims in a laissez-faire school environment? What were the results, and why did they occur?

12. In addition to the recurring themes of the great educators presented in this chapter, are there others you would list? Tell why you selected other themes.

13. List people, agencies, and legislation that are influencing early childhood education. Give specific examples. Do you think the influences will be long-lasting or short-lived?

14. What evidence can you find that Piaget has influenced early childhood programs?

15. List ways you have been or are being influenced by ideas and theories of the people and events discussed in this chapter. Do schools make a difference?

READINGS FOR FURTHER ENRICHMENT

Dewey, John. *Experience and Education:* (New York: Collier, 1938).

Dewey's comparison of traditional and progressive education.

Dropkin, Ruth, and Arthur Tobier, eds. *Roots of Open Education in America: Reminiscences and Reflections* (New York: City College Workshop Center for Open Education, 1976).

Papers that grew out of a 1975 conference at Lillian Weber's Center trace roots of open education back to the Mohawk nation. Settlement houses, one-room schoolhouses, Dewey, and progressivism are cited for their significant, or in some cases overrated, contributions.

Hymes, J. L., Jr. *Twenty Years in Review: A Look at 1971–1990* (Washington, D.C.: National Association for the Education of Young Children, 1991).

A treasure trove of detail about recent history in early childhood education. Each chapter chronicles a year's history.

Korn, Claire V. *Alternative American Schools: Ideals in Action* (Albany: State University of New York Press, 1991).

Examines alternative schools in the United States. Korn points out that perhaps the future of education depends on traveling off the beaten educational track. She looks at alternative schools that employ the philosophies of the great educators.

Montore, Will S. *Comenius and the Beginnings of Educational Reform* (New York: Arno, 1971).

The author traces the reform movement in education before and up to Comenius, who was responsible for the movement's most significant contributions. He also talks about the life of John Amos Comenius and his educational writings.

Winsor, Charlotte, ed. *Experimental Schools Revisited* (New York: Agathon, 1973).

A series of bulletins published by Bureau of Educational Experiments, a group of professionals dedicated to cooperative study of children, from 1917 to 1924. The book documents roots of modern education and relates the first serious attempts to provide educational programs for toddlers and experiences based on children's maturational levels. Chapters dealing with "Play School" and "Playthings" demonstrate philosophical and methodological bases for learning through play.

NOTES

1. From F. V. N. Painter, *Luther on Education,*© 1928 Concordia Publishing House, pp. 180–81. Used by permission.
2. John Amos Comenius, *The Great Didactic of John Amos Comenius,* ed. and trans. M. W. Keating (New York: Russell & Russell, 1967), p. 58.
3. Ibid., p 127.
4. John Locke, *An Essay Concerning Human Understanding,* ed. Peter H. Nidditch (Oxford: Oxford University Press, 1975), p. 104.
5. Jean-Jacques Rousseau, *Émile; Or, Education,* trans. Barbara Foxley (New York: Dutton, Everyman's Library, 1933), p. 5.
6. Jean-Jacques Rousseau, *Émile; Or, Education,* ed. and trans. William Boyd (New York: Teachers College Press, by arrangement with Heinemann, London, 1962), pp. 11–15.
7. Alexander S. Neill, *Summerhill* (New York: Hart, 1960), p. 4.
8. Roger DeGuimps, *Pestalozzi: His Life and Work* (New York: Appleton, 1890), p. 205.
9. Ibid., p. 196.
10. S. Bamford, *Passages in the Life of a Radical* (London: London Simpkin Marshall, 1844), n. p.
11. Friedrich Froebel, *The Education of Man* (Clifton, NJ: Kelley, 1974), pp. 7–8.
12. Friedrich Froebel, *The Education of Man,* trans. M. W. Hailman (New York: Appleton, 1887), p. 55.
13. Friedrich Froebel, *Pedagogics of the Kindergarten,* trans. Josephine Jarvis (New York: Appleton, 1902), p. 32.
14. Maria Montessori, *The Discovery of the Child,* trans. M. J. Costelloe (Notre Dame, IN: Fides, 1967), p. 22.
15. Maria Montessori, *The Montessori Method,* trans. Anne E. George (Cambridge, MA: Bentley, 1967), p. 38.
16. Montessori, *Discovery of the Child,* p. 28.
17. Ibid., p. 37.
18. Reginald D. Archambault, ed., *John Dewey on Education—Selected Writings* (New York: Random House, 1964), p. 430.
19. Henry Suzzallo, ed., *John Dewey's Interest and Effort in Education* (Boston: Houghton Mifflin, 1913), p. 65.
20. Archambault, *John Dewey on Education,* pp. 170–71.
21. Reprinted with permission of Simon & Schuster from *Democracy and Education* by John Dewey. Copyright 1916 by Macmillan Publishing Company, renewed 1944 by John Dewey.
22. Edwin G. Boring, ed., *A History of Psychology in Autobiography,* vol. IV (Worcester, MA: Clark University Press, 1952; New York: Russell & Russell, 1968), p. 244.
23. L. S. Vygotsky, *Mind in Society* (Cambridge, MA: Harvard University Press, 1978), p. 90.
24. Jonathan R. H. Tudge, "Processes and Consequences of Peer Collaboration: A Vygotskian Analysis," *Child Development* 63 (1992), p. 1365.
25. Ibid.
26. Vygotsky, *Mind in Society,* p. 90.
27. Tudge, "Processes and Consequences," p. 1365.
28. Howard Gardner, *Frames of Mind* (New York: Basic Books, 1983), pp. 60–61.

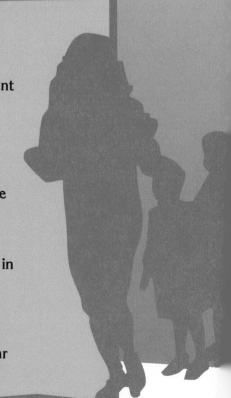

Montessori Education

Respect, Independence, and Self-Directed Learning

Focus Questions

1. Why are Montessori programs popular today?

2. What events in Maria Montessori's career influenced her educational methods?

3. How is Montessori's philosophy similar to and different from those of other early childhood education programs?

4. What are the main philosophical and pedagogical principles of the Montessori program?

5. What features of the prepared environment are unique to the Montessori method?

6. What materials are used in a Montessori program?

7. What are the essential roles of teachers and children in Montessori programs?

8. What are the basic characteristics of a good Montessori program?

9. How can the Montessori system be adapted to regular classroom settings?

f we were to single out one person to credit with a revival of early childhood education, it would be Maria Montessori. The Montessori method helped create and renew interest in early childhood education beginning about 1965. When parents and professionals were searching for exemplary early childhood programs, Montessori is one of the models they turned to.

WHY IS MONTESSORI SO POPULAR?

The Montessori system is intriguing for a number of reasons. First, Montessori education has always been identified as a quality program for young children. Second, parents who observe a *good* Montessori program like what they see: orderliness, independent children, self-directed learning, a calm environment, and *children* at the center of the learning process. Third, Montessori's philosophy is based on the premise that education begins at birth, and the idea of early learning has been and remains popular with parents. Fourth, public schools include Montessori in their magnet programs, giving parents choices in the kind of program their children will have at a particular school. It is also used as a means of desegregation.

Public school systems have implemented Montessori programs at increasing rates beginning in the 1980s. Montessori would probably smilingly approve of the contemporary use of her method to once again help change the nature and character of early childhood education.

PRINCIPLES OF THE MONTESSORI METHOD

The following principles are a synthesis of Montessori ideas and practices. They fairly and accurately represent how Montessori educators implement the Montessori method in many kinds of programs across the United States.

Respect for the Child

Respect for the child is the cornerstone on which all other Montessori principles rest. As Montessori said:

As a rule, however, we do not respect children. We try to force them to follow us without regard to their special needs. We are overbearing with them, and above all, rude; and then we expect them to be submissive and well-behaved, knowing all the time how strong is their instinct of imitation and how touching their faith in and admiration of us. They will imitate us in any case. Let us treat them, therefore, with all the kindness which we would wish to help to develop in them. And by kindness is not meant caresses. Should we not call anyone who embraced us at the first time of meeting rude, vulgar and ill-bred? Kindness consists in interpreting the wishes of others, in conforming one's self to them, and sacrificing, if need be, one's own desire.[1]

Because each child is unique, education should be individualized:

The educator must be as one inspired by a deep worship of life, and must, through this reverence, respect, while he observes with human interest, the development of the child life. Now, child life is not an abstraction; it is the life of individual children. There exists only one real biological manifestation: the living individual; and toward single individuals, one by one observed, education must direct itself.[2]

Children are not miniature adults and should not be treated as such. Montessori was firm in her belief that a child's life must be recognized as separate and distinct from that of the adult. She attributed most of the responsibility for restricting the education of young children to adults who impose their ideas and dreams on children, failing to distinguish between children's lives and their own.

In their dealings with children adults do not become egotistic but egocentric. They look upon everything pertaining to a child's soul from their own point of view and, consequently, their misapprehensions are constantly on the increase. Because of this egocentric view, adults look upon the child as something empty that is to be filled through their own efforts, as some-thing inert *and helpless for which they must do everything, as* something lacking an inner guide *and in constant need of direction. In conclusion we may say that the adult looks upon himself as the child's creator and judges the child's actions as good or bad from the viewpoint of his own relations to the child. The adult makes himself the touch stone of what is good and evil in the child. He is infallible, the model upon which the child must be molded. Any deviation on the child's part from adult ways is regarded as an evil which the adult hastens to correct.*

An adult who acts in this way, even though he may be convinced that he is filled with zeal, love, and a spirit of sacrifice on behalf of his child, unconsciously suppresses the development of the child's own personality.[3]

Educators and parents show respect for children in many ways. Helping children do things and learn for themselves, for example, encourages and promotes independence. At the same time, it also demonstrates a basic respect for their needs as individuals to be independent and self-regulating. When children have choices, they are able to develop the skills and abilities necessary for effective learning, autonomy, and positive self-esteem. These practices are so much more respectful of children than always doing for them or insisting that they do things as adults want them to. (The theme of respect for children resurfaces in our discussion of guiding behavior in Chap. 10.)

The Absorbent Mind

Montessori believed that children are not educated by others. Rather, one must educate oneself: "It may be said that we acquire knowledge by using our minds; but the child absorbs knowledge directly into his psychic life. Simply by continuing to live, the child learns to speak his native tongue."[4] This is the concept of the *absorbent mind.*

Montessori's philosophical and pedagogical ideas are evident in many early childhood programs. As much as any other single individual, Montessori influenced the nature and direction of American preschool education. Many parents and professionals consider it to be an ideal program as it encourages independence and responsibility in child-centered settings. What are three things about a Montessori program that appeal to parents?

There are unconscious and conscious stages in the development of the absorbent mind. From birth to three years, the unconscious absorbent mind develops the senses used for seeing, hearing, tasting, smelling, and touching. The child literally absorbs everything.

From three to six years, the conscious absorbent mind selects sensory impressions from the environment and further develops the senses. In this phase children are selective in that they refine what they know. For example, children in the unconscious stage merely see and absorb an array of colors without distinguishing among them; however, from three on, they develop the ability to distinguish, match, and grade colors. Montessori challenged the teacher to think through this concept of the absorbent mind:

How does a child, starting with nothing, orient himself in this complicated world? How does he come to distinguish things, by what marvelous means does he come to learn a language in all its minute details without a teacher but merely by living simply, joyfully, and without fatigue, whereas an adult is in constant need of assistance to orient himself in a new environment to learn a new language, which he finds tedious and which he will never master with the same perfection with which a child acquires his own mother tongue?[5]

Montessori wanted us to understand that children cannot help but learn. Simply by living, children learn from their environment. Jerome Bruner expresses this idea when he says that "learning is involuntary." Children learn because they are thinking beings. What they learn depends greatly on the people in their environment, what those people say and do, and how they react. In addition, available experiences and materials also help determine the type and quality of learning—and thus the type and quality of the individual.

Early childhood professionals are reemphasizing the ideas that children are born into the world learning and with constant readiness and ability to learn. We will discuss these concepts further in Chapter 6.

Sensitive Periods

Montessori believed there are sensitive periods when children are more susceptible to certain behaviors and can learn specific skills more easily:

A sensitive period refers to a special sensibility which a creature acquires in its infantile state, while it is still in a process of evolution. It is a transient disposition and limited to the acquisition of a particular trait. Once this trait or characteristic has been acquired, the special sensibility disappears. . . .

A child learns to adjust himself and make acquisitions in his sensitive periods. These are

like a beam that lights interiorly or a battery that furnishes energy. It is this sensibility which enables a child to come in contact with the external world in a particularly intense manner. At such a time everything is easy; all is life and enthusiasm. Every effort marks an increase in power. Only when the goal has been obtained does fatigue and the weight of indifference come on.

When one of these psychic passions is exhausted, another area is enkindled. Childhood thus passes from conquest to conquest in a constant rhythm that constitutes its joy and happiness.[6]

The secret of using sensitive periods in teaching is to recognize them when they occur. While all children experience the same sensitive periods (e.g., a sensitive period for writing), the sequence and timing vary for each child. Therefore, it becomes the role of the directress (as Montessori teachers are often called) or the parent to detect times of sensitivity and provide the setting for optimum fulfillment. Observation thus becomes crucial for teachers and parents. Indeed, many educators believe that information gained by observation of children's achievement and behavior is more accurate than that acquired through the use of tests (see Chap. 1).

The sensitive period for many learnings occurs early in life, during the time of rapid physical language and cognitive growth. Experiences necessary for optimum development must be provided at this time. Through observation and practice, for example, Montessori was convinced the sensitive period for development of language was a year or two earlier than originally thought.

Once the sensibility for learning a particular skill occurs, it does not arise again with the same intensity. For example, children will never learn languages as well as when the special sensitivity for language learning occurs. Montessori said, "The child grows up speaking his parent's tongue, yet to grownups the learning of a language is a very great intellectual achievement."[7]

Teachers must do three things: recognize that there are sensitive periods, learn to detect them, and capitalize on them by providing the optimum learning setting to foster their development. Much of what early childhood professionals mean by *readiness* is contained in Montessori's concept of sensitive periods.

The Prepared Environment

Montessori believed children learn best in a prepared environment, which can be any setting—classroom, a room at home, nursery, or playground. The purpose of the prepared environment is to make children independent of adults. It is a place in which children can *do things for themselves*. The ideal class-

rooms Montessori described are really what educators advocate when they talk about child-centered education and active learning. In many respects, Montessori was the precursor of many practices in use today.

Following their introduction to the prepared environment, children can come and go according to their desires and needs, deciding for themselves which materials to work with. Montessori removed the typical school desks from the classroom and replaced them with tables and chairs at which children could work individually or in small groups. In a modern Montessori classroom, much of a child's work is done on the floor. Montessori saw no reason for a teacher's desk, since the teacher should be involved with the children where they are doing their work. She also introduced child-sized furniture, lowered chalkboards, and outside areas

VIDEO VIEWPOINT

EMOTIONAL IQ

Researchers are now saying that the verbal intelligence of young children is not the only indicator of future success. Determining the emotional intelligence of people, including how they react when they are angry, having the ability to read others' non-verbal cues, and self-control, may better identify an individual who can adapt to societal pressures and the demands of the workplace. Parents and early childhood professionals can play a role in helping children develop healthy emotional attitudes.

Reflective Discussion Questions: Write down several examples of emotional intelligence. Give some examples of your personal emotional intelligence and how you manifest such emotions. Give examples. How would you explain emotional intelligence to a parent? Why is impulse control so important in children's lives?

Reflective Decision Making: How can you as an early childhood professional teach students about a healthy emotional intelligence? Give some examples of how you can role-play to demonstrate such emotions. What social skills can you help students learn in order to increase their emotional intelligence? What can you do to help children develop impulse control? Why is impulse control so important for success in life? What are some consequences of not being able to delay gratification and being able to exercise impulse control? As an early childhood professional, how can you help children control their anger? Make a list of children's books and other materials that you could use to help children "read other children's emotions." What are some things that you can do to be your students' emotional tutor?

A Montessori environment is characterized by orderliness, with a place for everything and everything in its place. The low shelving gives children ready access to materials to encourage their use. Why is it important to prepare such an organized environment?

in which children could, at will, take part in gardening and other outdoor activities.

Her concept of a classroom was a place in which children could do things for themselves, play with material placed there for specific purposes, and *educate themselves.* She developed a classroom free of many of the inhibiting elements in some of today's classrooms. Freedom is the essential characteristic of the prepared environment. Since children are free, within the environment, to explore materials of their own choosing, they absorb what they find there.

Many adults fear children will automatically abuse freedom or not know how to act in an environment in which they are responsible for governing their own actions. When a Montessori teacher anticipates inappropriate behavior, she quickly diverts the child to other materials or activities. Although the Montessori teacher believes in freedom for children

and children's ability to exercise that freedom, children's choices are not unlimited. For example, children must know how to use materials correctly before they are free to choose them. Students are free to pick within the framework of choices provided by the teacher. Choice, however, is also a product of discipline and self-control that children learn in the prepared environment.

Self- or Autoeducation

Montessori referred to the concept that children are capable of educating themselves as *autoeducation:*

The commonest prejudice in ordinary education is that everything can be accomplished by talking (by appealing, that is, to the child's ear), or by holding one's self up as a model to be imitated (a kind of appeal to the eye), while the truth is that the personality can only develop by making use of its own powers.[8]

Children who are actively involved in a prepared environment and exercising freedom of choice literally educate themselves. The role freedom plays in self-education is crucial:

And this freedom is not only an external sign of liberty, but a means of education. If by an awkward movement a child upsets a chair, which falls noisily to the floor, he will have an evident proof of his own incapacity; the same movement had it taken place amidst stationary benches would have passed unnoticed by him. Thus the child has some means by which he can correct himself, and having done so will have before him the actual proof of the power he has gained: the little tables and chairs remain firm and silent each in its own place. It is plainly seen that the child has learned *to command his movements.*[9]

Our universal perception of the teaching–learning act is that the teachers teach and children learn, a view that overlooks that everyone learns a great deal through their own efforts. Through the principle of auto-education, Montessori focuses our attention on this human capability. The art of teaching includes preparing the environment so that children, by participating in it, educate themselves. Think of the things you learned by yourself and the conditions and circumstances under which you learned them. Your reflections will remind you of the self-satisfaction that accompanies self-learning and its power to generate further involvement.

Obviously, it is sometimes quicker, more efficient, and more economical to be told or shown what to do and how to do it. Teachers and parents need to understand, however, that autoeducation should have a more dominant role in education than we have been willing to give it. In this sense, education should become more child centered and less teacher centered.

The Role of the Teacher

The Montessori teacher should demonstrate certain behaviors in order to implement the principles of this child-centered approach, including the following:

1. *Make children the center of learning.* As Montessori said, "The teacher's task is not to talk, but to prepare and arrange a series of motives for cultural activity in a special environment made for the child."[10]

2. *Encourage children to learn* by providing freedom for them in the prepared environment.

3. *Observe children* so as to prepare the best possible environment, recognizing sensitive periods, and diverting inappropriate behavior to meaningful tasks.

Montessori believed, "It is necessary for the teacher to guide the child without letting him feel her presence too much, so that she may be always ready to supply the desired help, but may never be the obstacle between the child and his experience."[11]

HOW DOES THE MONTESSORI METHOD WORK?

In a prepared environment, materials and activities provide for three basic areas of child involvement: *practical life* or motor education, *sensory materials* for training the senses, and *academic materials* for teaching writing, reading, and mathematics. All these activities are taught according to a prescribed procedure.

Practical Life

The prepared environment emphasizes basic, everyday motor activities, such as walking from place to place in an orderly manner,

BOX 4.1   Voices from the Field: A Montessori Teacher

In August 1980, I happened upon Montessori quite by accident. A friend suggested I volunteer in the classroom she was working in, to fill some of my summer afternoons.

I knew next to nothing about Maria Montessori and her methods but was immediately intrigued with what I saw in the classroom. I expected chaos; what I found was harmony. My curiosity had been aroused. After two years assisting full time in the classroom, I still was not satisfied with what I knew about Montessori, so I decided to pursue the formal training to become certified.

One of the fundamental tenets of my training was that, as Maria Montessori discovered through observation, children learn by doing. I have found the same to be true of myself. After I had completed my formal classroom training and read all my educational materials, I went into the classroom knowing I had many of the answers but I found I did not even know the questions. With all the knowledge I had gained, experience would prove to be the answer to the equation.

In a Montessori classroom, one of the primary responsibilities of the teacher is to become a catalyst between the materials and the child. This is achieved by giving lessons either individually or in a small group. But the lessons I provide are equal to the ones given to me by the children. For example, a coworker and I were struggling to get a printer hooked up to a new computer. As we did this, Travis, a four-year-old, walked up, looked at the back of the machine, and said, "Miss Susie, you need a different interface cable." My coworker and I looked at him then looked at one another in disbelief. After further investigation we found he was right. Through this and other experiences I learned not to take children for granted. Often they are much more aware than adults give them credit for.

The ability to laugh at disasters in the classroom and at oneself also is an important tool to possess. In addition to a sense of humor, one needs to have certain personality characteristics, including patience, understanding, enthusiasm, and dedication. In my opinion, one needs to possess all of these qualities to be successful in a career in early childhood education.

The unconditional love the children offer and the joy I receive in watching them grow have no equal. Becoming a Montessori teacher for me has proven to be not only a career choice but also a life choice. It has been a very eye-opening, rewarding, and fulfilling experience. While another career may have been more financially profitable, another career could never have given me the daily satisfaction I have received—satisfaction that money cannot buy.

Contributed by Susie Armstrong, teacher, three- to six-year-old primary class, Montessori at Greenwood Plaza, Englewood, CO.

carrying objects such as trays and chairs, greeting a visitor, learning self-care skills, and other practical activities. For example, the "dressing frames" are designed to perfect the motor skills involved in buttoning, zipping, lacing, buckling, and tying. The philosophy for activities such as these is to make children independent of the adult and develop concentration. Water activities play a large role in Montessori methods, and children are taught to scrub, wash, and pour as a means of developing coordination. Practical life exercises also include polishing mirrors, shoes, and plant leaves; sweeping the floor; dusting furniture; and peeling vegetables.

Montessori practitioners believe that without concentration and involvement through the senses, little learning takes place. They believe that as children become absorbed in an activity, they gradually lengthen their span of concentration; as they follow a regular sequence of actions, they learn to pay attention to details. Although most people assume that we learn practical life activities incidentally, a Montessori teacher shows children how to do these activities through precisely detailed instructions. Verbal instructions are minimal; the emphasis in the instructional process is on *showing how*—modeling and practice.

Montessori believed children's involvement and concentration in motor activities lengthens their attention span. In a Montessori classroom, it is not uncommon to see a child of four or five polish his shoes or scrub a table for twenty minutes at a time! The child finds the activity intrinsically rewarding and pleasurable.

Practical life activities are taught through four different types of exercises. *Care of the person* involves activities such as using the dressing frames, polishing shoes, and washing hands. *Care of the environment* includes dusting, polishing a table, and raking leaves. *Social relations* include lessons in grace and courtesy. The fourth type of exercise involves *analysis and control of movement* and includes locomotor activities such as walking and balancing. Figures 4.1, 4.2, and 4.3 are directions for some of the practical life activities in a Montessori classroom. Notice the procedures and the exactness of presentation.

Practical life activities help children learn about and practice everyday activities such as folding napkins, polishing, cleaning vegetables, and washing dishes. Children enjoy doing practical, useful activities. Why do you think they do?

Figure 4.1/*Pouring*

Materials: Tray, rice, two small pitchers (one empty, the other containing rice)

Presentation: The child must be shown how to lift the empty pitcher with the left hand and with the right, raise the pitcher containing rice slightly higher. Grasping the handle, lifting, and tilting are practiced. The spout of the full pitcher must be moved to about the center of the empty pitcher before the pouring begins. Set down both pitchers; then change the full one to the right side, to repeat the exercise.

When rice is spilled, the child will set the pitchers down, beside the top of the tray, and pick the grains up, one at a time, with thumb and forefinger.

Purpose: Control of movement.

Point of Interest: Watching the rice.

Control of Error: Hearing the rice drop on the tray.

Age: 2$\frac{1}{2}$ years.

Exercise: A container with a smaller diameter, requiring better control of movement. Control the amount of rice for the smaller container.

Note: Set up a similar exercise, using colored popcorn instead of rice.

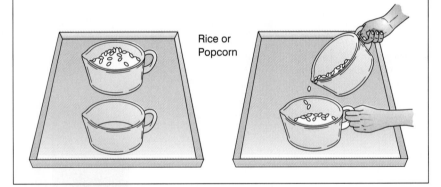

Rice or Popcorn

Sensory Materials

The following materials are among those found in a typical Montessori classroom (the learning purpose appears in parentheses):

- *Pink tower* (visual discrimination of dimension)—ten wood cubes of the same shape and texture, all pink, the largest of which is ten centimeters cubed. Each succeeding block is one centimeter smaller. Children build a tower beginning with the largest block.
- *Brown stairs* (visual discrimination of width and height)—ten blocks of wood, all brown, differing in height and width. Children arrange the blocks next to each other from thickest to thinnest so the blocks resemble a staircase.

Materials: Apron, green-leafed plant, sheet of white freezer paper, basket with small sponge, caster, bottle of plant polish, orange stick, cotton ball.

Presentation:
1. Lay out all the material in order of use from left to right.
2. Bring a plant to the table and place it on the paper.
3. Dampen the sponge at the sink and gently wipe off the top side of the leaf with forward strokes. Hold the leaf on the underside with the other hand. Stroke several leaves to remove the dust.
4. Pour small amount of polish into caster.
5. Wrap a small portion of the cotton ball on the orange stick.
6. Dip the stick in the polish and again stroke gently on the leaf in the manner described above.

Clean up:
1. Remove cotton from the stick and put it in the wastebasket.
2. Take the caster to the sink and wash and dry it.
3. Wash the sponge and bring it back to the table.
4. Place the material back in the basket.
5. Replace the plant on the shelf.
6. Fold the paper. Discard only if necessary.
7. Return basket and paper to the shelf.

Purpose: Coordination of movement; care of plants.

Point of Interest: Seeing the leaves get shiny.

Control of Error: Dull leaves and polish on white paper.

Age: 3 years and up.

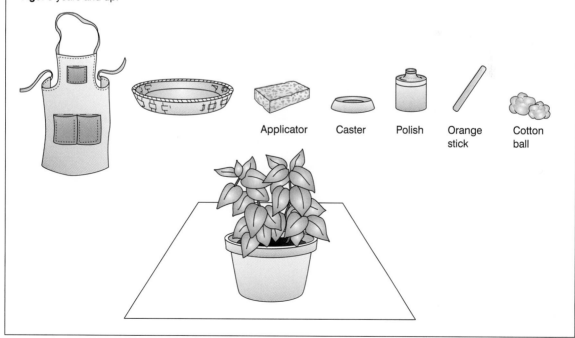

Applicator   Caster   Polish   Orange stick   Cotton ball

- *Red rods* (visual discrimination of length)—ten rod-shaped pieces of wood, all red, of identical size but differing in lengths from ten centimeters to one meter. The child arranges the rods next to each other from largest to smallest.

- *Cylinder blocks* (visual discrimination of size)—four individual wood blocks that

Figure 4.3/*Dusting*

Materials: Basket with a duster, soft brush, and feather duster; table to be dusted

Presentation:
Look for dust, with the eyes at the level of the surface of the table. Start with one half of the table, the one immediately in front of you.
Wipe the surface first, as most of the dust will be lying on the top and will give the greatest result.
Always dust away from the body, starting at one end working progressively to the other end, using circular movements.
After the top dust the sides, after the sides dust the legs. Don't forget the corners, the insides of the legs, and underneath the tabletop. The brush is to be used for the corners.
Shake the duster over the wastebasket or outdoors.

Purpose: Coordination of movements, care of the environment, indirect preparation for writing

Point of Interest: The dust to be found in the duster; shaking the dust off the cloth

Control of Error: Any spot of dust left behind

Age: 2½ to 4½ years.

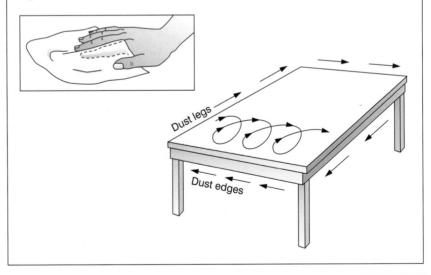

have holes of various sizes; one block deals with height, one with diameter, and two with the relationship of both variables. Children remove the cylinders in random order, then match each cylinder to the correct hole.

- *Smelling jars* (olfactory discrimination)—two identical sets of white, opaque glass jars with removable tops through which the child cannot see but through which odors can pass. The teacher places various substances, such as herbs, in the jars, and the child matches the jars according to the smells.

- *Baric tablets* (discrimination of weight)—sets of rectangular pieces of wood that vary according to weight. There are three sets—light, medium, and heavy—which children match according to the weight of the tablets.

- *Color tablets* (discrimination of color and education of the chromatic sense)—two identical sets of small, rectangular pieces of wood used for matching color or shading.

- *Sound boxes* (auditory discrimination)—two identical sets of cylinders filled with various materials, such as salt and rice. Children match the cylinders according to the sound the fillings make.

- *Tonal bells* (sound and pitch)—two sets of eight bells, alike in shape and size but different in color; one set is white, the other brown. The child matches the bells by tone.

- *Cloth swatches* (sense of touch)—two identical swatches of cloth. Children identify them according to touch, first without a blindfold but later using a blindfold.

- *Temperature jugs or thermic bottles* (thermic sense and ability to distinguish between temperatures)—small metal jugs filled with water of varying temperatures. Children match jugs of the same temperature.

Materials for training and developing the senses have these characteristics:

- *Control of error.* Materials are designed so that children can see if they make a mistake; for example, if a child does not build the blocks of the pink tower in their proper order, she does not achieve a tower effect.

- *Isolation of a single quality.* Materials are designed so that other variables are held constant except for the isolated quality or qualities. Therefore, all blocks of the pink tower are pink because size, not color, is the isolated quality.

- *Active involvement.* Materials encourage active involvement rather than the more passive process of looking.

- *Attractiveness.* Materials are attractive, with colors and proportions that appeal to children.

Basic Purposes of Sensory Materials

One purpose of Montessori sensory materials is to train children's senses to focus on some obvious, particular quality; for example, with the red rods, the quality is length; with pink tower cubes, size; and with bells, musical pitch. Montessori felt it is necessary to help children discriminate among the many stimuli they receive. Accordingly, the sensory materials help make children more aware of the capacity of their bodies to receive, interpret, and make use of stimuli. In this sense, the Montessori sensory materials are labeled *didactic,* designed to instruct.

Second, Montessori thought that perception and the ability to observe details were crucial to reading. The sensory materials help sharpen children's powers of observation and visual discrimination as readiness for learning to read.

A third purpose of the sensory materials is to increase children's ability to think, a process that depends on the ability to distinguish, classify, and organize. Children constantly face decisions about sensory materials: which block comes next, which color matches the other, which shape goes where. These are not decisions the teacher makes, nor are they decisions children arrive at by guessing; rather, they are decisions made by the intellectual process of observation and selection based on knowledge gathered through the senses.

Finally, all the sensory activities are not ends in themselves. Their purpose is to prepare children for the occurrence of the sensi-tive periods for writing and reading. In this sense, all activities are preliminary steps in the writing–reading process.

Academic Materials for Writing, Reading, and Mathematics

The third area of Montessori materials is academic; specifically, items for writing, reading, and mathematics. Exercises are presented in a sequence that encourages writing before reading. Reading is therefore an outgrowth of writing. Both processes, however, are introduced so gradually that children are never aware they are learning to write and read until one day they realize they are writing and reading. Describing this phenomenon, Montessori said that children "burst spontaneously" into writing and reading. Montessori anticipated contemporary practices such as the whole language approach in integrating writing and reading and in maintaining that through writing children learn to read.

Montessori believed many children were ready for writing at four years of age. Consequently, a child who enters a Montessori system at age three has done most of the sensory exercises by the time he is four. It is not uncommon to see four- and five-year-olds in a Montessori classroom writing and reading. Figures 4.4 and 4.5 show examples of children's writing. Following are examples of Montessori materials that lay the foundation for and promote writing and reading:

- *Ten geometric forms and colored pencils.* These introduce children to the coordination necessary for writing. After selecting a geometric inset, children trace it on paper and fill in the outline with a colored pencil of their choosing.

- *Sandpaper letters.* Each letter of the alphabet is outlined in sandpaper on a card, with vowels in blue and consonants in red. Children see the shape,

Sensory training plays a major role in the Montessori method. What knowledge, skills, and concepts is this child learning through her involvement with these materials?

Figure 4.4/*Writing Sample by Montessori Student José Roschetti*

The concert was very nice. The last song, the Firebird, was my favorite.

Figure 4.5/*Writing Sample by Montessori Student Alba Gosalbez*

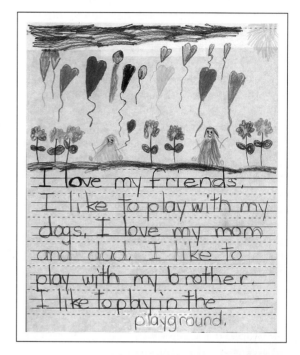

I love my friends. I like to play with my dogs. I love my mom and dad. I like to play with my brother. I like to play in the playground.

feel the shape, and hear the sound of the letter, which the teacher repeats when introducing it.

- *Movable alphabet, with individual letters.* Children learn to put together familiar words.

- *Command cards.* These are a set of red cards with a single action word printed on each card. Children read the word on the card and do what the word tells them to do (e.g., run, jump).

The following are examples of materials for mathematics:

- *Number rods.* A set of red and blue rods varying in length from ten centimeters to one meter, representing the quantities one through ten. With the help of the teacher, children are introduced to counting.

- *Sandpaper numerals.* Each number from one to nine is outlined in sandpaper on a card. Children see, touch, and hear the numbers. They eventually match

number rods and sandpaper numerals. Children also have the opportunity to discover mathematical facts through the use of these numerals.

- *Golden beads.* A concrete material for the decimal system. The single bead represents one unit. A bar made up of ten units in a row represents a ten; ten of the ten bars form a square representing one hundred; and ten hundred squares form the cube representing one thousand.

Additional Features

Other features of the Montessori system are mixed-age grouping and self-pacing. A Montessori classroom always contains children of different ages, usually from two-and-a-half to six years. This strategy is becoming more popular in many classrooms and has long been popular in the British Infant Schools. Advantages of mixed-age groups are that children learn from and help each other, a range of materials is available for all children, and older children become role models and collaborators for younger children. Contemporary instructional practices of student mentoring and cooperative learning have their roots in and are supported by multiage grouping.

In a Montessori classroom, children are free to learn at their own rate and level of achievement. They determine which activities to participate in and work at their own pace. However, children are not allowed to dally at a task. Through observation, the teacher determines when children have perfected one exercise and are ready to move to a higher level or different exercise. If a child does not perform an activity correctly, the teacher gives him or her additional help and instruction.

Table 4.1 outlines the basic characteristics of a good Montessori program that you can use as a guideline when you observe Montessori classrooms. Perhaps you can add other criteria you think would make a good early childhood program. Keep in mind that although details of educational programs vary from center to center, the basic constructs of a good Montessori program should be present.

MONTESSORI AS AN EDUCATIONAL SYSTEM

Montessori and the Public Schools

The first implementation of the Montessori program in the public schools occurred in Cincinnati, Ohio, in 1975. Since then, Montessori programs have been implemented in many public school programs, especially preschool programs and kindergartens. Currently more than fifteen hundred public school classrooms offer Montessori programs.[12]

A number of reasons account for the public school popularity of Montessori. First, Montessori is one of many programs of early childhood education that the public schools have used to *restructure,* or fundamentally change, the way they educate children. This restructuring of the schools is closely associated with the retraining of teachers; restructuring provides opportunities for retraining. So, a second reason for the growth of popularity of public school Montessori is that it is used as a means for retraining teachers. A successful Montessori program depends on well-trained teachers. Thus, by implementing a Montessori program, this provides the opportunity to train teachers in "new" and "alternative" approaches to educating young children.

Third, public school Montessori programs are often used as *magnet* schools. While the basic purpose of magnet schools is to integrate schools racially, at the same time they give parents a choice about what kind of program to give their children. Magnet schools as a means of integration have enabled professionals to use federal dollars that otherwise would not be available to them. Without a doubt the availability of federal dollars has been a major factor for public school implementation of the Montessori program. If Montessori is implemented *to the level it should be,* the cost can be $20,000 a classroom.

Fourth, inclusion of Montessori in the public schools is a way of giving parents choices in the kind of program their children will have at a particular school. Today, many early childhood and elementary programs specialize in a particular model, subject area, or program. This specialization enables many parents to select a school that teaches a curriculum they support.

Table **4.1**/*Basic Characteristics of a Montessori Program for Three- to Six-Year-Old Children*

Growth in the Child	Program Organization	Adult Aspects
Toward independence and problem solving	Ungraded three year age span: 2.6 to 6 years.	Certified Montessori teachers at the 3–6 year level
Toward the enjoyment of learning	Parental commitment to a three year cycle of attendance	Continuing professional development
Toward the development of order, concentration, and coordination	Five day week with a minimum daily three hour session	Observational skills to match students' developmental needs with activities
Toward skills in oral communication	Personal and group instruction	Strategies to facilitate the unique and total growth of each individual
Toward respect for oneself, other people, and the planet	Child:adult ratio of 15:1	Leadership skills to foster a nurturing environment supportive of learning
	Observational records of the child	
	Regularly scheduled parent conferences	A partnership developed with parents
Toward responsible group membership	Public observation policy	Supervision and education of auxiliary classroom personnel

Learning Environment	Program Emphasis	Administrative Support
Diverse set of Montessori materials, activities, and experiences	To encourage intrinsic motivation, spontaneous activity, and self-education	Organized as a legally and fiscally responsible entity
Schedule that allows large blocks of uninterrupted learning time	To provide sensory education for intellectual development	Non-discriminatory admissions policy
Classroom atmosphere that encourages social interaction	To encourage competencies through repetitive concrete experiences	Written educational policies and procedures
Space for personal, small group, and whole class learning activities	To encourage cooperative learning through peer teaching and social interaction	Adherence to state laws and health requirements
Lightweight, proportionate, movable child-sized furnishing	To provide learning opportunities through physical activity and outdoor work	Current school affiliation with AMS and other professional groups
Identifiable ground rules	To provide learning activities for creative expression	
Aesthetically pleasing environment		
Outdoor space to accommodate rigorous physical activity		

PROGRAM IN ACTION

A DAY IN A CHILDREN'S HOUSE

Billy Smith arrives at the Alexander Montessori School at 8:30 A.M. His mother drops him off at the entrance to the school on her way to work at the headquarters of a national airline. Billy is greeted by one of the classroom aides as he gets out of the car. Children who are new to the school are escorted to their classroom at the children's house by an aide until confident enough to go by themselves. Four-year-old Billy has gained a great deal of independence in his year and a half at the school and goes to his classroom by himself. Mrs. Collins, the classroom directress, greets Billy as he enters the classroom and engages him in a brief conversation about his baby sister.

Developing Independence

Mrs. Collins has the library, book cards, and the check-out and check-in systems arranged so the children do all the checking out and in of books, including writing their own name, without help. The key to this independence is the arrangement of the library. The previous day, Billy had checked out a book from the children's house library. This morning, Billy goes to the library card file and finds the card to the book he checked out. He places the card in the book and returns the book to the library.

Since Billy is the first child to arrive in the children's house this morning, he takes the chairs down from all the tables. He also puts down pieces of carpeting (approximately two by three feet) on the floor for each child and places a name card for each child on each piece of carpet. When the children come into the class, they will find their name card, pick it up, and place it on a pile. This is one way Mrs. Collins takes roll and at the same time helps the children learn their printed names.

Next, Billy goes to the language area, takes a set of geometric insets to a table (writing is always done on a table), and uses the frame and insets to make a geometric design of his choice on a sheet of paper. When his design is finished, he fills in the design with straight lines using colored pencils. Billy uses an ink stamp to stamp lines on the back of his paper, writes his name on the paper, and files his paper in his own file. The materials in his file will be made into a booklet that will be sent home at the end of the week.

Developing Writing

Billy is in the emergent, sensitive stage for writing. His motor skills make him capable of writing on paper, and he is always eager to write. Billy goes to the other side of the language corner to the movable alphabet cabinet and takes a set of word pictures to the carpet. Using the movable alphabet, he constructs a sentence using the picture card and movable alphabet letters. Billy's sentence is "The king is fat." After he has constructed his sentence, Billy takes paper and pencil and goes to a table where he writes this sentence. After he finishes writing, he puts the paper in his file.

Developing Responsible Behavior

At about 10:15 A.M., Billy takes a break for juice. The snack in the Montessori house is on an "as needed" basis, and Billy helps himself, pouring his own drink. Sometimes he and one of his friends take their break together. No attempt is made to force children to take a break or take it all at once or in groups.

After his snack, Billy goes to the practical life area and polishes a table. This activity takes about fifteen minutes. Billy gets all needed materials, completes the task, and puts things away by himself. Through exercises of practical life, Billy develops good work habits and extends his span of concentration. Polishing the table involves him in a gross-motor activity that must be performed in a certain way—setting up the material in a specific sequence (from left to right) and then polishing the table. It is Billy's responsibility when finished to replace the materials and return everything to the shelf.

Making Activity Choices

Billy, like all children, is very interested in writing and reading. He goes to the literacy area and writes a story about the concert he and his classmates attended the day before. Billy matches sounds to words as he writes. As part of the Montessori curriculum, he has learned sounds in relation to objects through the moveable alphabet. It is natural for him to "invent" the spelling of words he is interested in and that he needs in his writing. Mrs. Collins understands that left alone, and through the learning process, Billy will learn correct spelling.

From 11:00 to about 11:20, the children go outside, where they engage in free play for about ten minutes and then have a directed movement lesson consisting of jumping rope, throwing, or catching. In addition to free or directed play, children may use this outdoor time for nature walks and other kinds of field experiences.

Shared Learning Activities

When Billy comes in from outdoor play, he joins the other children in a circle activity with Mrs. Collins to learn songs and sing songs previously learned. The songs are usually based on a monthly theme Mrs. Collins selects. In addition to a song, the children also do finger plays, recite poems, and use rhythm band instruments. In the circle time (the children sit on a circle or ellipse marked on the floor), Billy holds the flag while the children say the Pledge of Allegiance, another child leads the group in song about good health habits, and each child is given an opportunity to share a personally important experience. Billy tells about his cousin visiting him over the weekend. The circle time also provides an opportunity to talk about matters of interest to the whole group. Children are free to join the circle time as they wish. The teacher respects children's personal independence and concentration on the task they are working on, so no one need stop what they are doing just to join. Because the circle time activities are so interesting, however, children generally want to join. The circle time provides an opportunity to all the children, who have been working at their own pace all morning, to come together.

When circle time is over, usually after about twenty minutes, the children eat their lunch. They wash their hands, get paper place mats and place them on a table, and set their lunch pails on them. At Billy's children's house, all the children bring their own lunch. Sometimes a child or several children who did not go outside during the recess time will set the tables.

In a children's house, children do everything they might normally do in their own homes: cleaning up, setting the table, getting a snack. Billy is responsible for helping clean up the table where he eats. After lunch, children can take part in games and songs, an activity directed by the teacher. Lunchtime usually lasts about an hour. During lunchtime, the children are also free to visit with each other and use materials of their choice.

After lunch, Billy checks his folder to see whether there is any unfinished work. If there is, he finishes it. If there is no work to be finished, the teacher suggests several things for him to do. On this particular day, Billy chooses to work with the geometry cabinet. This activity involves matching a set of cards to their corresponding geometric shapes. This matching activity takes Billy about twenty minutes. After he puts his materials away, Billy chooses easel painting. Again, Billy is responsible for putting on his own apron, getting the paper, putting it on the easel, and painting his own picture. This activity also encourages creativity.

Directed Instruction

In the children's house, there is no special time for rest. Children rest when they feel a need for it. Even with the two-and-a-half-year-olds, there is no attempt to force a nap time or rest period. The two-and-a-half- and three-year-old children go home for the day at noon, so there are only four- and five-year-olds in the school during the afternoon. Billy and his classmates, as a general rule, do not rest.

continued

When his art activity is finished, Billy's teacher offers him a new lesson with the hundred board. Billy is invited to a table, and the teacher brings the materials to the table. Part of Billy's task is to pay attention to the directed lesson so he will know how to do the lesson independently. When the teacher feels he is ready, Billy can begin to participate, and he gradually takes over the activity. This does not mean that Billy has entirely absorbed the lesson. If his teacher thinks it is necessary, she will give him another, or a more directed, lesson. This directed activity usually lasts about half an hour.

The last activity of the day is a birthday party for one of the classmates. The day ends at 3:00 P.M. Mrs. Collins says goodbye to Billy and tells him she is looking forward to seeing him tomorrow. Billy goes to the area where the children are picked up by their parents or other caregivers. Billy is picked up by a caregiver.

There is really no such thing as a "typical" day in a children's house. On any particular day, children may work only in the areas of math and practical life. Also, if children are undecided about what to do at any time, they will check their work folders to get ideas about what to do or to see what needs to be finished. They will also confer with the teacher or with one of the two classroom aides to get direction.

Keeping and Sharing Children's Records

Each child has a work folder with his or her name on it. Inside are four sheets listing the lessons from each of the four areas or avenues (practical life, sensorial, math, and language) of the Montessori system. Mrs. Collins marks each lesson with a yellow marker when she presents it to the child. When the child has mastered the lesson, she marks it in red, which indicates that the child is ready to go to another lesson. All written work, such as words, sentences, numbers, geometric shapes, and tracing, is kept in children's work folders. When a child has completed five papers of each activity, Mrs. Collins makes it into a booklet to take home.

Reports to parents are made in both conferences and writing. The Montessori program is explained to the parents before their children are enrolled. Periodic parent programs are also conducted to keep the parents informed and involved.

This account is based on the program and activities of the Alexander Montessori School in Miami, Florida. There are ten directresses at the Alexander School, all of whom are AMS certified.

Fifth, over the past decade parents who have had positive experiences with Montessori programs for their children have been strong advocates for the expansion of Montessori to public schools. This advocacy by parents has played a major role in both the popularity of Montessori and its growth.

Sixth, since Montessori developed her program for children with disabilities, some public schools see the Montessori method as an ideal way to meet the learning needs of today's children with disabilities.

The application of Montessori to the public school settings is so popular that these professionals have their own publication, the *Public School Montessorian* (published by Jola Publications, 2933 N. Second St., Minneapolis, MN 55411).

Thoroughly Modern Montessori

One of the many things that strikes a first-time observer of a Montessori classroom is how modern Montessori is both in terms of ideas and practice. Let us examine some features of Montessori that illustrate this.

1. *Integrated curriculum.* Montessori provides an integrated curriculum in which

children are actively involved in manipulating concrete materials across the curriculum—writing, reading, science, math, geography, and the arts. The Montessori curriculum is integrated in other ways, across ages and developmental levels. Montessori materials are age appropriate for a wide age range of children.

2. *Active learning.* In Montessori classrooms, children are actively involved in their own learning, as dramatized in the Program in Action feature, "A Day in a Children's House." Manipulative materials provide for active and concrete learning.

3. *Individualized instruction.* Curriculum and activities should be individualized for children. Montessori does this through individualizing learning for all children. Individualization occurs though children's interactions with the materials as they proceed at their own rates of mastery.

4. *Independence.* The Montessori environment emphasizes respect for children and promotes success, both of which encourage children to be independent. Indeed, independence has always been a hallmark of Montessori.

5. *Appropriate assessment.* Observation is the primary means of assessing children's progress, achievement, and behavior in a Montessori classroom. Well-trained Montessori teachers are skilled observers of children and are adept at translating their observation into appropriate ways for guiding, directing, facilitating, and channeling children's active learning.

6. *Developmentally appropriate practice.* From the preceding illustrations, it is apparent that the concepts and process of developmentally appropriate curricula and practice (see Chaps. 6 through 9) are inherent in the Montessori method. Indeed, it may well be that some of the most developmentally appropriate practices are conducted by Montessori practitioners. Furthermore, I suspect that quality Montessori practitioners understand, as Maria Montessori did, that children are much more capable than some early childhood education practitioners think.

Infant Montessori Programs

Montessori for children under age three is growing ever more popular, as illustrated by the rapidly expanding Montessori infant programs. The description of the Nido (Nest) on pages b–14 and b–15 in the second color insert, "Observing Programs in Action," provides an example of what is included in the Montessori infant program.

Frequently Asked Questions

Does attending a Montessori program stifle a child's creativity? People who ask this question for some reason think the prepared environment and didactic materials somehow keep or prohibit children from becoming or being creative. A Montessori program, in and of itself, does not inhibit children's creative impulses or activities. How parents and teachers encourage, support, and promote children's behaviors determines how "creative" they are. Oddly, this "creativity" question is seldom asked about other programs.

After attending a Montessori program, do children have trouble adjusting to a regular program? Embedded in this question is the belief that children who engage in active, independent learning inherent in a Montessori program will have trouble adjusting to a more "rigid" public school program. Fortunately, as described, increasing numbers of public schools are implementing the Montessori system. In addition, transition programs—programs designed to help children

PROGRAM IN ACTION

BILINGUAL MONTESSORI PRESCHOOL

A unique integration of native language instruction, preschool education, and the Montessori method is taking place in more than twenty child development centers throughout California. Administered by the Foundation Center for Phenomenological Research in Sacramento, the centers serve nearly 1,900 Spanish-speaking children six weeks to six years of age.

The Foundation Center provides a supportive learning environment for children through the Montessori method, home (i.e., native) language instruction, and multicultural environment. The staff relies exclusively on the child's primary language for instruction, interacting with the children only in Spanish throughout the day. Some children may respond occasionally in English, but staff members always use Spanish when communicating with the children.

"If you respect a child's home language, the transition to the second language will happen miraculously," comments Antonia López, director of education and staff development for the Foundation Center. "A lot of people think that if a child learns to speak English sooner, they'll be better off. But they don't realize what you're doing is separating the child from its parents."

All staff are recruited from the community the centers serve. After working as teaching assistants, they begin the process of being certified as Montessori teachers.

---

make smooth adjustments from one school program to another—are growing in popularity and use. Most Montessori programs have such transition programs for children and their families.

How long should a child attend a Montessori program? I was recently asked this question by a university student whose sister has her child in a Montessori program. The sister's worry is based on her fears that her daughter will have problems adapting to a public school setting.

Public school administrators and teachers are responding to parents' demands for Montessori programs for preschool through grade 6. Growing numbers of parents want the benefits of Montessori for their children throughout the elementary grades. So, some parents address the adapting question by advocating for elementary Montessori programs. The answer to the question rests then both with the availability of the program and with how satisfied children and parents are with it.

Guidelines for Selecting a Montessori School

Parents frequently ask early childhood professionals for advice about placing their children in a Montessori program. Unfortunately, there is no guarantee that a given Montessori program is of the kind and quality advocated by Maria Montessori. Selecting a Montessori preschool is like making other consumer choices; the customer must beware of being cheated. No truth-in-advertising law requires operators of a Montessori school to operate a quality program. Because the name has such appeal to parents, some schools call themselves Montessori without either the trained staff or facilities to justify their claim.

Not only do some schools misrepresent themselves, but some teachers do so as well. There is no requirement that a teacher must have Montessori training of any particular duration or by any prescribed course of instruction. The American Montessori Society (AMS) approves training programs that meet its standards for teacher training, and the Association Montessori International (AMI) approves teacher training programs that meet the standards of the international organization.

Early childhood professionals advise parents to consider the following points when selecting a Montessori program:

- Is the school affiliated with a recognized Montessori association (AMS or AMI)?

- Is the teacher a certified Montessori teacher or trained in the Montessori method?

- Are practices of the Montessori method part of the program?

- Contact parents of former students to determine their satisfaction with the program. Ask them, "Would you again send your child to this school? How is your child doing in first grade? How was the Montessori program beneficial to your child?"

- Compare tuition rates of the Montessori school to other schools. Is any difference in tuition worth it?

- Why do you want your child to attend a Montessori school? Is it social status? Prestige? Do you feel your child will achieve more by attending a Montessori school? Visit other preschool programs to determine whether a Montessori program is best for your child.

- Interview the director and staff to learn about the program's philosophy, curriculum, rules and regulations, and how the program differs from others that are not Montessori.

- Following enrollment, pay attention to children's progress through visits, written reports, and conferences to be sure they are learning what will be needed for an easy transition to the next grade, program, or school.

Criticisms of the Montessori Method

The Montessori system is not without critics. One criticism deals with the didactic nature of the materials and the program. Some say the system teaches a narrow spectrum of activities in which concepts are learned in a prescribed manner, following prescribed methods, using a prescribed set of material. Montessori believed children learn best from materials when shown how to use them, which seems to make sense, rather than just allowed to mess around with them. In many Montessori programs but by no means all, children are encouraged to use and experiment with the materials in creative ways after they have mastered them. One Montessori teacher related that she has seen children use the pink tower blocks in over a hundred ways!

Critics also claim the Montessori classroom does not provide for socialization. They cite the lack of group play, games, and other activities normally present in traditional kindergarten programs. This criticism, of course, is no truer for a Montessori setting than for any other classroom. No method or teacher can stop social interactions unless the teacher is determined to do so or the children are afraid of her. Many Montessori activities promote and offer opportunities for sharing tasks, cooperation, collaboration, and helping. Also, outdoor time and lunchtime (when children eat in pairs, threes, or small groups) afford ample opportunity for social interaction.

A related criticism is that children do not have opportunities to participate in dramatic make-believe and pretend play. Montessori believed that "play is the child's work." As such, children's play sets the stage for later roles and functions necessary for successful adult living. Thus, according to Montessori, fantasy play had little value. This is one Montessori area professionals must examine in terms of our *current* knowledge of children and learning.

The charge is frequently heard that Montessori schools represent an elitist or middle-class system. This claim likely stems from the fact that many Montessori schools were at one time operated by individuals for profit with high tuition. In most towns and cities, the Montessori program is now widely used in many Head Start, daycare, and public school programs.

One reason some parents and teachers feel the Montessori program is rigid is that its ideas and methodologies are so detailed. Another reason is that they have nothing to compare this system to other than the free-play programs they are more accustomed to. When parents and teachers compare the Montessori system, which organizes the environment and learning experiences in a specific, purposeful way, to a free-play setting, they tend to view the Montessori setting as rigid. Parents and teachers need to focus instead on the results of the system.

FURTHER THOUGHTS

In many respects, Maria Montessori was a person for all generations, and her method is proving to be a program for all generations. Montessori contributed greatly to early childhood programs and practices. Through her method she will continue to do so. Many of her practices—such as preparing the environment, providing child-size furniture, promoting active learning and independence, and using multiage grouping—have been incorporated into many early childhood classrooms. As a result, it is easy to take her contributions, like Froebel's, for granted. We do many things in a Montessorian way without thinking too much about it.

As we have noted, today Montessori education is enjoying another rebirth, especially in the public schools' embracing of its method. What is important is that early child-

hood professionals adopt the best of Montessori for children of the twenty-first century. As with any practice, professionals must adopt approaches to fit the children they are teaching while remaining true to what is best in that approach. Respect for children is never out of date and should be accorded to all children regardless of culture, gender, or socioeconomic background.

We have the tremendous benefit of hindsight when it comes to evaluating and analyzing educational thought and practice. In this process we need to consider what was appropriate then and determine what is appropriate today. When appropriate, early childhood professionals need to make reasoned and appropriate changes in educational practice. This is what growing the profession is all about.

More information about Montessori programs and training can be obtained by writing to the following organizations:

- The American Montessori Society, 150 Fifth Avenue, #203, New York, NY 10011; 212-924-3209

- Association Montessori International. (This is the oldest international Montessori organization, founded by Maria Montessori in 1929.) Address inquiries to AMI/USA, 410 Alexander St., Rochester, NY 14607; 716-461-5920

- North American Montessori Teachers' Association (NAMTA), 11424 Bellflower Rd. NE, Cleveland, OH 44106; 216-421-1905

ACTIVITIES FOR FURTHER ENRICHMENT

1. Write three or four paragraphs describing how you think Montessori has influenced early childhood educational practice.

2. Compare Montessori materials to those in other kindergartens and preschool programs. Is it possible for teachers to make Montessori materials? What advantages or disadvantages would there be in making and using these materials?

3. What features of the Montessori program do you like best? Why? What features do you like least? Why? What features are best for children?

4. After visiting a Montessori classroom and talking with teachers, evaluate the criticisms of the system given in the chapter. Are the criticisms valid? Are there any you would add? Why? In addition, make a list of the aspects of the Montessori classroom you liked and disliked and explain why.

5. A mother of a four-year-old asks your advice about sending her child to a Montessori school. What is your response?

6. Write to the AMS, AMI, and NAMTA for information about becoming a certified Montessori teacher. Compare the requirements for becoming a certified Montessori teacher with your university training. What are the similarities and differences?

7. Although there is a tremendous rise in the implementation of Montessori in the public schools, some educators think that this boom is not entirely good for either the Montessori system or the public schools. What do you think some of their concerns are?

8. Interview public and private school teachers about their understanding of the Montessori program. Do they have a good understanding of the program? What are the most critical areas of understanding or misunderstanding? Do you think *all* early childhood professionals should have knowledge of the Montessori program? Why?

9. Interview a Montessori school director to learn how to go about opening a Montessori school. Determine what basic materials are needed and their cost, then tell how your particular location would determine how you would "market" the program.

10. Multiage grouping is one of the aspects of the Montessori program that appeals to many early childhood professionals. List the advantages and disadvantages of multiage grouping. What conclusions can you draw from your list?

READINGS FOR FURTHER ENRICHMENT

Albanseia, Franco. *Montessori Classroom Management* (New York: Crown, 1990).

Provides insight on how to set up and manage a Montessori classroom. An asset for teachers who are hesitant about teaching in a Montessori setting but understand how a Montessori class can make a world of difference.

Britton, L. *Montessori Play and Learn: A Parent's Guide to Purposeful Play from Two to Six* (New York: Crown, 1992).

Designed for use by parents to further the emotional, social, and intellectual development of their two- to six-year-old children, this book describes the Montessori method of early childhood education and provides sample activities and games to develop children's skills in the home, the neighborhood, and the world.

Gordon, Cam. *Together with Montessori* (Minneapolis: Jola, 1993).

A practical guide to help teachers, administrators, and parents work cooperatively together in developing quality Montessori programs.

Kramer, Rita. *Maria Montessori* (New York: Putnam's, 1976).

Well-researched and documented biography.

Lillard, P. P. *Montessori Today: A Comprehensive Approach to Education from Birth to Adulthood* (New York: Shocken, 1996).

In detailed accounts of Montessori theory and practice, the author shows how children acquire the skills to answer their own questions, learn to manage freedom responsibly, and maintain a high level of intellectual curiosity. This is an essential handbook for parents and teachers interested in the Montessori alternative for older children.

Montessori, Maria. *Spontaneous Activity in Education,* trans. Arthur Livingston (New York: Schocken, 1965).

Continuation of ideas and methodologies begun in *The Montessori Method.* Deals with concepts of attention, intelligence, imagination, and moral development and discusses provisions for them in a Montessori setting.

Montessori, Mario M., Jr. *Education for Human Development: Understanding Montessori,* ed. Paula Polk Lillard (New York: Schocken, 1976).

Written by the grandson of Maria Montessori, essays in this book provide fresh insight into many Montessorian concepts. Addresses some traditional criticisms of the Montessori method and gives a modern approach to the Montessori system. Should be read after you have acquired knowledge of Montessori and her ideas.

Orem, R. C., and Marjorie Coburn. *Montessori Prescription for Children with Learning Disabilities* (New York: Putnam's, 1978).

Applies and adapts Montessori methods to the needs of the child with learning disabilities. There is much current interest in applying Montessori to programs for children with disabilities, so this book is timely despite its date.

Oriti, P., and D. Kahn, eds. *At Home with Montessori* (Cleveland Heights, OH: North American Montessori Teachers Association, 1994).

Based on Montessori's ideas about children's innate capabilities and potential, this book encourages restructuring the home environment to provide children, especially preschool children, with opportunities for self-directed activities and personal autonomy.

Standing, E. M., ed. *The Montessori Method* (New York: Shocken, 1962).

A foundational text in which Montessori describes her method and provides insight into her reasoning. Explains why she believed her method to be appropriate for all children.

NOTES

1. Maria Montessori, *Dr. Montessori's Own Handbook* (New York: Schocken, 1965), p. 133.
2. Maria Montessori, *The Montessori Method,* trans. Anne E. George (Cambridge, MA: Bentley, 1967), p. 104.
3. Maria Montessori, *The Secret of Childhood,* trans. M. J. Costello (Notre Dame, IN: Fides, 1966), p. 20.
4. Maria Montessori, *The Absorbent Mind,* trans. Claude A. Claremont (New York: Holt, Rinehart & Winston, 1967), p. 25.
5. Montessori, *The Secret of Childhood,* p. 48.
6. Ibid., pp. 46, 49.
7. Montessori, *The Absorbent Mind,* p. 6.
8. Ibid., p. 254.
9. Ibid., p. 84.
10. Ibid., p. 8.
11. Montessori, *Dr. Montessori's Own Handbook,* p. 131.
12. Interview 18 September 1996 with Denny Shapiro, editor of *The Public School Montessorian.*

C H A P T E R

5

Piaget

Constructivism
in Practice

Focus Questions

1. How is an understanding of Piaget's theory of intellectual development important to early childhood professionals?

2. What cognitive processes did Piaget consider integral to intellectual development?

3. What are the characteristics of children's thinking at each stage of intellectual development?

4. How do Piaget's stages of intellectual development relate to children's development of knowledge?

5. What are the major features and common concepts of educational curricula based on Piaget's theory?

6. What issues and controversies are associated with Piaget's theory?

ean Piaget developed the *cognitive theory* approach to learning. Piaget was interested in how humans learn and develop intellectually, beginning at birth and continuing across the life span. He devoted his life to conducting experiments, observing children (including his own), and writing about his theory. Piaget has enriched our knowledge about children's thinking, and his influence on early childhood education continues to be significant.

PIAGET'S DEFINITION OF INTELLIGENCE

Piaget developed an essentially logicomathematical theory of intelligence; that is, he perceived intelligence as consisting primarily of logical and mathematical abilities. (Compare this to Gardner's theory of multiple intelligences presented in Chap. 3.)

The term *intelligence* popularly suggests intelligence quotient or IQ—that which is measured on an intelligence test. Piaget, however, defined it as the *cognitive*, or mental, process by which children acquire knowledge; hence, *intelligence* is "to know." It is synonymous with *thinking* in that it involves the use of mental operations developed as a result of acting mentally and physically in and on the environment. Basic to Piaget's cognitive theory is the active involvement of children through direct experiences with the physical world. A second point is that intelligence develops over time, and a third premise is that children are *intrinsically motivated to develop* intelligence.

Piaget conceived of intelligence as having a biological basis; that is, all organisms, including humans, adapt to their environments. You are probably familiar with the process of physical adaptation, in which an individual, stimulated by environmental factors, reacts and adjusts to that environment; this adjustment results in physical changes. Piaget applied the concept of adaptation to the mental level and used it to help explain how intellectual development evolves through stages of thinking. Humans mentally adapt to environmental experiences as a result of encounters with people, places, and things; the result is cognitive development.

Constructivism and Intellectual Development

Piaget's theory is a *constructivist* view of development. Children literally construct their knowledge of the world and their level of cognitive functioning. "The more advanced forms of cognition are constructed anew by each individual through a process of 'self-directed' or 'self-regulated' activity."[1] The constructivist process

is defined in terms of the individual's organizing, structuring and restructuring of experience—an ongoing lifelong process—in accordance with existing schemes of thought. In turn, these very schemes become modified and enriched in the course of interaction with the physical and social world.[2]

Thus, "knowledge is built by an active child from the inside rather than being transmitted from the outside through the senses."[3]

LEARNING AS THE ADAPTION OF MENTAL CONSTRUCTS

Piaget used the term *schema* (scheme) to refer to any adaptive pattern of thought or action that an individual develops as a means of understanding the world. A newborn, for example, builds schemes based on reflective actions such as sucking and grasping. The child begins to build her concept and understanding of her world. When the child uses primarily reflexive actions to develop cognitive schemes, she is in what Piaget calls the *sensorimotor stage*, which begins at birth and usually ends between eighteen months and two years. (We discuss Piaget's stages of development in the next section of the chapter.) Reflexive actions help the child construct a mental scheme of what can and cannot be sucked, what sensations occur by sucking, what can and cannot be grasped. In infancy, the child uses these sensory schemes to know the world and to gain competence in acting on the environment. Schemes vary according to the environment in which the child is reared and the quality of her experiences in that environment. To a great extent, the environment establishes parameters for the development of intelligence. Children who have a variety of materials and a caring adult to help stimulate sensory responses are in a favorable environment for cognitive development.

Through this interaction with the environment that results in adaptation, children organize sensations and experiences. The resulting organization and processes of interaction are called *intelligence*. Obviously, therefore, the quality of the environment and the nature of children's experiences play a major role in the development of intelligence. For example, a child with various and differing objects available to grasp and suck, and many opportunities for this behavior, will develop differentiated sucking organizations (and therefore an intelligence) quite different from that of a child who has nothing to suck but a pacifier.

The Process of Adaptation

Piaget believed the adaptive process is composed of two interrelated processes, assimilation and accommodation, which ideally occur in equilibrium. Active learning is the key process by which children acquire their adaptive abilities.

Assimilation On the intellectual level, *assimilation* is the taking in of sensory data through experiences and impressions and incorporating them into knowledge of people and objects.

Every experience we have, whether as infant, child, or adult, is taken into the mind and made to fit into the experiences which already exist there. The new experience will need to be changed in some degree in order for it to fit in. Some experiences cannot be taken in because they do not fit. These are rejected. Thus the intellect assimilates new experiences into itself by transforming them to fit the structure

Caring for animals provides children opportunities to be physically and mentally involved. Piaget believed such active learning is necessary for mental development in the early years. What are some examples that you can give of how children's active involvement contributes to their learning?

which has been built up. This process of acting on the environment in order to build up a model of it in the mind, Piaget calls assimilation.[4]

Accommodation   Accommodation is the process by which individuals change their way of thinking, behaving, and believing to come into accord with reality. For example, a child who is familiar with cats because she has several at home may, upon seeing a dog for the first time, call it a cat. She has assimilated *dog* into her organization of *cat*. However, she must change (accommodate) her model of what constitutes "catness" to exclude dogs. She does this by starting to construct or build a scheme for *dog,* and thus for what "dogness" represents.

Now with each new experience, the structures which have already been built up will need to modify themselves to accept that new experience, for, as each new experience is fitted in to the old, the structures will be slightly changed. This process by which the intellect continually adjusts its model of the world to fit in each new acquisition, Piaget calls accommodation.[5]

The twin processes of assimilation and accommodation, viewed as an integrated, functioning whole, constitute *adaptation.*

Equilibrium   *Equilibrium* is a balance between assimilation and accommodation. Individuals cannot assimilate new data without to some degree changing their way of thinking or acting to fit those new data. People who always assimilate without much evidence of having changed are characterized as "flying in the face of reality." Yet, individuals cannot always accommodate old ideas to all the information they receive. If this were the case, no beliefs would ever be maintained. Balance is needed between the two. Diagrammed, the process would look something like that shown in Figure 5.1.

Upon receiving new sensory and experiential data, children assimilate or fit these data into their already existing schema of reality and the world. Equilibrium occurs if they can immediately assimilate the new data. If unable to assimilate the data, children try to accommodate and change their way of thinking, acting, and perceiving to account for the new data and restore equilibrium to the intellectual system. Data are rejected if they can neither be assimilated nor accommodated. Figure 5.2 illustrates this construction of a new concept.

Figure 5.1/*The Constructivist Process*

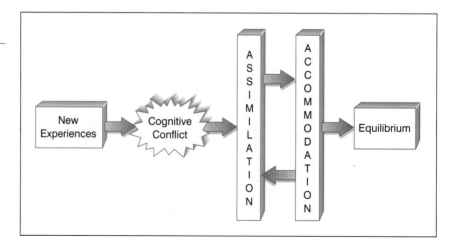

Consider three-year-old Betty, who meets cats in her neighborhood daily. From her observations, she is able to organize a mental category or concept built on cats' similarities, despite their differences. She can recall the category for use when needed. Organizing her observations in this way gives her an effective means of handling new observations. We can infer this from Betty's observed behavior.

One day she notices a squirrel for the first time . . .

Having focused on the squirrel's similarities with cats only, she mentally placed this new information from the environment into her category for cats. However, curiosity aroused, she approaches the squirrel and it runs off.

Later in the day, she is surprised to see a squirrel standing on its hind legs. After a momentary puzzlement her expression changes as she calls after the squirrel.

continued

Figure 5.2/*Continued*

Having focused on a difference between squirrels and cats, the child found the "cat" category was no longer useful here. She formed a new category based on the differences she observed. The squirrel can fit into this new category. Her facial expression suggests that she has reached a solution that is satisfying to her mental framework and is compatible with her experience.

On another occasion, when she used the "funny kitty" label in her mother's presence, she was given the correct label. The name "squirrel" fitted into her framework.

Source: The Piaget Primer: Thinking, Learning, Teaching by Ed Labinowicz, Reading, MA: Addison-Wesley, 1980, pp. 29, 30. © 1980 by Addison-Wesley Publishing Co., Inc. Used by permission.

Instances of rejection are common if what children (or, for that matter, adults) are trying to assimilate and accommodate is radically different from their past data and experiences. This partially accounts for Piaget's insistence that new experiences must have some connection or relationship to previous experiences. Present school experiences should build on previous life and school experiences.

Active Learning In this process of adaptation, Piaget ascribed primary importance to the child's physical activity. Physical activity leads to mental stimulus, which in turn leads to mental activity. Thus, it is not possible to draw a clear line between physical activity and mental activity in infancy and early childhood. Settings should provide for *active learning* by enabling children to explore and interact with people and objects. Early childhood professionals' understanding of this key concept helps explain their arranging infant and toddler settings so children can be active. It also helps explain the growth of programs that encourage and provide active learning for all children.

Active learning also means children will be mentally active and will engage in activities to promote thinking, problem solving, and decision making. Everyone recognizes that children should play, but we have not always recognized the importance of play as the context in which children construct mental schemes basic to all others. Play, to Piaget, is a powerful process in intellectual development. Parents seem to sense this intuitively in

wanting their children to play, particularly with other children. Many early childhood professionals understand the importance of play and include it in their curricula. NAEYC and the majority of early childhood professionals support active learning as the preferred practice in early childhood programs. Reggio Emilia is an outstanding example of children's active learning as well as constructivism in action. A description of Reggio Emilia in practice is found on pages b–4 and b–5 of the second color insert, "Observing Programs in Action."

STAGES OF INTELLECTUAL DEVELOPMENT

Table 5.1 summarizes Piaget's developmental stages and provides examples of stage-related characteristics. Piaget contended that developmental stages are the same for all children, including the atypical child, and that all children progress through each stage in the same order. The ages are only approximate and should not be considered fixed. The sequence of growth through the devel-

Table **5.1**/*Piaget's Stages of Cognitive Development*

Stage	Characteristic
Sensorimotor (Birth to 18 months/ 2 years)	Uses sensorimotor system of sucking, grasping, and gross-body activities to build schemes; begins to develop object permanency
Preoperational (2 to 7 years)	Dependent on concrete representations; uses the world of here and now as frame of reference; enjoys accelerated language development; internalizes events; is egocentric in thought and action; thinks everything has a reason or purpose; is perceptually bound; makes judgments primarily on basis of how things look
Concrete operations (7 to 12 years)	Is capable of reversal of thought process; able to conserve; still is dependent on how things look for decision making; becomes less egocentric; structures time and space; understands number; begins to think logically
Formal operations (12 to 15 years)	Is capable of dealing with verbal and hypothetical problems; can reason scientifically and logically; no longer is bound to the concrete; can think with symbols

opmental stages does not vary; the ages at which progression occurs do vary.

Sensorimotor Stage

During the period from birth to about two years, children use senses and motor reflexes to build knowledge of the world. They use their eyes to see, their mouths to suck, and their hands to grasp. Through these innate sensory and reflexive actions, they continue to develop an increasingly complex, unique, and individualized hierarchy of schemes. What children are to become physically and intellectually is related to these sensorimotor functions and interactions. As Furth says, "An organism exists only insofar as it functions."[6] This important concept stresses the necessity of an enriched environment for children.

The sensorimotor stage has the following major characteristics:

- Dependency on and use of innate reflexive actions

- Initial development of object permanency (the idea that objects can exist without being seen)

- Egocentricity, whereby children see themselves as the center of the world and believe events are caused by them

- Dependence on concrete representations (things) rather than symbols (words, pictures) for information

- By the end of the second year, children rely less on sensorimotor reflexive actions and begin to use symbols for things that are not present. (We will discuss intellectual development in infants, toddlers, preschoolers, and primary grade children in more detail in later chapters.)

Preoperational Stage

The preoperational stage begins at age two and ends at approximately seven years. Pre-operational children are different from sensorimotor children in the following ways:

- Language development begins to accelerate rapidly.

- Dependence on sensorimotor action decreases.

- There is increased ability to internalize events and think by utilizing representational symbols, such as words, in place of things.

Preoperational children continue to share common characteristics such as egocentricity with sensorimotor children. At the preoperational level, egocentricity is characterized by being perceptually bound. This is making judgments, expressing ideas, and basing perceptions mainly on an interpretation of how things are physically perceived by the senses. How things look to preoperational children is in turn the foundation for several other stage-related characteristics. First, children faced with an object that has multiple characteristics, such as a long, round, yellow pencil, will "see" whichever of those qualities first catches their eye. Preoperational children's knowledge is based only on what they are able to see, simply because they do not yet have operational intelligence or the ability to think using mental images.

Second, absence of operations makes it impossible to *conserve*, or determine that the quantity of an object does not change simply because some transformation occurs in its physical appearance. For example, show preoperational children two identical rows of checkers (Figure 5.3). Ask whether there are the same number of checkers in each row. The children should answer affirmatively. Next, space out the checkers in each row, and ask whether the two rows still have the same number of checkers. They may insist that there are more checkers in one row "because it's longer." These children base their judgment on what they can see, namely the spatial

Figure 5.3/Conservation of Number—A Lasting Equivalence

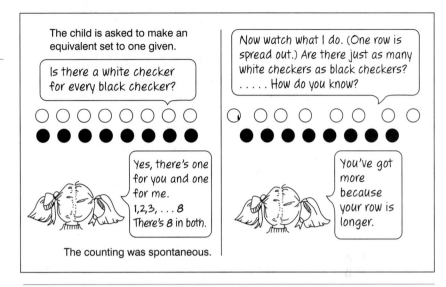

Source: *The Piaget Primer: Thinking, Learning, Teaching* by Ed Labinowicz, Reading, MA: Addison-Wesley, 1980, p. 101. ©1980 by Addison-Wesley Publishing Co., Inc. Used by permission.

Piaget's theory has many implications for how professionals interact with children and design learning experiences for them. Among the implications are that children think differently at different stages of cognitive development and that their thinking is not like adult thinking and should not be compared to it.

extension of one row beyond the other row. This is also an example of *reversibility;* in this case, the children are not capable of reversing thought or action, which would require mentally putting the row back to its original length.

Preoperational children act as though everything has a reason or purpose; that is, they believe every act of their parents and teacher or every event in nature happens for a specific purpose. This accounts for children's constant and recurring questions about why things happen, how things work, and the corresponding exasperation of adults in trying to answer these questions.

Preoperational children also believe everyone thinks as they think and therefore act as they act for the same reasons. Because preoperational children are egocentric, they cannot put themselves in another's place. To ask for sympathy or empathy with others is asking them to perform an operation beyond their developmental level.

Preoperational children's language illustrates their egocentrism. For example, in explaining to you about a dog that ran away, a child might say something like this: "And we couldn't find him . . . and my dad he looked . . . and we were glad." In this case, because of egocentrism, the child assumes you have the same point of view and know the whole story. The details are missing for you, not for the child. Young children's egocentrism also helps explain why they tend to talk at each other rather than with each other. This dialogue between two children playing at a day care center reveals egocentrism:

Jessica: My mommy's going to take me shopping.

Mandy: I'm going to dress this doll.

Jessica: If I'm good I'm going to get an ice cream cone too.

Mandy: I'm going to put this dress on her.

The point is that egocentrism is a fact of cognitive development in the early childhood years. Our inability always to see clearly someone else's point of view is evidence that egocentrism in one form or another is part of the cognitive process across the life span.

Concrete Operations Stage

Piaget defined *operation* as follows:

First of all, an operation is an action that can be internalized; that is, it can be carried out in thought as well as executed materially. Second, it is a reversible action; that is, it can take place in one direction or in the opposite direction.[7]

Unlike preoperational children, whose thought goes in only one direction (using the body and sensory organs to act on materials), children in the concrete operations stage begin to think using mental images and symbols and can reverse operations. Although children very much depend on the perceptual level of how things look to them, teachers can encourage children's mental development during this stage by using concrete or real objects as opposed to hypothetical situations or places.

Keep in mind, however, that telling is not teaching. Teachers often provide activities that are too easy rather than activities that are too difficult. Professionals should structure learning settings so children have experiences at their level with real objects, things, and people. For example, instead of just giving children a basket of small, plastic, colored beads to play with, ask them to sort the beads by color.

A characteristic of concrete operational children is the beginning of the ability to conserve. Unlike preoperational children, who think that because the physical appearance of an object changes it therefore follows that its quality or quantity changes (see Figure 5.3), concrete operational children begin to develop the ability to understand that change involving physical appearances does not necessarily change quality or quantity (Figure 5.4).

Figure 5.4/*Conservation*

PICK OUT THE TWO CLAY BALLS THAT HAVE THE SAME AMOUNT OF CLAY.	NOW WATCH WHAT I DO. I'M GOING TO MAKE THIS ONE INTO A SAUSAGE.	DO YOU STILL HAVE THE SAME AMOUNT OF CLAY, OR, DO YOU HAVE MORE IN ONE OF THE PIECES?	WHAT MAKES YOU THINK SO?
Equivalence Established	One Object Transformed	Child Judges Conservation	Child Justifies Response

Preoperational (2–7)

THE SAUSAGE IS MORE. IT'S LONGER.

Preoperational children are strongly influenced by appearances. When two dimensions are altered at the same time the preoperational child will center his attention on only one dimension and ignore the other. Most children younger than 7–8 years experience *centration* as they are unable to mentally hold two dimensions at the same time. They may have already constructed rules such as "longer is more" and "skinnier is less" but are unable to coordinate the rules.

When questioned, the children may agree that it's still the same clay. This knowledge of the *identity* of the clay is not enough to overcome the perceptual pull of the dominant dimension.

Children of this age tend to focus on the end result rather than on the act of transformation that neither adds nor subtracts any clay. Their responses reflect an *irreversibility* of such transformations to return to the original state. The children are unable to take a mental round trip back to the original shape of the clay.

Concrete Operational (7–11)

YOU MADE IT LONGER, BUT IT'S SKINNIER. IT'S STILL THE SAME AMOUNT.

IT'S THE SAME CLAY. YOU DIDN'T ADD ANY OR TAKE ANY AWAY.

IF YOU ROLLED IT BACK IT WOULD BE JUST AS BIG.

Seven to eight-year olds

Each child here justifies his conservation response with at least one of three logical arguments, as above. Children seldom offer more than two logical arguments in their justification. Children in the concrete operational stage have the following logical capacities:

Compensation: To mentally hold two dimensions at the same time (decenter) in order to see that one compensates for the other.
Identity: To incorporate identity in their justification. Identity now implies conservation.
Reversibility: To mentally reverse a physical action to return the object to its original state.

These related and reversible mental actions that operate in the presence of physical objects are called *concrete operations*.

Understanding of the conservation concept applied to most other properties requires more time and experience to develop.

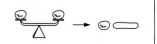

Does the clay ball weigh the same as the sausage, or does one weigh more?

Conservation of Weight (10 Years)

Will the water levels still be the same or will one be higher when the sausage is put in?

Conservation of Displacement Volume (11 Years)

Source: The Piaget Primer: Thinking, Learning, Teaching by Ed Labinowicz, Reading, MA: Addison-Wesley, 1980, p. 73. ©1980 by Addison-Wesley Publishing Co., Inc. Used by permission.

Children also begin to reverse thought processes, by going back over and "undoing" a mental action they have just accomplished. At the physical level, this relates to conservation. Children also are capable of other mental operations during this stage:

- One-to-one correspondence
- Classification of objects, events, and time according to certain characteristics
- Classification involving multiple properties of objects (Figure 5.5)

Figure 5.5/
Classification

Preoperational Stage (2–7)

Classification is the act of grouping objects according to their similarities. It is an activity in which young children naturally get involved.

"Put things together that are alike and go together."

Rather than arrange objects according to some chosen property, young children (four years) will arrange them according to the requirements of a picture.

Graphic representation

Children make piles of objects that look alike in one way.

Resemblance sorting

When two colors are present the child's grouping shows a lack of consistency. The child begins by grouping according to shape but soon loses track and allows color to become the basis for grouping.

Concrete Operational Stage (7–11)

Seven- to eight-year-old children can place objects in two overlapping classes and justify their choice.

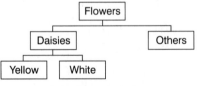

IT'S THE SMALL CIRCLE.
IT'S LIKE THE CIRCLE ⟷.
IT'S LIKE THE SQUARE ↕
BECAUSE IT'S SMALL.

Seven- to eight-year-old children can respond to the *class inclusion* tasks in the presence of objects, e.g., green + yellow chips.

Eight- to nine-year-old children demonstrate a refinement in approaching classification. When presented with groups of flowers they are able to respond correctly to the following questions:

(invisible relationship of groups)

"Which will make a bigger bunch, all the daisies or all the yellow daisies? . . . all of the flowers or all the daisies?"

"If you picked all the flowers in the garden would you have any daisies left?"

"Can you put a daisy in the box marked flowers without changing the label?"

"If you take all the daisies out of the box would you have any flowers left?"

- Class inclusion operations

- Complementary classes

Children are less egocentric during the concrete operations stage. They learn that other people's thoughts and feelings differ from their own. One of the more meaningful methods of helping children develop beyond this innate egocentrism is through interaction with other individuals, especially peers. The teacher's role is not to "teach" children to share or tell them when to apologize for something they have done. Children gradu-

ally become less egocentric through involvement with others, interacting and talking about social encounters.

Children do not suddenly emerge into the concrete operations stage after having been preoperational. It is rather a gradual, continual development over a period of time resulting from maturation and experiences. No simple sets of exercises will cause children to move up the developmental ladder. Experiences with people and objects result in activities that lead to conceptual understanding.

Piaget believed that, developmentally, after children were capable of making one-to-one correspondence and classifying and ordering objects they were ready for higher level thinking activities such as those that involve numeration and time and spatial relationships. How do these activities contribute to children's intellectual development?

Formal Operations Stage

The formal operations stage of development is the second part of operational intelligence. It begins at about eleven years of age and extends to about fifteen years. During this period, children become capable of dealing with increasingly complex verbal and hypothetical problems and are less dependent on concrete objects to solve problems. Children become free of the world of "things" as far as mental functioning is concerned, and can think abstractly over the past, present, and future. Children in this stage develop the ability to reason scientifically and logically, and they can think with all the processes and power of adults. How one thinks is thus pretty well established by the age of fifteen, although adolescents do not stop developing new schemes through assimilation and accommodation.

THE HIGH/SCOPE EDUCATIONAL APPROACH: A PIAGET-BASED PROGRAM

The High/Scope Educational Research Foundation is a nonprofit organization that sponsors and supports the High/Scope Educational Approach. The program is based on Piaget's intellectual development theory and

is an innovative, open-framework educational program that seeks to provide broad, realistic educational experiences for children. The curriculum is geared to the child's current stage of development to promote the spontaneous and constructive processes of learning and to broaden the child's emerging intellectual and social skills.[8]

Since part of the Piagetian theory of intellectual development maintains that children must be actively involved in their own learning through experiences and encounters with people and things, the High/Scope Educational Approach promotes children's active involvement in their own learning. The program identifies three fundamental principles:

- *Active participation of children in choosing, organizing, and evaluating learning activities, which are undertaken with careful teacher observation and guidance in a learning environment replete with a rich variety of materials located in various classroom learning centers*
- *Regular daily planning by the teaching staff in accord with a developmentally based curriculum model and careful child observations*
- *Developmentally sequenced goals and materials for children based on the High/Scope Key Experiences.*[9]

Objectives

The High/Scope program strives to

develop in children a broad range of skills, including the problem solving, interpersonal, and communication skills that are essential for successful living in a rapidly changing society. The curriculum encourages student initiative by providing children with materials, equipment, and time to pursue activities they choose. At the same time, it provides teachers with a framework for guiding children's independent activities toward sequenced learning goals.

The teacher plays a key role in instructional activities by selecting appropriate, developmentally sequenced material and by encouraging children to adopt an active problem-solving approach to learning. . . . This teacher–student interaction—teachers helping students achieve developmentally sequenced learning goals while also encouraging them to set many of their own goals—uniquely distinguishes the High/Scope Curriculum from direct-instruction and child-centered curricula.[10]

The High/Scope approach influences the arrangement of the classroom, the manner in which teachers interact with children, and the methods employed to assess children. The High/Scope curriculum can be defined by

Observation serves as a basis for assessing children's abilities and achievements. It also provides a basis for planning and for assuring that past learning is matched to present learning. What specific information can professionals gather through observation?

looking at the five interrelated components shown in Figure 5.6. Active learning forms the hub of the "wheel of learning" and is supported by the key elements of the curriculum.

The Five Elements of the High/Scope Approach

Adults who use the High/Scope Curriculum must be fully committed to providing settings in which children learn actively and construct their own knowledge. The child's knowledge comes from personal interaction with ideas, direct experience with physical objects, and application of logical thinking to these experiences. The adult's role is to supply the context for these experiences, to help the child think about them logically, and, through observation, to understand the progress the child is making. In a sense, children are expected to learn by the scientific method of observation and inference, at levels of sophistication consonant with their development.

Active Learning   At the center of the High/Scope curriculum is the idea that children are the mainspring of their own learning. The teacher supports children's active learning by stocking the classroom with a variety of materials, making plans and reviewing activities with children, interacting with and carefully observing individual children,

Figure 5.6/
*High/Scope Curricu-
lum Wheel*

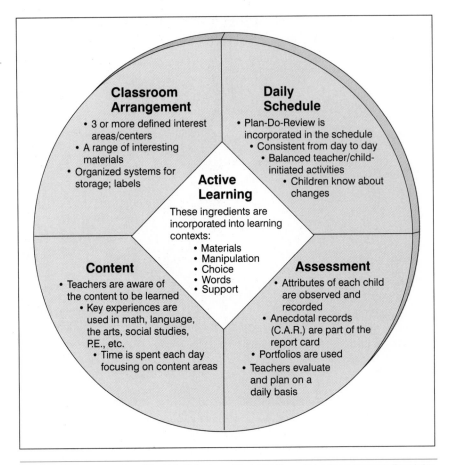

**Classroom
Arrangement**
- 3 or more defined interest
  areas/centers
- A range of interesting
  materials
- Organized systems for
  storage; labels

**Daily
Schedule**
- Plan-Do-Review is
  incorporated in the schedule
- Consistent from day to day
- Balanced teacher/child-
  initiated activities
- Children know about
  changes

**Active
Learning**
These ingredients are
incorporated into learning
contexts:
- Materials
- Manipulation
- Choice
- Words
- Support

Content
- Teachers are aware of
  the content to be learned
- Key experiences are
  used in math, language,
  the arts, social studies,
  P.E., etc.
- Time is spent each day
  focusing on content areas

Assessment
- Attributes of each child
  are observed and
  recorded
- Anecdotal records
  (C.A.R.) are part of the
  report card
- Portfolios are used
- Teachers evaluate
  and plan on a
  daily basis

Source: Used with permission of David P. Weikart, president, High/Scope Educational Research Foundation,
600 N. River St., Ypsilanti, Michigan 48198-2898.

and leading small- and large-group active
learning activities.

Classroom Arrangement The High/
Scope classroom arrangement invites children to engage in personal, meaningful, educational experiences. In addition, the classroom contains five or more interest areas
that encourage choice. Figure 5.7 shows a
room arrangement for kindergarten.

The plan-do-review process, detailed later
in the chapter, is the child-initiated experience
that implements the High/Scope Educational
Approach. The organization of materials and
equipment in the classroom supports the daily

routine—children know where to find materials
and what materials they can use, which
encourages development of self-direction and
independence. Small-group tables are used
for seating, independent work space, center
time activities, and teacher-directed instruction. Flexibility and versatility contribute to the
learning function. The floor plan in Figure 5.7
shows how room arrangement can support
and implement the program's philosophy,
goals, and objectives and how a center approach (books, blocks, computers, dramatic
play, art, construction) provides space for
large-group activities and meetings, small-
group activities, and individual work. In a

Figure 5.7/
A High/Scope Kinder-garten Classroom Arrangement

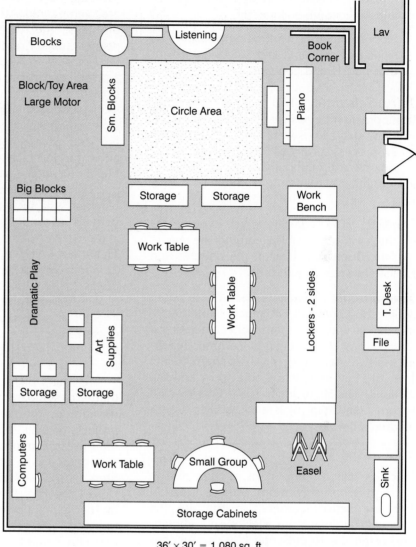

Blocks

Block/Toy Area
Large Motor

Sm. Blocks

Listening

Circle Area

Book Corner

Lav

Piano

Big Blocks

Storage   Storage

Work Bench

Dramatic Play

Work Table

Work Table

Lockers - 2 sides

T. Desk

File

Art Supplies

Storage   Storage

Computers

Work Table

Small Group

Easel

Sink

Storage Cabinets

36′ × 30′ = 1,080 sq. ft.

Source: Used with permission of David P. Weikart, president, High/Scope Educational Research Foundation, 600 N. River St., Ypsilanti, Michigan 48198-2898.

classroom where space is at a premium, the teacher must work at making one area serve many different purposes.

The teacher selects the centers and activities to use in the classroom based on several considerations:

- Interests of the children (e.g., kindergarten children are interested in blocks, housekeeping, and art)

- Opportunities for facilitating active involvement in seriation, number, time relations, classification, spatial relations, and language development

- Opportunities for reinforcing needed skills and concepts and functional use of those skills and concepts

Daily Schedule   The schedule considers developmental levels of children, incorporates a sixty to seventy-minute plan-do-review process, provides for content areas, is as consistent throughout the day as possible, and contains a minimum number of transitions.

Content   The High/Scope key experiences are lists of observable learning behaviors (see the discussion later in the chapter and the list shown in Figure 5.8).

Assessment   Teachers keep notes about significant behaviors, changes, statements, and things that help them better understand a child's way of thinking and learning. Teachers use two mechanisms to help them collect data, the key experience note form and the portfolio. The High/Scope Child Observation Record (see Chap. 8) is also used to assess children's development.

Role of the Teacher

Teachers play an important, unique role in the High/Scope curriculum. Just as the children are active learners, so too are the teachers. By daily team evaluation and planning using the High/Scope key experiences as a framework, teachers study their experiences with children and with classroom activities and strive to achieve new insights into each child's unique tapestry of skills and interests. Members of the teaching team challenge themselves by continually observing one another's performance and interacting in mutually supportive ways.

Another important aspect of the teacher's role concerns interaction with the child.

Although broad developmental milestones are employed to monitor youngsters' progress, the teacher does not teach a defined subject matter. Instead, she or he listens closely to what children plan and then actively questions and works with them to extend their activities to challenging levels, as appropriate. The teacher's questioning style emphasizes seeking information from the youngster—information that will help the adult to participate in the child's activity. "Test" questions, such as those about color, number, or size, are rarely used. Instead, the teachers ask such questions as, "What happened?" "How did you make that?" "Can you show me?" "Can you help another child?" This questioning style permits free conversation between adult and child and models language for child-to-child interaction. This approach permits the teacher and the child to interact as partners—as mutual thinkers and doers rather than as active teacher and passive pupil, the traditional school roles. All are sharing and learning as they work.

Teachers do not do a number of things that are standard in many classroom and daycare programs. They do not introduce projects for children to undertake. Neither do they use planned curriculum activities, such as workbooks or study guides, to train children in the alphabet or simple arithmetic skills. The High/Scope curriculum is based on the recognition that a group of three- and four-year-olds seldom would be able or wish to do the same thing at the same time and in the same manner without strong adult decision making, direction, and imposition of authority. Young children learn at different rates and from having a variety of experiences. Thus, the adults in a High/Scope program do not make the children pay attention, wait, perform tasks of little interest, or, most important, act on someone else's decisions. Rather, they develop and equip a stimulating environment, maintain a consistent daily routine, introduce ideas and activities as appropriate to extend child-developed plans or enable skill development, and interact naturally with children.

A Daily Routine to Support Active Learning

To create a setting in which children can learn actively, a consistent daily classroom routine is maintained that varies only when children have fair warning that things will be different the next day. Field trips are not sprung as surprises, nor are special visits or events planned for the classroom on the spur of the moment. This adherence to routine gives children the consistency they need to develop a sense of responsibility and at the same time enjoy opportunities for independence.

The High/Scope curriculum's daily routine is made up of a plan-do-review sequence and several additional elements. The plan-do-review sequence gives children opportunities to express intentions about their activities while keeping the teacher intimately involved in the whole process. The following paragraphs describe the elements of the daily routine.

Planning Time It is not unusual for young children to make choices and to make decisions about implementing the choices. But in most preschool programs, children seldom think about these decisions systematically or reflect on the possibilities and consequences of their choices. In the High/Scope approach, planning time gives children a structured, consistent chance to express their ideas to adults and to see themselves as individuals who can act on decisions. They experience the power of independence and the joy of working to be conscious of their intentions, and this supports the development of purpose and confidence.

The teacher talks with children about the plans they have made before the children carry them out. This helps children to clarify their ideas and think about how to proceed. Talking with children about their plans provides an opportunity for the teacher to encourage and respond to each child's ideas, to suggest ways to strengthen the plans so they will be successful, and to understand and gauge each child's level of development and thinking style. Both children and adults receive benefits: Children feel reinforced and ready to start their work, while adults have ideas of what opportunities for extension might arise, what difficulties children might have, and where problem solving may be needed. In such a classroom, all are playing appropriate and important roles.

Key Experiences The teacher must also continually encourage and support children's interest and involvement in activities, which occur within an organized environment and a consistent routine. Teachers plan from key experiences through which they may broaden and strengthen children's emerging abilities. Children generate many of these experiences on their own; others require adult guidance. Many key experiences are not limited to specific objects or places, but are natural extensions of children's projects and interests. Figure 5.8 lists key experiences that support learning in areas of speaking and listening, writing and reading.

Work Time This next part of the plan-do-review sequence is generally the longest single time period in the daily routine. Teachers new to the High/Scope curriculum sometimes find work time confusing because they are not sure of their role. Adults do not lead work-time activities—children execute their own plans of work—but neither do they just sit back and watch. The adult's role during work time is to observe children to see how they gather information, interact with peers, and

PROGRAM IN ACTION

HIGH/SCOPE IN PRACTICE

The High/Scope educational approach for three to five-year-olds is a developmental model based on the principle of active learning. The following beliefs underlie this approach:

- Children construct knowledge through their active involvement with people, materials, events, and ideas, a process that is intrinsically motivated.
- While children develop capacities in a predictable sequence, adult support contributes to children's intellectual, social, emotional, and physical development.
- Consistent adult support and respect for children's choices, thoughts, and actions strengthen children's self-confidence, sense of responsibility, self-control, and knowledge.
- Careful observation of children's interests and intentions is a necessary step in understanding their level of development and planning and carrying out appropriate interactions with them.

In High/Scope programs these principles are implemented throughout the day, both through the structure of the daily routine and in the strategies adults use as they work with children. Staff of each program plan for the day's experiences, striving to create a balance between adult- and child-initiated activity.

As they plan activities, the staff considers five "factors of intrinsic motivation" that research indicates are essential for learning. These factors are enjoyment, interest, control, probability of success, and feelings of competence. During greeting and small-group times, staff members actively involve children in decisions about activities and

materials as a way of supporting their intrinsic motivation to learn. This emphasis on child choice and control continues throughout the day, even during activities initiated by adults.

A Day at a High/Scope Program

Each program implements the High/Scope approach in a unique way. A typical day's activities at Giving Tree School follows:

The day begins with greeting time. Children gather as the teacher begins a well-known animal finger play, and join in immediately. Then the teacher suggests that the group make a circus of animals who are moving in many ways. Two children do not want to be animals, and the teacher suggests that these children may want to be the "audience." They get chairs and prepare to watch. Children suggest elephants, bears, and alligators as animals for the group to imitate. The children parade before the audience pretending to be animals and moving to the music. At the close of greeting time, the teacher suggests that children choose an animal to be as they move to the next activity, small-group time. During small-group time the children make "inventions" of their choice with recyclable materials a teacher has brought in and pine cones they collected the previous day.

As small-group time activities conclude, planning time begins. At this time, the teacher asks younger children to indicate their plans for work time by going to get something they will use in their play. She asks the older children to draw or copy the symbols or letters that stand for the area in which they plan to play (each play area is labeled with a sign containing both a simple picture symbol and words for the area).

solve problems, and then to enter into the children's activities to encourage, extend, and set up problem-solving situations.

Cleanup Time   Cleanup time is naturally integrated into the plan-do-review sequence

in the obvious place, after the "doing." During this time, children return materials and equipment to their labeled places and store their incomplete projects. This process restores order to the classroom and provides opportunities for the children to learn and

To indicate his plan, Charlie, age three, gets a small hollow block and brings it to the teacher. "I'm going to make a train. That's all," he says. Aja, age four, gets a dress and a roll of tape. "I'm going to the playhouse to be the mommy, and then I'm going to the art area to make something with tape," she explains. Five-year-old Ashley shows the teacher her drawing of the tub table and the scoops she will use with rice at the table.

During work time, the teachers participate in children's play. Riding on Charlie's "train," one teacher shows Tasha how to make the numerals 3 and 5 for train "tickets," joins two children playing a board game, and listens to Aja as she explains how she made a doll bed out of tape and a box. Another teacher helps Nicholas and Charlie negotiate a conflict over a block, encouraging them by listening and asking questions until they agree on a solution.

As children play, teachers occasionally jot down short notes about significant play episodes. During the morning, they record five or six brief anecdotes they will use later for planning and child assessment. As work time draws to a close, they move through the room, reminding the children that in a few minutes the cleanup bell will ring. Ashley suggests that for cleanup they make two trains, moving around the room to music and pausing when the music stops to clean up an area. The children really enjoy this activity and cleanup is accomplished quickly.

At recall time, the children gather with the same groups they met with at planning time. Standing in a circle, each group rotates a hula hoop through their hands as they sing a short song. When the song ends, the child nearest the tape is the first to recall his or her work time experiences. Charlie tells about the train they made out of blocks. Nicholas describes the special "speed sticks" he played with. Aja shows her doll bed, and Tasha describes her "tickets." After snack time, the children get their coats on and discuss what they will do outside. "Let's collect more pine cones. We can use them for food for the baby alligators." "Let's go on the swings. I just learned how to pump." "Let's see if we can find more bugs hiding under the rocks. They go there for winter." The teacher responds, "I'd like to help you look for bugs."

Key Experiences

As children play, they are actively involved in solving problems and participate in many of the High/Scope "key experiences." There are fifty-eight key experiences that fall into ten categories: *social relations and initiative, language, creative representation, music, movement, classification, seriation, numbers, pace,* and *time.* Teachers use the fifty-eight key experiences as guides for understanding development, planning activities, and describing the thinking and actions involved in children's play.

The High/Scope approach to learning supports developmentally appropriate, active learning experiences for each child as it encourages decision making, creative expression, problem solving, and other emerging abilities.

Contributed by Betsy Evans, Director and Teacher, The Giving Tree School, Gill, MA, and Field Consultant, High/Scope Educational Research Foundation.

use many basic cognitive skills. Of special importance is the way the learning environment is organized to facilitate children's use of materials. All materials in the classroom that are for children's use are within reach and on open shelves. Clear labeling is essential; this usually consists of easy-to-understand representations of the various objects on each shelf. With this organizational plan, children can realistically return all work materials to their appropriate places. Knowing where everything is located also gives

Figure 5.8/_Key Experiences in Language and Literacy for a High/Scope K–3 Curriculum_

SPEAKING AND LISTENING

Speaking their own language or dialect

Asking and answering questions

Stating facts and observations in their own words

Using language to solve problems

Participating in singing, storytelling, poetic and dramatic activities

Recalling thoughts and observations in a purposeful context

Acquiring, strengthening, and extending speaking and listening skills
  Discussing to clarify observations or to better follow directions
  Discussing to expand speaking and listening vocabulary
  Discussing to strengthen critical thinking and problem-solving abilities

WRITING

Observing the connections between spoken and written language

Writing in unconventional forms
  Scribbles
  Drawing
  Letters—random or patterned, possibly including elements of names copied from the environment
  Invented spelling of initial sounds and intermediate sounds

Writing in conventional forms

Expressing thoughts in writing

Sharing writing in purposeful context

Using writing equipment (e.g., computers, typewriters)

Writing in specific content areas

Acquiring, strengthening, and extending writing skills
  Letter formation
  Sentence and paragraph formation
  Capitalization, punctuation, and grammatical usage
  Editing and proofreading for mechanics, content, and style

Expanding the forms of composition
  Expressive mode
  Transactional mode—expository, argumentative, descriptive
  Poetic mode—narrative mode

Publishing selected compositions

READING

Experiencing varied genres of children's literature

Reading own compositions

Reading and listening to others read in a purposeful context

Figure 5.8/*Continued*

Using audio and/or video recordings in reading experiences

Acquiring, strengthening, and extending specific reading skills
  Auditory discrimination
  Letter recognition
  Decoding—phonetic analysis (letter/sound associations, factors affecting sounds, syllabication), structural
    analysis (forms, prefixes, suffixes)
  Vocabulary development

Expanding comprehension and fluency skills
  Activating prior knowledge
  Determining purpose, considering context, making predictions
  Developing strategies for interpreting narrative and expository text
  Reading varied genres of children's literature

children a sense of control, ownership, and even mastery.

Recall Time   Recall time, the final phase of the plan-do-review sequence, is the time when children represent their work time experience in a variety of developmentally appropriate ways. They might recall the names of the children they involved in their plan, draw a picture of the building they made, or describe the problems they encountered. Recall strategies include drawing pictures, making models, physically demonstrating how a plan was carried out, or verbally recalling the events of work time (Figure 5.9). The teacher supports children's linking of the actual work to their original plan.

This review permits children to reflect on what they did and how it was done. It brings closure to children's planning and work time activities, allowing them to express insight on what they have experienced. Putting their ideas and experiences into words also facilitates children's language development.

Small-Group Time   The general format of small-group time is familiar to most preschool teachers. The teacher presents a short activity

in which children participate for a given period of time. These activities may have to do with children's cultural backgrounds, field trips the group has taken, the seasons of the year, or age-appropriate aspects of music, movement, or art. In the High/Scope curriculum, the teacher introduces the activity and children are encouraged to contribute ideas and solve in their own way any problems presented. Activities follow no prescribed sequence but respond to children's needs, abilities, interests, and cognitive goals. Children work with materials in their own way and at their own rate.

In planning and implementing small-group time, active involvement by all children is important. The teacher extends children's ideas and actions by asking open-ended questions and by supporting additional problem-solving situations, and the activity that actually results may be different from that originally intended. An active small-group time gives children the chance to make choices, to explore materials and objects, and to talk and work with adults and other children.

Large-Group Time   In large-group time, the whole group meets together with an adult

Figure 5.9/*Representation of Work*

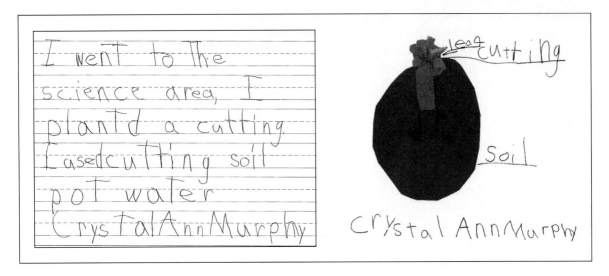

for ten to fifteen minutes to play games, sing songs, do finger plays, perform basic movement activities, play musical instruments, or reenact a special event. This time provides an opportunity for each child to experience a sense of community, to share and demonstrate ideas, and to take part in group problem-solving. Although the adult may bring the group together and initiate the activity, children act as leaders as well and are encouraged to make as many individual choices as possible.

Parent Involvement

Parent participation has been one of the High/Scope curriculum's hallmarks from the outset. The key to effective parent involvement is the two-way flow of information. Although the school and its staff have knowledge and training to provide to the family, the staff is also informed by the parents about the child, the family's culture, and their language and goals. The belief that parents and staff are each experts in their own domains is

essential to the success of the program and to its use in various settings.

Curriculum Themes

Four recurring themes based on Piaget's ideas appear in this curriculum. First, children's thinking is substantially different from that of adults, and adults must not try to impose their way of thinking on children. Adults should provide a setting in which children can think their own ideas and construct their own model of the world. Appropriate teacher behaviors include tolerance, support, acceptance of wrong answers, and encouragement to make hypotheses.

Second, children must be actively involved in learning. A child who is a passive recipient of information does not have the proper opportunity to develop intelligence to its fullest.

Third, learning should involve concrete objects and experiences with many children and adults, particularly at the sensorimotor and preoperational stages. Children are too often asked to deal with abstractions such as words and numbers when they have no idea what these symbols represent.

Finally, the fourth theme pertains to the quality and relatedness of experiences. What a child is like at a particular stage is largely a function of past experiences. Good experiences lead to intellectual development. Our job as teachers and parents is to maximize the quality of experiences. In addition, children's comprehension of an event depends greatly on the proximity of the event to the concepts involved. If children have nothing to associate an experience to, it is meaningless. Assimilation and accommodation cannot function unless experiences closely parallel each other.

PIAGET RECONSIDERED

Like all things designed to advance our knowledge and understanding of children, theories must stand the tests of time, criticism, and review. Theories are subject to the scrutiny, testing, and evaluation of professionals. This is the way theories are accepted, rejected, modified, and refined. Researchers have conducted thousands of studies to test the validity of Piaget's ideas. As a result of this constant review, professionals have challenged some of Piaget's ideas.

First, Piaget seems to have underestimated the ages at which children can perform certain mental operations. In fact, it appears that Piaget underestimated the intellectual abilities of all children, but particularly younger children. Children can understand more than Piaget believed based on the problems and tasks he gave them to perform. For example, children in the preoperational stage can perform tasks he assigned to the concrete operations stage. Additionally, recent advances in infant research (see Chap. 6) suggest that infants have more cognitive tools than Piaget or others thought.

Second, Piaget's emphasis on an undimensional view of intelligence as consisting primarily of logicomathematical knowledge and skills tends to de-emphasize other views. Professionals now recognize other definitions of intelligence and how it develops, such as Gardner's multiple intelligences (see Chap. 3). Early childhood professionals must consider varying definitions of intelligence when designing curricula and activities for children.

Third, Piaget's theory emphasizes that individual children are literally responsible for developing their own intelligence. In this regard, he likened children to "little scientists," engaged in a solitary process of intellectual development. With his emphasis on the role of the *individual child,* Piaget's approach to cognitive development tends to downplay the role of social interactions and the contributions of others to this process. On the other hand, Lev Vygotsky (see Chap. 3) believed that people play a major role in children's cognitive development and that children are not alone in their development of mental schemes. For Vygotsky, children develop knowledge, attitudes, and ideas through interactions with more capable others—parents, teachers, and peers. Early childhood professionals' embracing of Vygotsky's ideas helps explain the popularity of many social-based learning processes such as cooperative learning, multiage grouping, child-teacher collaboration, and peer-assisted teaching.

Fourth, one characteristic of children's language and cognitive development is that children talk to themselves. Perhaps you have observed a four-year-old busily engrossed in putting a puzzle together and heard her say, "Which piece comes next?" Piaget called this self-directed talk "ego-centric speech" and believed it furnished additional evidence of children's egocentrism, that children are more preoccupied with their own needs and concerns rather than the views of others. Vygotosky, on the other hand, believed that children's private speech plays an important role in cognitive development. He thought that children communicate with themselves to guide their behavior and thinking. As children develop, their audible private speech becomes silent inner speech and continues to serve the important functions of helping to solve problems and guide behavior. By being attentive to children's private speech, professionals can ask questions that will help children think and solve problems. Additionally, learning environments that permit children to be verbally active while solving problems support their cognitive development.

These and other views regarding the limitations of some of Piaget's ideas and observations do not invalidate his work. Rather, they mean that professionals must readjust their thinking and practices based on new discoveries about his ideas. While Piaget's theory is constantly reviewed and refined, and although other theories of intelligence are in the cognitive development spotlight, Piaget's contributions will continue to influence early childhood programs and professionals for decades to come. We have much more to learn from Piaget.

ACTIVITIES FOR FURTHER ENRICHMENT

1. Observe three children at the ages of six months, two years, and four years. Note in each child's activities what you consider typical behavior for that age. Can you find examples of behavior that correspond to one of Piaget's stages?

2. Observe a child between birth and eighteen months. Can you cite any concrete evidence, such as specific actions or incidents, to support the view that the child is developing schemes of the world through sensorimotor actions?

3. Figure 5.7 shows a floor plan for a High/Scope classroom. Design your own floor plan and provide a rationale for it. Tell how and why it differs from the plan in Figure 5.7.

4. The High/Scope approach is very popular in early childhood programs. What accounts for this popularity? Would you implement this curriculum in your program? Why?

5. Interview a trainer for the High/Scope approach, and identify the key issues in training professionals in the philosophy and methods of this program.

6. Compare Piaget's theory to another theory, such as Montessori's. How are they similar and different?

7. Plan a kindergarten lesson incorporating the plan-do-review process, using key experiences. What benefits for children does your lesson have?

8. List five concepts or ideas about Piaget's theory that you consider most significant for how to teach and rear young children. Explain how learning about Piaget's beliefs and methods may be influencing your philosophy of teaching.

9. Observe in a preschool program and record instances of children's private speech. How do children use private speech? What can you infer from what they are saying?

10. If an early childhood professional said she did not think it was important to know about Piaget's theory, how would you respond?

READINGS FOR FURTHER ENRICHMENT

Charbonneau, M., and B. Reider. *The Integrated Elementary Classroom: A Development Model of Education for the 21st Century* (Needham Heights, MA: Allyn & Bacon, 1996).

Targeting the elementary school-age child, (five to twelve), the book sets forth an integrated approach to developing classroom experiences using Piaget's theory as well as those of other theorists.

Hohmann, M. N., and D. P. Weikart. *Educating Young Children: Active Learning Practices for Preschool and Child Care Programs* (Ypsilanti, MI: High/Scope Press, 1995).

This is *the* High/Scope book and an excellent guide to understanding and employing the High/Scope Approach. It is the book professionals use.

Kamii, C., and R. DeVries. *Physical Knowledge in Preschool Education: Implications of Piaget's Theory* (Colchester, VT: Teachers College Press, 1993).

Guided by Piaget's constructivist theory on how children learn, the book explores an innovative approach to teaching physical knowledge in preschool.

NOTES

1. Deanna Kuhn, "The Role of Self-Directed Activity in Cognitive Development," in *New Directions in Piagetian Theory and Practice,* ed. Irving E. Sigel, David M. Brodzinsky, and Roberta M. Golinkoff (Hillsdale, NJ: Erlbaum, 1981), p. 353.

2. David M. Brodzinsky, Irving E. Sigel, and Roberta M. Golinkoff, "New Directions in Piagetian Theory and Research: An Integrative Perspective," in *New Directions in Piagetian Theory and Practice,* ed. Irving E. Sigel, David M. Brodzinsky, and Roberta M. Golinkoff (Hillsdale, NJ: Erlbaum, 1981), p. 5.

3. Constance Kamii, "Application of Piaget's Theory to Education: The Preoperational Level," in *New Directions in Piagetian Theory and Practice,* ed. Irving E. Sigel, David M. Brodzinsky, and Roberta M. Golinkoff (Hillsdale, NJ: Erlbaum, 1981), p. 234.

4. P. G. Richmond, *An Introduction to Piaget* (New York: Basic Books, 1970), p. 68.

5. Ibid.

6. Hans G. Furth, *Piaget for Teachers* (Upper Saddle River, NJ: Prentice Hall, 1970), p. 15.

7. Jean Piaget, *Genetic Epistemology,* trans. Eleanor Duckworth (New York: Columbia University Press, 1970), p. 21.

8. High/Scope Education Research Foundation, *The High/Scope K-3 Curriculum: An Introduction* (Ypsilanti, MI: Author, 1989), p. 1.

9. Ibid.

10. Ibid., p. 3.

Developmentally Appropriate Programs and Practices

PART THREE

> . . . play is never trivial; it is serious and deeply significant. It needs to be cherished and encouraged by the parents, for in his free choice of play a child reveals the future life of his mind to anyone who has insight into human nature.
>
> Friedrich Froebel

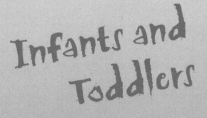

Infants and Toddlers

CHAPTER 6

Foundation Years for Learning

Focus Questions

1. Why has the number of infants and toddler programs increased?

2. What are milestones in infant and toddler development?

3. How does Piaget's cognitive theory explain infant and toddler development?

4. What are the major theories of infant and toddler language development and acquisition?

5. What are the major features of Erikson's theory of psychosocial development in the infant and toddler years?

6. What are the developmental differences between infants and toddlers?

7. How can professionals provide developmentally appropriate programs for infants and toddlers?

8. What features contribute to quality infant and toddler programs?

9. What issues are involved in quality care and education for infants and toddlers?

nterest in infant and toddler care and education is at an all-time high and will continue at this level into the twenty-first century. This growing demand stems primarily from the large number of women in the labor force. It is also fueled by parents who want their children to have an "early start" and get off on the "right foot" so they can have an even better life than their parents. The acceptance of early care and education is also attributable to a changing view of the very young and the discovery that infants are remarkably competent individuals. Parents and early childhood professionals have combined forces to give infants and toddlers quality care and education without harmfully and needlessly pushing and

153

hurrying them. This collaborative effort will continue.

PHYSICAL DEVELOPMENT

The infant and toddler years between birth and age three are full of developmental milestones and social events. Infancy, life's first year, includes the first breath, the first smile, first thoughts, first words, and first steps. Significant developments also occur during toddlerhood, the period between one and three years; two are unassisted walking and rapid language development. Mobility and language are the cornerstones of autonomy that enable toddlers to become independent. These unique developmental events are significant for children as well as those who care for and teach them. How early childhood professionals and parents respond to infants' firsts and toddlers' quests for autonomy helps determine how children grow and master the life events that await them.

To fully grasp their roles as educators and nurturers, early childhood professionals need to understand the major events and processes of normal growth and development. To begin, we must recognize that infants and toddlers are not the miniature adults many baby product advertisements picture them to be. Children need many years to develop fully and become independent. This period of dependency and professionals' responses to it are critical for the developing child. Professionals must constantly keep in mind that "normal" growth and development are based on averages, and the "average" is the middle ground of development. (Table 6.1 gives average heights and weights for infants and toddlers.) To assess children's progress, or lack of it, professionals must know the milestones of different stages of development. At the same time, to assess what is "normal" for each child, they must consider the whole child. They must look at cultural and family background, including nutritional and health history, to determine what is normal for that child. Professionals must also keep in mind that when children are provided with good nutrition, health care, and a warm, loving emotional environment, development tends toward what is "normal" for each child.

Table 6.1/*Average Height and Weight of Infants and Toddlers*

Age	Males		Females	
	Height (inches)	Weight (pounds)	Height (inches)	Weight (pounds)
Birth	19.9	7.2	19.6	7.1
3 months	24.1	13.2	23.4	11.9
6 months	26.7	17.3	25.9	15.9
9 months	28.5	20.2	27.7	18.9
1 year	30.0	22.4	29.3	21.0
1½ years	32.4	25.3	31.9	23.9
2 years	34.5	27.8	34.1	26.2
2½ years	36.3	30.1	35.9	28.5
3 years	38.0	32.4	37.6	30.7

Source: Based on data from P. V. V. Hamill et al., "Physical Growth: National Center for Health Statistics Percentiles," *American Journal of Clinical Nutrition* 32 (1979), pp. 607-629.

MOTOR DEVELOPMENT

Motor development is important to infants and toddlers because it contributes to intellectual and skill development. Human motor development is governed by certain basic principles:

- Motor development is sequential (Table 6.2).

- Maturation of the motor system proceeds from gross (large) to fine behaviors. When learning to reach, for example, an infant sweeps toward an object with the whole arm; as a result of development and experiences, gross reaching gives way to specific reaching and grasping.

- Motor development is from *cephalo* to *caudal*—from head to foot (tail). This process is known as *cephalocaudal* development. The head is the most developed part of the body at birth; infants hold their heads erect before they sit, and sitting precedes walking.

- Motor development proceeds from the *proximal* (midline or central part of the body) to the *distal* (extremities), known as *proximodistal* development. Infants are able to control their arm movements before they can control finger movements.

Motor development plays a major role in social and behavioral expectations. For example, toilet training (also called *toilet learning* or *toilet mastery*) is a milestone of the toddler period. This process often causes a great deal of anxiety for parents, professionals, and toddlers. American parents want to accomplish toilet training as quickly and efficiently as possible, but frustrations arise when they start too early and expect too much of children. Toilet training is largely a matter of physical readiness, and most child-rearing experts recommend waiting until children are two years old before beginning. Although some parents claim that their children are trained as early as one year, it is probably the parent rather than the child who is trained.

The principle of toilet training is that parents and professionals are helping children develop control over an involuntary response.

Table 6.2/Infant and Toddler Motor Milestones

Behavior	Age of Accomplishment for 90% of Infants/Toddlers
Chin up momentarily	3 weeks
Arms and legs move equally	7 weeks
Smiles responsively	2 months
Sits with support	4 months
Reaches for objects	5 months
Smiles spontaneously	5 months
Rolls over	5 months
Crawls	7 months
Creeps	10 months
Pulls self to stand	11 months
Walks holding onto furniture	13 months

Source: William K. Frankenburg, William Sciarillo, and David Burgess, "The Newly Abbreviated and Revised Denver Developmental Screening Test," *Journal of Pediatrics* 99 (Dec. 1981), p. 996. Used by permission.

Motor development plays a major role in cognitive and social development. Learning to walk enables young children to explore their environment which in turns contributes to cognitive development. What are some ways that motor development enhances young children's ability to learn?

When an infant's bladder and bowel are full, the urethral and sphincter muscles open. The goal of toilet training is to teach the child to control this involuntary reflex and use the toilet when appropriate. Training involves maturational development, timing, patience, modeling, preparing the environment, establishing a routine, and developing a partnership between the child and parents/professionals. Another necessary partnership is between parents and professionals who are assisting in toilet training, especially when parents do not know what to do, are hesitant about approaching toilet training, or want to start the training too soon.

HOW DOES INTELLECTUAL DEVELOPMENT OCCUR?

As we learned in Chapter 5, an individual's first schemata (schemes) are sensorimotor. According to Piaget, infants do not have "thoughts of the mind." Rather, they come to know their world by actively acting on it through their senses and motor action. According to Piaget, infants *construct* (as opposed to absorb) schemes using sensorimotor reflexive actions.

Infants begin life with only reflexive motor actions that they use to satisfy biological needs. In response to specific environmental conditions, they modify these reflexive actions through accommodation and adaptation to the environment. Patterns of adaptive behavior initiate more activity, which leads to more adaptive behavior, which in turn yields more schemes. Consider sucking, for example, an innate sensorimotor scheme. The child turns the head to the source of nourishment, closing the lips around the nipple, sucking, and swallowing. As a result of experiences and maturation, the infant adapts or changes this basic sensorimotor scheme to include both anticipatory sucking movements and nonnutritive sucking such as sucking a pacifier or blanket.

Children construct or create new schemes through the processes of assimilation and accommodation. Piaget believed children are active *constructors* of intelligence through assimilation (taking in new experiences) and accommodation (changing existing schemes to fit new information), which result in *equilibrium.*

Stages of Cognitive Development

Sensorimotor Intelligence   Sensorimotor intellectual development consists of six stages, shown in Table 6.3 and described in the following subsections.

Stage 1: Birth to One Month.   During this stage, infants suck and grasp everything. They are literally ruled by reflexive actions. Reflexive responses to objects are undifferentiated, and infants respond the same way to everything. Sensorimotor schemes help

Table 6.3/*Stages of Sensorimotor Intellectual Development*

Stage	Age	Behavior
I: Reflexive action	Birth to 1 month	Reflexive actions of sucking, grasping, crying, rooting, swallowing Through experiences, reflexes become more efficient (e.g., amount of sucking required for nourishment) Little or no tolerance for frustration or delayed gratification
II: Primary circular reactions	1 to 4 months	Acquired adaptations form Reflexive actions gradually replaced by voluntary actions Circular reactions result in modification of existing schemes
III: Secondary circular reactions	4 to 8 months	Increased responses to people and objects Able to initiate activities Beginning of object permanency
IV: Coordination of secondary schemes	8 to 12 months	Increased deliberation and purposefulness in responding to people and objects First clear signs of developing intelligence Continuing development of object permanency Actively searches for hidden objects Comprehends meanings of simple words
V: Experimentation (tertiary circular reactions)	12 to 18 months	Active expermentation begins through trial and error Spends much time "experimenting" with objects to see what happens; insatiable curiosity Differentiates self from objects Realization that "out of sight" is not "out of reach" or "out of existence" Beginning of understanding of space, time, and causality
VI: Representational intelligence (intention of means)	18 to 24 months	Development of cause–effect relationships Representational intelligence begins; can mentally represent objects Engages in symbolic imitative behavior Beginning of sense of time Egocentric in thought and behavior

infants learn new ways of interacting with the world, and the new ways of interacting promote cognitive development.

Grasping is a primary infant sensorimotor scheme. At birth, the grasping reflex consists of closing the fingers around an object placed in the hand. Through experiences and maturation, this basic reflexive grasping action becomes coordinated with looking, opening the hand, retracting the fingers, and grasping, thus developing from a pure, reflexive action to an intentional grasping action. As an infant matures in response to experiences, the grasping scheme is combined with a delightful activity of grasping and releasing things.

Stage 2: One to Four Months. The milestone of this stage is the modification of the reflexive actions of Stage 1. Sensorimotor behaviors not previously present in the infant begin to appear: habitual thumb sucking (indicates hand–mouth coordination), tracking moving objects with the eyes, and moving the head toward sounds (indicates the beginning of the recognition of causality). Infants start to direct their own behavior rather than being totally dependent on reflexive actions. The first steps of intellectual development have begun.

Primary circular reactions begin during Stage 2. A circular response occurs when an infant's actions cause a reaction in the infant or another person that prompts the infant to try to repeat the original action. The circular reaction is similar to a stimulus-response, cause-and-effect relationship.

Stage 3: Four to Eight Months. Piaget called this stage that of "making interesting things last." Infants manipulate objects, demonstrating coordination between vision and tactile senses. They also reproduce events with the purpose of sustaining and repeating acts. The intellectual milestone of this stage is the beginning of *object permanence.* When

infants in Stages 1 and 2 cannot see an object, it does not exist for them—" out of sight, out of mind." During later Stage 3, however, awareness grows that things that are out of sight continue to exist.

Secondary circular reactions begin during this stage. This process is characterized by an infant's repeating an action with the purpose of getting the same response from an object or person; for example, an infant will repeatedly shake a rattle to repeat the sound. Repetitiveness is characteristic of all circular reactions. *Secondary* here means that the reaction is elicited from a source other than the infant. The infant interacts with people and objects to make interesting sights, sounds, and events last. Given an object, the infant will use all available schemes, such as mouthing, hitting, and banging; if one of these schemes produces an interesting result, the infant continues to use the scheme to elicit the same response. Imitation becomes increasingly intentional as a means of prolonging an interest.

Stage 4: Eight to Twelve Months. During this stage, the infant uses means to attain ends. Infants move objects out of the way (means) to get another object (end). They begin to search for hidden objects, although not always in the places they were hidden, indicating a growing understanding of object permanence.

Stage 5: Twelve to Eighteen Months. This stage, the climax of the sensorimotor period, marks the beginning of truly intelligent behavior. Stage 5 is the stage of experimentation. Toddlers experiment with objects to solve problems, and their experimentation is characteristic of intelligence that involves *tertiary circular reactions*, in which they repeat actions and modify behaviors over and over to see what will happen. This repetition helps develop understanding of cause-and-effect relationships and leads to the discovery of new relationships through exploration and experimentation.

Physically, Stage 5 is also the beginning of the toddler stage, with the commencement of walking. Toddlers' physical mobility, combined with their growing ability and desire to experiment with objects, makes for fascinating and often frustrating child rearing. They are avid explorers, determined to touch, taste, and feel all they can. Although the term *terrible twos* was once used to describe this stage, professionals now recognize that there is nothing terrible about toddlers exploring their environment to develop their intelligence. Novelty is interesting for its own sake, and toddlers experiment in many different ways with a given object. For example, they will use any available item—a wood hammer, a block, a rhythm band instrument—to pound the pegs in a pound-a-peg toy.

Stage 6: Eighteen Months to Two Years.

This is the stage of transition from sensorimotor to symbolic thought. Stage 6 is the stage of symbolic representation. *Representation* occurs when toddlers can visualize events internally and maintain mental images of objects not present. Representational thought enables toddlers to solve problems in a sensorimotor way through experimentation and trial and error and predict cause-and-effect relationships more accurately. Toddlers also develop the ability to remember, which allows them to try out actions they see others do. During this stage, toddlers can "think" using mental images and memories, which enables them to engage in pretend activities. Toddlers' representational thought does not necessarily match the real world and its representations, which accounts for a toddler's ability to have other objects stand for almost anything: a wooden block is a car; a rag doll is a baby. This type of play, known as *symbolic play*, becomes more elaborate and complex in the preoperational period.

In summary, we need to keep in mind several important concepts of infant and toddler development:

1. The chronological ages associated with Piaget's stages of cognitive development are approximate. In fact, as we discussed in Chapter 5, children can do things earlier than the ages Piaget assigned. Professionals should not be preoccupied with children's ages but should focus on cognitive behavior, which gives a clearer understanding of a child's level of development. This is the true meaning of developmentally appropriate caregiving.

2. Infants and toddlers do not "think" as adults do; they come to know their world by acting on it and need many opportunities for *active* involvement.

3. Infants and toddlers are actively involved in *constructing* their own intelligence. Children's activity with people and objects stimulates them cognitively and leads to the development of mental schemata (schemes).

4. Parents and early childhood professionals need to provide *environments* and *opportunities* for infants and toddlers to be actively involved. These are two important conditions for intellectual development. Reflexive actions form the basis for assimilation and accommodation, which enable cognitive structures to develop. Professionals must ensure that infants and toddlers have experiences that will enable successful intellectual construction.

5. At birth, infants do not know that there are objects in the world and, in this sense, have no knowledge of the external world. They do not and cannot differentiate between themselves and the external world. For all practical

purposes, the infant *is* the world. All external objects are acted on through sucking, grasping, and looking. This acting on the world enables infants to construct schemes of the world.

6. The concept of *causality*, or cause and effect, does not exist at birth. Infants' and toddlers' concepts of causality begin to evolve only through acting on the environment.

7. As infants and toddlers move from one stage of intellectual development to another, later stages evolve from, rather than replace, earlier ones. Schemes developed in Stage 1 are incorporated into and improved on by the schemes constructed in Stage 2, and so forth.

HOW DOES LANGUAGE DEVELOP?

Language development begins at birth. Indeed, some argue it begins before birth. The first cry, the first coo, the first "da-da" and "ma-ma," the first word are auditory proof that children are participating in the process of language development. Language helps define us as human, and represents one of our most remarkable intellectual accom-

A major theme throughout this text is that all children are different. While we can clearly identify progressive stages of development, as in this photograph, early childhood professionals must always provide for the individual needs of every child. In what ways are these children similar? In what ways are they different?

Box 6.1   Voices from the Field: A View from the Classroom Door

What does good infant and toddler care and early education look like? Every center director spends at least some of her time each day looking into classroom doors or windows to see if things are going okay. What does she expect to see? What are the indicators that matter during this snapshot view? Here are some of those things for me.

Continuity of teachers and children in the group. By far the first thing I look for is a familiar scene. Is everyone who is supposed to be in the classroom there? Are the people present who are the most knowledgeable about the children in the group? Are all of the children in the group present?

Familiar faces of the adults who care for children and children who are in the group are crucial to high-quality care and early education for infants and toddlers. Continuity of caregiver and continuity of group together allow for an intense level of predictability and stability that facilitates children's adjustment to out-of-home care and increases the chance that the separation and reunion process will be predictable and pleasant.

I also look for continuity to remain stable over time. Keeping teachers and children together in primary groups for lengthy periods of time (up to three or more years) allows teachers of infants and toddlers to create an out of home caregiving experience that is compatible with their family experience.

A sense of peace and tranquility. Perhaps one of the most frightening aspects of out of home care for parents of infants and toddlers is the real concern that children's emotional needs will not be met. Parents report that they are afraid that their child will need attention and not get it because of the demands of having three or more infants and five or more toddlers in a group.

This fear is magnified by the separation and reunion process which, during the infant and toddler years, can often (and quite normally) be accompanied by crying and resistance. Parents may leave a crying child at the beginning of the day and return to a crying child at the end of the day—fueling fears that the time in the middle couldn't have been pleasant either.

So, classrooms for infants and toddlers need to have a sense of tranquility and peace—a sense that the underlying timbre of the classroom is calm and stable. I look for a classroom where crying children are getting a prompt response—at least a verbal connection ("I'm on my way as soon as I finish changing this diaper")—if not a physical one, and where actions speak as loud as words do. I look to see if teachers have ideas about what children need now as well as what they might need later. And, I look to see if teachers have planned for or are going about meeting those needs. (Are bottles being warmed? Are security items labeled and available?) I look for evidence that teachers know each child's individual daily routine and respect it by offering a bottle or lunch before the child is too hungry or beginning a calm-down routine before the child gets too tired. I also look for signs that the adults are calm, confident, relaxed, and unhurried.

A balance of novelty and predictability in a clean environment. In infant and toddler programs, cleanliness is crucial. Because infants and toddlers spend a great deal of time on the floor and exploring with their hands and mouths, the environment must be clean and without odors.

It must also be predictable, filled with familiar yet interesting things to look at and manipulate. Children need to be able to find things where they left them the last time they were here—the same place for sleeping, eating, and reading books. But I also look for novel and interesting things to do, objects to touch, places to be, things to dump and sort through, and things to be discovered by uncovering or unwrapping.

I look for space. Overcrowding is a real problem with infant and toddler care because required licensing standards often limit space, which in the infant environment particularly can be filled up with cribs and other furniture. Infants and toddlers need plenty of space—enough to always have another area to move or be moved to for exploration, visual and tactile stimulation, or experimentation, and they need to get away from stimulation and excitement to avoid over-stimulation.

Engagement between children and teachers. One of the most critical components of quality care and early education for infants and toddlers is the interactive environment.

I look for teachers to be where children are and children to be where teachers are. Sometimes this means physical engagement like sharing a book in a comfortable rocking chair or playing together on the floor. Sometimes this means emotional engagement such as that involving routine activities like diapering and eating.

It means seeing evidence of emotional contact and connectedness—quick responses to cries, looking where the child looks and commenting on what is seen, checking to see if you're needed, verbal exchanges that lead children to believe you mean what you say, and a sense of caring about what children are seeing, feeling, and doing.

I look to see if teachers treat children respectfully—asking a child if she is ready to be picked up before doing it, using language to talk "to" children rather than "at" them, narrating what is going to happen before it happens and as it happens, etc.

I also look to see if teachers are observing children. Careful observation is the source of recognition of developmental progress and the way to discover emergent skills and interests. It also ensures that teachers register and make changes as children change so that boredom does not set in.

Pace changes across the day. Because infants and toddlers in full day care and early education can spend a majority of their day in out of home care, pace changes are crucial—both for children and the adults who care for them.

I look to see that things change across the day. Positions are changed for young infants. All children get opportunities to go outside, music sometimes fills the air, window blinds are closed to create a sense of calm, then opened to let the sun shine in! I look to see if the pace picks up and becomes energetic and active and then quiets down to become intimate and soothing.

Help with social problem solving. Children under three in out of home care are not yet able to interact intensely for long periods of time in groups without facilitation and support. In the beginning this looks a lot like protection from others—keeping fingers out of mouths, helping children crawl around rather than over, supporting side by side play, and giving infants and toddlers opportunities to look at and watch other children doing interesting things. Later on, it includes facilitating emerging social skills like sharing re-sources, taking turns, perfecting skills like using an outstretched hand to ask for a toy nonverbally, and using language to communicate needs and wants.

To make this happen, teachers need to be close to where children are—physically near them—so they are available to model, guide, or support children's initial and subsequent interactions. So I look for teachers to be on the floor where children are, at the table when children are eating, participating in the process of picking up and putting down interesting toys, and supporting emerging skills by example as well as with verbal and physical guidance.

The view from the door is often a snapshot—and certainly not an in-depth program evaluation. But high quality care and early education for infants and toddlers is very observable—the components that create a positive experience for both children and their teachers can be seen in a view from the door.

Kay Albrecht, Ph.D. is the executive director of HeartsHome Early Learning Center, a nationally accredited care and early education program in Houston, Texas, which serves over 60 infants and toddlers.

plishments. How does the infant go from the first cry to the first word a year later? How does the toddler develop from saying one word to several hundred words a year later? While everyone agrees that children learn language, not everyone agrees how. How does language development begin? What forces and processes prompt children to participate in one of the uniquely human endeavors? Let us examine some of the explanations.

Language Acquisition

Heredity plays a role in language development in a number of ways. First, humans have the respiratory and laryngeal systems that make rapid and efficient vocal communication possible. Second, the human brain makes language possible. The left hemisphere is the center for speech and phonetic analysis and the brain's main language center. But the left hemisphere does not have the exclusive responsibility for language. The right hemisphere plays a role in our understanding of speech intonations, which enables us to distinguish between declarative, imperative, and interrogative sentences. Without these processing systems, language as we know it would be impossible. Third, heredity plays a role in language development in that some theorists believe that humans are innately endowed with the *ability* to produce language.

Noam Chomsky is one proponent of the theory that humans are born with the ability to acquire language. He hypothesizes that all children possess a structure or mechanism called a *language acquisition device* (LAD) that permits them to acquire language. The young child's LAD uses all the language sounds heard to process many grammatical sentences, even sentences never heard before. The child hears a particular language and processes it to form grammatical rules.

Eric Lenneberg has studied innate language acquisition in considerable detail in many different kinds of children, including the deaf. According to Lenneberg,

All the evidence suggests that the capacities for speech production and related aspects of language acquisition develop according to built-in biological schedules. They appear when the time is ripe and not until then, when a state of what I have called "resonance" exists. The child somehow becomes "excited," in phase with the environment, so that the sounds he hears and has been hearing all along suddenly acquire a peculiar prominence. The change is like the establishment of new sensitivities. He becomes aware in a new way, selecting certain parts of the total auditory input for attention, ignoring others.[1]

The fact that children generate sentences they have never heard before is often cited as proof of innate ability. What would language be if we were only capable of reproducing the sentences and words we heard? The ability of children in all cultures and social settings to acquire language at a relatively immature age tends to support the thesis that language acquisition and use is more than a product of imitation or direct instruction. Indeed, children learn language without formal instruction.

The idea of a sensitive period of language development makes a great deal of sense and had a particular fascination for Montessori, who believed there were two such sensitive periods. The first begins at birth and lasts until about three years. During this time, children unconsciously absorb language from the environment. The second period begins at three years and lasts until about eight years. During this time, children are active participants in their language development and learn how to use their power of communication. Milestones of language development for infants and toddlers are shown in Table 6.4.

Table 6.4/Language Development in Infants and Toddlers

Months of Age	Language
Birth	Crying
1½	Social smile
3	Cooing (long pure vowel sound)
5	"Ah-goo" (the transition between cooing and early babbling)
5	Razzing (child places tongue between lips and produces a "raspberry")
6½	Babbling (repetition of consonant sounds)
8	"Dada/Mama" (inappropriate)
10	"Dada/Mama" (appropriate)
11	One word
12	Two words
14	Three words
15	Four–six words
15	Immature jargoning (sounds like gibberish; does not include any true word)
18	Seven–twenty words
18	Mature jargoning
21	Two-word combinations
24	Fifty words
24	Two-word sentences
24	Pronouns (*I, me, you;* used inappropriately)

Source: A. J. Capute and P. J. Accardo, "Linguistic and Auditory Milestones during the First Two Years of Life," *Clinical Pediatrics* 17(11) (Nov. 1978), p. 848. Used by permission.

Environmental Factors   Theories about a biological basis of language should not be interpreted to mean that children are born with the particular language they will speak. While the ability to acquire language has a biological basis, the content of the language—syntax, grammar, and vocabulary—is acquired from the environment, which includes other people as models for language. Development depends on talk between children and adults, and between children and children. Optimal language development ultimately depends on interactions with the best possible language models. The biological process may be the same for all children, but the content of their language will differ according to environmental factors. Children left to their own devices will not learn a language as well as children reared in linguistically rich environments.

For example, Susan Curtiss writes of Genie, a modern-day "wild child." During her early days, Genie had minimal human contact, and her father and brother barked at her like dogs instead of using human language. She did not have an opportunity to learn language until she was thirteen-and-a-half years old, and even after prolonged treatment and care, Genie remained basically language deficient and conversationally incompetent.[2]

Behaviorism   One popular view of language development is that language is acquired through associations resulting from stimulus-response learning. Theorists who take this view see language acquisition as a product of parents' and the environment's rewarding children's language efforts. Parents, for example, reward children for their first sounds by talking to them and making sounds in response. First words are reinforced in the same way, with parents (and others) constantly praising and encouraging. Modeling and imitation also play important roles in this view of language acquisition. Children imitate the sounds, words, sentences, and grammar they hear other children and adults use. Children's parents reinforce or reward children when the sounds they make are a part of the language and do not reinforce sound patterns not in the language; in this way, children learn the language of their parents.

The question of innate language acquisition versus language acquisition based on environmental factors is similar to the controversy of nature versus nurture in intellectual development. One cannot reject one viewpoint at the expense of the other. We must consider language acquisition as the product of both innate processes and environmental factors.

Early Childhood Professionals and Language Learning

People who care for children and are around them in the early stages of language learning greatly influence how and what they learn. Children's language experiences can make the difference in their school success. Many children enter a preschool or child care setting without much experience in talking and listening to other children or adults in different social settings.

Parents and professionals should focus on the *content* of language: learning names for things, how to speak in full sentences, and how to use and understand language. Many of these language activities relate directly to success in preschool, kindergarten, and first grade. The following guide-

The process of language development begins at birth— perhaps even before. Parents, teachers, and others play powerful roles in children's language development. Communicating with children provides a rich linguistic environment for children to learn language. What are some specific things this caregiver can do to promote a child's language development?

lines will help you promote children's language development:

- Treat children as partners in the communication process. Many infant behaviors, such as smiling, cooing, and vocalizing, serve to initiate conversation, and professionals can be responsive to these through conversation.

- Conversations are the building blocks of language development. Attentive and caring adults are infants' and toddlers' best stimulators of cognitive and language development.

- Talk to infants in a soothing, pleasant voice, with frequent eye contact, even though they do not "talk" to you. Most mothers and professionals talk to their young children differently from the way they talk to adults. They adapt their speech so they can communicate in a distinctive way called *motherese*. Mothers' language interactions with their toddlers are much the same as with infants. When conversing with toddlers who are just learning language, it is a good idea to simplify verbalization—not by using "baby talk," such as "di-di" for diaper or "ba-ba" for bottle, but rather by speaking in an easily understandable way. For example, instead of saying, "We are going to take a walk around the block so you must put your coat on," you would instead say, "Let's get coats on."

- Use children's names when interacting with them, to personalize the conversation and build self-identity.

- Use a variety of means to stimulate and promote language development, including reading stories, singing songs, listening to records, and giving children many opportunities to verbally interact with adults and other children.

- Encourage children to converse and share information with other children and adults.

- Help children learn to converse in various settings by taking them to different places so they can use their language with a variety of people. This approach also gives children ideas and events for using language.

- Have children use language in different ways. Children need to know how to use language to ask questions, explain feelings and emotions, tell what they have done, and describe things.

- Give children experiences in the language of directions and commands. Many children fail in school settings not because they do not know language but because they have little or no experience in how language is used for giving and following directions. It is also important for children to understand that language can be used as a means to an end—a way of attaining a desired goal.

- Converse with children about what they are doing and how they are doing it. Children learn language through feedback—asking and answering questions and commenting about activities—which shows children that you are paying attention to them and what they are doing.

- Talk to children in the full range of adult language, including past and future tenses.

How Does Psychosocial Development Occur?

Erik H. Erikson (1902–1994) is noted for his *psychosocial theory* of development. According to Erikson, children's personalities grow and develop in response to social institutions such as families, schools, child care centers, and early childhood programs. Of course, adults are principal components of these environments and therefore play a powerful role in helping or hindering children in their personality development.

Stages of Psychosocial Development

Erikson's theory has eight stages, which he also classifies as *ego qualities*. These qualities emerge across the human life span. Erikson maintains psychosocial development results from the interaction between maturational processes such as biological needs and the social forces encountered in everyday living. Socialization provides the context for conflict and crisis resolution during the eight developmental stages. Four of these stages apply to children from birth to age eight (Table 6.5).

Stage 1: Basic Trust versus Mistrust (Birth to about Eighteen Months)
During this stage, children learn to trust or mistrust their environments and professionals. Trust develops when children's needs are met consistently, predictably, and lovingly.

Stage 2: Autonomy versus Shame and Doubt (Eighteen Months to about Three Years)
This is the stage of independence, when children want to do things for themselves. Lack of opportunities to become autonomous and independent and professional overprotection result in self-doubt and poor achievement. As a result, instead of feeling good about their accomplishments, children come to feel ashamed of their abilities.

Stage 3: Initiative versus Guilt (Three Years to about Five Years)
During the preschool years children need opportunities to respond with initiative to activities and tasks, which gives them a sense of purposefulness and accomplishment. Erikson believes children can feel guilty when they are discouraged or prohibited from initiating activities and are overly restricted in attempts to do things on their own.

Stage 4: Industry versus Inferiority (The Elementary School Years)
In this period, children display an industrious attitude and want to be productive. They want to build things, discover, manipulate objects, and find out how things work. Productivity is important during this stage. They also want recognition for their productivity, and adult response to children's efforts and accomplishments helps develop a positive self-concept. Feelings of inferiority result when children are criticized, belittled, or have few opportunities for productivity.

Basic Human Needs

Abraham Maslow (1890–1970) identified a hierarchy of basic human needs (Figure 6.1): (1) life essentials, (2) safety and security, (3) belongingness and love, (4) achievement and prestige, (5) aesthetic needs, and (6) self-actualization. All professionals must endeavor to provide the conditions, environments, and opportunities for children at all ages to have these basic needs met. Chapter 12 contains a comprehensive discussion of these needs and examples of how to provide for them, especially as a means of guiding children's behavior.

In Chapter 4 we discussed in detail the Montessori approach to educating young children and emphasized the use of Montessori educational materials. The description of the Montessori Nido on pages b-14 and b-15 of the second color insert, "Observing Programs in Action," illustrates the great respect Montessorians have for children and their development. Montessori believed children begin their mental development at birth and must receive active care in the first years of

Table 6.5/*Erikson's Stages of Psychosocial Development in Early Childhood*

Stage	Approximate Ages	Characteristics	Role of Early Childhood Educators	Outcome for Child
Basic trust vs. mistrust	Birth to 18 months or 2 years	Infants learn either to trust or mistrust that others will care for their basic needs, including nourishment, sucking, warmth, cleanliness, and physical contact.	Meet children's needs with consistency and continuity	Views the world as safe and dependable
Autonomy vs. shame	18 months to 3 years	Toddlers learn to be self-sufficient or to doubt their abilities in activities such as toileting, feeding, walking, and talking.	Encourage children to do what they are capable of doing; avoid shaming for any behavior	Learns independence and competence
Initiative vs. guilt	3 to 5 years (to beginning of school)	Children are learning and want to undertake many adultlike activities, sometimes overstepping the limits set by parents and thus feeling guilty.	Encourage children to engage in many activities; provide environments in which children can explore; promote language development	Able to undertake a task, be active and involved
Industry vs. inferiority	Elementary	Children actively and busily learn to be competent and productive or feel inferior and unable to do things well.	Help children win recognition by producing things; recognition results from achievement and success	Feelings of self-worth and industry

Figure 6.1/*Hierarchy of Needs*

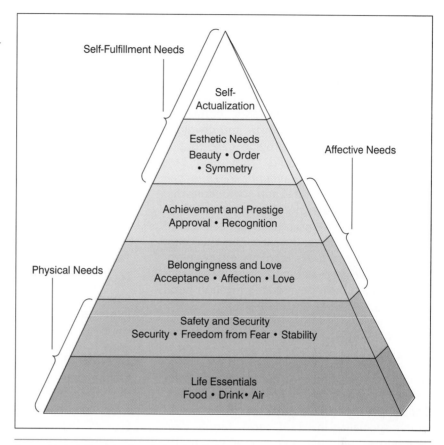

Self-Fulfillment Needs

Self-Actualization

Esthetic Needs
Beauty • Order • Symmetry

Affective Needs

Achievement and Prestige
Approval • Recognition

Physical Needs

Belongingness and Love
Acceptance • Affection • Love

Safety and Security
Security • Freedom from Fear • Stability

Life Essentials
Food • Drink • Air

Source: Maslow's hierarchy of needs data from *Motivation and Personality,* 3rd ed. by Abraham H. Maslow. Revised by Robert Frager et al. Copyright ©1954, 1987 by Harper & Row, Publishers, Inc. Copyright © 1970 by Abraham H. Maslow. Reprinted by permission of Addison-Wesley Educational Publishers, Inc.

life. Pay particular attention to the Nido as a prepared environment and the "knowledgeable care" provided.

CHARACTERISTICS OF EARLY CHILDHOOD PROFESSIONALS

Regardless of who provides care for infants and toddlers, professionals should have certain qualities to provide for children's *total* needs on all levels: physical, cognitive, language, social, and emotional. These traits include love of children, caring about children, warmth, kindness, patience, good physical and mental health, compassion, courtesy, dedication, empathy, enthusiasm, honesty, and intelligence. Some may think infants and toddlers are not capable of learning much in the early years, so it does not make much difference if caregivers do much with them. Infants and toddlers *are* very capable persons, and it does matter who takes care of and educates them. Alice Honig believes that *nurturing* is a necessary quality for all professionals: "The high-quality infant professional is a special kind of nurturing person, with keen observation skills. Flexible, creative, comforting—she or he has a calm style that radiates secure commitment to an infant's well-being."[3]

Quality professionals really *know* the children they care for. This knowledge, combined with knowledge of child growth and development, enables them to provide care that is appropriate for *each* child. They also *care* about the children. They accept and respect all children and their cultural and socioeconomic backgrounds. Furthermore, quality professionals *care about themselves*. This self-caring appears in their commitment to the child care profession and includes learning and developing the skills necessary to be a good care provider. It is further evidenced through good grooming, neatness, and cleanliness.

CHARACTERISTICS OF QUALITY INFANT AND TODDLER PROGRAMS

Infants and toddlers are cared for and educated in many kinds of programs and ways. These include child care centers (some of which specialize in infant care), family daycare homes, baby-sitting cooperatives, mothers' day-out programs, and the child's own home under a caregiver's supervision. Regardless of the type of program, a good-quality one has these basic features:

- *Quality professionals.* It is impossible to have a quality program without a quality staff. Those who are responsible for administering and conducting programs for the very young should make every effort to hire patient, warm adults who understand how infants and toddlers grow and develop. They are probably the most important factor in a developmentally appropriate early childhood program.

- *Acceptable staff–child ratios.* The NAEYC guidelines suggest ratios every program should strive to achieve. For infants (0–12 months) and toddlers (12–24 months), NAEYC recommends a staff–child ratio of 1:3 for a group of six and 1:4 for a group of eight. For two-year-olds (24–36 months), NAEYC recommends ratios of 1:4 for a group of eight, 1:5 for a group of ten, and 1:6 for a group of twelve.

- *Responsive environment.* An environment is responsive when it is sensitive to the unique needs of *all* children and not merely satisfied to meet the needs of the "average" child.

Developmentally Appropriate Programs

Many issues we have discussed in earlier chapters, particularly in Chapter 5, relate to infant and toddler education. First is the issue of developmental appropriateness. All early childhood professionals who provide care for infants and toddlers—indeed, for all children—must understand and recognize this important concept, which provides the solid foundation for any program. The NAEYC defines *developmentally appropriate* as having three dimensions:

- what is known about child development and learning—knowledge of age-related human characteristics that permits general predictions within an age range about what activities, materials, interactions, or experiences will be safe, healthy, interesting, achievable, and also challenging to children.
- what is known about the strengths, interests, and needs of each individual child in the group to be able to adapt for and be responsive to inevitable individual variation; and
- knowledge of the social and cultural contexts in which children live to ensure that learning experiences are meaningful, relevant, and respectful for the participating children and their families.[4]

As part of NAEYC's revised *Developmentally Appropriate Practice in Early Childhood*

Increasing numbers of children are in infant and toddler care. When making decisions about child care, parents and others must consider four essential factors that determine the quality of infant/toddler care: the environment, the caregivers, the nature of the care, and the curriculum.

Programs, the following guidelines for making decisions about developmentally appropriate practice will help staff plan for activities:

Guidelines for Decisions about Developmentally Appropriate Practice

An understanding of the nature of development and learning during the early childhood years, from birth through age 8, generates guidelines that inform the practices of early childhood educators. Developmentally appropriate practice requires that teachers integrate the many dimensions of their knowledge base. They must know

about child development and the implications of this knowledge for how to teach, the content of the curriculum—what to teach and when—how to assess what children have learned, and how to adapt curriculum and instruction to children's individual strengths, needs, and interests. Further, they must know the particular children they teach and their families and be knowledgeable as well about the social and cultural context.

The following guidelines address five interrelated dimensions of early childhood professional practice: creating a caring community of learners, teaching to enhance development and learning, constructing appropriate curriculum, assessing children's development and learning, and establishing reciprocal relationships with families. (The word teacher *is used to refer to any adult responsible for a group of children in any early childhood program, including infant/toddler caregivers, family child care providers, and specialists in other disciplines who fulfill the role of teacher.)*

1. Developmentally appropriate practices occur within a context that supports the development of relationships between adults and children, among children, among teachers, and between teachers and families.
   A. The early childhood setting functions as a community of learners in which all participants consider and contribute to each other's well-being and learning.
   B. Consistent, positive relationships with a limited number of adults and other children are a fundamental determinant of healthy human development and provide the context for children to learn about themselves and their world and also how to develop positive, constructive relationships with other people.
   C. Social relationships are an important context for learning. Each child has strengths or interests that contribute to the overall functioning of the group. When children have opportunities to play together, work on projects in small groups, and talk with other children and adults, their own development and learning are enhanced.
   D. The learning environment is designed to protect children's health and safety and is supportive of children's physiological needs for activity, sensory stimulation, fresh air, rest, and nourishment. The program protects children's psychological safety; that is, children feel secure, relaxed, and comfortable rather than disengaged, frightened, worried, or stressed.
   E. Children experience an organized environment and an orderly routine that provides an overall structure in which learning takes place; the environment is dynamic and changing but predictable and comprehensible from a child's point of view.
2. Adults are responsible for ensuring children's healthy development and learning.

   A. Teachers respect, value, and accept children and treat them with dignity at all times.
   B. Teachers make it a priority to know each child well.
   C. Teachers create an intellectually engaging, responsive environment to promote each child's learning and development.
   D. Teachers make plans to enable children to attain key curriculum goals across various disciplines, such as language arts, mathematics, social studies, science, art, music, physical education, and health.
   E. Teachers foster children's collaboration with peers on interesting, important enterprises.
   F. Teachers develop, refine, and use a wide repertoire of teaching strategies to enhance children's learning and development.
   G. Teachers facilitate the development of responsibility and self-regulation in children.
3. Constructing appropriate curriculum
   The content of the early childhood curriculum is determined by many factors, including the subject matter of the disciplines, social or cultural values, and parental input. In developmentally appropriate programs, decisions about curriculum content also take into consideration the age and experience of the learners. Achieving success for all children depends, among other essentials, on providing a challenging, interesting, developmentally appropriate curriculum. Constructing appropriate curriculum requires attention to at least the following guidelines for practice:
   A. Developmentally appropriate curriculum provides for all areas of a child's development: physical, emotional, social, linguistic, aesthetic, and cognitive.
   B. Curriculum includes a broad range of content across disciplines that is socially relevant, intellectually engaging, and personally meaningful to children.
   C. Curriculum builds upon what children already know and are able to do (activating prior knowledge) to consolidate their learning and to foster their acquisition of new concepts and skills.
   D. Effective curriculum plans frequently integrate across traditional subject-matter divisions to help children make meaningful connections and provide opportunities for rich conceptual

development; focusing on one subject is also a valid strategy at times.

E. Curriculum promotes the development of knowledge and understanding, processes and skills, as well as the dispositions to use and apply skills and to go on learning.

F. Curriculum content has intellectual integrity, reflecting the key concepts and tools of inquiry of recognized disciplines in ways that are accessible and achievable for young children, ages 3 through 8.

G. Curriculum provides opportunities to support children's home culture and language while also developing all children's abilities to participate in the shared culture of the program and the community.

H. Curriculum goals are realistic and attainable for most children in the designated age range for which they are designed.

I. When used, technology is physically and philosophically integrated in the classroom curriculum and teaching.

4. Assessing children's learning and development

Assessment of individual children's development and learning is essential for planning and implementing appropriate curriculum. In developmentally appropriate programs, assessment and curriculum are integrated, with teachers continually engaging in observational assessment for the purpose of improving teaching and learning.

A. Assessment of young children's progress and achievements is ongoing, strategic, and purposeful.

B. The content of assessments reflects progress toward important learning and developmental goals.

C. The methods of assessment are appropriate to the age and experiences of young children. Therefore, assessment of young children relies heavily on the results of observations of children's development, descriptive data, collections of representative work by children, and demonstrated performance during authentic, not contrived, activities. Input from families as well as children's evaluations of their own work are part of the overall assessment strategy.

D. Assessments are tailored to a specific purpose and used only for the purpose for which they have been demonstrated to produce reliable, valid information.

E. Decisions that have a major impact on children, such as enrollment or placement, are never made on the basis of a single developmental assessment or screening device but are based on multiple sources of relevant information, particularly observations by teachers and parents.

F. To identify children who have special learning or developmental needs and to plan appropriate curriculum and teaching for them, developmental assessments and observations are used.

G. Assessment recognizes individual variation in learners and allows for differences in styles and rates of learning. Assessment takes into consideration such factors as the child's facility in English, stage of acquisition, and whether the child has had the time and opportunity to develop proficiency in his or her home language as well as in English.

H. Assessment legitimately addresses not only what children can do independently but what they can do with assistance from other children or adults. Teachers study children as individuals as well as in relationship to groups by documenting group projects and other collaborative work.

5. Establishing reciprocal relationships with families

Developmentally appropriate practices derive from deep knowledge of individual children and the context within which they develop and learn. The younger the child, the more necessary it is for professionals to acquire this knowledge through relationships with children's families.

A. Reciprocal relationships between teachers and families require mutual respect, cooperation, shared responsibility, and negotiation of conflicts toward achievement of shared goals.

B. Early childhood teachers work in collaborative partnerships with families, establishing and maintaining regular, frequent two-way communication with children's parents.

C. Parents are welcome in the program and participate in decisions about their children's care and education. Parents observe and participate and serve in decision-making roles in the program.

D. Teachers acknowledge parents' choices and goals for children and respond with sensitivity and respect to parents' preferences and concerns without abdicating professional responsibility to children.

E. Teachers and parents share their knowledge of the child and understanding of children's development and learning as part of day-to-day communication and planned conferences. Teachers support families in ways that maximally promote family decision-making capabilities and competence.

F. To ensure more accurate and complete information, the program involves families in assessing and planning for individual children.

G. The program links families with a range of services, based on identified resources, priorities, and concerns.

H. Teachers, parents, programs, social service and health agencies, and consultants who may have educational responsibility for the child at different times should, with family participation, share developmental information about children as they pass from one level or program to another.[5]

The full text of the *NAEYC Position Statement on Developmentally Appropriate Practice in Early Childhood Programs* is found in Appendix C.

Early childhood professionals must also understand the importance of providing programs for infants and toddlers that are uniquely different from programs for older children. NAEYC states the following about the necessity for unique programming for infants and toddlers:

Developmentally appropriate programs for children from birth to age 3 are distinctly different from all other types of programs—they are not a scaled-down version of a good program for preschool children. These program differences are determined by the unique characteristics and needs of children during the first 3 years:

- *Changes take place far more rapidly in infancy than during any other period in life.*
- *During infancy, as at every other age, all areas of development—cognitive, social,*

emotional, and physical—are intertwined.
- *Infants are totally dependent on adults to meet their needs.*
- *Very young children are especially vulnerable to adversity because they are less able to cope actively with discomfort and stress.*

Infants and toddlers learn through their own experience, trial and error, repetition, imitation, and identification. Adults guide and encourage this learning by ensuring that the environment is safe and emotionally supportive. An appropriate program for children younger than three invites play, active exploration, and movement. It provides a broad array of stimulating experiences within a reliable framework of routines and protection from excessive stress. Relationships with people are emphasized as an essential contribution to the quality of children's experiences.[6]

Based on these dimensions, professionals must provide different programs of activities for infants and toddlers. To do so, early childhood professionals must get parents and other professionals to recognize that infants, as a group, are different from toddlers and need programs, curricula, and facilities specifically designed for them. It is then necessary to design and implement developmentally appropriate curricula. The early childhood education profession is leading the way in raising consciousness about the need to match what professionals do with children to children's development as individuals. We have a long way to go in this regard, but part of the resolution will come with ongoing training of professionals in child development and curriculum planning.

Finally, we will want to match professionals to children of different ages. Not everyone is emotionally or professionally suited to provide care for infants and toddlers. Both groups need adults who can respond to their particular needs and developmental characteristics. Infants need especially nurturing professionals; toddlers, on the other hand, need adults who can tolerate and allow for their emerging autonomy and independence.

Curricula for Infants and Toddlers

Curricula for infants and toddlers consist of all the activities and experiences they are involved in while under the direction of professionals. Consequently, early childhood professionals plan for *all* activities and involvements: feeding, washing, diapering/toileting, playing, learning and stimulating interactions, outings, involvements with others, and conversations. Professionals must plan the curriculum so it is developmentally appropriate. In addition to ideas derived from the NAEYC guidelines quoted previously, curriculum planning may include the following concepts:

- Self-help skills
- Ability to separate from parents
- Problem solving
- Autonomy and independence
- Assistance in meeting the developmental milestones associated with physical, cognitive, language, personality, and social development

Providing Multicultural Environments and Activities

As noted previously, NAEYC endorses multicultural experiences, materials, and equipment as an integral part of developmentally appropriate practices. NAEYC validates multicultural education in this way:

Providing a wide variety of multicultural, non-stereotyping materials and activities helps ensure the individual appropriateness of the curriculum and also

1. *enhances each child's self-concept and esteem,*
2. *supports the integrity of the child's family,*

VIDEO VIEWPOINT

First Three Years of Life

Children between the ages of zero to three change rapidly. The Carnegie Corporation has released a study of how important these years are for stimulation and nurturing and what being deprived of certain experiences and opportunities in the first three years of life can mean for the future of our children and our nation. This is called the "quiet crisis."

Reflective Discussion Questions: Why is the quiet crisis such an important issue for early childhood professionals? For parents? What is the consequence for our nation of not fully providing for children's development in the critical early years? How does poverty negatively influence children's environments and prevent them from fully developing in the early years?

Reflective Decision Making: What are some things that you can do to improve the quality of children's environments in the first three years of life? What advice would you give parents concerning the quality of their home environments or how they could improve the quality of their home environments? Review this and other chapters in *Early Childhood Education Today,* and list some things you can do to provide infants/toddlers with appropriate attention and stimulation. In Chapter 16, we discuss Early Head Start. How can this and other early intervention programs provide children with the stimulation and attention they need?

PROGRAM IN ACTION

A Day at HeartsHome Early Learning Center

Arrival

It is a chilly October morning. The day begins early for six-month-old Andrew. Before the sun has appeared he is dressed and sitting in a bouncy seat in the infant room of his child care early education program. The building is still quiet and Pam, his primary caregiver, is taking advantage of the early morning lull to spend some quality time with Andrew. Pam is the only full-time caregiver that Andrew has known since he began school at the age of six weeks. She is well tuned to his needs and preferences, so when he begins to squirm around in his seat and tip his head back she quickly puts his bottle in hot water to warm. His hunger anticipated, Andrew is spared having to cry for his bottle. As Andrew's formula warms, Pam narrates what she is doing, "I know Andrew, you're telling me you're beginning to get hungry—well, it's coming very soon."

As Pam is talking, twelve-month-old Fiona enters the room carried by her father, Jim. Pam looks up and greets them both. As she collects Fiona from her father's arms, Pam inquires about how the family's weekend had been. In the year that Fiona has attended school, Fiona's parents and Pam have scheduled several conferences—when Fiona first enrolled, every three months for a formal parent–teacher chat, and during regular "room" meetings. They have developed a relationship of trust and have an easy rapport with one another. After exchanging pleasantries, Jim begins to record information on Fiona's chart about her behavior and routines that morning. Pam sits Fiona down at the table for breakfast. Fiona is encouraged to develop self-help skills by being offered finger foods, such as French toast, for breakfast. In the same spirit, she is given a sippy cup—even though most of the juice still ends up on the floor. Fiona squeals with delight as she sends the cup careening across the table. Pam retrieves it from the floor, saying to Fiona, "Hey, you think that's pretty neat, huh? Why don't you try putting the cup in your mouth so you can have some juice?" She helps Fiona bring the cup to her mouth and take a drink. "Good job drinking," says Pam. Jim goes to the door and says good-bye to his daughter, assuring her that he will return later that day to pick her up. Fiona grimaces slightly, then looks to Pam for reassurance and returns to her breakfast.

"Fiona's just fine, as long as she's eating!" Pam says to her co-teacher John who has just arrived in the classroom. John and Pam each have primary responsibility for three infants, although each helps the other out when needed and is familiar with the routines of all the children. "Hi Don," beams Fiona. Pam asks John if he would mind feeding Andrew while she sits with Fiona. John picks up a smiling Andrew and settles down into a rocking chair with him in his lap. He sings and talks to him while Andrew drinks contently.

Activities

The rest of the children arrive over the course of the next hour. By nine o'clock, the room is still calm, but buzzing with activity. The teachers move quickly around the room, attending to crying children and presenting happy babies with new things to play and look at. Andrew has fallen asleep in a bouncer and is placed in his crib. Each child has their own spot. Andrew's is decorated with pictures of his parents and a small stuffed bear that he has cherished since birth. At about 11:00, John suggests he take the babies that are awake out on a stroller ride. Pam agrees that would be a good idea, but instructs John to leave Jasmine inside, so they can do a sensory activity. Three-month-old Jasmine is new to the center so Pam makes a special effort to spend extra time with her each day. This way Jasmine can make an emotional attachment to her caregiver—a relationship the center considers essential to a young child's optimum development. With two babies asleep and John outside with the others, Pam can devote all her attention to Jasmine. Today the activity is foot painting. A weekly curriculum is posted on the bulletin board—not all of the activities get done, but the teachers strive to do at least one art or sensory activity each day. Pam sets a large piece of paper underneath the jumper and dips Jasmine's feet into a saucer full of blue paint. "Pretty squishy, huh?" says Pam. Jasmine looks momentarily confused then giggles softly. Pam places her into the jumper and laughs and talks to her as she slides around on the paper. "I need to get a picture of this for mommy," Pam says and gets up to get the camera. "Hey, Jasmine. Are you having fun?" says Mary, the Director, as she makes her morning "rounds" through the center. Paul, an eighteen-month-old in John's care, wakes up and yells "Hi" from his crib. "Hi Paul," says the Director. "How are you today? Did you sleep well?" Pam leaves Jasmine in the jumper and goes to get Paul out of his crib. After a diaper change, Paul is set down in the music center, where he chooses a homemade rattle to play with.

John appears at the door with a buggy. "Look who's up," he says to Paul. Paul crawls quickly over to him. John picks him up in one arm and with the other reaches for the toddler's chart to see what time he woke up. John unloads the buggy and prepares to leave on his lunch break. He writes a detailed note of what each child will need during the next hour, even though Lori, the assistant teacher who is breaking him, is a familiar face around the room and knows the children well. When Lori enters, most of the children greet her happily, with the exception of Paul, who knows her arrival signals that John is leaving the room. John picks up a crying Paul and, assuring him he will return, passes him to Lori. Lori also reassures Paul and looks around the room for something fun to do. Paul's crying has disturbed Andrew, who is laying on the floor looking at mirrors. He startles and begins to wail. Pam, who is occupied with cleaning up Jasmine, looks over at Andrew and talks to him in a calm, soft tone. "I'm sorry I can't get to you right now. I know that scared you when Paul cried." Lori moves over to where Andrew is and manages to position a now calmer Paul in front of her while she picks up Andrew. "Boy. Sometimes you need six hands!" she exclaims to a smiling Pam.

Parent Information and Farewells

The rest of the afternoon follows basically the same pattern as the morning. Pam takes a group to play outside around three o'clock. She puts the non-mobile babies on sheepskins positioned around her on the ground, while she lets the crawlers get as dirty as they wish in the grass. Outside is one of Fiona's favorite places to be. Her parents consider a few dirty clothes a sign of a day well spent and Pam always makes sure Fiona's hands and face are cleaned as soon as they go back inside, Later, during a lull in the activity, Pam takes the time to write on her charts. She notes the mood of each child during the day and any special activities or occurrences. "Beware, blue feet!" she writes on Jasmine's chart. "Jasmine had a great time painting today. She was very content. Took her bottles well." In addition to being a valuable record for Pam, each child's chart is an important mode of communication with parents. Pam is especially careful to write detailed notes on Andrew's chart, as he is usually picked up after she has already left for the day.

Jasmine is the first to leave in Pam's group. She gives Mom a big smile as she picks her up to nurse her. Mom and Pam discuss Jasmine's day as Pam changes Fiona's diaper in preparation of her going home. Fiona, too, is happy to see her parent walk in the door, although she does take a moment to give Pam a big hug and kiss before she leaves. "Hugs like that make my job worth it!" says Pam as she tells the other children in the room good-bye. "See you all tomorrow!" she calls and closes the door behind her.

Contributed by Amanda Gorner, B.A., primary teacher, HeartsHome Early Learning Center.

3. enhances the child's learning processes in both the home and the early childhood program by strengthening ties,
4. extends experiences of children and their families to include knowledge of the ways of others, especially those who share the community, and
5. enriches the lives of all participants with respectful acceptance and appreciation of differences and similarities among them.

Multicultural experiences should not be limited to a celebration of holidays and should include foods, music, families, shelter, and other aspects common to all cultures.[7]

Early childhood professionals in all programs must endeavor to make their programs as multicultural and nonsexist as possible. The following ideas will help you achieve this goal:

Translating these theories and ideas into practice can be difficult at best. When you work in a program with a number of infants or toddlers it becomes very easy to get caught up in routine "custodial" duties and to forget you are dealing with unique individuals. The following suggestions will help bring multicultural education into the infant/toddler classroom:

- Create classrooms that are less conforming and more individualized. Is it really necessary for all toddlers to sit during "circle," or could there be a quiet option for those who would prefer it? Make an effort to recognize the special qualities of each child.
- Learn the background and culture of each family. The importance of continuity between center and home can't be overemphasized.
- Build self-esteem by allowing the child to feel competent. Encourage independence and allow the child to do things for him/herself. Plan this into the day—it takes twice as long but it's worth the effort.
- Encourage creativity. Allow children to do their own work regardless of how you think it looks. Allow them to be pleased and satisfied with their own work.

Encourage creative and unique responses to questions.
- Portray both genders in nurturing roles. Let toddlers visit and help with infants on a regular basis.
- Avoid gender-stereotyped toys, puppets, puzzles and books.
- Use different types of music in programs. Classical, country and popular music is often important in homes. Use music from other countries as well. Tapes of the parents singing or reading can also be effective.
- Talk about feelings often. Give labels to emotions. Research indicates that acquiring labels for emotions appears to be important for children to identify their own experiences as well as develop empathy for others.
- Be aware that toddlers from families whose first language is not English may be learning two languages simultaneously. Allow children to become competent in their first language. Expose them to English, but don't push. For example, write their names in both languages and ask parents to provide translations of frequently used phrases.
- Put up pictures of different experiences, ethnic groups and customs in the infant/toddler area. Show different ways of meeting the same needs.
- Encourage positive attention seeking behavior in both genders. Give boys the words to get their needs for nurturance met.
- Be sure your materials represent many cultures and lifestyles. Dolls, books, puppets, music and dramatic play materials are just some of the things that can be easily adapted.[8]

CHILDPROOFING HOMES AND CENTERS

As infants become more mobile and as toddlers start their constant exploration, safety becomes a major concern. Professionals can advise parents about childproofing the home. In addition, professionals must childproof centers and other settings.

Home

- Remove throw rugs so toddlers do not trip.
- Put breakable objects out of toddlers' reach.
- Cover electrical wall outlets with special covers.
- Remove electrical cords.
- Install gates in hallways and stairs (make sure gates are federally approved so the toddlers cannot get their heads stuck and strangle).
- Take knobs off stoves.
- Purchase medicines and cleaners with childproof caps.
- Store all medicines and cleaning agents out of reach; move all toxic chemicals from low cabinets to high ones (even things like mouthwash should be put in a safe place).
- Place safety locks that can be opened from the outside on bathroom doors.
- Cushion sharp corners of tables and counters with foam rubber and tape or cotton balls.
- If older children in the home use toys with small parts, beads, and so forth, have them use these when the toddler is not present or in an area where the toddler cannot get them.
- When cooking, turn all pot handles to the back of the stove.
- Avoid using cleaning fluids while children are present (because of toxic fumes).

- Place guards over hot water faucets in bathrooms so toddlers cannot turn them on.
- Keep wastebaskets on tops of desks.
- Keep doors to the washer and dryer closed at all times.
- Keep all plastic bags, including garbage bags, stored in a safe place.
- Shorten cords on draperies; if there are loops on cords, cut them.
- Immediately wipe up any spilled liquid from the floor.

Center

- Cover toddler area floors with carpeting or mats.
- Make sure storage shelves are anchored well and will not tip over; store things so children cannot pull heavy objects off shelves onto themselves.
- Use only safe equipment and materials, nothing that has sharp edges or is broken.
- Store all medicines in locked cabinets.
- Cushion sharp corners with foam rubber and tape.
- Keep doors closed or install gates.
- Fence all play areas.

IMPORTANT HEALTH ISSUES IN EARLY CHILDHOOD PROGRAMS

The spread of diseases in early childhood programs is a serious concern to all who care for young children (Figure 6.2). Part of the responsibility of all caregivers is to provide healthy care for all children. One of the most effective ways to control the spread of disease in early childhood programs and promote the

PROGRAM IN ACTION

A CHANGING CURRICULUM: A NECESSITY FOR THE TODDLER

The changing curriculum is a multifaceted environment consisting of an indoor play space designed to help children enjoy learning and an outdoor environment for extending learning opportunities. To produce happy, well-adjusted, intelligent young children, the daily environment, teachers, time frames, and schedules all must respond to children's developmental needs and desires. Children construct their knowledge by engaging in activities that are meaningful and purposeful to each unique individual. Each child becomes interested and absorbed in personally significant materials and ideas in achieving daily goals.

The Daily Environment

The indoor environment includes a covered walkway to the front door, a bridge of adjustment for toddlers as they prepare to say goodbye to mommy or daddy. The child enters the reception area with a parent where a caregiver takes health information.

A teacher or an aide greets children as they hang up their coats and escorts them to the main playroom. The room is divided into play areas for art, books, manipulative toys, small replicas and structures for role and dramatic play; indoor riding tracks, indoor wheel toys, small plastic construction sites, crawl-through play tunnels, slides, and a small indoor pond with toy ducks, frogs, and fish. Inviting pathways connect the areas to each other. Materials within areas are rotated often and changed frequently, with duplicates of "favorites" available.

Materials and play equipment should be open ended and suggestive rather than directive. A chest containing throwaways that suggest, but do not dictate, are recommended: empty boxes, plastic bottles, various shaped containers, tubes, different articles of clothing with unusual textures and colors. Toddlers like to form their own imaginative ideas, unlike older preschoolers, who like having structured activities imposed by an adult who suggests specific play or pretend situations. For example, four-year-olds like to have an adult suggest a tea party or a trip on a pirate ship. "Toddlers," "wad-dlers," and "talkers" prefer to create their own play situations.

Teachers here do not plan the curriculum, it is created each moment of the day as children respond to an environment carefully designed for interaction. The teacher observes, analyzes, and responds to each child's needs as the day progresses. As children are confronted with problems, the teacher attempts to answer or pose questions, select appropriate materials, and make suggestions to help children construct their own knowledge.

The following description of an imaginary child's morning in an ideal play center will help you to visualize how a changing curriculum would operate.

Libby's Day in the Changing Curriculum

Entering the Reception Area   A caregiver greets Libby and her mother at the door, saying, "Good morning, Libby. I'm glad to see you. Come, let me take your hand and we will talk with Miss Robyn. I know your mom wants to tell us what you had for breakfast, and how you slept last night." Miss Robyn is seated on a low chair so she can make eye contact and exchange smiles with all the arriving children. She writes on Libby's health chart (see Figure A) as Libby's mom speaks: ten hours of sleep; no bed wetting; bowel movement shortly after waking; no indication of fever, no rashes, eyes clear. Libby, while waiting, watches the water fountain nestled among the plants and walks over to pet a large toy pony statue on the head. As she becomes restless, an aide pulls a wagon in and Miss Robyn asks, "Libby, do you want to ride to the book corner?"

"I do," she responds.

The Day Begins   The wagon stops where books are on display and small chairs, pillows, and stuffed animals invite children into the area. From here, Libby can look out the window to see the rabbits in the cage on the patio, eating their break-

Figure A/*A Sample Health Card*

DAILY HEALTH CHECK

Date _____

Arrival Time: _____   Departure Time: _____

Accompanied By: _____

Breakfast: _____   Supper: _____ (previous evening)

No. Hours of Sleep:____   Bath: Yes____ No____   Wet Bed: Yes____ No____   No. of Times:_____

Any Sleep Disturbance: _____

Bowel Movement: Yes_____ No_____   Normal: Yes_____ No_____

Nausea: _____   Eyes: _____   Temperature: _____

Skin Rash: _____   Other: _____

Happy: _____   Reserved: _____   Other Emotional Behaviors: _____

Note: Health information is recorded on an 5" x 8" prepared information card. A health aide or teacher looks at eyes and takes temperature using an aural thermometer, such as those manufactured by Thermoscan, as the daily health check is completed.

fast of lettuce and chopped carrots. Libby watches for a very short time, then attends to the books.

Libby chooses one of her favorite books, *Good Night Moon,* stretches out on a large pillow, looks toward the ceiling, and calls out, "Can anyone get me a moon to play with?" At that moment, Brittany arrives and answers, "Sure, you know 'The Cow Jumped Over the Moon'? I bet she could." Libby jumps up from her pillow and says, "Where is that jumping cow, anyway?"

After about two minutes of searching, Libby finds a plastic cow used as a prop in the recital of the nursery rhyme, "The Cow Jumped Over the Moon." She says, "Hey, look, Miss Bone. He's dirty. A dirty cow can't find a moon if he is so dirty."

Miss Bone replies, "Why don't you go wash the cow?" Libby is on her way to the bathroom, the cow under her arm, when she observes Daniel and Jessie playing with blocks and cars and trucks carrying small people.

"Hey, let me play," says Libby.

"No! You don't have no people," replies Daniel. Libby throws the cow over a doll's bed and proceeds to take "people" away from the two boys. Daniel and Jessie rebuff her intrusion, and Libby begins to cry. Miss Bone, who has been watching, intercedes, asking, "Libby, what happened to the cow that jumped over the moon?"

Libby replies, "I don't know. I want to ride on the tricycle."

continued

The Day Continues   During the day, the teachers take children outside a few at a time to explore the great outdoors (see Figure B). A patio is the bridge from the indoor to the outdoor environment, which again is defined by pathways leading to expanding physical activities that are both safe and manageable for toddlers.

Many trees, small shrubs, blooming flowers, sandboxes with spades, trucks, cooking utensils, boats, things to climb on, crawl through, and wagons to pull are available. Best of all, there are places and spaces to hide, with or without a friend, where children can fantasize and invent their own worlds. Children may move to a climbing apparatus, enclosed play houses, old boats, shallow water with stepping stones, a water play area with hoses and sprinklers, or an imaginary play station. One covered area has wheel toys of various sizes, positioned adjacent to sand and water areas with plastic animals, trees, and barns. Nearby is a pen for live animals. These animals come to the center for short periods of time from pet stores or are brought by families to be shared.

One area has a garden, with fresh vegetables and flowers, and fruit trees for children to observe, and to sit beneath for rest periods or for private conversations. A tool shed here stores garden implements as well as other items that must be kept out of children's reach or protected from the weather. This shed has a large tub for washing toys and spaces for drying them, as well.

A few minutes after Libby goes outside, Miss Bone appears with two clay pots and a small spade and asks, "Libby, do you want to help me dig some dirt to put in these pots?"

"What we gonna do with the dirt?" Libby asks.

Miss Bone replies, "We are going to plant bean seeds and watch them grow."

After helping for a minute or so, Libby asks, "Is it time to go now?"

"It's almost time for lunch," replies Miss Bone. "Do you want to go by the rabbits' cage as we go inside?" Daniel, Jessie, Brittany, and Drew join Miss Bone and Libby as they walk toward the play-room. Each child waves and says, "Bye, Rabbit!"

The Changing Curriculum for Toddlers

We have shared our view of an ideal environment appropriate for toddlers both indoors and outdoors, a conceptual framework for the development of a curriculum unique to the individual programs and settings. You may adapt these suggestions to specific spaces and neighborhoods where programs exist for toddler care.

Your curriculum will not and cannot be successful with toddlers unless you understand the distinctive features of this special age group (16–36 months). You must carefully evaluate materials, activities, and encounters throughout the day, and must consider physical, social-emotional, and cognitive growth factors when constructing curricular opportunities.

For the curriculum to meet the needs of young children, content and presentation style must be modified to meet the rapid changes occurring in the structure of the brain, and to accommodate physical growth and personality adaption. To assist in this, your curriculum structure should be stable, to promote assurance and trust. The curriculum and environment also should promote autonomy and self-reliance.

The toddler is seeking to understand who he is, what he is able to do with his body, where he should be, and why he is requested to perform certain actions throughout the day. Toddlers are able to understand and are eager to learn much more than previously thought. A competent professional will be able to guide, give explanations, demonstrate, provide stimuli, ask questions and pose problems, thus allowing young children to embrace new horizons.

A toddler's perceptual development is changing rapidly and is affected by experiences and cognitive maturity. Sensation, presented by caregivers, and actions on and within the environment provide the basis for your curriculum. The interac-

Figure B/*A Typical Outdoor Environment*

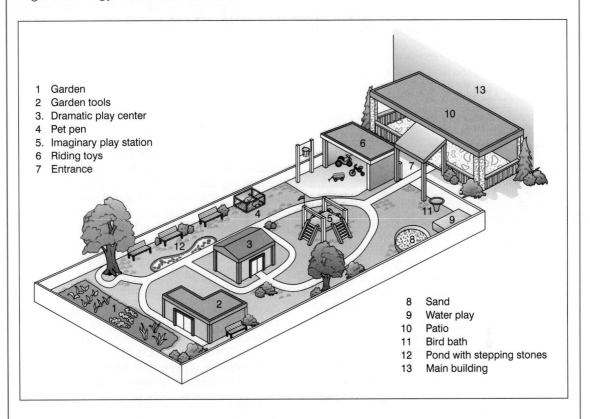

1 Garden
2 Garden tools
3. Dramatic play center
4 Pet pen
5. Imaginary play station
6 Riding toys
7 Entrance

8 Sand
9 Water play
10 Patio
11 Bird bath
12 Pond with stepping stones
13 Main building

tive physical, social, emotional, and cognitive stimulations should include sight, hearing, smell, taste, touch, as well as *proprioception* (body orientation, such as balance; ability to reach and stretch and to identify body parts; closing eyes and touching nose; sitting and standing with eyes closed; lifting, pushing, and pulling). Children begin to construct their own knowledge as they test information for validity. When a child validates her own sensations, she can expand knowledge in innumerable ways, such as by understanding how to use information that is similar or different to solve problems or to express herself creatively.

Toddlers as well as adults, live simultaneously in the worlds of reality and imagination. Children need to understand the fundamentals of their physical environment. Thus, the "real" world is the primary content source for a curriculum for young children.

The world of imagination and make-believe is just as important to young children as the real world. It is difficult for toddlers to tell when one ends and the other begins. The make-believe world is less threatening and offers more possibilities for pure or uncontaminated development to occur. It is easier for children to use their imagina-

continued

tion to deal with problems, thus creating their own learning and problem-solving techniques.

Connecting the Real and Imaginative Worlds Storybooks can be a bridge as the curriculum moves back and forth from the imaginative to the real world. Select books because they connect with home or community activities. Many connecting activities emerge from community, seasons, family-specific events or holidays, family relationships, hobbies, and daily living.

For example, the Walt Disney version of the story, *The Three Little Pigs,* where the pigs do not get eaten by the wolf, but run from one house to the other until they are all secure in the brick house, provides a nonthreatening, real-life situation. Large cardboard boxes may become symbols for the three houses; two should be collapsible. Children may examine real bricks, sticks, and straw before building the structures.

In this version of the story, each pig was musically talented: one played the piano, one the flute, and one the violin. You may present these musical instruments by having children role play the pigs. You also may include singing and movement activities, and may record them on videotape. You may wish to use other props, such as a large black pot of the kind used to make soup, to

hang in a make-believe fireplace. Another suggestion is to bring in a churn, which can be used to make butter to be served later.

Children may wish to become other storybook characters who visit the little pigs and eat soup. This activity may culminate with a celebration by extending an invitation to the "mother pig" to come and visit her three children. Children and teachers may also extend an invitation to parents and other significant individuals to share the butter and bread.

These cardboard box houses may later be used on the patio for different purposes, such as developing Our Town, consisting of toy stores, book and video stores, bakeries, banks, and doctors' offices. A vegetable stand could also be placed near the patio, thus linking the covered space with the outdoor environment.

Evaluation of Program Effectiveness and Children's Achievement

Authentic Data Files A variety of measurement tools are available to you. Your data collection for assessment must take place in a natural setting. The result should reflect your interpretation of each toddler's development based on the child's informal responses. Authentic assessment should

healthy care of young children is by washing hands. These are generally accepted procedures for hand washing:

1. Turn on the faucet. In some programs, faucets have control levers that can be turned on and shut off with the elbows. This is the preferable method since it eliminates the spread of germs and fecal matter by the hands.

2. Wet hands, wrists, and forearms.

3. Apply liquid soap. Liquid soap is preferred because cake soap can transmit germs and fecal matter.

4. Scrub hands, wrists, and forearms, making sure that enough pressure is applied to produce friction.

5. Rinse hands, wrists, and forearms.

6. Dry hands, wrists, and forearms completely with a disposable paper towel.

also include notating unsolicited responses and recording unanticipated events. Evidence of children's growth can be documented in a number of ways: pictorial, descriptive, audio, video, and in original samples of work.

Anecdotal Records Anecdotal records are a time-honored measurement device for young children. Anecdotal records are factual, nonjudgmental observations of a child's activity. Teachers and caregivers should record behaviors that relate to program and individual goals in addition to individual responses to the curriculum and environment. The anecdote should be kept in context, and include date, time, indoor or outdoor setting, and any other factual information necessary to facilitate understanding. For toddlers, the recording process must be kept simple.

Checklists and Rating Scales Checklists and rating scales that reflect program and individual objectives can be designed to collect specific information. Screening instruments and development scales will assist you in considering changes in curricular presentations and time frames.

Building the Toddler Data File The authentic data file of each toddler in the program may

include, but should not be limited to, the following:

- Birthdate; problems with pregnancies and early adjustments; note allergies, persons to contact in case of emergencies (giving relationship)
- Height, weight, and health status recorded at the initial registration and updated every three months
- Physical health, fine motor, gross motor, spacial orientation, with all data labeled and dated
- Children's scribbling and painting
- Photographs of play activities
- Videotapes of gross motor activities
- Audiotapes documenting the progression of language development through the waddler, toddler, and talker stages
- Teacher's notes from play encounters with children or from conversations and interviews conducted while playing games with children
- Videotapes of musical responses and sociodrama activities
- Special program, environment and/or curricular adaptations as discussed and mutually agreed upon by families, caregivers, and program directors

Contributed by Beverly M. Boals and Mildred B. Vance, professors of early childhood, Arkansas State University.

7. Use a disposable paper towel to turn off the faucet.

The spread of germs can also be greatly reduced through the use of sanitary diapering techniques. Diapering is another prime vehicle for germ transmission. It is imperative that sanitary procedures be followed while diapering children. NAEYC's guidelines for sanitary diaper changing are as follows:

1. *Place paper or other disposable cover on diapering surface.*
2. *Pick up the child. If the diaper is soiled, hold the child away from you.*
3. *Lay the child on the diapering surface. Never leave the child unattended. If you use them, put on disposable gloves now.*
4. *Remove soiled diaper and clothes. Fold disposable diapers inward and reseal with their tapes.*
5. *Put disposable diapers in a lined, covered step can. Put cloth diapers in a*

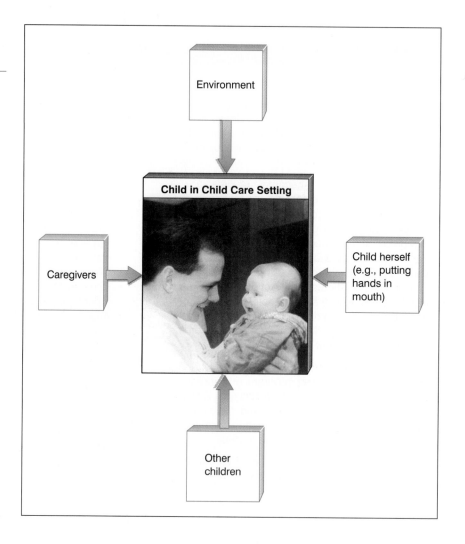

plastic bag securely tied, then put into a larger, labeled, plastic bag to go home. Do not put diapers in toilet. Bulky stool may be emptied into toilet.

6. Put soiled clothes in doubled, labeled plastic bags to be taken home.

7. Clean the child's bottom with a moist disposable wipe. Wipe front to back using towelette only once. Repeat with fresh wipes if necessary. Pay particular attention to skin folds. Pat dry with paper towel. Do not use any kind of powder, as inhaling it can be danger-

ous. Use a skin care product only on a parent's request.

8. Dispose of the towelette or paper towel in a lined, covered step can. If you used disposable gloves, discard them now.

9. Wipe your hands with a disposable wipe. Dispose of it in the lined, covered step can.

10. Diaper or dress the child. Now you can hold her or him close to you.

11. Wash the child's hands. Assist the child back to the group.

12. Remove disposable covering from the diapering surface.

13. *Wash and rinse the area with water (use soap if necessary), and sanitize it with bleach solution (quarter cup bleach to one gallon water) made fresh daily.*
14. *Wash your own hands thoroughly.*[9]

It is important for early childhood professionals to protect themselves and the children from AIDS. Here are some basic guidelines:

- *Staff and children should wash their hands before eating*
- *Staff and children should wash their hands before and after using the toilet*
- *Staff should wash their hands before and after changing a diaper*
- *Staff should wash their hands before and after treating a cut or wound*
- *Staff should wear gloves if there is contact with blood or blood-containing body fluids or tissue discharge*[10]

It sounds trite, but health in child care and preschool programs truly begins with the people who conduct the programs. Hand-washing policies, diapering procedures, and AIDS precautions, however well stated and intended, will do little good if not followed. It is important, therefore, for caregivers and teachers to do all that they can to protect and promote the health of children.

Infants and toddlers are interesting and remarkably competent individuals. The developmental and educational milestones of these years are the foundations of all that follow throughout life. All professionals must use their knowledge, understanding, energy, and talents to assure that this foundation is the best it can be.

ACTIVITIES FOR FURTHER ENRICHMENT

1. Visit at least two programs that provide care for infants and toddlers. Observe the curriculum to determine whether it is developmentally appropriate. What suggestions would you make for improving the curriculum? Explain what you liked most and least about the program.

2. Develop five activities professionals can do to promote children's basic trust needs.

3. You have been asked to speak to a group of parents about what they can do to promote their children's language development in the first two years of life. Outline your presentation, and list five specific suggestions you will make.

4. Observe children between the ages of birth and eighteen months. Identify the six stages of sensorimotor intelligence by describing the behaviors you observed. Cite specific examples of secondary and tertiary reactions. For each of the six stages, list two activities that would be cognitively appropriate.

5. In addition to the qualities cited in this chapter, list and explain five other qualities you think are important for professionals of infants and toddlers.

6. Why is motor development important in the early years? What are five things early childhood educators can include in their programs to promote motor development?

7. Identify customs that are passed down to infants and toddlers as a result of the family's cultural background. How do these customs affect young children's behavior?

8. Visit centers that care for young children of different cultures. List the differences you find. What areas are most similar?

9. Interview professionals who work in family day care homes and others who work in child care centers. How does the care for infants and toddlers differ in the two settings? In which kind of program would you prefer to be a professional? Why?

10. Identify at least ten games or activities that are beneficial to the developing infant and the growing toddler. Describe the benefits of each of the games or activities you list.

READINGS FOR FURTHER ENRICHMENT

Bornstein, M. *Parenting Infants* (Mahwah, NJ: Lawrence Erlbaum Associates, 1995).

This book features a brief history of interest in parenting infants followed by the theoretical significance attached to parenting infants. The book also describes the characteristics of infants and infant development that are meaningful for parenting.

Carnegie Task Force on Meeting the Needs of Young Children. *Starting Points: Meeting the Needs of Our Youngest Children* (New York: Carnegie Corporation of New York, 1994).

This report focuses attention on the "quiet crisis" affecting millions of children under three and their families. It challenges professionals to develop integrated programs for developing responsible parenthood, guaranteeing quality child care choices, ensuring basic health and protection and mobilizing communities to support young children and their families.

Dynerman, S. B. *Are Our Kids All Right? Answers to the Tough Questions about Child Care* (Princeton, NJ: Peterson's, 1994).

Examines over twenty years of research and shows that child care per se is not bad for children. In the process the author points out what is good and bad about child care today and provides suggestions for selecting and providing quality care.

Greenman, J. and A. Stonehouse. *Prime Times: A Handbook for Excellence in Infant and Toddler Care* (St. Paul MN: Redleaf, 1996).

Discusses all aspects of providing good care for infants and toddlers. Includes sample toddler needs and services plans, schedules, classrooms designs, parent handbook samples, and end-of-chapter exercises for staff development.

Jones, E. and J. Nimmo. *Emergent Curriculum* (Washington, D.C.: National Association for the Education of Young Children, 1994).

Chronicles an ongoing discussion among teachers in one center as they move through a yearly planning process and continuously change their plans in response to children's interests and activities.

Koop, C. (1993). *Baby Steps: The "Whys" of Your Child's Behavior in the First Two Years* (New York: Freeman, 1993).

In this book, the author begins with newborn and traces the changes that occur in physical, motor, mental, and social-emotional development.

Shatz, M. *A Toddler's Life: Becoming a Person* (New York: Oxford University Press, 1994).

This intimate account of a toddler's development from one to three is an odyssey conveyed through detailed and well-chosen observations as he participates in routine and special events.

NOTES

1. Eric H. Lenneberg, "The Biological Foundations of Language," in Mark Lester ed., *Readings in Applied Transformational Grammar* (New York: Holt, Rinehart & Winston, 1970), p. 8.
2. Susan Curtiss, *Genie: A Psycholinguistic Study of a Modern-Day "Wild Child"* (New York: Academic Press, 1977).
3. Alice C. Honig, "High Quality Infant/Toddler Care," *Young Children* 4 (Nov. 1985), p. 40.
4. Sue Bredekamp and Carol Copple, eds., *Developmentally Appropriate Practice in Early Childhood Programs,* revised edition. (Washington, D.C.: National Association for the Education of Young Children, 1997), p. 9 © 1997 by NAEYC. Used by permission.
5. Sue Bredekamp and Carol Copple, eds., *Developmentally Appropriate Practice in Early Childhood Programs,* revised edition (Washington, D.C.: National Association for the Education of Young Children, 1997), pp. 16–22.
6. National Association for the Education of Young Children, *Developmentally Appropriate Practice in Early Childhood Programs Serving Infants* (Washington, D.C.: Author, 1989), no. 547.
7. Sue Bredekamp, ed., *Developmentally Appropriate Practice in Early Chidhood*

Programs Serving Children from Birth through Age 8, expanded ed. (Washington, D.C., National Association for the Education of Young Children, 1987), p. 2.

8. Kimberlee Whaley and Elizabeth Blue Swadener, "Multicultural Education in Infant and Toddler Settings," *Childhood Education* 66 (4), pp. 239–40. Reprinted by permission of K. Whaley and E. B. Swadener and the Association for Childhood Education International, 11501 Georgia Ave., Suite 315, Wheaton, MD. Copyright 1990 by the Association.

9. A. Kendrick, R. Kaufmann, and K. Messenger, *Healthy Young Children: A Manual for Programs* (Washington, D.C.: NAEYC, 1988), p. 44.

10. National Academy of Early Childhood Programs, "Preventing HIV/AIDS Transmittal," *Newsletter of the National Academy of Early Childhood Programs* 66 (2), p. 5.

CHAPTER 7

Transitions and
New Encounters

Focus Questions

1. How has the history of preschool and nursery education influenced contemporary practice?

2. What reasons account for the current interest in preschool programs?

3. What are the characteristics of preschoolers' growth and development?

4. How does play promote children's learning?

5. What are the purposes of play in preschool programs?

6. What are important issues concerning preschool programs?

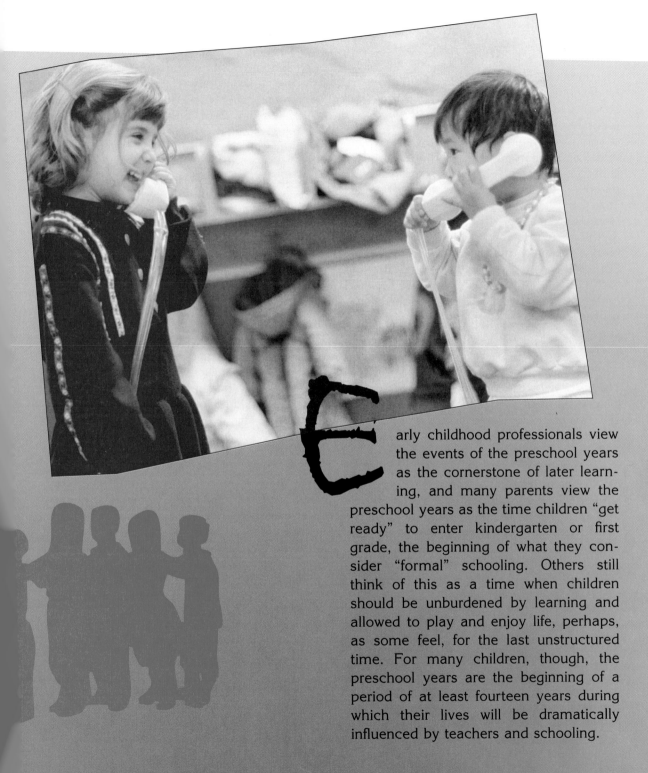

Early childhood professionals view the events of the preschool years as the cornerstone of later learning, and many parents view the preschool years as the time children "get ready" to enter kindergarten or first grade, the beginning of what they consider "formal" schooling. Others still think of this as a time when children should be unburdened by learning and allowed to play and enjoy life, perhaps, as some feel, for the last unstructured time. For many children, though, the preschool years are the beginning of a period of at least fourteen years during which their lives will be dramatically influenced by teachers and schooling.

WHAT IS PRESCHOOL?

The traditional use of the term *preschool years* to describe the period before children enter school is rapidly becoming obsolete. Today, it is common for many children to be in a school of some kind beginning as early as age two or three, and child care beginning at six weeks is becoming de rigueur for children of working parents. Additionally, many states, including Texas, Florida, California, New York, and North Carolina, have public preschool programs for four-year-olds; the term *preschool* hardly applies to threes and fours anymore. For our purposes, preschools are programs for two- to five-year-old children, before kindergarten. In this chapter we will also discuss *nursery schools*, programs for three- and four-year-olds.

The History of Preschool Education

The history of preschool education is really the history of nursery school education, which itself cannot be separated from the history of kindergarten education. Nursery schools as operated in the United States originated in Great Britain. In 1914, Margaret and Rachel McMillan started an open-air nursery emphasizing health care and healthy living, in which they also promoted cognitive stimulation. They also began a program of visiting homes to work with mothers. Their work led to the passage in 1918 of the Fisher Act, which provided national support for nursery education and led to the establishment of the first public nursery schools in Great Britain.

In 1914, Caroline Pratt opened the Play School (now the City & Country School; see Chap. 2) in New York City. One of the nation's first truly progressive schools, it was patterned on the philosophy of John Dewey and designed to take advantage of what Pratt called children's "natural and inevitable" desire to learn.

Patty Smith Hill, a champion of the nursery school movement in the United States, started a progressive laboratory school at Columbia Teachers College in New York in 1921. Abigail Eliot, another nursery school pioneer, studied in Great Britain for six months with the McMillan sisters, then started the Ruggles Street Nursery School in Boston in 1922. Meanwhile, also in 1922, the Merrill-Palmer Institute Nursery School opened in Detroit, under the direction of Edna White. The Institute and White were responsible for training many nursery school teachers.

A temporary impetus to nursery education occurred in 1933, when the federal Works Progress Administration provided funds to hire unemployed teachers in nursery school programs. In 1940, the Lanham Act provided money for child care for mothers employed in defense-related industries. For example, the Kaiser Child Service Centers were built by Edgar Kaiser to provide child care for children of workers in the Kaiser shipyards. Each center was designed to provide care for about one thousand children between the ages of eighteen months and six years. Open 364 days a year, 24 hours a day, these centers were staffed by people with degrees in child development. This support ended with the war in 1945.

From the 1940s to the present, many preschools have been private, sponsored by parent cooperatives, churches, and other agencies. Federal involvement in preschool education has been through Head Start and support for child care programs directed at low-income families and children. Interest and enrollment in preschools for all children, however, has increased since the 1980s.

Why Are Preschools Growing in Popularity?

The acceleration of preschool programs began with Head Start in 1965. This trend continues to grow, with greater numbers of four-year-olds entering preschools, many operated by public schools (Figure 7.1). In addition, children are entering preschool at a younger age.

Reasons for the rapid increase in and demand for preschool programs for three- and four-year-old children are best understood within the context of societal changes beginning in the 1970s as well as contemporary societal problems and concerns. Keep in mind that social events and issues determine the nature and kinds of both current educational programs and those we can expect to see in the next decade. Whenever we ask "why" about a particular educational program, we can always find the answer in societal needs and political concerns, because society traditionally and legitimately looks to educational institutions to help it address its short- and long-term goals. With these concepts in mind, we can identify the following reasons to explain the current popularity of preschool programs, particularly public programs for three- and four-year-olds:

- Changing family patterns, especially single-parent families

- Changing economic patterns, with more women in the work force

- Changing attitudes toward work and careers. The shift away from homemaking as a career to outside employment and careers causes the early childhood profession to provide more programs and services, including programs for threes and fours.

- The view by parents, public policy planners, and researchers that intervention

Figure 7.1/*Preschool Enrollment*

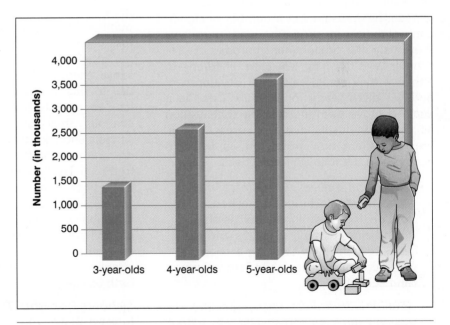

Source: U.S. Department of Education, National Center for Education Statistics, Primary Enrollment. (Table prepared July, 1995)

programs (to deal with such problems as substance abuse) work best in the early years. Research verifies the positive short- and long-term benefits to children and society of quality preschool programs.

- Growing concern on the part of corporations and businesses as to the quality of the contemporary and future work force. They see early education as one way of developing a literate work force.

- Advocacy for publicly supported and financed preschools as a means of preventing the exclusion of poor children and their families from the early education movement.

- The increasingly popular notion that three- and four-year-old children are ready, willing, and able to learn.

Paradigm shifts in preschool programs since the 1980s, and particularly in the past decade, have resulted in a number of significant changes in programs and purposes. Previously, the predominant purpose of preschools was to help socialize children—to enhance their social-emotional development and get them ready for school. There is a decided move away from using socialization as the sole justification for preschooling. Preschools are now promoted as ways to accomplish the following objectives:

- *Support and develop children's innate capacity for learning.* The responsibility for "getting ready for school" is shifted from being primarily a child's and parent's responsibility to being a cooperative venture between child/family/home and school.

- *Provide a centralized agency (i.e., the school) and a support system (i.e., school personnel) to deliver services at an early age to children and their families.*

- *Deliver a full range of health, social, economic, and literacy services to families.* Thus, *family welfare* is also seen as a justification for operating preschools.

- *Solve or find solutions for pressing social problems.* The early years are viewed as a time when interventions are most likely to have long-term positive influences. Preschool programs are seen as ways of lowering the number of dropouts, improving children's health, and reducing substance abuse and delinquency.

Should Public Schools Provide Preschool Services?

Many agencies provide services for preschool children, including child care programs, Head Start, cooperative preschools, and others. There is a growing consensus, however, that public schools should provide programs and services for three- and four-year-olds. This preference is based on several factors. First, public schools and their infrastructure (teachers, cafeteria workers, custodians, and administration) are already in place; it makes sense, therefore, for them to open their facilities to this younger population. Second, as long as parents pay taxes to support public schools, they often conclude that these schools should provide services for their children rather than their paying other programs to do so. Third, public schools are viewed as institutions that can offer all children equal access to educational and other services. If the public schools enroll three- and four-year-old children, other programs that traditionally offer programs to this age group will turn their attention to serving the needs of children from birth to age two.

Schools for the Twenty-First Century

Edward Zigler, one of the developers of the Head Start program, proposes an alternative model for preschool programs. Called

Schools for the Twenty-First Century, Zigler's model suggests that public schools serve as sites for a comprehensive child care system. These schools would provide developmental child care for children ages three to five, half-day care for kindergarten children, before- and afterschool care, and child care during vacations. Public school personnel would also provide parent education and training for family daycare providers. (A description of the Twenty-First Century School in Independence, Missouri, appears in Chap. 9.)

WHO IS THE PRESCHOOLER?

Today's preschoolers are not like the children of previous decades. Many have already attended one, two, or three years of child care or nursery school. They have watched hundreds of hours of television. Many have experienced the trauma of family divorces or the psychological effects of abuse. Both collectively and individually, the experiential backgrounds of preschoolers are quite different from those of previous generations. But it is precisely the impact and implications of this background that early childhood professionals must understand to meet preschoolers' needs effectively.

Observation is an excellent way for you to learn more about young children. Observation is a key method early childhood professionals use to find out what children think, know, feel; to assess their abilities and interests; and to assess learning styles. Information you gather through observation will enable you to develop educational plans for each of your children. Turn now to the first color insert, "Kidwatching: Developing Skills in Observation," and read how you can develop a systematic plan for observing children.

Physical and Motor Development

Understanding of preschoolers' physical and motor development enables you to acknowledge why active learning is so important. To begin with, a noticeable difference between preschoolers and their infant and toddler counterparts is that preschoolers have lost most of their baby fat and taken on a leaner, lankier look. This "slimming down" and increasing motor coordination enables the preschooler to participate with more confidence in the locomotor activities so vitally necessary during this stage of growth and development. Both girls and boys continue to grow several inches per year throughout the preschool years (Table 7.1).

Preschool children are in an age of rapid motor skill development. They are learning to use and test their bodies. It is a time for learning what they can do and how they can do it as individuals. *Locomotion* plays a large role in motor and skill development and includes activities of moving the body through space—

Table 7.1/*Average Height and Weight of Preschoolers*

| Age | Males | | Females | |
	Height (inches)	Weight (pounds)	Height (inches)	Weight (pounds)
3 years	38.0	32.4	37.6	30.7
4 years	40.5	36.8	40.0	35.2
5 years	43.3	41.2	42.7	38.9

Source: Based on data from P. V. V. Hamill et al., "Physical Growth: National Center for Health Statistics Percentiles," *American Journal of Clinical Nutrition* 32 (1979), pp. 607–629.

walking, running, hopping, jumping, rolling, dancing, climbing, and leaping. Children use these activities to investigate and explore the relationships between themselves, space, and objects in space.

Preschoolers demonstrate the principles of cephalocaudal and proximodistal development mentioned in Chapter 6. The cephalocaudal development enables the preschooler to participate in many physical activities; likewise, the concentration of motor development in the small muscles of the arms and hands lets them participate in fine-motor activities such as drawing, coloring, painting, cutting, and pasting. Consequently, preschoolers need programs that provide action and play, supported by proper nutrition and healthy habits of plentiful rest and good hygiene.

Good educational practices also dictate that preschool programs deemphasize activities that require preschoolers to wait or sit for extended periods of time. Although learning self-control is part of preschoolers' socialization process, developmentally appropriate practices call for activity. It is also important to incorporate health education and activities that promote good hygiene and nutrition into programs for three-, four-, and five-year-olds. Preschool and elementary curricula should incorporate lifelong goals and objectives for healthy living so children develop good habits early in life rather than grow up using bad habits.

Cognitive Development

Preschoolers are in the preoperational stage of intelligence. As we saw in Chapter 5, characteristics of the preoperational stage are (1) children grow in their ability to use symbols, including language; (2) children are not capable of operational thinking (an *operation* is a reversible mental action), which explains why Piaget named this stage *preoperational;* (3) children center on one thought or idea, often to the exclusion of other thoughts; (4)

Physical activities contribute to children's physical, social, emotional, linguistic, and cognitive development. It is essential that programs provide for children to engage in active play both in indoor and outdoor settings. What are some things that children can learn through participation in playground activities? What might these children be learning?

children are unable to conserve; and (5) children are egocentric.

Preoperational characteristics have particular implications for early childhood professionals. Early childhood professionals can promote children's learning during the preoperational stage of development by doing the following:

- *Furnish concrete materials to help children see and experience concepts and processes.* Children learn more from touching and experimenting with an actual object than they do from a picture, story, or video. If children are learning about apples, bring in a collection of apples for children to touch, feel, smell, taste, discuss, classify, manipulate, and explore.

- *Use hands-on activities that give children opportunities for active involvement in their learning.* When you encourage children to manipulate and interact with the world around them, they began to construct concepts about relationships, attributes, and processes. Through exploration, preoperational children begin to collect and organize data about the objects they manipulate. For example, when children engage in water play with funnels and cups, they learn about concepts such as measurement, volume, sink/float, bubbles and the prism, evaporation, and saturation.

- *Give children many and varied experiences.* Diverse activities and play environments lend themselves to teaching different skills, concepts, and processes. Children should spend time daily in both indoor and outdoor activities. Give consideration to the types of activities that facilitate large and fine motor, social, emotional, and cognitive development. For example, outdoor play activities and games such as tag, hopscotch, and jumprope enhance large motor development; whereas fine motor activities include using scissors, stringing beads, coloring, and writing.

- *Model appropriate tasks and behaviors, as the preoperational child learns to a great extent through modeling.* Children should see adults reading and writing daily. It is also helpful for children to view brief demonstrations by peers or

professionals on possible ways to use materials. For example, after children have spent a lot of time in free exploration with math manipulatives, teachers and others can show children patterning techniques and strategies they may want to experiment with in their own play.

- *Provide a print-rich environment to stimulate interest and development of language and literacy in a meaningful context.* The physical environment should display room labeling, class stories and dictations, children's writing, and charts of familiar songs and fingerplays. There should be a variety of literature for students to read including books, magazines, and newspapers. Paper and writing utensils should be abundant and assorted to motivate children to create. Daily literacy activities should include opportunities for shared, guided, and independent reading and writing; singing songs and fingerplays; and creative dramatics. Children should be read to every day.

- *Allow children periods of uninterrupted time to engage in self-chosen tasks.* Children benefit more from large blocks of time provided for in-depth exploration in meaningful play than they do from frequent, brief ones. It takes time for children to become deeply involved in play, especially imaginative and fantasy play. The morning afternoon schedule should each contain at least two such blocks of time.

Language Development

Children's language skills grow and develop rapidly during the preschool years. Vocabulary increases, and sentence length increases as children continue to master syntax and grammar. Infants or toddlers first use *holophrases,* single words that convey the meaning of a sentence. For example, a child may say "milk" to express, "I'd like some more milk, please."

At one year, infants know two or more words; by the age of two, about 275. During their second year, toddlers' language proficiency increases to include *telegraphic speech*—two- or three-word utterances acting as a sentence. "Amy go," for example, can mean that Amy wants her mother to take her for a walk in the stroller. During their third year or earlier, children add helping verbs and negatives to their vocabulary, for example, "No touch," or "I don't want milk." Sentences also become longer and more complex. During the fourth and fifth years, children use noun or subject clauses, conjunctions, and prepositions to complete their sentences.

During the preschool years, children's language development is diverse, comprehensive, and constitutes a truly impressive range of learning. An even more impressive feature of this language acquisition is that children learn intuitively, without a great deal of instruction, the rules of language that apply to words and phrases they use.

How Preschoolers Learn Through Play

There are many definitions of play and ideas about why children play. Children's play results in learning. Therefore, *play is the process through which children learn.* In this sense, play is a tool for learning.

The notion that children learn through play begins with Froebel, who built his system of schooling on the educative value of play. As discussed in Chapter 3, Froebel believed that natural unfolding (development) occurs through play. Since his time, most early childhood programs have incorporated play into their curricula or have made play a major part of the day.

Montessori viewed children's active involvement with materials and the prepared environment as the primary means through which they absorb knowledge and learn. John Dewey also advocated and supported active learning and believed that children learn through play activities based on their interests. Dewey thought too that children should have opportunities to engage in play associated with everyday activities (e.g., the house center, post office, grocery store, doctor's office). He felt that play helps prepare children for adult occupations. Many curriculum developers and teachers base play activities, such as a dress-up corner, around adult roles.

Piaget believed play promotes cognitive knowledge and was a means by which children construct knowledge of their world. He identified three kinds of knowledge: physical, logical-mathematical, and social. According to Piaget, through active involvement, children learn about things and the physical properties of objects; knowledge of the environment and their role(s) in it; and logical-mathematical knowledge—numeration, seriation, classification, time, space, and number. Piaget believed children learn social knowledge, vocabulary, labels, and proper behavior from others.

Unlike Piaget, Vygotsky viewed the social interaction that occurs through play as essential to children's development. He believed that children learn through social interactions with others (see Chap. 3) language and social skills—cooperation and collaboration—that promote and enhance their cognitive development. Viewed from Vygotsky's perspective, adults' play with children is as important as children's play with their peers. Thus, play promotes cognitive development and provides for a way to develop social skills.

Purposes of Play

Children learn through play, which occupies a major part of most children's lives. Play activities are essential to their development, helping them do the following:

- Learn concepts
- Develop social skills
- Develop physical skills
- Master life situations
- Practice language processes
- Develop literacy skills (see description later)
- Enhance self-esteem
- Prepare for adult life and roles (e.g., learn how to become independent, think, make decisions, cooperate/ collaborate with others)

Without the opportunity for play and an environment that supports it, children's learning is limited. Early childhood programs that provide time for play increase and enhance the limits of children's learning.

Montessori thought of play as children's work and of the home and preschool as "workplaces" where learning occurs through play. This linking of play and work is unfortunate in some respects because it attaches many of the negative connotations of adult work to children's play. However, the comparison does convey the total absorption, dedication, energy, and focus children demonstrate through their play activities. Children engage in play naturally and enjoy it; they do not select play activities because they intentionally set out to learn. A child does not choose to put blocks in order from small to large because she wants to learn how to seriate, nor does she build an incline because she wants to learn the concept of "down" or the principles of gravity; however, the learning outcomes of this play are obvious. Children's play is full of opportunities for learning, but there is no guarantee that children will learn all they need to know when they need to know it through play. Providing

opportunities for children to choose among well-planned, varied learning activities enhances the probability that they will learn through play.

Kinds of Play

Social Play Much of children's play occurs with or in the presence of other children. Social play occurs when children play with each other in groups. Mildred Parten developed the most comprehensive description and classification of the types of children's social play:

- Unoccupied play. *The child does not play with anything or anyone; the child merely stands or sits, without doing anything observable.*
- Solitary play. *Although involved in play, the child plays alone, seemingly unaware of other children.*
- Onlooker play. *The child watches and observes the play of other children; the center of interest is others' play.*
- Parallel play. *The child plays alone but in ways similar to and with toys or materials similar to those of other children.*
- Associative play. *Children interact with each other, perhaps by asking questions or sharing materials, but do not play together.*
- Cooperative play. *Children actively play together, often as a result of organization of the teacher (the least frequently witnessed play in preschools).*[1]

Social play supports many important functions. First, it provides the means for children to interact with others and learn many social skills. Play provides a context in which children learn: how to compromise ("OK, I'll be the baby first and you can be the mommy"), gain impulse control ("I can't always do what I want when I want to do it"), learn to be flexible ("We'll do it your way first and then my way"), resolve conflicts, and continue the process of learning who they are. Children learn what skills they have, such as those relating to leadership. Second, social

Puppets and plays provide many opportunities for children to learn and interact with others. Indeed, the props that professionals provide for children to play with contribute to all of children's learning, but in particular their literacy development. What literacy skills are these children learning?

play provides a vehicle for practicing and developing literacy skills. Children have others with whom to practice language and learn from. Third, play helps children learn impulse control; they realize they cannot always do whatever they want. And fourth, in giving a child other children with whom to interact, social play negates isolation and helps children learn the social interactions so vital to successful living.

Cognitive Play
Froebel, Montessori, and Piaget recognized the cognitive value of play.

Froebel through his gifts and occupations and Montessori through her sensory materials saw children's active participation with concrete materials as a direct link to knowledge and development. Piaget's theory influences contemporary thinking about the cognitive basis for play. From a Piagetian perspective, play is literally cognitive development (see Chap. 5 and the High/Scope curriculum description).

Piaget's Stages of Play   Piaget describes four stages of play through which children progress as they develop: functional play, symbolic play, playing games with rules, and constructive play.

Functional Play.   Functional play, the only play that occurs during the sensorimotor period, is based on and occurs in response to muscular activities and the need to be active. Functional play is characterized by repetitions, manipulations, and self-imitation. Piaget described functional play (which he also called *practice play* and *exercise play*) this way: "The child sooner or later (often even during the learning period) grasps for the pleasure of grasping, swings [a suspended object] for the sake of swinging, etc. In a word, he repeats his behavior not in any further effort to learn or to investigate, but for the mere joy of mastering it and of showing off to himself his own power of subduing reality."[2]

Functional play allows children to practice and learn physical capabilities while exploring their immediate environments. Very young children are especially fond of repeating movements for the pleasure of it. They engage in sensory impressions for the joy of experiencing the functioning of their bodies. Repetition of language also is common at this level.

Symbolic Play.   The second stage is symbolic play, which Piaget also referred to as the "let's pretend" stage of play. During this stage, children freely display their creative and physical abilities and social awareness in a number of ways, for example, by pretending to be something else, such as an animal. Symbolic play also occurs when children pretend that one object is another—that a building block is a car, for example—and may also entail pretending to be another person—a mommy, daddy, or caregiver. As toddlers and preschoolers grow older, their symbolic play becomes more elaborate and involved.

Playing Games with Rules. This third stage of play begins around age seven or eight. During this stage, children learn to play within rules and limits and adjust their behavior accordingly, and can make and follow social agreements. Games with rules are very common in middle childhood and adulthood.

Constructive Play. Piaget's fourth stage develops from symbolic play and represents children's adaptations to problems and their creative acts. Constructive play is characterized by children engaging in play activities in order to construct their knowledge of the world. They first manipulate play materials and then use these materials to create and build things (a sand castle, a block building, a grocery store) and experiment with the ways things go together.

The Value of Play

Play serves an important process for promoting children's learning and development. Play enhances social interaction and the development of social skills—learning how to share, getting along with others, taking turns, and generally learning how to live in a community. Play promotes physical development and body coordination and develops and refines small- and large-motor skills. Play helps children discover their bodies: how they function and how to use them in learning.

Lifetime attitudes toward play develop in early childhood. Children learn motor skills they will use as adults and discover that play can be restful, therapeutic, and satisfying. If children are taught that play is something one does only after all one's work is finished, or that it takes away from productive work, or is only for special occasions, children will have a negative attitude toward play, feel guilty about participating in it, and have a hard time integrating it into their adult lives.

Play assists in personality and emotional development because it enables children to try out different roles, release feelings, express themselves in a nonthreatening atmosphere, and consider the roles of others. Play enhances and promotes development in the cognitive, affective, and psychomotor areas. It helps children learn, acquire information, and construct their own intelligence. Through play, children develop schemes, find out how things work (and what will not work), and lay the foundation for cognitive growth. Because play activities are interesting, play becomes naturally, or intrinsically, rewarding, and children engage in it for its own value. Children's interest in their play also leads to a continually lengthened attention span.

Early Childhood Professionals' Roles in Promoting Play

Early childhood professionals are the key to promoting meaningful play, which promotes a basis for learning. What professionals do and the attitudes they have toward play determine the quality of the preschool environment and the events that occur there. Early childhood education professionals have the following responsibilities for supporting a quality play curriculum:

- Plan to implement the curriculum through play and integrating specific learning activities with play to achieve specific learning outcomes. Play activities should match children's developmental needs and be free of sex and cultural stereotypes. Professionals have to be clear about curriculum concepts and ideas they want children to learn through play.

- Provide time for learning through play and including it in the schedule as a legitimate activity in its own right.

- Structure time for learning through play. Create both indoor and outdoor environments that encourage play and support its role in learning

- Organize the classroom or center environment so that cooperative learning is possible and active learning occurs.

- Provide materials and equipment that are appropriate to the children's developmental level and support a nonsexist and multicultural curriculum.

- Educate assistants and parents in how to promote learning through play.

- Supervise play activities and participate in children's play. In these roles, professionals help, show, and model when appropriate and refrain from interfering when appropriate.

- Observe children's play. Teachers can learn how children play and the learning outcomes of play to use in planning classroom activities.

- Question children about their play, discuss what children did during play, and "debrief" children about what they have learned through play.

Informal or Free Play   Proponents of learning through spontaneous, informal play activities maintain that learning is best when it occurs in an environment that contains materials and people with whom children can interact. Learning materials may be grouped in centers with similar equipment: a kitchen center, a dress-up center, a block center, a music and art center, a water or sand area, and a free-play center, usually with items such as tricycles, wagons, and wooden slides for promoting large-muscle development.

The atmosphere of this kind of preschool setting tends to approximate a home setting, in which learning is informal, unstructured, and unpressured. Talk and interactions with adults are spontaneous. Play and learning episodes are generally determined by the interests of the children and, to some extent, professionals, based on what they think is best for children. The expected learning outcomes are socialization, emotional development, self-control, and acclimation to a school setting.

Three problems can result from a free-play format. First, some professionals interpret it to mean that children are free to do whatever they wish with whatever materials they want to use. Second, aside from seeing that children have materials to play with, some professionals do not plan for special play materials, how children will interact with the materials, or what children are to learn while playing. Third, sometimes professionals do not hold children accountable for learnings from free play. They rarely question children about concepts or point out the nature of the learning. Such professionals are seldom part of the play process. They act as disinterested bystanders, with their primary goal being to see that children do not injure themselves while playing. In a quality program of free play both indoors and outside, professionals are active participants. Sometimes they observe, sometimes they play with the children, sometimes they help the children, but they never intrude or impose. Avoiding the possible pitfalls of the free-play format enables children to learn many things as they interact with interesting activities, materials, and people in their environment.

Dramatic (Pretend) Play   Dramatic play allows children to participate vicariously in a wide range of activities associated with family living, society, and their and others' cultural heritage. Dramatic play is generally of two kinds: sociodramatic and fantasy. *Sociodramatic play* usually involves everyday realistic activities and events, whereas *fantasy play* typically involves fairy tale and superhero play. Dramatic play centers often include areas such as housekeeping, dress-up, occupations, dolls, school, and other situations that follow children's interests. A skillful professional can think of many ways to expand children's interests and then replace old centers with new ones. For

Dramatic play serves an important function of promoting children's understanding of concepts and processes. Here, play allows children to symbolically engage in health care procedures and helps alleviate their fears of doctors, nurses, and other medical practitioners as well as medical settings.

example, after a visit to the police station, a housekeeping center might be replaced by an occupations center.

In sociodramatic play, children have an opportunity to express themselves, assume different roles, and interact with their peers. Sociodramatic play centers thus act as a nonsexist and multicultural arena in which all children are equal. Professionals can learn a great deal about children by watching and listening to their dramatic play. For example, one professional heard a child remark to the doll he was feeding that "You better eat all of this 'cause it's all we got in the house." After investigating, the professional linked the family with a social service agency that helped them obtain food and assistance.

Professionals must assume a proactive role in organizing and changing dramatic play areas. They must set the stage for dramatic play and participate with children. They must also encourage those who "hang back" and are reluctant to play and involve those who may not be particularly popular with the other children. Surprisingly, because of their background and environment, some children have to be taught how to play. In other words, as in all areas of early childhood education, professionals must deal with children's dramatic play in an individual and holistic way.

Outdoor Play   Children's play outside is just as important as that inside. Unfortunately, many consider outdoor play relatively unimportant and needed only as an opportunity for children to let off steam and get rid of excess energy. Children do need to relieve stress and tension through play, and outdoor activities provide this opportunity; however, professionals should plan for what children will do and the equipment available. Outdoor play is not a chance for children to run wild.

Outdoor environments and activities promote large- and small-muscle development and body coordination as well as language development, social interaction, and creativity. Professionals should plan for a particular child or group of children to move through progressively higher skill levels of running, climbing, and throwing. The outdoor area is a learning environment, and as such, the playground should be designed according to learning objectives.

Many teachers also enjoy bringing the indoor learning environment "outdoors," using easels, play dough, or dramatic play props to further enhance learning opportunities. In addition, taking a group of children outdoors for story or music time, sitting in the shade of a tree, brings a fresh perspective to daily group activities. As with indoor activities, provisions for outdoor play involve planning, supervising, and helping children be responsible for their behavior.

Rough-and-Tumble Play   All children, to a greater or lesser degree, engage in rough-and-tumble play. One theory of play says that children play because they are biologically programmed to do so; that is, it is part of children's—and adults'—genetic heritage to engage in play activities. Indeed, there is a parallel in children's rough-and-tumble play and behaviors in the animal kingdom, for example, run-and-chase activities and "pretend" fighting. Rough-and-tumble play activities enable children to learn about themselves (e.g., lead/follow, develop physical skills, experiment and practice roles physically and vicariously).

Safety   Providing a safe and healthy environment is an important part of an early childhood professional's responsibilities and applies to the playground as well as to the inside facilities. Outdoor areas should be safe for children to play. Usually, states and cities have regulations requiring the playground to be fenced and have a source of drinking water, a minimum number of square feet of play area for each child, and equipment that

Observing Programs in Action

Nine Key Models

The Barnett Bank Child Development Center

Barnett Banks, Inc., founded in 1877, is Florida's leading financial institution and is headquartered in Jacksonville, Florida. The company houses several data processing and other support units at its Barnett Office Park, a modern, 9-building complex in suburban Jacksonville.

The Barnett Child Development Center was established with one goal in mind: to support Barnett employees by providing quality, convenient child care. The center is managed by Corporate Family Solutions, a company that works entirely in partnership with Barnett to create workplace family services. The 22,100-square-foot center can accommodate up to 300 children ages six weeks through five years. The center's location allows parents the convenience of being able to visit their child anytime during the day.

The center holds the belief that environment is critical to quality child care and offers a facility designed especially for growing children. Classrooms, outdoor play areas, and two large indoor play areas have been thoughtfully designed to create a safe environment for young children. A high emphasis is placed on learning acquired through play in an atmosphere of discovery.

In the infant department teachers work to develop warm, positive relationships so infants will feel secure and develop a sense of trust. Each baby has an assigned teacher who will respond to his or her special needs—rocking, talking, playing, and gently encouraging growth and progress. For toddlers, the world is an adventure. Teachers in the toddler program help young explorers discover their world in a reassuring and structured setting, encouraging them to learn and develop a sense of confidence and independence. In our preschool program, children are given the opportunity to learn on their own and at their own pace. Teachers provide enriching language experiences for children through a variety of interest centers and organized group activities. This comprehensive program allows children to develop socially, emotionally, physically, and intellectually. The Barnett Child Development Center is accredited by the National Association for the Education of Young Children.

Contributed by Susan Dittmer, Executive Director, Barnett Child Development Center, Jacksonville, Florida; photos © 1996 courtesy of Favorite Studio.

Texas A&M University–Corpus Christi Early Childhood Development Center

The Early Childhood Development Center (ECDC) is a 50,000-square-foot, two-story building on the TAMU-CC campus. All of the activities and programs in the Early Childhood Development Center are directly connected to the academic programs at the University.

The mission of the Texas A&M University–Corpus Christi Early Childhood Development Center is to be a *comprehensive educational facility,* collaborating with area school districts and demonstrating instructional excellence, integrated services and equity in an educational community for students, teachers, administrators, parents and University students. The Center's mission is facilitated using state-of-the-art instructional technology, dual-language proficiency, assessment and personalized education components, inclusion, interagency collaboration, parent education programs, wellness services, a curriculum materials resource center, staff development programs, and educational research and development.

A number of components comprise the Early Childhood Development Center. They include:

The **University Early Childhood School** in collaboration with the Corpus Christi Independent School District serves 132 children ages three through third grade. Children at this educational site are taught in Spanish and English. The Center features multi-age grouping, team teaching, instructional technology, and an integrated curriculum.

A **Companion Classroom** program links classrooms from neighboring school districts with the Early Childhood Development Center classrooms for replication purposes. The companion teachers take graduate courses in Early Childhood Education, allowing them to examine and consider current and exemplary instructional practice.

At the **Education Center** professionals and parents involve themselves in the education of their children and are encouraged to participate in seminars and programs offered by the University.

The **Teacher Resource Center** serves as a curriculum resource library lending instructional materials and software. It also serves as a demonstration site.

The **Diagnostic and Personalized Education Center** provides individual education assessment and prescription services for area school children focusing on reading, math, special education, language physiology, and counseling. This Center features

a counseling center linked to the College of Education graduate program in guidance and counseling.

The equivalent of an indoor gym, the **Motor Development Center** is designed for students in the school center to develop motor skills.

On site also is a **Wellness Center** which serves as a clinic to provide necessary health services. The Wellness Center also provides practical experiences and training for undergraduate and graduate nurse practitioners.

Especially unique to this early childhood program is the **CITGO Science Tower**. The Tower contains weather and environmental instrumentation for "hands on" application by all users of the Early Childhood Development Center. The instrumentation and equipment in the Tower is used to demonstrate the practical nature of science and mathematics.

Contributed by Ramón D. García-Barrios, Director, Early Childhood Development Center, Texas A&M University–Corpus Christi; photos provided by TAMU-CC Early Childhood Development Center.

Reggio Emilia

Reggio Emilia is a city in northern Italy. The excellent educational program the city offers its children, based on providing an educational environment that encourages learning, is known as the Reggio Emilia approach. Reggio Emilia sponsors infant programs for children three months to three years and programs for children three to six years.

Each of the Reggio schools can accommodate seventy-five children, with each group or class consisting of about twenty-five children with two coteachers. Children of single parents and children with disabilities have priority in admission. The other children are admitted according to a scale of needs. Parents pay on a sliding scale based on income.

The Reggio Emilia approach is unique in that children are encouraged to learn by investigating and exploring topics that interest them. Learning is a social and cultural process that does not occur in isolation from other children, adults, and the environment. The Reggio school environment is designed to accommodate the child's developmental culture and provide a wide range of stimulating media and materials for children to express their learning, such as words, sounds and music, movement, drawing, painting, sculpting and modeling clay or wire, making collages, using puppets and disguises, photography, and more.

Reggio children typically explore topics by way of group projects. This approach fosters a sense of community, respect for diversity, and a collaborative approach to problem solving—both important aspects of learning. Two coteachers are present during the project to guide the children and widen the range of learning. This is the way Carlina Rinaldi, pedagogista (consultant, resource person), describes a project:

> A project, which we view as sort of an adventure and research, can start through a suggestion from an adult, a child's idea, or from an event such as a snowfall or something else unex-

pected. But every project is based on the attention of the educators to what the children say and do as well as what they do not say and do. The adults must allow enough time for the thinking and actions of children to develop.[*]

The children pictured here are working on a special "Shadows" project. The exploration of shadows has great attraction for children and many implications for learning with pleasure. Children discuss their ideas about shadows and formulate hypotheses about shadows' origin and destiny. Exploration of shadows in the schools for Reggio Emilia continues to be a favorite theme for children and teachers. In this specific episode, after exploring shadows outside (at different times of day) and inside (with artificial light and flashlights), the teacher extends the interest of a child who has represented a little girl with full skirt by posing a question-problem to her.

Contributed by Lella Gandini, Northhampton, Massachusetts. Photos from the city of Reggio Emilia, teachers, and children of the preprimary schools Diana and Gulliver, *Tutto ha un'ombra meno le formiche* (Everything but the ant has a shadow) (City of Reggio Emilia, Italy: Department of Education Via Guido da Castello, 1990), p. 12; photos provided by Lella Gandini.

[*]Carlina Rinaldi, "The Emergent Curriculum and Social Constructivism," in Carolyn Edwards, Lella Gandini, and George Forman, eds., *The Hundred Languages of Children* (Norwood, NJ: Ablex, 1993), p. 108.

The Thurgood Marshall Child Development Center

The Thurgood Marshall Child Development Center is sponsored by the United States Supreme Court, the Administrative Office of the U.S. Courts, the Federal Judicial Center, the Judicial Panel on Multidistrict Litigation, and the U.S. Sentencing Commission. The Thurgood Marshall Child Development Center is built around a philosophy of caring, flexibility, and choice for children. The dynamic Marshall environment satisfies the young child's sense of wonder, sociability, and eagerness to explore. A bowl of water and a sponge, for instance, offer a chance for a child and teacher to talk, laugh, and explore together.

Marshall teachers are talented, highly trained, and academically credentialed. They nurture and facilitate integrated learning continuously, making sure to follow a child's own rhythms. Teachers understand that children are learning all the time through active and purposeful involvement with people, materials, and ideas.

An atmosphere of ongoing learning energizes and vitalizes the center, characterized by play-oriented, child-initiated curriculum. Moms and dads visit for story time or lunch. Children, staff, and parents take walks in the neighborhood and trips to museums and monuments.

The staff enjoys playing with the children on the carpet and feeding them while seated comfort-

ably on the sofa or in rocking chairs. Infants are on totally individual schedules as requested by their parents. Plenty of stimulating toys are available for the babies and their caregivers to enjoy. The staff understands the importance of talking and singing to the babies throughout the day.

There is a great respect for toddlers and two-year-olds. Each new step is applauded and cheered. The children are marching (or rather toddling!) toward more independence each day and need to have many choices of activities throughout the day. Toys and equipment such as soft building blocks are selected to help toddlers develop gross- and fine-motor skills.

The preschoolers' area provides preschoolers opportunities to explore and choose their own activities. Art, music, gross- and fine-motor activities, dramatic play, blocks, science, and books are some of the interesting centers around the room. The staff plans activities for the groups as well as for individual children in order to foster their development in all areas. The Marshall Center is a busy, happy place where children are respected and loved.

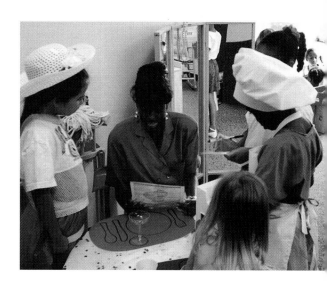

Contributed by Madeline Fried and Margery Sher, Fried & Sher, Inc., Herndon, Virginia; photos courtesy of Fried & Sher, Inc.

Bright Horizons Glaxo Wellcome Inc. Onsite Child Center

The standards at Bright Horizons Child Center focus on two primary aspects: the quality of our child-centered programming including interaction between faculty and families, and the quality of our faculty and the conditions in which they work. Guidelines have been created to continually assess our programs to assure that they exercise developmentally appropriate practices and that the delivery of our programs and design of our surroundings remain child-centered.

Developmentally appropriate standards, established by the National Association for the Education of Young Children, form the basis of our program's curriculum. To develop our curriculum, we not only recognize the universal patterns and milestones of child development but also work to find in each individual child their unique pattern of developmental capabilities, temperamental characteristics, and learning styles. The intent of our curriculum, therefore, is to provide learning activities and materials that are real, concrete, and relevant to the lives and experiences of our young children.

The teacher's role in classrooms at Bright Horizons is to provide a variety of challenging activity choices for children and then facilitate children's engagement in the activities they select. A teacher's thoughtful input at the right moment can advance a child's competence and challenge a child's thinking. Small group sizes, intensive teacher-child ratios, and highly qualified and trained teachers provide assurance that each child receives individual attention and develops a sense of belonging in the center. The development of self-esteem in each child is a fundamental goal. We believe that children develop a positive self-image when they are given opportunities to exercise the power of their own choices.

Essential to the Bright Horizons program is parent involvement and satisfaction. The center believes the systems created to support parent

communication and involvement form the cornerstone of the Bright Horizon–Parent Partnership. The center emphasizes the important role parents play in the early learning and development of their children. As teachers of young children, the center is able to share with parents aspects of the teachers' knowledge about child development and their particular insights about young children. To facilitate better communication, Bright Horizons issues a company-wide parent survey every year to solicit input with regard to all aspects of each center's program, such as program quality, faculty quality, and the level of satisfaction with the program. The faculty is surveyed as well.

In 1992, Bright Horizons established a task force to investigate the needs of families with both parents working and overall attitudes toward preschool education practices and school readiness. As a result of this undertaking, the center developed LANGUAGE WORKS!, a preschool program that is a whole language learning experience to address the key element that contributes to a child's readiness for school and lifelong learning: language proficiency. LANGUAGE WORKS! is an expansion in Bright Horizon's developmental preschool education pro-

gram to help children develop a foundation of social and cognitive skills. This program also offers opportunities for more parent participation, both in the classroom and at home, in order for children to enter elementary school "ready to learn."

Bright Horizons, based in Cambridge, Massachusetts, has managed Glaxo Wellcome Inc. child centers since late 1991. As a national childcare management company, it manages 130 childcare programs across the country. Photos provided by Bright Horizons.

b–9

The Stride Rite Intergenerational Day Care Center

Stride Rite's intergenerational day care center is the first center in American business to pair the care of children and the elderly.

On a Tuesday morning at the Stride Rite Corporation's headquarters in Cambridge, Massachusetts, an unusual scene is unfolding. Two elderly women, Eva DaRosa and Margaret Donovan, are ferrying preschoolers, two at a time, from their classroom to the lunchroom where the staff is working with the children and elders to make a handprint mural. Everyone is enjoying the project, but the real fun of the day has turned out to be the ride in Margaret's wheelchair. Each pair of children takes turns riding in her lap and pushing the chair with Eva's help. One child gets to ride on the way out, the other on the way back to their classroom. The women are enjoying the event almost as much, and after a dozen runs have dubbed themselves the pony express.

The center's design allows a traffic pattern that encourages the informal interaction between children and elders while also providing privacy for each group. It is divided into two separate wings that are connected through a large central area. The children's wing has four classrooms for different age groups; the elders' wing has three rooms designed for a variety of quiet and noisy activities. The central or middle core houses administrative offices, a kitchen and dining facility, and a resource center that includes conference rooms and a library. Among the special features of the facility are wide doorways to accommodate wheelchairs and floor surfaces that make mobility easier for frail elders. An outdoor space was built to accommodate and stimulate both groups of clients.

The Stride Rite program meets the physical, social, and intellectual needs of each group

b–10

through a carefully planned and supervised curriculum that fosters regular daily contact between the elders and children. Intergenerational curricula include (for children and elders separately and together) reading and writing stories, table games, celebrating holidays and birthdays, cooking and eating, arts and crafts, and taking field trips.

The intergenerational aspects are proving to be a great success for both children and elders. "The relationship between the children and the elders has really exceeded our expectations," says Karen Leibold, director, Work and Family Programs. "We thought we'd need to bring them together slowly, with a lot of staff direction and with specific projects to do. What we've found is that they're like magnets with each other. They just come together. They enjoy each other's company. Sometimes it can be for five minutes at the end of the day, when they meet in the entryway. Sometimes it's waving across the lunchroom at each other. Sometimes it can be an extended period of time, reading books together, or cooking, or making things with blocks or Play-Doh."

The intergenerational day care program is an outstanding example of how the needs of employees, employers, children, and elders can be met through collaborative planning.

Contributed by Stride Rite Corporation, Cambridge, Massachusetts; photos courtesy of Rick Friedman.

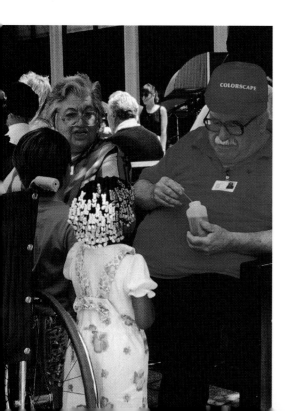

Voyager Expanded Learning, Inc.

An atmosphere of learning rich in opportunities for success, effective use of schools after traditional school hours, an exciting curriculum which infuses students with a lifelong love of learning, benefits which return to schools, communities, and families many times over . . . aren't these every educator's dream?

With the dual goals of increased learning time for children and innovative, extended-day support for working parents, Voyager Expanded Learning, Inc., is truly a new generation of partnership with public schools.

Because of the rapid changes in society and subsequent number of working parents, children often find themselves in unsupervised settings after school. In addition, statistics tell us that the school day itself for American schools is the shortest among industrialized nations. American schools are closed 50 percent of the time that parents must be at work. After-school hours is the ideal time to enrich and enhance the American educational experience while at the same time keeping children safe in school buildings until the end of the parental workday. The founders of Voyager Expanded Learning, Inc., have embraced this philosophy enthusiastically as the way to make a dramatic impact on the lives of children while directly supporting the schools they attend and their working parents. Begun in 1995 as extended-day programs in eleven Dallas-area schools spanning the socio-economic spectrum, Voyager is now available to schools and families in many locations nationwide.

Voyager is offered in schools to children in grades K through 6, and its curriculum reflects appropriate activity levels for different age groupings. Many Voyager teachers choose to group all children in grades K through 2

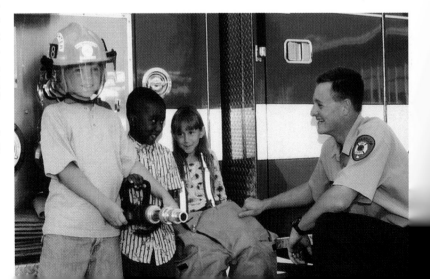

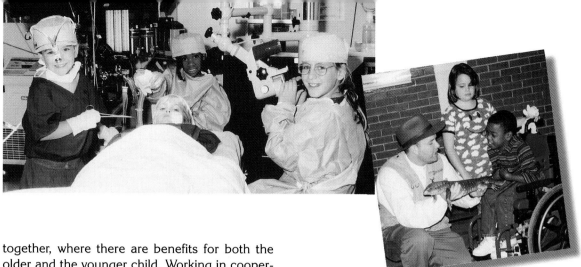

together, where there are benefits for both the older and the younger child. Working in cooperative groups and negotiating freely, children experience the high degree of social interaction necessary in the world at large. In Voyager, the curriculum is activity-based and therefore not limited by reading level. At the same time, depth of knowledge is achieved by the removal of time constraints and the absence of grades or tests. Learning for the fun of learning is the norm. Curriculum design teams are supported by partnerships with corporations and institutions to create learning programs of great value. In Success City, a Voyager learning module, the children explore the free enterprise system by forming their own companies, complete with executives, business plans, profit and loss columns, and final products. Teddy bears created by Voyager assembly lines have success-

fully passed through many small hands to reach the final quality control huggers.

Voyager curriculum is exciting, relevant, and appealing. It is a very defined change of pace from the regular school day, although it does build on skills previously introduced by the school and seeks most definitely to advance the school's mission. In Voyager, teachers act as facilitators, encouraging students to accept challenges and take risks. These same teachers are prepared for their Voyager duties and supported throughout the year with world-class training both in content and in instructional strategies.

Contributed by Susan Palmer; photos courtesy of Voyager.

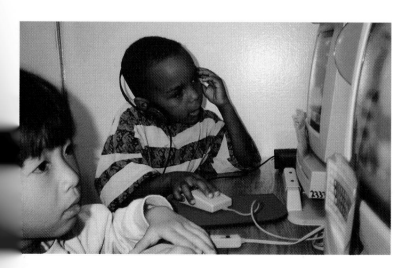

The Montessori Nido

A Nido consists of nine babies from two months to twelve to fourteen months (when the child is walking well). With three adults, a three-to-one child-caregiver ratio is maintained at all times. The Montessori Nido environment is divided into four main areas. The first area, the **movement area**, is equipped with a thin covered mattress with kiosks and bars the babies use for pulling up; other mattresses may be available around the room depending on the space. The movement area usually includes a stair as well.

The **sleeping area**, the second area of the Nido environment, is an isolated area with individual futons (the tiniest babies' futons are enclosed in a Plexiglas "crib" that sits on the floor). This area provides a quiet place for the babies to sleep whenever they need to, but it also has easy access to the rest of the environment so that when a baby awakens, he or she can crawl or walk to the adults. The children are free to go onto their futons when they are sleepy and come off when they awake.

The third area, the **eating area**, is equipped with low, heavy "weaning" tables and chairs instead of high chairs. The children are capable of getting into and out of the chairs with ease. The adults sit on low stools facing the children when feeding them. This area is not carpeted; the children are encouraged to feed themselves as soon as possible but are never left to eat alone as eating is a "social occasion." An area is provided for nursing moms to come and nurse their babies, and several adult areas are available for giving bottles to those babies who take them.

The last area, the **physical care area** (changing, bathing), is beside a water source. Elsewhere in the room there is a rocking chair for comforting babies. Most of the room is tiled—not carpeted—except for the sleeping area. This allows the babies to move around more easily and makes cleaning and sterilizing the floor possible. A low stool is used to accommodate children learning to change their own panties. Panties are used instead of diapers so that babies can move more easily and become more aware of their bodily functions. This environment has no walkers, swings, playpens, cribs, or high chairs—none of the devices sold to "aid" a baby's movement. Babies are placed on the floor and move everywhere.

There is no program, so to speak, in the Nido. The children spend their time as they would at home: sleeping, being awake and interacting with adults and other children, using the materials provided for their development, moving about the environment, going outside—either in the garden or on a walk, eating, bathing, and so forth.

Contributed by Judith Orion, director, A. M. I. Assistance to Infancy Training, Denver, Colorado; photos provided by The Montessori Institute, Denver, Colorado.

The Pacific Gas and Electric Company Children's Center

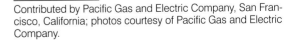

The Pacific Gas and Electric Company (PG&E) Children's Center is the first major corporate child care center to locate in downtown San Francisco. For PG&E, opening the Children's Center brings a new advantage to its downtown location, offering a way for employees to balance the demands for work and family.

The 9,000-square-foot Children's Center on the mezzanine floor of the headquarter building can accommodate up to sixty-six infants, toddlers, and preschoolers. The center's central location allows parents to leave their children in the morning, visit them at lunch or during breaks, and pick them up at the end of the day.

Inside the center, designers created an environment for learning, safety, and comfort. Classrooms and alcoves provide quiet space for reading, storytelling, or napping, while lofts and platforms offer ample practice for climbing and exploring—all in view of the center's professional caregivers.

Meeting individual needs is evident in the center's approach to physical activity. Opportunities for movement are a daily part of the indoor and outdoor environment.

The center upholds the premise that children learn by doing. Throughout the day, children have opportunities to participate in hands-on learning activities. Whether they are measuring sand, pouring water, or rattling instruments, children can feel, manipulate, and experiment with objects in an atmosphere of discovery. The center also places a high value on learning acquired through play. Development of language, problem-solving skills, and cooperation with others, as well as introductions to such cognitive concepts as mathematics, are all important outcomes of children's play.

Infants enjoy a homelike environment with soft lighting, colorful spaces, and comfortable furnishings. Activities such as feeding, holding, talking, and playing seek to meet individual needs and schedules.

Toddlers enjoy their own component of the curriculum, in which they have a primary caregiver who supports their growing independence while emphasizing eating, toileting, language, and movement. As toddlers become more independent, they are able to play and interact with others in a challenging and fun setting.

The final component of the center's curriculum concentrates on preschoolers. The preschool program promotes the development of creativity and self-esteem through play activities in science, art, music, reading, drama, cooking, and blocks. Such activities build emotional and social skills while enhancing learning and achievement.

Contributed by Pacific Gas and Electric Company, San Francisco, California; photos courtesy of Pacific Gas and Electric Company.

is in good repair. NAEYC advocates the following to assure that children get the most out of playgrounds:

- Children are carefully supervised. *The play area should be monitored by adults with a knowledge of injury prevention and first aid. Their responsibilities include scanning equipment, gates, and surfaces before children enter to check for stray animals, broken objects, and other hazards. Adults should set reasonable, appropriate rules for what children may do, such as sit down on the slide or wear sneakers to climb on monkey bars.*
- The space arrangement adds to children's safety. *Play areas should be inaccessible to streets, standing water, and other hazards. Equipment should be designed for a range of ages and abilities, and it should be installed with safety in mind. In a carefully constructed environment, children are able to roam between activities without getting into playground traffic jams.*
- Equipment is sturdy and engineered for safety. *The placement, size, height and complexity of equipment must be tailored to the children who use it. For example, climbing equipment should not be taller than the children who climb.*
- Landing surfaces are resilient. *Playground equipment should never be placed on concrete or asphalt. Choose a material that is impact-absorbing to cover all areas where children may jump or fall.*
- Routine maintenance is scheduled and budgeted. *Parts of equipment that move should be checked and repaired regularly.*
- Appropriate choices are offered. *Children's bodies are at work when they play outdoors, and they are ripe to practice and learn new skills.*[3]

Issues Associated with Play

The first issue is early childhood professionals' willingness, ability, and skill in explaining to parents in particular and the public in general the value of play and that children can and do learn through play. Early childhood professionals constantly must educate parents and the public about the function and value of play in preschool settings. When professionals do not do a good job of explaining, the value of play tends to lessen in the public's eye, which further encourages those who advocate a strictly academic approach to preschool programs.

Second, preschool professionals must plan for children's play to assure that they have time for play, the appropriate materials for play, and an appropriate environment that supports, promotes, and encourages developmentally appropriate play for all children. The unwillingness of some to do this or not do it well means that children will not gain from play the benefit that they need.

THE PRESCHOOL CURRICULUM

How do we determine an appropriate curriculum for three- and four-year-olds? Some say society determines the curriculum according to what its members think children should learn and do. For example, Western (Euro-American) society values academic skill related to reading, writing, and math as well as social skills and getting along with others. Therefore, in this society preschool activities that help children do these things should appear in the curriculum. Others say the curriculum should be based on what children will learn and do in kindergarten and first grade. This kind of preschool curriculum should, therefore, include many "readiness" activities. Still others say that individual children should determine the curriculum according to what each knows or does not know; thus, the starting place is the needs and interests of children.

Play as Curriculum

In this continuing debate, many people respond that play is the most appropriate curriculum. However, play is the *process* by which the curriculum is implemented. Al-

**VIDEO
VIEWPOINT**

IMPROVING INTELLIGENCE IN CHILDREN

Statistically speaking, children in grade 4 across the country are performing lower than ever academically, and improvement may mean helping children's brains grow larger. As scientists study how children's brains grow, they have discovered that if certain brain cells are not developed by certain ages the cells die off. Scientists offer solutions to the question of when it is critical to create an environment for children's brains to be better developed.

Reflective Discussion Questions: Why are we as a society suddenly interested in "growing the brains of young children"? What are some consequences for society and for children of not providing them with the early stimulation needed to grow their brains? How does the phrase "use it or lose it" apply to children's neurological and brain development? How early in life should parents begin to stimulate and promote language development in their children?

Reflective Decision Making: What are some things you can do as an early childhood professional to provide "nutrition" for children's brains? In Chapter 6 of *Early Childhood Education Today,* review the section on early language development. Make a list of things you can do to stimulate children's early language development. What advice would you give to parents about how they can promote language development in young children? Interview a music educator regarding how exposing children to music stimulates higher logical thought. What kind of music should children be exposed to? What are some math games you can teach your children that may promote higher thought processes?

though it is true that children learn *through* play, to say play is the curriculum begs the issue of what children are to learn.

What good preschool programs do—what any good educational program does—is to take *all* children at whatever point in their development, and provide a set of appropriate experiences enabling *each* child to go as far as possible *without* pushing, hurrying, or overstressing. The essence of early education is a set of guided experiences, both cognitive and affective. Early childhood educators should always start with children and base their curriculum on them. What we teach is and should be based on child development, the needs of children, and what they are like as individuals. If this is done, then the curriculum will be child centered and developmentally appropriate. As an example, the Program in Action feature on pages

208–209, "The Value of Play," illustrates how literacy may be promoted through play.

Appropriate Preschool Goals

All programs should have goals to guide activities and on which to base teaching methodologies. Without goals, it is easy to end up teaching just about anything without knowing why. Goals of individual preschools vary, but all programs should have certain essential goals. Simply because *programs* have goals, however, does not necessarily mean their teaching methods support or achieve those goals. Many preschools suffer this weakness—there is a difference between what they say they do and what they actually do. Most good preschools, however, plan goals in these areas: social and interpersonal skills, self-help and intrapersonal skills, building self-esteem, academics, thinking skills, learning readiness, language and literacy, and nutrition.

Social and Interpersonal Goals

- Helping children learn how to get along with other children and adults and how to develop good relationships with teachers
- Helping children learn to help others and develop caring attitudes

Self-Help Skills and Intrapersonal Goals

- Modeling for children how to take care of their personal needs such as dressing (tying, buttoning, zipping) and knowing what clothes to wear
- Eating skills (using utensils, napkins, and a cup or glass; setting a table)
- Health skills (how to wash and bathe, how to brush teeth)
- Grooming skills (combing hair, cleaning nails)

Self-Esteem Goals

- Promoting self-help skills to help children develop good self-image and high self-esteem
- Helping children learn about themselves, their family, and their culture
- Developing a sense of self-worth by providing experiences for success and competence
- Teaching about body parts and their function

Academic Goals

- Teaching children to learn their names, addresses, and phone numbers
- Facilitating children's learning of colors, sizes, shapes, and positions such as under, over, and around
- Facilitating children's learning of numbers and prewriting skills, shape identification, letter recognition, sounds, and rhyming
- Providing for small-muscle development

Thinking Goals

- Providing environments and activities that enable children to develop the skills essential to constructing schemes in a Piagetian sense—classification, seriation, numeration, and knowledge of space and time concepts. These form the basis for logical-mathematical thinking.
- Giving children opportunities to respond to questions and situations that require them to synthesize, analyze, and evaluate

Learning Readiness Goals

- Facilitating readiness skills related to school success, such as following directions, learning to work alone, listening to the teacher, developing an attention span, learning to stay with a task until it is completed, staying in one's seat, and controlling impulses

Language and Literacy Goals

- Providing opportunities for interaction with adults and peers as a means of developing oral language skills
- Helping children increase their vocabularies
- Helping children learn to converse with other children and adults
- Building proficiency in language
- Developing emergent literacy skills (prewriting and reading skills)

Nutrition Goals

- Providing experiences that enable children to learn the role of good nutritional practices and habits in their overall development

PROGRAM IN ACTION

THE VALUE OF PLAY

Early childhood educators have long recognized the value of play for social, emotional, and physical development. Recently, however, play has attracted greater importance as a medium for literacy development. It is now recognized that literacy develops in meaningful, functional social settings rather than as a set of abstract skills taught in formal pencil-and-paper settings.

Literacy development involves a child's active engagement in cooperation and collaboration with peers; it builds on what the child already knows with the support and guidance of others. Play provides this setting. During observations of children at play, especially in free-choice, cooperative play periods, one can note the functional uses of literacy that children incorporate into their play themes. When the environment is appropriately prepared with literacy materials in play areas, children have been observed to engage in attempted and conceptional reading and writing in collaboration with other youngsters. In similar settings lacking literacy materials, the same literacy activities did not occur.

To demonstrate how play in an appropriate setting can nurture literacy development, consider the following classroom setting in which the teacher has designed a veterinarian's office to go along with a class study on animals, focusing in particular on pets.

The dramatic play area is designed with a waiting room including chairs; a table filled with magazines, books, and pamphlets about pet care; posters about pets; office hour notices; a "No Smoking" sign; and a sign advising visitors to "Check in with the nurse when arriving." On a nurse's desk are patient forms on clipboards, a telephone, an address and telephone book, appointment cards, and a calendar. The office contains patient folders, prescription pads, white coats, masks, gloves, a toy doctor's kit, and stuffed animals for patients.

Ms. Meyers, the teacher, guides students in using the various materials in the veterinarian's office during free-play time. For example, she reminds the children to read important information they find in the waiting area or to fill out forms about their pet's needs, to ask the nurse for appointment times, or to have the doctor write out appropriate treatments or prescriptions. In addition to giving directions, Ms. Meyers also models behaviors by participating in the play center with the children when first introducing materials.

This play setting provided a literacy-rich environment with books and writing materials; modeled reading and writing by the teacher that children could observe and emulate; provided the opportunity to practice literacy in a real-life situation that had meaning and function; and encour-

---

- Providing food preparation experiences

- Introducing children to new foods, a balanced menu, and essential nutrients

Developing Independence Besides the goals of promoting the skill areas, but subsumed within them, are two other goals of the preschool experience: to foster independence and a positive attitude toward learning. In many respects, the major goal for all education from preschool to university is *to help students become independent.* In addi-

tion, children should develop an attitude of liking to learn and wanting to come to school. In a sense, the entire school program should help children do things for themselves, to become autonomous.

Unfortunately, some preschool programs and teachers foster an atmosphere of dependence, helplessness, and reliance on others by doing things for the children instead of helping them learn to do things for themselves. A good rule of thumb for all preschool professionals is to avoid doing anything for children that they

aged children to interact socially by collaborating and performing meaningful reading and writing activities with peers. The following anecdotes relate the type of behavior Ms. Meyers observed in the play area.

Jessica was waiting to see the doctor. She told her stuffed animal dog, Sam, not to worry that the doctor would not hurt him. She asked Jenny, who was waiting with her stuffed animal cat, Muffin, what the kitten's problem was. The girls agonized over the ailments of their pets. After a while they stopped talking, and Jessica picked up the book *Are You My Mother?* and pretended to read to her dog, Sam. Jessica showed Sam the pictures as she read.

Preston examined Christopher's teddy bear and wrote a report in the patient's folder. He read his scribble writing out loud and said, "This teddy bear's blood pressure is twenty-nine points. He should take sixty-two pills an hour until he is better and keep warm and go to bed." At the same time he read, he showed Christopher what he had written so he could understand what to do.

When selecting settings to promote literacy in play, choose those that are familiar to children and relate them to themes currently being stud-

ied. Suggestions for literacy materials and settings to add to dramatic play areas include the following:

- A fast-food restaurant, ice cream store, or bakery suggests menus, order pads, a cash register, specials for the day, recipes, and lists of flavors or products.
- A supermarket or local grocery store can include labeled shelves and sections, food containers, pricing labels, cash registers, telephones, shopping receipts, checkbooks, coupons, and promotional flyers.
- A post office to serve for mailing children's letters needs paper, envelopes, address books, pens, pencils, stamps, cash registers, and labeled mailboxes. A mail carrier hat and bag are important for children who deliver the mail and need to identify and read names and addresses.
- A gas station and car repair shop, designed in the block area, might have toy cars and trucks, receipts for sales, road maps for help with directions to different destinations, automotive tools and auto repair manuals for fixing cars and trucks, posters that advertise automobile equipment, and empty cans of different products typically found in service stations.

Contributed by Lesley Mandel Morrow, professor and Coordinator of Early Childhood Elementary Programs, Rutgers University.

can do or learn to do for themselves. We can encourage independence by having children take care of their own environment. Children should be responsible for dusting, cleaning, washing, wiping, polishing, emptying waste baskets, vacuuming, sweeping, and helping care for classroom pets. Figure 7.2 compares program practices that foster dependence and those that encourage independence.

Developing the Whole Child

Preschool professionals have always been concerned with the development of the whole child. This concern requires providing activities and experiences that promote growth in the physical, emotional, social, and cognitive realms. These areas are interrelated, *not* separate and mutually exclusive. Good programs try to balance activities to address these areas.

The Daily Schedule

Although there are various ways to implement a preschool's goals, most preschools operate according to a play-oriented pro-

Figure 7.2/*Preschool Environment Rating Scale for Independence*

PRACTICES THAT FOSTER DEPENDENCE	PRACTICES THAT ENCOURAGE INDEPENDENCE
Teachers put children's wraps on for them.	Teachers teach children how to put on their own wraps.
Adults set tables, put out napkins, pour drinks, etc.	Children set tables, put out napkins, pour their own drinks.
Adults serve children lunch, snacks.	Children serve themselves; preferably they eat family style.
Adults clean up after children.	Children clean up after themselves.
Adults feed children.	Children are taught how to feed themselves and other self-help skills.
Children have to ask adults for materials and equipment.	Children have reasonably free access to equipment and materials.
Adults pass out and collect materials.	Children are responsible for passing out, collecting, and organizing materials.
Adults clean up after children.	Children clean up after themselves and put away all materials.

gram that includes self-selection of activities and learning centers. The following sections illustrate a typical preschool daily schedule.

Opening Activities As children enter, the teacher greets each individually. Daily personal greetings make the child feel important, build a positive attitude toward school, and provide an opportunity to practice language skills. They also give the teacher a chance to check each child's health and emotional status.

Children usually do not arrive all at one time, so the first arrivals need something to do while others are arriving. Free selection of activities or letting children self-select from a limited range of quiet activities, such as puzzles, pegboards, or markers to color with, are appropriate. Some teachers further organize this procedure by having children use an "assignment board" to help them make choices, limit the available choices, and prac-

tice concepts such as colors, shapes, and recognizing their names. Initially, the teacher may stand beside the board when children come and tell each child what the choices are. The teacher may hand children their name tags and help them put them on the board. Later, children can find their own tags and put them up. At the first of the school year, each child's name tag can include her or his picture (use an instant camera) or a symbol or shape the child has selected.

Group Meeting/Planning After all children arrive, they and the teacher plan together and talk about the day ahead. This is also the time for announcements, sharing, and group songs.

Learning Centers After the group time, children are free to go to one of various learning centers, organized and designed to teach concepts. Table 7.2 lists types of learning cen-

Table 7.2/*Learning Centers*

Center	Concepts	Center	Concepts
• Housekeeping	Classification Language skills Sociodramtic play Functions Processes	• Woodworking (pinewood, cardboard, Styrofoam)	Following directions Functions Planning Whole/part
• Water/sand	Texture Volume Quantity Measure	• Art	Color Size Shape Texture Design Relationships
• Blocks	Size Shape Length Seriation Spatial relations	• Science	Identification of odors Functions Measure Volume Texture Size Relationships
• Books/language	Verbalization Listening Directions How to use books Colors, size Shapes Names	• Manipulatives	Classifications Spatial relationships Shape Color Size Seriation
• Puzzles/perceptual development	Size Shape Color Whole/part Figure/ground Spatial relations		

ters and the concepts each is intended to teach.

Bathroom/Hand Washing Before any activity in which food is handled, prepared, or eaten, children should wash and dry their hands.

Snacks After center activities, a snack is usually served. It should be nutritionally sound and something the children can serve (and often prepare) themselves.

Outdoor Activity/Play/Walking Ideally, outside play should be a time for learning new concepts and skills, not just a time to run around aimlessly. Children can practice climbing, jumping, swinging, throwing, and body control. Teachers may incorporate walking trips and other events into outdoor play.

Bathroom/Toileting Bathroom/toileting times offer opportunities to teach health, self-help, and intrapersonal skills. Children should also be allowed to use the bathroom whenever necessary.

Lunch Lunch should be a relaxing time, and the meal should be served family style, with professionals and children eating together. Children should set their own tables and decorate them with placemats and flowers they can make in the art center or as a special project. Children should be involved in cleaning up after meals and snacks.

Relaxation   After lunch, children should have a chance to relax, perhaps to the accompaniment of stories, records, and music. This is an ideal time to teach children breathing exercises and relaxation techniques.

Nap Time   Children who want or need to should have a chance to rest or sleep. Quiet activities should be available for those who do not need to or cannot sleep on a particular day. Under no circumstances should children be forced to sleep or lie on a cot or blanket if they cannot sleep or have outgrown their need for an afternoon nap.

Bathroom/Toileting   See the previous comments.

Snack   See the previous comments.

Centers or Special Projects   Following nap time is a good time for center activities or special projects. (Special projects can also be conducted in the morning, and some may be more appropriate then, such as cooking something for snack or lunch.) Special projects might be cooking, holiday activities, collecting things, work projects, art activities, and field trips.

Group Time   The day can end with a group meeting to review the day's activities. This meeting develops listening and attention skills, promotes oral communication, stresses that learning is important, and helps children evaluate their performance and behavior.

This preschool schedule is for a whole-day program; many other program arrangements are possible. Some preschools operate half-day, morning-only programs five days a week; others operate both a morning and afternoon session; others operate only two or three days a week. In still other programs, parents choose how many days they will send their children. Creativity and meeting parent needs seem to be hallmarks of effective preschool programs.

IMPORTANT CONSIDERATIONS FOR SELECTING A GOOD EARLY CHILDHOOD PROGRAM

Parents often wonder how to select a good early childhood program. Early childhood professionals can use the following guidelines to help others arrive at an appropriate preschool decision:

- What are the physical accommodations like? Is the facility pleasant, light, clean, and airy? Is it a physical setting you would want to spend time in? (If not, children will not want to, either.) Are plenty of materials available for the children to use?

- Do the children seem happy and involved or passive? Is television used as a substitute for a good curriculum and quality professionals?

- What kinds of materials are available for play and learning?

- Is there a balance of activity and quiet play and of individual, small-group, and group activities? Child-directed and professional-directed activities? Indoor and outdoor play?

- Is the physical setting safe and healthy?

- Does the school have a written philosophy, objectives, and curriculum? Does the program philosophy agree with the parents' personal philosophy of how children should be reared and educated? Are the philosophy and goals age appropriate for the children being served?

- Does the staff have written plans? Is there a smooth flow of activities, or do children wait for long periods "getting ready" for another activity? Does the curriculum provide for skills in self-help; readiness for learning; and cognitive, language, physical, and social-emotional development? Lack of planning indicates lack of direction. Although a program whose staff does not plan is not necessarily a poor program, planning is one indicator of a good program.

- What is the adult–child ratio? How much time do teachers spend with children one to one or in small groups? Do teachers take time to give children individual attention? Do children have an opportunity to be independent and do things for themselves?

- How does the staff relate to children? Are the relationships loving and caring?

- How do staff members handle typical discipline problems, such as disputes between children? Are positive guidance techniques used? Are indirect guidance techniques used, for example, through room arrangement, scheduling, and appropriate activity planning? Is there a written discipline philosophy that agrees with the parents' philosophy?

- Are staff personnel sensitive to the gender and cultural needs and backgrounds of children and families?

- Are there opportunities for outdoor activities?

- How is lunchtime handled? Are children allowed to talk while eating? Do staff members eat with the children?

- Is the staff stable?

- What kind of education or training does the staff have? The staff should have training in the curriculum and teaching of young children. The director should have at least a bachelor's degree in childhood education or child development (refer to Chap. 1, Figures 1.1 through 1.3).

- Is the director well trained? Can she or he explain the program? Describing a typical day can be helpful. Is she or he actively involved in the program?

- How does the staff treat adults, including parents? Does the program address the needs of children's families?

- Is the program affordable? If a program is too expensive for the family budget, parents may be unhappy in the long run. Parents should inquire about scholarships, reduced fees, fees adjusted to income level, fees paid in monthly installments, and sibling discounts.

- Are parents of children enrolled in the program satisfied?

- Do the program's hours and services match parents' needs?

- What are the provisions for emergency care and treatment? What procedures are there for taking care of ill children?

Preschool Education Issues

The eternal question about early childhood programs is, Do they do any good? During the last several years, a number of longitudinal studies were designed to answer this question. The Perry Preschool Study came to this conclusion:

Results to age 19 indicate lasting beneficial effects of preschool education in improving cognitive performance during early childhood; in improving scholastic placement and achievement during the school years; in decreasing delinquency and crime, the use of welfare assistance, and the incidence of teenage pregnancy; and in increasing high school graduation rates and the frequency of enrollment in post-secondary programs and employment.[4]

From an analysis of seven exemplary preschool programs, Schweinhart, Barnes, and Weikart reached the conclusion that "high quality, active-learning programs for young children living in poverty return $7.16 for every dollar invested, cut in half participants' crime rate through age 27, significantly increase participants' earnings and property wealth as adults, and significantly increase participants' commitment to marriage."[5]

Placement of Preschools in Public Schools   A major issue of preschool education is whether preschool programs should be operated by public schools. The fact remains, more and more four-year-olds are enrolled in preschool programs operated by the public schools. Some question whether public schools are the appropriate agencies to provide schooling for three- and four-year-olds. Many feel that public school professionals lack the training to meet the unique needs of this age group and that the public schools are motivated by a desire to gain control of this segment of education rather than to serve preschoolers' educational needs (see Chap. 2).

Developmentally Appropriate Curriculum   Many preschool programs are acade-

Although we want children to be involved in child-initiated and active learning, sometimes it is necessary to directly teach children certain concepts and skills. What concepts or skills is this teacher directly teaching the children?

mic in nature; the curriculum consists of many activities, concepts, and skills traditionally associated with kindergarten and first grade. Critics of public school programs for three- and four-year-old children think this kind of program puts too much pressure on them because they are not developmentally ready. A persistent and long-standing issue in early childhood education, "pushing" children usually revolves around overemphasis on learning basic skills and other skills associated with school success. The issue is complex. First, we need a precise understanding of what it means to "push" children. Some children are able to do more than others at earlier ages; some respond better to certain kinds of learning situations than others. Some parents and children are able to be involved in more activities than are others. So, we must always relate the topic of pushing to individual children and their family contexts. (Of course, when we feel parents may be pushing their child, we need to advise them of the potential harm they may be doing.)

Research data is emerging about the effects of pushing young children. Researchers at Temple University, for example, found that children of mothers "who pushed them to attain academic success in preschool were less creative, had more anxiety about tests, and, by the end of kindergarten, had failed to maintain their internal academic advantage over their less-pressured peers."[6] Given this kind of data, both parents and early childhood educators must remember to provide opportunities for children to learn and develop at their own rates.

In response to the developmentally appropriate issue, many public schools and early childhood educators are calling for a restructuring of preschool early childhood programs that would result in an early childhood unit.

Accessibility to Preschools

Accessibility to preschool is an issue facing children, families, and society. Currently, many children do not have access to preschools because there are not enough public preschools available. Many parents cannot afford to pay the tuition at private preschools (see also Figure 7.1). Rather than a comprehensive national program of preschools, children and families are confronted with a patchwork of fragmented public and private services that meet the needs of only some children. Additionally, available good programs are not equitably distributed.

Accordingly, the Carnegie Corporation proposes universal preschools for all three- and four-year-olds to promote their readiness and meet the need for school success. Their report said in part that "academic self-image is shaped between the ages of 3 and 10."[7] As preschools become more available and accessible to young children, they and their families will be included in the schools' programs. Parents are a vital link in creating the learning climate that all children need for life success.

Professional Training and Education

Another issue is the problem of providing quality early childhood education professionals. The growing number of preschools for three- and four-year-olds has created a need for more teachers and caregivers. Unfortunately, programs often hire unqualified personnel. In some cases this situation brings new revelations of child abuse in centers and makes more apparent inadequate screening of people who work with children. In our rush to provide programs, we must not cut corners or compromise standards. Professionals have moral, ethical, and legal obligations to protect children and provide them with teachers of the highest quality. Part of this issue involves teacher certification: people who work with or teach preschoolers should have specific training and/or certification for that age group. To allow someone with inappropriate education to teach preschoolers does an injustice to the concept of a developmentally appropriate curriculum. (See Chap. 1, especially Figures 1.1 through 1.4 and Table 1.3.)

Child-Centered Programs Quality in preschool programs is an issue in another way, focusing on how to provide a balance between the best of those characteristics we define as *quality:* desirable teacher–child ratios, encouraging independence, and a learning environment that promotes child-centered learning while providing children with the skills necessary for future academic success. Some preschool proponents tend to focus almost exclusively on the basic skills of reading, writing, and arithmetic, with an accompanying tendency to minimize the importance of nurturing development in children's social and emotional areas. As early childhood professionals, we must strive to provide a balance between academics and all areas of development.

Who Are Preschools For?

The question to ask is this: Should *all* three- and four-year-old children attend public preschools? As you might expect, there is more support for four-year-old attendance than for three-year-olds. Some think that preschool programs should be for all children, not just for those who are at risk for school failure. However, not all agree. Others believe that attendance of all children is too costly. (Some school districts, such as Dade County, Florida, provide public preschools for threes and fours, but they charge parents tuition for their children's attendance.) Still others think that inclusion of children with disabilities in public preschool programs places too many demands on other children and early childhood professionals. However, it is the *children* who are at risk for school failure and children with disabilities who are most likely to benefit from taxpayer support of public preschools.

The Future of Preschool Education

The further spread of public preschools for three- and four-year-old children is inevitable. This growth, to the point where all children are included, will take decades but *will* happen. Most likely, the public schools will focus more on programs for four-year-old children and then, over time, include three-year-olds. A logical outgrowth of this long-term trend will be for the public schools to provide services for even younger children and their families. One thing is certain: preschool as it was known a decade ago is not the same today, and ten years from now, it will again be different.

Activities for Further Enrichment

1. Visit preschool programs in your area. Determine their philosophies and find out what goes on in a typical day. Which would you send your children to? Why?

2. Piaget believed that children construct schemes through play. Observe children's play, and give examples of schemes developed through play.

3. Identify the basic purposes of a preschool program. Ask your classmates to rank these in order. What conclusions can you draw from their rankings?

4. Survey preschool parents to learn what they expect from a preschool program. How do parents' expectations compare to the goals of preschool programs you visited?

5. Tell how you would promote learning through a specific preschool activity. (For example, what learning outcomes would you have for a sand/water area?) What, specifically, would be your role in helping children learn?

6. Write a philosophy of a preschool program, and develop goals and objectives for it. Write a daily schedule that would support your goals.

7. Visit a preschool program, and request to see their program goals. How do they compare to those listed in this chapter? What would you change, add, or delete?

8. Read and review five articles that relate to today's trend in establishing quality preschool programs. What are the basic issues discussed? Do you agree with these issues?

9. Develop a file of activities you can use in a preschool program. Use the following headings to help organize your file: Activity Name; Objective; Description; Materials Needed. Is it easier to find materials for some areas than for others? Why?

10. How do parents and others "push" children? How can pushing harm children? Do you think some children need a push? What is the difference between constructive and destructive pushing?

READINGS FOR FURTHER ENRICHMENT

Homann, M., and D. Weikart. *Educating Young Children: Active Learning Practices for Preschool and Child Care Programs* (Ypsilanti, MI: High/Scope, 1995).

This book reviews the basic concepts of the High/Scope preschool curriculum and its development, implementation, and effectiveness.

Morrow, L. M. Literacy *Development in the Early Years: Helping Children Read and Write* (Boston: Allyn & Bacon, 1993).

An outstanding practical and informative book that provides the theory as well as the "how to" for promoting and helping children become literate.

Reynolds, E. *Guiding Young Children: A Child-Centered Approach* (Mountain View, CA: Mayfield, 1996).

Provides future child-care providers with practical problem-solving techniques that exclude the use of punishment, blame, or guilt. The author demonstrates how a problem-solving philosophy of freedom with responsibility can best address the development needs and abilities of young children.

Townsend-Butterworth, D. *Preschool and Your Child: What You Should Know* (New York: Walker, 1995).

This book answers the following questions: What is preschool about? What are appropriate parent expectations for the experience? Why should (or shouldn't) a child go to preschool? What are reasonable alternatives to preschool? The author also addresses other questions regarding preschool and children.

NOTES

1. Mildred Parten, "Social Play among Preschool Children," *Journal of Abnormal and Social Psychology* 27, pp. 243–69.
2. Jean Piaget, *Play, Dreams and Imitations in Childhood* (London: Routledge & Kegan Paul, 1967), p. 162.
3. National Association for the Education of Young Children, *Playgrounds: Keeping Outdoor Learning Safe* (Washington, D.C.: Author, 1996), n.p.
4. John R. Berrueta-Clement, *Changed Lives: The Effects of the Perry Preschool Program on Youths through Age 19* (Ypsilanti, MI: High/Scope, 1984), p. 1.
5. Lawrence J. Schweinhart, H. V. Barnes, and David P. Weikart with W. S. Barnett and A. S. Epstein. *Significant Benefits: The High/Scope Perry Preschool Study through Age 27* (Ypsilanti, MI: High/Scope, 1993), n.p.
6. *The New York Times,* 16 Sept. 1996, p. A13.
7. Ibid.

Kindergarten Education

CHAPTER 8

Learning All You Need to Know

Focus Questions

1. What is the history of kindergarten programs from Froebel to the present?

2. What are issues surrounding readiness for learning?

3. How does age influence entrance for kindergarten?

4. What are appropriate goals and objectives for kindergarten programs?

5. What is the nature of developmentally appropriate kindergarten curricula?

6. What are the strengths and weaknesses of kindergarten screening and assessment programs?

7. Why are transitions important for kindergarten children?

8. What issues confront kindergarten education today?

9. How does your personal philosophy of kindergarten education influence the way you will teach?

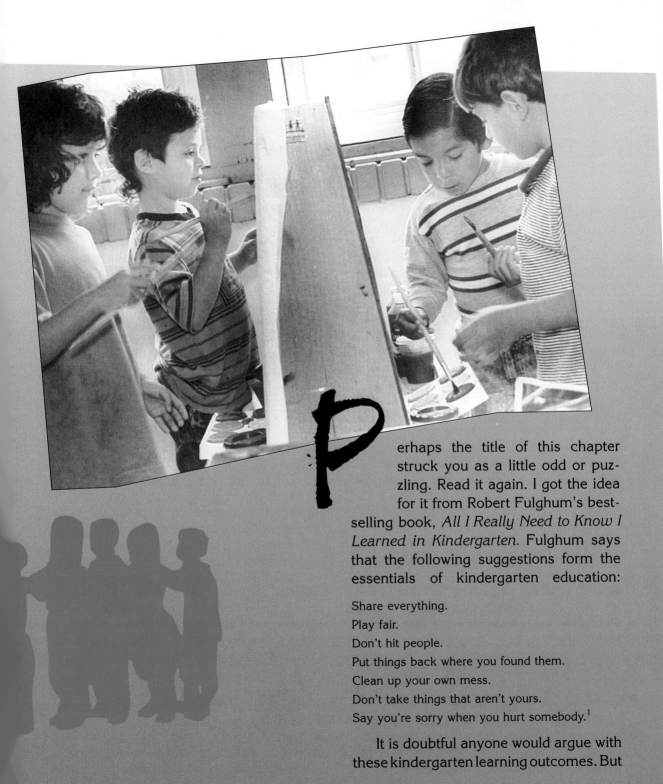

Perhaps the title of this chapter struck you as a little odd or puzzling. Read it again. I got the idea for it from Robert Fulghum's best-selling book, *All I Really Need to Know I Learned in Kindergarten*. Fulghum says that the following suggestions form the essentials of kindergarten education:

Share everything.
Play fair.
Don't hit people.
Put things back where you found them.
Clean up your own mess.
Don't take things that aren't yours.
Say you're sorry when you hurt somebody.[1]

It is doubtful anyone would argue with these kindergarten learning outcomes. But today, most people would expect *more* of kindergarten. Kindergarten is seen as an essential year, perhaps *the* essential year in the schooling experience. And it is for this reason that expectations are high for children to learn the essentials and be successful.

THE HISTORY OF KINDERGARTEN EDUCATION

Froebel's educational concepts and kindergarten program were imported into the United States in the nineteenth century virtually intact by individuals who believed in his ideas and methods. Froebelian influence remained dominant for almost half a century, until John Dewey and his followers challenged it in the early 1900s. While Froebel's ideas still seem perfectly acceptable today, they were not acceptable to those in the mid-nineteenth century who subscribed to the notion of early education. Especially innovative and hard to accept was that learning could be based on play and children's interests—in other words, that it could be child centered. Most European and American schools were subject oriented and emphasized teaching basic skills. In addition, Froebel was the first to advocate a communal education for young children *outside* the home. Until Froebel, young children were educated in the home, by their mothers. Although Froebel advocated this method too, his ideas for educating children as a group in a special place outside the home were revolutionary.

Credit for establishing the first kindergarten in the United States is accorded to Margarethe Schurz. After attending lectures on Froebelian principles in Germany, she returned to the United States and in 1856 opened her kindergarten at Watertown, Wisconsin. Schurz's program was conducted in German, as were many of the new kindergarten programs of the time, since Froebel's ideas of education appealed especially to bilingual parents. Schurz also influenced Elizabeth Peabody, the sister-in-law of Horace Mann, when, at the home of a mutual friend, Schurz explained the Froebelian system. Peabody was not only fascinated but converted.

Peabody opened her kindergarten in Boston in 1860. She and her sister, Mary Mann, also published a book, *Kindergarten Guide*. Peabody almost immediately realized that she lacked the necessary theoretical grounding to implement Froebel's ideas adequately. She visited kindergartens in Germany, then returned to the United States to popularize Froebel's methods. Peabody is generally credited as kindergarten's main promoter in the United States.

One event that also helped advance the kindergarten movement was the appearance of appropriate materials. In 1860, Milton Bradley, the toy manufacturer, attended a lecture by Peabody, became a convert to the concept of kindergarten, and began to manufacture Froebel's gifts and occupations.

The first *public* kindergarten was founded in St. Louis, Missouri, in 1873 by Susan E. Blow, with the cooperation of the St. Louis superintendent of schools, William T. Harris. Elizabeth Peabody had corresponded for several years with Harris, and the combination of her prodding and Blow's enthusiasm and knowledge convinced Harris to open a public kindergarten on an experimental basis. Endorsement of the kindergarten program by a public school system did much to increase its popularity and spread the Froebelian influence within early childhood education. In addition, Harris, who later became the U.S. commissioner of education, encouraged support for Froebel's ideas and methods.

Training for kindergarten teachers has figured prominently in the development of higher education. The Chicago Kindergarten

College was founded in 1886 to teach mothers and train kindergarten teachers. In 1930, the Chicago Kindergarten College became the National College of Education. In 1888, Lucy Wheelock opened a kindergarten training program in Boston. Known as the Wheelock School, it became Wheelock College in 1949.

The kindergarten movement in the United States was not without growing pains. Over a period of time, the kindergarten program, at first ahead of its time, became rigid and centered around methods and the teacher rather than the child. By the turn of the twentieth century, many kindergarten leaders thought that programs and training should be open to experimentation and innovation rather than rigidly following Froebel's ideas. The chief defender of the Froebelian status quo was Susan Blow. In the more moderate camp was Patty Smith Hill, who thought that while the kindergarten should remain faithful to Froebel's ideas, it should nevertheless be open to innovation. She believed that to survive, the kindergarten movement would have to move into the twentieth century and was able to convince many of her colleagues. More than anyone else, Hill is responsible for kindergarten as we know it today.

Hill's influence is evident in the format of many present-day preschools and kindergartens. Free, *creative* play, in which children can use materials as they wish, was Hill's idea and represented a sharp break with Froebelian philosophy. She also introduced large blocks and centers where children could engage in housekeeping, sand and water play, and other activities.

Were Froebel alive today, he would probably not recognize the program he gave his

Today, kindergarten is a universal part of schooling, enrolling children from different cultures and socioeconomic backgrounds and subsequently, different life experiences. Thus, kindergarten children are not all at the same level developmentally, so the kindergarten program should not be the same for all children. How can professionals help ensure that kindergarten experiences meet the unique needs of children?

life to developing. Many kindergarten programs are subject centered rather than child centered as Froebel envisioned them. Furthermore, he did not see his program as a "school" but a place where children could develop through play. Although kindergartens are evolving to meet the needs of society and families, we must not forget the philosophy and ideals on which the first kindergartens were based.

WHO IS KINDERGARTEN FOR?

Froebel's kindergarten was for children three to seven years of age; in the United States, kindergarten has been considered the year before children enter first grade. Since the age at which children enter first grade varies, the ages at which they enter kindergarten also differ. People tend to think that kindergarten is for five-year-old children rather than four-year-olds, and most professionals tend to support an older rather than a younger entrance age because they think older children are more "ready" for kindergarten and will learn better. Whereas in the past children had to be five years of age prior to December 31 for kindergarten admission, today the trend is toward an older admission age; many school districts require that children be five years old by September 1 of the school year.

Should Kindergarten Be Compulsory?

There is wide public support for compulsory *and* tax-supported public kindergarten. On one recent Gallup poll, 80 percent of respondents favored "making kindergarten available for all those who wish it as part of the public school system," 71 percent favored compulsory kindergarten attendance, and 70 percent thought children should start school at ages four or five (29 percent favored age four and 41 percent favored age five).[2] In

keeping with this national sentiment, most children attend kindergarten, though it is mandatory in only twelve states (Arkansas, Delaware, Florida, Oklahoma, South Carolina, Ohio, Kentucky, Maryland, New Mexico, Rhode Island, West Virginia, and Tennessee) and the District of Columbia.

Kindergarten has rapidly become universal for the majority of the nation's five-year-olds. Today, kindergarten is either a whole- or half-day program and within the reach of most of the nation's children. As with four-year-olds, the number of children attending kindergarten has risen steadily (Figure 8.1).

SCHOOL READINESS: WHO GETS READY FOR WHOM?

School readiness is a major topic of debate in discussions of preschool and kindergarten programs. Raising entrance ages for admittance to kindergarten and first grade is based on the reasoning that many children are "not ready," and teachers therefore have difficulty teaching them. The early childhood profession is reexamining "readiness," its many interpretations, and the various ways the concept is applied to educational settings and children.

For most parents, *readiness* means the child's ability to participate and succeed in beginning schooling. From this perspective, it includes a child's ability, at a given time, to accomplish activities and engage in processes associated with schooling, whether nursery school, preschool, kindergarten, or first grade. Readiness does not exist in the abstract—it must relate to something. Readiness is measured against the process of formal public schooling. By the same token, a child's lack of readiness may be considered a deficit and detriment, because it indicates a child does not have the knowledge and skills for success in kindergarten and first grade.

Figure 8.1/*Kindergarten Enrollment*

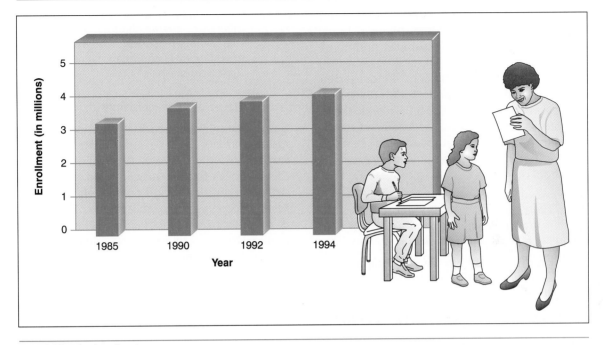

Note: Public school enrollment.

Source: U.S. Department of Education, National Center for Educational Statistics, Statistics of Public Elementary and Secondary School Systems.

However, as we discussed in Chapter 2, goal 1 of the Goals 2000: Educate America Act, the readiness goal, states, "Readiness for school: By the year 2000, all children in America will start school ready to learn." Goal 1 has three subgoals that merit our attention:[3]

- All children who are disadvantaged or who have disabilities will have access to high-quality and developmentally appropriate preschool programs that help prepare children for school.

- Every parent in the United States will be a child's first teacher and will devote time each day helping his or her preschool child learn; parents will have access to the training and support they need.

- Children will receive the nutrition and health care needed to arrive at school with healthy minds and bodies, and the number of low-birthweight babies will be significantly reduced through enhanced prenatal systems.

Discussions about readiness have changed our definition of it and attitude about what it means. Today, the term *readiness* is being replaced with the concept of *early development and learning*. Readiness is no longer seen as consisting of a predetermined set of capabilities children must attain before entering kindergarten or first grade. Furthermore, responsibility for children's early learning and development is no longer placed solely on the child or parents but rather is seen as a shared responsibility among children, parents, families, early childhood professionals, and communities.

The skills and behaviors kindergarten teachers believe are essential for kindergarten success are shown in Figure 8.2. How do these indicators compare to our discussion of readiness? To your beliefs about readiness? NAEYC has adopted the following position statement on school readiness:

The National Association for the Education of Young Children (NAEYC) believes that those who are committed to promoting universal school readiness must be committed to

1. *addressing the inequities in early life experience so that all children have*

   access to the opportunities which promote school success;
2. *recognizing and supporting individual differences among children; and*
3. *establishing reasonable and appropriate expectations of children's capabilities upon school entry.*[4]

Maturation and Readiness

Some early childhood professionals and many parents believe that time cures all things, including a lack of readiness. They think that as time passes, a child grows and develops physically and cognitively and, as a result, becomes ready to achieve. This belief is manifested in school admissions policies that advocate children's remaining out of school for a year if they are not ready for school as measured by a readiness test. Assuming that the passage of time will bring about readiness is similar to the concept of unfolding, popularized by Froebel. *Unfolding* implies that development is inevitable and certain and that a child's optimum degree of development is determined by heredity and a biological clock. Froebel likened children to plants and parents and teachers to gardeners whose task is to nurture and care for children so they can mature according to their genetic inheritance and maturational timetable. The concept of unfolding continues to be a powerful force in early childhood education, although many challenge it as an inadequate, outmoded concept.

The modern popularizer of the concept of unfolding was Arnold Gesell (1880–1961), whose ideas and work continue at the Gesell Institute of Human Development in New Haven, Connecticut. Gesell made fashionable and acceptable the notion of inherent maturation that is *predictable, patterned,* and *orderly.*[5] He also created a number of tests to measure this development, from which he constructed a series of developmental or behavioral norms that specify in detail chil-

Figure 8.2/What Kindergarten Teachers Believe Are Important Factors for Kindergarten Readiness

- Students are physically healthy, rested, and well nourished
- Able to finish task
- Can count to 20 or more
- Takes turns and shares
- Has good problem-solving skills
- Is enthusiastic and curious in approaching new activities
- Is able to use pencils or paint brushes
- Is not disruptive of the class
- Knows the English language
- Is sensitive to other children's feelings
- Sits still and pays attention
- Knows the letters of the alphabet
- Can follow directions
- Identifies primary colors and basic shapes
- Communicates needs, wants, and thoughts verbally in child's primary language

Source: U.S. Department of Education, National Center for Education Statistics, Kindergarten Teacher Survey on Student Readiness, 1995.

Children are born to learn. Learning is not something children "get ready for" but is a continuous process. What can professionals do to support children's learning? What factors do you think are critical to support children's readiness to learn?

dren's motor, adaptive, language, and personal-social behavior according to chronological age. Gesell also coined the concept of *developmental age* to distinguish children's developmental growth from chronological age; for example, a child who is five years old may have a developmental age of four because he demonstrates the behavioral characteristics of a four-year-old rather than a five-year-old. Gesell believed that parents make their greatest contribution to readiness by providing a climate in which children can grow without interference to their innate timetable and blueprint for development. The popularity of this *maturationist view* has led

to a persistent sentiment that children are being hurried to grow up too soon. More critics of early education say that we should let children be children, allow them to enjoy the only childhood they will ever have, and not push them into learning.

Play and Readiness

In addition to time and maturation, self-education through play and appropriate activities also promotes readiness. The self-education viewpoint stresses the roles children play in their own learning. In most discussions of readiness, people talk as though children take no part in it, giving all the credit to maturation and heredity. All great educators, however, have stressed the role children play in their own development. Froebel talked about unfolding, Montessori advocated auto- or self-education, and Piaget stressed the active involvement of the child in the process of cognitive development. Time alone is not sufficient to account for or provide children with the skills they need for school success.

For Froebel, play was the energizer, the process that promotes unfolding. He developed his gifts and occupations to help teachers involve children in play. Montessori believed the prepared environment, with its wealth of sensory materials specifically designed to meet children's interests, is the principal means to help children educate themselves. For Piaget, the physically and mentally active child in an environment that provides for assimilation and accommodation develops the mental schemes necessary for productive learning.

Self-education is child centered, not subject or teacher centered. Children play the star roles in the drama of learning; teachers are the supporting cast. Child-centered readiness programs provide children with enriched environments of material and human resources in which they can play and enhance their own development while they construct the cognitive schemes essential for readiness and, ultimately, school success. Concerning self-education, Caroline Pratt said about her famous Play School, "The attempt in the play school has been to place children in an environment through which by experiment with that environment they may become self-educated."[6]

For some children, the home is such an environment; for others, it is not. Unfortunately, some five-year-olds are denied admission to kindergarten programs because they are not "ready" and spend another year in a sterile home or program environment that has failed to support the growth and development necessary for them to be ready for the schooling experience. For these reasons, we now have an expanded vision of what readiness is and what is necessary to achieve this union.

Important Readiness Skills

In all the rhetoric associated with readiness, readiness skills and behaviors are frequently overlooked. These skills and behaviors include language, independence, impulse control, interpersonal skills, experiential background, and physical and mental health (see Figure 8.2).

Language　Language is the most important readiness skill. Children need language skills for success in both school and life. Important language skills include *receptive language,* such as listening to the teacher and following directions; *expressive language,* demonstrated in the ability to talk fluently and articulately with teacher and peers, the ability to express oneself in the language of the school, and the ability to communicate needs and ideas; and *symbolic language,* knowing the names of people, places, and things, words for concepts, and adjectives and prepositions.

Independence　Independence means the ability to work alone on a task, take care of oneself, and initiate projects without always being told what to do. Independence also includes mastery of self-help skills, including but not limited to dressing skills, health skills (toileting, hand washing, using a handkerchief, and brushing teeth), and eating skills (using utensils and napkins, serving oneself, and cleaning up).

Impulse Control　Controlling impulses includes working cooperatively with others and not hitting others or interfering with their work, developing an attention span that permits involvement in learning activities for a reasonable length of time, and being able to stay seated for a while. Children who are not able to control their impulses are frequently (and erroneously) labeled hyperactive or learning disabled.

Interpersonal Skills

Interpersonal skills are those of getting along and working with both peers and adults. Asked why they want their child to attend a preschool program, parents frequently respond, "To learn how to get along with others." Any child care or preschool program is an experience in group living, and children have the opportunity to interact with others so as to become successful in a group setting. Interpersonal skills include cooperating with others, learning and using basic manners, and most important, learning how to learn from and with others.

Experiential Background

Experiential background is important to readiness because experiences are the building blocks of knowledge, the raw materials of cognitive development. They provide the context for mental disequilibrium, which enables children to develop higher levels of thinking. Children must go places—the grocery store, library, zoo—and they must be involved in activities—creating things, painting, coloring, experimenting, discovering. Children can build only on the background of information they bring to a new experience. If they have had limited experiences, they have little to work with and cannot develop well.

Physical and Mental Health

Children must have good nutritional and physical habits that will enable them to participate fully in and profit from any program. They must also have positive, nurturing environments and caring professionals to help them develop a self-image for achievement.

Dimensions of Readiness

Readiness has many dimensions that make it much more than a skill-focused process.

Readiness is never ending. It does not exist only in the preschool and kindergarten years, although we often think of it this way. Readiness is not something children do or do not have but rather is a continuum throughout life—the next life event is always just ahead, and what experiences children are currently engaging in should prepare them for it.

All children are always ready for some kind of learning. Children always need experiences that will promote learning and get them ready for the next step. As early childhood educators, we should constantly ask such questions as, What does this child know? What can I do to help this child move to the next level of understanding?

Schools and professionals should promote readiness for children, not the other way around. In this regard, schools should get ready for children and offer a curriculum and climate that allows for children's inevitable differences. Rather than subscribe only to notions of what learning is about, early childhood professionals should rededicate themselves to the ideal that schools are for children. Public schools that want children to be ready for predetermined programs have their priorities reversed. Schools should provide programs based on the needs of children and families, not on preconceived notions of what children ought to be able to do.

Children's readiness for learning should be viewed as a collaborative effort among children, the school, early childhood professionals, families, and the community. (In this regard we can define the "community" as local, state, and national.) No longer can we or should we place the primary responsibility for children's readiness solely on children themselves or on their families. We all, individually and collectively, are responsible for helping children gain all they can from the process of schooling while assuring that they can be all they are capable of becoming.

Readiness is individualized. Five- and six-year-old children exhibit a range of abilities. While we have said previously that all

Sometimes, some children can benefit from spending more time in developing skills that come more rapidly to other children. Additionally, children can benefit from individualized attention and help with learning specific skills. How can early childhood professionals help assure that children progress at their own pace so that they learn and achieve well?

children are ready for particular learning experiences, not all children are ready for the same thing. It is not abnormal for some children to be behind in certain skills and behaviors and others to be ahead. What is abnormal is to expect all children to be the same.

Readiness is a function of culture. Professionals have to be sensitive to the fact that different cultures have different values regarding the purpose of school, the process of schooling, children's roles in the schooling process, and what the family's and culture's roles are in promoting readiness. Professionals must learn about other cultures, talk with parents, and try to find a match between the process and activities of schooling and fami-

lies' cultures. (See Chapters 7, 12, and 14 for a discussion of culturally sensitive caregiving.)

Making Readiness a National Agenda

Ernest L. Boyer (1928–1995) and the Carnegie Foundation for the Advancement of Teaching have set a national agenda for helping assure that all children will enter school ready to learn. They propose a seven-step agenda for achieving this goal.[7] The steps are listed here with some of the suggested subgoals:

Step 1: *A Healthy Start.* Good health and good schooling are inextricably interlocked, and every child, to be ready to learn, must have a healthy birth and be well nourished and protected in the early years of life. As part of step 1, Boyer proposes a network of neighborhood-based Ready-to-Learn Clinics in every underserved community to assure basic health care for all mothers and preschool children.

Step 2: *Empowered Parents.* The home is the first classroom. Parents are the most essential teachers; all children, as a readiness requirement, should live in a secure environment in which empowered parents encourage language development. Boyer recommends a new Ready-to-Learn Reading Series with recommended books for preschoolers, prepared under the leadership of the American Library Association.

Step 3: *Quality Preschool.* Since many young children are cared for outside the home, high-quality preschool programs are required that not only provide good care but also address all dimensions of school readiness. Boyer suggests that every school district establish a preschool program as an optional service for all three- and four-year-olds not participating in Head Start.

Step 4: *A Responsive Workplace.* If each child in the United States is to come to school ready to learn, we must have workplace policies that are family-friendly, ones that offer child care services and give parents time to be with their young children.

Step 5: *Television as Teacher.* Next to parents, television is the child's most influential teacher. School readiness requires television programming that is both educational and enriching. In this area, Boyer proposes a Ready-to-Learn cable channel, working collaboratively with public television, to offer programming aimed exclusively at the educational needs and interests of preschool children.

Step 6: *Neighborhoods for Learning.* Since all children need spaces and places for growth and exploration, safe and friendly neighborhoods are necessary. Efforts to achieve this

goal would include a network of well-designed outdoor and indoor parks in every community to give preschoolers opportunities for exercise and exploration.

Step 7: *Connections across the Generations.* Connections across the generations will give children a sense of security and continuity, which will contribute to their readiness in the fullest sense. Boyer envisions a "Grand-teacher Program" in communities across the country in which older people participate as mentors in daycare centers and preschools.

The readiness goal is a popular one with professionals and parents. Popularity is not enough, however. It will take the concerted efforts of all—professionals, parents, communities, state governments, the federal government, business, and citizens—to move from rhetoric to reality.

What Should Kindergarten Be Like?

When making decisions about what kindergarten should be like, we can apply the critical ideas and philosophies of the historic figures discussed in Chapter 2 to contemporary practice. Consider Froebel, for example:

The Kindergarten is an institution which treats the child according to its nature; compares it with a flower in a garden; recognizes its threefold relation to God, man and nature; supplies the means for the development of its faculties, for the training of the senses, and for the strengthening of its physical powers. It is the institution where a child plays with children.[8]

By comparing Froebel's vision of the kindergarten to today's kindergartens, we see that many of today's kindergartens are much different than what Froebel envisioned. This situation is entirely appropriate in many ways, for society is vastly different today than is was in Froebel's time. However, we still need to remember Froebel's and others' visions of what kindergartens can be like.

Additionally, NAEYC identifies the following ten signs of a good kindergarten:

1. *Children are playing and working with materials or other children. They are not aimlessly wandering or forced to sit quietly for long periods of time.*

2. *Children have access to various activities throughout the day, such as block building, pretend play, picture books, paints, and other art materials, and table toys such as legos, pegboards, and puzzles. Children are not all doing the same things at the same time.*

3. *Teachers work with individual children, small groups, and the whole group at different times during the day. They do not spend time only with the entire group.*

4. *The classroom is decorated with children's original artwork, their own writing with invented spelling, and dictated stories.*

5. *Children learn numbers and the alphabet in the context of their everyday experiences. Exploring the natural world of plants and animals cooking, taking attendance, and serving snack are all meaningful activities to children.*

6. *Children work on projects and have long periods of time (at least one hour) to play and explore. Filling out worksheets should not be their primary activity.*

7. *Children have an opportunity to play outside every day that weather permits. This play is never sacrificed for more instructional time.*

8. *Teachers read books to children throughout the day, not just at story time.*

9. *Curriculum is adapted for those who are ahead as well as those who need additional help. Because children differ in experiences and background, they do not learn the same things at the same time in the same way.*

10. *Children and their parents look forward to school. Parents feel safe sending their child to kindergarten. Children are happy; they are not crying or regularly sick.*[9]

Developmentally Appropriate Practice

This book has emphasized that in all things early childhood professionals do for and with children, their efforts should be *developmentally appropriate.* Developmentally appropriate practice—that is, teaching and caring for young children—facilitates learning that is in accordance with children's physical, cognitive, social, and linguistic development. Understanding professionals will help children learn and develop in ways that are compatible with their age and who they are as individuals (e.g., their background of experiences, culture). Those early childhood professionals who embody the qualities of good kindergarten teachers (Box 8.1) will tend to be those who teach in developmentally appropriate ways.

Talking about developmentally appropriate practice is one thing; putting it into practice is another. Here are some of the implications of such practice for kindergarten programs (indeed, all programs involving young children):

- Learning must be meaningful to children and related to what they already know. Children find things meaningful when they are interesting to them and they can relate to them.

- Children do not learn in the same way or are interested in learning the same thing as everyone else all the time. Thus, teachers must individualize their curriculum as much as possible. Montessori understood this point (see Chap. 4), and the High/Scope educational approach provides for it (see Chap. 5).

BOX 8.1 Qualities of a Good Kindergarten Teacher

1. Loves children (acceptance of various backgrounds and ability levels), respects children and parents
2. Patient, kind, caring, and understanding
3. Is a good listener
4. Promotes active learning, includes children's interests in the curriculum
5. Keeps up with current/new trends in education
6. Attends workshops and seminars regarding early childhood
7. Has a love for teaching kindergarten
8. Plans for learning, has a daily schedule, and is a short- and long-range planner
9. Is well organized
10. Has good classroom management
11. Has a good rapport with colleagues, parents, and children
12. Uses learning centers and has a child-centered classroom
13. Is innovative/creative
14. Can provide for all levels of students from enrichment to remedial
15. Instills a love of learning in students
16. Willing to give many extra hours
17. Has a desire and motivation to do a good job
18. Has a goal of wanting to ensure that each child is successful

---

Contributed by the kindergarten teachers at Croissant Park Elementary School, Broward County, FL.

• Learning should be physically and mentally *active;* that is, children should be actively involved in learning activities by building, making, experimenting, investigating, and working collaboratively with their peers.

• Children should be involved in *hands-on* activities with concrete objects and manipulative. Emphasis is on real-life activities as opposed to workbook and worksheet activities.

Developmental Kindergartens   The developmental kindergarten is a prekindergarten for developmentally or behaviorally delayed kindergarten children. It is seen as one means of helping at-risk children succeed in school. There is a specific procedure and rationale for placing children in such a program:

  • *Test kindergarten-eligible children prior to their entrance to kindergarten to determine which children are at risk (developmentally delayed).*

  • *Give at-risk children an extra year to develop by placing them in a less cognitively oriented kindergarten classroom in which developmental needs can be addressed.*
  • *Promote them to a regular kindergarten classroom the following year.*
  • *As a result of having had an extra year to mature in the developmental kindergarten, a reduction in later school failure will be achieved.*[10]

Transition Classes   A *transition class* is designed to give children the time they need to achieve what is required for entry into another grade. Children are really getting two years to achieve what they normally would achieve in one. A transition class is different from a nongraded program in that the transition class consists of children of the same age, whereas the nongraded classroom has multiage children.

The concept and practice of transition classes implies and should involve linear progression. Children are placed in a transition

Today there is a great deal of emphasis on literacy development. The nation has set a goal of having all children read and write at or above level by grade 3. What are some activities and practices you can implement that will help ensure that all children achieve this national goal?

class so that they can continue to progress at their own pace. The curriculum, materials, and teaching practices should be appropriate for each child's developmental age or level.

Proponents of transitional programs believe they offer the following advantages:

- Placement in a transition program promotes success, whereas retention is a regressive practice that promotes failure.

- The program provides for children's developmental abilities.

- Children are with other children of the same developmental age.

- The program provides children with an appropriate learning environment.

- The program puts children's needs ahead of the need to place a child in a particular grade.

- The program provides time for children to integrate learning. This extra time is often referred to as "the gift of time."

On the other hand, opponents of such programs make these points:

- Transition programs are another form of failure and are really retention in disguise.

- Transition programs are really another form of tracking in which the less ready children are removed from their more able peers.

- Transition programs can reinforce a basic skills orientation to kindergarten. Some school districts have eliminated or prohibit transitional programs.

Full- or Half-Day Kindergarten

Both half- and full-day kindergarten programs are available. A school district that operates a half-day program usually offers one session in the morning and one in the afternoon, so that one teacher can teach two classes. Although many kindergartens are half-day programs, there is no general agreement that this system is best. Those who argue for it say that this is all the schooling the five-year-old child is ready to experience and that it provides an ideal transition to the all-day first grade. Those in favor of full-day sessions generally feel that not only is the child ready for and capable of a program of this length but also that such an approach allows for a more comprehensive program. Kindergartens are about evenly divided between whole- and half-day programs across the United States (thus, descriptions of both appear in this chapter).

The general trend is toward full-day kindergarten programs for all five-year-old children. However, essentially two factors stand in the way of a more rapid transition to full-day programs: tradition and money. Kindergartens are historically and traditionally half-day programs, although there is ample evidence of full-day programs for four- and five-year-old children. As time passes and society's needs begin to point to full-day programs to prepare children for living in an increasingly complex world, more kindergarten programs will become full-day.

Money is the most important obstacle to the growth of full-day kindergarten programs. Without a doubt, it takes twice as many teachers to operate full-day programs as half-day programs. But as society continues to recognize the benefits of early education and as kindergartens and early childhood programs are seen as one means for solving societal problems, more funding will be forthcoming.

ASSESSMENT IN KINDERGARTEN

Because of federal mandates and state laws, school districts usually evaluate children in some way before or at the time of their entrance into school. Also, some type of screening occurs at the time of kindergarten entrance to evaluate learning readiness.

Unfortunately, children are often classified on the basis of how well they perform on these screenings. When assessment is appropriate and the results are used to design developmentally appropriate instruction, it is valuable and worthwhile. Assessment tests serve basically seven purposes:

- Identify what children know
- Identify special needs
- Assist in referral decisions
- Determine appropriate placement
- Help develop lesson plans and programs
- Identify behavioral and developmental levels as opposed to chronological level
- Inform parents about their children's developmental status

Screening Processes

Screening measures give school personnel a broad picture of what children know and are able to do, as well as their physical and emotional status. As gross indicators of children's abilities, screening procedures provide much useful information for decisions about placement for initial instruction, referral to other agencies, and what additional testing may be necessary to pinpoint a learning or health problem. Many school districts conduct a comprehensive screening program in the spring for children who will enter kindergarten in the fall, which can involve the following:

- Gathering parent information about health, learning patterns, learning achievements, personal habits, and special problems
- Health screening, including a physical examination, health history, and a blood sample for analysis
- Vision, hearing, and speech screening

PROGRAM IN ACTION

EVALUATING THE LEARNING PROCESS

I have used student portfolios to evaluate my kindergarten students for fifteen years. Over time, however, I have redefined their purpose and identified several criteria to make more effective use of portfolios. I believe that the value of student portfolios is to provide a record of each student's process of learning and therefore collect student work based on the following criteria:

- Portfolio entries reflect a student's cognitive, social, emotional, and physical development.
- They provide a visual record of student process of learning over time.
- They encourage input from students, teacher, and parents.

My students and I together select the work samples. Each portfolio also includes a parent questionnaire, parent responses to conferences, individual assessment profiles, and anecdotal records. Because the volume of materials that can accumulate in a portfolio can become overwhelming, I use a table of contents in the format of a checklist stapled inside the folder, which makes examining the contents more practical and efficient. As work is added, I check the table of contents and can determine at a glance what data I have to make wise instructional decisions and what information I still need.

The success of student portfolios as an evaluation tool depends on the appropriate assessment of individual students, and accurate, conscientious documentation of student growth.

Appropriate Assessment

Appropriate assessment is the process of observing, recording, and documenting the work children do and how they do it. In my classroom, assessments are ongoing and occur as children perform daily classroom routines and participate in group time, share time, center time, and recess. I note which activities the children choose, how long they work on specific activities, and their process for completing activities. I observe students' learning styles, interest levels, skill levels, coping techniques, strategies for decision making and problem solving, and interactions with other children. Observations, however, have little value unless they are accurately documented.

Accurate Documentation

To manage documentation more accurately and efficiently, I have developed or adapted a variety of forms to make *systematic assessments*. Throughout the year, I use these assessment tools to systematically record information on individual children in each area of their development. I use a symbol system to date the occurrence of behaviors and describe and document skill proficiency as appropriate. Emphasis is on what each child can do, and each child's progress is com-

---

- Collecting and analyzing data from former programs and teachers, such as preschools and child care programs
- Administering a cognitive and/or behavioral screening instrument

Comprehensive screening programs are conducted in one day or over several days. Data for each child are usually evaluated by a team of professionals who make instructional placement recommendations and, when appropriate, advise additional testing and make referrals to other agencies for assistance.

Screening Instruments and Observational Records

Several screening instruments provide information for grouping and planning instructional strategies. Most can be administered by people who do not have specialized train-

pared with his or her prior work. As I review these individual assessments I am able to quickly detect areas of growth.

Symbol System

+ = Progress is noted

✓ = Needs more time and/or experience

∗ = See comments

In addition to the individual student profiles, I have also developed several class evaluation forms that allow me flexibility in recording observations quickly yet accurately. These forms are especially useful in planning group and/or individual instruction and they provide additional documentation that supports the individual assessment records. For example, I make *anecdotal records* (on Post-It® notes) of unanticipated events or behaviors, a child's social interactions, and problem-solving strategies. I transfer these Post-Its® to a class grid so I can determine at a glance which children I have observed. The anecdotal records, along with the individual assessment profiles, become a part of each student's portfolio to be used for instructional planning and communicating with parents.

Throughout the year *samples of students' work* are dated and included in the portfolios.

Quarterly work samples that I select include some illustrating abilities with cutting activities, writing numbers (each child decides how far he or she can write), writing letters of the alphabet, and any words or stories a child can write independently (using either invented or conventional spelling). The children select samples of artwork and creative writing (e.g., journal entries, letters or drawing they have done for parents).

Use of Information

I use the information from student portfolios to plan classroom instruction for individuals and groups, to identify children who may need special help, and to confer with parents and colleagues. During conferences, I share with parents the student's assessment profile for the different areas of development, and together we examine samples of the child's work that supports the assessment. Even though the progress is visually obvious, I can also point out less obvious progress as we view the samples. I give parents conference response forms and ask for comments or suggestions for additional portfolio entries. Using the portfolio, I am satisfied that I have gleaned an accurate assessment of and appreciation for each child's total development.

Contributed by Linda Sholar, Sangre Ridge Elementary School, Stillwater, OK.

---

ing in test administration. Parent volunteers often help administer screening instruments, many of which can be administered in about thirty minutes.

BRIGANCE® K and 1 Screen The BRIGANCE® K and 1 screen is an evaluation instrument for use in kindergarten and grade 1. The kindergarten pupil data sheet for the BRIGANCE® K and 1 screen shows the skills, behaviors, and concepts evaluated in the

kindergarten portion of the screening instrument (Figure 8.3).

DIAL-R The DIAL-R (Developmental Indicators for the Assessment of Learning—Revised) is an instrument designed for screening large numbers of prekindergarten children. Requiring approximately twenty-five to thirty minutes to administer, it involves individual observation for motor skills, concepts, and language skills. The screening

Figure 8.3/A Completed Kindergarten Pupil Data Sheet from BRIGANCE® K and 1 Screen

A. Student's Name Colin Killoran

Parents/Guardian Kristin Killoran

Address 310 Locke Street

	Year	Month	Day
Date of Screening	97	6	15
Birth date	92	1	10
Age	5	5	5

School/Program Vinal School

Teacher Leslie Feingold

Assessor Dennis Dowd

B. Basic Screening Assessments

Page	Assessment Number	Skill (Circle the skill for each correct response and make notes as appropriate.)	C. Scoring Number of Correct Responses	Point Value	Student's Score
3	1A	**Personal Data Response:** Verbally gives: (1) first name (2) full name (3) age 4. address (street or mailing) 5. birth date (month and day)	3×	2 points each	6/10
4 & 5	2A	**Color Recognition:** (1) red (2) blue (3) green (4) yellow (5) orange 6. purple (7) brown (8) black (9) pink 10. gray	8×	1 point	8/10
6	3A	**Picture Vocabulary:** Recognizes and names pictures of: (1) dog (2) cat (3) key (4) girl (5) boy (6) airplane (7) apple (8) leaf 9. cup 10. car	8×	1 point each	8/10
7	4A	**Visual Discrimination—Forms and Uppercase Letters:** Visually discriminates which one of four symbols is different:(1) (2) (3)□ (4)○ (5)△ (6)○ 7. I (8) P 9. V 10. X	7×	1 point each	7/10
8	5A	**Visual-Motor Skills:** Copies:(1) — (2)○ (3)+ (4)□ 5. △	4×	2 points ea.	8/10
9 & 10	6A	**Gross-Motor Skills:** (1) Hops two hops on one foot. (3) Stands on one foot for five seconds. (5) Stands on one foot for five seconds. (7) Walks forward heel-to-toe four steps. (9) Stands on one foot momentarily with eyes closed. (2) Hops two hops on the other foot (4) Stands on the other foot momentarily. (6) Stands on the other foot for five seconds. 8. Walks backward toe-to-heel four steps. 10. Stands on the other foot momentarily with eyes closed.	8×	1 pt. ea.	8/10
11	7A	**Rote Counting:** Counts by rote to: (Circle all letters prior to the first error.) (1) (2) (3) (4) (5) (6) (7) 8 9 10	6×	.5 point each	3/5
12	8A	**Identifies Body Parts:** Identifies by pointing to or touching: (1) chin (2) fingernails (3) heels (4) ankles (5) jaw (6) shoulders (7) elbows 8. hips (9) wrists 10. waist	8×	.5 point each	4/5
13 & 14	9A	**Follows Verbal Directions:** Listens to, remembers, and follows: (1) one-step direction 2. two-step direction	1×	2.5 points each	2.5/5
15	10A	**Numeral Comprehension:** Matches quantity with numerals:(2) (1) (4) (3) 5	4×	2 points ea.	8/10
16	11A	**Prints Personal Data:** (Prints first name) Reversals: Yes No ✓	1×	5 points	5/5
17	12A	**Syntax and Fluency:** (1) Speech is understandable. (2) Speaks in complete sentences.	2×	5 points ea.	10/10
				Total Score:	77.5/100

D. Observations:

1. Handedness: Right ✓ Left _____ Uncertain _____
2. Grasps pencil with: Fist _____ Fingers ✓
3. Hearing appeared to be normal: (See p. vii) Yes _____ No _____ Uncertain _____
4. Vision appeared to be normal: (See p. vii) Yes _____ No _____ Uncertain _____
5. Record other observations on another sheet.

E. Recommendations:

Ask nurse to check hearing. Below cutoff (<92).

Factor score 13.5 below at-risk guideline (<18).

Presence of risk factors. Rescreen in 6–9 months.

Source: From BRIGANCE ® K & 1 Screen (revised–1997), Curriculum Associates, Inc. BRIGANCE ® is a registered trademark of Curriculum Associates, Inc. Used by permission.

team consists of a coordinator, an operator for each of the skills areas screened, and aides or volunteers to register parents and children.

The High/Scope Child Observation Record The High/Scope Child Observation Record (COR) for Ages 2½ to 6 is used by teachers or other observers to assess young children's development by observing their typical classroom activities.[11] The COR measures young children's progress in all facets of their development, whether or not the teacher is using the High/Scope curriculum.

The High/Scope COR assesses the full variety of processes of young children's development of initiative, social relations, creative representation, music and movement, language and literacy, and logic and mathematics. It is not limited, as typical tests are, to language and mathematics questions that each have only one right answer. The teacher directs a test; using the COR, the teacher observes young children's self-initiated activities.

The teacher using the COR begins by observing children's activities throughout both the program day and the classroom, writing notes to describe these activities in developmental terms. In addition to identifying the date and the child, each note describes an activity succinctly but with relevant details. A typical note under "Initiative," for example, would be as follows:

> (10/25) La Tanya wrote her name three times on the turn list so she could have three turns at the new mask computer game.

The teacher collects these notes throughout the reporting period, which could be as brief as a month or as long as a semester, recording them on forms supplied for this purpose or, in the computer version, in easily retrievable data files. Using a Parent Report Form, the teacher reports to parents selected notes about young children's development.

This report is an opportunity for conversations with parents about what their children are doing in the classroom and at home and how parents and teachers can work together as partners to contribute to young children's development.

After collecting the notes, the teacher also uses them to rate each child's development from level 1 to level 5 on each of 30 items. These items encompass the various aspects of development, from engaging in complex play and making friends to showing interest in reading, sorting, and counting objects. The item on expressing choices, for example, has the following five levels:

1. Child does not yet express choices to others.

2. Child indicates a desired activity or place of activity by saying a word, pointing, or some other action.

3. Child indicates desired activity, place of activity, materials, or playmates with a short sentence.

4. Child indicates with a short sentence how plans will be carried out ("I want to drive the truck on the road").

5. Child gives detailed description of intended actions ("I want to make a road out of blocks with Sara and drive a truck on it.")

The resulting scores indicate children's development in the various areas. Comparing children's developmental status at the beginning and end of a period indicates the progress during that period. In a study of 64 Head Start teaching teams, the High/Scope COR demonstrated evidence of its reliability and concurrent validity.[12]

Developmentally Appropriate Assessment

A great deal of controversy exists in the early childhood professions about appropriate and inappropriate uses of assessment. According to NAEYC, developmentally appropriate assessment of young children should incorporate the following features:

- *Assessment of young children's progress and achievements is ongoing, strategic, and purposeful.*
- *The content of assessments reflects progress toward important learning and devined goals.*
- *The methods of assessment are appropriate to the age and experiences of young children.*
- *Assessments are tailored to a specific purpose and used only for the purpose for which they have been demonstrated to produce reliable, valid information*
- *Decisions that have a major impact on children, such as enrollment or placement, are never made on the basis of a single developmental assessment or screening device.*
- *Assessment recognizes individual variation in learners and allows for differences in style and rates of learning.[13]*

Portfolios Today many teachers use portfolios, a compilation of children's work samples, products, and teacher observations collected *over time* as a basis for assessment. Decisions about what to include in portfolios vary, but examples include written work, artwork, audiotapes, pictures, models, and other materials that attest to what children are able to do. Some teachers let children put their best work in their portfolios; others decide with children what will be included; still others select for themselves what to include. An important point to remember, and one often overlooked, is that portfolios are only one part of children's assessment.

LITERACY EDUCATION AND YOUNG CHILDREN

Literacy education is an "in" phrase; we hear it in virtually all educational circles, and almost every early childhood educator is talking about how to promote it. It has replaced reading readiness as the main objective of many kindergarten and primary programs. *Literacy* means the ability to read, write, speak, and listen, with emphasis on reading and writing well. To be literate also means reading, writing, speaking, and listening within the context of one's cultural and social setting.

Literacy education is a hot topic in educational circles for a number of reasons. First, the National Adult Literacy Survey estimates that over 50 million Americans are functionally illiterate—at or below a fifth grade reading level. Furthermore, when we compare the U.S. literacy rate to that of other countries, we do not fare too well—many industrialized countries have higher literacy rates.[14] Consequently, educators and social policy planners are always concerned about the inability of the schools to teach all children to read at more than a functional level.

Second, as discussed in Chapter 2, businesses and industry are concerned about how unprepared the nation's work force is to meet the demands of the workplace. Critics of the educational establishment maintain that many high school graduates do not have the basic literacy skills required for many of today's high-tech jobs. Therefore, schools, especially at the early grades, are feeling the pressure to adopt measures that will give future citizens the skills they will need for productive work and meaningful living.

Cultural and Social Processes of Literacy Education

Literacy is viewed as a process that involves *both* cognitive and social activities. Some reading and writing practices focus primarily on the cognitive—they are designed to give children mental skills such as word recognition or sound–word relationships. Teachers teach children to read using methods such as whole-word and phonetic analysis; these methods constitute the major portion of the reading program. Reading and writing are frequently taught as isolated, separate subjects and skills. Furthermore, reading and writing are often taught in ways that give them little meaning to children. Treating reading and writing as processes and skills that are separate from children's daily and immediate lives can lead to failure and retention. Fortunately, this approach to literacy is changing.

Emergent Literacy

Today, early childhood professionals use the term *emergent literacy* when talking about reading, writing, speaking, and listening. Professionals view literacy as a process that begins at birth, perhaps before, and contin-

ues to develop across the life span, through the school years and into adulthood. Thus, with the first cry, children are considered to begin language development (see Chap. 6 for a discussion of linguistic development).

Emergent literacy themes emphasize using environmental and social contexts to support and extend children's reading and writing. Children want to make sense of what they read and write. The meaningful part of reading and writing occurs when children talk to each other, write letters, and read good literature or have it read to them. All of this occurs within a print-rich environment, one in which children see others read, make lists, and use language and the written word to achieve goals. Proponents of whole language maintain that this environment is highly preferable to previous approaches to literacy development.

The process of becoming literate is also viewed as a *natural* process; reading and

The emergent literacy model views reading and writing acquisition as a continuum of development. Hence, children are always thought of as being on a continuous journey towards gaining full literacy development. How is this philosophy similar to or different from a philosophy that views some children as nonreaders and illiterate?

writing are processes that children partici-pate in naturally, long before they come to school. No doubt you have participated with or know of toddlers and preschoolers who are literate in many ways. They "read" all kinds of signs (McDonald's) and labels (Campbell's soup) and scribble with and on anything and everything.

The concept of emergent literacy, then, is based on the following beliefs about literacy and about how children learn:

- Reading and writing involve cognitive and social abilities that children employ in the processes of becoming literate and gaining meaning from reading, writ-ing, speaking, and listening.

- Most children begin processes involved in reading and writing long before they come to school; they do not wait until someone teaches them. They should not have to wait to be taught. (Remem-ber what Montessori said about early literacy.)

- Literacy is a social process that devel-ops within a context in which children have the opportunity to interact with and respond to printed language and to other children and adults who are using printed language. In this context, chil-dren bring meaning to and derive meaning from reading and writing. Teachers and classrooms should encourage discussing and sharing knowledge and ideas through reading and writing.

- The cultural group in which children become literate influences how literacy develops and the form it takes. Children should also have opportunities to read the literature of many cultural groups in addition to their own.

Developing Literacy in Young Children

Literacy is certainly a worthy national and educational goal, not only for young children, but everyone. However, how best to promote literacy has always been a controversial topic. One popular approach is "skill and drill," which involves repeated teaching of carefully planned sequential lessons. Many *basal reading* programs (fundamental mate-rials used to teach literacy) that use this approach are still widely used in early child-hood classrooms.

Basal approaches and materials used for literacy development often emphasize a par-ticular method. One of the most popular methods is the *sight word* approach (also called *whole-word* or *look-say*) in which chil-dren are presented with whole words (*cat, bat, sat*) and develop a "sight vocabulary" that enables them to begin reading and writ-ing. Many early childhood professionals label objects in their classrooms (door, bookcase, etc.) as a means of teaching a sight vocabu-lary.

A second popular basal approach is based on *phonics* instruction, which stresses teaching letter-sound correspondence. By learning these connections, children are able to combine sounds into words (C–A–T). The proponents of phonics instruction argue that letter-sound correspondences enable chil-dren to make automatic connections be-tween words and sounds and, as a result, are able to sound out words and read them on their own. From the 1950s up until the pre-sent time (see Chap. 3) there has been much debate about which of these two approaches to literacy development is best. Today, there is a decided re-emphasis on the use of phon-ics instruction.

Another method of literacy development, the Language Experience Approach, follows the philosophy and suggestions inherent in progressive education philosophy (see Chap. 3). This approach is child centered and maintains that literacy education should be meaningful to children and should grow out of experiences that are interesting to them. Children's own experience is a key element in such child-centered approaches. Many teachers transcribe children's dictated "experience" stories and use them as a basis for writing and for reading instruction.

Beginning about 1980, early childhood practitioners in the United States were influenced by literacy education approaches used in Australia and New Zealand as well as by approaches from Great Britain that were popular during the open education movement of the 1960s. These influences gradually developed into what is known as the *whole language* approach to literacy development. Since whole language is a philosophy rather than a method, its definition often depends on who is using the term. This approach nonetheless advocates using all aspects of language—reading, writing, listening, and speaking—as the basis for developing literacy. Children learn about reading and writing by speaking and listening; they learn to read by writing and they learn to write by reading. Basic philosophical premises of whole language follow:

- It is *child-centered*—children, rather than teachers, are at the center of instruction and learning. Thus, children's experiences and interests serve as the context for topics and as a basis for their intrinsic motivation to read, write, and converse. In this way, literacy learning becomes meaningful and functional for children.

- Social interaction is important and part of the process of becoming literate. Lev Vygotsky (see Chap. 3) stressed the social dimensions of learning. He pro-

posed that through interaction with others, especially with more confident peers and through interactions and conversations with teachers, children are able to develop higher cognitive learning. This process of learning through social interaction is referred to as *socially constructed knowledge.*

- Spending time on the processes of reading and writing is more important than spending time on learning skills for getting ready to read. Consequently, from the moment they enter the learning setting children are involved in literacy activities, that is, being read to, "reading" books, pamphlets, magazines, etc., scribbling, "writing" notes and so forth.

- Reading, writing, speaking, and listening are taught as an integrated whole, rather than in isolation.

- Writing begins early (see previous).

- Children's written documents are used as reading materials.

- Themes or units of study are used as a means of promoting interests and content. Generally, themes are selected cooperatively by children and teachers and are used as means of promoting ongoing intrinsic interest in literary processes. (See the Program in Action, "Exploring Our World Through Discovery.")

Whole language dominated early childhood practice from about 1990 through 1995. However, growing numbers of critics of this approach, including parents and the public, maintain that because it is a philosophy rather than a specific approach, it does not teach children skills necessary for good reading. Additionally, some teachers have difficulty explaining the whole language approach to

PROGRAM IN ACTION

EXPLORING OUR WORLD THROUGH DISCOVERY

Burleigh Elementary School is located in Brookfield, a western suburb of Milwaukee, Wisconsin. It houses 800 kindergarten through sixth grade students, with five sections of kindergarten. The kindergarten children are taught by four teachers (three regular education teachers and one special education teacher) and teaching assistants. All the early childhood students with special needs are also located at Burleigh. Students are mainstreamed as much as possible. In the morning, one of the kindergarten teachers team teaches with an early childhood teacher to provide an integrated setting for regular and special needs children. Burleigh also is part of a program offering opportunities for city children to attend suburban schools. Presently African American and Hmong students are in the kindergarten classes.

Integrated Themes

One of the main focuses of the school is integrated thematic teaching and learning. Each year the staff chooses an all-school theme to explore. This year the theme is "Dare to Discover." Each grade level chooses its own subtheme to explore. The kindergarten staff, during summer curriculum writing, wrote an all-year plan, "Exploring My World Through Discovery," which includes units of study such as Life Cycles, Changes, Animals, Community, Underground, Healthy Me, Safety Town, The Arts, and Measuring in Math and Science. The staff works as a team to select topics based on district outcomes. All through the year students are discovering themselves and the world around them. The theme of Underground, for instance, starts with a Nutrition unit. Students will explore plants growing underground such as peanuts and potatoes, with a discussion of habitats, such as burrows. This topic will be revisited during Groundhog Day activities. The underground is also explored during a later unit, Digging Up the Past, in which children can explore rocks and fossils. Later underground topics center on the water cycle, rabbits, earthworms, and insects.

Home projects also can be a part of the units. During an Egg Unit, children and parents created an "egg-creation" at home which was then shared and displayed at school. During the Underground unit, children were asked to go home and dig a hole and "discover" what was in it. Children started with the question "What's in My Hole?" and then recorded their answers in words and pictures. The children's discoveries were shared and feedback was given from friends and families. In the spring, the entire school's focus on the discovery theme will culminate in a Family Night when children share what they have learned.

The kindergarten year starts out with all three teachers using cooperative planning. All classes participate in a program called "Safety Town." This program had been previously offered by the Junior Women's League in the summer with a limited enrollment. Because the program was so beneficial, Burleigh's kindergarten staff decided to incorporate it as part of their kindergarten curriculum. The program covers daily lessons on such things as bus safety, pedestrian safety, fire safety, and saying No to strangers. Field trips to the city's police and fire stations are part of the program, and police officers and fire fighters come to our classes to present lessons on safety.

Each day the children also get to practice being pedestrians and motorists. We painted a city with streets and sidewalks on the playground. Big-wheel trike riders are the motorists. While half the children practice being pedestrians (walking on the sidewalks, stopping at corners and stop signs, and looking both ways), the other half ride on the trikes, also stopping at corners and stop signs. There is also a working traffic light so that children can practice stopping on red and starting on green. Parent volunteers and teachers work together to manage the "traffic." Safety Town activities ended by inviting parents to come and see the children demonstrate their skills as good pedestrians and motorists.

Other units of study include a water cycle theme in which the process of scientific inquiry is developed. Children are young scientists who ask questions, experiment to find answers, and record their findings. Children work cooperatively in small groups, to make discoveries about absorption, how water changes form, sinking and floating, and evaporation. Sometimes I team with a first grade teacher in many activities. The whole unit is integrated also through language arts. We read books and poems about rain and water. Art activities and daily projects are based on the books read that day. Big books on sinking and floating are read during the shared book time. Oral language is encouraged during small-group activities. Children utilize writing and drawing to record their discoveries each day. Science units are always presented in a "hands-on discovery" approach. This active involvement is a natural motivator and helps children be enthusiastic about their learning.

Literacy Activities

Reading and writing activities occur daily. When children come into school at 12:40, they sit down and write in their journals. This is free writing—children choose what and how they want to write. There are many stages of writing that children go through as emergent literacy learners including scribbling, copying environmental print, writing classmate's names, and using temporary spelling (writing down the sounds they know). All children are working at their own developmental level.

The room is immersed in print—alphabet letters, words based on the theme, children's names, schedules, and so forth, are displayed around the room. We also have a Word Wall. The alphabet is displayed and as children become interested in words, such as "dog," "pumpkin," or "dinosaur," we add them to the world wall. Eventually, high frequency words such as "the" and "and" are added. I always draw a picture next to the word so children can remember what it is. The rule is, once a word is up on the wall you need to find it yourself or with help from peers. Last year I went to a week-long conference in May. When I returned, I noticed the children had added about twenty new

words with matching pictures, all by themselves. They were learning alphabetizing and beginning dictionary skills. Children talk to each other a great deal during journal time and do a lot of sharing with each other. About 90 percent of composing in kindergarten is oral. A child might tell his peers a detailed story about his dog. He then writes "dog" and draws a picture.

Observing and Assessing   I individually assess each child at the beginning of the year on such things as letter and sound recognition, concepts of print and book handling, and attitudes about reading and writing. I use this information to guide children individually in their quest to make sense of written language. Assessment guides instruction, so I repeat these assessments throughout the year and modify my lessons in order to meet children's needs. During journal time I walk around the room observing children and jotting down notes. When children are finished with their journal writing, they individually "read" it to me. This sharing of their work is actually a daily conference with me and gives me daily information I need to guide the children's growth.

As children finish writing, they sit on the carpet for "noisy reading" time. It is called noisy reading time because children at this age usually retell stories, read aloud, or read with buddies. During this time, I engage in "kid watching" or observing the reading behaviors of the children. I may be looking to see whether a child can retell a story using pictures, is paying attention to the print, or has voice-print match (can point to each word when reading). I use this information, again, to guide children individually in their reading development.

Sharing   At 1:00 the children gather together as a group on the carpet. During the first part of this group time, children can share their writing with the whole class. I select four or five children based on their table arrangement. Each table gets to share weekly. This sharing is an important part of the writing process in kindergarten. Children feel

continued

good about themselves, and the other children learn different strategies to use in their own journals.

I use the next part of group time to introduce the concepts that the children will be learning that day. During this time, children also participate in calendar and math activities on counting. About 1:20 we have large-group shared book reading time when I read a big book to the children. Children usually join in on repetitive phrases.

When children are done with their project, they then can choose discovery learning centers. Individual choice and learning time is highly valued. They usually have thirty minutes of free-choice time. The reading corner is set up with lots of books, big books, pillows, rocking chairs, and stuffed animal book characters to read to.

Sharing is encouraged. Children share their journals with the whole class. We also publish books. Parent volunteers and teachers help children make books by writing down children's ideas and encouraging them to illustrate. We give the books a title, copyright date, dedication page, and family comment sheet for positive feedback. We have an all-school publishing center; our fifth grade buddy class helps us with our rough drafts. When the books are done, we practice reading them to each other. The culminating activity is an author's tea. Children share their books with peers and parents in small groups. This activity is very rewarding for parents, children, and teachers.

A Balanced Reading Program Our balanced reading program also involves reading quality literature to children daily. "Take home" books are available for students. Lots of emergent-level books are available in baskets. Children can choose to take one home each night and read it to or with their family. A note accompanies the book so parents can communicate back to me how their child performed. I also have small guided reading groups, of five children at a time. We first "walk through" a book, looking at the pictures and sharing ideas from our experiences. I then model reading the book as I point to the words to reinforce voice-print match. Next, the group reads it together and then two pairs of children partner-read while I listen to the fifth child read, taking notes or making a running record.

Another part of our balanced reading program is our literature circle, which we do about six times a year. Children choose a book to take home. Their parents read it to them, discuss it, and do an activity such as, "Draw the main character and tell why you think he/she is the main character." We then discuss the books in small cooperative groups with parent volunteers as leaders. These books have strong story mapping elements—characters, setting, action, problem, solution. The children also record their responses in literature logs.

We also have incorporated Author Studies. We purchased four collections of books from different authors. We then study an author each quarter of the year. The children really get to know the authors very well and can identify their style and illustrations. As we explore our world in kindergarten, we discover books and authors, and learn that language is everywhere.

Contributed by Chris Holicek, kindergarten teacher, Burleigh Elementary School, Brookfield, WI.

parents, and some find it difficult to implement as well. Further, some research has indicated that whole language approaches do not result in the high levels of reading achievement claimed by its supporters. As a result, proponents of phonics instruction are aggressively advocating a return to this approach as one which will best meet the needs of parents, children, and society. As with most things, a balanced approach is probably the best and many early childhood advocates are encouraging literacy approaches that provide a balance between whole language methods and phonics instruction and which meet the specific needs of individual children. It is likely that as the debate over "the best approach" will continue. At the same time, there will be increased efforts to integrate the best of *all* approaches into a unified whole in order to make literacy education a reality for all children.

KINDERGARTEN CHILDREN AND TRANSITIONS

A *transition* is a passage from one learning setting, grade, program, or experience to another. Young children face many such transitions in their lives. They are left with baby-sitters and enter child care programs, preschools, kindergarten, and first grade. Depending on how adults help children make these transitions, they can be either unsettling and traumatic or happy and rewarding experiences.

The transition from home to preschool to kindergarten influences positively or negatively children's attitudes toward school. Under no circumstances should the transition from preschool to kindergarten or from kindergarten to first grade be viewed as the beginning of "real learning." Leaving kindergarten to enter first grade is a major transition. The transition may not be too difficult for children whose kindergarten classroom is housed in the same building as the primary grades. For others whose kindergarten is separate from the primary program or who have not attended kindergarten, the experience can be unsettling. Children with special needs who are making a transition from a special program to a mainstreamed classroom need extra attention and support, as we will discuss in Chapter 13.

Parents and kindergarten professionals can help children make transitions easily and confidently in several ways:

- Educate and prepare children ahead of time for any new situation. For example, children and teachers can visit the kindergarten or first grade program the children will attend. Also, toward the end of the preschool or kindergarten year or as time to enter the kindergarten or first grade approaches, children can practice certain routines as they will do them when they enter their new school or grade.

- Alert parents to new and different standards, dress, behavior, and parent–teacher interactions. Preschool professionals, in cooperation with kindergarten teachers, should share curriculum materials with parents so they can be familiar with what their children will learn. Kindergarten professionals can do the same with first grade teachers.

- Let parents know ahead of time what their children will need in the new program (e.g., lunch box, change of clothing, etc.).

- Provide parents of special needs children and bilingual parents with additional help and support during the transition.

- Offer parents and children an opportunity to visit programs. Children will better understand the physical, curricular, and affective climates of the new programs if they visit in advance. Professionals can then incorporate methods into their own program that will help children adjust to new settings.

- Cooperate with the staff of any program the children will attend, to work out a "transitional plan." Continuity between programs is important for social, emotional, and educational reasons. Children should see their new setting as an exciting place where they will be happy and successful.

PROGRAM IN ACTION

TEACHING IN THE KINDERGARTEN

"Mrs. Sholar, look. I lost my tooth. . . ."

"Teacher, you'll never guess what I have in here [as a ten-inch grass snake appears from a plastic butter tub], and it's not even slimy!"

"Who's the leader today?"

So begins a typical morning kindergarten class at Sangre Ridge Elementary School in Stillwater, Oklahoma.

Teaching involves establishing a classroom environment that promotes optimal learning and growth. For this to be done effectively, it is essential to identify basic beliefs about children and how they learn. These beliefs are reflected in the physical environment, academic agenda, and social climate of the classroom and the ones I use to structure my classroom and guide children are highlighted in the following text.

• *My challenge as a teacher is to create an environment in which the children feel safe and welcome so they are free to be risk takers in learning.* Class rules established by the children, clearly displayed on the walls and referred to as needed, promote a feeling of physical safety and fairness among the children. Children's drawings on the classroom walls reflect current units of study and imply this room belongs to children whose work and ideas are valued. Scissors, glue, staplers, tape, and crayons are accessible to the children so they can exercise independence in helping themselves and assume responsibility for caring for themselves. Low tables are arranged to encourage easy movement from one learning activity to the next and to allow for individual and small group participation.

As the kindergarten children begin to feel comfortable in their classroom, I get to better know and understand them. They come from diverse backgrounds and enter the classroom at different stages of development and with unique learning styles. Regardless of how each child learns, I want the children to see themselves as successful readers, writers, artists, mathematicians, and scientists. Children need an introduction and organized exposure to new information followed by opportunities to manipulate and interact with the new information. They learn best when they are actively involved in the learning process and when they are encouraged to wonder, for example, what will happen to the pumpkin seed if it is planted; to then experience planting and nurturing it; and to finally discover the network of roots just before the sprout pokes through the soil.

• *In kindergarten, I want my class to share experiences and develop as a community of learners in which my children and I learn from each other in a noncompetitive environment.* The process a child goes through to complete a task or learn a new concept is important. Answers are not automatically given, do not always come from the teacher, and often lead to more questions. As I question a child about how he made the green color on his picture when he had only red, yellow, and blue paint, he is encouraged to think about the process, experiment, and reach a conclusion. Other children learn from his explanation or may have their own explanation.

• *I want my children to experience learning as whole and natural and meaningful.* Thematic units, carefully developed to integrate curriculum and skill areas, are adapted to class needs and interests. Concepts are presented in context, and it is often difficult to determine whether we are learning math or science or reading or writing. Learning is not preparation for the next grade in school; it is not even preparation for life. Rather, learning is life, and the classroom consists of real-life situations in which problem solving and learning occur because of real and obvious needs. When a child tells me she has made pictures for all her friends,

I ask her to count them to see whether she has enough for everyone. When someone discovers the soap dispenser is out of soap, I suggest that child write a note for the custodian to remind him of the need. When the class disagrees about which book to read, we vote and experience democracy in action.

• *My experience has shown how valuable it is to involve children in making decisions about their own learning.* Time is scheduled each day for children to select learning activities of their choice. All activities promote quality experiences and are supportive of current concepts and skills, so any choice is appropriate. As a child chooses, he decides what he is going to do first and how long he will work in the area. He may need a second plan of action if his first choice is already taken. He may decide to practice in the same area several days or to try a new activity each day or several activities in one day. His best work is a natural outcome since he is controlling what he does, when he does it, and how long he spends on the activity.

• *Teaching is enhanced if children see their parents as an integral part of their learning experience; with teachers and parents working as a team.* Parents need and often want to be involved in their child's school experience. Parent meetings and conferences, K News (our class newsletter), informal notes, and a parent bulletin board are useful tools of parental involvement in my classroom. An active "Helping Hands" program also encourages regular parent participation. In the classroom, parents interact with the children during center activities, read to individual children, or assist with special class events. A slide show set to music during our kindergarten class open house provides parents, who otherwise could not get into the classroom during the school day, the opportunity to see their children in action.

• As we in education are bombarded with "new" ideas, commercial programs, and "easy" solutions or "cure-alls" for educating our youth, *it is critical that we be authorities in our fields.* We must be creative in the classroom, read professionally, attend workshops, discuss and share with colleagues, and most importantly continue to learn. We must learn from the very ones we teach and selectively make changes that are consistent with sound educational principles, personal philosophy, and results from classroom research. We must recognize our influence in the lives of children and be responsible to them.

As a teacher, I am continually challenged and rewarded. I am challenged to assess and plan for thirty-five unique individuals every day, helping them experience community without losing individuality. I am rewarded when I observe my five- and six-year-old children working together, offering another help or celebrating another's success. I am challenged to channel the energies and emotions of thirty-five sometimes fragile and sometimes not so fragile young spirits, knowing when to step in and guide and when to wait and watch. I am rewarded when I see these children developing self-control and working out conflicts in mutually acceptable ways. I am challenged to be genuine and "real" to my students. I am rewarded when middle school and junior high students return to my classroom to let their kindergarten teacher know what is happening in their lives because they know I care. As a teacher and the decisive factor in the classroom, I am challenged to be the best that I can be. I am rewarded daily when I observe my five- and six-year-old eager and trusting learners becoming the best that they can be.

Contributed by Linda Sholar, Sangre Ridge Elementary School, Stillwater, OK.

Additionally, what happens to children *before* they come to kindergarten influences the nature and success of their transitions. Three areas are particularly important in influencing the success of transitional experiences: children's skills and prior school-related experiences; children's home lives; and preschool and kindergarten classroom characteristics. Research demonstrates the following in relation to these three areas:[15]

- Children who are socially adjusted have better transitions. For example, kindergarten children whose parents initiate social opportunities for them are better adjusted socially.

- Rejected children have difficulty with transitions.

- Children with more preschool experiences have fewer transition adjustments to make.

- Children whose parents expect them to do well in kindergarten do better than children whose parents have low expectations for them.

- Developmentally appropriate classrooms and practices promote easier and smoother transitions for children.

The nature, extent, creativity, and effectiveness of transitional experiences for children, parents, and staff will be limited only by the commitment of all involved. If we are interested in providing good preschools, kindergartens, and primary schools, then we will include transitional experiences in the curricula of all these programs.

ISSUES RELATED TO KINDERGARTEN

In addition to readiness and transition issues, a number of other issues swirl around kinder-

garten practices and challenge professionals to make the kindergarten experience a meaningful one for all children.

The Pushed-Down Curriculum

Perhaps you have visited a kindergarten program and left thinking, "Wow, a lot of what they're doing in kindergarten I did in first grade!" Many early childhood professionals would agree. The "pushed-down curriculum" is what happens when professionals teach kindergarten children as first graders and expect them to act like first graders and when the kindergarten curriculum resembles that of first grade. The kindergarten curriculum should challenge all children to do their best and provide them with social and cognitive skills they need for success, but it should also be appropriate for them.

A number of reasons account for the pushed-down (or "escalated") curriculum. First, beginning in the 1980s there has been a decided emphasis on "academics" in U.S. education, particularly early childhood education (see Chap. 3). Second, some parents believe an academic approach to learning is the best way to succeed in school and the work world. They may also see academics as one of the ways to compensate for the lack of experiences and opportunities prior to their child's school entry. The challenge for early childhood professionals in this regard is to educate parents about what is and is not appropriate for young children's learning. Third, some first grade teachers are demanding children who are grounded in academics. And fourth, more teachers prepared to teach elementary and upper elementary grades are teaching in kindergarten.

Retention

Along with the benefits of early education and universal kindergarten come disturbing and potentially disastrous side effects for children. Retained children, instead of participating in kindergarten graduation ceremonies with their classmates, are destined to spend another year in kindergarten. Many of these children are retained or failed because teachers judge them to be immature, or they fail to measure up to the district's or teachers' standards for promotion to first grade. Children are usually retained in the elementary years because of low academic achievement or low IQ. (In comparison, reasons for retention are different at the junior high level, at which students are generally retained because of behavior problems or excessive absences.)

When well-meaning early childhood education professionals fail children, they do so in the belief that they are doing them and their families a favor. These professionals feel that children who have an opportunity to spend an extra year in the same grade will do better the second time around. Teachers' hopes, and consequently parents' hopes, are that these failed children will go on to do as well as (many teachers hold out the promise that they will do even better than) their nonretained classmates. But is this true? Do children do better the second time around?

Despite our intuitive feelings that children who are retained will do better, the research evidence is unequivocally to the contrary: children do not do better the second time around. In addition, parents report that retained children have a more pessimistic attitude toward school, with a consequently negative impact on their social-emotional development.[16]

The ultimate issue of retention is how to prevent failure and promote success. To achieve those goals, professionals will have to change their views about what practices are best for children and how to prevent the risk factors that create a climate for unsuccessful school experiences. Some school districts have banned retention in kindergarten and first grade. As alternatives to retaining

children in a grade, many school districts are implementing two kinds of programs, discussed earlier: One is the developmental kindergarten, which, in essence, gives children two years to complete one year of kindergarten work. The second is transitional classes between kindergarten and first grade. However, as discussed, these programs are controversial.

High-Stakes Testing

Some kindergarten children still face *high-stakes testing*—a test that determines whether they will be promoted to first grade. Such tests, also known as *benchmark* tests, are an effort to reduce *social promotion,* in which children are promoted so they can keep up with their age mates, their social peers. There are a number of reasons for movement away from high-stakes testing. First, such tests do not fit well with the newer curriculum approaches such as whole language and with assessment processes such as portfolios. Second, high-stakes tests do not necessarily test what children really know. Third, these tests may be inappropriate for children of particular cultures. Fourth, many early childhood professionals believe it is not fair to children or their families to make a decision for or against promotion on the basis of one test.

The Graying of Kindergarten

There is a growing tendency for upwardly mobile parents to hold their children (especially sons) out of kindergarten for a year, for several reasons. First, when boys, who tend to be less mature than girls, have a birthday that makes them one of the youngest children in the class, they may not do as well as their parents expect. These parents want their children to be the oldest members of the kindergarten class, not the youngest. They reason that the older children will be the class leaders, will get more attention from

LONGFELLOW ELEMENTARY SCHOOL FOR THE VISUAL AND PERFORMING ARTS

An excellent example of restructuring at work in the early childhood arena is Longfellow Elementary School in Kansas City, Missouri, a magnet school for the visual and performing arts. Yvonne Clay's twenty-two kindergartners engage in an all-day program of basic skill instruction and drama, dance, music, and movement. Visual arts include painting, sketching, modeling with clay, and creative writing; the performing arts entail music, theater, and dance.

Drama plays a significant role in the curriculum and life of the kindergarten classroom. As Yvonne explains, "Drama and the other performing arts give children exposure to and experience with topics and people they would not otherwise have. Drama is in many ways a mirror of real-life events. I use drama to help children learn many important skills, concepts, and values. Drama is also a natural way of helping children learn through their bodies."

Yvonne gives these examples of drama activities in her kindergarten: "One of my groups reads in their basal reader a story of the rabbit and the hare. After the reading, the children acted out the story. We emphasized expression and how the human voice—their voices—sounds in certain situations. Also, during Black History Month in February, the children did a 'Readers Theater' of the Rosa Parks Story. One group read the story and another group acted out the events. The children had a lot of fun getting ready. They made bus stop signs, made costumes out of clothing from the Salvation Army, and made a bus out of cardboard boxes with chairs for seats. I revised an existing script for the children and worked with the parents of the children who had reading parts. It was a great learning activity!"

Yvonne teaches readiness skills, reading (many of the children are reading at a first grade level or above by the end of the school year), math, social studies, science, writing, and creative movement—all integrated with drama. Support teachers provide instruction in art, music, physical education, computers, and Suzuki violin.

"I integrate academics into everything I do," explains Yvonne. "The visual and performing arts give children experiences to build their academics

on. The arts also give children a chance to appreciate their self-worth at many levels and in different ways. Take, for example, a child like Alex, who struggles in reading. He really excels in dance. The experiences of being good in this area are a great benefit to him."

A number of important activities support the curriculum and make this kindergarten program unique.

Artist-in-Residence Program

The school district has an artist-in-residence program through which artists come into the school and classrooms to perform and teach. For example, a local, well-known puppeteer gave a performance, then taught the children about puppets. He worked with the children in making puppets and helped them give a performance with their puppets.

Field Trips

The kindergarten children go every other month to various performing arts functions. These include trips to the ballet, symphony orchestra, plays, and other performances throughout the Kansas City area. Following the field trips, children's experiences are integrated into the curriculum. For example, after a trip to the zoo, some children may create an art product and others may choose to write about the experience.

Community support for the Longfellow Magnet School is strong. According to Dee Davis, coordinator, early childhood, for the Kansas City Public Schools, "Families are enthusiastic about schools of choice for their children. They want and like to make choices on behalf of their children. Parents feel children do better in school when they study what interests them most."

The curriculum of the kindergarten program, with its focus on song and dance, is in many ways reminiscent of that supported by Froebel and other great educators. It is also significant that a school named for one of the nation's most celebrated poets—Henry Wadsworth Longfellow—should be involved in promoting learning through the arts.

the teacher, and have another year of school under their belt and therefore will be able to better handle the pushed-down curriculum. In other words, these children will be at the top of their class in all respects.

Second, parents who keep their children out of kindergarten for a year can afford to do this. Less well-to-do parents, on the other hand, want their children in school because they cannot afford daycare or baby-sitters.

Until society and schools really implement goal 1 of Goals 2000 ("Every child will enter school ready to learn") and until schools commit themselves to providing every child with the opportunity to learn to his or her fullest potential, the graying of kindergarten will likely continue.

THE FUTURE OF KINDERGARTEN

From our discussions in this chapter, you may have several ideas about how kindergarten programs will evolve as we move into the twenty-first century. Add your ideas to the ones cited here:

- The trend in kindergarten education is toward full-day, cognitive-based programs. Kindergartens give public schools an opportunity to provide children with the help they need for later success in school and life. Children come to kindergarten programs knowing more than their counterparts of twenty years ago. Children with different abilities and a society with different needs require that kindergarten programs change accordingly.

- Kindergarten curricula will include more writing and reading. This literacy emphasis is appropriate and flows naturally out of whole language programs. The challenge for all professionals is to keep literacy development from becoming a rigid, basic skills approach.

- Technology (see Chap. 11) will be included more in both preschool and kindergarten programs. This technology inclusion is in keeping with the current growth of technology in all grade levels. However, as with many things, we think that earlier is better, so introducing technology early is seen as one way of making children in the United States computer literate. The description of the kindergarten instructional program at the Alexander D. Henderson University School on pages c–1 and c–2 of the third color insert, "Observing Technology Programs in Action," illustrates and emphasizes the following points: (1) technology *as an instructional model* exists in growing numbers of early childhood programs, (2) technology is no longer something that can be feared or ignored by early childhood professionals, and (3) children are and can be very comfortable with and adept at technological applications to their lives and learning.

- Kindergarten will be viewed less as a place in which children get ready for school—and fail if they are not ready—and more as a place in which children learn and develop as part of the pre-K–12 schooling process.

ACTIVITIES FOR FURTHER ENRICHMENT

1. Interview parents to determine what they think children should learn in kindergarten. How do their ideas compare to the ideas in this chapter and to your ideas?

2. Do you think as a teacher you are oriented toward cognitive skills or social-emotional play? Explain your reasons, and compare your response to those of your classmates.

3. As a teacher, would you support an earlier or later entrance age to kindergarten? If

your local legislator wanted specific reasons, what would you tell him or her? Ask other teachers and compare their viewpoints.

4. How might culture, socioeconomic background, and home life affect what should be taught to children in kindergarten?

5. Give examples from your observations of kindergarten programs to support one of these opinions: (1) Society is pushing kindergarten children; (2) Many kindergartens are not teaching children enough.

6. List special services school districts should provide to kindergarten children.

7. Compare the curriculum of a for-profit kindergarten, a parochial school kindergarten, and a public school kindergarten. What are the similarities and differences? Which would you send your child to? Why?

8. Do you think kindergarten should be mandatory for all five-year-old children? At what age should it be mandatory?

9. Should the results of a readiness test be the final word on whether a child is admitted to kindergarten? Explain your answer.

10. What are reasons for the current interest in helping children make transitions from one setting or agency to another? What are other transitions that early childhood educators should help children make, besides those mentioned in this chapter?

11. You have been asked to speak to a parent group about the pros and cons of contemporary approaches to literacy development in kindergarten. What major topics would you include?

12. Develop a list of suggestions for how parents can promote literacy in the home.

READINGS FOR FURTHER ENRICHMENT

Fromberg, D. *The Full-Day Kindergarten: Planning and Practicing a Dynamic Themes Curriculum.* Early Childhood Education Series,

2nd ed. (New York: Teachers College Press, 1995).

This book examines problems and questions related to full-day kindergarten. It deals with early childhood curriculum design and development, also suggests specific step-by-step ways to plan and emergent curriculum based on integrated, dynamic themes that grow out of children's diverse personal and cultural experiences.

Graue, M. *Ready for What? Constructing Meanings of Readiness of Kindergarten* (Albany, NY: State University of New York Press, 1993).

This book examines the issue of school readiness, focusing on children's readiness to enter into kindergarten and promotion to first grade.

Walmsley, B. B., A. M. Camp, and S. A. Walmsley. *Teaching Kindergarten: A Developmentally Appropriate Approach* (Portsmouth, NH: Heinemann, 1993).

Not a book, but rather a package of activities for the kindergarten teacher who wants to implement a developmentally appropriate program but does not know where to begin.

NOTES

1. From *All I Really Need to Know I Learned in Kindergarten* by Robert L. Fulghum (New York: Villard, 1988), p. 6. Copyright© 1986, 1988, by Robert L. Fulghum. Reprinted by permission of Villard Books, a division of Random House, Inc.

2. Alec M. Gallup, "The 18th Annual Gallup Poll of the Public's Attitudes toward Public Schools," *Phi Delta Kappan* 68 (1), pp. 55–56.

3. *Goals 2000: Educate America Act* (Washington, D.C.: U.S. Government Printing Office, 1994).

4. National Association for the Education of Young Children, "NAEYC Position Statement on School Readiness," *Young Children* 46 (1) (Nov. 1990), p. 21.

5. Arnold Gesell and Catherine Amatrudda, *Developmental Diagnosis: Normal and Abnormal Child Development* (New York: Harper & Row, 1941).

6. Caroline Pratt and Lucile C. Deming, "The Play School," in *Experimental Schools Revisited,* ed. Charlotte Winsor (New York: Agathon, 1973), p. 23.

7. Ernest L. Boyer, *Ready to Learn: A Mandate for the Nation* (Princeton, NJ: Carnegie Foundation for the Advancement of Teaching, 1992), pp. 136–43. Used by permission.

8. Friedrich Froebel, *Mother's Songs, Games and Stories* (New York: Arno, 1976) p. 136.

9. Copyright © 1996 by the National Association for the Education of Young Children, Early Years are Learning Years Series, "Top Ten Signs of a Good Kindergarten Classroom," on NAEYC Website at http://www.naeyc.org/naeyc.

10. Jeffrey Burkart, "Developmental Kindergarten—In the Child's Best Interest?" *National Association of Early Childhood Teacher Educators* 10 (1989), pp. 9–10.

11. High/Scope Educational Research Foundation. (1992). *High/Scope Child Observation Record (COR) for Ages 2 ½ to 6* (Ypsilanti, MI: Author).

12. L. J. Schweinhart, S. McNair, H. Barnes, and M. Larner, "Observing Young Children in Action to Assess Their Development: The High/Scope Child Observation Record Study," *Educational and Psychological Measurement,* 53 (Summer), pp. 445–55.

13. Sue Bredekamp and Carol Copple, eds., *Developmentally Appropriate Practice in Early Childhood Programs,* revised edition. (Washington, D.C.: National Association for the Education of Young Children, 1997) p. 21 © 1997 by NAEYC. Used by permission.

14. Literacy Volunteers of America, *Facts on Literacy* (Syracuse, NY: Literacy Volunteers of America, 1994).

15. K. L. Maxwell and S. K. Elder, "Children's Transition to Kindergarten," *Young Children* 49 (6), pp. 56–63.

16. P. Mantzicopoulos and D. Morrison, "Kindergarten Retention: Academics and Behavioral Outcomes through the End of Second Grade," *American Educational Research Journal* 29 (1), pp. 182–98.

The Primary Grades

CHAPTER

9

Preparation for
Lifelong Success

Focus Questions

1. How are the primary years important for children, families, and the profession?

2. What are the similarities and differences among preschool, kindergarten, and primary grade children?

3. What are the physical, cognitive, language, psychosocial, and moral developmental characteristics of primary children?

4. How do the instruction and learning processes used in the primary grades influence teaching and learning?

5. How is the assessment of young children an important part of teaching and learning?

6. What are contemporary issues involved in primary education?

7. How is education in the primary years changing?

In contrast to the renewed interest in infants and preschoolers discussed in the previous chapters, one might almost say that the years from six to eight are the forgotten years of early childhood. In many ways, primary children are frequently overlooked in terms of early childhood education. Although the profession defines *early childhood* as the period from birth to age eight, children from birth through kindergarten receive most of the attention; primary grade children are more often thought of as belonging to the elementary years. Indeed, the years from six to twelve are often referred to as the *middle years* or *middle childhood*, the years between early childhood and adolescence.

255

Accordingly, one of the major challenges facing the early childhood profession is to reclaim the years from age six through eight. We cannot focus research and training almost exclusively on the years up to age five as we presently do. Lives are shaped in not only the early years, but in the primary years as well.

WHAT ARE PRIMARY CHILDREN LIKE?

Throughout this text, we stress the uniqueness and individuality of children. Although we discuss in this and other chapters what children are like, and the common characteristics they share, as an early childhood professional you must always remember that each child is unique.

Physical Development

Two words describe the physical growth of primary age children: *slow* and *steady*. Children at this age do not make the rapid and obvious height and weight gains of the infant, toddler, and preschooler. Instead, they experience continual growth, develop increasing

control over their bodies, and explore the things they are able to do.

From ages five to seven, children's average weight and height approximate each other. For example, at six years, boys weigh forty-six pounds and are forty-six inches tall, while girls weigh forty-three pounds and are forty-five inches tall. At age seven, boys weigh fifty pounds and are forty-eight inches tall and girls, forty-eight pounds and forty-eight inches (Table 9.1). The weight of boys and girls tends to be the same until about age nine, when girls pull ahead of boys in both height and weight. Wide variations appear in both individual rates of growth and development and among the sizes of children in each classroom. These differences in physical appearance result from genetic and cultural factors, nutritional intake and habits, health care, and experiential background.

Motor Development

Primary children are adept at many motor skills. The six-year-old is in the *initiative* stage of psychosocial development; seven- and eight-year-old children are in the *industry* stage. Not only are children intuitively driven to initiate activities, they are also learning to be competent and productive

Table 9.1/*Average Height and Weight for Primary School-Age Children*

Age	Males		Females	
	Height (inches)	Weight (pounds)	Height (inches)	Weight (pounds)
6.0 years	46	46	45	43
6.5 years	47	48	46	45
7.0 years	48	50	48	48
7.5 years	49	53	49	51
8.0 years	50	56	50	55
8.5 years	51	59	50	58

Source: Based on data from P. V. V. Hamill et al., "Physical Growth: National Center for Health Statistics Percentiles," *American Journal of Clinical Nutrition* 32 (1979), pp. 607–29.

individuals. The primary years are thus a time to use and test developing motor skills. Children at this age should be actively involved in activities that enable them to use their bodies to learn and develop feelings of purpose and competence. Their growing confidence and physical skills are reflected in games of running, chasing, and kicking. A nearly universal characteristic of children in this period is their almost constant physical activity.

Differences between boys' and girls' motor skills during the primary years are minimal—their abilities are about equal. Teachers therefore should not try to limit based on gender either boys' or girls' involvement in activities. We see evidence of continuing refinement of fine-motor skills in children's mastery of many of the tasks they previously could not do or could do only with difficulty. They are now able to dress themselves relatively easily and attend to most of their personal needs, such as using utensils, combing their hair, and brushing their teeth. They are also more proficient at school tasks that require fine-motor skills, such as writing, artwork, and using computers.

Cognitive Development

Children's cognitive development during the primary school years enables them to do things as first, second, and third graders that they could not do as preschoolers. A major difference between these two age groups is that older children's thinking has become less egocentric and more logical (see Chap. 7). The cognitive milestone that enables children between seven and eleven to think and act as they do is *concrete operational thought*. Logical operations, although more sophisticated than in preoperational children, still require concrete objects and referents in the here and now. Abstract reasoning comes later, in the *formal operations stage* during adolescence.

Moral Development

Jean Piaget and Lawrence Kohlberg are the leading proponents of a developmental concept of children's moral growth. Piaget identified the two stages of moral thinking typical of children in the elementary grades as *heteronomy*—being governed by others regarding right and wrong—and *autonomy*—being governed by oneself regarding right and wrong. As Piaget points out:

Society is the sum of social relations, and among these relations we can distinguish two extreme types: relations of constraint, whose characteristic is to impose upon the individual from outside a system of rules with obligatory content, and relations of cooperation, whose characteristic is to create within people's minds the consciousness of ideal norms at the back of all rules. Arising from the ties of authority and unilateral respect, the relations of constraint therefore characterize most of the features of society as it exists, and in particular the relations of the child to its adult surrounding. Defined by equality and mutual respect, the relations of cooperation, on the contrary, constitute an equiliberal [sic] limit rather than a static system.[1]

Heteronomy is characterized by *relations of constraint*. In this stage, children's concepts of good and bad and right and wrong are determined by the judgments pronounced by adults. An act is "wrong" because a parent or teacher says it is wrong. Children's understanding of morality is based on the authority of adults and those values that "constrain" them.

Gradually, as children mature and have opportunities for experiences with peers and adults, moral thinking may change to *relations of cooperation*. This stage of personal morality, autonomy, is characterized by exchange of viewpoints among children and between children and adults as to what is right, wrong, good, or bad. This level is not achieved by authority but rather by social experiences within which children may try

Although children in the primary years do not grow as rapidly physically as when they were younger, the years between six and eight are important ones for cognitive growth. Children in the primary grades need lots of opportunities to think, do, and become competent and self-assured persons. What role should professionals play in these formative years for children?

out different ideas and discuss moral situations. Autonomous behavior does not mean that children agree with other children or adults but that autonomous people exchange opinions and try to negotiate solutions.

Recall that in Chapter 3 we discussed Lev Vygotsky's zone of proximal development and the importance of having children collaborate with more competent peers and adults for cognitive and social development. According to Vygotsky, social interactions provide children opportunities for "scaffolding" to higher levels of thinking and behavior. Furthermore, Vygotsky said that part of the professional's pedagogical role was to challenge and help children move to higher levels of thinking and, in this case, moral development.

The stage of relations of constraint is characteristic of children up through first and second grades, while the stage of relations of cooperation is characteristic for children in the middle and upper elementary grades.

The real criterion for determining which developmental stage a child is operating in, however, is how that child is thinking, not how old she is.

We can also see in Kohlberg's theory the importance of social interactions and collaboration of adults and peers in children's moral development. Kohlberg, a follower of Piaget, believed children's moral thinking occurs in developmental levels. Kohlberg conceptualized the levels and substages of moral growth as preconventional, conventional, and postconventional.[2]

1: Preconventional Level (Ages Four to Ten)
Morality is basically a matter of good or bad, based on a system of punishments and rewards as administered by adults in authority positions. In stage 1, the *punishment and obedience orientation,* children operate within and respond to physical consequences of behavior. Good and bad are

based on the rewards they bring, and children base judgments on whether an action will bring pleasure.

In stage 2, the *instrumental-relativist* orientation, children's actions are motivated by satisfaction of needs. Consequently, interpersonal relations have their basis in arrangements of mutual convenience based on need satisfaction. ("You scratch my back; I'll scratch yours.")

2: Conventional Level (Ages Ten to Thirteen)
Morality here is doing what is socially accepted, desired, and approved. Children conform to, support, and justify the order of society. Stage 3 is the *interpersonal concordance* or *"good boy/nice girl"* orientation. Emphasis is on what a "good boy" or "nice girl" would do. The child conforms to images of what good behavior is.

In stage 4, the *law-and-order* orientation, emphasis is on respect for authority and doing one's duty under the law.

3: Postconventional Level (Age Thirteen and Older)
Morality consists of principles beyond a particular group or authority structure. The individual develops a moral system that reflects universal considerations and rights.

Stage 5 is the *social contract–legalistic* orientation. Right action consists of the individual rights agreed on by all society. In addition to democratic and constitutional considerations, what is right is relative to personal values.

At stage 6, the *universal ethical principle* orientation, individuals determine what is right by applying universal principles of justice, reciprocity, and equality. The actions of the individual are based on a combination of conscience and these ethical principles.

Just as Piaget's cognitive stages are fixed and invariant for all children, so too are Kohlberg's moral levels. All individuals move through the process of moral development beginning at level 1 and progress through each level. No level can be skipped, nor does an individual necessarily achieve every level. Just as intellectual development may become "fixed" at a particular level of development, so may an individual become fixed at any one of the moral levels.

Implications for Classrooms The theories of Piaget and Kohlberg and programs for promoting affective education have the following implications for primary grade classroom practice:

- All professionals must like and respect children.

- The classroom climate must support individual values. Respect for children means respect for and acceptance of the value systems children bring to school.

- Professionals and schools must be willing to deal with issues, morals, and value systems other than those they promote for convenience, such as obedience and docility.

- A sense of justice must prevail in the schools, instead of the injustice that arises from imposing arbitrary institutional values.

- Children must have opportunities to interact with peers, children of different age groups and cultures, and adults to enable them to move to the higher levels of moral functioning.

- Students must have opportunities to make decisions and discuss the results of decision making. Children do not develop a value system through being told what to do or through infrequent opportunities for making choices and decisions.

THEY ARE WHAT THEY EAT

Children are not born with a taste for high fat foods. It is a learned behavior. But, often, children are not given better choices. Let loose in a supermarket to make their own choices, parents are appalled at what their children do not know about good nutrition and at food manufacturers who do not necessarily offer the healthiest of choices in their kid-attractive packages.

Reflective Discussion Questions: Why do you think it is that when given the opportunity, children select high calorie, high fat foods rather than "healthy foods"? Why do you think it is that manufacturers produce and sell foods with higher fat content for children than adults? How are children's cartoons and cartoon characters used to market children's foods? How does television advertising steer children toward "bad food choices"? What are some reasons that children are eating more "unhealthy" foods? What is your reaction to the comment that "there are no good or bad foods, that eaten in moderation, any food is part of a well-balanced diet"?

Reflective Decision Making: Visit a local supermarket and read the fat, salt, and sugar content for foods marketed specifically for children. Make a list of the top fat, salt, and sugar foods for children. How can you work with parents to help them provide good nutritional meals for their children and other family members? What can you do in preschool and other early childhood settings to help children learn good nutritional practices? Conduct a survey of the foods that young children eat during the day. How many total grams of fat do you estimate they eat during a typical day? How does this compare with the 50 to 60 grams of fat recommended by nutritionists? Give specific examples of how manufacturers use food to promote and sell a particular product. What could you do as an early childhood educator to get children to eat more fruits and vegetables rather than fatty snacks?

The Significance of the Primary Years

The primary years of early childhood education are significant because children are further inducted into the process of formal schooling. The preschool experience is often viewed as preparation for school, whereas with kindergarten (and increasingly with first grade) the process of schooling begins. How this induction goes will, to a large extent, determine how well children learn and whether they like school.

Children's attitudes toward themselves and their lives are determined at this time. The degree of success now sets limits on lifelong success as well as school success. Preparation for dealing with, engaging in, and successfully completing school tasks begins long before the primary grades, but it is during the primary grades that children encounter failure, grade retention, and negative attitudes. Negative experiences during this period have a profound effect on their efforts to develop a positive self-image. Primary children are in Erik Erikson's *industry versus inferiority* stage (see Chap. 6). They want and need to be competent, and they should be given the opportunities to be so.

HOW RESTRUCTURING IS AFFECTING THE PRIMARY GRADES

In Chapter 2 we discuss the *restructuring* of early childhood programs in the United States today. Nowhere is this restructuring more evident than in the primary grades. Grassroots efforts, led by parents, teachers, and building- or program-level administrators are aimed at changing how schools operate and are organized, how teachers teach, how children are taught and evaluated, and how schools involve and relate to parents and the community. Accountability and collaboration are in; schooling as usual is out.

One such effort to help schools restructure is that developed by James P. Comer of the Yale Child Study Center. This nationally acclaimed approach is detailed in the Program in Action feature, "The School Development Program: The Comer Process."

Reasons for Restructuring Primary Education

Education in the primary grades is changing. Schooling in the elementary years in the United States has become a serious enterprise, for political, social, and economic reasons. First, educators, parents, and politicians are realizing that solutions to illiteracy, a poorly prepared work force, and many social problems begin in the first years of school or even before. Second, the public is not happy about continuing declines in educational achievement. It wants the schools to do a better job teaching children the skills business and industry will need in the twenty-first century. Third, parents and the public in general want the schools to help solve many of society's problems (substance abuse, crime, violence, etc.) and turn around what many see as an abandonment of traditional American and family values.

THE CONTEMPORARY PRIMARY SCHOOL

A lot of change has occurred in the primary grades since the 1980s, with more on the way. Single-subject teaching and learning are out; integration of subject areas through such practices as whole language, thematic ap-

proaches, and literature-based programs are in. Students sitting in single seats, in straight rows, solitarily doing their own work are out; cooperative learning is in. Textbooks are out; projects and hands-on, active learning are in. Paper-and-pencil tests are out; student work samples and collaborative discussion of achievements are in. The teacher as director of all and "the sage on center stage" is out; facilitation, collaboration, cooperative discipline, and coaching are in. Letter grades and report cards are out; narrative reports, in which professionals describe and report on student achievement, checklists, which describe the competencies students have demonstrated, parent conferences, and other ways of reporting achievement are in.

In many respects, Dewey's progressive education ideas are finding fertile ground once again in the hearts and minds of early childhood professionals and parents who desire more personalized and developmental programs for young children. Additionally, in Chapter 2 and in several of the model programs described in the second color insert, "Observing Programs in Action," we read about the creative and exemplary accomplishments of business and industry operating child care and preschool programs. Why can't they accomplish the same things for public education? Why not, indeed! This is but one of the many questions you should ask as you read about the model programs and consider how public agencies are helping change how schools operate. In the answers to your questions lie the future directions of many early childhood programs and the future of your career, as well.

The New Curriculum for the Primary Grades

In Chapters 1, 7, and 8, we identified child-centered practices and programs. The child-centered movement also is alive and well in the primary grades. We discuss some of these practices in this section.

PROGRAM IN ACTION

THE SCHOOL DEVELOPMENT PROGRAM: THE COMER PROCESS

The School Development Program (SDP) model was established in 1968 in two elementary schools as a collaborative effort between the Yale Child Study Center and the New Haven Public Schools. The two schools involved were the lowest achieving in the city, with poor attendance and serious relationship problems among students, staff, and parents. Staff morale was low. Parents were angry and distrustful of the school. Hopelessness and despair were pervasive.

Because of preschool experiences in families under stress, a disproportionate number of low-income children presented themselves to the schools in ways that were understood as "bad," undermotivated, or appropriate on the playground, at home, or other places outside the school but inappropriate in school.

The school staffs lacked training in child development and behavior and understood school achievement solely as a function of genetically determined intellectual ability and individual motivation. Because of this, the schools were ill prepared to modify behavior or close the developmental gaps of their students. The staffs usually responded with low expectations.

To understand how such misalignments occur and how to overcome them in order to promote educational development, we began with the fact that a child develops a strong emotional bond to competent caretakers—usually parents—that enables them to help that child develop. Adequate development in social, psychological, emotional, moral, linguistic, and cognitive areas are critical for future academic learning. The attitudes, values, and behavior of the family and its social network strongly affect such development. A child whose development meshes with the mainstream

values encountered at school will be prepared to achieve at the level of his or her ability. In addition, the meshing of home and school fosters further development. When a child's social skill are considered appropriate by the teacher, they elicit positive reactions. A bond develops between the child and the teacher, who can now join in supporting the overall development of the child.

By contrast, a child from a poor, marginal family is likely to enter school without adequate preparation. The child may arrive without ever having learned such social skills as negotiation and compromise. A child who is expected to read at school may come from a home in which no one reads, in which no parent ever read a bedtime story. It is because such circumstances differ from mainstream expectations that these children are often considered aggressive or "bad" and judged to have low academic potential.

Parents, for their part, take such problems as a personal failure or evidence of animosity from the mainstream. They lose hope and become less supportive of the school. Some parents, ashamed of their speech, dress, or failure to hold jobs, may become defensive and hostile, avoiding contact with the school staff. The result is a high degree of distrust between home and school. This degree of alienation between home and school makes it difficult to nurture a bond between child and teacher that can support development and learning.

We found that even when there was a desire to work differently, no mechanism was in place at the *building level* to allow parents, teachers, and administrators first to understand the needs, then to collaborate with and help each other address them in an integrated, coordinated way. In response to this discovery, we worked collaboratively with parents

The Self-Esteem Movement   In Chapter 6, we examined Maslow's hierarchy of needs. One of these needs is for *self-esteem,* a positive feeling of self-worth and self-image. The self-esteem movement began in the 1980s

as a way of improving children's achievement. The argument is that children do not or cannot achieve because of poor self-worth. Proponents maintain that programs and practices to enhance self-esteem are

and staff to develop a nine-component model that includes three mechanisms, three operations, and three guiding principles.

The three mechanisms consist of the following:

- A governance and management team, which includes representative parents, teachers, administrators, and support staff
- A mental health or support staff team
- A parents' program

The governance and management team carries out the following three operations:

- The development of a comprehensive school plan with specific goals to improve the social climate and academic areas
- Staff development activities based on building-level goals in these areas (social and academic)
- Periodic assessment, which allows the staff to modify the program to meet identified needs and opportunities

The following three principles and agreements guide all individuals and teams:

- Participants of the governance and management team cannot paralyze the leader. On the other hand, the leader cannot use the group as a rubber stamp.
- Decisions are made by consensus to avoid "winner–loser" feelings and behavior.
- A *no-fault problem-solving* approach is used by all the working groups within the school

because we believe that eventually these attitudes permeate the thinking of most individuals.

As the governance and management team systematically addresses the problems and opportunities in the school students, staff, and parents begin to function more effectively. At the same time, the staff development program helps teachers gain the skills necessary to promote personal, social, and academic growth among students. As the hope and energy levels of all staff members go up, so do the opportunities and motivation to devote time to planning, which leads to improved curriculum development and instruction.

Goals to promote the overall development of students, including significant gains in academic and social behavior skills provide enriched school experiences.

Participation in both the day-to-day program in the classroom as well as in school governance builds parents' confidence and competence as contributors to, and decision makers in, the school community. Such enhancement of parents' social and academic skills has motivated many to return to school and complete their own high school, and in some cases college, education, which improves their employment opportunities.

The School Development Program is not a "quick fix," nor is it an "add-on." It is a different way of conceptualizing and working in schools and completely replaces traditional organization and management.

Contributed by James P. Comer, M.D., Director, School Development Program, Yale Child Study Center.

particularly important for certain groups of children: minorities, females, and those at risk. Further, they maintain that children's self-esteem is lessened by uncaring teachers and an indifferent school system.

Efforts to enhance students' self-esteem have resulted in a number of practices:

- Praise is used as a means of recognizing and rewarding achievement. It also is used to make children feel special and

Today there is a great emphasis on teaching children self-esteem, a positive feeling of self-worth and self-image. Self-esteem is based on achievement and motivation. A critical factor, then, in promoting children's self-esteem is to help them achieve and be successful. Teaching about self-esteem is less important than enabling children to learn how to assume responsibility for their learning and to succeed through their own efforts. What are some things that you can do to help students be successful?

comfortable with learning and to try to get children to do their best. Advocates of praising as a means of promoting self-esteem say it places less importance on the product and more on children's efforts. Unfortunately, in some cases, teachers have used praise too much, too often, and without a basis in solid achievement.

- Schools have been established specifically designed to promote self-esteem and increase achievement through identity with one's culture.
- Mentoring, role modeling, and "shadowing" programs have begun, in which students are given opportunities to interact with successful people of their culture and socioeconomic background.

However, not everyone agrees that the self-esteem movement is in children's best interests. Critics claim that teachers over-praise children, reward them for little effort and achievement, and substitute praise and rewards for teaching. Further, they maintain that true self-esteem results from achievement, not from hollow praise.

Prosocial and Peace Education   There is a growing feeling among early childhood professionals that the ill effects of many societal problems, including war and violence, can be reduced or avoided. They believe efforts to achieve this goal should begin in the primary and preschool years. Consequently, emphasis is placed on *prosocial behaviors*—teaching children the fundamentals of peaceful living, kindness, helpfulness, and cooperation. Educators can do several things to foster development of prosocial skills in the classroom:

- *Be a good role model for children.* You must demonstrate in your life and relationships with children and other adults the behaviors of cooperation and kindness that you want to encourage in children.

- *Provide positive feedback and reinforcement when children perform prosocial behaviors.* When children are rewarded for appropriate behavior, they tend to repeat that behavior. ("I like how you helped Tim get up when you accidentally ran into him. I bet that made him feel better.")

- *Provide opportunities for children to help and show kindness to others.* Cooperative programs between primary children and nursing and retirement homes are excellent opportunities to practice helping and kind behaviors. (See the description of the Stride Rite Intergenerational Center on pages b–10 and b–11 in the second color insert, "Observing Programs in Action.")

- *Conduct classroom routines and activities so they are as free as possible of conflict.* Provide opportunities for children to work together and practice skills for cooperative living. Design learning centers and activities for children to share and work cooperatively.

- *When real conflicts occur, provide practice in co flict resolution skills.* These skills inc ide taking turns, talking through problems, compromising, and apologizing. A word of caution regarding apologies: too often, an apology is a perfunctory response on the part of

teachers and children. Rather than just saying the often empty words, "I'm sorry," it is far more meaningful to help one child understand how another is feeling. Encouraging empathic behavior in children is a key to the development of prosocial behavior.

- *Conduct classroom activities based on multicultural principles and that are free from stereotyping and sexist behaviors* (see Chap. 12).

- *Read stories to children that exemplify prosocial behaviors, and provide such literature for them to read.*

- *Counsel and work with parents to encourage them to limit their children's television viewing, especially concerning programs that contain violence.*

- *Help children feel good about themselves, build strong self-images, and be competent individuals.* Children who are happy, confident, and competent feel good about themselves and are more likely to behave positively toward others.

Teaching Thinking The back-to-basics movement has been a dominant theme in U.S. education and will likely continue as a curriculum force. We generally think of basic skills as reading, writing, and arithmetic, and many elementary schools allot these subjects the lion's share of time and teacher emphasis. Yet some critics of education and advocates of basic education do not consider the "three Rs" the ultimate "basic" of sound education. Rather, they feel, the real basic of education is *thinking.* The rationale is that if students can think, they can meaningfully engage in subject matter curriculum and the rigors and demands of the workplace and life. Increasingly, thinking and problem-solving skills are coming to be regarded as no less "basic" than

PROGRAM IN ACTION

LEARNING ABOUT PARTNERSHIPS, TEAMS, AND SHARING LEARNING

Sharing the responsibility of educating our youth is an emphasis goal at Lexington Park Elementary School in St. Mary's County, MD. Because we are located near the Naval Air Warfare Center Aircraft Division at Patuxent River, MD, we are involved in a community partnership with the Naval Aviation Depot Operations Center (NADOC). Personnel from NADOC volunteer time at our school as tutor buddies. Students identified under Chapter 1 are placed with tutors initially. However, any student showing need can receive support and assistance from a NADOC volunteer. For example, tutors will reread stories with children, listen to stories children read, and review comprehension questions.

Partnerships are also evident within our school in the way teachers team together to coordinate teaching efforts and learning experiences. Music, media/computer lab, physical education, and art teachers coordinate their lessons with studies developed in individual classrooms. For example, the art teacher will help us make handmade paper from egg cartons because, in our study of Japan, we learned that papermaking was a Japanese enterprise.

Partnerships, teams, and *sharing* are terms used frequently throughout our school. In addi-

tion to team teaching experiences, students benefit from a program entitled *Roots and Wings* from the New American Schools Development Corporation. The goal of the New American School Development Corporation is to support school restructuring efforts. *Roots and Wings* is one of eight grants funded nationally, and St. Mary's County Schools and Johns Hopkins University were jointly awarded a grant to initiate the program in our schools.

Math Wings is a pilot component of the *Roots and Wings* program. Piloting this math program provides for a unique teaching and learning experience. The units and lessons are sent from Johns Hopkins, and the program involves cooperative learning teams. The daily plan includes class discussion, team investigation, partnered practice, and individual reinforcement with homework. The program allows students to invent their own methods to solve problems. Students have begun to accept ownership of Math Wings because their comments and concerns are welcomed and encouraged from Johns Hopkins. Students are free to provide constructive criticism about the lessons. Most students support the program. They are particularly fond of the use of manipulatives to reinforce the skills taught.

math facts, spelling, knowledge of geography, and so on.

As a result, teachers are including the teaching of thinking in their daily lesson plans, using both direct and nondirect methods of instruction to teach learning skills. A trend in curriculum and instruction today is to infuse the teaching of thinking across the curriculum and to make thinking a part of the culture of a classroom.

To talk about a classroom culture of thinking *is to refer to a classroom environment in which several*

forces such as language, values, expectations, and habits work together to express and reinforce the enterprise of good thinking. In a classroom culture of thinking, the spirit of good thinking is everywhere. There is the sense that "everyone is doing it," that everyone including the teacher is making the effort to be thoughtful, inquiring, and imaginative, and that these behaviors are strongly supported by the learning environment.[3]

In classrooms that emphasize thinking, students are encouraged to use their power of analysis and teachers ask higher-level

In the afternoon, our theme of partnership extends from individual classrooms to every third, fourth, and fifth grade classroom. All three grade levels work together to teach Cooperative Integrated Reading and Composition (CIRC), yet another component of the *Roots and Wings* program. This program, involving the use of cooperative learning teams, allows third, fourth, and fifth grade students to be placed in a group at their individual reading level. My own third graders enjoy working with students at different age and grade levels. Once students are grouped, their focus is to work together to achieve a common goal. The hour-and-a-half CIRC block involves whole-class discussion, cooperative groupings, partnering activities, as well as individual assignments. This component of *Roots and Wings* has been in place for two years. Teaching and reading and writing through the CIRC process has proven to be effective in increasing student self-esteem as well as student achievement.

Our day has just about come to a close. Students return to their homeroom classrooms and prepare for dismissal. In the last few minutes of the school day, students unwind with a book, debrief with a friend, or jot down events of the day in their journals. Unless a child is picked up by a parent, all students ride a bus home from school. As the last bus is called, a few students are left behind who are involved in after-school programs. Still another component of *Roots and Wings* is available for students who want and can be involved in afterschool programs. These students may enroll in a computer club, homework center, tutoring, and even drama club, all of which are made available four days a week.

As a third grade teacher, I expect to see children go through remarkable changes as they grow and learn. I have observed how the partnerships, teamwork, and shared learning experiences my students are able to engage in at Lexington Park Elementary help them develop strong roots grounded in effective instructional practice. I also have witnessed how students grow in self-esteem, learn to respect one another's ideas, and find their wings as they discover who they are and what the world has to offer them.

Contributed by Barbara Lord, Lexington Park Elementary School, Lexington Park, MD.

questions. Teachers are being encouraged to challenge their children to think about classroom information and learning material rather than to merely memorize acceptable responses. Instead of asking children to recall information, teachers are asking them to think critically about information, solve problems, and reflect, teaching them skills such as those on the following list:

Commonly Taught Thinking Skills

- Analyzing—*examining something methodically; identifying the parts of something and the relationships between those parts*
- Inferring—*drawing a reasonable conclusion from known information*
- Comparing and contrasting—*noting similarities and differences between two things or events*
- Predicting—*forecasting what will happen next in a given situation, based on the circumstances*
- Hypothesizing—*developing a reasonable explanation for events, based on an analysis of evidence*

- Critical thinking—*examining evidence and arguments carefully, without bias, and reaching sound conclusions*
- Deductive reasoning—*applying general principles to specific cases*
- Inductive reasoning—*deriving general principles from an analysis of individual cases*
- Organizing—*imposing logical order on something*
- Classifying—*putting things into groups based on shared characteristics*
- Decision making—*examining alternatives and choosing one, for sound reasons*
- Problem solving—*analyzing a difficult situation and thinking creatively about how to resolve it*[4]

Inductive and Deductive Reasoning. Other basic building blocks are reasoning skills, which include the following intellectual activities:[5]

- Enumeration; listing

- Grouping

- Labeling; categorizing

- Identifying critical relationships

- Making inferences

- Predicting consequences; explaining unfamiliar phenomena; hypothesizing

- Explaining and/or supporting the predictions and hypotheses

- Verifying predictions

These skills are used in *inductive reasoning,* thinking from the particular to the general or drawing a logical conclusion from instances of a case, and in *deductive reasoning,* inferring specifics from a general principle or drawing a logical conclusion from a premise.

Critical Thinking Skills. Critical thinking skills are used in everyday life activities to help determine the accuracy of information and to make decisions regarding choices. *Critical thinking* is the process of logically and systematically analyzing problems, data, and solutions in order to make rational decisions about what to do or believe. Skills involved in critical thinking include the following:

- *Identify central issues or problems.*
- *Compare similarities and differences.*
- *Determine which information is relevant.*
- *Formulate appropriate questions.*
- *Distinguish among facts, opinion, and reasoning judgment.*
- *Check consistency.*
- *Identify unstated assumptions.*
- *Recognize stereotypes and cliches.*
- *Recognize bias, emotional factors, propaganda, and semantic slanting.*
- *Recognize different value systems and ideologies.*
- *Evaluate the adequacy of data.*
- *Predict probable consequences.*[6]

The goal of teaching critical thinking is to encourage students to question what they hear and read and to examine their own thinking. Teachers cultivate critical thinking by providing learning environments in which divergent perspectives are respected and free discussion is allowed.

Creative Problem-Solving Strategies. Problem solving in any content area rests on thinking skills and critical thinking. Problem-solving skills can be taught directly through process strategies. For example, one system teaches problem-solving strategies using the acronym IDEAL as a mnemonic for a five-step process:

I	*Identify the problem.*
D	*Define and represent the problem.*
E	*Explore possible strategies.*
A	*Act on the strategies.*
L	*Look back and evaluate the effects of your activities.*[7]

Other effective problem-solving strategies include teaching students brainstorming techniques, imaging strategies, and ways to represent problems visually as an aid to finding a solution.

Implications for Professionals. Professionals who want to promote critical and creative thinking in children need to be aware of several things. First, children need the freedom *and* security to be creative thinkers. Many teachers and school programs focus on helping children learn the *right* answers to problems, so children soon learn from the process of schooling that there is only one right - answer. Children may be so "right answer" oriented that they are uncomfortable with searching for other answers or consider it a waste of time.

Second, the environment must support children's creative efforts. Teachers must

Critical thinking is necessary for successful participation in many life- and work-related activities. Critical thinking skills are useful in almost every life situation. Teaching critical thinking should be integrated throughout the entire early childhood curriculum. What are some ways that you will integrate the teaching of critical thinking in your curriculum?

create classroom cultures in which children have the time, opportunity, and materials with which to be creative. Letting children think creatively only when all their subjects are completed, or scheduling creative thinking for certain times, does not properly encourage it.

Third, creative *and* critical thinking must be *integrated* into the total curriculum, so that children learn to think across the curriculum, the entire school day, and throughout their lives.

Cooperative Learning You can probably remember how, when you were in primary school, you competed with other kids. You probably tried to see whether you could be the first to raise your hand. You leaned out over the front of your seat, frantically waving for your teacher's attention. In many of today's primary classrooms, however, the emphasis is on cooperation, not competition. Cooperative learning is seen as a way to boost student achievement and enhance self-esteem.

Cooperative learning is an instructional and learning strategy that focuses on instructional methods in which students are encouraged or required to work together on academic tasks. Students work in small, mixed-ability learning groups of usually four members wherein each member is responsible for learning and for helping all members learn. In one form of cooperative learning, called "Student Teams–Achievement Division," four students—usually one high achiever, two average students, and one low achiever—participate in a regular cycle of activities, such as the following:[8]

- The teacher presents the lesson to the group.

- Students work to master the material using worksheets or other learning materials. Students are encouraged not

Research shows that higher achievement results when children are engaged in cooperative learning tasks. Also, cooperative learning results in helping children see the world from other people's point of view. What are ways that you can include cooperative learning in your classroom practices?

only to complete their work but also to explain their work and ideas to group members.

- Students take brief quizzes.

Children in a cooperative learning group are assigned certain responsibilities; for example, there is a group *leader,* who announces the problems or task; a *praiser,* who praises group members for their answers and work; and a *checker.* Responsibilities rotate as the group engages in different tasks. Children are

also encouraged to develop and use interpersonal skills, such as addressing classmates by their first names, saying "Thank you," and explaining to their groupmates why they are proposing an answer. On the classroom level, teachers must incorporate five basic elements into the instructional process for cooperative learning to be successful:[9]

1. *Positive independence.* The students have to believe they are in the learning process together and that they care about one another's learning.

2. *Verbal, face-to-face interaction.* Students must explain, argue, elaborate, and tie what they are learning now to what they have previously learned.

3. *Individual accountability.* Every member of the group must realize that it is his or her own responsibility to learn.

4. *Social.* Students must learn appropriate leadership, communication, trust-building, and conflict resolution skills.

5. *Group processing.* The group has to assess how well its members are working together and how they can do better.

Proponents and practitioners of cooperative learning are enthusiastic about its benefits:[10]

- It motivates students to do their best.

- It motivates students to help one another.

- It significantly increases student achievement.

Supporters of cooperative learning maintain that it enables children to learn how to cooperate and that children learn from each other. And because schools are usually such competitive places, it gives children an opportunity to learn cooperative skills.

Not all teachers agree that cooperative learning is a good idea, however. They maintain that it is too time-consuming, because a group may take longer than an individual to solve a problem. Other critics charge that time spent on cooperative learning takes away time from learning the basic skills of reading, writing, and arithmetic.

Given the new approaches in primary education, it makes sense that professionals would want to use a child-centered approach that increases student achievement. Furthermore, school critics say that classrooms are frequently too competitive and that students who are neither competitive nor high achievers are left behind. Cooperative learning would seem to be one of the better ways to reduce classroom competitiveness and foster "helping" attitudes.

Character Education

Character education is back in many elementary classrooms (and middle and senior high schools as well) across the United States, for several reasons. As a society, we are alarmed by what we see as a decline in moral values and abandonment of ethical values. The character education movement is also a reaction to the "anything goes" 1980s characterized by the savings and loan scandals and the "me first" and "I want everything—now" attitudes. Of course, we are also alarmed by substance abuse, teenage pregnancies, violence, and juvenile delinquency. Character education is seen as a way of reducing, and possibly, preventing these societal problems.

Character education programs seek to teach a set of traditional core values that will result in civic virtue and moral character, including honesty, kindness, respect, responsibility, tolerance for diversity, racial harmony, and good citizenship.

Efforts to promote character qualities and values are evident in statewide efforts. For example, the state of Georgia has identified the following core values it wants all children to exhibit:

Citizenship

Democracy: government of, by and for the people, exercised through the voting process

- *Respect for and acceptance of authority: the need for and primacy of authority, including the law, in given circumstances*
- *Equality: the right and opportunity to develop one's potential as a human being*
- *Freedom of conscience and expression: the right to hold beliefs, whether religious, ethical or political, and to express one's views*

PROGRAM IN ACTION

THEY WON'T SEE BOUNDARIES

When anyone walks into our classroom, there are always four things I hope are immediately apparent to them: the children and the physical environment exude a sense of cheerfulness; the children's work is not only proudly displayed but is always used over teacher-prepared or commercially prepared materials; the children are busy at learning; and the children are enveloped in a nonthreatening sense of community. The observer won't see boundaries established by straight rows of desks and chairs. Reading areas spill over into science areas that spill over into computer areas that spill over into writing areas, and so on. . . . Shelves are placed around the room, none higher than thirty inches so that all supplies, tools, and materials are easily available to the children. There is no teacher's desk—we don't waste the "real estate"!

Developing Literacy

From the time we start the morning letter until the day's last activity I try to think of ways to extend children's thinking and learning. Our morning letter is filled with information about what is going to happen during the day. I have found this to be a way to give reading meaning to these emergent learners. This letter is like having minilessons: Children are provided phonetic and contextual strategies to decode, observe word repetition and patterns, increase their sight vocabulary, and identify a one-to-one correspondence while reading as the "leader" moves a pointer from one word to another. This latter activity appears to be very helpful for my English as a Second Language (ESL) children. All of the children can "read" our morning letter, even my nonreaders, and you can hear them happily reading it all the way down the hall.

Our administrative staff offers our school a reading program constructed of anthologies of children's literature. I say offers because we are fortunate enough to be in a district that allows teachers to choose and use appropriate material at our own discretion. The stories are real children's stories and children learn to use picture, contextual, and phonetic clues to decode, as well as rhyming word, pattern, and prediction strategies. A strength to this program is that it allows my more developed readers opportunities for growth as well. These more accomplished readers can learn developmentally appropriate punctuation and capitalization and strengthen and blend their own reading strategies. It's very exciting to hear an advanced reader explain to a grade-level reader, "You can tell this word is fish 'cause you can see them fishing and you can see that it starts with an 'f' and ends with a 'sh' sound."

I use small groups a lot in the classroom and we are quite flexible in our grouping while working with our reading stories. Puppet shows and plays are wonderful ways of getting all children involved. This year we performed a puppet show after only two weeks in school. Each child had a script written from the book with his or her part highlighted. With practice and a little help from home, each child knew their lines though only a quarter of them could actually read their script. During the shows, however, I noticed that every child used the script (it was optional), and read or mimicked reading from it. There was no difference in how successful those children felt as readers when it was over.

Trade books are another way I meet individual reading needs. They're great for developed readers, who find their comfortable reading level with books that interest them. Sometimes children are peer grouped so they can discuss, write about, and enjoy developmentally appropriate stories with others. And, since many children at this age can enjoy far more sophisticated stories than they can read, some children might listen to and follow the story at the listening center and are then able to discuss it with other children who read the story. Also, a trade book library can allow children to experiment and develop tastes for certain types of books or authors based on their interests.

Our reading corner is carpeted, well illuminated by a window, has shelves that display the books so children can see the covers, and is filled with pillows and stuffed animals. If a child is not feeling great, is tired, or has had a bad day, this comforting area is usually where a child chooses to go.

Hopefully, what the reading corner extends in comfort, the math corner extends in excitement. The children have at their grasp bright, colorful, interesting manipulatives in easy-to-use tubs. In fact, one of the most popular math activities is "tubbing." Children are partnered, sometimes deliberately, but usually randomly, and then select a tub and freely explore, hands on. If you walk in on a "tubbing" activity, your initial impression might be that the children are at play, but on closer inspection you might notice two children grouping teddy bear counters by color; two children sorting and classifying sea shells by type, size, color, or likes; two children using nonstandard forms of measurement such as seeing who is taller or how wide the room is in unifix cubes; children creating beautiful flowers and patterns from colorful geometric shapes; or two children discovering that a block tower is structurally sounder when the base is wider and the structure narrows as it grows taller.

Math in Action

I try to involve the children in their learning at all times. During our estimating activities the children get to handle, shake, or walk around whatever we are estimating. If it's our weekly estimating, we have a beginning estimate, count out around half of the objects, and then have an opportunity to revise our estimates. We counted out 233 objects last week. I am convinced it was the first time many of those children ever said most of those numbers, but they were so excited afterwards they had me write down the number so they could take it home and show their parents how high they counted.

Other estimating might come from what we are working on in other areas of the curriculum. A couple of our stories have bears, boats, and water in them, so we would estimate how many teddy bear counters it will take to sink the milk carton boats we made. Or during the apple unit and money unit the children estimate how many nickels it would take to equal an apple on the balance scale.

Graphing is another area that is integrated across the curriculum. Whether we are tasting apples or apple byproducts, choosing our favorite bear or favorite genre of literature, learning about syllables, counting the number of pockets we have, or finding out which Teddy Graham© shapes are most prevalent in the box, we graph our results and share the information we can generalize from the data.

Though a lot of our math education is experienced through exploration and discovery, there are still skills that we need to practice once the concepts are introduced. Giving children many real possibilities to practice is essential in creating a purpose to learning or practice skills. Purchasing items with coins, adding groups together to see totals, or cutting pizzas, cakes, and pies to use fractions all add to the excitement and meaning of math learning.

Each year during our addition unit, we construct a miniature golf course in the classroom. The hole is considered zero and then we tape outward at one-foot intervals. If we have one fancy hole, we hit as partners. Each child hits twice. The children pick which shot they want to use and then add them together. One partner writes and calculates the problem horizontally, the other vertically on the blackboard and then each tells why they chose the shot they did. An emergent learner might choose smaller numbers because they are easier to add. A child developed further might choose a number by a "sum of 10" strategy, a "doubles," or "doubles plus one" strategy. And yes, children can identify what strategy they use if they are taught to communicate their math reasoning.

Even taking slateboards outside to practice addition facts and strategies is more exciting than doing paper-and-pencil tasks at a desk. It also

continued

aids those children still developing fine-motor coordination even though they may be competent to think the work through as quickly as others.

Making Curricular Connections

Our science and social studies curriculum is thoroughly blended into our language arts program to keep it real, interactive, and interesting. The children learn to organize and communicate things they are able to observe. One of our early small-group projects is to create "sense" poems about different types of apples. Each group is given an apple and as a group must describe it visually. Then each member is assigned a remaining sense to describe. These observations are recorded and put into a format for writing poetry.

Making connections is also important. Last year our class constructed a "Spider Island." A very cooperative *orb weaver* spider was the sole inhabitant and created beautiful webs for us. Unfortunately, we noticed that no insects were being caught in the web. We decided to figure out why. At first the children thought there were no insects landing in the web because the island was inside. One of the children brought up the point that other spiders live inside so there must be something to eat for them. Another child suggested that maybe the insects were afraid of water. This was quickly countered by another child saying that there are always bugs flying around when she and her family are on their boat fishing. After a few more sug-

gestions, ruled out by other children, one of the children suggested that there was something wrong with the web or the spider's ability in making a "good one." How could we find out (a question my students are constantly asking)? We quickly decided we should catch some flies and force them to hit the web. After three flies were thrown into the web and were then able to fly away, we decided something was wrong with the web. The thrill came when the third fly, one of those big hairy ones that just seem to appear in the middle of winter, hit the web. The children who were sitting closest noticed a puff of dust come off the web. The children quickly brainstormed the possible sources of dust and concluded that the chalkboard was causing the problem. The children also concluded that since the web wasn't sticky, the spider wouldn't be able to catch the food necessary to sustain life and quickly voted on letting the spider go the next day. There is a sad sidebar to this story: the next morning when I came to school, I found our spider floating belly-up in the water. To this day I don't know if it was an accident, starvation, suicide, or foul play. Needless to say, I told the kids that he must have escaped overnight. I didn't want to dampen the humane climate they had created.

One might ask at this point about writing. Although I haven't yet mentioned it, writing is an integral part of each area of instruction. As part of the reading program the children write about their reading. They might write about story parts one

- *Justice: equal and impartial treatment under the law*
- *Liberty: freedom from oppression, tyranny or the domination of government*
- *Tolerance: recognition of the diversity of others, their opinions, practices and culture*

Patriotism: support of and love for the United States of America with zealous guarding of its welfare

- *Courage: willingness to face obstacles and danger with determination*
- *Loyalty: steadfastness or faithfulness to a person, institution, custom or idea to which one is tied by duty, pledge or a promise*

Respect for the Natural Environment: care for and conservation of land, trees, clean air and pure water and of all living inhabitants of the earth

day, likes and dislikes another, add different endings to stories another, or create their own storybooks on the computer or through our school's publishing center. Finished books are always shared with the class. With our science experiments we might write our predictions, record certain data, or communicate to others our findings and conclusions. And with math we might communicate how we solved a problem, which only helps to strengthen our discovered concepts and uses of strategies.

Our class uses a temporary (inventive) spelling approach, which in the beginning of the year is very difficult for some children (and parents) to accept. Children often come to school believing they have to spell every word correctly, and if they can't, they don't want to write. To release them from this mentality is imperative to help them learn to express themselves in a developmentally appropriate way. To hear a child who is ready to use the words "hurricane" and "circumstance" in a spoken sentence and then see them unafraid to write them is an exhilarating experience.

One other thing our class learns from the start is that there are different purposes for writing and that the purpose determines how far we take the writing process. If the children are brainstorming, making predictions, or listing living things on a nature walk, their writing would stay in the prewriting or rough copy stage. If they are writing a script for a play or presenting the findings of a science experiment to the class, we might revise it to make sure the message is clear. If we are sending something to the publishing company or writing letters to pen pals, we will take the piece to final copy.

This way we are also able to collect the children's writing in a variety of forms, not just "showcase" certain pieces, which gives great insight into children's development. We place both self-selected and teacher-selected pieces in each child's portfolio for us to use to monitor growth, pinpoint areas for improvement, celebrate successes, and describe the child's learning.

Children's individual portfolios house more than just their writing. They also store running records, interest inventories, developmental checklists, story webs, math charts, district tests, handwriting practice sheets, and anything else relevant to their learning. Portfolios are invaluable when it comes to marking period conferences. The reporting system our district uses is developmental in the primary grades and it is difficult for many parents to understand a developmental summary. Using their children's actual work, I have always been able to communicate to parents both growth and problem areas.

Contributed by Paul E. Hochschwender, first grade teacher, Ithan Elementary School, Radnor, PA.

- *Conservation: avoiding waste and pollution of natural resources*

Respect for Others

Altruism: concern for and motivation to act for the welfare of others

- *Civility: courtesy and politeness in action or speech*

- *Compassion: concern for suffering or distress of others and response to their feelings and needs*
- *Courtesy: recognition of mutual interdependence with others resulting in polite treatment and respect from them*

Integrity: confirmed virtue and uprightness of character; freedom from hypocrisy

- *Honesty: truthfulness and sincerity*
- *Truth: freedom from deceit or falseness; based on fact or reality*
- *Trustworthiness: worthy of confidence*

Respect for Self

Accountability: responsibility for one's actions and their consequences

- *Commitment: being emotionally, physically or intellectually bound to something*
- *Perseverance: adherence to action, belief or purpose without giving way*
- *Self-Control: exercising authority over one's emotions and actions*
- *Frugality: effective use of resources; thrift*

Self-Esteem: pride and belief in oneself and in achievement of one's potential

- *Knowledge: learning, understanding, awareness*
- *Moderation: avoidance of extreme views or measures*
- *Respect for physical, mental and fiscal health: awareness of the importance of and conscious activity toward maintaining fitness in these areas*

Work Ethic: belief that work is good and that everyone who can, should work

- *Accomplishment: appreciation for completing a task*
- *Cooperation: working with others for mutual benefit*
- *Dependability: reliability, trustworthiness*
- *Diligence: attentiveness, persistence; perseverance*
- *Pride: dignity; self-respect; doing one's best*
- *Productivity: supporting one's self; contributing to society*
- *Creativity: exhibiting an entrepreneurial spirit; inventiveness; originality; not bound by the norm[11]*

It is likely that there will be a great deal more emphasis in the near future on teaching character traits because parents and society are increasingly concerned about the life direction of children and youth.

The Naturalness of Literacy Development

Educators today stress the "naturalness" of children's literacy development. The case is made that many children learn to write and read in natural ways, many times on their own and without formal instruction. The example *par excellence* of this naturalness at work in literacy development is the many kindergarten and first grade children who come to school with rather well-developed writing and reading skills. Of course, Maria Montessori discussed this process as part of her program (see Chap. 4).

The naturalness with which many children develop an interest in reading and writing *and* read and write at home and in preschool settings is frequently sharply contrasted with what many critics maintain are less natural approaches to teaching language arts. These "less than natural" approaches include what is frequently referred to as "sit-down instruction," in which teachers teach children how to read and write. Other practices that critics label unnatural include the use of photocopies, worksheets, and mindless, repetitive exercises. For example, story starters, a technique by which teachers give children sentences to begin stories, can discourage writing and creativity if used unimaginatively. If teachers start every story with, "Today is [the day of the school week], and it is cold outside. . . ," should it come as a surprise that students soon lose interest in learning to write?

Efforts to promote a "natural" approach to reading and writing are seen in programs to involve parents in reading to their children at home, encouraging children and their families to use public libraries, and the growth of children's book clubs. The process of "being read to" in home and school is gaining in attention and popularity. Children who have been read to:

- *have developed crucial insights about written language being essential for learning to read and write;*
- *realize that written language, while related to it, is not the same as spoken language;*
- *have discovered that both spoken and written language can serve the same function; and*
- *have learned to follow plot and character development.*[12]

Reading, Writing, and Literature

Learning to write and improving students' writing through reading is also receiving renewed emphasis today, which is why so many students are encouraged to read *good literature* as part of their reading/writing programs. This concept is affecting not only how children are taught (e.g., through literature), it is also influencing publishing companies, who are including more literature in their reading books.

The inclusion of literature in the reading/language arts curriculum is characterized by several important features:

- The inclusion of literature by well-known authors (e.g., Cynthia Rylant, A. A. Milne, Langston Hughes)

- The inclusion of the *unabridged* works of famous authors. Critics of the status of children's literacy have complained that rather than reading the "real thing," students have been subjected to the watered-down versions of famous authors. They cite this as one more example of the "dumbing-down" of textbooks and the curriculum.

- The use of literature as the context within which to teach reading and language arts skills

The Whole Language Curriculum

A whole language literacy program has a number of important components:[13]

- It uses and incorporates *functional language;* that is, children are offered involvement with written language in and from the environment. Examples of the involvement of children in functional language include making signs and posters, writing letters, and making lists.

- It uses *predictable materials* such as signs, nursery rhymes, poems, as well as classical and contemporary children's stories. Predictable books are especially important because of their repetitive language, match between text and illustration, and familiar content.

- It incorporates *language experience* stories that evolve from the children's interests and activities.

- It uses *shared reading.* This is essentially a process in which teachers read favorite stories to children. This emphasis on shared reading has lead to the development of "big books." These oversized books enable teachers to involve children in a shared reading experience so they can see, participate, and feel that they are part of the process.

- It involves *story reading* in which children are read to one-on-one by older children, then the younger child reads to the older child. This process can also incorporate adults reading to children and vice versa.

- It uses *sustained silent reading,* which is a process in which a brief period of time is set aside daily so that everyone—children, teacher, principal, and in some schools custodians and cafeteria workers—read by themselves.

- It encourages children to *control their own learning* by initiating reading and writing activities. For example, they determine what books to read and when to read them.

A Holistic Approach

As discussed in Chapter 8, more professionals are adapting a balanced approach to promoting children's literacy development. One such approach is *holistic literary education,* which advocates a complete system to assume children's literacy development. The following are characteristic of the holistic approach:

- *Teachers integrate the teaching of the language arts into a single period. They recognize the interrelatedness of reading, writing, speaking, and listening. . . . Holistic teachers therefore provide children with opportunities to talk, write, listen, and speak to each other, and to the teacher. . . .*
- *Teachers use children's oral language as the vehicle for helping them make the transition to the written language. Children are given opportunities to write messages, letters, and stories, using their own words and sentence patterns, even before they can accurately read, write, or spell.*
- *Teachers encourage students to write as soon as they enter school. Children may dictate experiences or stories for others to write, as is done in the Language Experience Approach to reading instruction; however, holistic teachers emphasize children's doing their own writing, following their belief that children's writing skills develop from scribbling to invented spellings to eventual mature writing.*
- *In addition to using children's written documents as reading material, holistic teachers frequently use literature books, rejecting vocabulary-controlled, sentence-controlled stories in favor of those containing predictable language patterns. They choose the best children's literature available to read to and with children.*

- *Holistic teachers organize literacy instruction around themes or units of study relevant to students. Children use all of the language arts (listening, speaking, reading, and writing) as they study a particular theme. Many teachers also integrate the teaching of music, art, social studies, and other subjects into these units of study.*
- *Holistic teachers believe in intrinsic motivation, and when children enjoy good literature, create stories, write letters, keep personal journals, and share their written documents with others, language learning becomes intrinsically rewarding.*
- *Holistic teachers believe that literacy development depends on having opportunities to communicate. Since communication is not possible without social interaction, these teachers give children opportunities to read other children's compositions, and to write, listen, and speak to each other.*
- *Holistic teachers give children opportunities to both teach and learn from each other. They often work collaboratively on a common interest or goal. They react to each other's written products, and they share favorite books with each other.*
- *Holistic teachers control literacy instruction. It may be student centered, but it is also teacher guided. . . . [H]olistic teachers recognize that some direct instruction, including instruction in phonics, is not incompatible with student empowerment.*
- *Teachers emphasize holistic reading and writing experiences—children spend most of the classroom time available on meaningful reading and writing experiences. . . .*[14]

Authentic Writing

As a result of whole language and holistic literacy education, writing is becoming more *authentic;* that is, it is more concerned with the real world. Children are writing about real-life topics and

Much of literacy development involves engaging children in authentic practices. These include using materials from the environment, such as magazines, menus, posters, advertisements, and so forth as a means of becoming literate. What are the advantages of using authentic materials to promote children's interest and involvement in reading and writing?

issues—the environment, violence, how to help the homeless, and so forth. In today's contemporary classrooms, contrived writing is out the window and the real world is open for discussion and writing.

The Integrated Curriculum   The integrated curriculum is a natural progression from whole language, or whole language may be the result of attempts to integrate the curriculum. The integrated curriculum is an attempt to break down barriers between subject matter areas and help children make connections among all content areas. In integrated learning, for example, children write in their journals about life in the United States or construct bar graphs about the height and weight of their classmates.

ASSESSMENT

Much of the primary school child's life is influenced by assessment of achievement. What children study, how they study it, and the length of time they study it are all evaluated in some way. Decisions about promotion are also made from assessment results. With so much emphasis on tests, it is understandable that the issue raises many concerns. Critics maintain that the standardized testing movement reduces teaching and learning to the lowest common denominator—teaching children what they need to know to get the right answers. Many early childhood professionals believe that standardized tests do not measure children's thinking, problem-solving ability, or responsibility for their own learning. Furthermore, these critics believe that the group-administered, objectively scored, skills-focused tests that dominate much of U.S. education do not support (indeed, may undermine) many of the curricular reforms taking place today.

In response to such criticisms, testing and evaluation have undergone much change. We discuss some of these changes here.

Authentic Assessment

Also referred to as *performance-based assessment,* authentic assessment is carried out through activities that require children to demonstrate what they know and are able to do. Meaningless facts and isolated information are considered unauthentic. Authentic assessment has the following traits:

- *Assesses children on the basis of their actual work.* Work samples—often in a portfolio—exhibitions, performances, learning logs, journals, projects, presentations, experiments, and teacher observations are essential processes in authentic assessment.

- *Provides for ongoing assessment, over time, over the entire school year.* Children's performance and achievement are continuously assessed, not just at the end of a grading period or at the end of the year through a standardized achievement test.

- *Is curriculum embedded.* Children are assessed on what they are actually doing in and through the curriculum.

- *Is a cooperative and collaborative process involving children, teachers, and in many cases parents.* This is an attempt to move away from teacher-focused assessment and make assessment more child centered.

- *Is intended to help professionals and parents learn more about children.* All areas—social-emotional, language, cognitive, and physical—are assessed. The whole child is evaluated rather than a narrow set of skills. In this sense, it is child centered and humane.

- *Assesses what individual children are able to do.* Authentic assessment evaluates what they as individuals are learning as opposed to measuring or comparing one child to another or children to children, as is so often the case.

- *Makes assessment part of the learning process.* For example, third grader Haydee Bolado, as part of a project on the community, visited the recycling center. She made a presentation to the class and used the overhead projector to illustrate her major points, and displayed a poster board with pictures she had taken of the center, and several graphs to show which products are recycled most. In this way, she was able to demonstrate a broader range of what she had learned.

While early childhood professionals are enthusiastic about authentic assessment, some professionals are quick to point out inherent drawbacks:

- Authentic assessment takes a lot more of the teacher's time to plan for and participate in.

- Professionals need training to help them understand and apply it.

- Some parents see the schools' shift away from the traditional—traditional grading practices, traditional grades, and traditional testing—as a another sign of the faddism that schooling periodically

undergoes. They want to stay with traditional ways of doing things.

See Box 9.1 for guidelines for implementing appropriate assessment.

Promotion

Not surprisingly, with the new directions in primary education there is also a new look at grade failure and retention practices. Retention as a cure for poor or nonachievement is popular, especially with many professionals and the public. Despite the use of retention as a panacea for poor achievement, "the evidence to date suggests that achievement-

---

BOX 9.1 Guidelines for Appropriate Assessment

From a Position Statement of the National Association for the Education of Young Children and the National Association for Early Childhood Specialists in State Departments of Education:

1. Curriculum and assessment are integrated throughout the program; assessment is congruent with and relevant to the goals, objectives and content of the program.
2. Assessment results in benefits to the child, such as needed adjustments in the curriculum or more individualized instruction and improvements in the program.
3. Children's development and learning in all domains—physical, social, emotional, and cognitive—and their dispositions and feelings are informally and routinely assessed by teachers observing children's activities and interactions, listening to them as they talk, and using their constructive errors to understand their learning.
4. Assessment provides teachers with useful information to successfully fulfill their responsibilities: to support children's learning and

development, to plan for individuals and groups, and to communicate with parents.
5. Assessment involves regular and periodic observation of the child in a wide variety of circumstances that are representative of the child's behavior in the program over time.
6. Assessment relies primarily on procedures that reflect the ongoing life of the classroom and typical activities of the children. Assessment avoids approaches that place children in artificial situations, impede the usual learning and developmental experiences in the classroom, or divert children from their natural learning processes.
7. Assessment relies on demonstrated performance during real, not contrived, activities, for example, real reading and writing activities rather than only skills testing.
8. Assessment utilizes an array of tools and a variety of processes, including, but not limited to, collections of representative work by children (artwork, stories they write, tape recordings of their reading), records of systematic observations by teachers, records of conver-

sations and interviews with children, and teachers' summaries of children's progress as individuals and as groups.

9. Assessment recognizes individual diversity of learning and allows for differences in styles and rates of learning. Assessment takes into consideration children's ability in English, their stage of language acquisition, and whether they have been given the time and opportunity to develop proficiency in their native language as well as English.

10. Assessment supports children's development and learning; it does *not* threaten children's psychological safety or feelings of self-esteem.

11. Assessment supports parents' relationships with their children and does not undermine parents' confidence in their children's or their own ability, nor does it devalue the language and culture of the family.

12. Assessment demonstrates children's overall strengths and progress, what children *can* do, not just their wrong answers and what they cannot do or do not know.

13. Assessment is an essential component of the teacher's role. Since teachers can make maximal use of assessment results, the teacher is the *primary* assessor.

14. Assessment is a collaborative process involving children and teachers, teachers and parents, school and community. Information from parents about each child's experiences at home is used in planning instruction and evaluating children's learning. Information obtained from assessment is shared with parents in language they can understand.

15. Assessment encourages children to participate in self-evaluation.

16. Assessment addresses what children can do independently and what they can demonstrate with assistance since the latter shows the direction of their growth.

17. Information about each child's growth, development, and learning is systematically collected and recorded at regular intervals. Information such as samples of children's work, descriptions of their performance, and anecdotal records is used for planning instruction and communicating with parents.

18. A regular process exists for periodic information sharing between teachers and parents about children's growth and development and performance. The method of reporting to parents does not rely on letter or numerical grades but rather provides more meaningful, descriptive information in narrative form.

based promotion does not deal effectively with the problem of low achievement."[15] Better and more helpful approaches to student achievement include the following strategies:

- Use promotion combined with individualized instruction.

- Promote to a transition class in which students receive help to master skills not previously achieved.

- Use afterschool and summer programs to help students master skills.

- Provide children specific and individualized help in mastery of skills.

- Work with parents to teach them how to help their children work on mastery skills.

- Identify children who may need help before they enter first grade so that developmental services are provided early.

- Use multiage grouping as a means of providing for a broader range of children's abilities and to provide children the benefits that come from multiage grouping.

- Have a professional teach or stay with the same group of children over a period of several years as a means of getting to know children and their families better and, as a result, provide better for children's educational and developmental needs. This approach is also called *sustained instruction*.

- Use a nongraded classroom. The nongraded classroom and *nongraded institution* go hand in hand. In the nongraded classroom, individual differences are recognized and accounted for. The state of Kentucky mandates that grades 1 through 3 be nongraded. Advocates of nongraded classrooms offer the following advantages:

Opportunities for individualized instruction
An enhanced social atmosphere because older children help younger children and there are more opportunities for role modeling
Reduced or few, if any, retentions
Students do not have to progress through a grade-level curriculum in a lock-step approach with their age peers

Any effort to improve student achievement must emphasize helping children rather than using practices that threaten to detract from their self-image and make them solely responsible for their failure.

CHARACTERISTICS OF PRIMARY EDUCATION PROFESSIONALS

When all is said and done, it is the professional who sets the tone and direction for classroom instruction and learning. Without quality professionals, a quality program is impossible. Quality primary education professionals must be humane, loving, and caring people. In addition, they must be capable of interacting with very energetic young children. Unlike upper elementary children, who are more goal oriented and self-directed, primary children need help in developing the skills and personal habits that will enable them to be independent learners. To help them develop these skills and habits should be primary education professionals' foremost goal. The following guidelines will help you implement that goal:

- *Plan for instruction.* Planning is the basis for the vision of what professionals want for themselves and for children. Professionals who try to operate without a plan are like builders without a blueprint. Although planning takes time, it *saves* time in the long run, and it provides direction for instruction.

- *Be the classroom leader.* A quality professional leads the classroom. Some professionals forget this, and although children at all ages are capable of performing leadership responsibilities, it is the professional who sets the guidelines within which effective instruction occurs. Without strong leadership—*not* overbearing or dictatorial leadership—classrooms do not operate well. Planning for instruction helps a professional lead.

- *Involve children in meaningful learning tasks.* To learn, children need to be

PROGRAM IN ACTION

THE TWENTY-FIRST CENTURY PROGRAM IN INDEPENDENCE, MISSOURI

The Twenty-First Century Schools Program is a comprehensive child care program designed by Edward Zigler of Yale University's Bush Center for Child Development and Social Policy. It has served children from birth to twelve years of age and their families through a variety of services in the Independence, MO, school district since 1988.

Six components define the Twenty-First Century program:

1. Before- and after-school care for elementary school children (including half-day, flip-flop care for kindergartners)
2. Child care for three- to five-year-olds
3. Parents as Teachers for parents with children birth to three years old
4. Neighborhood daycare providers network
5. Information and referral
6. Medical screenings and referrals (Medicaid)

Through these six components the Independence School District strives to provide for the social, emotional, physical, and intellectual growth of each child, and offers safe, high-quality child care that is accessible and affordable for families of children from two to twelve years of age. Parents pay a maximum of $26 per week for schoolage child care and $63 per week for daycare for preschoolers.

The Twenty-First Century program operates from 6:30 A.M. to 6:00 P.M. Before- and afterschool care is provided in all thirteen Independence School District elementary buildings and one for-

mer elementary school building. The schoolage child care program strives to build self-esteem and enhance the personal development of each child through crafts, physical activities, fine arts, music, field trips, computer work, and special events. Each child chooses from a variety of daily curriculum choices. For example, an older child might spend thirty minutes doing supervised homework, then decide to work on the computer. A younger child might participate in group exercises one day and outside team sports another. The curriculum is child centered, which enables each child to engage in activities that are of benefit physically, socially, and emotionally. A child's choice is the key.

Seven elementary school sites and one former elementary school building offer child care for children three to five. The Cognitively Oriented Curriculum/Project Construct approach is used in these daycare programs. This approach focuses on the development of self-help skills, social skills, problem solving, and language. Children make choices from activity centers located around each room. Breakfast, lunch, and snack are included in the cost of the program.

More information on the Twenty-First Century Schools Program may be obtained by writing or calling school district superintendent Robert Watkins or school board president Phillip Parrino, Independence School District, 1231 S. Windsor, Independence, MO 64055; 816-833-3433.

---

active and involved. To learn to read they must read; to learn to write, they must write. Although these guidelines may seem self-evident, they are not always implemented. To learn,

children need to spend time on learning tasks.

- *Provide individualized instruction.* A range of abilities and interests is apparent in any classroom of twenty-five or more children. The early education professional must provide for these differences if children are going to learn to their fullest. There is a difference between *individual* and *individualized* instruction; it is impossible to provide individual attention to all children all the time, but providing for children at their individual levels is both possible and necessary. Educators are often accused of teaching to the average, boring the more able, and leaving the less able behind. This criticism can be addressed with individualized instruction. (See Chap. 1 for more information about professionalism and becoming a professional.)

THE FUTURE OF PRIMARY EDUCATION

Although the educational system in general is slow to meet the demands and dictates of society, it is likely the dramatic changes seen in primary education will continue in the next decade. The direction will be determined by continual reassessment of the purpose of education and attempts to match the needs of society to the goals of schools. Drug use, child abuse, the breakup of the family, and illiteracy are some of the societal problems the schools are being asked to address in significant ways.

Increasingly schools are asked to prepare children for their places in the world of tomorrow. All early childhood programs must help children and youth develop the skills necessary for life success. Even with the trend toward having children spend more time in school, we know that learning does not end with school and that children do not learn all they will need to know in an acade-

mic setting. It makes sense, therefore, to empower students with skills they can use throughout life in all kinds of interpersonal and organizational settings. Such skills include the following:

- The ability to communicate with others, orally and in writing

- The ability to work well with people of all races, cultures, and personalities

- The ability to be responsible for directing one's behavior

- The desire and ability for success in life—not as measured by earning a lot of money but by becoming a productive member of society

- The desire and ability to continue learning throughout life

ACTIVITIES FOR FURTHER ENRICHMENT

1. Interview parents and teachers to determine their views pro and con of nonpromotion in the primary grades. Summarize your findings. What are your opinions on retention?

2. List five things primary teachers can do to promote positive assessment in the primary years.

3. In addition to the characteristics of primary teachers listed in this chapter, what others do you think are desirable? Recall your own primary teachers. What characteristics did they have that had the greatest influence on you?

4. You have been asked to submit ten recommendations for changing and improving primary education. Provide a rationale for each of your recommendations.

5. What other issues of primary education would you add to those mentioned in this

chapter? How would you suggest dealing with them?

6. Identify five contemporary issues or concerns facing society, and tell how teachers and primary schools could address each of them.

7. Explain how first grade children's cognitive and physical differences make a difference in how they are taught. Give specific examples.

8. Of the three primary grades, decide which you would most like to teach, and explain your reasons.

9. What do you think are the most important subjects of the primary grades? Why? What would you say to a parent who thought any subjects besides reading, writing, and arithmetic were a waste of time?

READINGS FOR FURTHER ENRICHMENT

Stiggins, Richard J. *Student-Centered Classroom Assessment,* 2nd ed. (Upper Saddle River, NJ: Merrill/Prentice Hall, 1997).

Outlines a comprehensive philosophy of classroom assessment that places students at the center of the assessment process. Provides guidelines for the thoughtful and sensitive use of assessment within the instructional environment.

Tishman, Shari, David N. Perkins, and Ellen Jay. *The Thinking Classroom: Learning and Teaching in a Culture of Thinking* (Boston: Allyn & Bacon, 1995).

Offers a clear and informed view of the nature of good thinking, along with straightforward guidelines for how to teach it. Shows how to transform the classroom into a culture of thinking.

Wadsworth, Barry J., *Piaget's Theory of Cognitive and Affective Development* (White Plains, NY: Longman, 1996).

Provides a clear and interesting introduction to Piaget's theory and how to apply concepts and ideas to primary school practice. Helps teachers develop a better understanding of children and the education process.

NOTES

1. Jean Piaget, *The Moral Judgment of the Child,* trans. Marjorie Gabin (New York: Free Press, 1965), p. 395.
2. Lawrence Kohlberg, "The Claim to Moral Adequacy of a Highest Stage of Moral Judgment," *Journal of Philosophy* 70 (18), pp. 630–46.
3. S. Tishman, D. Perkins, and E. Jay, *The Thinking Classroom* (Boston: Allyn & Bacon 1995), p. 2.
4. Adapted from "You CAN Teach Thinking Skills," by Scott Willis from *Instructor,* February 1993. Copyright © 1993 by Scholastic, Inc. Reprinted by permission.
5. Hilda Taba, *Teacher's Handbook for Elementary Social Studies* (Reading, MA: Addison-Wesley, 1967), pp. 92–109.
6. P. Kneedler, "California Assesses Critical Thinking." In A. Costa (ed.), *Developing Minds: A Resource Book for Teaching Thinking* (Alexandria, VA: Association for Supervision and Curriculum Development, 1985), p. 277.
7. A. Woolfolk, *Educational Psychology* (Boston: Allyn & Bacon, 1995), p. 292.
8. R. E. Slavin, "Cooperative Learning and the Cooperative School," *Educational Leadership* 45 (1987), pp. 7–13.
9. R. Brandt, "On Cooperation in Schools: A Conversation with David and Roger Johnson," *Educational Leadership* 45 (1987), pp. 14–19.
10. Slavin, "Cooperative Learning," pp. 8–9.
11. Georgia Board of Education, Office of Instructional Services, Division of Student Support, *List of Core Values* (Atlanta: Author, 1992). Used by permission.
12. Judith M. Newman, "Using Children's Books to Teach Reading," in Judith M. Newman, ed., *Whole Language: Theory in Use*

(Portsmouth, NH: Heinemann Educational Books, 1985), p. 61.

13. Ibid, pp. 62–63.

14. J. Lloyd Eldredge, *Teaching Decoding in Holistic Classrooms,* © 1995, pp. 5–6. Adapted by permission of Prentice Hall, Upper Saddle River, New Jersey.

15. Monica Overman, "Practical Applications of Research: Student Promotion and Retention," *Phi Delta Kappan* 67 (April 1986), p. 612.

Guiding Children

CHAPTER 10

Creating Environments for Prosocial Behavior

Focus Questions

1. How do guidance, discipline, and punishment differ?

2. Why is it important to help children develop an internal locus of control?

3. How is a rationale for guiding children's behavior important?

4. What role does positive reinforcement play in developing appropriate behaviors in children?

5. Why is developing a philosophy of guiding children's behavior important?

6. What are different theories of guiding children's behavior?

7. What are the essential characteristics of effective behavior guidance?

8. Why is it important to become conversant about issues related to discipline and young children?

9. What are important trends in children's behavior guidance?

As early childhood professionals, we recognize that if we and
parents do a good job today
society will have fewer youth-
related problems tomorrow. Reading the
daily newspapers, we understand why
there is so much interest in how to guide
children's behavior. U.S. juvenile crime
statistics illustrate the seriousness of the
problem. For example:

*Thirty-six percent of juvenile arrests involved
youths below the age of 15. These young juve-
niles were involved in 11% of all juvenile murder
arrests, 38% of forcible rape, 28% of robbery, 32%
of aggravated assault, 415 of burglary, 45% of
larceny-thefts, 29% of motor vehicle theft, 45% of
runaway, 30% of weapon, and 15% of drug law
violation arrests.*[1]

This information paints a pretty grim picture of the nation's youth. Local and national news media underscore public and professional interest in children's behaviors at home, on the streets, and in early childhood programs. The public sees children, at ever younger ages, being mean and nasty to their peers and adults. They also see young children as victims of violence and crime by ever-younger children.

Who is to blame? Certainly parents receive their share. But the public also blames the educational system for allowing and even promoting uncivilized behavior. Parents interpret children's misbehavior as one indicator that educators have gone "soft" on discipline. Educators are accused of not managing children's behavior and not teaching them the manners, morals, and behavior necessary for living in civilized society.

Contemporary society also receives its share of blame for the way children act. There is national concern about the breakup of the family, the breakdown of moral standards, violence on television, widespread substance use, rampant crime, and general disrespect for authority. These trends are seen as evidence of parental and societal erosion of authority and discipline beginning in the earliest years. Again, many believe that current social ills are caused by parents' and educators' failures to discipline children.

The present and future behavior and misbehavior of children is the subject of much debate. Parents and the public look to early childhood professionals for assistance in helping children learn how to live in a democratic society.

WHAT IS GUIDING BEHAVIOR?

As a society, we believe discipline by parents and teachers is one solution to children's misbehavior. But what does the term *discipline* mean? *Discipline* comes from the Latin *disciplina,* which means to instruct or teach. And this is what all who have any responsibility for children should do—*teach* them how to guide and direct their own behavior and get along with others. The emphasis is on *teaching* children how to become responsible for guiding and directing their own behavior.

Guiding children's behavior is not an end in itself or a punitive process, but is a process of helping children build positive behaviors. Discipline is not about compliance and control but involves *behavior guidance,* a process by which *all* children learn to control and direct their own behavior and become independent and self-reliant. In this view, behavior guidance is a process of helping children develop skills useful to them over a lifetime. Professionals' and parents' roles are to (1) help children solve problems, (2) help children be problem solvers, (3) guide children toward developing self-control, (4) encourage children to be independent, (5) meet children's intellectual and emotional needs, (6) establish expectations for children, (7) organize appropriate behaviors and arrange environments so self-discipline can occur, and (8) change their own behavior when necessary.

The goal of most parents and early childhood professionals is to have children behave in socially acceptable and appropriate ways that contribute to and promote living in a democratic society. Professionals should view guidance of children's behavior as a process of learning by doing. Children cannot learn to develop appropriate behaviors and learn to be responsible by themselves. Just as no one learns to ride a bicycle by reading a book on the subject, children do not learn to guide themselves by being told what to do all the time. Maria Montessori often remarked that "discipline is not telling." Children must be shown and taught through precept and example. Children need opportunities to develop, practice, and perfect their abilities to control

Parents and early childhood professionals have an obligation to help children learn correct behaviors and how to guide their actions. Hoping someone else or some other agency will do it is not satisfactory. Professionals must conceptualize their rules in modeling appropriate behavior and provide guidance, support, and encouragement so children can do the same.

and guide their own behavior. They need the guidance, help, support, and encouragement of parents and early childhood professionals.

Thus, effective guidance of children's behavior at home and in early childhood programs consists of these essential elements:

- Know yourself
- Know child development
- Meet children's needs in individually and culturally appropriate ways
- Help children build new behaviors and skills of independence and responsibility
- Establish appropriate expectations
- Arrange and modify the environment so that appropriate, expected behavior and self-control are possible
- Model appropriate behavior

- Provide guidance
- Avoid creating or encouraging behavior problems
- Involve parents and families
- Promote empathy and prosocial behavior
- Teach cooperative living and learning
- Use conflict management and resolution techniques

Let us take a closer look at each of these essential elements in guiding children's behavior.

Know Yourself

The first rule in guiding children's behavior is to *know yourself*. Unless you know your attitudes toward discipline and behavior, it will be hard to practice a rational and consistent program of guidance and discipline. So, develop a philosophy about what you believe about childrearing, discipline, and children.

Knowing yourself and what you believe makes it easier for you to share with parents, help them guide behavior, and counsel them about discipline. Today, many parents find the challenges of childrearing overwhelming. They do not know what to do and consequently look to professionals for help. Knowing what you believe, based on sound principles of how children grow, develop, and learn, enables you to work with parents confidently.

Know Child Development

It may be overstating the obvious, but the foundation for guiding all children is to know what they are like. Unfortunately, not all early childhood professionals are as knowledgeable about children as they should be, and expect some children to behave in ways that are more appropriate for younger or older children. Here lies part of the problem of not being able to help children guide their behavior: Children cannot behave well when adults expect too much or too little of them based on their development or when they expect them to behave in ways inappropriate for them as individuals. So, a key for guiding children's behavior is to know—really *know*—what they are like. This is one reason we present in this text child development information for all children to age eight (see, for example, the Program in Action features concerning infants and toddlers in Chap. 6).

Meet Children's Needs

Part of knowing children and child development is knowing and meeting their needs. Abraham Maslow felt that human growth and development was oriented toward *self-actualization,* the striving to realize one's potential. He felt that humans are internally motivated by five basic needs that constitute a hierarchy of motivating behaviors, progressing from physical needs to self-fulfillment. Maslow's hierarchy (see Figure 6.1 for a graphic representation of the hierarchy) moves through physical needs, safety and security needs, belonging and affection needs, and self-esteem needs, culminating in self-actualization. Let us look at an example of each of these stages and behaviors to see how we can apply them to guiding children's behavior.

- *Physical needs.* Children's abilities to guide their behavior depends in part on how well their physical needs are met. Children do their best in school, for example, when they are well nourished. Thus, parents should provide for their children's nutritional needs by giving them breakfast. Early childhood professionals should also stress the nutritional and health benefits of eating breakfast. The quality of the environment is also important. Children cannot be expected to "behave" if classrooms are dark and

noisy and smell of stale air. Children also need adequate rest to do and be their best. The amount of rest is an individual matter, but many young children need eight to ten hours of sleep. A tired child cannot meet many of the expectations of schooling.

- *Safety and security.* Children should not have to fear parents or professionals and should feel comfortable and secure at home and at school. Asking or forcing children to do school tasks for which they do not have the skills makes them feel insecure, and children who are afraid and insecure are under a great deal of tension. Consider also the dangers many urban children face, such as crime, drugs, and homelessness, or the insecurity of children who live in an atmosphere of domestic violence. So, in addition, part of guiding children's behavior includes providing safe and secure communities/neighborhoods.

- *Belonging and affection.* Children need love and affection and the sense of belonging that comes from being given jobs to do, being given responsibilities, and helping make classroom and home decisions. Love and affection needs are also satisfied when parents hold, hug, and kiss their children and tell them, "I love you." Professionals meet children's affectional needs when they smile, speak pleasantly, are kind and gentle, treat children with courtesy and respect, and genuinely value each child for who she or he is. An excellent way to show respect for children and demonstrate to them belonging and affection is to greet them personally when they come into the classroom, center, or home. A personal greeting helps children feel wanted and secure and promotes feelings of self-worth. In fact, all early childhood programs should begin with this daily validation of each child.

- *Self-esteem.* Children who view themselves as worthy, responsible, and competent act in accordance with these feelings. Children's views of themselves come primarily from parents and early childhood professionals. Experiencing success gives them feelings of high self-esteem, and it is up to parents and professionals to give all children opportunities for success. The foundation for self-esteem is success and achievement.

- *Self-actualization.* Children want to use their talents and abilities to do things for themselves and be independent. Professionals and parents can help children become independent by helping them learn to dress themselves, go to the restroom by themselves, and take care of their environments. They can also help children set achievement and behavior goals ("Tell me what you are going to build with your blocks") and encourage them to evaluate their behavior ("Let's talk about how you cleaned up your room").

These points highlight the basic needs professionals and parents must consider when guiding children and helping them develop responsibility for their behavior.

Help Children Build New Behaviors

Helping children build new behaviors means that we help them learn that they are primarily responsible for their own behavior, and that the pleasures and rewards for appropriate behavior are internal, coming from within them as opposed to always coming from outside (i.e., from the approval and praise of others). This concept we refer to as *locus of*

control—the source or place of control. The preferred and recommended locus of control for young and old alike is internal.

Children are not born with this desired inner-directed locus of control. The process of developing an internal locus of control begins at birth, continues through the early childhood years, and is a never ending process throughout life. We want children to control their own behavior. When their locus of control is external, children are controlled by others; they are always told what to do and how to behave. Parents and professionals must try to avoid developing an external locus of control in children.

One criticism of programs and practices in which children's behaviors are constantly reinforced through praise and rewards is that this approach promotes an external locus of control (i.e., the person providing the reinforcement and the reinforcement itself). The argument goes that children behave only because someone else is telling them to and rewarding them for the behavior. However, rewards, such as genuine praise and other means of reinforcement, are entirely proper when used wisely and appropriately. Everyone likes praise, and there should be praise for honest efforts. We will discuss this point further shortly.

Empower Children Helping children build new behaviors creates a sense of responsibility and self-confidence. As children are given responsibility, they develop greater self-discipline, so that early childhood professionals and parents have to provide less guidance. Some professionals and parents hesitate to let children assume responsibilities, but without responsibilities, children are bored and frustrated and become discipline problems—the very opposite of what is intended. Guidance is not a matter of adults getting children to please them by making remarks such as,

"Show me how perfect you can be," "Don't embarrass me by your behavior in front of others," "I want to see nice groups," or "I'm waiting for quiet."

To reiterate, guiding behavior is not about compliance and control. Rather, it is important to instill in children a sense of independence and responsibility for their own behavior. For example, you might say, "You have really worked a long time cutting out the flower you drew. You kept working on it until you were finished. Would you like some tape to hang it up with?"

Parents and early childhood professionals can do a number of things to help children develop new behaviors that result in empowerment:

- *Give children responsibilities.* All children, from an early age, should have responsibilities, that is, tasks that are their job to do and for which they are

Helping children become more independent by warmly supporting their efforts is one of the most effective forms of guidance. Developing a sense of responsibility empowers children and enables them to become self-confident. Identify some ways professionals can support children's efforts to do things for themselves.

responsible. Being responsible for completing tasks and doing such things as putting toys and learning materials away promotes a positive sense of self-worth and conveys to children that in a community people have responsibilities for making the community work well.

- *Give children choices.* Life is full of choices—some require thought and decisions; others do not. But every time you make a decision, you are being responsible and exercising your right to decide. Children like to have choices, and choices help them become independent, confident, and self-disciplined. Learning to make choices early in life lays the foundation for decision making later. Guidelines for giving children choices are as follows:

    Give children choices when there are valid choices to make. When it comes time to clean up the classroom, do not let children choose whether they want to participate, but let them pick between collecting the scissors or the crayons.

    Help children make choices. Rather than say, "What would you like to do today?" say, "Sarah, you have a choice between working in the woodworking center or the computer center. Which would you like to do?"

    When you do not want children to make a decision, do not offer them a choice.

    In the High/Scope curriculum (Chap. 5), children select what activities they will participate in and then are accountable for their choices. Making choices is key for children developing responsible behavior that internalizes their locus of control.

- *Support children.* As an early childhood professional, you must support children

In a High/Scope classroom (see Chap. 5), children are encouraged to make choices about what activities they will engage in and how they will accomplish the activity. Giving children choices is an excellent way to help them develop independence and responsibility.

in their efforts to be successful. Arrange the environment and make opportunities available for children to be able to do things. Successful accomplishments are a major ingredient of positive behavior.

Establish Appropriate Expectations

Expectations relate to and set the boundaries for desired behavior. Expectations are the guideposts children use in learning to direct their own behavior. Like everyone, children need guideposts along life's way.

Early childhood professionals and parents need to set appropriate expectations for children, which means they must decide what behaviors they expect of children. When children know what adults expect, they can better achieve those expectations. Up to a point, the more we expect of children, the more and better they achieve. Generally, we expect too little of most children.

However, having expectations for children is not enough. Early childhood professionals have to help children know and understand what the expectations are and help them meet these expectations. Some children will need little help in meeting expectations; others will need demonstration, explanation, encouragement, and support as they learn.

Set Limits   Setting limits is closely associated with establishing expectations and relates to defining unacceptable behavior. For example, knocking over a block tower built by someone else and running in the classroom are generally considered unacceptable behaviors. Setting clear limits is important for three reasons:

1. It helps you clarify in your own mind what you believe is unacceptable *based on your knowledge of child development, children, their families, and their culture.* When you do not set limits, inconsistency can occur.

2. Setting limits helps children act with confidence because they know which behaviors are acceptable.

3. Limits provide children with security. Children want and need limits.

As children grow and mature, the limits change and are adjusted to developmental levels, programmatic considerations, and life situations.

Classroom Rules   Although I like to talk about and think in terms of expectations and limits, some early childhood professionals think and talk about rules. This is fine, but here are some additional guidelines.

Plan classroom rules from the first day of class. As the year goes on, you can involve children in establishing classroom rules, but in the beginning, children want and need to know what they can and cannot do. For example, rules might relate to changing groups and bathroom routines. Whatever rules you establish, they should be fair, reasonable, and appropriate to the children's age and maturity. Keep rules to a minimum; the fewer the better. For example, the following would be appropriate guidelines for four-year-olds:

1. Be gentle with your friends.

2. We are all friends at nursery school.

3. Use an inside voice.

4. Use your words when you have a problem.

You would remind children of these rules and encourage them to conform to them. Four-year-olds can realistically be expected to follow these guidelines, so there is less chance for misbehavior. Children are able to become responsible for their own behavior in a positive, accepting atmosphere where they know what the expectations are. Review the rules, and have children evaluate their behavior against the rules. You can have expectations without having rules. If you have activities ready for children when they enter the classroom, you establish the expectation that on arriving, they should be busy.

Arrange and Modify the Environment

Environment plays a key role in children's ability to guide their behavior. For example, if parents want a child to be responsible for taking care of his room, they should arrange the environment so he can do so, by providing shelves, hangers, and drawers at child height. Similarly, arrange your classroom so children can get and return their own papers and materials, use learning centers, and have time to work on individual projects.

In child care centers, early childhood classrooms, and family daycare homes, early childhood professionals arrange the environment so that it supports the purposes of the program and makes appropriate behavior possible. Room arrangement is crucial to guiding children's behavior and appropriate room arrangements signal to children that they are expected to guide and be responsible for their own behavior. Additionally, the appropriate environment enables teachers to observe and provide for children's interests through their selection of activities. Furthermore, it is easier to live and work in an attractive and aesthetically pleasing classroom or center. We all want a nice environment—children should have one, too. The following guidelines can be helpful to you as you think about and arrange your classroom or program area to support your efforts toward helping children guide their own behavior.

- Have an open area in which you and your children can meet as a whole group. This area is essential for story-time, general class meetings, and so on. Starting and ending the day with a class meeting allows children to discuss their behavior and say how they and others can do a better job.

- Center areas should be well defined, accessible to children, and have appropriate and abundant materials for children's use. Also, center boundaries should be low enough so that you and others can see over them for proper supervision and observation.

- Provide for all kinds of activities, both quiet and loud. Try to locate quiet areas together (reading area and puzzle area) and loud centers together (woodworking and blocks).

- Locate materials so that children can easily retrieve them. When children have to ask for materials, this promotes dependency and can lead to behavior problems.

- Materials should be easily stored, and children should put them away. A general rule of thumb is that there should be a place for everything and everything should be in its place when not in use.

- Provide children with guidelines for how to use centers and materials.

The Classroom as Reinforcer You also can apply behavior modification strategies to the physical setting of the classroom, arranging it so that it is conducive to the behaviors you want to reinforce. If you want to encourage independent work, you must provide places and time for children to work alone. Disruptive behavior is often encouraged by classroom arrangements that force children to walk over other children to get to equipment and materials. You may find that your classroom actually contributes to misbehavior. The atmosphere of the classroom or the learning environment must be such that new behaviors are possible.

The same situation applies in the home. If a parent wants a child to keep her room neat and clean, it must be possible for the child to do so. The child should also be shown how to take care of her room. The parent may have to lower shelves or install clothes hooks. When the physical arrangement is to the child's size, the child can learn how to use a clothes hanger and where to hang certain clothes. A child's room should have a place for everything, and these places should be accessible and easy to use.

A Rewarding Environment The classroom should be a place where children can do their best work and be on their best behavior. It should be a rewarding place to be. The following are components of an environmentally rewarding classroom:

- Opportunities for children to display their work

- Opportunities for freedom of movement (within guidelines)

- Opportunities for independent work

- A variety of work stations and materials based on children's interests

Time and Transitions   Generally more important to adults than children, time plays a major role in every program. The following guidelines relate to time and its use:

1. *Do not waste children's time.* They should be involved in interesting, meaningful activities from the moment they enter the center, classroom, or family daycare home.

2. *Do not make children wait.* When children have to wait for materials, their turn, and so forth, provide them with something else to do, such as listening to a story or playing in the block center. Problems can occur when children have to wait, because children like to be busy and involved.

Transitions are times when children move from one activity to another. They should be made as smoothly as possible. In one program, teachers sing, "It's Cleanup Time!" as a transition from one activity to cleanup and then to another activity.

Routines   Establish classroom routines from the beginning. Children need the confidence and security of a routine that will help them do their best. A routine also helps prevent discipline problems, because children know what to do and can learn to do it without a lot of disturbance. Parents need to establish routines in the home; a child who knows the family always eats at 5:30 P.M. can be expected to be there. As an early childhood professional, you must also be consistent. Consistency plays an important role in managing behavior in both the home and classroom. If children know what to expect in terms of routine and behavior, they will behave better.

Model Appropriate Behavior

We have all heard the maxim, "Telling is not teaching." Nevertheless, we tend to teach by giving instructions. Professional educators soon realize, however, that actions speak louder than words.

Children see and remember how other people act. Observing another person, the child tries out the behavior. If this new action brings a reward of some kind, the child repeats it. Proponents of the modeling approach to learning believe that most behavior people exhibit is learned from the behavior of a model or models. They think children tend to model behavior that brings rewards from parents and early childhood professionals.

A model may be someone whom we respect or find interesting and whom we believe is being rewarded for the behavior he or she exhibits. Groups may also serve as models. For example, it is common to hear a teacher in an early childhood classroom comment, "I like how Cristina and Carlos are sitting quietly and listening to the story." Immediately following such a remark, you can see the group of children settle down to listen quietly to the story. Models children emulate do not necessarily have to be from real life; they can come from books and television. In addition, the modeled behavior does not have to be socially acceptable to be reinforcing.

You can use the following techniques to help children learn through modeling:

- *Show.* Show children where the block corner is and how and where the blocks are stored.

- *Demonstrate.* Perform a task while students watch. For example, demonstrate the proper way to put the blocks away

Demonstrating for children how to act and react are two of the most important things for children to observe. Modeling appropriate behavior is an easily accomplished means of helping children learn to guide their behavior.

and how to store them. Extensions of the demonstration method are to have the children practice the demonstration while you supervise, and to ask a child to demonstrate to other children.

- *Model.* Modeling occurs when you practice the behavior you expect of the children. Also, you can call children's attention to the desired behavior when another child models it.

- *Supervise.* Supervision is a process of reviewing, insisting, maintaining standards, and following up. If children are not performing the desired behavior, you

will need to *review* the behavior. You must be consistent in your expectations of desired behavior. Children will soon learn they do not have to put away their blocks if you allow them not to do it even once. Remember, you are responsible for setting up the environment to enable the children's learning to take place.

As an early childhood professional, you will need to model and demonstrate social and group-living behaviors as well, including using simple courtesies (saying, "Please," "Thank you," "You're welcome," etc.) and practicing cooperation, sharing, and respect for others.

Provide Guidance

Children need help to act their way out of undesirable behavior. Parents and early childhood professionals may say, "You know how to act," when indeed the child does not know. Teachers also often say, "He could do better if he wanted to." The problem, however, is that the child may *not* know what he wants to do or may not know what is appropriate. In other words, he needs an organized procedure for how to act. Building new behavior, then, is a process of getting children to act in new ways.

A common approach to behavior management is "talking to" and reasoning. As children often do not understand abstract reasoning, it does not generally have the desired effect. The child is likely to behave the same way, or worse. This often leads to a punishment trap, in which the early childhood professional or parent resorts to yelling to get the desired results. The behavior we want children to demonstrate must be within their ability. For instance, children cannot pay attention to and be interested in a story that is based on concepts that are too advanced for their comprehension or that is read in a monotonic, unenthusiastic voice. Although *Charlotte's Web* is a children's classic, we cannot expect a group of three-year-olds to sit still and listen attentively while we read it aloud.

Avoid Problems

Parents and early childhood professionals can encourage children's misbehavior. Frequently, professionals see too much and ignore too little. Parents expect perfection and adult behavior. If we focus on building responsible behavior, there will be less need to solve behavior problems.

Ignoring inappropriate behavior is probably one of the most overlooked strategies for managing an effective learning setting and guiding children's behavior. Ironically, many early childhood professionals feel guilty when they use this strategy. They believe that ignoring undesirable behaviors is not good teaching. While ignoring some inappropriate behavior can be an effective strategy, it must be combined with positive reinforcement of desirable behavior. Thus, one ignores inappropriate behavior and at the same time reinforces appropriate behavior. A combination of positive reinforcement and ignoring can lead to desired behavior.

When children do something good or are on task, reward them. Use verbal and nonverbal reinforcement and privileges to help assure that the appropriate behavior will continue. Catch children being good; that is, look for good behavior. This helps improve not only individual behavior but group behavior as well.

Writing contracts for certain work experiences is a great way to involve children in planning their own work and behavior. Follow these rules when contracting: (1) keep contracts short and uncomplicated, (2) make an offer the child cannot refuse, (3) make sure the child is able to do what you contract for, and (4) pay off when the contract is completed.

Involve Parents and Families

Involving parents and families is a wonderful way to gain invaluable insights about children. Furthermore, parents and early childhood professionals must be partners and work cooperatively in effectively guiding children's behaviors.

Another important rule in guiding behavior is to *know your children*. A good way to learn about the children you care for and teach is through home visits. If you do not have an opportunity to visit the home, a parent conference is also valuable. Either way, you should gather information concerning the child's health history and interests; the child's attitude toward schooling; the parents' educational expectations for the child; what school support is available in the home (e.g., books, places to study); home conditions that would support or hinder school achievement (such as where the child sleeps); parents' attitudes toward schooling and discipline; parents' support of the child (e.g., encouragement to do well); parents' interests and abilities; and parents' desire to become involved in the school.

The visit or conference offers an opportunity for you to share ideas with parents. You should, for example, express your desire for the child to do well in school; encourage parents to take part in school and classroom programs; suggest ways parents can help children learn; describe some of the school programs; give information about school events, projects, and meetings; and explain your beliefs about discipline.

Working with and involving parents also provides early childhood professionals with opportunities to help parents with parenting skills and child-related problems. The foundation for children's behavior is built in the home, and some parents unwittingly encourage and promote children's misbehavior and antisocial behavior. In many ways, parents promote antisocial behavior in their children by using punitive, negative, and overly restrictive punishment. In particular, when children are enrolled in child care programs at an early age, professionals have an ideal opportunity to help parents learn about and use positive discipline approaches to childrearing. (Chap. 15 is devoted entirely to parent, family, and community involvement.)

Promote Empathy and Prosocial Behavior

A trend in early childhood education since the 1980s is for professionals to focus on helping children learn how to share, care for, and assist others. We call these and similar behaviors *prosocial behaviors.*

Parents and early childhood professionals want to encourage *altruistic behavior* in children, that is, intentional behaviors that benefit others. Part of altruistic behavior involves *empathy,* the ability to vicariously feel another person's emotions and feelings. As mentioned in Chapter 5, Piaget believed that young children are egocentric, which prevents them from having empathy for others. This is another area in which Piaget's theory is being modified and updated based on continuing research. We now know that children as young as two and three years of age are quite capable of empathy.

You can do a number of things to promote prosocial behaviors that will enable children to show concern for others; to help others through acts of kindness and sharing; and to respond to the conditions of others through affection, comfort, sympathy, joy, and love:

1. *Model behaviors that are caring, loving, and helping.* When young children see adults helping others, sharing with others, and comforting others in distress, then they too learn that such behaviors are important and worthwhile. Provide children opportunities to see other children and adults modeling prosocial behaviors. Organizations such as Junior Girl Scouts, Brownies, Cub Scouts, and others that traditionally engage in helping activities offer a social context for children to see people helping others and for them to do the same.

2. *Provide opportunities to engage children in helping and service to others.* For

PROGRAM IN ACTION

POSITIVE DISCIPLINE: RESPONSIBLE, MOTIVATED, SELF-DIRECTED LEARNERS

When Grapevine (Texas) Elementary School opened in the fall of 1994, its staff had a vision. This vision emphasized the desire to encourage all learners to be responsible, intrinsically motivated, and self-directed in an environment of mutual respect. As we looked for a discipline management system that fit this philosophy, we recognized that we needed one that emphasized personal responsibility for behavior and cooperation instead of competition, and that focused on developing a community of supportive members. We also discovered that we held several beliefs in common that should be the foundation for our discipline management plan:

1. All human beings have three basic needs—to feel connected (the ability to love and be loved), to feel capable (a sense of "I can" accomplish things), and to feel contributive (I count in the communities in which I belong).
2. Natural and logical consequences for poor choices encourage responsible behavior. Punishment, on the other hand, encourages rebellion and resentment.
3. Children can be creative decision makers and responsible citizens when given opportunities to direct the processes that affect the day-to-day environment in which they live.

Our desire was, and is, to address the needs of the whole child as we educate our children to be responsible citizens.

Adopting the Discipline Plan

After much research and deliberation, we, as a faculty and staff, decided to implement "Positive Discipline" as a discipline management system. The training of the staff occurred during the summer before the school opened. As we studied the book *Positive Discipline in the Classroom* by Jane Nelsen, Lynn Lott, and Stephen Glenn, teachers spontaneously began to discuss several rituals that normally occur in school routines which did not seem to fit the philosophy of the environment we were attempting to create. One of these was the concept of "rules." Teachers decided to establish a set of *Grapevine Star Responsibilities* in the place of the more traditional concept of rules:

I will be responsible for myself and my learning.

I will respect others and their property.

I will listen and follow directions promptly.

I will complete my class work and homework in a quality manner.

Furthermore, we decided that rewards, whether in the way of stickers, pencils, or award ceremonies were not, on the whole, consistent with encouraging intrinsic motivation and a belief that all children should continuously monitor their own learning and behavior. Rather, reward for success should be based on what children find personally significant. Reward should come from within as children and classes celebrate achievement of personal and class goals.

In the summer before school began, teachers discussed the understanding that they should be role models. It was understood that the decision to implement "Positive Discipline" would require a change in thinking and a change in behavior for teachers. Teachers would have to change from the role of arbitrator/referee to mediator; they would become facilitators of decision-making sessions instead of "generals in command"; and they would have to consistently challenge themselves to think in terms of consequences instead of punishment. Instead of demanding, they would encourage and invite, and instead of constantly evaluating the behavior and work of students, they would use questioning strategies to encourage self-evaluation by students. For example, teachers might ask, "What would responsible second-grade behavior look like in this situation?" Teachers knew that the atmosphere of caring they created in their classrooms would determine whether their classrooms would build or hinder the development of community within each class and, in a larger context, the school.

Engaging Students

Throughout the course of the year, students set goals each six-week period (usually one academic goal and one behavioral goal) and conferred with their teachers at the end of the six weeks to determine the extent of their achievement toward that goal. At the end of our first year, students participated in a celebration of achievement. Each student chose the goal that held the most personal significance and received a certificate that detailed the goal. The principal read each chosen goal in grade-level celebrations as the student walked across the stage and shook hands with the principal. One second grader chose a goal that included developing two new friendships; a third grader chose a goal that reflected learning all of his multiplication facts; a kindergartner expressed delight in overcoming his fear of the class pet, a rat! Teachers, parents, and students all enjoyed this ceremony that emphasized the worth of each individual and that learning was, and is, the ultimate goal of education and school (as opposed to a grade or series of marks on a report card).

Class meetings are the cornerstone of "Positive Discipline." The format of a class meeting is forming a circle, giving compliments, and addressing items that students or teachers have placed on the agenda. In the primary grades, agenda items include problems that students are having with one another or a teacher, decisions the class has to make, and concerns that the teacher might have. Before a class can begin to have meetings, children need to learn effective communication skills and must begin to develop a basic understanding of the difference between *consequences* and *punishment.* Teachers must practice with their students skills such as active listening, the use of I-messages, and brainstorming solutions to problems.

One of the most amazing and critical parts of a class meeting is the compliment time at the beginning. Children are encouraged to compliment others for specific actions of character traits, not the generic, "I like Joan because she's my friend." In any Grapevine Elementary kindergarten class, one could observe children as they pass a stuffed animal around the circle (whoever holds the stuffed animal is the speaker) and compliment one another with statements such as, "Thanks, Tim for helping me pick up all the crayons I dropped this morning." If indeed the deepest craving of every soul is the need to be appreciated, this part of the class meeting proves magical. Children beam as their classmates compliment them. We often note that children who normally are left out become the target of compliments by responsible, caring leaders in the class without any prompting from teachers. This part of class meetings is beneficial in and of itself because it encourages the atmosphere in which children can feel they are connected, capable contributors!

Problems identified by students or teachers are addressed in the meeting's agenda section. Each teacher has their own individualized method for developing a class agenda. In kindergarten, the children draw pictures on a class tablet to remind them of what the problem is; in second grade, children are able to write the problem on a slip of paper and place it in the agenda box. The focus during the agenda section of the class meeting is on addressing problems and finding solutions; not placing blame or punishing. When the school year began, it was not unusual for children to suggest that others be "sent to the principal" for some act of unkindness or lack of responsibility. Gradually, children became extremely creative and often decided on solutions that astounded teachers.

In one third grade class, the children were having a continual problem with one student who was using inappropriate language and embarrass-

continued

ing students. The students took turns telling this boy how his language and behavior was making them feel. The boy began to cry quietly. Rather than stopping the process, the children continued. When everyone had a turn at sharing, they each walked by the young boy, touched him gently on the knee or shoulder and told him something they appreciated about him and how glad they were that he was in the class. The boy's behavior changed, and students were empowered by taking responsibility for communicating respectfully and for helping a fellow classmate.

Irene Boynton, a mixed-age (K–1) teacher, notes that a great deal of teaching and work is required to make class meetings successful. She spends time brainstorming feeling words because children often get stuck on the words *good* and *bad*. Role playing is used successfully in her class meetings to focus on issues such as pushing in line and "bothering" other students. Occasionally, she will purposefully tailor a cooperative learning activity immediately before a class meeting so that everyone can discuss issues of cooperation in the meeting itself while the experiences are fresh on the students' minds. Mrs. Boynton comments that "Positive Discipline" allows children to experience the rewards of feeling confident and healthy about making respectful, responsible choices because it is the "right" thing to do, not because they will receive something for their choice.

The Benefits

At Grapevine Elementary, it took children a while to move past wanting the teacher to make decisions for them, as had been done in the past, toward an understanding that they had the skills to solve their own problems. Now, teachers consistently respond that the use of class meetings encourages children to be responsible for personal problem solving. When asked by a child to referee or arbitrate, they are often able to respond with, "Have you tried to work it out yourselves?" or, "Is this something that you need to place on the class agenda?" Tattling, too, has decreased dramatically as we continue to emphasize the difference between tattling and important telling and the use of "I-Care" language.

Kindergarten teacher Carol Matthews believes that class meetings are an excellent tool for teaching problem solving. Meetings encourage children to talk about their own feelings and to be aware of the feelings of others. For her, seeing children carry over skills outside of the classroom is exciting. A mother of one of her students once told Mrs. Matthews that her daughter responded in an interesting way when she and some other girls were squabbling over how to accomplish a task during an Indian Princess camp out, declaring, "C'mon you guys, we've got to solve this problem ourselves." The children went off to the side and talked through the problem without help from an adult. The process empowers children!

Teachers at Grapevine Elementary, when asked to comment on "Positive Discipline," say such things as, "Is there any other way to teach?" and, "We would never go back to playing referee again!" Students no longer ask, "What am I going to get?" in response to a request to go to the extra mile for another student or while working on a project. They are developing respect for themselves and for the rights and needs of others. The skills learned in class meetings extend into academic areas where we find that students are becoming more thoughtful, introspective, self-motivated, and effective problem solvers. We believe that we are fostering a safe, respectful community where children and adults thrive together in an atmosphere of mutual respect.

Contributed by Nancy Robinson, Grapevine Elementary, Grapevine, TX. For more detailed information on implementing "Positive Discipline," refer to *Positive Discipline in the Classroom,* by Jane Nelsen, Lynn Lott, and H. Stephen Glenn (see Readings for Further Enrichment). Our implementation of this program was based on teachers' understanding of the book and other programs, not from direct training from any of the authors.

example, beginning in the toddler years, children can visit with the elderly, bringing them treats and artwork. What is important is to offer children the chance to engage in helping others in meaningful ways.

3. *Help children "put themselves in someone else's place." Ask them how they think about a particular situation or event.* For example, you might ask, "How do you think Laura feels because you won't share your toys with her?"

Parents and professionals want to promote the intrinsic development of empathy, that is, a desire to engage in sympathetic behaviors because it is the right and good thing to do. They should avoid rewarding children for these behaviors. When rewards are the consequences of empathy and helping, then children learn that acts of helping or kindness are based on these external rewards. Certainly children can and should be complimented for doing good things, and they should be encouraged to assist others. However, they should not learn that the reward is the reason for helping others. Helping and kindness are themselves rewards.

Teach Cooperative Living and Learning

Early childhood professionals can do a lot to promote cooperative living in which children help each other direct their behavior. Recall from Chapter 3 our discussion of Vygotsky's theory of social relations. Children are born seeking social interactions, and social relations are necessary for children's learning and development. Peers help each other learn.

Children's natural social groups and play groups are ideal and natural settings in which to help children assist each other in learning new behaviors and being responsible for their own behavior. The classroom as a whole is

an important social group. Classroom meetings in which early childhood professionals and children talk can serve many useful functions. They can talk about expected behaviors from day to day ("When we are done playing with toys, what do we do with them?"), review with children what they did in a particular center or situation, and help them anticipate what they will do in future situations ("Tomorrow morning when we visit the Senior Citizen Center . . ."). In all these situations, children are cooperatively engaged in thinking about, talking about, and learning how to engage in appropriate behavior. Furthermore, children can help identify a particular problem or misbehavior and discuss appropriate behavior.

Teachers and children also form an important social group that influences behavior. You can model a particular behavior, engage a child in a discussion of behavior, and compliment the child on behavior.

Early childhood professionals must initiate, support, and foster a cooperative, collaborative learning community in the classroom in which children are involved in developing and setting guidelines and devising classroom and, by extension, individual norms of behavior. Professionals "assist" children but do not do things for them, and they ask questions that make children think about their behavior—how it influences the class, themselves, and others. This process of cooperative living occurs daily. Discussions grow out of existing problems, and guidance is provided on needs of children and the classroom.

The account of the Stride Rite Intergenerational Daycare Center on pages b–10 and b–11 in the second color insert, "Observing Programs in Action," illustrates the importance and benefits of social interactions across age ranges. There are many social, cognitive, and behavioral benefits to children helping the elderly and the elderly helping children.

Use Conflict Management and Resolution Techniques

Quite often, conflicts result from children's interactions with others. Increasingly, early childhood professionals are advocating teaching children ways to manage and resolve their own conflicts.

Teaching conflict resolution strategies is important for several reasons. First, it makes sense to give children the skills they need to handle and resolve their own conflicts. Second, teaching conflict resolution skills to children enables them to use these same skills as adults. Third, the peaceful resolution of interpersonal conflicts contributes, in the long run, to world peace. In this sense, peace curricula and attempts to teach children behaviors associated with peacemaking begin with harmony in the child care and preschool classroom families. Children who are involved in efforts to resolve interpersonal behavior problems peacefully intuitively learn that peace begins with them.

Strategies used to teach and model conflict resolution include the following:

- *Talk it over.* Children can learn that talking about a problem often leads to a resolution and reveals that there are always two sides to an argument. Talking also helps children think about other ways to solve problems. Children can and should be involved in the solution of their interpersonal problems *and* classroom and activity problems.

- *Model resolutions.* Professionals can model resolutions for children: "Erica, please don't knock over Shantrell's building because she worked hard to build it"; "Barry, what is another way (instead of hitting) you can tell Pam that she is sitting in your chair?"

- *Teach children to say "I'm sorry."* Saying "I'm sorry" is one way to heal and

resolve conflicts. It can be a step toward good behavior. Piaget maintained that prior to the stage of concrete operations (before the age of seven), young children do not have the cognitive maturity to take another's point of view. Since they cannot "decenter," it is difficult for them to know how others feel and therefore to be sorry for something. Thus, the very young are not cognitively able to learn to say "I'm sorry" and have real conviction that they indeed are sorry. Nevertheless, children need to be reared in an environment in which they see and experience others being sorry for their inappropriate actions toward others.

- *Do something else.* Teach children to get involved in another activity. Children can learn that they do not always have to play with a toy someone else is playing with. They can get involved in another activity with a different toy. They can do something else now and play with the toy later. Chances are, however, that by getting involved in another activity they will forget about the toy they were ready to fight for.

- *Take turns.* Taking turns is a good way for children to learn that they cannot always be first, have their own way, or do a prized activity. Taking turns brings equality and fairness to interpersonal relations.

- *Share.* Sharing is good behavior to promote in any setting. Children have to be taught how to share and how to behave when others do not share. Children can be helped to select another toy rather than hitting or grabbing. Again, keep in mind that during the early years children are egocentric, and acts of sharing are likely to be motivated by expectations of a reward or approval such as being thought of as a "good" boy or girl.

BEHAVIOR MODIFICATION APPROACHES TO GUIDING BEHAVIOR

A popular approach to guidance based on behavior rather than on feelings is *behavior modification.* An important concept of behavior modification is that all behavior has a cause. Everyone acts the way they do for reasons, although the reasons may not always be apparent; individuals themselves do not always know why they behave a certain way. How often have you heard the expressions, "He didn't know what he was doing," "I don't know why she acts like she does," "I can't understand why I did that," and "I didn't know what I was doing"?

A second basic concept is that behavior results from reinforcement received from the environment. American psychologist Edward L. Thorndike (1874–1949) observed that the consequences of one's behavior influence future behavior. He formalized this observation in his learning principle, the *law of effect:* If a satisfying condition follows a behavior, the individual tends to repeat that behavior, and the strength of the stimulus–response connection increases. If an unsatisfying condition follows a behavior, the individual tends not to repeat that behavior, and the stimulus–response connection weakens or disappears. The law of effect points out how important the quality of feedback is for behavior.

This law has gradually come to be known as the *imperial law of effect,* which says that the consequences of particular responses determine whether the response will be continued and therefore learned. In other words, what happens to a child *after* acting in a particular way determines whether he or she continues to act that way. If a child cries and is immediately given a cookie, and this happens several times, that youngster will probably learn that crying is a good way to get cookies. And the cycle continues: receiving cookies reinforces crying behavior. We should understand that this behavior is not always planned; a child does not necessarily think, "I'm going to cry because I know Mom will give me a cookie." The child may have cried, the mother gave a cookie to stop the crying, and the child associated the two events.

B. F. Skinner (1904–1990) is given credit for many of the technological and pedagogical applications of behavior modification, including programmed instruction. Skinner also emphasized the role of the environment in providing people with clues that reinforce their behavior.

In behavior management, we are concerned with behavior modification, or changing behavior. As used in our discussion, *behavior modification* means the *conscious* application of the methods of behavioral science, with the intent of changing children's behavior. Early childhood professionals and parents have always been concerned with changing children's behavior, but it is implicit in the term *behavior modification* that we mean the conscious use of techniques to change behavior.

Behaviorists maintain that all behavior is learned and, in this sense, all behavior is caused by reinforcers from which individuals gain pleasure of some kind. The problem, however, is that early childhood professionals and parents have usually changed children's behavior without realizing it. We must be more aware of the effect we have on children's behavior. To use power ignorantly and unconsciously to achieve ends that are basically dehumanizing to children is not good teaching practice. For example, when a child first comes to school, she may not understand that sitting quietly is a desirable behavior that many schools and teachers have established as a goal. The teacher may scold the child until she not only sits quietly but sits quietly and bites her nails. The teacher did not intentionally set out to reinforce nail biting, but this is the child's terminal behavior, and the teacher is unaware of how it happened.

Reinforced Misbehavior

We must recognize that our behavior, attitudes, predisposition, and inclinations can cause a great deal of child misbehavior. Many children misbehave because their misbehavior is reinforced. For example, children enjoy receiving attention; therefore, when a child receives any kind of attention, it reinforces the behavior the child exhibited to get that attention. A child who is noisy receives attention by being scolded. The chances of his exhibiting the same behavior (such as talking to the child beside him) to elicit attention is greatly increased as a result of the reinforcement.

We sometimes encourage children to do sloppy work or hurry through an activity when we emphasize finishing it. We may give children a paper with six squares on it to color and cut out and say, "After you color all the squares, I will give you a pair of scissors so you can cut the squares out." The child may hurry through the coloring to get to the cutting. We would do better to concentrate on coloring first, then cutting.

Positive Reinforcement

When we talk about positive reinforcement, we are talking about providing *rewards* or *reinforcers* that promote behaviors we decide are desirable. *Positive reinforcement* is maintaining or increasing the frequency of a behavior following a particular stimulus. What the child receives, whether candy, money, or a hug, is the *reinforcer,* the *reinforcement,* or the *reward.* Generally, a positive reinforcer is any stimulus that maintains or increases a particular behavior.

Verbal reinforcers include "Good," "Right," "Correct," "Wonderful," "Very good," "I like that," "That's great!" and "I knew you could do

it." You can also use nonverbal behavior to reinforce children's behavior and learning; for example, a nod, smile, hug, pat on the head or shoulder, standing close to someone, eye contact, paying attention, or even a wink show children that you approve of their behavior or are proud of what they are doing.

You can set up your classroom as a positively reinforcing environment. If it is organized to help make desired behaviors possible, provides opportunities for novelty and children's control over their environment, and reflects children's desires, interests, and ideas, children will tend to try to live up to the expectations the setting suggests.

Understanding Behavior

Another extremely important concept of behavior modification focuses on external behavior rather than the causes of behavior; that is, professionals and parents should generally not be concerned with *why* a child acts as he or she does. This idea usually takes some getting used to, because it is almost the opposite of what we have been taught. Early childhood professionals particularly feel it is beneficial to know why children act the way they do, and they spend a great deal of time and effort trying to determine motivations. If Gloria is fidgety and inclined to daydream, for example, her teacher may spend six weeks investigating the causes. He learns that Gloria's mother has been divorced three times and ignores her at home. On the basis of this information, he concludes that Gloria needs help but may be no closer to solving her problem than he was six weeks previously. As educators, our time and energy should be spent developing strategies to help children with their behavior. Sometimes underlying causes help us deal with the behavior we wish to modify, but we need to recognize that the *behavior* a child exhibits is the problem, and it is behavior that we need to attend to.

REINFORCING BEHAVIOR

Appropriate Reinforcers

A reinforcer is only as effective as the child's desire for it. In other words, if the reinforcer has the power to reinforce the behavior that precedes it, then it will work. One method used to determine the nature of a reinforcer is the *Premack principle.* David Premack determined that behaviors with a high probability of occurrence can be used to reinforce behaviors with a low probability of occurrence. For example, activities children participate in when they have free time are often what they like to do best. You can use these activities to reinforce desired behaviors.

Using the chalkboard or art easels is a highly desirable activity in many early childhood classrooms. Therefore, you can provide extra time to use them to reinforce desired behavior. Rewards that children help select are most likely to have a desired effect on behavior. Privileges children often choose are watering the plants, feeding classroom pets, washing chalkboards, running errands, going outside, playing games with friends, leading games, enjoying extra recess, passing out papers and supplies, using audiovisual equipment, doing flash cards, and cutting and pasting. Figure 10.1 shows typical reinforcers in an early childhood setting.

Praise as a Reinforcer

Praise is probably the most frequent method of rewarding or reinforcing children's behavior. Praise is either general or specific. Specific praise is more effective because it describes the behavior we want to build. The child has no doubt that she is being praised and what she is being praised for. For example, if a child picks up her blocks and you say, "Good, Laura," she may or may not know what you are referring to, but if you say "Laura, you did a nice job of putting your blocks away," Laura knows exactly what you are talking about.

Parents and early childhood professionals should approach children positively. A positive approach builds self-esteem. We help build positive self-images and expectations for good behavior by complimenting children and praising them for the things they do well. Every child has praiseworthy qualities.

Contingency Management

Early childhood professionals frequently find it helpful to engage in *contingency contracting* or *contingency management* to reinforce behavior. With this strategy, you might tell a child, "If you put the materials away when you're done with them, you can use the chalkboard for five minutes." Sometimes contingency management is accompanied by a written contract between teacher and student, depending, of course, on the child's age and maturity.

When parents or early childhood professionals manage a contingency, they must be sure they have thought through its consequences. For example, if a parent says, "If you don't clean up your room, you have to stay there until you do," the child may choose not to clean up his room but to stay there and play with his toys. In this case, he does not have to do as he was told and is rewarded for not doing it.

Token System

Reinforcement works best when it occurs at the time of the behavior we want to reinforce. Also, the sooner reinforcement follows the desired behavior, the better it works. Particularly when building new skills or shaping new behaviors, it is important to reinforce the child immediately. To provide immediate reinforcement, some professionals use tokens, such as plastic disks, buttons, trading stamps, or beans, which the child later trades for an activity. If children like to use the art easel, the teacher might allow them to exchange ten tokens for time at the easel.

Figure 10.1/*Reinforcers Used in Early Childhood Settings*

PRIMARY REINFORCERS	CONDITIONED REINFORCERS		
Reinforce behavior without the respondent's having much previous expreience with an item	Reinforce as a result of experiences the respondent has had with the reinforcer		

Food

Juice	Raisins
Celery	Cheese
Carrots	Fruit

Verbal—praise

"I like the way you . . ."			"Good job!"
"Great"	"Wow"	"Excellent"	"Tremendous"
"Right on"	"Way to go"	"Fantastic"	"Awesome"
"Beautiful"	"Super"		"Cool"
"Terrific"			"You're working hard"

Nonverbal

Facial	*Gestures*	*Proximity*
Smile	Clapping of hands	Standing near someone
Wink	Waving	
Raised eyebrow	Forming an okay sign (thumb + index finger)	Shaking hands
Eye contact		Getting down on child's level
	Victory sign	Hugging, touching
	Nodding head	Holding child's arm up
	Shrugging shoulders	

Social (occur in or as a result of social consequences)

Parties

Group approval

Class privileges

The child receives a token for performing appropriate tasks and exhibiting teacher-specified behavior.

Time-Out

Time-out is another practice early childhood professionals and parents often use. In fact, it is the most favored form of discipline used by parents (Table 10.1). *Time-out* is the removal of a child from an activity because that child has done something wrong. Pre-

sumably, the time-out gives the child an opportunity to think about the misbehavior. After a set amount of time or when the child says he or she can behave (which, of course, *all* children say), the child is allowed to return to the activity.

Early childhood professionals should use time-out only when it is appropriate to children's developmental levels. This strategy is inappropriate for infants' and toddlers' developmental levels, but infrequent use is some-

Learning how to get along with others is a major life task. It makes sense for early childhood professionals to help children to learn how to resolve their differences and work cooperatively together. Because of this, curricula for helping children to peaceably resolve conflicts is growing in popularity.

times effective with preschoolers. Time-out is generally not effective as a guidance technique, because it is debatable whether young children will "think" about what they did wrong. Additionally, time-out is usually irrelevant to the inappropriate behavior, so children do not make a connection between the poor behavior and the punishment.

Children are energetic and impulsive, so it is effective to use *preventive guidance* techniques that catch problems before they happen, or "prevent" them. Examples of preventive guidance are appealing room ar range-

ment, effective scheduling, minimal waiting time, and an interesting, active curriculum. These approaches are far more effective than using "band-aid" strategies to guidance such as time-out.

DEVELOPMENT OF AUTONOMOUS BEHAVIOR

Implicit in guiding children's behavior is the assumption that they can be, should be, and will be responsible for their own behavior. The ultimate goal of all education is to

Table 10.1/*Methods of Discipline Favored by Parents*

Type of Discipline	Percentage of Parents
Using time-out	38
Lecturing (in a nice way)	24
Spanking	19
Taking away television privileges	15
Scolding (not in a nice way)	15
"Grounding" them	14
Taking away allowance	2

Note: Percentages do not add up to one hundred because parents use more than one method.
Source: "Parental Discipline," *Education Week,* May 9, 1993, p. 3. Reprinted with permission from *Education Week.*

develop *autonomy* in children, which means "being governed by oneself."

Early childhood educators need to conduct programs that promote development of autonomy. One aspect of facilitating autonomy is exchanging points of view with children.

When a child tells a lie, for example, the adult can deprive him of dessert or make him write 50 times "I will not lie." The adult can also refrain from punishing the child and, instead, look him straight in the eye with great skepticism and affection and say, "I really can't believe what you are saying because. . . ." This is an example of an exchange of points of view that contributes to the development of autonomy in children. The child who can see that the adult cannot believe him can be motivated to think about what he must do to be believed. The child who is raised with many similar opportunities can, over time, construct for himself the conviction that it is best eventually for people to deal honestly with each other.[2]

The ultimate goal of developing autonomy in children is to have them regulate their own behavior and make decisions about good and bad, right and wrong (when they are mature enough to understand these concepts), and how they will behave in relation to themselves and others. Autonomous behavior can be achieved only when children consider other people's points of view, which can occur only if they are presented with viewpoints that differ from their own and are encouraged to consider them in deciding how they will behave. The ability to take another person's point of view is largely developmental. It is not until around age eight, when children become less egocentric, that they are able to decenter and see things from other people's points of view. Autonomy is reinforced when professionals and parents allow sufficient time and opportunities for children to practice and perform tasks for themselves. Independence is also nurtured when children are allowed to use problem-solving techniques and to learn from their mistakes.

Rewards and punishment tend to encourage children to obey others without helping them understand how their behavior was appropriate or inappropriate. Even more importantly, they have not had an opportunity to develop rules of conduct to govern their behavior. Children can be encouraged to regulate and be responsible for their own behavior through what Piaget referred to as "sanctions by reciprocity." These sanctions "are directly related to the act we want to sanction and to the adult's point of view, and have the effect of motivating the child to construct rules of conduct for himself, through the coordination of viewpoints."[3]

Examples of sanctions by reciprocity include exclusion from the group, when children have a choice of staying and behaving or leaving; taking away from children the materials or privileges they have abused, such as not allowing them to use certain materials while leaving open the opportunity to use them again if they express a desire to use them appropriately; and helping children fix things they have broken and clean up after themselves. A fine line separates sanctions by reciprocity and punishment. The critical ingredients that balance the scales on the side of reciprocity is your respect for children and your desire to help them develop autonomy rather than blind obedience.

PHYSICAL PUNISHMENT

Is it possible to guide children's behavior without punishment? More and more, early childhood professionals agree that it is. Whether parents and professionals should spank or paddle as a means of guiding behavior is an age-old controversy. Some parents spank their children, following a "No!" with a slap on the hand or a spank on the bottom. This form of punishment can be an effective means of controlling a child's behavior when used in moderation immediately following the misbehavior. Some parents and religious groups base their use of physical punishment on their religious beliefs. Yet, what some parents do with their child in the home is not acceptable for others to do outside the home, where spanking is considered an inappropriate form of guidance. In fact, in some places, such as Florida, physical punishment in child care programs is legislatively prohibited.

Several problems with spanking and other forms of physical punishment persist. First, physical punishment is generally ineffective in building behavior in children. Physical punishment does not show children what to do or provide them with alternative ways of behaving. Second, adults who use physical punishment are modeling physical aggression. They are, in effect, saying that it is permissible to use aggression in interpersonal relationships. Children who are spanked thus are more likely to use aggression with their peers. Third, spanking and physical punishment increase the risk of physical injury to the child. Spanking can be an emotionally charged situation, and the spanker can become too aggressive, overdo the punishment, and hit the child in vulnerable places. Fourth, parents, caregivers, and teachers are children's sources of security. Physical punishment takes away from and erodes the sense of security that children must have in order to function confidently in their daily lives. In short, the best advice regarding physical punishment is to avoid it; use nonviolent means for guiding children's behavior. For more information on Physical Punishment, see the online website (http://www.parentsplace.com).

In the long run, parents and early childhood professionals determine children's behavior. In guiding the behavior of children entrusted to their care, professionals and others must select procedures that are appropriate to their own philosophies and children's particular needs. Guiding children to help them develop their own internal system of behavior control benefits them more than a system that relies on external control and authoritarianism. Developing self-discipline in children should be a primary goal of all professionals.

TRENDS IN BEHAVIOR GUIDANCE

As we look toward the twenty-first century we can clearly see trends in to the guidance and discipline of young children. As an early childhood professional, you can expect to be involved in the following:

1. *Development of democratic learning environments.* In our efforts to help prepare all children to live effectively and productively in a democracy, we are placing increasing emphasis on giving students experiences that will help promote behavior associated with democratic living. As a result, more professionals are making efforts to run their

classrooms as democracies. The idea of teaching this behavior through classrooms that are miniature democracies is not new. John Dewey was an advocate of this approach and championed democratic classrooms as a way of promoting democratic living. However, running a democratic classroom is easier said than done. It requires a confident professional who believes it is worth the effort. Democratic learning environments require that students develop responsibility for their and others' behaviors and learning, that classrooms operate as communities, and that all children are respected and respectful of others.

2. *The use of character education as a means of promoting responsible behavior.* In Chapter 9 we discussed reasons for character education and its importance and role in the contemporary curriculum. Character education will continue to grow as a means of promoting fundamental behaviors early childhood professionals and society believe are essential for living in democratic society.

3. *Teaching civility.* Civil behavior and how to promote civility are of growing interest at all levels of society. The specific teaching of *civil behavior,* how to treat others well and in turn be treated well, is seen as essential for living well in contemporary society. At a minimum, civil behavior includes manners, respect, and the ability to get along with people of all races, cultures, and socioeconomic backgrounds.

4. *Early intervention.* We all know habits are hard to break and that a behavior once set is difficult to change. Early childhood professionals believe it is essential to help develop appropriate behaviors in the early years by working with parents and families to help them guide their children's behavior. Waiting to address delinquent behavior is much more costly than promoting right behavior from the beginning of children's lives.

As we have emphasized in this and other chapters, cognitive and social development and behavioral characteristics are interconnected. More early childhood professionals recognize that it does not make sense to teach children reading, writing, and arithmetic and not also teach them skills necessary for responsibly guiding their own behavior.

ACTIVITIES FOR FURTHER ENRICHMENT

1. List five advantages and disadvantages of using rewards to stimulate and reinforce desired behaviors.

2. What is the difference between *normal* behavior and *acceptable* behavior? Give an example of when normal behavior may not be acceptable and another when acceptable behavior may not be normal.

3. Observe an early childhood classroom. What reinforcement system (implicit or explicit) does the teacher use to operate the classroom? Do you think the teacher is aware of the systems of reinforcement in use?

4. Behavior modification is sometimes practiced by parents and early childhood professionals without their being aware of what they are doing or the processes they are using. Observe a mother–child relationship for examples of parental behavioral management. What rewards does she offer? What was the child's resultant behavior? After further observation, answer these questions for the early childhood professional–child relationship. In both situations, what are the ethical implications of the adult's actions?

5. Observe an early childhood classroom to see which behaviors earn the teacher's attention. Does the teacher pay more attention to positive or negative behavior? Why do you think the teacher does this?

6. Observe in a primary classroom and identify aspects of the physical setting and atmosphere that could influence classroom behavior. Can you suggest improvements?

7. List ten behaviors you think are desirable in toddlers, ten for preschoolers, and ten for kindergartners. For each behavior, give two examples of how you would encourage and promote development of that behavior.

8. Interview five parents of young children to determine what they mean when they use the word *discipline*. What implications might these definitions have for you if you were their children's teacher?

9. List five methods for guiding children's behavior. Tell why you think each is effective, and give examples.

10. Explain, with examples, why it is important for early childhood professionals and parents to agree on a philosophy of behavioral guidance.

READINGS FOR FURTHER ENRICHMENT

Gordon, A., and K. Browne. *Guiding Young Children in a Diverse Society* (Needham Heights, MA: Allyn & Bacon, 1996).

This book features an eclectic view of discipline. The authors provide a large range of theoretical perspectives as well as techniques and strategies drawn from all major models of discipline.

Marion, M. *Guidance of Young Children,* 4th ed. (Upper Saddle River, NJ: Merrill/Prentice Hall, 1995).

This book gives the reader a solid theory and research that will help in the understanding of the child guidance process.

Nelsen, Jane, Lynn Lott, and H. Stephen Glenn. *Positive Discipline in the Classroom* (Rocklin, CA: Prima, 1993).

Given the varied background of children and the many intrusive influences on the classroom, how can teachers foster the essential skills and attitudes for success in the students? This book addresses the popular concept of class meetings, where students and teachers discuss moral, ethical, and behavioral issues and work together to solve problems.

Reynolds, E. *Guiding Young Children: A Child-Centered Approach* (Mountain View, CA: Mayfield, 1996).

This text gives child care professionals practical problem-solving techniques that eliminate the use of blame, guilt, and punishment.

NOTES

1. United States Department of Justice, 1995. *Juvenile Arrests.* Internet address www.ncjrs.org/ojjhom.html.

2. Constance Kamii, *Number in Preschool and Kindergarten* (Washington, D.C.: National Association for the Education of Young Children, 1982), p. 23.

3. Ibid., p. 77.

Developing Curricula to Meet the Special Needs of Young Children

PART FOUR

The intellectual environments offered to children by today's cultures are poor in opportunities to bring their thinking about thinking into the open, to learn to talk about it and to test their ideas by externalizing them. Access to computers can dramatically change this situation.

Seymour Papert

317

Technology and Young Children

11

Education for the Information Age

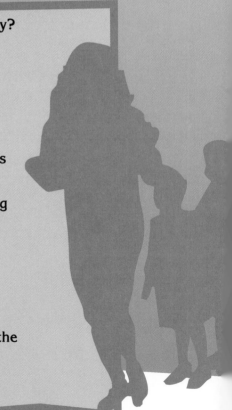

Focus Questions

1. How is technology important in contemporary society?

2. What is technological literacy and what are its implications for young children and early childhood professionals?

3. What is the role, place, and scope of technology in early childhood programs?

4. How does technology support and facilitate children's learning and thinking?

5. What is the role of assistive technology in supporting the learning of children with disabilities?

6. How does technology influence how early childhood professionals teach and how children learn?

7. What are critical issues relating to children's use of and involvement in technology?

8. What are the roles of professionals for providing for the developmentally appropriate use of technology?

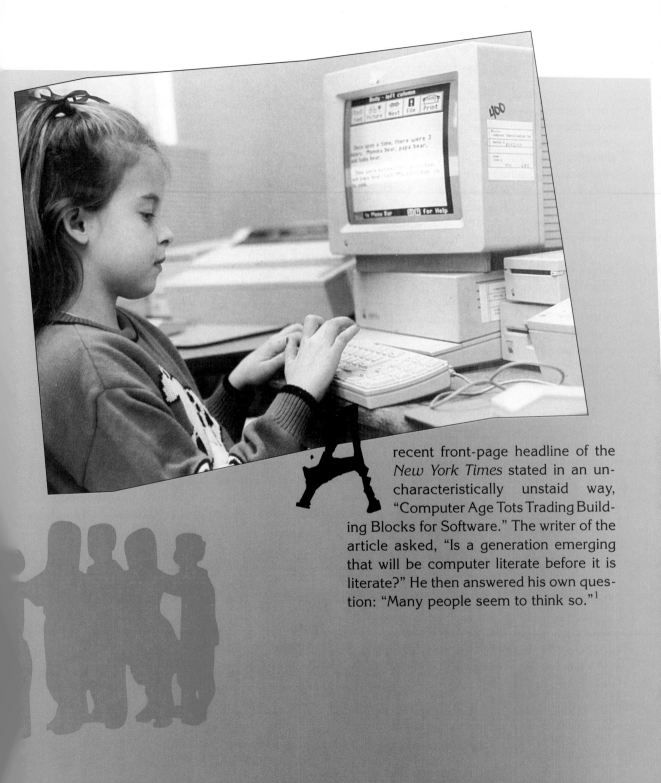

recent front-page headline of the *New York Times* stated in an uncharacteristically unstaid way, "Computer Age Tots Trading Building Blocks for Software." The writer of the article asked, "Is a generation emerging that will be computer literate before it is literate?" He then answered his own question: "Many people seem to think so."[1]

THE COMPUTER GENERATION

Children today are technological persons. Their growth and development consist of large doses of television, videos, electronic games, and computers in the home and shopping center. Every day, newspapers, television, and other forms of popular media chronicle the latest technological benefits to society. What once was exceptional is now commonplace. Computers were once huge, power-hungry machines that filled rooms the size of small houses. Today, powerful computers are small enough to sit on students' desks, and more and more students have laptop computers they easily carry back and forth from home to school. Tables 11.1 and 11.2 show children's computer use at home and school. Note how computer use varies by gender, culture, and socioeconomic background. These have serious implications for children, families, and professionals.

Home computing has grown in popularity during the 1990s. A host of computer manufacturers have introduced computers targeted for the home market. Manufacturers design software to entertain and educate adults and children at home. Publishers of educational software for school use now design many of their newest titles with families in mind as well.

John Dewey said that education is a process of living, not a process of preparing students for the future. Dewey's observation is as meaningful now as it was then. Early childhood professionals must incorporate computers and other technology into their programs and children's lives.

Technology: A Definition

Technology is the application of scientific, material, and human resources to the solution of human needs. Technology is of immense benefit to all humankind. Using this definition, technology goes beyond computers and video games. Part of children's becoming technologically literate requires that they have experiences with the full range of available technological resources.

Technology is applied to early childhood programs through computers, computer programs, television, videodiscs, tape recorders, cassettes, and assistive technology. These forms of technology have many teaching applications. Consequently, as an early childhood professional, you must consider the full range of technology that is

Table 11.1/*Children's Computer Use at Home*

Household Income	Prekindergarten and Kindergarten (%)	Grades 1 to 8 (%)	Grades 9 to 12 (%)
Less than $5,000	1.1	4.1	6.8
$5,000 to $9,999	0.9	4.5	6.8
$10,000 to $14,999	4.6	6.4	8.7
$15,000 to $19,999	6.9	10.9	14.1
$20,000 to $24,999	7.4	13.1	17.9
$25,000 to $29,999	12.3	19.3	22.0
$30,000 to $34,999	18.7	20.5	29.1
$35,000 to $39,999	13.0	26.3	28.1
$40,000 to $49,999	21.6	32.9	33.9
$50,000 to $74,999	25.5	45.3	46.4
$75,000 or more	38.2	62.3	61.0

Source: U.S. Department of Commerce, Bureau of the Census, 1994.

Table 11.2/*Children's Computer Use at School*

Group	Prekindergarten and Kindergarten (%)		Grades 1 to 8 (%)	
	1991	1993	1991	1993
Male	13.9	25.9	52.9	69.5
Female	15.6	26.5	51.7	68.4
White	17	29.4	58.4	73.7
Black	7.4	16.5	35.7	56.5
Hispanic	10.1	19.2	40.2	58.4

Source: U.S. Department of Commerce, Bureau of the Census, 1994.

applicable to your classroom, learning centers, and activities. You also must be conversant with technological terminology (Figure 11.1) if you wish to become technologically literate.

Technological Literacy

We cannot speak or think about technology as though it were apart from what goes on in the everyday world, and children are aware of this. Many children are very savvy about technology and its use. (Read how a

Computers are fast becoming a common part of the home environment. Many children come to school familiar with computers and other technology. Other children have very limited exposure. Professionals have to accept the challenge of meeting all children's technological needs.

Figure 11.1/*Glossary*

Bit: The smallest unit of information in a computer. It is an abbreviation for *binary digit.*

Byte: A string of eight bits. A byte represents a number or character. *K* is used to stand for 1,024 bytes. (*K* means 1,000.) *Megabyte* equals 1,000 K. (*Mega* means a million.) This designation is important because it is how the power of computers is determined. (*See also* RAM.)

CD-ROM (compact disc—read-only memory): A disk that looks like an audio CD. Includes color graphics, text, sound, and full-motion video.

Digital: Computers perform their operations with quantities represented by electronic digits (0s and 1s representing on and off) in the RAM memory.

Electronic bulletin board: Electronic networks in which people can leave messages for anyone accessing that network. Literally, electronic public bulletin boards.

E-mail: An electronic computer network that enables individuals to exchange information and create electronic ties with others. For example, my e-mail address is morrison@coefs.coe.unt.edu. Any person linked to the *Internet* (see definition) can communicate with me electronically through e-mail. E-mail and electronic bulletin boards are often linked together. As a result, persons can "post" notices on electronic bulletin boards and read the responses through their e-mail.

Floppy disk: A recordable, removable magnetic data storage device.

Hard disk: A sealed disk used to store data. It stores more information and runs (works) faster than a floppy disk. Hard disks come in many sizes, and the bigger the better, because much of today's software takes large amounts of disk space.

Hardware: The equipment of technology. Hardware includes computers, monitors, keyboards, VCR players, disk drives, mice, and printers.

Hypermedia: Software that enables the user to access or link to other media such as graphics, audio, video, animations, and so forth, through a process known as *branching.* For example, you could read a small biography on Mozart, click a button to hear a symphony, and click another button to read about the influence of his music on the film industry.

Interactive: When a person is communicating one-on-one with the computer. The person operating the computer gives the computer a command, the computer reacts, the operator gives another command, and so forth. An example of a *noninteractive* process is when the computer operator gives a command and the computer finishes the task, process, or program without further instructions from the operator. Typically, drill-type software for young children is considered noninteractive, or *passive.* An open-ended product, such as a software drawing program, would be considered interactive.

preschooler solved a teacher's computer problem in the vignette in Chap. 4, Box 4.1.)

As a society, we increasingly feel that *technological literacy,* the ability to understand and apply technology to meet personal goals, is as important as the traditional components of literacy—reading, writing, speaking, and listening. Advocates of technological literacy maintain that students need to be able to read and write online as well as with books and paper and pencil, that they need to speak on the phone and with voice mail and to participate in video conferencing as well as in face-to-face conversations, and that they must develop

Internet: A worldwide computer network that links nodes (computer systems) at participating government agencies, educational institutions, and commercial and private entities. The Department of Defense started the network in 1969. Today, the Internet consists of thousands and thousands of interconnected networks. Quite an electronic highway!

Megabyte: One million bytes.

Modem: Hardware, either internal or external, that connects to a telephone line and converts computer language to be sent over telephone lines. The modem transforms the computer's digital signals (0s and 1s) to analog signals (sound).

Mouse: An attachment that enables users to manipulate the cursor by hand—by moving the mouse and clicking a switch—rather than by using keyboard commands. A *trackball* performs the same function but is stationary.

Multimedia: The integration of still pictures, motion pictures, text, and sound with reading, writing, drawing, problem solving, searching, and creating. This definition is different from a common use of the word to mean the use of various media hardware such as television, computers, projectors, and so forth.

RAM: Acronym for *r*andom *a*ccess *m*emory, to cite how much memory a computer has (e.g., 640 K of RAM). RAM is important because software packages specify how many megabytes of RAM are required to run them.

Scanner: An input device that copies pictures and words into the computer by turning the visual representations (analog) into digital information that can be reproduced on the computer screen or printed.

Software: The programs, systems, data, games, and information that are stored on disks and tapes used in computers and other hardware.

Soundboard: Hardware, either built into the computer or an additional accessory, used to digitize speech or music.

Telecommunications: The process of using telephone lines and a computer(s) to communicate with another computer. *Satellite dishes* play an important role in telecommunications and in *distance learning*, that is, the delivery of classes in which the teacher is not physically present. Telecommunications, such as E-mail, involves a computer, modem, telephone line, and telecommunications software.

Virtual reality: A computer-based simulated environment that users seem to enter and that seems real for the participant.

skills in presenting their knowledge and products with multimedia. In fact, many educators fear that the United States may be creating a new class of illiterates—children who do not have access to computers and other technology and who do not know how to use and apply technology. Table 11.2 indicates that many children still do not use computers in the public schools, with African American children in particular using computers less than other children. It may be that students do not use computers because they do not have access to them and/or their teachers do not incorporate their use in curricula and activities.

The Technology of Teaching and Learning

Much of the application of technology to curriculum and instruction, especially as applied to children with special needs, is attributable to B. F. Skinner. Skinner introduced to education and teaching the concept of *programmed learning,* in which what students are to learn is programmed or arranged in a progressive series of small steps from simple or basic to complex. Students are rewarded or reinforced with the right answer after each small step, a concept in keeping with Skinner's belief that knowing that one has answered a question correctly (in other words, *positive feedback*) is a powerful motivating force.

Advantages of programmed learning are that learning is broken down into small, manageable units; when software based, students can use the program themselves; and students progress at their own rate. Today, software programs designed to teach colors, numbers, and numerous other concepts use many of Skinner's ideas. As students select a response, they are "rewarded" with the right answer, and, in many software programs, a voice responds saying, "Good job, [name of child]." In other programs, a musical tone or other sound signals a right answer. The software is programmed so that a right answer advances the program to the next frame, story, or problem. If the student responds incorrectly, the software is programmed to ask the same question again or provide a review scenario and ask another question. Well-written software provides for appropriate feedback, reinforcement of concepts, and review.

However, many early childhood professionals question whether Skinner's approach to learning is developmentally appropriate for young children, especially when applied to software programs as described here. They stress the need to avoid drill-type software and lessons, frequently referred to as "electronic ditto sheets." Rather, they advocate that children be involved in open-ended software that promotes discovery learning. Further, they stress that developmentally appropriate software enables children to be "in command" rather than being controlled by the software, as often happens in drill-type software.

COMPUTERS IN EARLY CHILDHOOD PROGRAMS

Computer literacy is knowledge about, understanding of, and the ability to use computers. Computer literacy also includes an understanding of the social and educational implications of computers; of the fact that computers play an important part in daily living and can help us learn. Computers are used for many different things and in many different ways. Children can explore and understand the way computers are used and can learn that people build and program them. Critical to computer literacy is a child's attitude toward computers and their applications. This feeling should be one of confidence and willingness to learn more about and become involved with computers and computer technology. Such an attitude comes naturally when children are involved in appropriate activities and software.

Three problems confront early childhood teachers in implementing an effective program of computer instruction: their personal acceptance of computers, decisions about how to use computers in early childhood programs and classrooms, and assuring themselves that computers do not have a negative influence on children. Teachers cannot afford to decide not to use computers and technology. When they do, they risk having technologically illiterate children; denying children access to skills, knowledge, and learning; and not promoting an attitude of acceptance of technology into their everyday lives. Rather, they must promote access to technology and develop creative ways to involve children.

Appropriate Use of Technology

Decisions about how to use technology in early childhood programs must always be based on developmentally appropriate practice. The NAEYC Position on Developmentally Appropriate Practice is found in Appendix C. Additionally, highlights of NAEYC's Position Statement on Technology and Young Children are found in Appendix D. Also, Figure 11.6 provides guidelines for evaluating children's software. It would be helpful for you to review these three resources now as a means of developing your awareness about the use of technology and as background for making decisions about how to best provide for the technological needs of children. As in all areas of the curriculum, it is you the professional who makes decisions about how and the extent to which children will be involved in activities that involve technology. Also, you will be called on every day to make decisions regarding the selection and use of technological resources and materials.

In addition to making curriculum decisions about the use of technology, professionals must also make decisions about instructional applications as well. Young children must be encouraged and facilitated in the use of technology. Some children will need more help and encouragement than others, and some will intrinsically want to be more involved because of their learning style preference for using technology to learn. You will want to take children's individual differences into account when making decisions about how to best involve them in learning activities with computers and other technology.

Another consideration in your use of computers with young children is how to best arrange the classroom to make computers an integrated part of the program and ensure they are available and accessible to children. An important part of the classroom environment is the comfort level children have with computers. One way to demonstrate that computers are an important part of the classroom is for early childhood teachers to use and be involved with computers. You can demonstrate your own comfort and confidence in using computers in the classroom. As you use computers to access information through the Internet, send e-mail, and keep records of children's accomplishments, children will come to understand that computers are a natural part of the process of schooling and learning.

Computers and other technology have had and will continue to have a dramatic impact on young children, early childhood professionals, and the profession. In order for this impact to be productive and meaningful, four factors are essential:

- Early childhood teachers must be aware of the potential benefits of computers and technology.

- Early childhood professionals must be open to the use of technology to help children learn new knowledge and skills.

- Early childhood teacher education and staff development programs must provide training in how to integrate technology into all areas of the early childhood curriculum.

- Early childhood programs must make computers available to all teachers and programs.[2]

Four interesting processes are apparent in the growth of technological applications in early childhood programs. First, computer technology is being used in unique ways to help children learn. Second, more hardware and software is used to assist professionals to help children learn. Third, early childhood professionals are embracing technology as a way of helping them *manage* instruction, keep records, report to parents, and communicate with colleagues and other professionals. For example, some teachers and children keep a daily computer record of each child's activities, achievement, and progress. This is used as one basis for planning, assessment, and reporting to parents. Software packages are also available that help professionals build portfolios for each child.

Fourth, technology can help children with special needs learn and can help their teachers teach. Technology helps children with vision impairments see and children with physical disabilities read and write. Technology helps developmentally delayed children learn the skills they need to achieve at their appropriate levels and enables children with disabilities to substitute one ability for another and receive the special training they need. Technology permits children with special needs to enjoy, through the process of learning, knowledge, skills, and behaviors that might otherwise be inaccessible to them. Technology *empowers* children with special needs; that is, it enables them to exercise control over their lives and the conditions of their learning. It enables them to do things previously thought impossible.

In addition, technology changes people's attitudes about children with disabilities. For example, some may view children with disabilities as not being able to participate fully in regular classrooms, they may now recognize that instead of being segregated in separate programs, these children can be fully included with the assistance of technology.

Different educators have varying approaches to and philosophies of facilitating and promoting children's learning through computers. In the Program in Action, "Writing to Read," children are involved in learning literacy through the use of a somewhat structured approach. The computer and software are seen as a central element of teachers teaching and children learning. On the other hand, in the Program in Action, "The Computer-Enriched Kindergarten," computers are seen as a means of providing open-ended discovery learning, problem solving, and computer competence.

BOX 11.1 The Pros and Cons of Computers in Early Childhood Programs

Using technology in the classroom with young children is still open for debate. The advantages of using computer technology in the classroom must be weighed against the resources available, the appropriateness of the media, and the way computers are used in the classroom. Before integrating computers into classroom instruction, early childhood teachers must reflect on the following issues:

- Will instructional programming come from computers located within the classroom or from a centrally located computer somewhere else in the building?
- What is the cost of the computers weighed against the educational benefits?
- What software programs are appropriate for young children?
- How can the technology be utilized to enhance the effectiveness of your classroom planning, management, and instruction?
- How should computer use be scheduled for young children; how much time should children spend using the computers?
- How do you provide a balance of instruction using computers and more traditional teaching practices?
- How can you provide low-income children with computer experience that will decrease the gap between children who have or do not have access to a computer at home?

The following is a list of arguments supporting or opposing the use of computers in the classroom. You as an early childhood professional need to address these issues when initiating plans for computer use in classrooms designed for young children:

	Advantages	Disadvantages
The influence of technology on preoperational children's *cognitive* development	• Computers can provide meaningful experiences for children, often in ways not possible with concrete materials or in real life. For example, children can fly in a plane or see what it is like to live in an environment that gets a lot of snow. • Through using open-ended software, activities are self-chosen by children and are therefore enjoyable and more meaningful. • Children can manipulate things on the computer in an endless number of ways. • Children receive immediate feedback for their efforts and experimentation on the computer. • Cognitive conflict results out of experimentation with open-ended software. • On the computer, if something does not turn out how the child wants it, he can "undo" it and continue experimenting. • Children are highly motivated to interact with the computer and deem what they are doing as play. Such motivation and enjoyment lead to persistance with tasks and a higher level of skill mastery than children who believe the activities they are doing is "work." • When children work in groups on the computer, conflict often arises that spurs children to create rules to govern their play and turn-taking behavior. Vygotsky believed that optimum levels of cognitive growth occur in such situations when children have cultural interaction with media and peers in a situation surrounding conflict.	• The use of the computer will not provide the preoperational child with hands-on experiences, opportunities to interact with concrete materials, or meaningful learning and may actually conflict with assimilation and accommodation of new information in a child's cognitive processing. • Computers are an abstract tool. Young children would be better off spending their time manipulating concrete tools and materials.
The influence of technology on preoperational children's *social* development	• The computer can be used by individuals, pairs, or groups. More and more software is being developed that encourages more than one person to participate in computer games and activities.	• The computer is better suited for solitary activities. Children will be substituting time they could spend interacting with adults and peers for time spent in isolation.

continued

	Advantages	Disadvantages
	Children are very social and will want to have their peers around them as they work. • Because of the high level of interest in the computer and the high ratio of students to computers in the class-room today, students will want and ask to share the computer. • As children work together using computer-assisted instruction (CAI) or open-ended software, conflict and differing perspectives often emerge. As children work through their problems of how to share the computer fairly, who gets to do what, and the deci-sions about how things should be done, they are developing social skills in areas of conflict resolution, problem solving, rule making, social equality, supply and demand, and compromis-ing for the good of the group. • The computer can serve as a media tool to aid children in their Interactions with others and with information. • The computer plays a significant role in our current social matrix. Children should be familiar with forces that are driving our society.	• Children will gain no social skills from time spent on the computer.
The appropriate-ness of using high-tech computers with children	• As computers have increased their level of sophistication, they have become easier for everyone to use, including young children. • Turning the computer on and choos-ing the software to run has become so simple that a child as young as three years of age can do this without assis-tance. The mouse is also easy to manipulate and children become profi-cient with this quickly. • Computer programs for young chil-dren are designed so reading and writing skills are not necessary. Chil-dren learn which buttons and icons to click in one or two sessions in order to achieve the outcomes they desire.	• Computers are complicated, techni-cal pieces of equipment. Therefore, children cannot and should not oper-ate them.

	Advantages	Disadvantages
	• Parents, teachers, caregivers, and peers can provide the scaffold for young children, supplying them with aid and assistance to successfully have more advanced interactions with the computer.	
	• The computer and early childhood software can serve as a scaffold in itself. For example, "Living Books" software programs read books to children that they are not able to read to themselves. Additionally, children who do word processing on the computer are not held back by their fine-motor limitations.	
	• Computers can be used in appropriate, nonstressful ways that do not set inappropriately high expectations. As with anything else in our lives, it is often not the tool itself that is inappropriate, but the way in which the tool is used. Positive cognitive growth will occur when children are given appropriate software to use.	
The concerns associated with introducing children to the Internet	• The Internet provides children with access to a wealth of information they may not otherwise be able to acquire.	• Children should not have access to the computer, and specifically the Internet, due to information available on the Internet that is inappropriate for young children.
	• The Internet can be used even when the library is closed.	• E-mail should not take the place of more traditional forms of communication. Attention must be given to handwriting, traditional letter writing, and verbal communication.
	• Filters are available that provide parents with controls to "block out" inappropriate information found on the Internet.	
	• Children can communicate with others easily through the use of e-mail and chat rooms designed for them.	

Contributed by Christi Turner, graduate assistant, University of North Texas, Denton, TX.

Multicultural Technology

The United States is a changing society. By 2010, one-third of all U.S. youth will live in California, Florida, Texas, and New York. In Texas and California, 57 percent of these youth will be nonwhite; in New York and Florida, 53 percent.[3] What are the implications of the growing multicultural nature of the United States? One is that the *appropriate* use of technology can help promote children's literacy development, especially the learning of both English and their native language. Technology has to do more than provide children skills they can use in shopping center arcades and on home video games. It has to help students learn the social, language, and cognitive skills they need for successful learning and living.

PROGRAM IN ACTION

WRITING TO READ (*VOY A LEÉR ESCRIBIENDO*)

Writing to Read is a computer-based reading and writing program for kindergarten and first grade students. Combining technology with educational techniques, Writing to Read is based on the assumption that children best learn to read by being taught how to write. With this program, young children learn to write what they can say and read stories they have written. The program builds on a child's natural language growth, which typically includes a 2,000- to 4,000-word vocabulary when entering kindergarten. In many traditional programs, the kindergartner is expected to learn to read only six to eight words, but in Writing to Read, the child is able to write any word in his or her vocabulary.

Methods and Expectations

This instructional method builds writing and reading skills before a youngster has mastered all the complexities of spelling. A phonemic spelling system is used in which the sounds of spoken English are represented by a selected set of forty-two phonemes. To learn these phonemes, five learning stations are provided that address visual, auditory, and tactile modalities. Once children have learned these phonemes, they can write anything they can say, including such motivating words as *tyrannosaurus rex, boa constrictor,* and *skateboarding.* A distinction is made between invented and standard spelling, but while in the Writing to Read Center, children spell words the way they sound without worrying about correct spelling. Children make a natural transition to conventional spelling as they read standard spelling in textbooks and literature. Five learning stations work together to provide an active and motivating learning environment: Computer, Work Journal, Writing/ Typing, Listening Library, and Make Words.

Educators expect several specific outcomes for children involved in this program. First, children become fluent and productive writers. Students are expected to write words, sentences, or stories every day while in the center. By the end of first grade, a number of children are writing multi-

chapter books. Children become confident about their writing ability, and writing becomes a part of their basic repertoire of skills at a very young age.

Program Sequence

We will follow a typical kindergarten child during her daily hour in the Writing to Read Center. Cecilia is in a class of thirty-three kindergarten children in South Bay Union School District, located in California on the Mexican border. The district has a substantial percentage of low-income, single-parent families, as well as a high level of limited English-speaking students. (Students who are being taught in Spanish participate in the Spanish version of Writing to Read, Voy a Leér Escribiendo, or VALE.) Cecilia began the program in December after a two-week orientation.

Learning Stations   The Writing to Read Center is located in a separate room not far from the kindergarten. I had already passed out the small books called Work Journals to all the children in the classroom before they entered the center. Children have been assigned their first station while in the classroom, and they proceed directly to that station to begin work. Cecilia and her partner John have been assigned first to the Computer station. Ms. Allas, the lab assistant, has already loaded the correct disk into the computer. At this station, Cecilia will work with her partner while responding to instructions given by the computer "voice." The computer will instruct the partners to say and type the sounds of one of the thirty words, called "cycle words," included in the lesson. Cecilia works at this station for approximately fifteen minutes, which provides enough repetition to learn the sounds in a cycle word such as *cat.*

After Cecilia and John have completed their work at this station, they proceed to the Work Journal station. Here they listen to a taped lesson that reinforces the sounds they have just learned. They write sounds and words in their Work Journal. After the partners have completed the Work Journal station, they are free to choose their next station. An important goal of the Writing to Read program is to help children become responsible for their own learning.

Cecilia decides she would like to write something on the computer today, so she goes to the typing section of the Writing/Typing station, which contains eight word processors. She finds her own story disk and loads it into the computer. She recently had a birthday and wants to write about the ring she received as a gift. Cecilia is a very independent kindergartner and writes her story without assistance. When she has finished, she prints her story on the printer, removes her disk, and puts it away.

The next stop is the Writing Table, where Cecilia proudly reads her story to me. Cecilia receives a lot of specific praise for her creation (see Figure A).

Cecilia has just enough time to go to the Make Words station, where she can select manipulatives (hands-on learning materials) to form words. Today she chooses letter stamps and a stamp pad to write her mom a note. She stamps "I love you, Mom" and draws lots of hearts around the edge of the paper.

There are usually groans when I signal that it is time to clean up the center to go back to the classroom. Children, while actively learning, also have a great deal of fun.

Tomorrow, when the class comes to Writing to Read, Cecilia will probably be assigned to the Listening Library station because she did not have time to go to that station today. There she will listen to high-quality children's literature (written by famous authors) while tracking the story in a book. This process helps reinforce the sound-symbol relationship in context and teach standard spelling because children see correct spelling in the books. Cecilia will also have a chance to go to the Writing Table, which is part of the Writing/Typing Station. Here, she will work with pencil and paper while I encourage her writing.

Figure A/*Cecilia's Story*

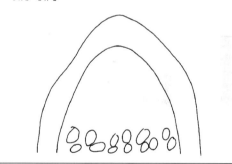

I see many strengths in the Writing to Read program. First, it provides for all the readiness levels of the students in my kindergarten class by encouraging developmentally appropriate activities that can be adjusted to meet students' needs. Self-esteem is enhanced because children are not categorized into high, middle, and low groups, and they develop a "can-do" attitude. Children can progress and review at their own rate because the computer allows for individualized learning.

Contributed by Kathie W. Dobberteen, former kindergarten teacher, South Bay Union School District, Imperial Beach, California.

Second, school districts are searching for ways to teach basic skills to an increasingly diverse population of students. Increasingly, they look to technology for ways to achieve their goals of literacy learning for all children and their families. They are collaborating with computer companies to develop hardware and software to assist them in this task.

Bilingual Education Technology

The Florida Department of Education, the Dade County, Florida, Public Schools, and the Jostens Learning Corporation in San Diego, California, cooperatively developed "Technology-Assisted Language Learning for K–12 ESOL Students." The program was designed so it would also be appropriate for English for Speakers of Other Languages (ESOL) programs across the nation. Total development cost of this program exceeded $6 million.

One part of this program is designed to help Spanish-speaking students in kindergarten and primary grades become fluent in English. It introduces them to the sounds and rhythms of the English language through literature, rhymes, and songs. Eight thematic units include on- and off-line activities that work together to help nonindependent and beginning-level students acquire the basic vocabulary and concepts they need to succeed in the English-speaking classroom. These units use animation, full-color graphics, sound, role plays, games, small-group activities, and collaborative groups. Figure 11.2 depicts the contents of the K–3 component and shows the steps to English language development.

Such collaborative efforts between a software company and school districts are commonplace. Whereas the bilingual/multicultural software market was once somewhat ignored, businesses now realize there is growing need for programs and software to meet the needs of a diverse population.

Technology and Children with Special Needs

Computer technology is a valuable tool to those who work with children with special needs. A child with cerebral palsy speaks his first words by choosing words on a communication speech board that is under his control. A speech synthesizer then pronounces the words. Deaf children learn to hear as speech vibrations are transformed into tactile patterns they can feel. An autistic child, assumed to be deaf and without speech, speaks her first words after manipulating the Logo turtle. (*Logo* is a programming language developed for children that enables them to produce screen graphics.)

The number of such applications grows daily. For example, the 1995 Lekotek *Software Resource Guide* lists over three hundred sixty software programs suited for children aged two through fourteen with mental, physical, behavioral, sensory, and learning disabilities.[4] The guide is available from the publisher, the National Lekotek Center, 2100 Ridge Ave., Evanston, IL 60201; 847-328-0001.

Assistive Technology Assistive technology covers a range of products and applications. Figures 11.3, 11.4, and 11.5 illustrate some of the applications of assistive technology in early childhood settings. In Figure 11.3 we see how alternative keyboards can be used to emulate joystick and mouse inputs. The large keyboard in front of the girl is used to produce up, down, left, and right cursor movement and mouse button action.

Assistive technology for children with special needs ranges from such simple devices as adaptive spoons and switch-adapted, battery-operated toys to complex devices such as computerized interactive language systems. Single switches, the most common, are used with software that scans available options. All the child needs to do is hit the switch. There are all kinds of switches, such as pads, puff, and eyebrow (see Figure 11.4). Figure 11.5

Technology Programs in Action
Teaching and Learning with Computers

The Alexander D. Henderson University School

Technology is rapidly changing the way we conduct our daily lives. School systems across the country are incorporating technology into their instructional programs for young children. The Alexander D. Henderson University School, a K–8 public school in Boca Raton, Florida, is the perfect example of the successful incorporation of computers to foster learning. Learning at this school is accomplished through a series of related computer activities that involve all the child's senses. The program is called "Teach-

ing and Learning with Computers," or TLC, and is a complete instructional model. At Henderson, students first encounter computers in kindergarten.

In Elaine Lewis's kindergarten class, students work with the literacy program *Writing to Read 2000*, which includes using books and audio tapes. They also spend time in a "Make Words" center that contains tactile letters of plastic and felt or stencils for creating letters and words.

c–1

The program at this stage is a useful diagnostic tool. Lewis says she often observes children as they work at the various centers to see eye-hand coordination, audio discrimination, and if they are following directions.

In the first grade and higher, the TLC program expands to include science and mathematics programs as well. The incorporation of computers in these grades is more comprehensive.

Suzanne Sturrock, one of Henderson's first grade teachers, says her children are in learning centers all day. In the morning, she talks to the whole class for about thirty minutes to review what they did the day before. Then the students form small groups and begin moving through the room's five centers. At the end of the rotation, everyone gathers to talk about what they have done. At this point Sturrock evaluates the effectiveness of the tasks and assigns enrichment or review tasks for students as needed.

Additionally, Sturrock likes the integrated nature of the program, which addresses social, educational, and technological learning skills simultaneously. "It seems to meet the needs of all children by using a variety of activities. I can remediate slower learners and provide enrichment for gifted ones," she says. As the children progress through each grade, the program grows and changes with them to suit their needs. The technology component in the program provides an element of recency other educational materials cannot maintain.

Contributed by Barbara Bittner, Director, Alexander D. Henderson University School, Boca Raton, Florida; photos supplied by International Business Machines Corporation.

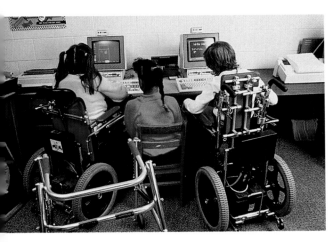

VistaKids Computer Literacy Program

Hispanics consider education one of the keys to the future. Unfortunately, report after report reveals the high school dropout rate and underachievement of Hispanic children. One solution to these problems is the VistaKids program. It is designed to boost the reading, writing, and math skills of low-income Hispanic children and improve their sense of competence and self-esteem through the use of computers.

Another issue facing Hispanic children is technological literacy. Research shows that Hispanic children are less likely to have access to computers than their non-Hispanic counterparts. Technological literacy is a primary goal of VistaKids.

VistaKids is a project sponsored by VISTA magazine in collaboration with SER-Jobs for

Progress, a nonprofit educational and employment training organization serving Hispanics.

The VistaKids program is located at Shenandoah Elementary School in Miami, Florida, an innercity school with an enrollment of 1,295 students in grades 1 through 5. (The pre-K and kindergarten children are in a satellite facility at a nearby middle school.) The school serves many recently arrived families from Cuba, Nicaragua, Guatemala, and El Salvador. When the children enter school, they speak little if any English. Most are eligible for free breakfast and lunch programs.

The VistaKids program is an after-school program that begins at 2:00 P.M. and runs until 5 P.M. The children in the 2 P.M. to 3 P.M. class ride the buses home. The children in the 3 P.M. to 5 P.M. classes are in the after-school child care program. The program also operates on Saturday from 10 A.M. to noon, and the parents are actively involved in bringing their children, learning to assist in the program, and learning the value their English fluency plays in their children's lives. Parents also realize the importance of learning English and supporting their children's English use in out-of-home settings.

Enrollment in VistaKids is open to all children. However, space and the number of computers are limited, so only 60 children are enrolled at one time. Approximately 240 children are served throughout the school year. Enrollment is based on a child's English for Speakers of Other Languages (ESOL) level. All children in VistaKids are at the lowest ESOL level, which means they do not know enough English to get by.

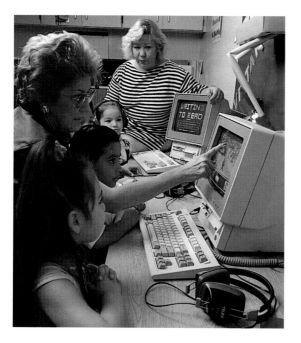

is to make sure that all kids enrolled in the program enter third grade at the level of learning at least equal to that of their more affluent Anglo counterparts." And Teresa continues, "The results so far have been outstanding and even beyond our expectations. The minds of those recently arrived children are like sponges, and it is incredible how much and how fast they learn under the proper learning environment. We are very encouraged and feel confident that VistaKids is a program that is making a difference."

Children such as Licet Ramirez, Carlos Ortiz, Jeanette Martinez, and Katrine Arauz are enthusiastic about the program, too. As Carlos says, "I want to come all the time." Katrine has bigger plans: "I want my parents to get me a computer so I can work at home!"

Principal Maria Llerena wishes there were more space and more computers and says, "When our young students join the VistaKids program, they begin to see school as a positive place to be, and they soon realize that learning can be fun."

Used with permission of VISTA magazine, 999 Ponce de Leon Blvd., Coral Gables, Florida; photos by Michael Upright.

Becky Bolivar, director of the program, and eight aides work with the children after school and on Saturdays. As Becky explains, "To promote comprehension and to help the children to become English-proficient as soon as possible, we avoid translating into Spanish, and the VistaKids program is entirely in English."

Teresa Estrada, a VISTA director and the driving force behind the program, explains: "When underprivileged immigrant children start the early grades with practically no knowledge of English because in most cases they do not even hear English at home, unless they get some specialized attention at school, they are likely to fall well behind their learning potential. If the trend continues beyond third grade, it becomes in many cases a hopeless situation, and by the time they enter high school they are at-risk students very likely to drop out. The objective of our program

Figure 11.2/*Steps to English Language Development*

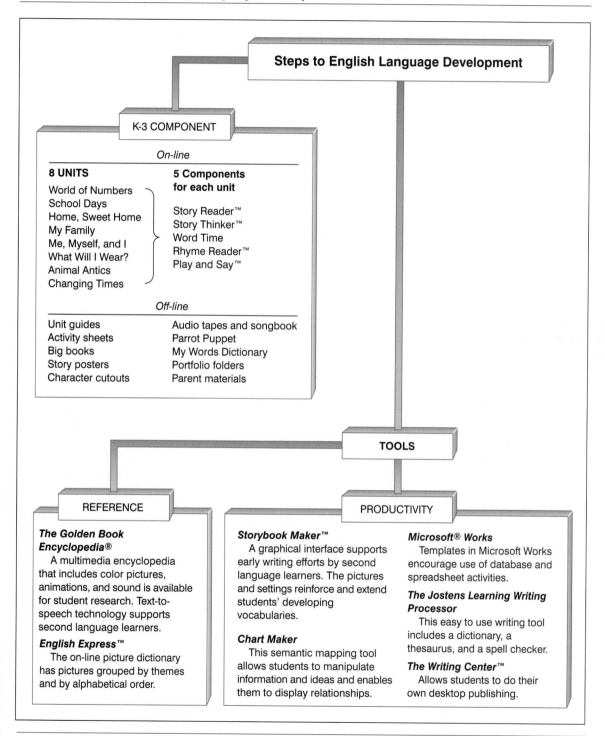

Steps to English Language Development

K-3 COMPONENT

On-line

8 UNITS
World of Numbers
School Days
Home, Sweet Home
My Family
Me, Myself, and I
What Will I Wear?
Animal Antics
Changing Times

**5 Components
for each unit**

Story Reader™
Story Thinker™
Word Time
Rhyme Reader™
Play and Say™

Off-line

Unit guides
Activity sheets
Big books
Story posters
Character cutouts

Audio tapes and songbook
Parrot Puppet
My Words Dictionary
Portfolio folders
Parent materials

TOOLS

REFERENCE

***The Golden Book
Encyclopedia®***
A multimedia encyclopedia
that includes color pictures,
animations, and sound is available
for student research. Text-to-
speech technology supports
second language learners.

English Express™
The on-line picture dictionary
has pictures grouped by themes
and by alphabetical order.

PRODUCTIVITY

Storybook Maker™
A graphical interface supports
early writing efforts by second
language learners. The pictures
and settings reinforce and extend
students' developing
vocabularies.

Chart Maker
This semantic mapping tool
allows students to manipulate
information and ideas and enables
them to display relationships.

Microsoft® Works
Templates in Microsoft Works
encourage use of database and
spreadsheet activities.

***The Jostens Learning Writing
Processor***
This easy to use writing tool
includes a dictionary, a
thesaurus, and a spell checker.

The Writing Center™
Allows students to do their
own desktop publishing.

Source: Courtesy of Jostens Learning, 9920 Pacific Heights Blvd., Suite 500, San Diego, California 92121-4330. Used by permission.

Figure 11.3/*Emulators for Joystick and Mouse. (a) The joystick and mouse shown require a certain amount of manual dexterity. So other devices, such as the emulator boards shown in (b) and (c), enable a child to achieve the same purpose possible with a mouse or joystick.*

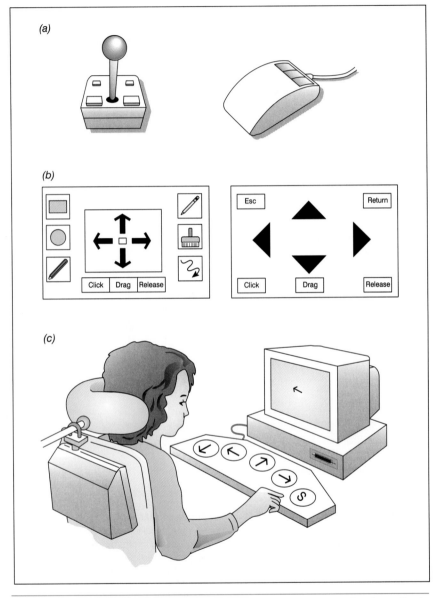

Source: Gregory Church and Sharon Glennen, *The Handbook of Assistive Technology* (San Diego: Singular Publisher Group, 1992), p. 150. Used by permission.

shows how professionals can create and use activity choice boards to help children learn how to make selections and take turns.

The field of early childhood education is undergoing dramatic changes through integration with the field of special education. As a result, early childhood professionals are adopting assistive technology to help children and their families. Opportunities for using many forms of technology are available to very young children, from birth to age three. Some of these include powered mobility,

Figure 11.4/*Switches for Children with Paralysis. Eye blinks activate (a), the switch, (b), a sip-and-puff switch, and (c) a muscle tension switch.*

Source: Gregory Church and Sharon Glennen, *The Handbook of Assistive Technology* (San Diego: Singular Publisher Group, 1992), p. 181. Used by permission.

335

Figure 11.5/*Play Activity Choice Boards*

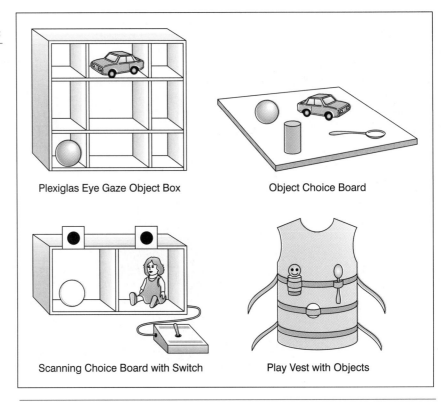

Plexiglas Eye Gaze Object Box

Object Choice Board

Scanning Choice Board with Switch

Play Vest with Objects

Source: Gregory Church and Sharon Glennen, *The Handbook of Assistive Technology* (San Diego: Singular Publisher Group, 1992), p. 186. Used by permission.

myoelectric prostheses, and communication devices. Infants as young as three months have interacted with computers, eighteen-month-old children have driven powered mobility devices and used myoelectric hands, and two-year-olds have talked via speech synthesizers. Children with severe physical disabilities learn how to use switches and scanning techniques.

Technology is particularly important for children with disabilities who depend on and need assistive technology to assist them to communicate, learn, and be mobile. Public Law 100–407, the Technology Related Assistance for Individuals with Disabilities Act of 1988, defines *assistive technology* as "any item, device or piece of equipment that is used to increase, maintain, or improve the functional abilities of persons with disabilities."[5]

An extremely important issue in the use of assistive technology with young children is the appropriateness of such technology. It is considered appropriate if it meets the following criteria:

First, a technology should respond to (or anticipate) specific, clearly defined goals that result in enhanced skills for the child.

Second, a technology should be compatible with practical constraints, such as available resources or the amount of training required to enable the child, his family, and the early childhood educator to use the technology.

Third, a technology should result in desirable and sufficient outcomes. Some basic considerations for children with disabilities are related to (1) ease of training the child and his family to use and care for the technology; (2) reasonable maintenance and repair, with regard to time and expense; and (3) monitoring of the technology's effectiveness.[6]

Assistive technology enables children with disabilities to participate in regular classrooms and to learn skills and behaviors not previously thought possible. Technology will play an even greater role in children's learning in the years to come.

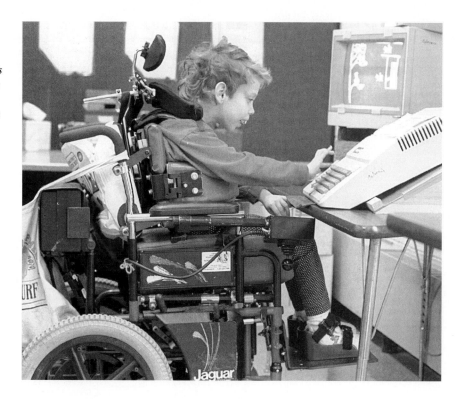

The mere application of technology is therefore not enough. Early childhood professionals have to be sensitive to the above criteria as they work with children, families, and other professionals in applying technology to learning settings and children's special needs.

Software for Young Children

The quantity and quality of software for children is growing. More children are coming "online" as part of their learning to read, write, and compute.

Not all software is good software. Good teachers have always evaluated the materials they use with their children. Now they must also assess the software that children use. Figure 11.6 provides one set of evaluative criteria that teachers may use. Table 11.3 lists examples of software deemed exceptional by Susan Haugland, one of the developers of the Haugland/Shade Developmental Scale shown in Figure 11.6.

Integrated Learning Systems

Integrated learning systems (ILS's) are networked systems that present groups of children with lessons on their individual computers from programs of lessons and activities stored in a central computer. They are frequently criticized as electronic workbooks with an emphasis on rote learning. As Clements and his colleagues point out, "Evaluations of these systems show moderate effect on basic skill; however, one must question other aspects of ILS's, especially diminished teacher and learner control. In too many cases ILS's represent a triumph of bureaucratic efficiency over young children's development."[7]

Proponents, however, maintain that contemporary versions are more sophisticated,

Figure 11.6/*Haugland/*
Shade Developmental
Scale, Revised Edition

HAUGLAND/SHADE DEVELOPMENTAL SCALE
REVISED EDITION

Title [   ] Ages [   ]
Publisher [   ] Cost [   ]
Date Evaluated [   ] Hardware Eval. On [   ] Updated [   ]
Evaluated by [   ] Multiple Platforms [   ] Copyright [   ]

Description

[   ]

Comments

PICTURE

[   ]

Age Appropriate [   ] ☐ Realistic Concepts
                             ☐ Appropriate Methods

Child in Control [   ] ☐ Actors not Reactors
                             ☐ Can Escape
                             ☐ Children Set Pace
                             ☐ Trial & Error

Clear Instructions [   ] ☐ Picture Choices
                               ☐ Simple, Precise Directions
                               ☐ Verbal Instructions

Expanding Complexity [   ] ☐ Low Entry, High Ceiling
                                 ☐ Learning Sequence is Clear
                                 ☐ Teaches Powerful Ideas

Independence [   ] ☐ Adult Supervision Not Needed After Initial Exposure

Non-Violence [   ] ☐ Software is free of violent characters and actions
                         ☐ Software models positive social values

Process Orientation [   ] ☐ Discovery Learning, Not Skill Drilling
                                ☐ Intrinsic Motivation
                                ☐ Process Engages, Product Secondary

Real World Model [   ] ☐ Concrete Representations
                             ☐ Objects Function
                             ☐ Simple, Reliable Model

Technical Features [   ] ☐ Animation
                               ☐ Colorful
                               ☐ Installs Easily
                               ☐ Operates Consistently
                               ☐ Prints
                               ☐ Realistic Corresponding Sound Effects or Music
                               ☐ Runs Quickly
                               ☐ Saves Children's Work
                               ☐ Uncluttered Realistic Graphics

Transformations [   ] ☐ Objects and Situations Change
                            ☐ Process Highlighter

Multiple Languages [   ] ☐ Multiple Languages

Universal Focus [   ] ☐ Universal Focus

Mixed Gender and Role Equity [   ] ☐ Mixed Gender and Role Equity
                                         ☐ Exempt

People of Diverse Cultures [   ] ☐ People of Diverse Cultures
                                       ☐ Exempt

Differing Ages and Abilities [   ] ☐ Differing Ability or Age
                                         ☐ Exempt

Diverse Family Styles [   ] ☐ Diverse Family Styles
                                  ☐ Exempt

Subscore [   ]
Anti-Bias [   ]
TOTAL [   ]

Source: Revised by Susan W. Haugland, director, Kids Interacting with Developmental Software, Department of Human Environmental Sciences, Southeast Missouri State University, Cape Girardeau, Missouri. Used by permission.

Table 11.3/*Haugland's 1996 Developmental Software Awards, Ages 3 to 8*

Category	Software	Publisher
Creativity	Name: Blocks in Motion Desc: An extensive shape builder program full of drawing, building, and movement options. Numerous background templates included such as Arctic trek, Middle Ages, rain forest, and space. Children can type text related to their creation.	Don Johnson
Language	Name: Stanley's Sticker Stories Desc: Children animate stories, write text, and/or create alphabet and counting books. They select from 300 stickers to compose their stories, record sounds, and/or write words and sentences.	Edmark Corp
Math and Science	Name: Math Keys: Unlocking Probability Desc: Software provides "hands-on" learning experiences focusing on the laws of probability. Children explore coins, spinners, cubes, marbles, and/or play three games: Crazy Creatures, Change Crossing, and Cloud Hop. After finishing a problem, children write about their findings.	MECC
Thematic Focus	Name: Let's Explore the Airport with Buzzy Desc: Children explore 40 locations at the airport. They investigate the ticket counter, the cockpit, the parking garage, the baggage processing area, the rental car area, etc. A functioning microworld in which children control their computer experiences.	Humongous Entertainment

Source: Provided courtesy of Susan W. Haugland. Used by permission.

with graphics and lessons that pace each individual's learning. The popularity of ILS's seems to be growing. For example, in 1994, the Palm Beach County, Florida, school district spent $25 million to install 7,500 computer work stations in the district's seventy-five elementary schools. This project, in conjunction with Computer Curriculum Corporation, represents the largest installation of a computer-based learning system in the nation. The software, Success Maker™, includes full-motion video, animation, computer graphics, and digitized sound to provide an interactive learning environment in mathematics, reading, language arts, writing, science, and life skills.

Other Technological Applications

Synthesizers   During the 1990s, technology has had an expanding impact on music education. New technologies, such as the synthesizer, help children learn music better. Synthesizers are capable of producing sounds from 120 different instruments and contain many songs built into the system. A synthesizer makes it possible to easily teach many skills, such as instrument recognition, and gives children the ability to play simple melodies.

CD-ROM   A CD-ROM disc is exactly like an audio compact disc; it is made of aluminum with an acrylic cover. Data are recorded as tiny pits in tracks in the aluminum layer and are read by a laser beam reflecting off those pits. About 660 megabytes fit on one disk, which corresponds to more than 250,000 typed pages! A new technology, DVD, promises storage capacities ranging from 4.7 to 17 *gigabytes* (one gigabyte equals one thousand megabytes) on the same size disc.[8]

PROGRAM IN ACTION

THE COMPUTER-ENRICHED KINDERGARTEN

It is time to begin the day, and twenty energetic five-year-olds sit cross-legged on the group-time rug. "Our calendar person today is Sharla!" Nancy Edwards, master teacher of the University of Delaware kindergarten, announces. With Nancy's guidance, Sharla announces the day and date and determines from the month's calendar pattern the color of today's square. "Pink, white, red, red, pink, white, red, red," Sharla points to the previous days. "Today has to be pink!" *Sharla has followed the program of the calendar in the same way the computer follows a preset program.*

After calendar time, Nancy draws the children's attention to the various activities available to them for the day, including several related to the week's theme of beavers. She then dismisses them to the different areas of the room. Christine, Joshua, and Will enter the cardboard beaver lodge in dramatic play, Christopher and Orion set about constructing their City of Doom in the block area, Sharla and Catherine put on smocks before painting, and Ronnie heads for the Macintosh near the front of the room.

Kids Using Computers

Ronnie holds the computer's mouse comfortably and navigates through Kid Desk (the file manager that organizes programs that students may access) and into Spelunx, his favorite program. As soon as Xavier hears the familiar drum rhythms that accompany the program, he rushes to fill the empty seat next to Ronnie. "I can get into every cave in this program. You want me to show you?" Xavier offers. "Do you know how to get to the room that shows Pluto and Saturn and the planets?" Ronnie asks. Xavier nods vigorously, "Yeah, you got to click on the left tunnel. No, this left tunnel," pointing to the screen as Ronnie controls the mouse.

Spelunx is *a software program that combines state-of-the-art graphics and sound with an open-ended, exploration design, which allows children to exercise problem-solving abilities and commu-*

nication skills while developing computer competence. Children refine their cognitive and social skills just as when they engage in more traditional activities. "I had heard all about using the computer to create 'microworlds' for kids to explore, but it never really made sense to me until I saw this program," Nancy comments. "When the kids are moving through the various caves and tunnels in Spelunx, their language is no different from what I hear them use when they're in a dramatic play setting, like the beaver lodge. They are *using the computer to play,* I mean *really play, in the way that lets them explore an entirely new environment."*

At a nearby table, Amy is arranging colored Popsicle sticks to match the patterns suggested on the direction board. The student teacher designed this activity to foster small-motor coordination, but by simply propping up the direction board against an empty shoe box, *the teacher has re-created the horizontal–vertical situation common to the computer keyboard–screen relationship.* Mastering this activity will help Amy feel more comfortable using the computer, as well as increase her fine-motor dexterity.

Fun Shawn has discovered the Macintosh in the rear of the room. Clicking on the picture of his teacher, he smiles as he hears Nancy's recorded voice welcome the kindergartners to the computer. "I'm the skateboard," Shawn whispers as he selects his icon from a class list in Kid Desk. "This is my desk," he declares proudly as a colorful dinosaur-decorated desktop is displayed. "Listen to this!" Shawn clicks on the representation of an answering machine, and Nancy's voice again is heard, "Hi, Shawn! Have fun on the computer today." Shawn laughs, "She's talking to me!"

A student teacher approaches the computer with Hannah in tow. "Shawn, Hannah would like to play on the computer, too, and since there is still one chair empty here, there is room to share with her, OK?" Shawn scoots his chair slightly, and Hannah takes a seat. After watching silently for a few moments, Hannah requests that Shawn open up the jellybean game. "Which is that?" Shawn asks, and Hannah offers to show him. Taking the mouse, Hannah selects Millie's Math House and navigates to the appropriate game. "Here, see, you gotta put that many jellybeans on the cookie," indicating the number on the screen.

After several correct responses, Hannah pushes the mouse to Shawn so he can try. "I don't want to put that many on. I don't like jellybeans." With Hannah's assistance, Shawn contentedly creates cookies that match his preferences rather than the computer's, and he continues with the game. *Unlike drill-and-practice programs, a developmentally appropriate piece of software allows children to experiment with various responses without being "punished" by a buzzing sound or negative reply.* The children have the chance to ask, "What would happen if . . . ?" and then are able to test their hypotheses.

Versatility Computers are probably the most versatile material a kindergarten room can have. Nancy agrees. "A computer can provide activities that promote language development, or art, or math skills, or all of them at once," she says. In an appropriate program, while the children are playing the game, they are also engaged in problem solving and discussion with peers.

Several minutes later, Shawn decides to move to the block area. Hannah immediately exits the math game and navigates to her own desk icon on the Macintosh. Opening the program Storybook Weaver, she declares, "I have this one at home, so I'm really good at it. I like it 'cause I like to draw pictures, and I can't draw a Pegasus by myself, but with the computer, I can."

Exploration After a short snack break, the children assemble on the rug to share the objects they have brought from home. Today's designated object is a favorite book, so the group circle is filled with proud readers, holding well-loved copies of such classics as *Where the Wild Things Are* and *The Cat in the Hat*. Stephen waves his book

happily. "Look, Nancy! My book is the same one we have on the computer!" And, indeed, the paperback copy of Mercer Mayer's *Just Grandma and Me* that Stephen holds is the same story that is told through an *interactive CD-ROM literature program*. Available in the classroom since the first day in September, this program *allows the children to explore inside the animated illustrations while the computer reads the text aloud in a selected language,* such as English, Spanish, or Japanese.

Programs like Just Grandma and Me and A Silly Noisy House (another CD-ROM program) provide a welcoming introduction to computers for young children, since they allow unlimited exploration with no predetermined right or wrong answers. The child can place the cursor on almost any object on the screen and get a positive response, in the form of character animation or music. "It gives the child a feeling of immediate success," Nancy says. "That's especially important for those children who may be hesitant to try something new. It gets them on the computer, and there is no chance to fail."

Dr. Daniel Shade, director of the Technology in Early Childhood Project, believes that *good pieces of software,* like A Silly Noisy House, do just that: *put the child in control, allow exploration, and offer success.* Mastering these pieces of software gives children a strong sense of power; now they can use a tool that grown-ups use in the real world—not a scaled-down version or a pretend computer, but a real, working piece of technology.

In this area of technology, the boundaries that have traditionally separated the child's world from the adult's are fading. For instance, Jill brought to share time a minibook she created: a single page of information on beavers she printed out from an online encyclopedia on her home computer. "More and more of our share times include some kind of computer activity," Nancy notes. "It could be a picture or story the child creates on the computer, or an experience he or she had using technology at home." Hannah illustrates this by sharing, along

continued

with her book, a bookmark she designed on her home version of Storybook Weaver.

Computers Supporting Curriculum

Before dismissing the children to free-choice time, the teacher directs their attention to the Apple II computer near the door. "Boys and girls, some of you might have noticed today that we've put out a new piece of software. It's called Tracks, and I know that Josh tried it this morning. Josh, can you tell us what this program does?" Josh squirms under the class's attention and responds quietly, "I built a beaver lodge." "You did? Just like we're doing in the dramatic play area? That's great!" Nancy encourages. "Boys and girls, maybe some of you would like to look at the program and see how it can help you build a beaver lodge on the computer. Or, you can take apart the lodge that the computer built and see what's inside. Since Josh is the expert at Tracks, you can ask him for help if you need it." *With the wide range of early childhood software available, almost every topic covered in the classroom can be supported on the computer*—including beavers.

While several children move to examine the new program, others approach the art table to complete a beaver puppet. By "reading" the rebus cards provided, the young students are practicing early literacy skills, as well as developing their abilities to follow picture directions and process step-by-step instructions. The refinement of these *emergent literacy skills, part of any developmentally appropriate early childhood classroom, is also necessary for successful computer use.* With minimal adaptation, the beaver puppet construction becomes a way to foster computer accom-plishment. "The last thing this activity is," the teacher remarks, "is an art project."

Scaffolding While Xavier and Catherine build their puppets, Maria and Tara are busily working on an Apple computer. At the request of a teacher, Maria is showing Tara how to make her own story with the Stone Soup program. Maria is the class expert for Stone Soup.

After reading the book to the class and having them act out the story, Nancy introduced the children to the software program of the same name. Maria decided she would create her own Stone Soup book, and has diligently devoted some time of every day for two weeks to her project. Each day, Maria independently loads the program, chooses a page of the animated story, rearranges, adds and removes objects, and types invented text to build her own story. When asked why she decided to use the computer for her project rather than crayons or paints, Maria replies, "The computer makes it an easier time. Crayons don't know what I want the picture to look like, and I can't make them look right. The computer knows how I want it to look, and then I can make it do what I want." Daniel Shade describes this as *scaffolding;* like Hannah with her Pegasus, Maria is using the computer as a tool to assist her in producing a picture that she can describe and understand but cannot yet create on her own. *The computer extends the child's natural abilities* and will support her *until she develops the physiological and cognitive skills necessary to master the task independently.*

Confidence Although the computer is assisting the child, it does not *control* her. As our expert Maria explains, "The computer helps me start, but

---

The potential of the CD-ROM in the schools is practically unlimited in terms of function and content. Excellent CD-ROM programs are available for classroom use, such as The Golden Book Encyclopedia and The San Diego Zoo Presents the Animals. Both these make use of pictures, sound, and animation in addition to text and are very easy to use. As another example, Joint Education Initiative developed an educational CD-ROM in cooperation with NOAA and NASA. Their philosophy is that the best way to learn sci-

I tell it what to do, 'cause I use the command keys." The emphasis this classroom's teacher places on the computer as a tool, operated by the child and helpless without the child's direction, is evident in Maria's explanation; this child knows that *she* is in control of the *machine,* not the other way around.

Mary Minker, a teacher in the University of Delaware Preschool, has recently begun to use computers in her classroom of four-year-olds and can already see the impact of their sense of control. "After the children are exposed to some programs where they can feel successful, they are really confident in their status as computer users. In the beginning of the year, I made sure all my student teachers were thoroughly familiar with the programs so they could help the children. Well, now I have a brand new group of student teachers, and it's the children who are teaching them how the computers work! The children are very proud of what they can do on the machines."

Pride in Learning These children should be proud of their accomplishments. Often, they master complex computer skills that adult users find difficult. For example, Sharla ends her activity time on KidPix, a graphics program. Rather than being content with the simple painting and drawing options, Sharla chooses to take a predrawn graphic and alter it to her own specifications. Selecting the picture of a horse, Sharla uses the Stamp Editor function to enlarge the picture and change the color, one pixel at a time. She rushes to the ImageWriter* to watch the color printout emerge.

As the day's session comes to an end, the children proudly display the work they have completed. In this technology-enriched classroom, the students are fortunate enough to include computer printouts along with the traditional finger paintings and puppets. But more than just creating printouts, these children are developing the confidence and abilities of computer users, which allow them to say, "Look what I did! I did it all by myself with the computer!"

Software References

Explore-a-Classic: Stone Soup (William K. Bradford, 1989)

Explore-a-Science: Tracks (William K. Bradford, 1989)

Just Grandma and Me by Mercer Mayer (Brøderbund Software, 1992)

Kid Desk (Edmark Software, 1992)

Kid Pix (Brøderbund Software, 1991)

Millie's Math House (Edmark Software, 1992)

Silly Noisy House by Peggy Weil (The Voyager Company, 1991)

Spelunx (Brøderbund Software, 1992)

Storybook Weaver (MECC, 1992)

Contributed by Bernadette Caruso-Davis, University of Delaware Kindergarten.

ence is by doing science, no matter the grade level. The user is introduced to such material as earthquakes, voyager imagery, comets, and Yellowstone forest fires. Brøderbund Software has developed a title for children called Kid Pix Studio. Children can create productions that combine animation, photographs, special effects, video, music, and sound effects. Nordic Software has created Language Explorer, with 500 animated picture titles covering 42 topics in Spanish, French, German, and English.

Videodiscs Videodiscs are similar to musical compact discs. They are larger, about twelve inches, and store pictures, charts, and other information as well as words and music in stereo. Students watch the program on the classroom television using an appropriate player. When the videodisc is attached to a computer, the program becomes "interactive"; that is, students can pinpoint and replay specific information in response to their individual questions and learning needs.

Another advantage of videodiscs is that the disc player can access two different soundtracks, a digital and an analog track. Each track in turn has a right and a left channel. Videodisc manufacturers use this availability of multiple audio channels to add the soundtrack in other languages, music, or a combination, or to add supplemental information. DVD systems will ultimately replace this technology.

Videodisc manufacturers are responding to the growing need for multilingual and multicultural software. The Optical Data Corporation of Warren, New Jersey, developed the first electronic textbook. Called Windows on Science, a science curriculum for grades K through 6, it has a separate Spanish soundtrack and is also available in an all-Spanish version. Texas adopted this electronic textbook, gaining the distinction of being the first state to use such material.

Audio Audio support for computers provides many important instructional advantages. It helps students' reading skills development in a way that was previously possible only by means of the human voice. It supports understanding of vocabulary and onscreen text and can provide additional background or setting information. Audio is also essential for teaching phonetic features of language. Audio feedback gives students immediate information about their lesson responses. Not only are correct answers acknowledged, but the reasons why they are correct are often reinforced.

In the event of an incorrect response, audio guidance often suggests approaches that may lead to a right answer.

Television Joan Ganz Cooney, originator of *Sesame Street* and chair of the executive committee of Children's Television Workshop, believes that the technology of television has three important strengths: it is accessible, it is cost effective, and it works.[9] An example of the strengths of television applied to early childhood education is the Sesame Street Preschool Education Program Initiative (PEP). PEP is a national educational program for preschool children in child care centers and family day-care homes. Created around *Sesame Street* viewing, PEP uses storybook reading and related activities to promote and stimulate children's natural curiosity for learning. It is estimated that 2.3 million children participate in PEP.

EARLY CHILDHOOD PROFESSIONALS AND TECHNOLOGY

Early childhood professionals have to make decisions about their roles in and use of technology. Clements and his colleagues believe professionals have three choices:

An important decision must be made among three paths that differ in the goals and types of computer applications. Those traveling the first path use simple computer games for "rewards" or occasionally use drill software but do not integrate it into their wider educational program. Those traveling on the second path integrate drill and other structured software activities into their programs. Those traveling on the third path use problem-solving software and tools such as word processors, Logo, and drawing programs to extend and enrich their children's education.

Research suggests that the first path leads nowhere: teachers might better invest efforts and resources elsewhere.

The second path is educationally plausible. Well-planned, integrated computer activities can increase achievement in cost-effective ways. . . .

The third path is more challenging—in time, in effort, in commitment, and in vision. This path alone, however, offers the potential for substantive educational innovation consonant with NAEYC guidelines and those of other professional organizations.[10]

Research on Technology and Education

Research provides us with much valuable information about the influence of technology on children, their responses to technology,

---

BOX 11.2 You, Your Students, and Technology

With a personal computer, a *modem,* a device that enables computers to communicate over telephone lines, and the appropriate access software, you and your students can be on the Internet.

GETTING ON THE INTERNET

You can gain access to the Internet through university links, commercial agencies, regional networks, state networks, and freenets. Most colleges and universities are connected to the Internet and give students access through personal accounts, often for free or at a modest cost per term. In addition, some colleges and universities provide access to local school districts.

Commercial companies, such as America Online, CompuServe, Prodigy, and direct Internet service providers (ISPs) provide software that provides access to the Internet for a monthly fee. It is through these companies that many parents and students have Internet access in their homes. Many large school districts, government agencies, and corporations provide access through their own networks. Many communities provide *freenets* for use by educators and community members. These freenets are generally operated and supported by local and regional libraries and are paid for out of local tax revenues. For example, the Fernnet is operated by the Broward County (Florida) library system, and access is provided free by dialing a special telephone number. Contact your local library system, to determine if there is a freenet in your area. Many of the commercial networks offer many services to their subscribers. For example, America Online offers education discussion groups, online homework help for students, software library with programs in science,

mathematics, language arts, and social studies, and access to National Geographic's educational resources.

USING THE INTERNET

E-mail, the sending and receiving of electronic messages, is the most widely used of all Internet applications. Through e-mail you and your students will be able to communicate with teachers and students in your and other school districts, and at schools across the country and throughout the world. You will also be able to communicate with your students at home. Some teachers provide help with homework and other class work via e-mail. You and your students can also participate in *newsgroups,* a cross between a bulletin board and discussion group. In fact, you can start a discussion group on a particular classroom topic and invite other teachers and students to participate.

The information contained on the Internet is vast and extensive. One source of help is a *gopher,* a server software developed at the University of Minnesota (Gophers) to provide access to resources and databases. A gopher organizes information into menus that allow you to browse and select the information you want. The *World Wide Web* (WWW) is a database and information format that includes multimedia such as prints, photos, video clips, and sound recordings.

You can use networks to access databases containing useful information. For example, The U.S. Department of Education supports the Educational Resource Information Center (ERIC) which seeks to provide access to all literature in the field of education. AskERIC is an Internet service of the ERIC system for anyone interested in education.

continued

AskERIC is coordinated by the ERIC Clearing house on Information and Technology (ERIC/IT) at Syracuse University. To use AskERIC, e-mail your question to **askeric@ericir.syr.edu.** PARENTS AskERIC, at the same e-mail address, is that part of AskERIC specifically designed for parents and others who have questions about the development, education, and care of children from birth to the high school years. The ERIC Clearing House on Elementary and Early Childhood Education (ERIC/EECE) maintains a gopher and World Wide Web Server (computers on which information is stored). Through the gopher menu, you can access the National Parent Information Network (NPIN), a national electronic network for parents and parent educators, community planners, professional associations, and others who work with parents and families. The gopher address is **ericps.ed.uiuc.edu.**

To begin your electronic journey, you must (1) learn how to operate a computer; (2) have a computer with a modem and telecommunications software; (3) gain access to the Internet through your college or university, school district, commercial service, or freenet; and (4) learn the use and protocol of the Internet. You can use the following electronic addressees to access additional information:

The Awesome Lists
**http://www.clark.net/pub/journalism/
awesome.html**

Berit's Best Sites for Children
http://db.cochran.com/db_HTML:theopage.db

Department of Education
http://www.ed.gov/pubs/parents

Information on The Solar System
http://bang.lanl.gov.solarsys

Kid's Web
http://www.npac.syr.edu/textbook/kidsweb/

Links to Educational Websites
http://www.mebbs.com/tenny/educate.htm

Online Educator
http://ole.net/ole/

OSC Young Person Guide to the Internet
http://www.osc.on.ca:kids.html

Sounds of the World's Animals
**http://www.georgetown.edu/cball/animals/
animals.html**

Steve Linduska's K-12 Resources
**http://www.public.iastate.edu/~linduska/
homepage.html**

TENET Web
http://www.tenet.edu/education/main.html

and how technology helps them learn. In one study involving kindergarten and third grade children, researchers found that computers cultivated and sustained children's attention and concentration. Even while using television as a distractor during a twenty-seven-minute lesson, kindergarten children spent 69 percent and third graders 86 percent of their time attending to the computer. The researchers concluded the following:

Computers can provide an intrinsically interesting learning environment for children that promotes attention, concentration to the task at hand, and reduced distractibility to competing environmental stimuli. Like television, computers appear to sustain attention by a rather effortless process. This effortless attentional process can be directed towards educational computer content that is worthy of children's sustained attention.[11]

Researchers have conducted many studies regarding the effects of technology on children's behavior, achievement, and literacy development. This research shows that technology and appropriate software, used in the right ways, promotes active learning, problem solving, literacy, and social-emotional development.[12] Furthermore, children exposed to developmental software—that is, software specifically identified as having the potential to support children's development—

demonstrated gains in intelligence, nonverbal skills, structural knowledge, long-term memory, and complex memory. In addition, when developmental software is reinforced with supplemental activities, then children also show gains in verbal skills, problem solving, abstractions, and conceptual skills.[13]

The "Technology Programs in Action" color insert, found after page 332, features early childhood professionals in two programs—The Alexander D. Henderson University School and the VistaKids program—who use technology to help their children learn. What are some features about these two programs that make them unique? How are these two programs using technology to meet the needs of their children?

ISSUES IN TECHNOLOGY

As an early childhood professional, you must consider a number of issues related to the selection and use of hardware and software.

Equity

All children must have equitable access to technology that is appropriate for them. While some may think that a worthy goal is to see that all children spend the same amount of time on the computer, all children may not *need* the same amount of time. Some children may have to spend more time to master the objectives.

Equity consists of more than access and time. Equity also includes the idea that all children will learn how to use technology and appropriate software to become technologically literate. Having one group, socioeconomic class, or gender be more comfortable with, skillful with, and proficient in technology means that inequities and *technological illiteracy* result. We must avoid creating a generation of "have nots" of technology.

Equity also means that all children have opportunities to use good software. In partic-

ular, it means that children are not drilled to death with electronic worksheets as a means of attempting to raise their or their school's achievement test scores.

Antibias

As discussed in Chapter 12 and elsewhere throughout this text, all professionals must take into consideration the diversity present in contemporary society. When professionals select materials, *including computer software, videos, films, and other technologically based applications,* they must make sure these materials include depictions of children and adults with differing abilities, ages, and ethnic backgrounds, and that these materials are nonstereotypic of gender, culture, and socioeconomic class. The software industry has made progress in this regard but still has a long way to go in order to meet antibias criteria in their products. Professionals must evaluate all software they purchase and continually advocate for nonbiased software.

Haugland offers the following suggestions when evaluating software:

- *Software should be available in multiple languages.*
- *Software should portray diverse environments and cultures as well as characteristics of all environments.*
- *Software should maintain gender equity; that is, both sexes are represented and there should be equity in their roles.*
- *Software should have heterogeneous representation, African-Americans, Hispanics, Asians, etc.*[14]

Integration

Technology should be integrated as fully as possible into the early childhood curriculum and learning environment so its use can help promote cooperative learning and achieve learning outcomes for children. For example, you could create a computer/technology learning center in your classroom that children have access to as they would any other center. In this way, the technology would be used as much as possible. And, just as important, such a center should have software that enables children to work independently, with little or minimal adult supervision.

Appropriate Use

Educational technology should not be something children get to use only when they have completed other tasks. It should not be used as a reward, nor should it be a supplemental activity. Technology should be an integrated part of your early childhood program.

Drill versus Discovery

A major controversy among early childhood professionals involves the purpose of computers in the classroom. On the one hand, some say that drill-and-practice programs that emphasize helping children learn colors, numbers, vocabulary, and skills such as addition have no place in the early childhood program. They say that only software that encourages learning by discovery and exploration is appropriate. On the other hand, some professionals see drill-and-practice software as a valuable means for children to learn concepts and skills they so desperately need to succeed in school. The VistaKids program (on pp. c–3 and c–4 of the "Technology Programs in Action" color insert) is an example of using skill-based software to help children develop literacy and English language competency.

Of course, in this case, as with so many things, a middle ground offers an appropriate solution. Many children like drill-and-practice programs and the positive feedback that often comes with them. Also, some children spend long periods of time working on such programs. However, not all children like or do well with skill-drill programs. Technological aids, as with other learning materials, require early childhood professionals to identify and address children's learning styles. What is important is

that all children should have access to a variety of software and instructional and learning activities that are appropriate to them as individuals. This is what a developmentally appropriate curriculum is all about, and it applies to technology and software as well.

Higher-Order Learning

Technology can support and facilitate critical educational and cognitive processes such as cooperative learning, group and individual problem solving, critical thinking, reflective practices, analysis, inquiry, process writing, and public speaking. Also, technology can promote *metacognition,* that is, thinking about thinking.

Computer Literacy

Children and their teachers need to be computer literate, and this goal should direct the computer program of the primary grades. You can develop an effective program of computer literacy using the following guidelines:[15]

1. "Computer literacy must be defined comprehensively, including two general areas: learning *with* computers and learning *about* computers."[16]

2. However, decisions concerning what children learn about computers should be made not by asking, "What can we teach kids about computers?" but rather by asking, "What understandings about computers, their impact on our world, and their uses are *developmentally appropriate* for, and *educationally relevant* to, young children?" This question implies that lectures on the history of computers or rote memorization of computer components terminology should not be included in the curriculum. Only when meaningful concepts can be actively learned should they be considered for inclusion.

Computers play a large role in teaching and learning. Technology allows children to explore different worlds, access resources, and engage in learning activities. From the preschool years, many children have used computers for word processing, graphic design, and game playing. How can you appropriately support children's learning through the use of computers and other technology?

3. For both general areas, educators should (a) decide first how and when to use computers to accomplish the goals of early education and (b) integrate these uses into the curriculum, while (c) remaining consistent with the beliefs, principles, and practices of the program.

These guidelines have several important ramifications. For example, they imply that the development of the "whole child" will be given first and primary consideration; there will not be a "computers" unit that is separate from work in social studies, science, language arts, and so on; and *individual children will have different needs, interests, and abilities and, therefore, will learn different things about computers and will use them in different ways.* This should be welcomed as well as accepted; no effort should be made to force all children to "master" all aspects of computer literacy. Instead of one definition of computer literacy for all, teachers should determine what computers can do to help a particular child reach a particular goal.

The Future

Undoubtedly you have heard the saying "You haven't seen anything yet." This remark applies to technology and its application to all school settings from prekindergarten through grade 12. The vision that each child will acquire the foundational skills and competencies to succeed as an adult in the information age begins in the early years.

What will have to happen in order to bring tomorrow to the classrooms today? First, early childhood professionals must decide themselves to use technology and gain the training necessary to be computer literate. Second, professionals must dedicate themselves to the developmentally appropriate use of technology and software. Third, professionals must recognize that technology and all its applications are not just add-ons to the curriculum or activities to do only when there is time or as rewards for good behavior or achievement. Technology, hardware and software, is here to stay, and can, like text-based materials, help children learn to their fullest potential.

Activities for Further Enrichment

1. Visit classrooms in your local school districts. What evidence of the integration of technology into the curriculum can you find? What conclusions can you draw from your data?

2. Interview early childhood professionals in your school district. What barriers do they say they must contend with in their efforts to include technology in the curriculum? What implications do these barriers have for what early childhood professionals can accomplish?

3. Read the two Program in Action features in this chapter, "Writing to Read" and "The Computer-Enriched Kindergarten." List at least three ways they are similar and three ways they are different. Write a paragraph explaining which approach you support.

4. Select at least four commercial educational software programs. Using the criteria from Figure 11.6, rate their suitability for use with children.

5. Develop a plan for how you would use Vygotsky's views (see Chap. 3) to promote children's social interaction through computers.

6. Some teachers and parents think children should not be introduced to computers at an early age. List reasons why they might feel this way. Then, interview five parents and teachers. Ask them the following questions:

   a. Should young children be introduced to computers?

   b. At what age should young children be introduced?

   c. Why do you feel this age to be the best?

7. Visit a center or program that provides services to children with disabilities. Cite five ways in which technology is used to implement the curriculum, help teachers teach, and promote children's learning.

8. Choose a particular theme, and write a lesson plan to show how you would integrate technology relating to that theme into a kindergarten classroom.

9. Write a four-paragraph report in which you explain your views of the use of technology in early childhood programs. Present this to a center director, school principal, or similar person for feedback. Set up a conference for discussion and reaction.

Readings for Further Enrichment

Beynon, J., and H. Mackay, eds. *Computers into Classrooms: More Questions Than Answers* (Bristol, PA: Falmer, 1993).

Critically examines computers and their use in teaching and learning. Provides much interesting information and raises many issues that need to be addressed by teachers who wish to bring themselves and their children into the technological age.

Buckleitner, W. *High/Scope Buyer's Guide to Children's Software 1995* (Ypsilanti, MI: High/Scope, 1996).

High/Scope's annual survey of programs for children aged three to seven. Over five hundred software programs reviewed. Includes descriptions, ratings, award-winning programs, a glossary, and a national directory of software producers.

Geisert, P., and M. Futrell. *Teachers, Computers, and Curriculum: Microcomputers in the Classroom,* 2nd ed. (Needham Heights, MA: Allyn & Bacon, 1995).

This book focuses on curriculum and teaching. Its aim is to help teachers incorporate microcomputers into their teaching, not to provide a survey of computers in education.

Maddux, C., Johnson, D., and J. Willis. *Educational Computing: Learning with Tomorrow's Technologies* (Needham Heights, MA: Allyn & Bacon, 1997).

This book gives general concepts and the theory and research on teaching, learning, and technology rather than hands-on assignments at the computer. The text also links actual practice to underlying theories of both teaching and learning. It helps students develop their own framework for thinking about educational computing.

Merrill, P., K. Hammons, B. Vincent, and P. Reynolds. *Computers in Education,* 3rd ed. (Needham Heights, MA: Allyn & Bacon, 1996).

This book helps teachers who use computer technology to increase the efficiency and effectiveness of the educational process.

Papert, S. *The Children's Machine: Rethinking School in the Age of the Computer* (New York: Basic Books, 1993).

Papert is the popularizer of Logo; in this book he envisions a future for education in which computers restore the wonder to learning.

NOTES

1. Joshua Mills, "Computer Age Tots Trading Building Blocks for Software," *New York Times,* 13 Feb. 1994, p. A1.
2. S. Haugland, "Will Technology Change Early Childhood Education?" *Day Care and Early Education* (Summer 1995), pp. 45–46.
3. U.S. Bureau of the Census, 1991.
4. P. Ross, ed., *Software Resources Guide* (Evanston, IL: National Lekotek Center, n.d.).
5. The Technology Related Assistance for Individuals with Disabilities Act of 1988 (PL 100–407). Available online at Internet address http://pursuit.rehab.uiuc.edu.
6. L. Holder-Brown and H. Parette, "Children with Disabilities Who Use Assistive Technology: Ethical Considerations," *Young Children* (Sept. 1992), pp. 74–75.
7. D. H. Clements, B. K. Nastasi, and S. Swaninathan, "Young Children and Computers: Crossroads and Directions from Research," *Young Children* (Jan. 1993), p. 57.
8. Rik Myslewski, "Apple, Power to Take DVD Lead," *MacUser* 13 (March 1997), pp. 30–31.
9. J. G. Cooney, "Not a Moment to Waste," *Electronic Learning* 12 (1993), p. 54.
10 Clements et al., p. 63.
11. Sandra L. Calvert, Caitlin Brune, Maria Eguia, and Jean Marcato, "Attention Inertia and Distractibility during Children's Educational Computer Interactions." Poster session presented at the biennial meeting of the Society for Research in Child Development, Seattle, WA, April 1991.
12. Clements et al., pp. 56–64.
13. Susan W. Haugland, "The Effects of Computer Software on Preschool Children's Developmental Gains," *Journal of Computing in Childhood Education* 3 (1992), pp. 15–30.
14. Susan W. Haugland, "Maintaining an Anti-Bias Curriculum," *Day Care and Early Education* (Winter 1992), pp. 44–45.
15. Douglas H. Clements, *Computers in Early and Primary Education* (Needham Heights, MA: Allyn & Bacon, 1985), pp. 52–53.
16. Ibid.

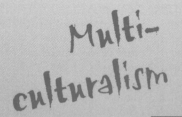

CHAPTER 12

Multiculturalism

Education for Living in a Diverse Society

Focus Questions

1. What is the language and terminology associated with multicultural education?

2. What are the implications of a multicultural contemporary society for schooling?

3. How do early childhood professionals infuse multicultural content in curriculum, programs, and activities?

4. How would you develop and defend a philosophy of teaching for multicultural awareness and understanding?

5. How do early childhood professionals implement multicultural programs and practices in centers and classrooms?

6. What contemporary issues relate to multiculturalism?

7. How would you educate both yourself and young children for living in a diverse society?

n its simplest form, *multicultural* awareness is the appreciation for and understanding of peoples' cultures, socioeconomic status, and gender. It also includes understanding one's own culture. Some early childhood professionals assume they are promoting multicultural awareness when they are actually presenting only a fragment of the concept.

Multicultural awareness in the classroom is not the presentation of other cultures to the exclusion of the cultures represented by children in the class. Rather, multicultural awareness programs and activities focus on other cultures while at the same time making children aware of the content, nature, and richness of their own. The terms and concepts for describing multicultural education and awareness (Figure 12.1) are not as important as the methods, procedures, and activities for developing meaningful early childhood programs. Learning about other cultures concurrently with their own culture enables children to integrate commonalities and appreciate differences without inferring inferiority or superiority of one or the other.

WHO ARE MULTICULTURAL CHILDREN?

The population of young children in the United States reflects the population at large, and represents a number of different cultures and ethnicities. Thus, many cities and school districts have populations that express great ethnic diversity, including Asian Americans, Native Americans, African Americans, and Hispanic Americans. For example, the Dade County, Florida, school district has children from 122 countries of the world, each with its own culture.

The great diversity of young children creates interesting challenges for early childhood educators. Many children speak languages other than English, behave differently reflective of cultural customs and values, and come from many socioeconomic backgrounds. Because of the multicultural composition of society, as an early childhood educator, you will want to promote multicultural awareness in your classroom.

In Chapter 2 we stressed the diverse nature of U.S. society. We emphasize it again here. The reality today is that the United States is a multicultural country, as conveyed in Figure 12.2. Early childhood professionals must prepare themselves and their children to live happily and productively in this society.

Yet how to prepare children of all cultures for productive living is a major challenge for everyone. VistaKids programs represent one attempt to address some basic fundamental challenges of educating the United States' increasingly diverse population (see pages c–3 and c–4 of the "Technology Programs in Action" color insert). For instance, how can early childhood professionals use technology to help millions of immigrant children become literate both in their native language and English? How can professionals help ensure that multicultural children will not become technological illiterates? The answers to these questions are not easy to give or implement, but programs such as VistaKids are trying.

VistaKids programs also represent another reality: the willingness of the private sector and special interest groups to fund and support programs for young children. In fact, this continuing trend is one of the great changes in early childhood education over the last quarter of the twentieth century.

Promoting multiculturalism in an early childhood program has implications far beyond the program itself. Multiculturalism influences and affects work habits, interpersonal relations, and a person's general outlook on life. Early childhood professionals must take these multicultural influences into consideration when designing curriculum and instructional processes for the impressionable children they will teach. One way to accomplish the primary goal of multicultural education—to positively change the lives of children and their families—is to infuse multiculturalism into early childhood activities and practices.

Figure 12.1/*Glossary*

The following terms will assist you as you study this chapter:

Antibias: An active/activist approach to challenging prejudice, stereotyping, bias, and the "isms"*

Bias-free: Programs, activities, materials and behaviors that are free from biased perceptions, language, attitudes, and actions

Bilingual education: "The use of two languages for the purposes of academic instruction with an organized curriculum that includes, at a minimum, (1) continued primary language (language 1) development, (2) English (language 2) acquisition, and (3) subject matter instruction through (language 1) and (language 2). Bilingual education programs assist limited-English-proficient (LEP) students in developing literacy both in English and the primary language to a level at which they can succeed in an English-only classroom. Programs may also include native speakers of English [these are children whose primary language is English and are learning a second language]."

Diversity: Describes various cultures, ethnic groups, socioeconomic groups, languages, and gender indentities that exist in society at large and early childhood programs in particular. Diversity is seen as a positive rather than negative state. Consequently, diversity is celebrated, studied, and respected. Additionally, early childhood professionals try to ensure that cultural diversity exists in curriculum, teaching, caregiving practices, and acitivites.

Infusion: A process of integrating multicultural perspectives into the curriculum, as well as promoting content awareness, sensitivity, knowledge, and behaviors. Infusion is used as a means of transforming existing or new curricula so that they are truly multicultural.

Language maintenance: "The preservation of a native language when a second language is learned as opposed to displacement of the native language by the second language"

Limited-English-proficient (LEP) parents: "Parents whose children have been identified as limited-English-proficient and/or who are also limited in their proficiency in English"

Limited-English-proficient (LEP) student: "A student whose primary language is other than English and who does not comprehend, speak, read, or write at a level necessary to receive instruction only in English with native English-speaking peers"

Mainstream: "In the field of bilingual education, this term refers to the monolingual English curriculum or classroom." (See Chap. 13 for a full discussion of mainstream and mainstreaming.)

Multicultural education: Multicultural education is education that prepares students to live, learn, communicate, and work to achieve common goals in a culturally diverse world by fostering understanding, appreciation, and respect for people of other ethnic, gender, socioeconomic, language, and cultural backgrounds.

Nonsexist: Attitudes and behaviors that convey that the sexes are equal.

---

*Quoted definitions are from the Division of Human Resource Development, Florida Atlantic University Multifunctional Resource Center, *Empowering ESOL Teachers: An Overview*, vol. 2 (Tallahassee, FL: Florida Department of Education, 1993), Appendix A, Glossary, sections VII-X, pp. i-vi.

Figure 12.2/Resident Population of the United States

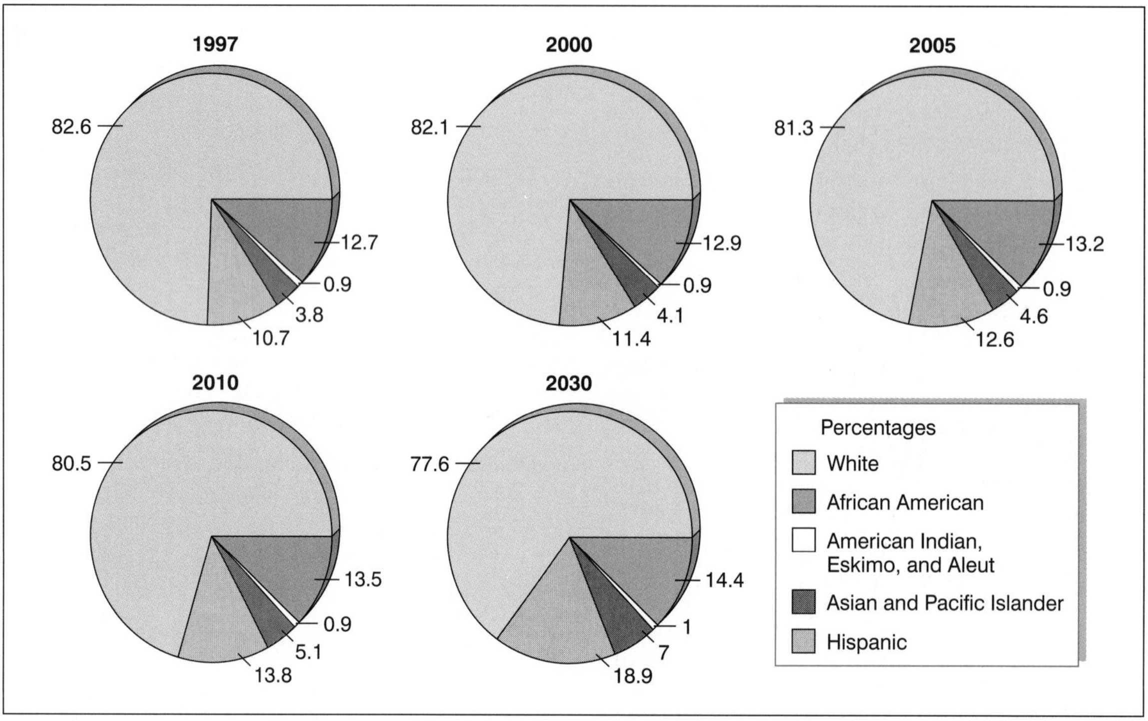

Source: Estimated from the U.S. Bureau of the Census, Current Population Reports, Series P25-1130; consistent with the 1990 Census, as enumerated, 1995.

WHAT IS MULTICULTURAL INFUSION?

Infusion means that multicultural education permeates the curriculum to alter or affect the way young children and teachers look at diversity issues. In a larger perspective, infusion strategies are used to assure that multiculturalism becomes a part of the entire center, school, and home. Infusion processes used by early childhood programs encompass a range of practices that embody the following precepts:

1. Foster cultural awareness
2. Teach to children's learning styles
3. Encourage cooperative learning
4. Promote and use conflict resolution strategies
5. Welcome parent and community involvement

We will discuss each of these practices in detail so you may fully understand how to apply them to your life and program. Keep in mind that as an early childhood professional, you will want to be constantly in a process of developing your multicultural awareness, attitude, knowledge, and skills.

Foster Cultural Awareness

Assess Your Attitudes Toward Children

Before working with children to influence their multicultural awareness and education

Today's society is multiculturally pluralistic. Early childhood professionals must consider the diverse needs of students, including gender, ethnicity, race, and socioeconomic factors, when planning learning opportunities in activities and programs.

it is important for early childhood professionals to first assess their own attitudes toward young children and their families to help ensure that they are multiculturally sensitive. The following will help you assess your own multicultural awareness level.

- *Do you have different expectations of children from different neighborhoods? For example, do you expect a higher level of work from students who live in affluent neighborhoods than from those who live in trailer parks?*
- *With which children do you feel most comfortable? Are you influenced by what children wear? The positions their parents hold? The color of their skin? Some people believe men have higher levels of intelligence than women and that those with lighter skin colors are smarter than those with dark skin. Some people perceive those with an affluent, white-collar lifestyle as being "smarter, better, and more civilized" than those from working-class communities.*
- *What do you know about children's communities? In order to provide schooling relevant to students' lives, teachers need a sense of children's worldviews. What is it like living in the community? What roles and relationships are most important? Do you understand the nuances of student verbal and nonverbal communication?*

- *What connections do you feel to the children's community? Society has changed drastically in the past quarter-century. Few children attend neighborhood schools in large urban districts; instead, many students of all ethnicities have become accustomed to long bus rides. In addition, few teachers teach in their own neighborhoods; they may instead drive ten miles or more to another community.*

- *Do you expect children to learn through your ways of teaching only, or do you find out in which modes of instruction children learn best? When teaching in a multicultural manner, do not try to mold children to fit your manner of teaching. Instead, learn about them and change your teaching to affirm them. As one effective strategy, use culturally familiar examples when discussing new concepts. For example, a teacher was giving a les-*son *in how people can provide themselves with complete proteins every day without eating meat. The teacher asked her predominantly Mexican American class what they ate for dinner. Some of the kids said, "pizza." Other students said, "spaghetti," while others yelled out, "tortillas and beans." The teacher then explained that when they ate tortillas, which are made from grains, with their beans, they were getting a complete protein. The example helped to make connections between an abstract scientific concept and students' personal lives.*[1]

Guidelines and Processes for Fostering Awareness   As an early childhood professional, you must keep in mind that you are the key to a multicultural classroom. The following guidelines can help you in teaching multiculturalism:

Not all children learn in the same way. Some children have individual styles of learning. It is important to assess each child's learning style and teach each child appropriately. What style of learning do you use to learn best?

- Recognize that all children are unique. They all have special talents, abilities, and styles of learning and relating to others. Provide opportunities for children to be different and use their abilities.

- Promote uniqueness and diversity as positive.

- Get to know, appreciate, and respect the cultural backgrounds of your children. Visit families and community neighborhoods to learn more about cultures and religions and the ways of life they engender.

- Infuse children's culture (and other cultures as well) in your teaching.

- Use *authentic* situations to provide for cultural learning and understanding. For example, a field trip to a culturally diverse neighborhood of your city or town provides children an opportunity for understanding firsthand many of the details about how people conduct their daily lives. Such an experience provides wonderful opportunities for involving children in writing, cooking, reading, and dramatic play activities. What about setting up a market in the classroom?

- Use authentic assessment activities to assess fully children's learning and growth. Portfolios (see Chaps. 8 and 9) are ideal for assessing children in nonbiased and culturally sensitive ways. The point is that early childhood professionals should use varied ways of assessing children.

- Infuse culture into your lesson planning, teaching, and caregiving. Use all subject areas—math, science, language arts, literacy, music, art, and social studies—to relate culture to all the children and all you do.

- Use children's interests and experiences to form a basis for planning lessons and developing activities. This approach makes students feel good about their backgrounds, cultures, families, and experiences. Also, when children can relate what they are doing in the classroom to the rest of their daily lives, their learning is more meaningful to them.

- Be knowledgeable about, proud of, and secure in your own culture. Children will ask about you, and you should share your background with them.

The following six processes will help you and other professionals assure that you and they conduct authentic multicultural programs and activities:

1. Building multicultural programs. *This means that teachers will seek to develop and conduct programs that are multicultural. Teachers and caregivers must truly want to have a classroom, center, and program that is multicultural in materials, programs, and attitudes. Such programs should include the similarities and differences in peoples and culture.*

2. Showing appreciation of differences in others. *To achieve this goal, early childhood educators must model the behavior they want in their children and colleagues. For example, professionals should respond positively to children's language, avoid correcting, and show appreciation and encouragement. In authentic classrooms—as opposed to unaware ones—professionals demonstrate appreciation of other cultures and viewpoints.*

3. Avoiding stereotypes. *The culturally aware professional realizes that, for example, "Hispanic" is not one culture but that it includes children from many countries and cultures. The culturally sensitive professional does not predict failure for certain cultural groups but has high hopes, aspirations, and expectations for all*

children and believes all children are capable of learning.

4.   Acknowledging differences.   *Professionals must believe children are different, acknowledge children are different, and plan curriculum and programs that reflect and authentically demonstrate that children are different. Children's cultures and family backgrounds are viewed as assets, not deficits.*

5.   Discovering diversity within the classroom.   *Professionals really get to know children and their families by visiting in their homes, by talking to them, by exploring the communities in which they live, and by involving parents, family members, and the community in the program.*

6.   Avoiding pseudomulticulturalism.   *Authentic professionals address the needs of all children and are sensitive to all cultures of all children. Sometimes people mistakenly think they are promoting multiculturalism by focusing exclusively on teaching about and infusing one culture into the curriculum and program.*[2]

Select Appropriate Instructional Materials

In addition to assessing your own attitudes and instituting guidelines for infusing personal sensitivity into a multicultural classroom, you need to carefully consider and select appropriate instructional materials to support the infusion of multicultural education. The following sections offer suggestions.

Multicultural Literature.   Choose literature that emphasizes people's habits, customs, and general living and working behaviors. This approach stresses similarities and differences regarding how children and families live their *whole* lives, and avoids merely noting differences or only teaching about habits and customs. Multicultural literature today is more representative of various cultural groups than in the past, and provides a more authentic language experience for young children. This literature is written by authors from particular cultures and contains more true-to-life stories and culturally authentic writing styles. The following books are representative of the rich selection now available:

- *The Last Princess,* by Fay Stanley (New York: Four Winds Press, 1991). This is a biography of nineteenth-century Hawaiian Princess Ka'iulani and her efforts to keep business interests from taking over Hawaii.

- *Nine-In One Grr! Grr!,* by Blia Xiong (San Francisco: Children's Book Press, 1989). A story of the Hmong tribe. When the great god Shao promises Tiger nine cubs each year, Bird comes up with a clever trick to prevent the land from being overrun by tigers.

- *Family Pictures,* by Carmen Lomas Garza (San Francisco: Children's Book Press, 1990). The author describes in illustrations and bilingual text her experiences growing up in a Hispanic community in Texas.

- *The Invisible Hunters,* by Harriet Rohmer (San Francisco: Children's Book Press, 1987). Set in seventeenth-century Nicaragua, this Miskito Indian legend illustrates the impact of the first European trader on traditional life.

- *Tar Beach,* by Faith Ringgold (New York: Crown, 1991). A young girl dreams of flying above her Harlem home, claiming all she sees for herself and her family. Based on the author's quilt painting of the same name.

- *Bigmama's,* by Donald Crews (New York: Greenwillow, 1991). Visiting Bigmama's house in the country, young Donald Crews finds his relatives full of news and the old place and its surroundings, just the same as the year before.

Themes. Early childhood professionals may select and teach through thematic units that help strengthen children's understanding of themselves, their culture, and the cultures of others. Thematic choices from a variety of cultures can help children identify cultural similarities and encourage understanding and tolerance, as with the following suggestions:

Getting to Know Myself, Getting to Know Others

What Is Special About You and Me?

Growing Up in the City

Growing Up in the Country

Tell Me About Africa (South America; China, etc.)

Contributions. Add to classroom activities, as appropriate, the accomplishments of people from different cultural groups, women of all cultures, and individuals with disabilities.

The following criteria are most important when picking materials for use in a multicultural curriculum for early childhood programs:

1. Make sure people of all cultures are represented fairly and accurately.

2. Make sure to represent people of color, many cultural groups, and people with exceptionalities.

3. Make sure that historic information is accurate and nondiscriminatory.

4. Make sure the materials do not include stereotypical roles and language.

5. Make sure there is gender equity—that is, that boys and girls are represented equally and in nonstereotypical roles.

Avoid Sexism and Sex-Role Stereotyping

Current interest in multiculturalism in general and nondiscrimination in particular has also prompted concern about sexism and sex-role stereotyping.

The Civil Rights movement and its emphasis on equality provides the impetus for seeking more equal treatment for women as well as for minority groups. Encouraged by the Civil Rights Act of 1964, which prohibits discrimination on the basis of race or national origin, civil rights and women's groups successfully sought legislation to prohibit discrimination on the basis of sex. Title IX of the Education Amendments Acts of 1972, as amended by Public Law 93–568, prohibits such discrimination in the schools: "No person in the United States shall, on the basis of sex, be excluded from participation in, be denied the benefits of, or be subjected to discrimination under any education program or activity receiving Federal financial assistance."[3]

Since Title IX prohibits sex discrimination in any educational program that receives federal money, early childhood programs as well as elementary schools, high schools, and universities cannot discriminate against males or females in enrollment policies, curriculum offerings, or activities.

The women's movement (see Chap. 1) has encouraged the nation, educational institutions, and families to examine how they educate, treat, and rear children in relationship to sex roles.

There is yet another reason for the nation's interest in sexism. A recent survey conducted by the American Association of University Women (AAUW) reveals that four out of five students in grades 8 to 11 are sexually harassed in school. Sexual harassment was defined as "unwanted and unwelcome sexual behavior which interferes with your life."[4] The AAUW research further revealed that

- *girls receive significantly less attention from classroom teachers than do boys;*
- *African American girls have fewer interactions with teachers than do white girls, despite evidence that they attempt to initiate interactions more frequently;*

PROGRAM IN ACTION

THE BAY AREA HISPANO INSTITUTE FOR ADVANCEMENT

For over twenty-one years, the Bay Area Institute for Advancement, Inc. (BAHIA) has provided child care to the Latino community, a service that remains unduplicated and very much in demand in Berkeley, CA. BAHIA meets the needs of the Latino community by creating an environment in which working families know their children are cared for in a place of learning that is clean, safe, warm, affordable, and most importantly, bilingual.

Parents of BAHIA children, diverse in their professions, are linked by their desire for their children to be bilingual. Services offered by BAHIA are directly linked to giving children and families different and consistent opportunities to be bilingual.

What Are Highlights of the BAHIA Program?

Bilingual Emphasis BAHIA's services are enhanced by its resolution to be 100 percent bilingual in every child, parent, and staff activity; written communication, meetings, and the hiring of individuals from youth workers to the Executive Director exemplify the value of bilingualism in the community. BAHIA's philosophy is that success as a bilingual person does not come at the expense of a child's first or second language. Instead, language is used as a gateway to understand and build a broader cultural sensitivity through activities and environment planning that promote diversity, identity, and understanding. Evidence of a successful bilingual program is observed in children learning and playing games in Spanish, practicing their English with friends, or writing or dictating stories in Spanish to share with their parents.

Service to Familias At BAHIA, *familias* are looked upon as an integral part of a child's healthy and positive development. Support for *familias* is therefore a high priority for the BAHIA program.

For example, parents are provided a continuum of services for their children from two to ten years of age including referrals to social services as needed. Parents are able to hold down jobs, seek employment, receive training and/or improve their education by attending school. Additionally, BAHIA provides an opportunity for parents to participate in bilingual parenting workshops and parent–teacher conferences scheduled twice a year.

Servicing Two Age Groups To further help Latino families the BAHIA program provides subsidized and full-cost child care at two sites: Centro VIDA preschool offers full-time care for 64 children ages two to five years; BAHIA School-age Program serves 65 children ages five to ten years by providing afterschool care during the regular school year and full-time care during holidays and the summer months.

Linking Familias Latinos have been the majority, culturally and linguistically, in BAHIA's programs. However, a more diverse community of children is now enrolling in BAHIA, so Latino parents and children have a greater exposure to *familias* that are not Latino. Specifically, in this environment, Latino parents have opportunities to meet, share, and work alongside *familias* who are African American, Asian, gay, single father, single mother, biracial, Anglo parents with adopted Latino children, and grandparents rearing children. Their link to one another as *familias* is that they all value Spanish, bilingualism, and the services provided by BAHIA.

How Do You Know Your Program Is Successful?

Success and results are reflected in many forms. It is seen in

- The children who grow up to become successful and proud bilingual individuals as a result of early and positive learning experiences

- *Familias* connecting with one another and staying connected over the years
- Recognition received from the City of Berkeley for serving the Latino community for the past twenty years
- Annually surpassing the administration and management standards for child development set by the California State Department of Education
- Recognition in 1996 by the National Latino Children's Agenda as an exemplary program serving children

BAHIA also considers itself successful because of the support it receives from parents in all its endeavors to improve its program. Parent collaborators help raise funds to purchase supplies and materials and even help write grants to support new program ideas. Additionally, parent contributions have helped reduce costs to improve and expand services by donating time and labor, including the construction of two new specialized classrooms for math and science and the landscaping and maintenance of a play yard for schoolage children at both sites.

Parents once served by BAHIA (over the past twenty-one years) often return to donate time, money, or labor to continue the tradition of caring that they experienced when BAHIA served them. Parents and children especially like being able to still see themselves in the colorful picture collages that are displayed in the child care centers. Volunteers from the community have provided over 500 hours of time to the children's programs.

What Barriers Has BAHIA Had to Overcome?

In society, bilingual child care continues to be high in demand, yet limited, underfunded, and undervalued. Certain professional requirements for bilingual child care teachers sometimes create a barrier for native speaking, credentialed teachers from Mexico and Latin America. Thus, BAHIA has had some difficulty filling teacher job openings because prospective teachers do not have the units in child development required by the State of California. To overcome this limited supply of teachers, BAHIA provides stipends to teacher assistants each year to help them in their professional development, paying for classes, conferences, books, and supplies. This plan includes young Latino men and women who were not previously interested in college, but who demonstrate leadership, interest, and an understanding of working with children. Providing these stipends for professional development and job training results from the belief that the quality of bilingual learning experiences for children is of the utmost importance to the long-term development of children.

The need to nurture bilingualism is not only particular to Latinos, but also to *familias* that see the value of two languages in building crosscultural understanding, and is what prompted the events leading to BAHIA's creation in 1974. Its growth and improvements since that time have been inspired and reinspired by the parents, staff, and a committed Board of Directors to keep BAHIA, and its bilingual children's program, vital and active assets to the community.

Contributed by Beatriz Leyva-Cutler, BAHIA, Inc.

- *sexual harassment of girls by boys—from innuendo to actual assault—in our nation's schools is increasing.*[5]

The AAUW results have many implications for early childhood professionals. First, the findings reveal the extent of sexual harassment. Second, 85 percent of girls surveyed and 76 percent of boys said that they have been sexually harassed. Some may have thought or think that sexual harassment is something only girls experience, but this data indicate the extent to which boys are also harassed. Third, the data from the survey reveal that the psychological effects of sexual harassment are more profound for girls than for boys; 70 percent of girls and 24 percent of boys reported that the experience made them very or somewhat upset.

These data should cause early childhood professionals to be concerned about the roots of sexism and sexual harassment and to realize that these practices have their beginnings in practices found in children's early years in homes, centers, and preschools. Early childhood professionals must continue to examine personal and programmatic practices, evaluate materials, and work with parents for the purpose of eliminating sexism and to assure that girls—indeed, all children—will not be shortchanged in any way.

The *Federal Register* defines *sexism* as, "the collection of attitudes, beliefs, and behaviors which result from the assumption that one sex is superior. *In the context of schools,* the term refers to the collection of structures, policies, practices and activities that overtly or covertly prescribe the development of girls and boys and prepare them for traditional sex roles."[6]

On the basis of sex, parents and society begin at a child's birth to teach a particular sex role. Probably no other factor plays such a determining role in life as does this sex-role identification. It was once thought that certain characteristics of maleness or femaleness were innate; but it is now generally recognized that sex roles are products of socialization, role modeling, and conscious and unconscious behavior modification. Culturally, certain role models are considered appropriate for males and certain ones suitable for females, centering around cultural definitions of masculinity and femininity.

Society imposes and enforces certain sex roles. Schools, as agents of socialization, encourage different behaviors for boys and girls. Parents, by the way they dress their children, the toys they give them, and what they let them do, encourage certain sex-role behaviors. Parents also model behaviors for their children and tell them to act "like your mother" or act "like your father." Parents and teachers also modify, shape, and reinforce sex-role behavior: "Don't act like a girl"; "Don't play with that—it's for boys"; "Boys don't cry"; "Don't behave that way—it's not ladylike."

Educators disagree as to whether children can or should be reared in a nonstereotyped environment. Some say children have a right to determine their own sex roles and should therefore be reared in an environment that does not impose arbitrary roles. Other educators say it is impossible not to assign sex roles. In addition, they argue that sex-role development is a difficult task of childhood and that children need help in this process.

It is too simplistic to say one will not assign or teach a particular sex role. As society is now constituted, differentiated sex roles are still very much in evidence and are likely to remain so for the foreseeable future. Parents and teachers should provide children with less restrictive options and promote a more open framework in which sex roles can develop. Following are some ways to provide a non–sex-stereotyped environment:

- *Provide opportunities for all children to experience the activities, materials, toys, and emotions traditionally associated with both sexes.* Give boys as well as girls opportunities to experience tenderness, affection, and the warmth of close parent–child and teacher–pupil relationships. Conversely, girls as well as boys should be able to behave aggressively, get dirty, and participate in what are typically considered male activities, such as woodworking and block building.

- *Examine the classroom materials you are using and determine whether they contain obvious instances of sex-role stereotyping.* When you find examples, modify the materials or do not use them. Let publishers know your feelings, and tell other faculty members about them.

- *Examine your behavior to see whether you are encouraging sex stereotypes.* Do you tell girls they cannot empty wastebaskets, but they can water the plants? Do you tell boys they should not play with dolls? Do you tell girls they cannot lift certain things in the classroom because they are too heavy for them? Do you say that "boys aren't supposed to cry"? Do you reward only females who are always passive, well behaved, and well mannered?

- *Have a colleague or parent observe you in your classroom to determine what sex-role behaviors you are encouraging.* We are often unaware of our behaviors, and self-correction begins only after someone points out the behaviors to us. Obviously, unless you begin with yourself, eliminating sex-role stereotyping practices will be next to impossible.

- *Determine what physical arrangements in the classroom promote or encourage sex-role stereotyping.* Are boys encouraged to use the block area more than girls? Are girls encouraged to use the quiet areas more than boys? Do children hang their wraps separately—a place for boys and a place for girls? All children should have equal access to all learning areas of the classroom; no area should be reserved exclusively for one sex. In addition, examine any activity and practice that promotes segregation of children by sex or culture. Cooperative learning activities and group work offer ways to assure that children of both sexes work together.

- *Counsel with parents to show them ways to promote nonsexist childrearing.* If society is to achieve a truly nonsexist environment, parents will be the key factor, for it is in the home that many sex-stereotyping behaviors are initiated and practiced.

- *Become conscious of words that promote sexism.* For example, in a topic on community helpers, taught in most preschool and kindergarten programs at one time or another, many words carry a sexist connotation. *Fireman, policeman,* and *mailman,* for example, are all masculine terms; nonsexist terms are *firefighter, police officer,* and *mail carrier.* You should examine all your curricular materials and teaching practices to determine how you can make them free from sexism.

- *Examine your teaching and behavior to be sure you are not limiting certain roles to either sex.* Females should not be encouraged to pursue only roles that are subservient, submissive, lacking in intellectual demands, or low paying. You can do the following specific things in your teaching:

  Give all children a chance to respond to questions. Research consistently shows that teachers do not wait long enough after they ask a question for most children, especially girls, to respond. Therefore, quick responders—usually boys—answer all the questions. By waiting longer you will be able to respond to more girls' answers.

Be an active professional. Just as we want children to engage in active learning, so too professionals should engage in active involvement in the classroom. This helps ensure that you will get to interact with and give attention to all children, not to just a few.

Help all children become independent and do things for themselves. Discourage behaviors and attitudes that promote helplessness and dependency. Discourage remarks such as "I can't because I'm not good at . . ."

Examine your classroom management and behavioral guidance techniques (see Chap. 10). Are you treating both sexes and all cultures fairly and in individual and culturally appropriate ways?

Use portfolios, teacher observations, and other authentic means of assessing children's progress (see Chap. 9) in order to provide bias-free assessment. Involving children in the evaluation of their own efforts also is a good way of promoting children's positive images of themselves.

- *Do not encourage children to dress in ways that lead to sex stereotyping.* Females should not be encouraged to wear frilly dresses, then forbidden to participate in an activity because they might get dirty or spoil their clothes. Children should be encouraged to dress so they will be able to participate in a range of both indoor and outdoor activi-

ties. This is an area in which you may be able to help parents if they seek your advice by discussing how dressing their child differently can contribute to more effective participation.

Implement an Antibias Curriculum and Activities The goal of an *antibias* curriculum is to help children learn to be accepting of others regardless of gender, race, ethnicity, socioeconomic status, or disability. Children participating in an antibias curriculum are comfortable with diversity and learn to stand up for themselves and others in the face of injustice. Additionally, in this supportive, open-minded environment, children learn to construct a knowledgeable, confident self-identity.

Young children are constantly learning about differences and need a sensitive teacher to help them form positive, unbiased perceptions about variations among people. As children color pictures of themselves, for example, you may hear a comment such as, "Your skin is white and my skin is brown." Many teachers are tempted, in the name of equality, to respond, "It doesn't matter what color we are—we are all people." While this remark does not sound harmful, it fails to help children develop positive feelings about *themselves*. A more appropriate response might be, "Tabitha, your skin is a beautiful dark brown, which is just right for you; Christina, your skin is a beautiful light tan, which is just right for you." A comment such as this positively acknowledges each child's different skin color, which is an important step for developing a positive self-concept.

Through the sensitive guidance of caring teachers, children learn to speak up for themselves and others. By living and learning in an accepting environment, children find that they have the ability to change intolerable situations and can have a positive impact on the future. This is part of what empowerment is all about, and it begins in the home and in early childhood programs. It is important, then, that an antibias curriculum starts in early childhood and continue throughout the school years.

Teach to Children's Learning Styles

Every person has a unique learning style. Although every person's learning style is different, we can cluster learning styles for instructional purposes. It makes sense to consider these various styles and account for them in early childhood programs when organizing the environment and developing activities.

Different Children, Different Learning Styles

Every person has a unique learning style. Educators can broadly categorize individual learning styles for instructional purposes. It makes sense to consider these various styles and account for them in early childhood programs when organizing the environment and developing activities.

What do we mean, exactly, by learning styles? "Learning style is the way that students of every age are affected by their (1) immediate environment, (2) own emotionality, (3) sociological needs, (4) physical characteristics, and (5) psychological inclinations when concentrating and trying to master and remember new or difficult information or skills. Children learn best *only* when they use their learning style characteristics advantageously; otherwise they study, but often forget what they tried to learn."[7] Early childhood professionals categorize learning styles as consisting of the following elements (graphically depicted in Figure 12.3):

- *Environmental*—sound, light, temperature, and design

- *Emotional*—motivation, persistence, responsibility, and the need for either structure or choice

- *Sociological*—learning alone, with others, or in a variety of ways (perhaps including media)

- *Physical*—perceptual strengths, intake, time of day or night energy levels, and mobility

- *Psychological*—global/analytic, hemispheric preference, and impulsive/reflective

Providing for children's learning styles helps you respond appropriately to diversity in your program. One of the most effective ways to begin is by diagnosing each individual student's learning style. A useful device for doing this is the *Learning Style Inventory,* developed by Dunn, Dunn, and Price.[8] You also should provide for children's individual learning styles through classroom practices and adaptations. For example, Dunn et al. suggest the following ways to adapt the learning environment to children's individual learning styles.

Noise Level. Provide music on earphones or earplugs (to avoid distractions for those who need quiet); create conversation areas or an activity-oriented learning environment separately from children who need quiet. *Or* establish silent areas: provide individual dens or alcoves with carpeted sections; suggest earphones or earplugs without sound to insulate against activity and noise.

Light. Place children near windows or under adequate illumination; add table or desk lamps. *Or* create learning spaces under indirect or subdued light away from windows; use dividers or plants to block or diffuse illumination.

Authority Figures Present. Place children near appropriate professionals and schedule periodic meetings with them; supervise and check assignments often. *Or* identify the child's sociological characteristics, and

Figure 12.3/*Diagnosing Learning Styles*

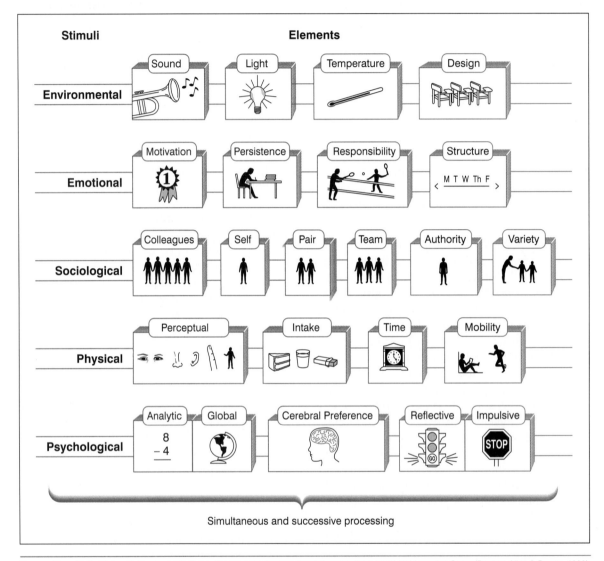

Source: From M. C. Carbo, R. Dunn, and K. Dunn, *Teaching Students to Read Through Their Individual Learning Styles* (Boston: Allyn & Bacon, 1986), p. 3. Copyright © 1986 by Allyn & Bacon. Reprinted by permission.

permit isolated study if self-oriented and peer groupings if peer oriented, or multiple options if learning in several ways is indicated; interact with collaborative professional.

Visual Preferences. Use pictures, filmstrips, films, graphs, single-concept loops, transparencies, computer monitors, diagrams, drawings, books, and magazines; supply resources that require reading and seeing; use programmed learning (if student needs structure) and written assignments and evaluations. Reinforce knowledge through tactile, kinesthetic, and then auditory resources. *Or* use resources prescribed under the perceptual preferences that are strong. Use several multisensory resources such as videotapes, sound-filmstrips, television, and tactile/ kinesthetic material. Introduce information through child's strongest perceptual preference.

Tactile Preferences. Use manipulative and three-dimensional materials; resources should be touchable and movable as well as readable; allow such children to plan, demonstrate, report, and evaluate with models and other real objects; encourage them to keep written or graphic records. Reinforce through kinesthetic, visual, and then auditory resources. *Or* use resources prescribed under the perceptual preferences that are strong. Use several multisensory resources such as videotapes, sound-filmstrips, television, and

real-life experiences such as visits, interviewing, building, designing, and so on. Introduce information through activities such as baking, building, sewing, visiting, or acting; reinforce through visual, auditory, and kinesthetic methods. Introduce information through child's strongest perceptual preference.

Kinesthetic Preferences. Provide opportunities for real and active experiences in planning and carrying out objectives; visits, projects, acting, and floor games are appropriate activities for such individuals. Reinforce through tactile, visual, and then auditory resources. *Or* use resources prescribed under the preferences that are strong. Use several multisensory resources such as videotapes, sound-filmstrips, television, and tactile / manipulative materials. Introduce information through "real-life" activities (e.g., planning a part in a play or a trip); reinforce through tactile resources such as electroboards, task cards, learning circles, and

Cooperative learning provides an ideal way for children to work together. Additionally, working together helps children learn more about themselves and others. Cooperative learning supports the multicultural goals of today's classrooms. What multicultural understandings can children learn by working together?

so forth; then reinforce further visual and auditory resources.

Mobility. Provide frequent breaks, assignments that require movement to different locations, and schedules that permit mobility in the learning environment; require results, not immobility. *Or* provide a stationary desk or learning station where most of the child's responsibilities can be completed without requiring excessive movement.

Different Children, Different Intelligences Piaget's theory of intelligence (see Chap. 5) is based primarily on one intelligence, logical-mathematical. In his book *Frames of Mind,* Gardner hypothesizes that rather than one overall intelligence, there are at least seven distinct intelligences (see Chap. 3):[9]

- linguistic
- logical-mathematical
- spatial
- musical
- bodily kinesthetic
- interpersonal
- intrapersonal

Further, Gardner maintains that all children possess all seven of these intelligences, although some intelligences may be stronger than others. This accounts for why children have a preferred learning style, different interests, likes and dislikes, habits, preferred lifestyles, and career choices.

These seven intelligences imply that students have unique learning styles appropriate to the particular intelligences. Consequently, early childhood professionals must consider children's learning styles and make efforts to accommodate their teaching styles, activities, and materials to them. Table 12.1 will help you make the connection using Gardner's theory.

Encourage Cooperative Learning

Cooperative learning is a popular child-centered approach. As a tool to infuse multi-cultural education, an early childhood educator can form small cooperative groups to engage in discussions about a number of cultural issues including prejudice, stereotyping, discrimination, and segregation. Using role playing or puppets in these groups can promote communication and create a sense of equity. Some discussions may be initiated through the use of good multicultural literature. (See Chaps. 8 and 9 for an expanded discussion of cooperative learning.)

Promote and Use Conflict Resolution Strategies

We all live in a world of conflict. Television and other media bombard us with images of violence, crime, and international and personal conflict. Unfortunately, many children live in homes where conflict and disharmony are ways of life rather than exceptions. Increasingly, early childhood professionals are challenged to help children and themselves resolve conflicts in peaceful ways. For this reason, *conflict resolution strategies* seek to help children learn how to solve problems, disagree in appropriate ways, how to negotiate, and live in harmony with others.

Part of your goal is to have children reach mutually agreeable solutions to problems without the use of power (fighting, hitting, pushing, shoving, etc.). You may wish to adopt the following strategies for helping children resolve conflicts:

Steps in using the "no-lose" method of conflict resolution:

1. *Identify and define conflict in nonaccusatory way (e.g., "Vinnie and Rachael, you have a problem. You both want the green paint . . .").*
2. *Invite children to participate in fixing problem ("Let's think of how to solve the problem").*

Table 12.1/*Seven Styles of Learning*

Type	Likes To	Is Good At	Learns Best By
Linguistic Learner *"The Word Player"*	read write tell stories	memorizing names, places, dates and trivia	saying, hearing, and seeing words
Logical/Mathematical Learner *"The Questioner"*	do experiments figure things out work with numbers ask questions explore patterns and relationships	math reasoning logic problem solving	categorizing classifying working with abstract patterns/relationships
Spatial Learner *"The Visualizer"*	draw, build, design and create things daydream look at pictures/slides watch movies play with machines	imagining things sensing changes mazes/puzzles reading maps, charts	visualizing dreaming using the mind's eye working with colors/pictures
Musical Learner *"The Music Lover"*	sing, hum tunes listen to music play an instrument respond to music	picking up sounds remembering melodies noticing pitches/rhythms keeping time	rhythm melody music
Bodily/Kinesthetic Learner *"The Mover"*	move around touch and talk use body language	physical activites (sports/dance/acting) crafts	touching moving interacting with space processing knowledge through bodily sensations
Interpersonal Learner *"The Socializer"*	have lots of friends talk to people join groups	understanding people leading others organizing communicating manipulating mediating conflicts	sharing comparing relating cooperating interviewing
Intrapersonal Learner *"The Individual"*	work alone pursue own interests	understanding self focusing inward on feelings/dreams following instincts pursuing interests/goals being original	working alone individualized projects self-paced instruction having own space

3. *Generate possible solutions with children. Accept a variety of solutions. Avoid evaluating them (". . . Yes, you could both use the same paint cup . . . you could take turns . . .").*

4. *Examine each idea for merits and drawbacks. With children, decide which to try. Thank children for thinking of solutions (". . . You want to both use the green paint at the same time . . .").*

5. *Put plan into action ("You might have to take turns dipping your brushes into the paint. . . . Try your idea").*

6. *Follow up. Evaluate how well the solution worked (Teacher comes back in a few minutes, ". . . looks like your idea of how to solve your green paint problem really worked").*[10]

Welcome Parent and Community Involvement

As an early childhood professional, you will work with children and families of diverse cul-

tural backgrounds. As such you will need to learn about the cultural background of children and families so that you can respond appropriately to their needs. For example, let's take a look at the Hispanic culture and its implications for parent and family involvement (see also Box 12.1).

Throughout Hispanic culture there is a widespread belief in the absolute authority of the school and teachers. In many Latin American countries it is considered rude for a parent to intrude into the life of the school. Parents believe that it is the school's job to educate and the parent's job to nurture and that the two jobs do not mix. A child who is well educated is one who has learned moral and ethical behavior.

Hispanics, as a whole, have strong family ties, believe in family loyalty, and have a collective orientation that supports community life; and have been found to be field dependent with a sensitivity to nonverbal

All classrooms must be places where peoples of all cultures, races, socioeconomic backgrounds, religion, and gender backgrounds are welcomed and accepted. parents and other family members can and should be encouraged to help make all early childhood settings places where everyone is valued and respected. How can you work with parents to assure that your classroom supports a multicultural community?

indicators of feeling.[11] Culturally this is represented by an emphasis on warm, personalized styles of interaction, a relaxed sense of time, and a need for an informal atmosphere for communication. Given these preferences, a culture clash may result when Hispanic students and parents are confronted with the typical task-oriented style of most American teachers.

When an understanding of the general cultural characteristics of Hispanics is helpful, it is important to not overgeneralize. Each family and child is unique, and care should be taken to not assume values and beliefs just because a family speaks Spanish and is from Latin America. It is important that teachers spend the time to discover the particular values, beliefs, and practices of the families in the community.

Based on this knowledge, you can use the following guidelines to involve Hispanic parents:

- *Use a personal touch.* It is crucial to use face-to-face communication in the Hispanic parents' primary language when first making contact. Written flyers or articles sent home have proven to be ineffective even when written in Spanish. It may also take several personal meetings before the parents gain sufficient trust to actively participate. Home visits are a particularly good way to begin to develop rapport.

- *Use nonjudgmental communication.* In order to gain the trust and confidence of Hispanic parents, teachers must avoid making them feel they are to blame or are doing something wrong. Parents need to be supported for their strengths, not judged for perceived failings.

- *Be persistent in maintaining involvement.* To keep Hispanic parents

actively engaged, activities planned by the early childhood program must respond to a real need or concern of the parents. Teachers should have a good idea about what parents will get out of each meeting and how the meeting will help them in their role as parents.

- *Provide bilingual support.* All communication with Hispanic parents, written and oral, must be provided in Spanish and English. Many programs report that having bicultural and bilingual staff helps promote trust.[12]

- *Provide strong leadership and administrative support.* Flexible policies, a welcoming environment, and a collegial atmosphere all require administrative leadership and support. As with other educational projects or practices that require innovation and adaptation, the efforts of teachers alone cannot bring success to parent involvement projects. Principals must also be committed to project goals.

- *Provide staff development focused on Hispanic culture.* All staff must understand the key features of Hispanic culture and its impact on their students' behavior and learning styles. It is the educator's obligation to learn as much about the children and their culture and background as possible.

- *Conduct community outreach.* Many Hispanic families could benefit from family literacy programs, vocational training, ESL programs, improved medical and dental services, and other community-based social services. A school or early childhood program can serve as a resource and referral agency to support the overall strength and stability of the families.

BOX 12.1 Implications of Latino Child Development for Early Childhood Professionals

In order to provide appropriate programs and services to Latino populations (i.e., people whose origins are Mexican, Puerto Rican, Cuban, Central or South American, or some other Spanish origin) residing in the United States, early childhood professionals must begin to understand what aspects of the developmental process are "culturally specific" and what aspects are universal or common to all humans regardless of cultural background. This differentiation is not easily made. One of the primary reasons for our lack of understanding is the absence of systematic research targeting minority children in general. Much of what we know is often based on data that implicitly or explicitly compares low-income minority children against middle-class Anglo populations.

The problem with this approach is that minority children's development tends to be viewed as less optimal when compared to their middle-class counterparts. Rather, an understanding of minority children's development must be based within the contextual parameters of a particular culture. Given this guideline, what, as early childhood professionals, do we know about the Latino child's growth and development that is "culturally specific" and what implications does that knowledge have for how programs and services should be structured?

First, we know that cultural background and socioeconomic background are highly interrelated so that what we think may be "culturally specific" may be more a function of the group's adaptation to their socioeconomic conditions. When social class is similar, differences between middle-income Anglos and middle-income Latinos may decrease. For example, research shows that maternal teaching strategies are different when comparing low-income Latinos and middle-income Anglos. However, differences substantially comparisons are made between middle-income Latinos and middle-income Anglos.

Social class standing is an important indicator of available resources such as the quality of housing, employment opportunities, medical services, and, most importantly, the quality of educational programs. For Latinos residing in the United States, level of acculturation also plays an important role. *Acculturation* refers to the degree to which an individual is able to function effectively in the dominant culture. This quality includes the ability to speak the language and knowledge of the dominant group's values and cultural expressions (e.g., foods, art). These factors play a major role in determining an individual's ability to adapt to the society. The early childhood professional must appreciate the relationship between social class standing and acculturation and those behaviors that stem from living in different socioeconomic situations.

Second, in understanding Latino child development, it is important to cultivate an awareness of Latino parents' orientation to children and examine how this affects the goals of childrearing. Previous research on parental beliefs suggest that cultural background is an important determinant of parental ideas. The type of competence parents expect of young children may vary from culture to culture. For low-income immigrant Latino parents, expectation for their children's skill development may differ from Latinos born in the United States; foreign-born Latinos perceive the behavioral capabilities of young children as developing later than do U.S.–born Latinos. It may be that low-income immigrant Latinos have a more maturational orientation to children's development so that the early emphasis on cognitive stimulation promoted in the United States is somewhat inconsistent with their expectations.

A maturational approach to childrearing may stem from the social and historic backgrounds of Latino groups living in the United States. In cultures in which children are expected to take part in the cultural activities of adults, such as sibling caretaking and economic maintenance of the family, certain parent–child interaction patterns will emerge. Thus, in more rural, traditional culture, parents may socialize their children by stressing observation and immediate assistance in task development rather than explicit instruction, which tends to be valued by middle-class U.S. parents. On the other hand, in U.S. culture children are segregated into age-graded classrooms in which information is given in bits and pieces over an extended period.

Early childhood professionals need to consider how parental orientation may differ from the specific goals and objectives of a particular intervention program. When working with immigrant families it is sometimes appropriate to indicate how the expectations of the school explicitly differ from the group's orientation. For many immigrant families, adaptation and innovation are a way of life, and accepting different ways of doing things is part and parcel of the immigrant experience. However, for second-generation or more acculturated groups reared in the United States, such explicit contrast may not suffice. In these instances, practitioners must become familiar with the degree of acculturation that characterizes the group and adjust their services accordingly.

Third, Latinos hold certain values and beliefs that are important for childhood socialization. The following sections present an overview of important core values and beliefs that will vary in individual families depending on their acculturation level, socioeconomic standing, and ethnic loyalty. It is very important to see these core values as broad generalizations subject to adaptations to local conditions.

FAMILIALISM

This value is viewed as one of the most important culture-specific values of Latinos. *Familialism* refers to strong identification and connections to the immediate and extended family. Behaviors associated with familialism include strong feelings of loyalty, reciprocity, and solidarity. Familialism is manifested through the following: (1) feelings of obligation to provide both material and emotional support to the family, (2) dependence on relatives for help and support, and (3) reliance on relatives as behavioral and attitudinal referents.

RESPETO

Associated with familialism is the cultural concept of *respeto,* which is an extremely important underlying tenet of interpersonal interaction. Basically, *respeto* (respect) refers to the deference ascribed to various members of the family or society because of their position. Generally speaking, respect is accorded to the position and not necessarily the person. Thus, respect is expected toward elders, parents, older siblings within the family, and teachers, clergy, nurses, and doctors outside the family. With respect comes deference; that is, the person will not question the individual in the authority position, will exhibit very courteous behavior in front of them, and will appear to agree with information presented to them by the authority figure.

BIEN EDUCADO

If a person exhibits the characteristics associated with *respeto,* then they are said to be *bien educado.* What is important here is that the term *educado* (education) refers not to formal education but to the acquisition of the appropriate social skills and graces within the Latino cultural context. For traditional Latinos, someone having honors from Harvard University, but who did not conform to this system, would be considered badly educated.

Incorporation of important cultural values and beliefs into the early childhood professional's interpersonal conduct provides families with a semblance of cultural continuity and maintains feelings of self-respect. The professional can accomplish this by demonstrating high degrees of courtesy, by understanding that indirect communication on the part of the child and parent is a reflection of *respeto* to teachers as authority figures, and by viewing the broader family configuration as an important resource for understanding Latino family dynamics. Within this general framework, the professional must accommodate individual differences and local community conditions.

Contributed by Marlene Zepeda, California State University, Los Angeles, CA.

PROGRAMS THAT SUPPORT MULTI-CULTURAL EDUCATION

In Chapter 1 we stressed the diverse nature of U.S. society. We emphasize it again here. The reality today is that the United States is a multicultural country, as shown in Figure 12.2. Early childhood professionals must prepare both themselves and the children they work with to live happily and productively in this society.

Bilingual Education

For most people, *bilingual education* means that children (or adults, or both) will be taught a second language. Some people interpret this to mean that a child's native language (often referred to as the *home language*)—whether English, Spanish, French, Italian, Chinese, Tagalog, or any of the other 125 languages in which bilingual programs are conducted—will tend to be suppressed. For other people, bilingual education means that children will be taught in both the home language and the primary language. The Bilingual Education Act, Title VII of the Elementary Secondary Education Act (ESEA), sets forth the federal government's policy toward bilingual education:

The Congress declares it to be the policy of the United States, in order to establish equal educa-

---

PROGRAM IN ACTION

PROMISE, POWER, PROSPERITY©

In the Socorro Independent School District, in El Paso, Texas, a two-way dual language/multiage program has begun practicing additive bilingualism for its students. Classroom teachers Antonio A. Fierro and Olga Escobar-Mendoza teach English and Spanish to a classroom of 38 five and six-year-old students. Using thematic units, they teach concepts in the primary language and reinforce them in the second language through additional teacher-directed instruction, thematic boards, and homogeneous and heterogeneous groupings. (Homogeneous groups have children who speak only one language; heterogeneous groups have a mixture of English speakers and Spanish speakers.)

Separate language groupings introduce the children to a new language, a new instructional program, and new cultures. Research has indicated that the most productive dual language instruction is one that maintains the students together for the majority of the instructional day. Because of this research, students receive same-language instruction depending on the language of the week. Since this program is utilizing a 50/50 language development model, language instruction is given biweekly (two weeks in English followed by two weeks in Spanish). Throughout the learning process, the instructional team will be sensitive to students' native language and scaffolding techniques may be utilized to ensure comprehension. The switch from one language to the other will occur, not for direct interpretation, but to aid children's ability to fully comprehend the content.

Fierro and Mendoza use such holistic strategies as the language experience approach, webbing, wordless books, dramatizations, total physical response, and shared reading. These strategies allow their students to be challenged and to become risk takers. To further complement their instructional design, they have set up fourteen learning centers and workstations in the classroom with activities that target a range of ages and learning possibilities. Most importantly, the classroom environment respects individual language and cultural differences.

Early childhood programs must develop and support programs that value the linguistic diversity of all students. "Promise, Power, Prosperity©" does just that.

Contributed by Antonio Fierro, 1996 Texas kindergarten teacher of the year, Socorro Independent School District, El Paso, TX.

tional opportunity for all children and to promote educational excellence (A) to encourage the establishment and operation, where appropriate, of educational programs using bilingual educational practices, techniques, and methods, (B) to encourage the establishment of special alternative instructional programs for students of limited English proficiency in school districts where the establishment of bilingual education programs is not practicable or for other appropriate reasons, and (C) for those purposes, to provide financial assistance to local educational agencies.[13]

Now would be a good time to read about the Early Childhood Development Center at Texas A&M University on pages b–2 and b–3 of the second color insert, "Observing Programs in Action."

Reasons for Interest in Bilingual Education

Diversity is a positive aspect of U.S. society. Ethnic pride and identity have caused renewed interest in languages and a more conscious effort to preserve children's native languages. In the nineteenth and early twentieth centuries, foreign-born individuals and their children wanted to camouflage their ethnicity and unlearn their language because it seemed unpatriotic or un-American; today, however, we hold the opposite viewpoint.

A second reason for interest in bilingual education is an emphasis on civil rights. Indeed, much of the concept of providing children with an opportunity to know, value, and use their heritage and language stems from people's recognition that they have a right to them. Just as extending rights to children with disabilities is very much evident today, so it is with children and their languages, as part of the view of children as people with rights (see Chap. 2).

Yet another reason for bilingual interest is the number of people who speak a language other than English. According to the Census Bureau, 31.8 million, or one in seven, residents of the United States speak a language other than English, with Spanish now the second most common language other than English. Table 12.2 shows the twenty-five most common languages (other than English) spoken in U.S. homes. Pay particular note to the fastest-growing languages, such as Mon-Khmer, spoken by Cambodians. Taken as a group, the Asian schoolage population is expected to double by the year 2020.

These data show that the chances are increasing that you will work with parents, children, and families in a language other than English. They also give you some idea what languages parents and children you work with will speak. Moreover, these increases will necessitate a need to develop culturally appropriate material and activities. As individual professionals and as a body, we cannot ignore the need for appropriate curriculum materials for children of all cultures. To do so adds to the risk of language-minority children being cut off from mainstream life and from the "American dream." Finally, there is a need to develop training programs for early childhood professionals that will enable them to work in culturally sensitive ways with parents, families, and children.

Programs for Students with Limited English Proficiency

Early childhood programs and schools can make several responses to language learning for children with limited English proficiency (LEP). First, they can use an *immersion* program, in which children typically are placed in a program in which English is the exclusive language and all instruction is conducted in English. A teacher may or may not know the child's native language. The goal of an immersion program is to have children learn English as quickly and fluently as possible. Little if any effort is made to maintain or improve the child's native language ability.

Other than immersion, there are three broad categories of programs aimed at LEP

Table 12.2/*The Twenty-Five Languages Other Than English Most Commonly Spoken at Home*

Language	Total Speakers over 5 Years Old	Percentage Change from 1980
Spanish	17,339,172	50.1
French	1,702,176	8.3
German	1,547,049	−3.7
Italian	1,308,648	−19.9
Chinese	1,249,213	97.7
Tagalog	843,251	86.6
Polish	723,483	−12.4
Korean	626,478	127.2
Vietnamese	507,069	149.5
Portuguese	429,860	19.0
Japanese	427,657	25.0
Greek	388,260	−5.4
Arabic	355,150	57.4
Hindi, Urdu, and related	331,484	155.1
Russian	241,798	38.5
Yiddish	213,064	−33.5
Thai	206,266	131.6
Persian	201,865	84.7
French Creole	187,658	654.1
Armenian	149,694	46.3
Navajo	148,530	20.6
Hungarian	147,902	−17.9
Hebrew	144,292	45.5
Dutch	142,684	−2.6
Mon-Khmer	127,441	676.3

Source: "U.S. Census Bureau, "Detailed Language Spoken at Home and Ability to Speak English for Persons 5 Years and Older" (Washington, D.C.: U.S. Government Printing Office, 1995).

students: English as a second language programs, transitional bilingual education programs, and maintenance bilingual education programs. While there are variations within each, the first two place value only on developing English language competency, and the third tries to create bilingual, biliterate students. (Note that bilingual programs may have different names in different states.)

English as a second language (ESL) programs generally provide a special English class for students learning the language along with sheltered English approaches to other subjects. *Sheltered English* involves a high degree of visualization of subject matter and a vocabulary adapted to the student's level of English proficiency.

Transitional bilingual programs have an ESL component and use the native language as a medium of instruction in the other subjects. As students learn more English, the native language use is de-emphasized until students fully adapt to a curriculum that uses English only.

Maintenance bilingual programs, like transitional ones, also teach English while using the native language to teach other subjects. As students learn more English, it is woven into content area instruction. What makes maintenance bilingual programs unique is that native language instruction is continued after students are fully functional in English. The goal of maintenance bilingual programs is to create students who are not only bilingual, but also biliterate.

Research on Second Language Learning

Research increasingly points toward a consensus: Children learn English faster and are more likely to excel academically if they are given several years of instruction in their native language first. A study endorsed by the National Academy of Sciences that followed two thousand Hispanic American school children concluded that "it is a myth that if you want children to learn English, you give them nothing but English."

Another commonly held misconception about acquiring English as a second language is that instruction in the student's first language will impair the acquisition of English. Research indicates that students who are literate and who understand grammar in their first language are more efficient learners of a second language than students who are not literate in their first language.

Research in second language acquisition since the 1970s has shown some surprising results:

- Early childhood is not necessarily the optimum period in which to acquire a second language; older children and adults can actually be better learners. Thus, the rush to immerse very young children in a second language may be inappropriate.

- Language proficiency is a configuration of many different kinds of language abilities. Though children may quickly acquire simple, everyday, social English, the English they need for academic success will take much longer to develop.

- Skills learned in one language transfer to another. Children with a good academic foundation in their first language will do better in a second language in the long run.

- Reading, especially for at-risk children, should first be taught in the native language. These skills will ultimately transfer into higher achievement in the second language.

- Children are not handicapped cognitively by bilingualism; some types of intelligence, such as creativity, may actually be enhanced by the child's being bilingual.

Issues in Bilingual Education

As you might expect, programs for helping children learn English are controversial. Critics of immersion programs assert that when the focus is only on teaching English, children are at risk for losing the ability to speak and use their native language. On the other hand, proponents of immersion programs maintain that English is the language of schooling and U.S. society, and it is in children's best interests to learn English as quickly and fluently as possible. Further, they maintain that it is the parents' responsibility to help maintain native language and culture. For their part, parents want their children to be successful in both school and society. Some regret that their children have not maintained their native language because of the role it plays in culture and religion.

Critics of transitional bilingual programs maintain that it takes children too long to learn English and that it is too costly to try and maintain a child's native language. On the other hand, proponents of transitional programs say it makes sense to help children learn English while preserving native language and culture.

Native American and Native Alaskan Education

Many Native American groups have revived their concern for preservation and teaching of native languages, in part because of (1) a resurgence of general interest in Native American issues and concerns, (2) a national report, and (3) the passage of several federal laws. The national report of the Indian Nations at Risk Task Force states that if Native American children are to succeed, then barriers such as "the loss of native-language ability and the wisdom of the older generations" must be overcome.[14] The report also encourages that native languages be used in the home and reinforced in the schools. In addition, the Native American Languages Act of 1990 urges "all educational institutions serving Indians to include native-language instruction in their curricula."[15]

Head Start and Multicultural Programming

Head Start has identified the following principles as a framework for multicultural programming:[16]

- Every individual is rooted in culture.

- The cultural groups represented in the communities and families of each Head Start program are the primary sources for culturally relevant programming.

- Culturally relevant and diverse programming requires learning accurate information about the culture of different groups and discarding stereotypes.

- Addressing cultural relevance in making curriculum choices is a necessary, developmentally appropriate practice.

- Every individual has the right to maintain his or her own identity while acquiring the skills required to function in our diverse society.

- Effective programs for children with limited English-speaking ability require continued development of the primary language while the acquisition of English is facilitated.

- Culturally relevant programming requires staff who reflect the community and families served.

- Multicultural programming for children enables children to develop an awareness of, respect for, and appreciation of individual cultural differences. It is beneficial to all children.

- Culturally relevant and diverse programming examines and challenges institutional and personal biases.

- Culturally relevant and diverse programming and practices are incorporated in all components and services.

TRENDS IN MULTICULTURAL EDUCATION

As with most areas of early childhood education, we can identify trends that will affect multicultural curricula, programs, and practices. The following trends, and others to come, will affect how you teach young children:

- Multicultural curricula are becoming more pluralistic and are including knowledge and information about many cultures. Children learn to look at the world through the eyes of other cultures and ethnic groups. As a result, more children will examine a full range of cultures rather than looking at only two or three, as is often the current practice.

- More early childhood teachers are recognizing that just because children are young does not mean that they cannot learn about multicultural perspectives. Consequently, multicultural activities and content are being included in curricula from the time children enter preschool programs. For example, kindergarten children might be encouraged to look at Thanksgiving through the eyes of both Native Americans and Pilgrims instead of being taught only the Pilgrims' point of view.

- Many early childhood professionals are being challenged to preserve children's natural reactions to others' differences before they adopt or are taught adult stereotypical reactions. Young children are, in general, understanding and accepting of differences in others.

- Since the 1980s increasing amounts of materials have become available to aid in teaching multicultural education. The amount and kind of multicultural materials will continue to increase so that teachers will have ever more decisions to make regarding what kind of materials they want and can use. Because not all materials are of equal value or worth, this abundance will mean that professionals will need to be increasingly diligent when selecting appropriate materials for young children.

- There is a growing recognition that effective multicultural education is good for all. Whereas in the past some teachers and parents have resisted multicultural teaching, more and more the public is accepting and supportive of teaching multicultural education to all children.

- You have read in this chapter about methods and strategies for teaching multicultural curricula to young children. Early childhood professionals will continue to create classroom environments that accommodate cultural and personal differences among students. These accommodations are and will continue to take place through the use of specific teaching strategies designed to address children's cultural and learning needs, including cooperative team learning, peer and cross-age tutoring, and involving all children in multiage, multigender, and multicultural group learning.

While we have a long way to go to ensure that all classrooms and curricula provide for children's multicultural needs, we are making progress. You can be at the forefront of making even greater advances.

ACTIVITIES FOR FURTHER ENRICHMENT

1. Choose ten children's books and evaluate them for multicultural content. Decide how you would use these materials to promote awareness and acceptance of diversity.

2. Interview students with field experience regarding their ethnic origins and positive classroom experiences relating to culture. Explain how these comments would influence the curriculum you would teach and how you would present it.

3. Interview people in your community to determine typical attitudes toward and means of punishment of children in different cultures. Be specific, so you can be aware of similarities and differences. What

implications do these have for the teacher's role in reporting child abuse?

4. Examine children's readers and supplemental materials to determine instances of sexism. What recommendations would you make to change such practices?

5. Observe children in both school and non-school settings for examples of how dress reflects sex stereotyping and how parents' behaviors promote sex stereotyping.

6. The classroom environment and certain educational materials may promote sexism, and play a powerful role in sex-role stereotyping. Examine the environment of selected classrooms and homes to determine the extent of sexist practices. Make recommendations based on your findings for minimizing or eliminating any such practices you find.

7. Stories and literature play an important role in transmitting to children information about themselves and what to expect in life.

   a. What books and literature played an important role in your growing up? Why?

   b. Identify five children's books and state why you think they would be good to use with children.

8. Survey ten teachers and your classmates, asking them what the term *multicultural* means. What are the similarities and differences among their responses? What recommendations would you make based on these definitions?

9. Interview at least three local principals to discover how they are dealing with issues of multiculturalism in their schools. What are they doing to actively promote a truly multicultural setting?

10. Cite at least five ways in which culture determines different childrearing patterns. Identify five implications these patterns have for early childhood professionals.

READINGS FOR FURTHER ENRICHMENT

Banks, J. A., ed. *Multiethnic Education: Theory and Practice,* 2nd ed. (Boston: Allyn & Bacon, 1994).

   The book presents articles on bilingual education, multicultural education, and the educational values, learning styles, and experiences of various American ethnic minorities.

Banks, James A., and Cherry McGee Banks. *Multicultural Education: Issues and Perspectives,* 2nd ed. (Boston: Allyn & Bacon, 1995).

   Two of the country's leading authorities on multicultural issues and programming provide a comprehensive and informative discussion of many issues involved in multicultural education today.

Barruth, L. G., and M. L. Manning. *Multicultural Education of Children and Adolescents* (Boston: Allyn & Bacon, 1994).

   Focuses on multicultural education theory and methods and their applications in classroom practice across the curriculum at all grade levels.

Bennett, C. *Comprehensive Multicultural Education: Theory and Practice,* 3rd ed. (Boston: Allyn & Bacon, 1995).

   Bennett offers an in-depth research-based treatment of the history of education for diversity in the United States and contemporary theory and methods in multicultural education.

Grant, C. A., ed. *Educating for Diversity* (Boston: Allyn & Bacon, 1995).

   Grant offers perspectives on the theme of your role as a teacher in diverse communities, schools, and classrooms. This book provides a base of information about the learning needs of students from a variety of cultures.

Grossman, H., ed. *Gender Issues in Education* (Boston: Allyn & Bacon, 1995).

   Contains articles on the influence of gender on the educational experience. It reports research, theory, practice, and controversies in the quest for gender equity in education.

Robles de Melendez, W., and V. Ostertag. *Teaching Young Children in Multicultural Classrooms* (Albany, NY: Delmar, 1997).

This book is a comprehensive study of the historical, theoretical, and practical aspects of multicultural education as it relates to young children. It addresses current and future trends of multicultural education and provides many practical classroom ideas for implementation.

NOTES

1. Valerie Ooka Pang and Jesus Nieto, "Multicultural Teaching," *Kappa Delta Pi Record* 29 (1) (Fall 1992), pp. 25–27.
2. Gloria S. Boutte and Christine B. McCormick, "Authentic Multicultural Activities: Avoiding Pseudomulticulturalism," *Childhood Education* (Spring 1992), pp. 140–44. Reprinted by permission of the Association for Childhood Education International, 11501 Georgia Ave., Suite 315, Wheaton, MD. Copyright © 1992 by the Association.
3. *Federal Register* (4 June 1975), p. 24128.
4. Millicent Lawton, "Four of Five Students in Grades 8 to 11 Sexually Harassed at School, Poll Finds," *Education Week* (9 June 1993), p. 5.
5. American Association of University Women, "What the Research Reveals," *The AAUW Report: How Schools Shortchange Girls: Executive Summary* (Washington D.C.: Author, 1992), p. 2. Copyright © 1992, the American Association of University Women Educational Foundation.
6. *Federal Register* (11 Aug. 1975), p. 33803.
7. Marie Cabo, Rita Dunn, and Kenneth Dunn, *Teaching Students to Read Through Their Individual Learning Styles* (Boston: Allyn & Bacon, 1991), p. 2.
8. Rita Dunn, Kenneth Dunn, and Gary Price, *Learning Styles Inventory (LSI)* (Lawrence, KS: Price Systems, 1987), pp. 14–19. Adapted by permission.
9. Howard Gardner, *Frames of Mind* (New York: Basic Books, 1983).
10. Marian Marion, *Guidance of Young Children*, 4th ed. (Upper Saddle River, NJ: Merrill/Prentice Hall, 1995), pp. 290–91.
11. N. Williams, *The Mexican American Family* (Dix Hills, NY: General Hill, 1990).
12. L. Espinosa, *Hispanic Parent Involvement in Early Childhood Programs* (Washington, D.C.: Office of Educational Research and Improvement, 1995).
13. Statute 2372, Section 703. Bilingual Education Act, Title VII of the Elementary Secondary Education Act, Statute 2268, Vol. 92 (Nov. 1978).
14. *Indian National Risk: An Educational Strategy for Action; Final Report of the Indian Nation at Risk Task Force* (Washington, D.C.: U.S. Department of Education, 1991), n.p.
15. Public Law 101–477, 104 Stat. 1152, Title I (30 Oct. 1991).
16. U.S. Department of Health and Human Services, Administration for Children, Youth, and Families, *Multicultural Principles for Head Start Programs,* CYF-IM-91-03 (Washington, D.C.: U.S. Government Printing Office, March 1991), pp. 5–6.

Children with Special Needs

CHAPTER 13

Providing
Appropriate
Education for All

Focus Questions

1. What are the appropriate terminology for and legal definitions of children with special needs?

2. What are reasons for contemporary interest in children with special needs?

3. What constitutes the legal, political, moral, and social bases for mainstreaming and full inclusion of children in early childhood programs?

4. What are the major provisions of federal laws affecting children with special needs?

5. What issues relate to teaching children with special needs?

6. What are methods for involving parents of special needs children in educational programs?

7. How do programs for the gifted meet children's needs?

8. What is the role of the early childhood professional in identifying and reporting child abuse?

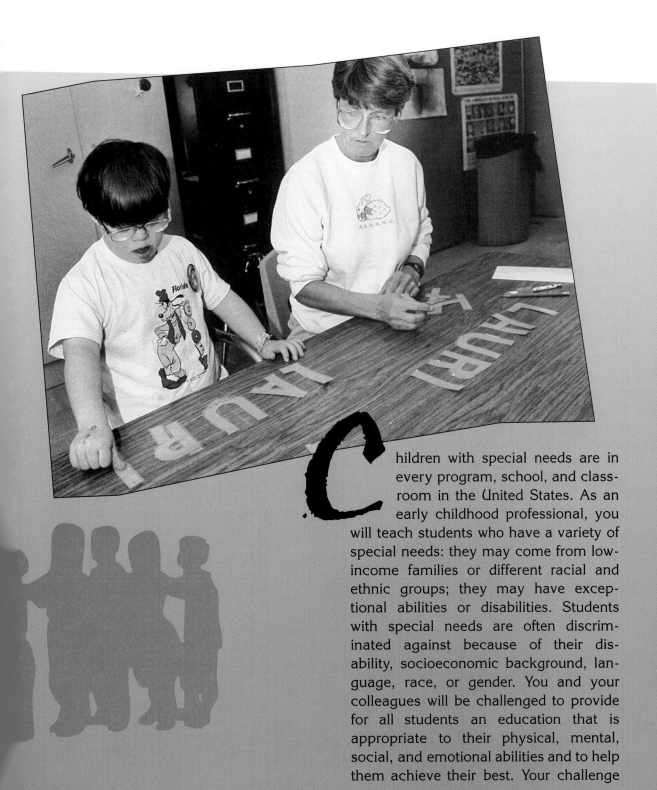

Children with special needs are in every program, school, and classroom in the United States. As an early childhood professional, you will teach students who have a variety of special needs: they may come from low-income families or different racial and ethnic groups; they may have exceptional abilities or disabilities. Students with special needs are often discriminated against because of their disability, socioeconomic background, language, race, or gender. You and your colleagues will be challenged to provide for all students an education that is appropriate to their physical, mental, social, and emotional abilities and to help them achieve their best. Your challenge

385

includes learning as much as you can about the special needs of children and collaborating with other professionals to identify and develop teaching strategies, programs, and curricula for them. Most of all, you need to be a strong advocate for meeting all children's individual needs.

CHILDREN WITH DISABILITIES

As a professional who works with children with special needs, you will need to know about laws that define terms and give special rights to children with special needs and their families. You will also use terms that apply to children and to services provided for them. It is important for you to know these terms and to use them properly (Figure 13.1). For example, *children with disabilities* replaces terms such as *handicapped children.* Avoiding the reversals of phrases, such as *disabled children,* communicates to parents, children, and other professionals that you are sensitive to using more people-first language.

The Individuals with Disabilities Education Act (IDEA)

The Individuals with Disabilities Education Act (IDEA) defines children with disabilities as those children

with mental retardation, hearing impairments including deafness, speech or language impairments, including blindness, serious emotional disturbance, orthopedic impairments, autism, traumatic brain injury, other health impairments, or specific learning disabilities; and who, by reason thereof, need special education and related services.[1]

The Americans with Disabilities Act (ADA) of 1990, defines *disability* as "a physical or mental impairment that substantially limits one or more of the major life activities."[2] This act mandates equal access by individuals with disabilities to both public and private schools. This law has had and will continue to have a profound effect on school architecture and equipment. For example, more schools and classrooms are wheelchair accessible and more playgrounds now have wheelchair-accessible equipment such as swings.

Table 13.1 shows the number of persons birth to age twenty-one with disabilities in the various categories. About 10 to 12 percent of the nation's students have disabilities.

Disabilities Covered under IDEA As an early childhood educator, you will have children with special needs in your classroom. The following disabilities qualify children for special education services under IDEA:

1. *Autism: A developmental disability significantly affecting verbal and nonverbal communication and social interaction, generally evident before age three, that adversely affects educational performance.*
2. *Deafness: A hearing impairment which is so severe that a child is impaired in processing linguistic information through hearing, with or without amplification, which adversely affects education performance.*
3. *Deaf-blindness: Simultaneous hearing and visual impairments, the combination of which causes such severe communication and other developmental and educational problems that a child cannot be accommodated in special education programs solely for children with deafness or children with blindness.*
4. *Hearing Impairment: A hearing impairment, whether permanent or fluctuating, which adversely affects a child's educational performance but which is not included under the definition of "deafness."*

Figure 13.1/Glossary

Adaptive education: An educational approach aimed at providing learning experiences that help each student achieve desired educational goals. The term *adaptive* refers to the modification of school learning environments to respond effectively to student differences and to enhance the individual's ability to succeed in learning in such environments.[*]

Children with disabilities: Replaces former terms such as *handicapped.* To avoid labeling children, do not use the reversal of these words (*i.e., disabled children*).

Co-teaching: The process by which a regular classroom professional and a special educator or a person trained in exceptional student education team teach, in the same classroom, a group of regular and mainstreamed children.

Disability: A physical or mental impairment that substantially limits one or more major life activities.

Early education and care settings: Promotes the idea that all children learn and that child care and other programs *should* be educating children birth to age eight.

Early intervention: Providing services to children and families as early in the child's life as possible in order to prevent or help with a special need or needs.

Exceptional student education: Replaces the term *special education;* refers to the education of children with special needs.

Full inclusion: The mainstreaming or inclusion of all children with disabilities into natural environments such as playgrounds, family daycare centers, child care centers, preschool, kindergarten, and primary grades.

Individualized education program (IEP): A written plan for a child stating what will be done, how it will be done, and when it will be done.

Integration: A generic term that refers to educating children with disabilities along with typically developing children. This education can occur in mainstream, reverse mainstream, and full-inclusion programs.

Least restrictive environment (LRE): Children with disabilities are educated with children who are not disabled, and that special classes, separate schooling, or other removal of children with disabilities from the regular educational environment occurs only when the nature of severity of the disability is such that education in regular classes with the use of supplementary aids and services cannot be achieved satisfactorily.[†]

Limited English proficiency (LEP): Describes children who have limited English skills.

Mainstreaming: The social and educational integration of children with special needs into the general instructional process; usually a regular classroom program.

Merged classroom: A classroom that includes—merges—children with special needs and children without special needs and teaches them together in one classroom (see Program in Action feature, "The Merged Classroom").

Natural environment: Any environment it is natural for any child to be in, such as home, child care center, preschool, kindergarten, primary grades, playground, and so on.

Normalized setting: A place that is "normal" or best for the child.

Reverse mainstreaming: The process by which typically developing children are placed in programs for children with disabilities. In reverse mainstreaming, children with disabilities are in the majority.

Typically developing children: Children who are developing according to and within the boundaries of normal growth and development.

---

[*]Margaret C. Wang, *Adaptive Education Strategies: Building on Diversity* (Baltimore: Brooks, 1992), pp. 3–4.
[†]Public Law 101–476, 30 October 1990, Stat. 1103.

Table 13.1/*Children Served in Federally Supported Programs by Type of Disability*

	Numbers Served	Percent of Total Students Enrollment
All disabilities	5,125,000	11.97
Specific learning disabilities	2,354,000	5.50
Speech or language impairments	996,000	2.33
Mental retardation	519,000	1.21
Serious emotional disturbance	401,000	0.94
Hearing impairments	60,000	0.14
Orthopedic impairments	52,000	0.12
Other health impairments	65,000	0.15
Visual impairments	23,000	0.05
Multiple disabilities	102,000	0.24
Deaf and blind	1,000	0.004
Autism and other	19,000	0.04
Preschool disabled	531,000	1.24

Note: Based on the enrollment in public schools, kindergarten through twelfth grade.
Source: U.S. Department of Education, Office of Special Education and Rehabilitation Services, *Annual Report to Congress on the Implementation of The Individuals with Disabilities Education Art,* various years, and unpublished tabulations; and National Center for Education Statistics, Common Core of Data survey. (Table prepared June 1995.)

5. *Mental Retardation: Significantly subaverage general intellectual functioning existing concurrently with deficits in adaptive behavior and manifested during the developmental period, which adversely affects a child's educational performance.*

6. *Multiple Disabilities: Simultaneous impairments (such as mental retardation/ blindness, mental retardation/ orthopedic impairment, etc.), the combination of which causes such severe educational problems that the child cannot be accommodated in a special education program solely for one of the impairments.*

7. *Orthopedic Impairment: A severe orthopedic impairment which adversely affects a child's educational performance. The term includes impairments caused by a congenital anomaly (e.g. clubfoot, absence of some member, etc.), impairments caused by disease (e.g.*

poliomyelitis, bone tuberculosis, etc.), and impairments from other causes (e.g., cerebral palsy, amputations, and fractures or burns which cause contractures).

8. *Other Health Impairment: Having limited strength, vitality or alertness, due to chronic or acute health problems such as a heart condition, tuberculosis, rheumatic fever, nephritis, asthma, sickle cell anemia, hemophilia, epilepsy, lead poisoning, leukemia, or diabetes, which adversely affects a child's educational performance. According to the Office of Special Education and Rehabilitative Services' clarification statement of September 16, 1991, eligible children with ADD may also be classified under "other health impairment."*

9. *Serious Emotional Disturbance: A condition exhibiting one or more of the following characteristics over a long period of time and to a marked degree, which*

adversely affects educational performance: (A) an inability to learn which cannot be explained by intellectual, sensory, or health factors; (B) an inability to build or maintain satisfactory interpersonal relationships with peers and teachers; (C) inappropriate types of behavior or feelings under normal circumstances; (D) a general pervasive mood of unhappiness or depression; or (E) a tendency to develop physical symptoms or fears associated with personal or school problems. The term includes children who have schizophrenia. The term does not include children who are socially maladjusted, unless it is determined that they have a serious emotional disturbance.

10. *Specific Learning Disability:* A disorder in one or more of the basic psychological processes involved in understanding or in using language, spoken or written, which may manifest itself in an imperfect ability to listen, think, speak, read, write, spell, or to do mathematical calculations. The term includes such conditions as perceptual disabilities, brain injury, minimal brain dysfunction, dyslexia, and developmental aphasia. The term does not include children who have learning problems which are primarily the result of visual, hearing, or motor disabilities, of mental retardation, of emotional disturbance, or of environmental, cultural, or economic disadvantage.

11. *Speech or Language Impairment:* A .communication disorder such as stuttering, impaired articulation, a language impairment, or a voice impairment, which adversely affects a child's educational performance.

12. *Traumatic Brain Injury:* An injury to the brain caused by an external physical force, resulting in total or partial functional disability or psychosocial maladjustment, or both, which adversely affects educational performance. The term does not include brain injuries that are congenital or degenerative, or brain injuries induced by birth trauma.

13. *Visual Impairment, Including Blindness:* A visual impairment which, even with correction, adversely affects a child's educational performance. The term includes both children with partial sight and those with blindness.[3]

State definitions of eligibility for special services under IDEA vary; many states are still in the process of developing their exceptional education programs. Therefore, depending on the state, services for children with certain disabilities may be fully available or are still in the process of developing. State governments are working in accordance with the six principles described in the following subsection.

IDEA's Six Principles   The Individuals with Disabilities Education Act (IDEA) sets guidelines for providing for the needs of students with disabilities. The law states:

It is the purpose of this Act to ensure that all disabled children have available to them . . . a free appropriate public education which emphasizes special education and related services designed to meet their unique needs, to assure that the rights of disabled children and their parents or guardians are protected, to assist States and localities to provide for the education of all disabled children, and to assess and assure the effectiveness of efforts to educate disabled children.[4]

IDEA establishes the following six principles for professionals to follow as they provide educational and other sources to children with special needs:[5]

1. *Zero reject:* a rule against excluding any student.

2. *Nondiscriminatory evaluation:* requiring schools to evaluate students fairly to determine if they have a disability and, if so, what kind and how extensive a disability they have.

BOX 13.1 Timeline: Special Needs Programs

1963 PL 88–156 Maternal and Child Health Program is expanded.

1965 PL 89–313 Payments are made to states for children with disabilities, from birth to age twenty, in state-operated programs.

1965 PL 89–97 Medicaid Program is established.

1967 PL 90–248 Early and Periodic Screening, Diagnosis, and Treatment Program (EPSDT) is added to Medicaid program.

1968 PL 90–538 Handicapped Children's Early Education Assistance Act creates Handicapped Children's Early Education Program (HCEEP); provides for model demonstration programs to acquaint public with problems and potentials of children with special needs.

1970 PL 91–230 Education of the Handicapped Act (EHA) is created; HCEEP is folded into part C of EHA.

1974 PL 93–644 Head Start program is amended to require that 10 percent of enrollment opportunities be made available to children with disabilities.

1975 PL 94–142 The Education for All Handicapped Children Act guarantees a free and appropriate education to children with disabilities ages five through twenty-one.

1983 PL 98–199 EHA is amended to allow use of funds for services to children with disabilities from birth.

1986 PL 99–457 authorizes the Federal Preschool Program, which extends rights under PL 99–142 to children age three through five,

and the Early Intervention Program, which establishes a state grant program for children from birth to two years old.

1990 Americans with Disabilities Act (ADA) requires access to public accommodations for all individuals regardless of disability. These public accommodations include child care centers and family child care homes.

1990 PL 101–476 Individuals with Disabilities Education Act (IDEA) provides services to children with disabilities from birth through age five.

1991 PL 102–119 Part H of IDEA is reauthorized and amended.

1992 Americans with Disabilities Act (ADA) establishes equal rights for people with disabilities in employment, state and local public services, and public accommodations including preschools, child care centers, and family child care homes.

1994 Improving America's School Act provides federal support for at-risk children to help them achieve challenging standards in core academic subjects.

1995 IDEA Amendments of 1995 specify in part that it be the policy of the United States that all children with disabilities have the opportunity to (1) meet developmental goals and, to the maximum extent possible, those challenging standards that have been established for all children; and (2) be prepared to lead productive, independent adult lives, again to the maximum extent possible.

---

3. *Appropriate education:* requiring schools to provide individually tailored education for each student based on the evaluation and augmented by related or supplementary services.

4. *Least restrictive environment:* requiring schools to educate students with disabilities with nondisabled students to the maximum extent appropriate for the students with disabilities.

5. *Procedural due process:* providing safeguards for students against schools' actions, including a right to sue in court.

All early childhood programs should serve children with a broad range of disabilities. When children with varying disabilities are learning together, it is possible to provide a wider range of activities. Additionally, programs can provide opportunities for families to come together and share ideas and information. How can you help assure that children with disabilities are meaningfully involved under conditions that are as normal as possible?

6. *Parental and student participation:* requiring schools to collaborate with parents and adolescent students in designing and carrying out special education programs.

Guaranteeing a Free and Appropriate Education

IDEA mandates a free and appropriate education (FAPE) for all persons between the ages of three and twenty-one. To guarantee students a free appropriate public education, IDEA provides federal money to state and local educational agencies to help educate students in the following age groups:

1. From birth to age three (early intervention)

2. From age three to age six (early childhood special education)

3. From age six to age eighteen

4. From age eighteen to age twenty-one (transition or aging out of school)

The state and local agencies, however, must agree to comply with the federal law or else they will not receive federal money. Exceptional education and related services specified by IDEA are shown in Figure 13.2.

Creating an Individualized Education Program

Exceptional student education laws currently mandate the creation of an Individualized Education Program (IEP), which requires a plan for the *individualization* of each student's instruction. This requires creating learning objectives, and basing each student's learning plan on their specific needs, disabilities, and preferences, as well as on those of their parents. A collaborative team of regular and special educators creates these objectives. The Individualized Education Plan (IEP) must specify what will be done for the child, how and when it will be done, and by whom, and this information must be in writing. In developing the IEP, a person trained in diagnosing

Figure 13.2/*Services Provided by IDEA*

1. "Audiology" includes identification of children with hearing loss; determination of the range, nature, and degree of hearing loss; and creation and administration of programs for [treatment and] prevention of hearing loss.
2. "Counseling services" means services provided by qualified social workers, psychologists, guidance counselors, or other qualified personnel.
3. "Early identification and assessment of disabilities in children" means the implementation of a formal plan for identifying a disability as early as possible in a child's life.
4. "Medical services" means services provided by a licensed physician to determine a child's medically related disability that results in the child's need for special education and related services.
5. "Occupational therapy" includes improving, developing, or restoring functions impaired or lost through illness, injury, or deprivation.
6. "Parent counseling and training" means assisting parents in understanding the special needs of their child and providing parents with information about child development.
7. "Physical therapy" means services provided by a qualified physical therapist.
8. "Psychological services" includes administering psychological and educational tests, and other assessment procedures; interpreting assessment results; obtaining, integrating, and interpreting information about child behavior and conditions relating to learning; consulting with other staff members in planning school programs to meet the special needs of children as indicated by psychological tests, interviews, and behavioral evaluations; and planning and managing a program of psychological services, including psychological counseling for children and parents.
9. "Recreation" includes assessment of leisure function, therapeutic recreation services, recreation programs in schools and community agencies, and leisure education.
10. "Rehabilitative counseling services" means services that focus specifically on career development, employment preparation, achieving independence, and integration in the workplace and community of a student with a disability.
11. "School health services" means services provided by a qualified school nurse or other qualified person.
12. "Social work services in schools" includes preparing a social or developmental history on a child with a disability, group and individual counseling with the child and family, working with those problems in a child's living situation (home, school, and community) that affect the child's adjustment in school, and mobilizing school and community resources to enable the child to learn as effectively as possible in his or her educational program.
13. "Speech pathology" includes identification, diagnosis, and appraisal of specific speech or language impairments, provision of speech and lauguage services, and counseling and guidance of parents, children, and teachers regarding speech and language impairments.
14. "Transportation" includes travel to and from school and between schools, travel in and around school buildings, and specialized equipment (such as special or adapted buses, lifts, and ramps), if required to provide special transportation for a child with a disability.
15. Assistive technology and services are devices and related services that restore lost capacities or improve capacities.

Source: Exceptional Lives: Special Education in Today's Schools by Turnbull/Turnbull/Shank/Leal, © 1995. Reprinted by permission of Prentice-Hall, Inc., Upper Saddle River, NJ.

disabling conditions, such as a school psychologist, must be part of the IEP team, as well as the parent, and when appropriate, the child.

Function of the IEP Using an individualized education plan with all children, not just those with disabilities, is gaining acceptance with all early childhood professionals. Individualizing objectives, methodology, and teaching helps ensure that the teaching process will become more accurate and accountable.

The IEP has several purposes. First, it protects children and parents by ensuring that planning *will* occur. Second, the IEP guarantees that children will have plans tailored to their individual strengths, weaknesses, and learning styles. Third, the IEP helps professionals and other instructional and administrative personnel focus their teaching and resources on children's specific needs, promoting the best use of everyone's time, efforts, and talents.

Fourth, the IEP helps ensure that children with disabilities will receive a range of services from other agencies. The plan must not only include an educational component, but also specify how the child's total needs will be met. If a child can benefit from special services such as physical therapy, for example, it must be written into the IEP. This provision is beneficial not only for children but for classroom professionals as well, because it broadens their perspective of the educational function.

Fifth, the IEP helps clarify and refine decisions as to what is best for children—where they should be placed, how they should be taught and helped. It also assures that children will not be categorized or labeled without discussion of their unique needs.

Finally, review of the IEP at least annually encourages professionals to consider how and what children have learned, to determine whether what was prescribed is effective, and to prescribe new or modified strategies.

IDEA for Infants and Toddlers Under Part H of IDEA, funds are provided for infants and toddlers to receive early intervention services for the following purposes:

- *Enhance the child's development and minimize the potential for any developmental delays.*
- *Reduce the costs of educating the child by minimizing the need for special education when the child reaches school age.*
- *Minimize the likelihood that the family will institutionalize the child and increase the chances that the child, when an adult, will live independently.*
- *To enhance the family's capacities to meet the child's special needs.*[6]

Services that can be provided under Part H include (but are not limited to) those shown in Figure 13.3.

Figure 13.3/*Services That Can Be Provided under Part H*

Assistive Technology Devices and Services
Audiology
Family Training, Counseling, and Home Visits
Health Services
Medical Services for Diagnosis or Evaluation
Nursing Services
Nutrition Services
Occupational Therapy
Physical Therapy
Psychological Services
Service Coordination Services
Social Work Services
Special Instruction
Speech-Language Pathology
Transportation and Related Costs
Vision Services

Source: From 34 *Code of Federal Register* (CFR) §303.12(d).

Parents must be involved in helping plan objectives and curricula for their children with disabilities. Parents have a great deal of knowledge and information about their children which is invaluable in planning for children's education. What are some things this teacher and parent may be discussing as they consider what is best for the child?

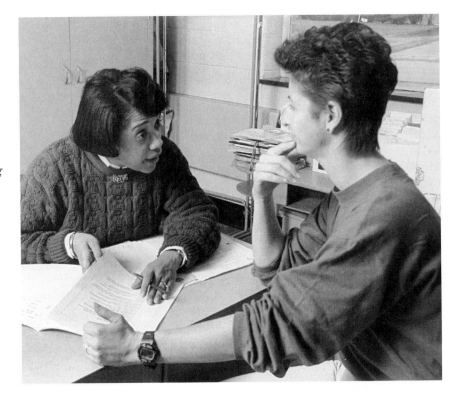

The Individualized Family Service Plan. Under Part H, infants, toddlers, and their families have the right to an individualized family service plan (IFSP), which specifies what service children and their families will receive. Also, the IFSP is designed to help families reach the goals they have for themselves and their children. The IFSP provides for the following:

- Multidisciplinary assessment developed by a multidisciplinary team and the parents. Planned services must meet developmental needs and can include special education, speech and language pathology and audiology, occupational therapy, physical therapy, psychological services, parent and family training and counseling services, transition services, medical diagnostic services, and health services.

- A statement of the child's present levels of development; a statement of the family's strengths and needs in regard to enhancing the child's development; a statement of major expected outcomes for the child and family; the criteria, procedures, and timeliness for determining progress; the specific early intervention services necessary to meet the unique needs of the child and family; the projected dates for initiation of services; the name of the case manager; and transition procedures from the early intervention program into a preschool program.

Table 13.2 shows one page from an IFSP developed for one child by Child Development Resources in Norge, VA. Note that the IFSP is for the beginning implementation stage, which accounts for why the section "Parents' Report of Progress Toward Outcome" is not yet filled in. As the plan is put into practice, this section will be completed. The entire IFSP is presented in Appendix E. An important document that merits close examination and study, this IFSP is a prototype and reflects the latest thinking in early childhood professionals' efforts to provide for special needs children and their families.

Benefits of Family-Centered Services. As we have discussed, family-centered services are an important component of early childhood programming. They will become more important. Programs that embrace and utilize family center services report results in the following areas:

- *improving child developmental and social adjustment outcomes;*
- *decreasing parental stress as a result of support and assistance in accessing needed services of their child and themselves;*
- *recognizing the family's role as decision maker and partner in the early intervention process on behalf of their children and themselves;*
- *helping families to make the best choices for their children by providing comprehensive information about the full range of formal and natural resources in their communities;*
- *accommodating individual child, family, and community differences through*

Table 13.2/*A Partial IFSP*

Outcome	Course of Action	Review/Modify (date)	Parents' Report of Progress Toward Outcome (date)
1. Kevin will have a smooth transition from CDR to the public schools (Fall 1995).	1a. Kevin's family and Lara will visit the Play Center to observe classrooms, therapies, and to meet the staff.	Feb. 1995	
	1b. Kevin will be referred to the Play Center by Lara with parent's permission.	Mar. 1995	
	1c. Kevin's parents and Lara will attend eligibility and IEP meetings as needed.	May/June 1995	
	1d. Kevin will attend Developmental Play Group more frequently in the spring to help him prepare for transition, if his parents desire.	Ongoing (starting late Spring 1995)	

Source: Child Development Resources, P.O. Box 280, Norge, VA 23127. Used by permission.

*creative, flexible, and collaborative
approaches to services;*

- *valuing children and families for their
  unique capacities, experiences, and
  potential;*
- *seeking meaningful and active family
  involvement in the planning and implementation of family-centered and community-based services; and*
- *obtaining potential health care savings
  due to ongoing monitoring of health
  status and referral for primary health
  care and nutritional services.*[7]

The following points should be kept in
mind when striving for effective individual
and family service plans:

- Methods and techniques of diagnostic
  and prescriptive teaching are essential
  as a basis for writing and implementing
  the IEP and the IFSP.

- Working with parents is an absolute
  must for every classroom professional.
  You should learn all you can about parent conferences and communication,
  parent involvement, and parents as volunteers and aides (see Chap. 15).

- Working with all levels of professionals
  offers a unique opportunity for the
  classroom professional to individualize
  instruction. Since it is obvious that all
  professionals need help in individualizing
  instruction, it makes sense to involve all
  professionals in this process.

- As individual education becomes a reality for *all* children and families, early
  childhood professionals will need skills
  in assessing student behavior and family
  background and settings.

**VIDEO
VIEWPOINT**

TEACHER'S LITTLE HELPER

As more children become more difficult for teachers to teach and control, teachers are
increasingly recommending that children be placed on medication to control their
behavior. This use of using drugs to control children's behavior, rather than teaching
children to control their own behavior, is a growing concern for many early childhood
professionals. Growing numbers of professionals object to medication being part of the
teacher's "bag of tricks."

Reflective Discussion Questions: What are the controversies surrounding the use
of Ritalin to control children's behaviors? What are some reasons why teachers would
recommend that children should be placed on Ritalin? Would you as an early childhood
professional consider Ritalin an appropriate alternative for use with young children? Do
you think the use of Ritalin is an epidemic?

Reflective Decision Making: Interview parents whose children are on Ritalin. Why
was the child placed on Ritalin? Do the parents believe that Ritalin is helping their
child? How? What advice would you give to a parent who asked you if you thought
Ritalin is an appropriate response to children's destructive/aggressive/hyperactive
behavior? What would be some activities you could recommend for controlling children's behavior without medication? Interview early childhood teachers and ask their
opinions regarding the use of Ritalin. Based on your discussions with teachers, do you
think they are pressuring parents into having Ritalin prescribed for their children?

Including Children with Disabilities
Natural Settings Provide a Key

A visitor asked Andrea, the kindergarten teacher, what it was like having a child with a disability in her classroom. When Andrea looked puzzled, the visitor continued, "I mean, do you think he belongs here?" Andrea replied, "He's five, isn't he?"[1]

Andrea's response is a wonderful demonstration of her commitment to equitable inclusion for young children with disabilities into regular classrooms. For Andrea, it is not whether the child has disabilities that become the criterion for her acceptance or nonacceptance. The needs of the child dictate her choices.

In the past, many teachers concluded that children's disabilities prevented them from taking advantage of experiences that promote typical child development.[2] Research studies, however, indicate that young children with disabilities need developmentally appropriate services just as typically developing children do. Intervention services including preventative, remedial, and compensatory efforts provided during the preschool years increases the developmental and educational gains for young children with disabilities.[3] In addition to intervention services, studies also indicate that when young children with disabilities are enrolled in integrated educational settings, they make greater gains in language, cognitive, and motor development.[4] These children also demonstrate higher levels of social play and more appropriate social interactions than children with disabilities who are in special, self-contained classes.[5] Young children with disabilities need to experience inclusive practices in preschool programs.

What Are Practices for Inclusion in Preschool Settings?

Inclusion is...the underlying supposition that all children will be based in classrooms they would attend if they did not have a disability.[6] Inclusive practices accommodate the diverse needs of all children by "including" them in physical, social, and academic activities with typically developing children in regular classrooms or physical education environments—natural environments to the maximum extent possible. Natural environments are identified as any environment in which it would be natural for any young child to be such as child care centers, family daycare centers, preschools, kindergartens, primary grades, and playgrounds. Inclusion of young children with disabilities in natural environments is an example of best practice.

Introduce Yourself to Cory

Cory is a young child with an orthopedic impairment who is included in a regular preschool program. Observe Cory as he moves from his wheelchair to his walker. What do you notice about his ability to be included in natural childhood settings? His autonomy? What early intervention strategies do you think allow Cory to be so independent now?

What are the other children's relationships to Cory? How does Cory seem to relate to other children? What do you think other children can learn by and through their interactions with Cory? What would you encourage them to learn from their interactions with Cory?

What can you say about Cory's ability to engage in physical activities? List five activities Cory is able to do. What positive contributions does Cory bring to the learning settings? What modifications in the learning environment has the teacher made that make it possible for Cory to fully participate?

 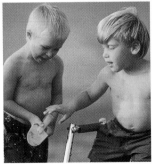 

How does this field trip to the beach encourage the use of language for Cory? What additional strategies would you use during this field trip to further encourage Cory's language and social development?

Best practices in early childhood programming for children with disabilities have traditionally been based on a special education perspective.[7,8] As early childhood educational practice moves toward a more equitable inclusion of children with disabilities, professionals must integrate Early Childhood Special Education (ECSE) practices with Early Childhood Education (ECE) practices.[9] ECSE programs are oriented more toward teacher-directed activities, with a focus on behavioral learning, and are designed to meet individualized goals and objectives. Implicit in the ECSE design is the fact that children with disabilities may not get to take advantage of typical environmental experiences and child-initiated activities promoted as more developmentally appropriate practice by professional organizations such as NAEYC. Thus, by its very nature and language, "best practices" generated by the field of special education has inadvertently communicated that what professionals do for children with disabilities must be somehow very different from the goals set for typically developing children by the rest of the early childhood profession.[10] Early childhood professionals increasingly are proposing the creation of one system of early childhood education for all. Essentially this system would frame a plan based on what it takes to allow all young children to succeed. Practices that seem to be working for all children focus on developing language in inclusive, natural settings.

Inclusion and the Acquisition of Language

The acquisition of language forms the basis of all other forms of symbolic activity by humans.[11] When children in the first few years of life are given appropriate literacy opportunities they make a remarkable, effortless acquisition of language. Conversely, delayed language development can be calamitous as it crosses over into other domains of development. Children learn what language is by learning what language can do.[12,13] In isolated settings we cannot expect children with disabilities to learn what language can do or how to use it well.

For some children with disabilities the greatest chance for success may be the implementation of specialized interventions within natural environments. In these environments children could be engaged in language development both through *milieu teaching* and *responsive interaction*. Milieu teaching differs from a didactic teaching methodology in that the topic and reinforcement used for communication is based on the child's immediate interest.[14] Thus, milieu teaching follows a child's attentional lead and is based on the premise that a child's language production can be prompted, either indirectly through environmental arrangement or directly through explicit prompts. For example, an explicit prompt (called a *mand*, like demand) would have an adult say to a child who is handling a plastic dinosaur, *"This is a dinosaur. Say dinosaur."*

Responsive interaction focuses on increased responsiveness and decreased "directedness" of an adult in a conversation between an adult and a child. It also follows a child's lead but promotes more of a balance in the responsibility of a conversation between an adult and a child. For example, if a child who is physically able to enter and play in a home center picks up a cup, the adult might say, *"Let's pretend we are having tea. Do you want me to pour tea into your cup? Tell me when you have enough."*

One other strategy that also promises to engage children in typical childhood opportunities for language and play is *activity-based intervention*. Activity-based intervention asks the

teacher to prepare an environment that is not only stimulating for all students but also considers how the classroom arrangement can develop functional skills and generalizable goals. In this approach, managing the environment to promote requests or comments by children is critical. One example of purposely setting up the environment to promote language might be: A preschool teacher arranges a center or physical environment with attractive materials and a high interest activity. In this environmental arrangement, she prepares an activity that children have done previously with some frequency, such as cut and paste. However, this time as the teacher sets up the activity she purposely leaves out some portion of the materials needed such as scissors. Children have to request their need of scissors to complete the activity. By providing the materials requested by the child, the adult reinforces the child's use of language. In this kind of intervention strategy it becomes critical for the teacher or other adults to encourage children to initiate language as a means of gaining access to materials and getting help.[15]

Other activity-based intervention strategies can also be used to increase the chances that a child will use language skills. These might include: (1) any activity or material that increases the likelihood that children will get excited and need to talk about what is going on, (2) activities and materials that prompt children to respond to nonverbal teacher cues, (3) materials that are slightly out of reach, (4) attractive materials that require adult assistance to use, (5) "sabotage," where materials are inadequate or missing, (6) activities that require children to make choices, and (7) activities or events that are unusual, discrepant, or silly. (One silly event might have a teacher putting a child's coat on inside out or a similar event that is inconsistently absurd compared with normal daily events.)[16]

Keys to success for these kinds of interventions are to use the environment to focus on making it a part of children's routines, provide adult and peer models who not only encourage children to use language but also respond to their attempts to do so, and establish a conditional relationship between access to materials and a need for assistance.[17] Activity-based intervention strategies involve planning activities or centers that help all children negotiate their environment satisfactorily, develop independence, and practice skills they will use in many different settings.

In Summary

All children benefit when children with and without disabilities are included in the same natural environment. Children with disabilities learn personal, language, cognitive, and social skills they might not otherwise learn in separate classrooms. Children who do not have disabilities demonstrate an increased self-concept, growth in social cognition, tolerance of others, and a decreased fear of differences in people.[18]

The references can be found after the Chapter 13 endnotes.

- Professionals must know how to identify sources of, and how to order and use, a range of instructional materials, including the various media technologies. One cannot hope to individualize without a full range of materials and media. Professionals must regularly be concerned with students' visual, auditory, and tactile/kinesthetic learning styles. Some children in a classroom may learn best through one mode, others through another. The classroom professional can utilize media technologies in particular, to help make teaching styles congruent with children's learning modalities.

Inclusion

Inclusion is the practice of ensuring that all students with disabilities participate with other students in all aspects of the educational setting of which they are a part, including playgrounds, family daycare centers, child care centers, preschools, and general education classrooms. IDEA specifies that

To the maximum extent appropriate, children with disabilities . . . are educated with children who are not disabled, and that special classes, separate schooling, or other removal of children with disabilities from the regular environment occurs only when the nature or severity of the disability is such that education in regular classes with the use of supplementary aids and services cannot be attained satisfactorily.[8]

Services formerly provided in separate special education programs are now provided in inclusion programs in the natural environment by special educators and other special service providers.

Inclusion receives a lot of attention and is the subject of great national debate for a number of reasons. First, court decisions and state and federal laws mandate, support, and encourage full inclusion. Many of these laws and court cases relate to extending to children and parents basic civil rights. For example, in the 1992 case, *Oberti v. Board of Education of the Borough of Clementon School District,* the judge ruled that Rafael, an eight-year-old with Down syndrome, should not have to earn his way into an integrated classroom but that it was his right to be there from the beginning.

Second, some parents of children with disabilities are dissatisfied with their children's attending separate programs. They view separate programs for their children as a form of segregation. In addition, they want their children to have the social benefits of attending classes in general education classrooms. On the other hand, some parents believe their children are best served in separate special education settings.

Third, some teachers feel they do not have the training or support necessary to provide for the disabilities of children who will be placed in their classrooms as a result of full inclusion. They also believe that they will not be able to provide for children with disabilities even with the assistance of aides and special support services.

Fourth, some people believe that the cost of inclusion outweighs the benefits. On the other hand, some professionals think the cost involved in separate special education facilities and programs can better be used in inclusion programs. There is no doubt that educating students with disabilities costs more. The average cost of educating a regular classroom student nationally is $5,623, compared to $12,932 (2.3 times) for an exceptional education student. This cost can be higher for some individual students and in some school districts.

A Continuum of Inclusive Services
The policy of the Council for Exceptional Children (CEC), a professional organization of special educators, is as follows:

text continued on page 401

PROGRAM IN ACTION

THE MERGED CLASSROOM

What It Is

The merged classroom is an innovative approach that allows all students to meet their full potential without pullout programs or segregation. This environment merges general education students and students with special needs together in one classroom, with the general education teacher and the special education teacher co-teaching all students. In *co-teaching,* or *cooperative teaching,* general and special educators jointly teach academically and behaviorally heterogeneous groups of students in an educationally integrated setting. Both teachers are simultaneously present in the classroom and maintain joint responsibility for instruction.

Merging special education and general education students is the best way to meet individual needs. The focus is on the students' strengths, not their disabilities. The overall effectiveness of the merged program is based not only on the acquisition of academic skills but also on the quality of interactions and friendships fostered among the children throughout the year.

The difference between this approach and mainstreaming or fully including isolated students in the general classroom is that all merged students work at their ability level within the core curriculum to acquire academic skills and at the same time are truly part of the class.

Why It Came About

Before developing this program, one of us taught first grade and the other a self-contained special education class. We frequently discussed our frustrations with our system's limitations. Kari, the general educator, felt mainstreamed students were "visitors" in her classroom. It was difficult for her to meet their needs, and she believed they often missed connections due to their limited involvement. As the special educator, Julie had always felt uncomfortable simply mainstreaming individual students into general education classrooms for a limited time each day. The students found it difficult to feel like true members of the classroom, and it

was difficult for the general education teacher to assume ownership for their education.

We attempted merging our classrooms daily on a limited basis, initially for opening exercises and physical education, although we also planned thematic units together. After experiencing some success with limited integration, we planned cooperative group activities related to our study theme and grouped our students heterogeneously for those activities.

Our success led to a pilot summer school program, fully merging a general education class of kindergarten and first grade students with a special education class of students with nonsevere disabilities in kindergarten, first, and second grades. The special education students included children with Down syndrome, cerebral palsy, childhood schizophrenia, learning disabilities, and Apert's syndrome. We received positive feedback from administrators, parents, and children throughout the summer. We then began a regular school year program, and are now in our second year of co-teaching in a merged classroom.

How It Operates

Throughout the day, we group our students in a variety of ways for instruction including large groups, split groups, cooperative groups, enrichment and remediation groups, and skill groups. Most groups are heterogeneous, containing both general education and special education students, although we do create homogeneous instructional groups to teach specific skills.

At the beginning of the year, we individually assessed each child's developmental skill levels in reading, math, and writing, forming flexible instructional groups based on this data. Ongoing assessment and teacher observations are used to change student groupings as the needs arise. Our program is based on the whole-language model, which enables us to meet the wide range of developmental levels in our classroom.

We jointly plan the week's activities, and each of us assumes responsibility for our own heterogeneous reading and math groups. This approach allows us to focus on the specific learning needs of each child. The weekly planning sessions are imperative to our success as we make adaptations, discuss children's progress, and attend to the program's many necessary details.

Another necessary ingredient for us is a well-articulated behavior management program. We teach the students appropriate social skills and behavior and make them accountable through the use of a "star card" system that monitors behavior on a half-hour basis.

Overall, our merged program is highly successful. As with any experiment, we have found the program to have both positive and negative aspects.

Pros

- Cooperative teaching partners provide each other with professional support to celebrate successes and to help with those inevitable less-than-positive circumstances.
- The potential for burnout of the special education teacher is all but eliminated in the merged classroom.
- The synergy, or collective energy, created when co-teaching ignites ideas and provides endless possibilities for teachers and students. Cooperative teaching awakens each teacher's unique talents and abilities. As Nancy Cozen, a parent of a student in our program, states, "Dedication, enthusiasm, and consistency are the attributes that make these teachers a powerful team."
- Co-teaching is a natural peer coaching situation as we practice new teaching strategies. The general education students benefit from smaller instructional groups geared toward meeting their individual needs. This approach allows them to gain a keen understanding of the unique qualities and differences in others. They learn to value others for what they can do, not dismiss them for what they cannot do.

- The merged classroom allows us to serve at-risk students who do not qualify for designated programs.
- Students with exceptional needs benefit from being part of a school community, forming relationships with regular education peers that transcend the walls of the classroom.
- The classroom provides these students with appropriate role models for behavior, social, and language skills. Teachers may move forward with the curriculum while supporting each student at their level within that curriculum.

Cons

- The co-teachers must commit a great deal of time for joint planning and program development and to maintain a quality program.
- Differences in opinion may arise between the co-teachers. Both teachers need to be willing to change the way they have done things in the past.
- Some people raise the objection that students with exceptional needs should be merged with students who are at the grade-appropriate level only. We feel that each student needs to be looked at as an individual and that for some, grade-appropriate merging creates frustration both academically and socially. Many students with special needs find their greatest success when working with general education students who are one to two years younger. Our ideal is a multiage setting for both general and special education students.
- Not all children with special needs can succeed in a merged classroom. Some students' physical, emotional, or behavioral disabilities are simply too severe for the classroom to meet their needs.

What Life Is Like for the Children

Our classroom has two teachers and a full-time instructional aide, a larger class size than normal,

continued

and two full-size classrooms. Diversity is seen as a strength, not as a weakness or a problem. If you are a student in our classroom, the child sitting beside you may have autism, Down syndrome, cerebral palsy, a brain injury, or no disabilities at all.

Laura Carpenter, a student in our class, states her feelings succinctly: "This is a very fun class. It makes me happy!" Jim and Anne-Marie Roach, parents of a general education student in our program, put it this way: "We really feel that it is important for children to develop an awareness of people with different backgrounds, be it ethnic, physical, religious, etc. Your classroom setting has helped Danny toward this awareness. It is rewarding to see children integrated in such a stimulating learning environment."

Overall, we have found the merged classroom to be a successful alternative to mainstreaming and integration of individual students with exceptional needs into general education classes. Co-teaching in such a program is a viable method of instruction designed to meet the needs of diverse groups of children.

Matthew

As an example, Julie describes her experience with Matthew, a young boy with Down syndrome:

Matthew joined my self-contained special education class when he was five. He was a very enthusiastic child with some preschool-level skills. His speech was unintelligible, but he still tried to converse with peers and adults. He manifested some behavior problems when involved in physical activities with other children.

Matthew functioned very well in the self-contained setting, but needed to be involved with his general education peers. He was mainstreamed into a kindergarten class for forty-five minutes per day. He experienced some success, but if activities were unstructured, he tended to become too rough with other children and the materials.

Before the next school year began, I searched for a kindergarten teacher who would integrate Matthew full time. I was fortunate to find someone willing to take on such a responsibility even though she had over thirty other kindergartners. Matthew proved ready and able to handle a kindergarten curriculum. Through the year, I provided behavioral support and his kindergarten teacher was in charge of his academic skills.

The year brought many successes. Matthew was accepted as a peer by the other children. He was able to function well within the academic setting. However, his behavior problems continued to occur on the playground during physical activities.

Unfortunately, Matthew soon became treated as a mascot. The girls all tended to mother him, and the boys tended to cater toward him. This was something I had feared from the start. Matthew's teacher tried not to foster these behaviors, but the kids adored Matthew and saw him as needing their help. As a result, Matthew became lazy. He continually looked to others for help, even when he did not need it, and the quality of his work diminished greatly. While the year was seen as an overall success, I felt frustrated with the status thrust on Matthew, and I knew I had some bad habits to break.

The following year, Matthew became a part of our merged classroom. It was the perfect placement for him, and he thrived in this environment from the start. We set our initial expectations high in order to break the bad habits he had developed the past year.

Matthew had not made the academic progress in kindergarten I felt he was capable of, so we designed a special curriculum to help him. Through the year, he learned to read emergent-level books with confidence, and currently is doing his best at written language. He still struggles greatly with oral language skills.

He has continued in the merged class this year and is a model student. He is now an independent worker and is treated by his peers as just another friend, not as a mascot or as someone who needs guidance. He still experiences some behavior problems on the playground, but not everyone can be perfect. Matthew is truly a merged classroom success story.

Contributed by Kari Hull and Julie Morse, Lemon Avenue Elementary School, La Mesa, CA.

CEC believes that a continuum of services must be available for all children, youth, and young adults. CEC also believes that the concept of inclusion is a meaningful goal to be pursued in our schools and communities. In addition, CEC believes children, youth, and young adults with disabilities should be served whenever possible in general education classrooms in inclusive neighborhood schools and community settings. Such settings should be strengthened and supported by an infusion of especially trained personnel and other appropriate supportive practices according to the individual needs of the child.[9]

A *continuum of services* means that a full range of services is available for individuals from the most restrictive to the least restrictive placements. This continuum implies a graduated range of services with one level of services leading directly to the next. For example, a continuum of services for stu-

dents with disabilities would define institutional placement as the most restrictive and a general education classroom as the least restrictive (Figure 13.4). There is considerable debate over whether or not providing such a continuum is an appropriate policy. Advocates of inclusion say that the approach works against developing truly inclusive programs. Figure 13.5 presents the policy on inclusion for the Division for Early Childhood of the Council for Exceptional Children.

There are many benefits for children in inclusive classrooms. They demonstrate increased acceptance and appreciation of diversity; develop better communication and social skills; show greater development in moral and ethical principles; create warm and caring friendships; and demonstrate increased self-esteem.

Given the great amount of interest in inclusion, discussions regarding its appropri-

Figure 13.4/A Continuum of Services

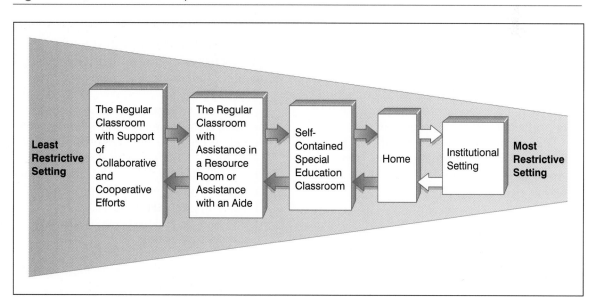

Source: G. S. Morrison, *Teaching in America* (Needham Heights, MA: Allyn & Bacon, 1997) p. 171. Copyright © 1997 by Allyn & Bacon. Reprinted by permission.

Figure 13.5/ *The Division for Early Childhood's Position Statement on Inclusion*

Inclusion, as a value, supports the right of all children, regardless of their diverse abilities, to participate actively in natural settings within their communities. A *natural setting* is one in which the child would spend time had he or she not had a disability. Such settings include, but are not limited to, home and family, play groups, child care, nursery schools, Head Start programs, kindergartens, and neighborhood school classrooms.

DEC believes in and supports full and successful access to health, social service, education, and other supports and services for young children and their families that promote full participation in community life. DEC values the diversity of families and supports a family-guided process for determining services that are based on the needs and preferences of individual families and children.

To implement inclusive practices DEC supports:

a. The continued development, evaluation, and dissemination of full inclusion supports, services, and systems *so that options for inclusion are of high quality;*

b. The development of preservice and inservice training programs to prepare families, administrators, and service providers to develop and work within inclusive setttings;

c. Collaboration among all key stakeholders to implement fiscal and administrative procedures in support of inclusion;

d. Research that contributes to our knowledge of state of the art services; and

e. The restructuring and unification of social, education, health, and intervention supports and services to make them more responsive to the needs of all children and families.

Source: Division for Early Childhood of the Council for Exceptional Children, adopted April 1993, revised December 1993. Used by permission.

ateness and how best to implement it will continue for some time. As an early childhood professional, you will have many opportunities to participate in this discussion and to help shape the policies of implementation and classroom practice. You should fully participate in such processes.

The websites shown in Figure 13.6 will help you access information you can use in your work with children and their families.

Strategies for Teaching Children with Disabilities

Sound teaching strategies work well for all students, including those with disabilities. You must plan how to create inclusive teaching environments. The following ideas will help you teach children with disabilities and create inclusive settings that enhance the education of all students.

- *Accentuate the positive.* One of the most effective strategies is to emphasize what children can do rather than what they cannot do. Children with disabilities have talents and abilities similar to other children and by exercising professional knowledge and skills, you can help these and all children reach their full academic potential.

- *Use appropriate assessment including work samples, cumulative records, and appropriate assessment instruments.* Dis-

---

Figure 13.6/Websites

---

http://www.ed.gov/offices/OSERS

http://www.census.gov/

http://www.cfoc.org/

http://www2.ari.net/home/nch/////families.html

http://www.medaccess.com/abuse/
   abuse_toc.html

http://child.cornell.edu/capn.html

http://www.aed.org:80/nichcy/

http://curry.edschool.virginia.edu/curry/dept/cise
   /ose

cussions with parents and other professionals who have worked with the individual child are sources of valuable information and contribute to making accurate and appropriate plans for children.

- *Use concrete examples and materials.*

- *Develop and use multisensory approaches to learning.*

- *Model what children are to do rather than just telling them what to do.* Have a child who has mastered a certain task or behavior model it for others. Ask each child to perform a designated skill or task with supervision. Give corrective feedback.

- *Let children practice or perform a certain behavior,* involving them in their own assessment of that behavior.

- *Make the learning environment a pleasant, rewarding place to be.*

- *Create a dependable classroom schedule.* Young children develop a sense of security when daily plans follow a consistent pattern. Allowing for flexibility also is important, however.

- *Encourage parents to volunteer at school and to read to their children at home.*

- *Identify appropriate tasks children can accomplish on their own* to create in them an opportunity to become more independent of you and others.

- *Use cooperative learning.* Cooperative learning enables all students to work together to achieve common goals. Cooperative learning has five components:
  1. *Positive interdependence.* Group members establish mutual goals, divide the prerequisite tasks, share materials and resources, assume shared roles, and give joint rewards.
  2. *Face-to-face interaction.* Group members encourage and facilitate each other's efforts to complete tasks through direct communication.
  3. *Individual accountability/personal responsibility.* Individual performance is assessed, and results are reported back to both the individual and the group. The group holds each member responsible for completing his or her fair share of responsibility.
  4. *Interpersonal and small-group skills.* Students are responsible for getting to know and trust each other, communicating accurately and clearly, accepting and supporting each other, and resolving conflicts in a constructive manner.
  5. *Group processing.* Group reflection includes describing which contributions of members are helpful or unhelpful in making decisions and which group actions should be continued or changed.

- *Use Circle of Friends.* This technique helps students develop friendships with their classmates. Classmates volunteer to be part of a student's circle, and the

PROGRAM IN ACTION

PRESCHOOL TREATMENT SERVICES: A COMMUNITY TEAM APPROACH TO THERAPY NEEDS FOR INFANTS AND CHILDREN IN COMMUNITY-BASED PROGRAMS

Alberta Children's Hospital in Calgary, Alberta, Canada, operates a unique outreach program using mobile therapy teams to provide therapeutic intervention to children with special needs in mainstreamed community settings.

Three community teams, each staffed by a speech/language pathologist, a physiotherapist, and an occupational therapist, travel daily throughout the city from their hospital base. While each team provides some direct treatment, their focus is on collaborative goal setting and program implementation with primary caregivers (parents, teachers, and aides), formulating individual service plans (ISPs) for each child. A psychologist and family support worker are available to provide support, education, and consultation to the team members, families, and community daycare centers.

The program caseload consists of 150 infants and children with a range of disabilities and functional levels. Intervention takes place in homes, family daycare homes, daycare centers, nursery schools, and preschool and school programs.

A significant feature of the program is the collaborative network established with seventy-five high-quality, community-based daycare centers. A solid four-way partnership exists among the hospital teams, families, daycare centers, and government funding agencies involved with special services for children with disabilities.

Philosophy

Central to the program philosophy is the belief that children with disabilities reach their maximum potential with minimal separation from family and community life. Merging the knowledge and skills of therapists and primary caregivers eases the transfer of responsibility to family and community for integrating therapy techniques into children's daily activities.

The preschool treatment services program believes in the principles of family-centered care, and in the values and benefits of early intervention. Program members believe it is important to include children with special needs in family and community life, and strive to strengthen their working relationship with the community to achieve children's optimal functioning.

Objectives

The outreach program has the following objectives:

- Provide therapeutic intervention by direct treatment, demonstration teaching, and consultation.
- Share knowledge and skills with primary caregivers and facilitate transfer of responsibility for therapy to family and community.

circle meets as a team on a regular basis. The teacher coordinates the circle and helps the group solve problems or concerns that arise. Students in the circle provide friendship and support so that no student is isolated or alone in the class.[10]

- *Use Classwide Peer Tutoring Program (CWPT).* CWPT involves whole classrooms of students in tutoring activities that improve achievement and student

engagement, particularly for at-risk, low-income students. Having opportunities to teach peers appears to reinforce students' own learning and motivation, according to Charles R. Greenwood, the program developer.[11]

- *Develop a peer buddy system.* In a peer buddy system, classmates serve as peer buddies (friends, guides, or counselors) to students who are experiencing problems.

- Help primary caregivers integrate treatment into daily routines.
- Provide parents, professionals, and related community staff with services, one-on-one consultation, and dialogue leading to increased knowledge and skills.
- Support, educate, and encourage parents to become informed advocates for their children.
- Provide educational presentations directed at increasing public awareness, knowledge, and involvement.

Program Model

The program provides coordinated, continuous services for children from infancy to six years of age. The purpose, quantity, and type of assessment and intervention vary according to each child's needs. It is essential, therefore, that the program and model of service delivery remain flexible. A case manager oversees each child's intervention needs, which may include therapy, education/coaching, family support, and community education and support.

The program emphasizes collaboration. Everyone involved with each child is an integral member of the team. The team approach varies between interdisciplinary and transdisciplinary according to the circumstances. To fully integrate children's programs into daily routine, the community team emphasizes teaching the necessary skills to parents and community caregivers. Sharing knowledge takes the form of demonstration teaching, writing skill-specific programs, providing disability-specific materials, and peer evaluation of skill acquisition. Sharing practical alternatives and creative responses to programming problems are the essence of frequent, short, and specific teaching sessions.

The community team has pioneered the concept of integrating children with special needs into regular nonspecialized community settings. The model, initially developed for an urban setting, has been adapted to the needs of several smaller regional cities and rural areas. Over the past eighteen years, the program has assisted in developing a strong cadre of enthusiastic, dedicated community daycare and preschool program staff.

Contributed by Ruth Cripps, former director, Community Outreach Services; Shirley Crozier, former coordinator of the community team; and M. Shirley Wormsbecker, program manager, Preschool Treatment Services, Alberta Children's Hospital, Calgary, Alberta, Canada.

Variations are to pair an older student with a younger one who is experiencing a problem and to pair two students who are experiencing similar problems.[12]

The color insert, "Including Children with Disabilities: Natural Settings Provide a Key," will help you prepare to provide for all children in your program or classroom. As you read about providing for the needs of children with disabilities, reflect about what you will need to do to prepare yourself for such a role and the specific things you will want to learn.

A Transdisciplinary Team For young children with special needs, a *transdisciplinary* team approach consists of interdisciplinary involvement across and among various health and social services disciplines. Members of this team can include any of the following professionals: early childhood educator, physical therapist, occupational therapist, speech communication therapist, psychologist, social worker, and pediatrician. The rationale for the transdisciplinary team is that a unified and holistic approach is the most effective way to provide resources and deliver services to children and their families.

Members of the team diagnose, prescribe, share information, and work cooperatively to meet children's needs. One of the members, usually the early childhood educator, heads the team, and other members act as consultants. The team leader carries out the instructions of other team members. A variation of this model is to have members of the team, such as the physical therapist, work directly with the child at specified times (e.g., twice a week) and provide activities and suggestions for the early childhood educator to implement at other times.

Making Transitions Transitional experiences from one setting to another are a must for all special needs children, especially those who have attended preschool in a special setting or a separate public school facility from the elementary school. To help the special needs child make a transition, the staffs of the sending and receiving agencies must cooperate in arrangements, activities, and plans. Consider the following suggestions:

- Try to approximate certain features of the receiving environment. If the new classroom has a larger child–adult ratio, gradually get children used to working and functioning in larger groups.

- Help children become accustomed to social skills appropriate to the new environment. If children have been using a restroom inside the classroom but will have to go outside the classroom in the new school, help them practice this new routine.

- Use materials and activities as children will encounter them in the new setting. For example, get a set of textbooks and familiarize the child with the format and activities.

- Approximate the kind and length of instructional activities children will be expected to participate in and complete.

- Visit the new school with children and their parents.

- Communicate with the receiving professional to share information about the child.

- Structure a social setting in the receiving classroom. Arrange a "buddy system" with a child in the new classroom.

- After the child has made the transition, visit the classroom to demonstrate a supportive, caring attitude to the receiving professional, parents, and child.

- The receiving professional has reciprocal responsibilities to make the transition as stress free and rewarding as possible. Successful transitions involve all concerned—children, parents, professionals, administrators, and support personnel. (Other suggestions for transitional experiences are given in Chap. 8.)

Figure 13.7 provides further information about what you will need to know and be able to do to be an effective teacher of children with disabilities.

GIFTED AND TALENTED CHILDREN

In contrast to children with disabilities, children identified as gifted or talented are not

Figure 13.7/*Knowledge and Skills for Effective Teaching in Inclusive Classrooms*

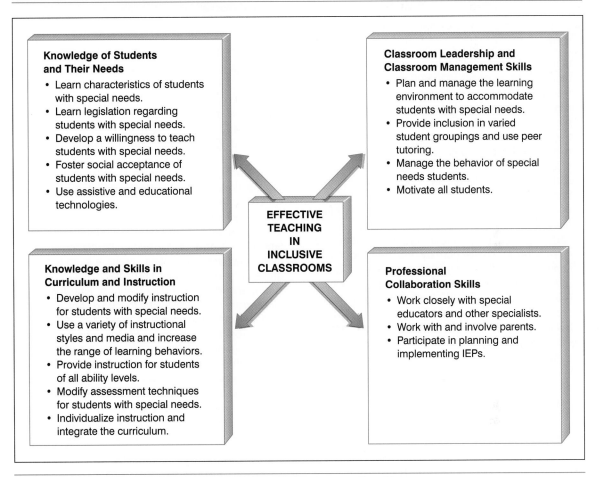

Source: G. S. Morrison, *Teaching in America* (Needham Heights, MA: Allyn & Bacon, 1997), p. 173.
Copyright © 1997 by Allyn & Bacon. Reprinted by permission.

covered under IDEA's provisions, and Congress has passed other legislation specifically to provide for these children. The Jacob K. Javits Gifted and Talented Students Education Act of 1988 defines *gifted and talented children* as those who "give evidence of high performance capabilities in areas such as intellectual, creative, artistic, or leadership capacity; or in specific academic fields, and who require services or activities not ordinarily provided by the school in order to fully develop such capabilities."[13] The definition distinguishes between *giftedness,* characterized by above-average intellectual ability, and *talented,* referring to individuals who excel in such areas as drama, art, music, athletics, and leadership. Students can have these abilities separately or in combination. A talented five-year-old may be learning disabled, and a student with orthopedic disabilities may be gifted. Gifted and creative children may

PROGRAM IN ACTION

THE SUNRISE CHILDREN'S CENTER

The Sunrise Children's Center is an inclusionary center that serves children ages two to six years old. Sunrise, currently a 10,600 square-foot facility with eight classrooms, began as a self-contained regional preschool program housed within a local elementary school. As the need for inclusion became evident, teachers surveyed the area for existing child care programs or preschools that would "mainstream" children. Several challenges surfaced. Developmentally appropriate centers had long waiting lists and would not change their policy for children with special needs (who often are not identified until September). Many classes had large teacher–student ratios, and teachers were already challenged by the behaviors and concerns of their "typical" population. When approached, teachers often overreacted to children with special needs, feeling the need to do something "special" with their program. Sunrise began by hiring teachers and welcoming parents that believed in full inclusion. Their philosophy is that all children have strengths and areas of concerns, all children deserve individual educational programs, and that typically developing children benefit in an inclusionary model as much, if not more than, do children with special needs.

A Child's View of the Sunrise Center

Consistency is essential for all children. Every morning when I arrive I know exactly what is expected of me. I hang up my coat, put my lunch away, and get a big smile and greeting from my teacher and friends. *The room is sunny and well organized. Centers may change, but not without warning and preparation.* I like it when I know about changes. One day we talked about changing the dress-up corner to a hospital, and before we did it we all talked about what we wanted to do. *Everything in the room has its place and there is lots of room to play.* I look around the room and see a block area, a housekeeping center, a fine-motor play area, a reading corner, a sand table, a dress-up corner, and an art center.

Teachers always give plenty of time for transition from one activity to the next. My teacher starts singing the clean-up song and turns the timer over. The timer helps me know how long we have. Johnny isn't helping to clean up today, so my teacher starts to help me and encourages Johnny to put one block away. When he does she says, "Thank you!" so he wants to help more!

Circle should be at the same time every day. Many children benefit from preteaching before cir-

---

display characteristic behaviors, as identified in Figure 13.8.

Although children may not display all these signs, the presence of several of them can alert parents and early childhood professionals to make appropriate instructional, environmental, and social adjustments. Additionally, Figure 13.9 outlines characteristics displayed in each of the areas of giftedness. You can also use these to help you identify gifted children in your program.

Nature or Nurture?

When identifying gifted and talented children, there is always the issue of how much gifted-

ness is attributed to nature (genetic and biological factors), and how much is attributed to nurture (the environment). While experts agree that giftedness is attributable to both nature and nurture, they do not agree on what percentage each contributes. The following environmental factors, among others, contribute to giftedness—and to all good childrearing:

- *Excellent early opportunities with encouragement from family and friends*
- *Superior, early, and continuing guidance and instruction*
- *Frequent and continual opportunity to practice and extend children's special abilities and to progress as they are able*

cle begins. It's circle time and my teacher has the chairs out with our names on them. I have trouble with this but an assistant helps me. She sits in back of me during circle because I have trouble sitting still. She rubs my back hard (I like it!) and helps me when I get confused. Before circle we went over the songs, fingerplays, and book so I feel great that I know it. *The assistant needs to be discrete and nonverbal during circle to not distract from the teacher.* I like the assistant in back of me, she's very quiet and not too pushy. After circle it's time to have snack. *Snack is a great time to encourage language.* During snack I practice talking to my friends. My assistant asks me lots of questions.

Therapy should be incorporated into daily group routine. Children should never feel singled out, different, or isolated from their peers. I have an oral motor program, but everyone does it with me. The teacher makes it into a game for all of us, saying, "Bring your tongue to the top of the house, to the basement," and so on.

Therapy should be provided in the setting that challenges the child. It's time for the bath-

room and to get ready to go outside. I have trouble with the bathroom, but the assistant takes me in and asks me to use the toilet. My friends are there, too. I watch them and want to try! Getting my coat on is hard, but my teacher showed us all an easy way. The assistant helps me a little and I do the rest. We go out to the playground and a lady helps me play games with my friends. Our teachers warn us before it's time to line up and come inside.

Now it's time for activity centers. We gather on the rug and the teacher tells us about the different activities we can do. I feel overwhelmed, but the assistant suggests a table. I go to the table and another special person is playing a game that helps me with my speech. I have three other friends with me at the table. A bell rings and I go to another table where I learn to cut and paste. Sometimes I get to take friends to a special room and work with helper people.

It's time to go home now and we get back into a circle and sing, "It's time to say goodbye to our friends."

Contributed by Joanna Bogin, director, Sunrise Children's Center, Amherst, NH.

Figure 13.8/*Characteristics of Gifted/Creative Children*

A. High sensitivity.
B. Excessive amounts of energy.
C. Bores easily and may appear to have a short attention span.
D. Requires emotionally stable and secure adults around him/her.
E. Will resist authority if it not democratically oriented.
F. Have preferred ways of learning; particularly in reading and mathamatics.
G. May become easily frustrated because of his/her big ideas and not having the resources or people to assist him/her in carrying these tasks to fruition.
H. Learns from an exploratory level and resists rote memory and just being a listener.
I. Cannot sit still unless absorbed in something of his/her own interest.
J. Very compassionate and has many fears such as death and loss of loved ones.
K. If they experience failure early, may give up and develop permanent learning blocks.

Source: The National Foundation for Gifted and Creative Children, 1997. Used with permission.

Figure 13.9/*Characteristics of Various Areas of Giftedness*

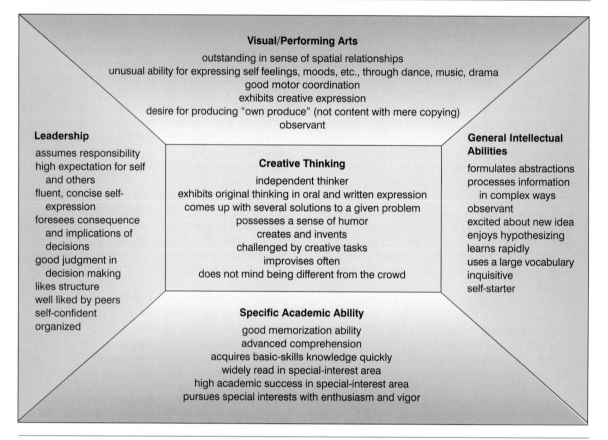

- *Close association with others of similar ability*
- *Opportunities for real accomplishment within their capabilities but with increasing challenge*
- *Provision for strong success experiences and recognition of successes.*[14]

Educating the Gifted and Talented

Professionals tend to suggest special programs and sometimes schools for the gifted and talented, which would seem to be a move away from providing for these children in regular classrooms. Regular classroom professionals can provide for gifted children in their classrooms through enrichment and acceleration. *Enrichment* provides an opportunity for children to pursue topics in greater depth and in different ways than planned for in the curriculum. *Acceleration* permits children to progress academically at their own pace.

In regular classrooms, early childhood professionals can encourage gifted children to pursue special interests as a means of extending and enriching classroom learning.

They can use parents and resource people to tutor and work in special ways with these children and provide opportunities for children to assume leadership responsibilities themselves. For example, they may be interested in tutoring other students who need extra practice or help. Tutoring can cut across grade and age levels. Students can also help explain directions and procedures to the class. Professionals can also encourage them to use their talents and abilities outside the classroom by becoming involved with other people and agencies and can foster creativity through classroom activities that require divergent thinking ("Let's think of all the different uses for a paper clip").

Professionals must challenge children to think through the use of higher-order questions that encourage them to explain, apply, analyze, rearrange, and judge. Many schools have resource rooms for gifted and talented students, in which children can spend a half-day or more every week working with a professional who is interested and trained in working with them. There are seven primary ways to provide for the needs of gifted and talented children:[15]

Enrichment classroom. The classroom professional conducts a differentiated program of study without the help of outside personnel.

Consultant professional. A program of differentiated instruction is conducted in the regular classroom with the assistance of a specially trained consultant.

Resource room pullout. Gifted students leave the classroom for a short period of time to receive instruction from a specially trained professional.

Community mentor. Gifted students interact with an adult from the community who has special knowledge in the area of interest.

Independent study. Students select projects and work on them under the supervision of a qualified professional.

Special class. Gifted students are grouped together during most of the class time and are instructed by a specially trained professional.

Special schools. Gifted students receive differentiated instruction at a special school with a specially trained staff.

Of the seven methods, resource room pullout is the most popular.

CHILDREN WHO HAVE BEEN ABUSED OR NEGLECTED

Many of our views of childhood are highly romanticized. We tend to believe that parents always love their children and enjoy caring for them. We also envision family settings full of joy, happiness, and parent–child harmony. Unfortunately for children, their parents, and society, these assumptions are not always true. The extent of child abuse is far greater than we might imagine. In 1995, an estimated 3.1 million incidents were reported to Child Protective Services (CPS) agencies as alleged victims of child maltreatment (e.g. physical abuse, neglect, sexual abuse, emotional maltreatment). This means that forty-five children per thousand are reported each year; this number represents a 6 percent increase per year over the last decade. Figure 13.10 shows the number of substantiated abuse cases by category.

Child abuse is not new, although it receives greater attention and publicity now than previously. Abuse, in the form of abandonment, infanticide, and neglect, has been documented throughout history. The attitude that children are property partly accounts for the history of abuse. Parents have believed,

Figure 13.10/
Substantiated Abuse and Neglect Cases

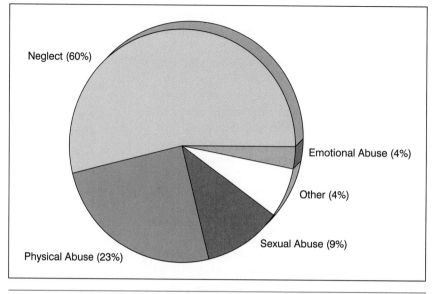

Neglect (60%)

Emotional Abuse (4%)

Other (4%)

Sexual Abuse (9%)

Physical Abuse (23%)

Source: National Committee to Prevent Child Abuse, 1996.

and some still do, that they own their children and can do with them as they please.

The extent to which children are abused is difficult to ascertain but is probably much greater than most people realize. Valid statistics are difficult to come by because the interest in reported child abuse is relatively new. In addition, definitions of child abuse and neglect differ from state to state and reports are categorized differently. Probably as many as one million incidents of abuse occur a year, but it is estimated that only one in four cases is reported.

Because of the increasing concern over child abuse, social agencies, hospitals, child care centers, and schools are becoming more involved in identification, treatment, and prevention of this national social problem. To do something about child abuse, those who are involved with children and parents have to know what abuse is. Public Law 93–247, the Child Abuse Prevention and Treatment act, defines *child abuse* and *neglect* as the "physical or mental injury,

sexual abuse, negligent treatment or maltreatment of a child under the age of eighteen by a person who is responsible for the child's welfare under circumstances which indicate that the child's health or welfare is harmed or threatened thereby as determined in accordance with regulations prescribed by the Secretary."[16]

In addition, all states have some kind of legal or statutory definition for child abuse and treatment. Many states are defining penalties for child abuse. Just as debilitating as physical abuse and neglect is *emotional abuse,* which occurs when parents, teachers, and others strip children of their self-esteem and self-image. Adults take away children's self-esteem through continually criticizing, belittling, screaming and nagging, creating fear, and intentionally and severely limiting opportunities. Emotional abuse is difficult to define legally and, most certainly, difficult to document. The unfortunate consequence for emotionally abused children is that they are often left in a debilitating environment. Both abuse and neglect adversely affect children's growth and development.

The guidelines in Table 13.3 may help you identify abuse and neglect, and provide for children's needs. However, you must remember that the presence of a single characteristic does not necessarily indicate abuse. You should observe the child's behavior and appearance over a period of time, and should also be willing to give parents the benefit of the doubt about a child's condition.

Causes of Abuse

Why do parents and guardians abuse children? Those who have been responsible for a group of young children will better understand the reasons for child abuse than those who do not know young children. Childrearing is hard work; it requires patience, self-control, understanding, and restraint. It is entirely likely that most parents, at one time or another, have come close to behavior that could be judged abusive.

Stress is one of the most frequent cases of child abuse. Stressful situations arise from employment, divorce or separation, income, quality of family life, moving, death of a family member, violations of law, sickness or injury, and other sources. We are learning more about stress and its effect on health and the general quality of life. Parenting and teaching are stressful occupations, and parents and teachers often need support from professionals to manage stress.

Lack of parenting information is another reason parents abuse or neglect their children. Some parents do not know what to do or how to do it; these cases more frequently result in acts of omission or neglect than in physical violence. Frequently, the child does not receive proper emotional care and support because the parent is ignorant of this need. Lack of parenting information is attributable to several factors.

First, in this mobile population, young parents often live apart from their own parents so grandparents have little opportunity to share childrearing information.

Second, the greater number of teenage parents means that many parents are neither emotionally nor cognitively ready to have children; they are really children themselves. We need a national effort to put parenting information into the curricula of every elementary and high school. Fortunately, a trend is beginning in this area.

A third reason for child abuse is the parent's cognitive and emotional state. How people are reared and what parenting attitudes were modeled for them have a tremendous influence on how they will rear their own children. Methods of childrearing are handed down from generation to generation, and people who were abused as children are often abusive parents.

A fourth cause of abuse relates to unwanted and unloved children. We like to assume that every child is wanted and loved, but this is not the case. Some parents take out their frustration on their children, whom they view as barriers to their dreams and self-fulfillment. Or a parent may dislike a child because the child is a constant reminder of an absent spouse.

Some people believe a fifth reason for child abuse is the amount of violence in our society. Opponents of violence on television cite it as an example of people's callousness toward each other and decry it as poor role modeling for children.

A sixth cause of abuse can be attributed to parental substance abuse. Substance abuse creates a chaotic environment in which children cannot tell what to expect from their parents. Children of parents who use or abuse alcohol or drugs are often neglected because the parent is emotionally or physically absent when drunk or high. Substance-abusing parents may forget to go to the store for a week

Table 13.3/*Guidelines for Detecting Abuse and Neglect*

Kind of Abuse	Child's Appearance	Child's Behavior	Parent or Caregiver's Behavior	Suggested Responses to Suspected Abuse
Physical	Unusual bruises, welts, burns, or fractures Bite marks Frequent injuries, explained as "accidental"	Reports injury by parents Unpleasant, hard to get along with, demanding, often disobeys, frequently causes trouble or interferes with others; breaks or damages things; or is shy, avoids others, is too anxious to please, too ready to let other people say and do things to him or her without protest Frequently late or absent, or comes to school too early or hangs around after school Avoids physical contact with adults Wears long sleeves or other concealing clothing Version of how a physical injury occurred is not believable (does not fit type or seriousness of the injury) Seems frightened of parents Shows little or no distress at separation from parents May seek affection from any adult	History of abuse as a child Uses unnecessarily harsh discipline Offers explanation of child's injury that does not make sense, does not fit injury, or offers no explanation Seems unconcerned about child Sees child as bad, evil, a monster, etc. Misuses alcohol or other drugs Attempts to conceal child's injury or protect identity of responsible party	You should be aware of the official policy and specific reporting procedures of your school system, and should know your legal obligations and the protections from civil and criminal liability specified in your state's reporting law. (All states provide immunity for mandated, good-faith reports.) Although you should be familiar with your state's legal definition of abuse and neglect, you are not required to make legal distinctions in order to report. Definitions should serve as guides. If you suspect that a child is abused or neglected, you should report. The teacher's value lies in noticing conditions that indicate that a child's welfare may be in jeopardy. Be concerned about the rights of the child—the rights to life, food, shelter, clothing, and security. But also be aware of the parents' rights—particularly their rights to be treated with respect and to be given needed help and support. Bear in mind that reporting does not stigmatize a parent as "evil." The report is the start of a rehabilitative process that seeks to protect the child and help the family as a whole. A report signifies only the *suspicion* of abuse or neglect. Teachers' reports are seldom unfounded. At the very least, they tend to indicate a need for help and support to the family.

Emotional	Less obvious signs than other types of mistreatment; behavior is best indication	Unpleasant, hard to get along with, demanding; frequently causes trouble, will not leave others alone Unusually shy, avoids others, too anxious to please, too submissive, puts up with unpleasantness from others without protest Either unusually adult or overly young for age (e.g., sucks thumb, rocks constantly) Behind for age physically, emotionally, or intellectually	Blames or belittles child Cold and rejecting Withholds love Treats children unequally Seems not to care about child's problems
Neglect	Often dirty, tired, no energy Comes to school without breakfast, often does not have lunch or lunch money Clothes dirty or inappropriate for weather Alone often, for long periods Needs glasses, dental care, or other medical attention	Frequently absent Begs or steals food Causes trouble in school Often hasn't done homework Uses alcohol or drugs Engages in vandalism, sexual misconduct Withdrawn or engages in fantasy or babyish behavior	Misuses alcohol or other drugs Disorganized, upset home life Seems not to care what happens Isolated from friends, relatives, neighbors Does not know how to get along with others Long-term chronic illnesses History of neglect as a child
Sexual	Torn, stained, or bloody underclothing	Poor relationships with other children	Protective or jealous of child

If you report a borderline case in good faith, do not feel guilty or upset if it is dismissed as unfounded upon investigation. Some marginal cases are found to be valid.

Don't put off making a report until the end of the school year. Teachers sometimes live with their suspicions until they suddenly fear for the child's safety during the summer months. A delayed report may mean a delay in needed help for the child and the family. Moreover, by reporting late in the school year, you remove yourself as a continued support to both the child protective agency and the reported family.

If you remove yourself from a case of suspected abuse or neglect by passing it on to superiors, you deprive child protective services of one of their most competent sources of information. For example, a teacher who tells a [children's protective services] worker that the child is especially upset on Mondays directs the worker to investigate conditions in the home on weekends. Few persons other than teachers are able to provide this kind of information. Your guideline should be to resolve any question in favor of the child. When in doubt, report. Even if you, as a teacher, have no immunity from liability and prosecution under state law, the fact that your report is made in good faith will free you from liability and prosecution.

In the absence of guidance from the protective agency, the teacher can rely on several general rules for dealing with the abused or neglected child:

continued

Table 13.3/ *Guidelines for Detecting Abuse and Neglect* *(Continued)*

Kind of Abuse	Child's Appearance	Child's Behavior	Parent or Caregiver's Behavior	Suggested Responses to Suspected Abuse
	Pain or itching in genital area Has veneral disease	Unwilling to participate in physical activities Engages in deliquent acts or runs away Says has been sexually assaulted by parent/caregiver	Encourages child to engage in prositution or sexual acts in presence of caregiver Misuses alcohol or other drugs Frequently absent from home	• Try to give the child additional attention whenever possible. • Create a more individualized program for the child. Lower your academic expectations and make fewer demands on the child's performance—he or she probably has enough pressures and crises to deal with presently at home. • Be warm and loving. If possible, let the child perceive you as a special friend to whom he or she can talk. By abusing or neglecting the child, someone has said in a physcial way, "I don't love you." You can reassure the child that someone cares. • Most important, remember that in identifying and reporting child maltreatment, you are not putting yourself in the position of autocrat over a family. The one purpose of your actions is to get help for a troubled child and family: the one goal is to reverse a situation that jeopardizes a child's healthy growth and development.

Source: U.S. Department of Health, Education, and Welfare, Office of Human Development Services. Administration for Children, Youth, and Families, Head Start Bureau, Indian and Migrant Programs Division, *New Light on an Old Problem,* DHEW Publication No. (OHDS) 78-31108 (Washington, D.C.: Author, 1978). pp. 8–11.

Children today are subjected to many stressful situations, including community environments, home life, and television. As early childhood professionals, we must seek ways to reduce or eliminate stress in children's lives that imperils their lives and learning. How can you advocate for reducing violence in children's environments?

to buy food. Because children of drug-using parents may not be physically abused, the signs of abuse may be subtle. A teacher might pick up clues that something is wrong at home if the child is not bringing lunch, is wearing either the same clothes over and over again or clothes that do not fit, or has worn-out shoes because the parents have not noticed that new ones are needed. In general, drug use renders parents dysfunctional and unable to care for their children adequately.

To fully understand the causes and symptoms of abuse of children, we must consider the entire context of the family setting. Most abused children live in families that are dysfunctional. *Dysfunctional* families are characterized by parental mental instability, confused roles (a parent may function in the role of a child, which thus necessitates that the child function at an adult level), and a chaotic, unpredictable family structure and environment. Adults in such families are not functioning at a healthy level and are generally unable to care for and nurture a child's growth and development adequately.

Seeking Help

What can be done about child abuse? There must be a conscious effort to educate, treat, and help abusers or potential abusers. The school is a good place to begin. Another source of help is the federal government's National Center on Child Abuse and Neglect, which helps coordinate and develop programs and policies concerning child abuse and neglect. For information, call or write to any of the following:

- The National Center on Child Abuse and Neglect, Children's Bureau, Office of Child Development, Office of Human Development, Department of Health and Human Services, 200 Independence Avenue, W., Washington, D.C. 20201.

- Child Help USA handles crisis calls and provides information and referrals to every county in the United States. Their hotline is 1-800-422-4453.

- The National Committee to Prevent Child Abuse (NCPCA) is a volunteer organization of concerned citizens that works with community, state, and national groups to expand and disseminate knowledge about child abuse prevention. The NCPCA has chapters in all states; the address for its national office is National Committee to Prevent Child Abuse, 332 S. Michigan Avenue, Suite 1600, Chicago, IL 60604; telephone 312-663-3520.

Child Abuse Prevention Curricula

Many curricula have been developed to help teachers, caregivers, and parents work with children to prevent abuse. The primary purposes of these programs are to educate children about abuse and to teach them strategies to avoid it. Before using an abuse prevention curriculum with children, staff and parents should help select the curriculum and learn how to use it. Parent involvement is essential. As with anything early childhood professionals undertake, parents' understanding, approval, and support of a program make its goals easier to achieve. Parents and caregivers should not assume, however, that merely teaching children with an abuse prevention curriculum ends their responsibilities. A parent's responsibility for a child's care and protection never ends. Likewise, professionals have the same responsibility for the children entrusted to them.

Homeless Children

Walking down a city street, you may have encountered homeless men and women, but have you seen a homeless child? Homeless children are the neglected, forgotten, often abandoned segment of the growing homeless population in the United States. The National Coalition for the Homeless estimates there are between 500,000 and 750,000 homeless youth, living either in homeless families or on their own. Figure 13.11 provides information about homeless children and families.

Homelessness has significant mental, physical, and educational consequences for children. Homelessness results in developmental delays and can produce high levels of distress. Homeless children observed in day-care centers exhibit such problem behaviors as short attention spans, weak impulse control, withdrawal, aggression, speech delays, and regressive behavior. Homeless children are at greater risk for health problems. It is estimated that over 40 percent of homeless children do not attend school. If they do enter school, they face many problems relating to their previous school problems (grade failure) and attendance (long trips to attend school). Fortunately, more agencies are responding to the unique needs of homeless children and their families.

Public Law 100–77, the Stewart B. Mc-Kinney Homeless Assistance Act of 1987,

---

Figure 13.11/ *Homeless Children and Families*

- Average age of a homeless person in America is nine.
- Children and families make up the fastest growing segment of the homeless population.
- One-third of homeless families have an open case for child abuse or neglect; one out of five have lost at least one child to foster care.
- More than half of homeless children either have witnessed or have been subjected to violence in their home.
- Half of all homeless children have never lived in their own home. Over 40 percent have been homeless more than once.
- The fastest growing segment of the homeless population is families with children. Families with children constitute approximately 40 percent of people who become homeless, while on any given night, an estimated 20 percent of the homeless population are families.
- A survey of 29 U.S. cities found that in 1996, children accounted for 27 percent of the homeless population.
- Requests for emergency shelter by families with children in 29 U.S. cities increased by an average of 7 percent between 1995 and 1996. The same study found that 24 percent of requests for shelter by homeless families were denied in 1996 due to lack of resources. Moreover, every city surveyed expects an increase in the number of requests for emergency shelter by families with children in 1997.

Source: National Coaltion for the Homeless, 1997.

---

provides that "each State educational agency shall assure that each child of a homeless individual and each homeless youth have access to a free, appropriate public education which would be provided to the children of a resident of a State."[17] PL 100–77 was amended in 1994 to extend the right to free, appropriate public preschool education to homeless preschoolers. It further provides that services to homeless children are not to replace a regular academic program or to segregate homeless children.

Childhood Stress

The scene of children being left at a child care center or preschool for the first time is familiar to anyone who has worked with young children. Some children quickly become happily involved with new friends in a new setting; some are tense, clinging fearfully to their parents. For many children, separation from the ones they are attached to is a stressful experience. Crying, fear, and tension are the *stress responses,* the symptoms or outward manifestations of children's stress.

Young children are subjected to an increasing number of situations and events that cause them fear and stress (Figure 13.12). Some of the *stressors* include their parents' divorce, being left at home alone before and after school, parents who constantly argue, the death of a parent or friend, being hospitalized, living in a dangerous neighborhood, family violence, poverty, and child abuse.

Parents and early childhood professionals are becoming aware of the effects stress can have on children: sickness, withdrawal, shyness, loss of appetite, poor sleep patterns, urinary and bowel disorders, and general behavior and discipline problems.

Many early childhood educators believe that one way to alleviate stress is through

PROGRAM IN ACTION

THE TONE SCHOOL, TACOMA, WASHINGTON

The Tone School, in Tacoma, Washington, was established on 1988 to offer homeless students educational and support systems that address their current needs and that ease their transition back into a permanent school setting. Program goals include the following:

1. Provide a safe, nurturing educational environment for homeless children in the Tacoma school district.
2. Provide homeless children with individual academic assessments and appropriate teaching methods.
3. Offer a full complement of support services to assist homeless students and their families in coping with the social, emotional, and physical impact of homelessness, including counseling, social work, and health services.
4. Assist in placing students in a permanent school setting once permanent housing is found, and to provide services such as school supplies and clothing to ease their transition.
5. Provide transition services to families as they move into permanent housing through follow-up or referrals to community agencies and services.

The Tacoma area shelters require that all children residing at the shelters attend school. Children who do not attend a traditional Tacoma school attend the Tone School. Enrollment is streamlined to take place at the shelter. Bus transportation is provided to each of the shelters. Breakfast and lunch are provided. Students receive clothing from the Tone clothing bank and school supplies. These items are provided through community donations.

The curriculum includes math, reading, social studies, health, art, music, physical education, swimming, and computer literacy. The average length of stay is twenty-one days. The Tone School services approximately 140 Head Start children (three- to four-year-olds) and 350 kindergarten through eighth-grade students per year.

The overwhelming needs of these homeless children are for physical and psychological safety and security. Recognizing these needs, the staff has established a safe, nurturing, and stimulating environment, with predictable routines and engaging developmental activities. Services are comprehensive, incorporating education, nutrition, health, mental health, family support, and parent and community involvement.

Because children typically stay in the program for only two to three weeks, their needs must be assessed and addressed quickly. A family advocate works with the classroom staff to assist each child in selecting new clothing within two days of entry. While the classroom staff and nurse are assessing and meeting children's social, emotional, physical, and cognitive needs, including special education support services, the family advocate and nurse are working in the shelters with the families to help them acquire the resources to meet their immediate needs and to take the next steps toward self-sufficiency. The classroom staff also visits the families at the shelters, talking with them about their children's development and offering ideas for learning activities they may do together. As families leave the shelters, staff continue to work with them as their children transfer into a new school situation. For children and families dealing with the trauma of homelessness, the Tone School and its Head Start program are beacons of hope and caring.

Contributed by Tamie Williams, the Tone School, Tacoma, WA.

Figure 13.12/*Indicators of Fear and Stress in Children*

Children who are exposed to stressful situations, such as violence, either in person or through the media, can suffer both short- and long-term development problems. Indicators of developmental problems include:

- Nightmares, inability to sleep, or loss of appetite, especially in younger children
- Unusual crying, even over minor upsets
- Headaches, stomachaches, or unexplained fever
- Increased aggressive or disruptive behavior
- Inability to concentrate and declining achievement at school
- Anxiety, fearfulness, emotional distress, a tendency to be "clingy." This can include regressive behavior, such as bed wetting and thumb sucking.
- Depression and social isolation

Situations that include fear vary from age to age and developmental level. Some common fears and when to expect them in early childhood education are these:

Infants	*Toddlers*	*Preschool*	*School Age*
Strangers	Separation	Monsters	School
Separation	Toilets	Animals	Injury
Noises	Noises	Bedtime	Bullies
Falling	Bedtime	Daycare	Teachers
	Daycare	Death	Tests
			Getting lost

Sources: Mark Rubinstein, "What Children Fear the Most," *Child* 4 (July/Aug. 1989), p. 42;. Sandra Dark, "When Terror Strikes Innocence," *Kiwanis* (Feb 1997), p. 32. Used with permission.

---

play. They feel children should be encouraged to play as a therapeutic antidote to the effects of stress. A second way to relieve stress in children is to stop hurrying and pressuring them. Many think children should be free from parental and social demands so they can enjoy their childhood. Unfortunately, society is as it is; we cannot and should not want to return to the "good old days." The tempo of life in the United States will continue to be hectic, and demands for individual achievement are increasing. As a result, the emphasis must be on helping children manage stress in their lives.

From preschool on, children should be taught stress reduction techniques, including relaxation and breathing exercises, yoga, physical exercises, meditation, and regular physical activity. Since we cannot slow the pace of society, we need to teach children coping skills. The amount and kinds of stress on children and its effect are causing more early childhood professionals to become involved in programs and agencies that work for solutions to societal issues that cause stress. In fact, reducing stress is one of the premier issues in early childhood education.

ACTIVITIES FOR FURTHER ENRICHMENT

1. Visit several public schools to see how they are providing individualized and appropriate

programs for children with disabilities. What efforts are being made to involve parents?

2. Interview parents of children with disabilities. What do they feel are their greatest problems? What do they consider the greatest needs for their children? List specific ways they have been involved in educational agencies. How have educational agencies avoided or resisted providing for their or their children's needs?

3. Spend some time in mainstreamed inclusive classrooms. What specific skills would you need to become a good professional in such settings?

4. Visit agencies and programs that provide services for people with disabilities. Before you visit, list specific features, services, and facilities you will look for.

5. What programs does the federal government support for children with special needs in your area? Give specific information.

6. Discuss with people of another culture their culture's attitudes toward children with disabilities. How are they similar or different from your attitudes?

READINGS FOR FURTHER ENRICHMENT

Aefsky, F. *Inclusion Confusion: A Guide to Educating Students with Exceptional Needs* (Thousand Oaks, CA: Corwin, 1995).

Provides guidelines, strategies, and techniques for developing and implementing inclusion programs. Discusses current legal cases and explains how these issues pertain to the classroom, and contains practical suggestions for application to inclusive programs.

Chenoweth, K., ed. *Creating Schools for All Our Students: What 12 Schools Have to Say* (Reston, VA: Council for Exceptional Children, 1995).

A report of findings by a team of educators and parents brought together at the Working Forum on

Inclusive Schools, a pioneering effort of ten major national educational organizations.

Davis, G. A., and S. B. Rimm. *Education of the Gifted and Talented,* 3rd ed. (Boston: Allyn & Bacon, 1994).

Provides an overview of the gifted and talented field, including an introduction to giftedness, characteristics, program types, curriculum, identification, and program evaluation.

Friend, M., and W. Bursuck. *Including Students with Special Needs* (Boston: Allyn & Bacon, 1996).

A practical guide for classroom teachers on teaching all students in inclusive classrooms. This book explains how to modify curricula, textbooks, classrooms, student groupings, assessments, and instruction to meet all students' learning needs.

Giangreco, M. F., J. C. Chigee, and V. S. Iverson. *Choosing Options and Accommodations for Children: A Guide to Planning Inclusive Education* (Baltimore, MD: Paul H. Brookes, 1993).

This book about children with disabilities in general education classrooms offers a step-by-step process, specific instruction, scheduling helps, and master forms. An introduction describes the COACH (Choosing Options and Accommodations for Children) approach identifying such assumptions as educational planning and the importance of collaborative teamwork.

Lewis, Rena B., and Donald H. Doorlag. *Teaching Special Students in the Mainstream,* 4th ed. (Upper Saddle River, NJ: Merrill/Prentice Hall, 1995).

Presents practical strategies for adapting standard instruction to meet the learning needs of all children in a mainstreamed classroom. Clear and informative account of providing for children with special needs; includes tips and practical advice.

McLaughlin, M. W., Merita Irby, and J. Langman. *Urban Sanctuaries: Neighborhood Organizations in the Lives and Futures of Inner-City Youth* (San Francisco: Jossey-Bass, 1994).

Examines the importance of "safe havens," community-based organizations that put the needs of youth first, in the lives of inner city youth. The authors explain how these "sanctuaries" have succeeded in weaning youths away from gangs. These successful community agencies resemble a family in which individuals are valued and rules of membership are clear.

Morton-Young, T. *After-School and Parent Education Programs for At-Risk Youth and Their Families* (Springfield, IL: Charles C Thomas, 1995).

A guide to organizing and operating a community-based center for basic educational skills reinforcement, homework assistance, culture enrichment, and a parent involvement focus.

Siegel, L. *Least Restrictive Environment: The Paradox of Inclusion* (Horsham, PA: LRP Publications, 1994).

Illustrates when need may be more important than placement. Also included, why, for children with hearing impairments, the benefits of age- and language-appropriate peers may outweigh the benefits of exposure to nondisabled children and the dangers of "generic" placement for all children.

Smith, D. D., and R. Luckasson. *Introduction to Special Education: Teaching in an Age of Challenge,* 2nd ed. (Boston: Allyn & Bacon, 1995).

A well-written and understandable discussion of the field of special education. Provides many useful examples of educational procedures that can be applied to classrooms. Addresses in separate chapters all the special needs of students and their families.

NOTES

1. Public Law 101–476, 30 October 1990, Stat. 1103.
2. 42 U.S.C. 12101, 26 July 1990.
3. Public Law 101–476, 30 October 1990, Stat. 1103.
4. Ibid.
5. A. Turnbull, H. Turnbull III, M. Shank, and D. Leal, *Exceptional Lives* (Upper Saddle River, NJ: Merrill/Prentice Hall, 1995), pp. 64–71.
6. Ibid., p. 84.
7. National Early Childhood Technical Assistance System, *Helping Our Nation's Infants and Toddlers with Disabilities and Their Families, A Briefing Paper on Part H of the Individuals with Disabilities Education Act (IDEA),* (Author, 1996). Internet address http://www.nectas.unc.edu/index.html
8. Public Law 101–476, 30 October 1990, Stat. 1103.
9. Council for Exceptional Children, 1996. Internet address http://www.cec.sped.org/
10. J. Burnette, "Including Students with Disabilities in General Education Classrooms: From Policy to Practice," *The Eric Review* 4 (1996), pp. 2–11.
11. Ibid.
12. Ibid.
13. Jacob K. Javits Gifted and Talented Students Education Act of 1988.
14. B. Clark, *Growing Up Gifted,* 4th ed. (Upper Saddle River, NJ: Merrill/Prentice Hall, 1992), pp. 73–76.
15. J. Gallagher, P. Weiss, K. Oglesby, and T. Thomas, *The Status of Gifted/Talented Education: United States Survey Needs, Practices, and Policies* (Los Angeles: National/State Leadership Training Institute on the Gifted and Talented, 1983).
16. United States Statutes at Large, vol. 88, pt. 1 (Washington, D.C.: U.S. Government Printing Office, 1976), p. 5.
17. Public Law 100–77, the Stewart B. McKinney Homeless Assistance Act, Title VII-B—Subtitle B-Education for Homeless Youth, July 1987.

REFERENCES FOR "INCLUDING CHILDREN WITH DISABILITIES" INSERT

1. Christine L. Salisbury, "Mainstreaming During the Early Childhood Years," *Exceptional Children,* Oct./Nov. 1991, p. 146.
2. Karen E. Diamond, Linda L. Hestenes, and Caryn O'Connor, "Integrating Children with

Disabilities into Preschool," June 1994, EJ 365 981.

3. B. J. Smith and P. S. Strain, "Does Early Intervention Help?", 1988, EJ 455.

4. R. R. Fewell and P. L. Oelwein, "The Relationship Between Time in Integrated Environments and Developmental Gains in Young Children with Special Needs," *Topics in Early Childhood Special Education* 10 (2, Summer), 1990, EJ 413 316.

5. C. A. Peck, P. Carlson, and E. Helmsetter, "Parent and Teacher Perceptions of Outcomes for Typically Developing Children Enrolled in Integrated Early Childhood Programs: A Statewide Study," *Journal of Early Intervention* 16(1, Winter) 1993, EJ 445 822.

6. Salisbury, 1991, p. 147.

7. A. McDonnell and M. Hardman, "A Synthesis of 'Best Practice' Guidelines for Early Childhood Services," *Journal of the Division for Early Childhood* 12(4), 1988.

8. L. H. Meyer, J. Eichinger, and S. Park-Lee, "A Validation of Program Quality Indicators in Educational Services for Students with Severe Disabilities," *Journal of the Association for Persons with Severe Handicaps* 12(4), 1987.

9. Gerald Mahoney, Cordelia Robinson, and Amy Powell, "Focusing on Parent–Child Interaction: The Bridge to Developmentally Appropriate Practices," 12(1, Spring), 1992, EJ 449 978.

10. Salisbury, 1991.

11. Steven F. Warren and Paul J. Yoder, "Communication and Language Intervention: Why a Constructivist Approach Is Insufficient," *The Journal of Special Education* 28(3), 1994, p. 248.

12. E. Bates, *The Emergency of Symbols: Cognition and Communication in Infancy* (New York: Academic Press, 1979).

13. B. Hart, "Naturalistic Language Training Techniques," in S. F. Warren and A. Rogers-Warren (Eds.), *Teaching Functional Language* (Baltimore: University Park Press, 1985).

14. Mary Louise Hemmeter and Ann P. Kaiser, "Enhanced Milieu Teaching: Effects of Parent-Implemented Language Intervention," *Journal of Early Intervention, 18*(3), 1994.

15. Michaelene M. Ostrosky and Ann P. Kaiser, "Preschool Classroom Environments That Promote Communication," *Teaching Exceptional Children,* Summer, 1991.

16. Ibid., pp. 8–9.

17. Ibid., p.7.

18. C. A. Peck, J. Donaldson, and M. Pezzoli, "Some Benefits Nonhandicapped Adolescents Perceive for Themselves from Their Social Relationships with Peers Who Have Handicaps," *Journal of the Association for Persons with Severe Handicaps 15*(2), 1990.

The Role of Families and the Federal Government in Developing Early Childhood Programs

PART FIVE

The belief in the promise of high-quality care to positively influence a child's life underlies the recent growth in public support for programs such as Head Start. But this promise must encompass more than academic achievement and "assimilation" into the mainstream culture. Solid family communication, connection to community, and a strong sense of self are also important in fostering a child's success and happiness.

California Tomorrow

425

CHAPTER 14

Child Care

Meeting the Needs of Children, Parents, and Families

Focus Questions

1. What are families' needs for child care services?

2. What is the terminology used with child care?

3. What are the purposes of child care programs?

4. What is quality child care and how do quality programs operate?

5. What are the types of child care services and programs?

6. How is child care funded?

7. How effective are child care programs in meeting the needs of children, parents, and families?

8. What are the reasons for the growth of proprietary child care?

9. What issues are associated with child care?

10. What are future trends in child care services and needs?

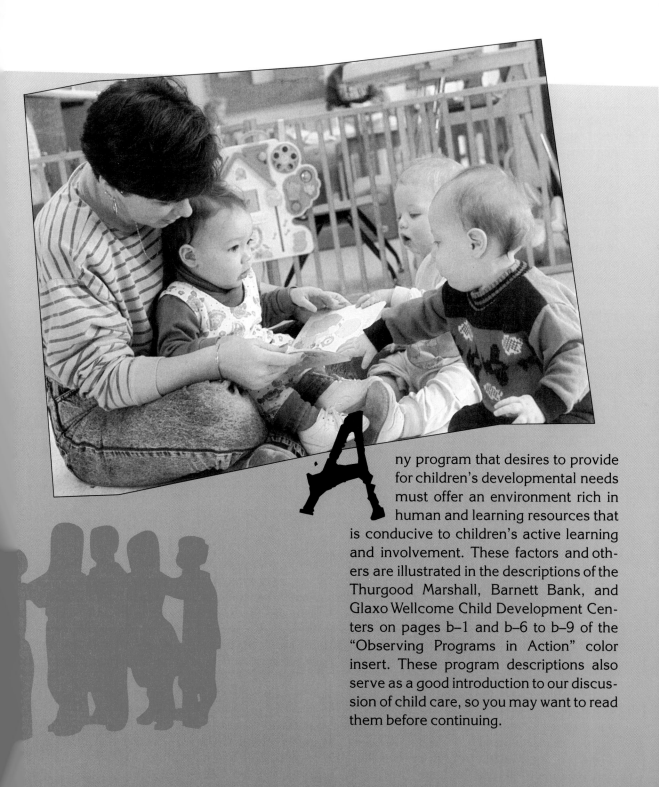

ny program that desires to provide for children's developmental needs must offer an environment rich in human and learning resources that is conducive to children's active learning and involvement. These factors and others are illustrated in the descriptions of the Thurgood Marshall, Barnett Bank, and Glaxo Wellcome Child Development Centers on pages b–1 and b–6 to b–9 of the "Observing Programs in Action" color insert. These program descriptions also serve as a good introduction to our discussion of child care, so you may want to read them before continuing.

WHY IS CHILD CARE SO POPULAR?

The need for child care is high and will continue to grow, owing to maternal employment, dual-career families, changing family patterns, and changes in child care practices by U.S. families. Over 62 percent of mothers with children under six are employed (see Chap. 2).

Also, there is an increasing need for child care for infants. Although about 54 percent of mothers with children under three years of age work, infant care is not readily available; and when it is available, it is expensive.

While more programs are available for three-, four-, and five-year-olds, many operate part time only. Most parents do not work part time. Unavailable full-time child care necessitates alternate care arrangements in the course of a day, which is inconvenient and expensive, and disrupts children's need for continuity.

Changing family patterns also create a need for child care (see Chaps. 2 and 15). Both men and women are deciding to become parents—natural or adoptive—without marrying. Nearly 26 percent of women who had a child in 1994 were single.[1] This increase contrasts sharply with a 15 percent (one in seven) birth rate by single women in 1982. Interestingly, the sharpest increase in single parenthood is among affluent and well-educated women. For example, the percentage of unmarried women with one or more years of college who gave birth rose from 5.5 percent in 1982 to 13.3 percent in 1994. The implications of these social conditions are obvious: children need care by people other than their parents, frequently in places other than their homes. As more women enter the labor force and as the demand for child care increases, the challenge is clear. Early childhood professionals must advocate for and participate in the development of quality, licensed child care programs.

TERMINOLOGY OF CHILD CARE

Sometimes the term *child care* is used interchangeably with other terminology such as *family daycare, baby-sitting,* and *early childhood education.* The term *child care* is preferable to *daycare,* because children are the central focus of any program provided for them.

The currently accepted concept of child care is that it is a *comprehensive* service to children and families that *supplements* the care children receive from their families. Care is supplemental in that parents delegate responsibility to caregivers for providing care and appropriate experiences in their absence. Care is comprehensive in that, although it includes custodial care such as supervision, food, shelter, and other physical necessities, it goes beyond these to include activities that encourage and aid learning and are responsive to children's health, social, and psychological needs. A comprehensive view of child care considers the child to be a whole person; therefore, the major purpose of child care is to facilitate optimum development.

TYPES OF CHILD CARE PROGRAMS

Child care is offered in many places, by many types of persons and agencies who provide a variety of care and services. A program may operate twenty-four hours a day, with the center or home open to admit children at any hour. There are also whole-day programs that usually operate on a 6:30 A.M. to 6:00 P.M. schedule to accommodate working parents. Half-day programs, such as those operated in many Head Start centers, usually run from 8:30 or 9:00 A.M. to 1:00 or 2:00 P.M., although many are becoming full-day programs. Parents who work usually supplement half-day programs with other forms of child care or with a baby-sitter.

Full-Service Child and Family Programs

While child care programs have traditionally focused on children's needs, the trend is toward providing a range of services to children and their families. Family-centered programs go beyond providing child care. They help parents cope with daily living problems (e.g., finding adequate housing) and enhance their parenting skills (e.g., providing parenting classes), and otherwise assist parents (e.g., connecting parents with health services). In this regard, child and family programs are linking up with other agencies, such as health clinics, so that they can meet children's, parents', and families' needs.

Child Care by Family and Relatives

Child care is most commonly arranged within nuclear and extended families or with friends (see Figure 14.1). Parents handle these arrangements in various ways. Some mothers and fathers work different shifts, so one parent cares for the children while the spouse is at work. These families do not need out-of-home care. In some cases, children are cared for by grandparents, aunts, uncles, or other relatives. These arrangements satisfy parents' needs to have their children cared for by people with similar lifestyles and values. Such care may be less costly, and compensation may be made in ways other than direct monetary payments. For example, one couple converted part of their house into an efficiency apartment where an elderly aunt lives rent-free in return for caring for the couple's two-year-old child. These types of arrangements allow children to remain in familiar environments with people they know. Child care by family members provides children with continuity and a sense of safety and security.

Figure 14.1/*Caregivers of Children Under Age 5 Whose Mothers Work*

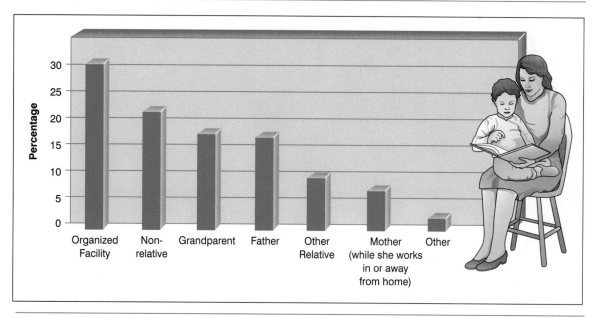

Source: U.S. Department of Education, National Center for Educational Statistics, 1996.

The number of children who are cared for through informal arrangements exceeds the number enrolled in centers or family care for two primary reasons. First, there is a lack of available quality child care programs. Second, many parents simply prefer to take care of their own children. When people search for child care, they often turn out of necessity to people who are available and willing to take care of children. These two criteria, however, are not the best or only ones that people who provide child care or baby-sitting services should meet. There is a tremendous difference between placing a child in a high-quality, comprehensive program and placing that child with an individual who provides primarily custodial care.

Family Daycare

When child care is provided in a child's own family or familylike setting, it is known as *family daycare.* In this arrangement an individual caregiver provides care and education for a small group of children in her or his home. Eleven percent of children under five in child care are in family daycare. Family daycare generally involves three types of settings: homes that are unlicensed and unregulated by a state or local agency, homes that are licensed by regulatory agencies, and homes that are licensed and associated with an administrative agency.

Many parents leave their children at unregulated and unlicensed homes, and the

Family daycare is the preferred method of child care. Parents like a program for their children that approximates a homelike setting. What are some characteristics of a homelike setting that you can incorporate into your classroom?

kind of care a child then receives depends on the skill, background, and training of the person who offers it. Some family daycare providers are motivated to meet state or local standards for child care so they can be licensed. Family daycare providers may also be associated with a child care agency. They meet state and agency standards for care and, in return, receive assistance, training, and referrals. The agency usually subsidizes the cost of children's care when parents are eligible for subsidies.

In the past, there was a tendency to equate family care with custodial care. Care providers today, however, are becoming more diligent about interacting with and stimulating the children they care for. The quantity and quality of specific services provided in family homes varies from home to home and from agency to agency. However, almost 50 percent of caregivers spend a substantial amount of their time in direct interaction with children. After you have read the Program in Action, "Patrick's Day at Family Daycare," it will be obvious that good family daycare is much more than baby-sitting. Undoubtedly, one reason parents prefer it is that it offers a family atmosphere, especially for younger children.

Intergenerational Child Care

Intergenerational child care programs take two forms. One kind integrates children and the elderly into an early childhood and adult care facility. The elderly derive pleasure and feelings of competence from helping care for and interact with children, and young children receive attention and love from older caregivers. In today's mobile society, families often live long distances from each other, and children may be isolated from the care that grandparents can offer. Intergenerational programs blend the best of two worlds: children and the elderly both receive care and attention in a nurturing environment.

For example, the Stride Rite Intergenerational Daycare Center, located in Cambridge, Massachusetts, enables children and elders to come together for activities including reading, baking, and painting. The Intergenerational Center is the daytime home (7:30 A.M. to 5:30 P.M.) for elders over the age of sixty and children aged fifteen months to six years (see pages b–10 and b–11 of the "Observing Programs in Action" color insert).

A second type of intergenerational child care utilizes older adults, often retirees, as employees and volunteers to help care for children. Older citizens are valuable and often untapped resources of skills and knowledge who have much to offer children and programs.

Center Child Care

Care of children in center settings, also called *center child care* or *group child care,* is conducted in specially designed and constructed centers, churches, YMCAs and YWCAs, and other such settings. Each state has its own definition of a center-based program; for example, the definition in Florida is as follows:

[to] serve groups of six (6) or more children. It utilizes subgrouping on the basis of age and special need but provides opportunity for experience and learning that accompanies a mixing of ages. Group daycare centers may enroll children under two years of age only if special provisions are made for the needs of the infants to be consistently met by one person, rather than a series of people; and which permits the infant to develop a strong, warm relationship with one mother figure. This relationship should approximate the mothering the infant would receive in a family daycare home.[2]

In Texas, on the other hand, "[a] daycare center is a child care facility that provides care less than twenty-four hours a day for more than twelve children under age fourteen."[3]

PROGRAM IN ACTION

PATRICK'S DAY AT FAMILY DAYCARE

I enjoy being a child care provider because I realize I can enhance a good family situation but cannot replace it. My home is open from 7:00 A.M. to 5:00 P.M. If these hours are not convenient for a family, other child care homes in my city have more flexible hours. I encourage parents to interview with as many care providers as possible before they make a decision about a particular home.

The Day

7:45 A.M. Patrick is four and a half years old and has been coming to my family daycare home since he was ten weeks old. He is dropped off by his dad. Melanie, three and a half years; Bret, two and a half years; and Marina, four months, have already arrived. Marina has been fed and is napping. Bret and Melanie are playing with puzzles or stringing beads at the kitchen table. Patrick's dad chats a moment with Patrick and me, gives Patrick a kiss, and says goodbye. (I do not like sneak-out goodbyes; these can lead to distrust.) Patrick joins the activities at the table and after fifteen to twenty minutes goes to the blocks, as he loves to build. Tyler, twenty-three months, arrives and is fussy. He has been out ill for several days and has a rough time getting into the swing of things. I recommend that Tyler's dad make his goodbye quick and firm to end Tyler's turmoil. Tyler gets a hug and love from Dad and me, and tells me he would like to take a little rest. Five minutes later he wants to get up and play with his friends.

8:40–9:00 A.M. The children have breakfast. Patrick and Melanie help set the table, and everyone, even Tyler, helps clean up their own places after eating. Patrick leads everyone to the bathroom for wash-up time.

9:10 A.M. The children all help pick up toys, so we can get ready for music time, approximately twenty to thirty minutes of dancing, shaking, stomping, singing, and music making. I encourage the children to express their creativity, and each child gets a chance to perform individually. Melanie and Patrick love to use the wooden microphones and sing solo or duet. Tyler wants to copy everything anyone else does.

9:40 A.M. We have circle time, when everyone reviews the calendar, weather, shapes, and colors. Patrick reminds us he wants to do the alphabet mystery draw, where each child reaches into a bag and draws out a letter of the alphabet. One of the children draws a letter, and everyone tries to name it, even Tyler. Everyone helps him guess! Patrick loves this game and excels.

We then do fingerpaints, poster paints, felt pens, crayons, and chalking. Paper cutting and pasting is a constant favorite. Patrick will stick to a project until completed and then will "teach" a younger child how to complete his work. He is very kind and sincere in his efforts, and Bret appreciates the thoughtfulness. Tyler has to be included in all activities, or he will fuss until he is. His efforts are sincere, and he is very proud of himself. So are we all.

Many center programs are comprehensive, providing a full range of services. Some are baby-sitting programs, while some offer less than good custodial care. The quality of daycare services among settings depends on those who provide the services, which makes conclusively defining child care difficult. Variations from state to state also make it hard to do anything but generalize.

Employer-Sponsored Child Care Programs

Today, almost everyone is expected to work, including women with young children. But many of society's institutions were designed during an era of male breadwinners and female homemakers. What we need now are child care programs and workplace policies

10:30 A.M. We go outdoors, play in the yard, go for a hike, or ride bikes around the block. The yard is large and fenced, and the children utilize all the territory. One area has climbing apparatus, another has kitchen equipment, and another has a playhouse. An easel occupies a creative area. Patrick loves to paint as well as dig and plant. Of course, digging is the best part, according to Melanie. All the children come in rough-and-tumble clothes so I do not spend a lot of time worrying about staying clean.

12:00 Noon. At lunch, Patrick once again leads the way to wash-up and helps supervise the younger ones. Melanie, Bret, and Patrick set the table, and lunch is served. Everyone again cleans their place.

12:15 P.M. Baby Ben, six months old, arrives and joins the lunch crowd.

12:45 P.M. Wash-up and nap time. Everyone appreciates this quiet time of day. The children's day has started early at home and has been busy in our home. They sleep in separate beds but are two or three to a room. Patrick and Melanie may wake up early, go potty, and back to bed. Sometimes they whisper back and forth until it is time to wake up. "Shush, here comes Mary Ann," says Patrick.

3:00 P.M. Diapers, potty, wash-up, and baby bottles for the two infants and snack time for the older children. We read stories until my voice cracks, and then we go outside again. Baby, toddler, and preschooler—all together we swing, crawl, run, jump, hop, learn simple games, do finger plays, explore the garden, work, and play. We check the progress of our butterfly cocoons and what flowers are blooming.

4:00 P.M. Patrick's mom arrives, we visit for five to ten minutes, and they leave. The rest of the children play outdoors, or we come back inside and read. The remainder of the time is spent in free play; by 5:00 everyone is gone. The last few minutes are spent in picking up and cleaning up.

Conclusion

Over the course of a year we visit museums, aquariums, zoos, and parks, take train rides, and learn to cooperate with and respect each other. I try to keep my group small and stable, raising over 50 percent of the children to kindergarten age. Some leave the area or want extended hours, so I can no longer meet their needs. Once they go to school they are welcome to come visit, but I think at that point they need a different caregiver. It is terrific to see the development and personal growth of a six-week-old infant as he or she matures to happy, competent living. What a wonderful process life is. This is a very satisfying and rewarding way to make a living.

Contributed by Mary Ann Coulson, past president, California Federation of Family Day Care Associations, Inc., and chair of the Federation of FDCA Education Project.

---

that ensure that both women and men can participate fully in their jobs and careers and still have time and resources to invest in their children.

New responses to child care arise as more and more parents enter the work force. The most rapidly growing segment of the work force, in fact, is married women with children under one year of age. To meet the needs of working parents, employers are increasingly called on to provide affordable, accessible, quality child care. Corporate-supported child care is one of the fastest-growing employee benefits, as identified by the U.S. Chamber of Commerce.

Since the 1980s, employer-sponsored child care has become one of the more talked-about and most frequently implemented child care programs. Although not new (the Stride Rite Corporation started the first on-site corporate child care program in Boston in 1971), there is currently a surge in these services. Of the 44,000 U.S. employers with a hundred or more workers, the number of employer-sponsored child care programs has grown from 110 in 1972 to over 4,500 in 1993, partly because of the increase of mothers in the work force but also because of the realization that child care is good business. Yet, despite its numerous advantages, child care remains the least frequently offered employee benefit.

Employers can provide child care services in a number of ways:

- *Resource and referral services.* Corporations supply several services in this area, such as information and counseling for parents on selecting quality care and referrals to local child care providers. These services can be offered in-house (i.e., on site) or through a community or national resource and referral agency.

- *On-site or near-site child care centers for employees' children.* The corporation supplies space, equipment, and child care workers. Some corporations contract with an outside agency to provide child care service. Some corporations also maintain a list of family daycare homes and contract for spaces. They may also assist in equipping the providers' homes for child care services.

- *Direct aid.* Some companies provide a flat subsidy—a specific amount to their employees to help cover the cost of child care. For example, NationsBank, the largest bank in the South, pays its associates with limited incomes up to $35 per week to pay for child care.

- *Voucher systems.* Corporations give employees vouchers with which to purchase services at child care centers.

- *Vendor systems.* Corporations purchase spaces at child care centers and make them available to employees either free or at reduced rates.

- *Consortium.* Two or more corporations share the cost of on-site or near-site child care.

- *Contributions to a child care center* where many of the corporation's employees place their children. The subsidy results in reduced rates for employees and/or priority on a center waiting list.

- *Parent-family leave.* A corporation provides a paid or subsidized leave of absence for the parent in lieu of specific child care services.

Employers who do not extend direct child care benefits can make arrangements easier for their employees in other ways. They can offer a flexible work schedule, so parents may need less or no child care. They may also offer maternity leave extensions and paternity leaves, and allow sick leave use to include absence from work for a sick child.

Payroll Deductions for Child Care   Federal tax law allows employee payroll deductions for a flexible spending account for child care. The employee reimbursement system works either as a direct employee benefit or as a salary reduction plan, and does not limit the type of child care the employee can use.

As a benefit, the employee sets aside a certain amount of salary to be paid directly by the employer to the child care provider. Employee salary reductions are more common, which allow child care payments to be made from pretax earnings, often at a considerable discount for most employees. This plan provides a significant benefit to workers in higher tax brackets.

Under such plans, present tax law requires that employees forfeit any of the amount specifically set aside that they do not spend on child care by the end of the calendar year. Employees pay no federal or social security taxes on money spent for child care. The maximum salary reduction allowed is $5,000 per year.

Advantages of Employer-Sponsored Child Care

Many advantages accrue to corporations that sponsor or support child care. The presence of a corporate child care program can be an excellent recruiting device; hospitals, in particular, find child care services to be an added incentive.

Corporate-sponsored child care also promotes employee morale and reduces absenteeism. A possible side benefit is that the corporation may be eligible for a variety of tax benefits through business expenses, charitable gifts, and depreciation. Knowing they need not worry about child care may motivate employees to stay with a company. In fact, employees may view corporate child care as a family support system, which tends to encourage positive feelings toward the company and may perhaps offset negative feelings about other factors, such as pay and working conditions. Employees may also be more inclined to work different shifts when child care is available.

Similarly, there are advantages to employees. Parents can be more relaxed and confident about their children's care. Many parents can visit their children during breaks or even eat lunch with them. Being near their children is particularly advantageous for nursing mothers. Also, if a child becomes ill, the employee is immediately available. When parents have long commuting distances, parents and children get to spend more time together.

Financial benefits to employees of employer child care include (1) the possibility of deducting the cost of child care from salary, which represents a forced means of budgeting; (2) employers can usually provide high-quality care at reasonable cost; and (3) when child care is provided as part of an employee's work benefits package, the cost is not taxable.

What's New in Corporate Involvement?

Corporations increasingly recognize that they have both a social responsibility and a responsibility to their future work forces to be involved in child care and early childhood programs. They are more proactive in outreach efforts to involve the community in two ways. First, they are inviting the community to reserve slots for children in their child care programs. Second, corporations are providing monies to programs in the community to train personnel and upgrade child care services.

Corporations are collaborating with private and governmental agencies to address issues of supply, demand, and quality. For example, the DuPont Company, through its Flying Colors Program, encourages and supports child care programs to become NAEYC accredited. To date, seventy-five programs have been accredited through the program.

Corporations here in the United States are looking at child care programs in other industrialized countries, to determine what unique and beneficial features they can apply to their own programs. As companies examine how other countries excel in world economic markets, it is only natural that they should also look at how those nations care for and educate their future work force.

As a group, corporations are interested in investing in quality. They want quality programs for their employee's children and families. Corporations also want to promote quality child care in communities,

PROGRAM IN ACTION

NATIONSBANK CHILD CARE CENTER

NationsBank, the South's largest banking company, has earned national recognition as a leader in developing progressive and flexible programs for working parents. The results of an employee survey in the mid-1980s revealed child care to be the number one need. The company responded with an expanding and evolving array of work-family programs. The NationsBank Child Care Center in Charlotte, North Carolina, is a model representing an added dimension in the company's efforts to aid employees.

The center is designed with its primary users in mind: children. Natural lighting and play space are given priority. Each classroom opens directly to one of six outdoor playgrounds. Large, interior central foyers turn into recreational areas on foul-weather days.

The capacity for full-year care is 160 children. Forty spaces (25 percent) are reserved for children of eligible tenants of the NationsBank Corporate Center. Also, there are thirty Back-Up Care spaces and ten Get Well Care spaces. Capacity may change based on enrollment demands. However, the anticipated enrollment structure is forty-eight infants (six groups of eight children), forty toddlers (four groups of ten children), and seventy-two preschoolers (four groups of eighteen children).

The Curriculum

Children enrolled in the center participate in a developmentally appropriate, individualized curriculum. Teachers understand the variety of learning styles and paces in children's normal development. Their job is to respond to each child's own style and pace.

At the heart is a warm, nurturing relationship with caring adults in a stimulating, developmentally designed environment. Thus, much of the teachers' planning revolves around the needs of the children—individually and as a group. Each day there is both indoor and outdoor activity, small-group and independent projects, and active and quiet play.

The program begins with an understanding that children are active learners and that there is no clear separation between learning and caring, play and work. The NationsBank Child Care Center is committed to promoting all aspects of development, including the following:

Motor development—using large muscles for skills such as throwing and running as well as small muscles for activities such as stacking and writing

Perceptual development—for example, learning to look deliberately, thinking about what one sees, and distinguishing parts of a whole scene

Social/emotional development—how to be a constructive member of a group as well as an individual; recognizing and understanding feelings, how to act on or cope with them; allowing each child to develop their unique, individual talents; developing a foundation that promotes success in school, including problem-solving skills, a high self-

particularly those in which they have plants and offices.

Corporations are becoming more involved in programs for older children. They are investing in before- and afterschool care programs, summer camps, and institutes, especially those that focus on math, science, and technology.

Corporations believe that they are laying the groundwork for the future work force.

More and more, corporate executives discuss the need to invest in the quality of the future work force by investing in children today. In this sense, corporations are becoming more oriented not only to their future needs but to the needs of society as well.

The description of the Pacific Gas and Electric Company Children's Center on page b–16 of the "Observing Programs in Action" color insert illustrates how business and

esteem, and a love of learning; providing an environment that is free of racial and gender bias or stereotypes

Language development—using words to express and understand needs, feelings, and ideas; reading and prereading skills; and appreciation for books and other written language

The center's yard, enclosed by a brick and wrought iron fence, has playground equipment for children to enjoy during recreation time. The ample exterior play space allows children to crawl, run, jump, skip, and enjoy outdoor activities on sunny days. Each of the six play areas serves as the "backyard" for children at their daytime home away from home.

Get Well Care   A program for children who are mildly ill is included among the services of the Full-Year Care. Parents receive detailed guidelines for Get Well Care on enrollment. When children in Full-Year Care are under the weather and not up to the demands of their regular activity, but well enough to leave home, care can be provided in Get Well Care. This is a separate area, staffed by a full-time registered nurse.

Parent Involvement

NationsBank is committed to promoting active parent participation in the center. Parents are encouraged to visit the center and are welcome at any time. Extensive communication with parents about

their child, their child's room, and the center is an important part of the program.

In addition to many written and verbal means of communication with parents, the parent representative system (parent reps) is a formal way parents can give feedback and input. Each month volunteer parent reps call other parents to learn how things are going and obtain ideas, questions, or suggestions about the center. Parent reps meet monthly to discuss these comments; these meetings are open to all parents.

Administration

Resources for Child Care Management (RCCM) manages and supervises NationsBank Child Care Center. RCCM's unique approach to the management of workplace child care centers assures NationsBank will have a strong influence on the program and policy at its center. This partnership is based on a mutual commitment to well-accepted standards of high-quality care.

Providing for children in developmentally appropriate ways is a major goal of NationsBank Child Care Center. Professionals respond to children's interests and learning styles in warm, nurturing ways. Corporations across the country are including child care in the benefits provided employees and their families and are leading the way in designing environments and programs that are child centered and family focused.

---

industry are fast becoming leaders in setting the standards for child care programming. These straightforward and extensive involvements of companies in providing child care and family-related services are a primary example of the restructuring occurring in the nation's business sector and how these changes in turn change the child care landscape. As you read and study these descriptions, think about how such pro-

grams are changing how businesses take care of employees' children. Also, develop a list of such changes and predict how you think business-supported and -sponsored child care will continue to change over the next decade.

Proprietary Child Care

Some child care centers are run by corporations, businesses, and individual proprietors for the purpose of making a profit. Some for-profit centers provide custodial services and preschool and elementary programs as well. Many of these programs emphasize their educational component and appeal to middle-class families who are willing to pay for the promised services. About 35 percent of all child care centers in the United States are operated for profit, and the number is likely to grow. Child care is a big service industry, with more and more entrepreneurs realizing that there is money to be made in caring for the nation's children. Figure 14.2 shows the percentage of types of agencies that operate child care programs.

Foster Child Care

Almost every state uses foster child care. Children are placed in foster care because their parents cannot or will not take care of them, or because they have been abused or abandoned. As many as 429,000 children live in foster care homes or foster group homes.[4] Many children in foster care facilities have some disability that makes them less attractive to some for adoption.

A growing phenomenon in the United States is the number of hand-me-down children; many parents find they cannot afford to raise their children or can no longer discipline them effectively, so they simply turn them over to the courts, which in turn place them in foster care.

Baby-sitters

Children are their parents' most valuable assets, so parents should not seek the lowest common denominator either in quality or pay when deciding about the kind of person to whom they will entrust their children. Early childhood professionals should encourage parents to look for the following important qualities in anyone who acts as a baby-sitter:

Figure 14.2/Center Care by Auspices

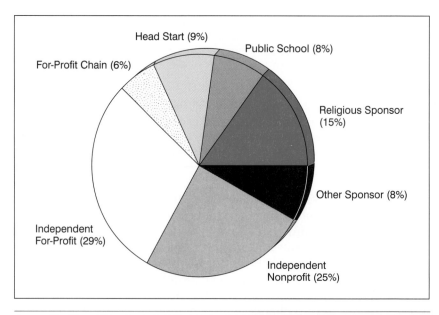

Head Start (9%)
Public School (8%)
For-Profit Chain (6%)
Religious Sponsor (15%)
Other Sponsor (8%)
Independent For-Profit (29%)
Independent Nonprofit (25%)

Source: Ellen Eliason Kisker, Sandra L. Hofferth, Deborah A. Phillips, and Elizabeth Farquhar, *A Profile of Child Care Settings: Early Education and Care in 1990,* vol. 1 (Princeton, NJ: Mathematica Policy Research, 1991), p. 36. Used by permission.

- *The necessary age and maturity to provide basic care for children.* While no particular chronological age makes a person qualified to give basic care, a certain degree of maturity is necessary.

- *Education in providing child care.* Training might come through a course offered by a school or service organization or through caring for younger brothers and sisters. In any case, a sitter should know how to diaper, feed, and interact with children.

- *Basic training in first aid and emergency procedures.*

- *Trustworthiness.*

- *Childrearing values that agree with those of the parents.* Parents must tell babysitters how they want certain situations handled and how they want their children disciplined.

- *Neatness, good grooming, and acceptable verbal skills.*

- *Good recommendations and references from others* who know and/or have used the sitter.

Additionally, professionals should share the following guidelines with parents for specific rules children and sitters should follow:[5]

1. Lock all doors when the parents leave.

2. Watch carefully while children are awake and protect them from dangerous objects, chemicals, and household accidents.

3. Don't permit visitors or guests.

4. Don't leave the children alone in the house at any time.

5. Check the children regularly while they are asleep.

6. Stay awake during your stay in the house.

7. Do not tell telephone callers that the children are alone with a baby-sitter. Ask the caller to leave a message for the parents.

8. Do not open the door to anyone unless parents have given permission. Ask to take a message.

9. If you take the children outside, watch them carefully. Ask parents if the children may play outside and who they can or cannot visit.

10. If you take the children to a public place, watch them carefully and do not permit them to wander. Avoid sending the children to public restrooms alone. Make sure that you lock all windows and doors before you leave. When you return, if something seems suspicious (broken window or door), call the police immediately from another house.

Drop-In or Casual Child Care

Many parents with part-time jobs or flexible schedules need a place to leave their children. Some child care services meet such needs with storefront child care centers, child care services in shopping centers, and parents who do occasional baby-sitting in their homes. These services are convenient, but do have drawbacks. First, the quality of care may be low simply because the children are transient, and it is difficult to build continuity into a program whose population base is unstable. In addition, such sporadic contact with strangers can be stressful to children.

Military Child Care

The Army, Navy, Air Force, Marine Corps, and Coast Guard operate Child Development Programs at over seven hundred locations within the United States and throughout the world. The armed services are the United States's largest providers of employer child care services. The programs offer care of all kinds—hourly, part-day, full-day, before- and afterschool, evening, and weekend—to children of military families and other Department of Defense personnel. The services operate center programs ranging in size from 29 to 450 children. Infant care accounts for 40 percent of all child care services provided. These programs help family members meet their military responsibilities secure in the knowledge that their children are receiving quality care.

Military child care programs are funded through Defense Department appropriations, participant fees, and funds from local programs. Department of Defense funds usually cover the costs of facilities, utilities, supplies, and equipment; participant fees cover the cost of staff salaries.

The armed forces provide great career opportunities for early childhood professionals. It offers one of the best job opportunities in the world; in fact, the military offers many job opportunities around the world. A socalled *horizontal employment pathway* is the opportunity to be a teacher in a center or a home child care provider. A *vertical pathway* is entering as a teacher, moving up to assistant center director, then center director, and so on (see Figure 14.3).

The military also offers professional training that enables personnel to assume a range of jobs; in other words, the military grows its own professionals. The needs of military child care are simply too vast for the services to rely on other agencies (i.e., community colleges, colleges, universities). Consequently, the military trains its personnel and promotes from within.

Child Care for Children with Medical Needs

As child care becomes more popular, it also is becoming more specialized. Consequently,

more and more programs are providing care for children with medical needs.

Ill Child Care

For most parents, balancing the demands of a job and the obligations of parenthood is manageable as long as children are healthy. But when children get sick, parents must find someone who will take care of them or must stay home. The National Child Care Survey data reveal that 35 percent of mothers employed outside the home reported that in the month previous to the survey their child was sick on a day they were supposed to work. Fifty-one percent of these women missed an average of 2.2 days of work per month because of sick children.[6]

Fortunately, working parents increasingly have flexible employee benefits that enable them to stay home with sick children; however, many still do not. Also, when children are only mildly ill or do not have a contagious illness, parents feel there should be other options to losing a day's work. Child care providers have begun to respond to parents' needs. Some centers provide care for sick children as part of their program, and other providers are opening centers exclusively for the care of ill children. Ill children are cared for in the following ways:

- *In the home*—Child care aides go into homes to care for ill children.

- *Hospital based*—Some hospitals have programs for providing for sick children.

- *Center based*—Ill child care is part of a center's program of services, usually in a separate room.

- *A separate facility* is specifically designed, built, and staffed to provide child care as needed for sick children.

- *Family care*—Ill children are provided for in a family daycare home.

Figure 14.3/*Army Child Development Services*

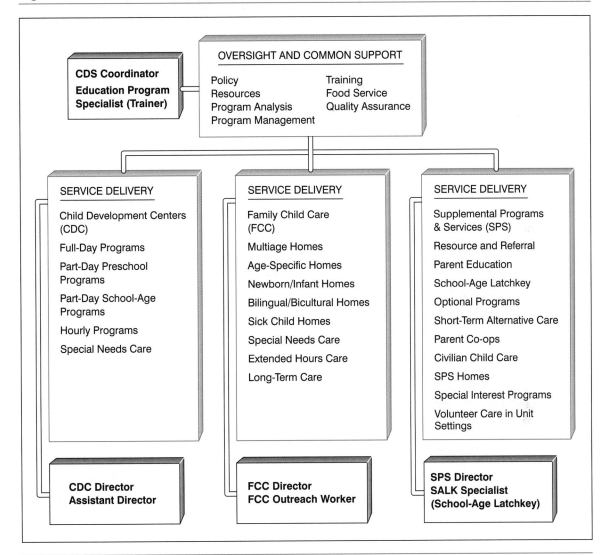

Source: U.S. Army Community and Family Support Center, 2461 Eisenhower Ave., Alexandria, Virginia 22331. Used by permission.

Staff training for those who provide care for ill children is also a critical concern. Factors in training include the following:

- What caregivers and parents can expect in behaviors and symptoms of typical childhood illnesses

- How to care for ill children according to different kinds of illnesses

- How to respond to the needs of ill children

- When to exclude the child from ill child care

PROGRAM IN ACTION

THE SICK CHILD CARE CENTER

The Sick Child Care Center in San Jose, California, is one of a growing number of programs that provide care for mildly ill children. Before using its services, parents are asked to register their children while they are well. The Sick Child Care Center provides care for children ages 2 months to 14 years. Once they have registered, parents need only to call for care when their child is ill. One of the staff members conducts a phone triage survey to determine if The Sick Child Care Center is appropriate for that child for that day, if they can come directly from home, or whether he or she must first see a physician. When parents bring their children in, a registered nurse does a health assessment to determine the nature of the symptoms and confirms whether they can attend. Care at The Sick Child Care Center is partially subsidized by United Way and the City of San Jose. Cost to the parent is determined by a sliding scale for family size and income. Employers can also elect to subsidize the program to make the sliding scale available to their employees.

The Sick Child Care Center will not admit children with measles, mumps, or chicken pox; otherwise, children with almost any other illness can be admitted. The Sick Child Care Center will accept children with fevers, ear infection, vomiting, diarrhea, or colds; it will also accept an asthmatic child who has seen a doctor and whose asthma is under control; postsurgical children who have had, for example, an appendectomy or tonsillectomy; and children in casts who have sprains or fractures.

Although children can stay at The Sick Child Care Center for as long as they need ill care, the average stay is two days. The Sick Child Care Center can care for fifteen children each day; the daily average is six to nine. During their stay children are involved in developmentally appropriate activities that take into consideration their illness and physical condition. The nurse and the teacher decide on the appropriate activities in the beginning of the day. If needed, the diet will be modified, treatments will be carried out, medicines will be administered, and the condition will be monitored. At the end of the day the parent receives a copy of the child's records for further care.

San Juan Bautista Child Development Agency is the parent organization of The Sick Child Care Center as well as a number of regular child care centers. The Sick Child Care Center shares a site with one of the child care centers. In addition to a registered nurse, the staff includes a fully qualified director/teacher and teaching and nursing assistants. The staff takes special precautions to assure that the furniture, equipment, and materials are disinfected daily to control infections, yet at the same time they allow the children to use the environment freely. Parents are delighted to bring their children back time and again for a healthy dose of TLC.

Contributed by The Sick Child Care Center, San Jose, CA.

- Curriculum—how to provide learning opportunities for ill children within the limits of their illness and in mixed age groups

- Administering first aid and CPR

- Infection control

The National Association of Sick Child Daycare (NASCDC) offers the following recommendations for programs that offer sick-child care:

- Programs should be medically safe and sound.

- A health professional who is well versed in ambulatory pediatric care and familiar with the child care field should be represented in the operation of the service.

- Children should have many opportunities to be involved in play and in school-related activities. Children's development does not end just because they are ill.

- Programs should screen children prior to admittance for diseases that are too contagious or serious.

- When medically fragile and technologically dependent children are admitted to the rest program, a clinical nurse should be on site.

- Parents should visit a program and evaluate it prior to using its services. Some things to look for:

   Is the facility clean, and does the staff disinfect furniture, materials, and equipment?

   Does the staff meet the needs of children quickly, pleasantly, and respectfully?

   Are licenses, staff qualifications, menus, and daily schedules clearly posted?

   Does each child have a written record of his or her medical and developmental progress while in the program?

According to Gail D. Gonzalez, past president of NASCD, "Every program, despite its design, should have a yearly evaluation to assure that there are appropriate procedures in place to prevent contamination and infections. In any quality sick daycare program, children are happy, parents are trustful of the care, and health professionals are comfortable with the services."[7]

Daycare for Children with AIDS   What do you do for child care if you and/or your child has AIDS? One solution is to send your child to a child care center designed especially for children with AIDS. Although children with AIDS are covered under the provisions of the Americans with Disabilities Act (see Chap. 13), some child care centers take children with AIDS and others will not. Both these situations pose a problem if a parent with AIDS must work, is sick, or needs to go to the doctor (see the Program in Action feature, "Caring for Children with AIDS").

Before- and Afterschool Care

In many respects, public schools are logical places for before- and afterschool care. They have the administrative organization, facilities, and staff to provide such care. Many taxpayers and professionals have always believed that schools should not sit empty in the afternoons, evenings, holidays, and summers. Using resources already in place for child care makes good sense. This is why in many communities public schools are helping meet the need for afterschool child care.

The Dade County, Florida, public schools provide afterschool care for 20,300 students in 200 elementary schools. The school district operates 103 afterschool centers with its own personnel; 59 are operated by the YMCA; 17 by the YWCA; and 21 by the Family Christian Association of America. The district also operates 102 before-school care sites; 34 are operated by the YMCA, 5 by the YWCA, and 63 are school based.

Special-needs students are mainstreamed at 83 schools with over 700 students in afterschool care. Parents pay from $15 to $25 per week depending on the per-child cost at the individual school. Because the programs are school based and managed, the costs of services vary depending on the nature and cost of each program. Services begin at dismissal and end at 6:00 P.M. The curriculum includes Boy and Girl Scouts, 4-H, fun activities based on skills and concepts measured by state assessment tests for grades 3 and 5, drama, and ballet.

In other localities, afterschool care may be no more than baby-sitting, with large groups of children supervised by a few adults. The cost

PROGRAM IN ACTION

CARING FOR CHILDREN WITH AIDS

A unique program for some families is a child care center for children who have AIDS or whose parents have AIDS. One such center is operated by Children's Home Society of Florida, Southeastern Division, in Miami, Florida. After New York, Florida has the highest number of children with AIDS. The daycare center enrolls ten children between the ages of eighteen months and five years. Eight are HIV positive or have AIDS; two are HIV negative.

Roger Croteau, a registered nurse, established the center with the help of a state grant because parents who have AIDS or whose children have AIDS have few options regarding child care. As Roger says, "Although times are changing and people are more understanding about AIDS, the fact remains that especially in children, AIDS carries a stigma."

The program is a social and academic development one modeled after Head Start. The daycare contracts with a local health agency for special services such as speech and hearing therapy and developmental assessment. Field trips are conducted once a week. Roger believes getting children out into the community is a good way to provide for their needs. As he says, "It is important for the children go on field trips once a week to provide the emotional, physical, and social stimulation that a lot of the families can't provide for their children due to the family conditions and parents' failing health."

In addition to Roger, the program is staffed by a certified teacher and teacher aide, providing a five-to-one child–staff ratio.

Christopher

When three-year-old Christopher entered the program, he had a mother and father. However, he lived with his mother and grandmother. His mother was having kidney failure as a result of AIDS and had trouble taking care of him, so his grandmother helped. His father was working twelve-hour days and lived alone in their apartment.

Christopher is HIV infected and has AIDS. When he entered the daycare program, he did not exhibit any signs of infection and took AZT (an antiviral drug) four times a day. Socially, Christopher was introverted and shy and would cling to his parents. His grandmother was also working full time, and his mother could not spend much time with him because of her condition. The need for child care was obvious.

Six months after enrolling in the daycare program, Christopher's mother died. Prior to her death, she was as involved in Christopher's daycare as much as her illness would allow her. She volunteered in the classroom and attended parent meetings. She was a strong advocate for the children. She attended a conference of the Association for the Care of Children's Health in Washington, D.C., and took part in a parent networking weekend. At such conferences, parents learn about similar programs and are encouraged to return to their hometown and build a

of afterschool care may be more than parents can afford. Also, when the program follows the school calendar, parents are left to find other care when school is not in session.

According to the National Study of Before and After School Programs, about 1.7 million children in kindergarten through grade 8 are enrolled in 49,500 programs.[8] The three most common sponsors of before-

and afterschool child care are the public schools, for-profit corporations, and nonprofit organizations. Nationally, as with the Dade County program described earlier, most care is provided after school. The study states that the ability of agencies to serve more poor families and to enhance the developmental nature of the programs is hampered by a reliance on paid tuition, a lack of access to

support network and advocate for chronically ill children.

Christopher's father is involved in his care and is supportive of his attendance at the child care center. He may be HIV positive but refuses to be tested.

Christopher has blossomed as a result of being in the program. He gets along well with other children and adults, is very talkative, and is no longer as shy as he used to be. Christopher is a very bright child and cognitively is developmentally above average.

The Program

A number of things make this child care program unique:

- It provides a nondiscriminatory environment for children with AIDS. Although child care programs cannot legally discriminate, some nonetheless do. The staff acknowledges from the beginning the HIV status of the children. They are willing to administer AZT to the children, with parental consent.
- The staff makes a point of academically stimulating the children to try to maintain their developmental levels. They feel this is important because the children may be absent because of their illness.
- The staff meets once a month with a special immunology team from a local hospital to discuss families' and children's health status and medical treatments.

- At monthly parent meetings, the agenda is family focused and parents set the topics of discussion, such as emphasizing infection control and disease reduction. For example, they discuss the do's and don'ts of home hygiene, such as the need for cleanliness and the types and uses of solutions that kill HIV. They address the dangers of the fact that children with AIDS are much more vulnerable to the side effects of childhood diseases such as chicken pox. These children require additional medication to help them battle the diseases' effects. They also talk about topics that other parents might not consider important, such as not allowing their children to play in sandboxes, which are bacteria breeding grounds.
- The staff helps parents learn the necessity of providing a balanced nutritional program that is appropriate for their children's HIV symptoms.

A primary goal of the program is to mainstream the children into Head Start, early intervention programs, and other pre-K programs. Roger and the staff work for full inclusion of the children in regular programs. Roger believes there is currently a need for child care for children with AIDS, but the long-term goal is to not have such programs. "Kids need to be with kids and have as normal a childhood as possible," he explains.

"child friendly" space, high staff turnover, and inadequate programming for children beyond third grade.

The profile on Voyager Expanded Learning shown in the "Observing Programs in Action" color insert on pages b–12 and b–13 illustrates how private corporations are working in partnership with schools in order to meet the before- and afterschool educational

needs of children and families. Voyager seeks to further instill in children a love of learning and a desire to excel.

Latchkey Children Every day, many children stay home by themselves until it is time to go to school or until their parents return from work. Children who care for themselves before and/or after school are referred to as *latchkey* or *self-care* children. While there are risks associated with young children providing themselves self-care, one reality of contemporary life is that thousands do, as many as 2.5 million children between the ages of 5 and 13. Some states have laws against leaving children under a certain age (usually 12) alone without supervision. Many parents may not be aware of these laws or may feel they really have no choice. In fact, for some parents, self-care for their children is a positive choice. The following example illustrates that some children are successful in the process of self-care.

Eight-year-old Myra Martinez, an only child, takes the school bus home each day from school. With the housekey hung around her neck, she lets herself in and cares for herself from approximately 3:15 until 6:30 P.M., when her parents arrive home.

Myra follows a routine she and her parents have worked out for her well-being and safety. When she gets home, Myra immediately "beeps" her mother at work. This way, her mother knows Myra is home and returns her call. Myra stays in the house, does not answer the door for strangers, and does not have friends over while her parents are not home. In addition, Myra and her parents have rehearsed what to do in an emergency. Myra is very happy and self-confident about taking care of herself. As she says, "I feel very independent, and I like being able to take care of myself."

As an early childhood professional, you are in a unique position to advise and work with parents about the self-care of their children. Guidelines to share with parents follow:

- Do not expect children to assume more responsibilities than they are capable of. Some children are more responsible than others. Parents and professionals can help children assume responsibilities by helping them learn to do things for themselves.

- Establish rules that children must follow when they are caring for themselves. You must decide what to do in the following circumstances:

  Whether children may leave the house.
  Who is in charge when more than one child is involved.
  Whether other children or adults are allowed to visit.

Many children come home after school to homes without parents or others to provide care and supervision. In order to help address this problem of latchkey children, more school districts are providing before- and afterschool child care programs. What are some advantages of these before- and afterschool programs?

Whether children are not to answer the door for anybody or whether they may answer the door for relatives and previously approved adults, such as the next-door neighbor.

- Set up emergency procedures.

  Post a list of all emergency numbers: police, fire, 911.
  Instruct children about what to do in an emergency.

- Show children how to do certain things or tell them they cannot do certain things. If children can fix a snack, what kind? Can they use the stove? The microwave? Some parents have children do chores such as washing clothes. Other parents view this time as a good time for children to do their homework.

- When possible, have children call a parent when they get home from school. Parents, friends, and relatives can periodically check on their children. In addition, consider joining or forming a volunteer-run telephone network to monitor neighborhood latchkey children.

LOCATING CHILD CARE

The majority of parents (66 percent) find child care for their children through friends, neighbors, and relatives. Parents obviously feel more comfortable using this informal system, probably believing they can trust these people's judgments.

Thirteen percent of parents locate their child care through newspaper advertisement and bulletin boards; 9 percent use a resource and referral system.[9] The use of such information and referral systems is increasing.

These systems, usually computer based and operated by municipal governments, universities, corporations, and nonprofit agencies, help parents gain access to information about competent, convenient, and affordable care. Information supplied to parents includes names, addresses, and phone numbers of providers and basic information about the services, such as hours of operation, ages of children cared for, and activities provided.

FUNDING AND SUPPORT FOR CHILD CARE

The following are the most common sources for funding and support for child care:

- Parents, who pay all or part of the cost

- State programs, especially Health and Human Services

- Federal agencies (Administration for Children, Youth, and Families; Social Security Administration; Child Care Food Program of the USDA)

- Private and charitable foundations (United Way, Easter Seal Society)

- Organizations (YMCA, YWCA, YMHA), and religious groups that provide care to members and to the public, usually at reduced rates

- Employers

- Parent cooperatives

After food, housing, and taxes, child care is the fourth largest budget item for an average working family. Many families spend at least 10 percent of their income on child care, and the average single mother may spend up to one-fourth of her income (see Figure 14.4). Families with employed mothers

Figure 14.4/*Weekly Child Care Costs for Children Under Age 5*

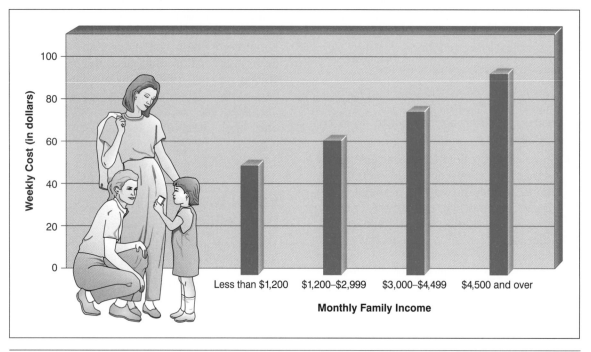

Source: U.S. Census Bureau, 1994.

spend over $21 billion per year on child care services. The average weekly expenditure for child care by employed mothers with preschool children is $63.[10]

Who Should Pay for Child Care?

The federal government's support for child care services has been shrinking over the past decade, although Head Start receives enhanced funding (see Chap. 16). This means that the three other available sources for child care support—state agencies, private agencies, and consumers—will, of necessity, have to increase their support.

As fewer and fewer federal dollars become available, more parents will be called on to help pay the real cost of their children's care. Yet the fact remains that most parents who have to work probably cannot and will not be able to afford the cost of quality child care programs. Efforts to have child care subsidized by employers, foundations, and charitable groups will have to increase.

How Much Should Child Care Cost?

Traditionally, child care has been a low-cost and low-paying operation. Many programs emphasize keeping costs low so that working and low-income parents will not be overburdened; this results in a very low pay scale for child care workers. Thus, as the cost of child care is kept low, the true cost is subsidized by low-paid workers. Yet, if child care costs rise to provide workers with fairer wages, many families who can hardly afford what they now pay would be priced out of the services. Also, as more public schools offer programs for four-year-olds, many child care workers with degrees will be attracted to these programs by the higher salaries. This shift could tend to lower the quality of child care programs and further decrease salaries.

Two noteworthy efforts are currently underway to help address issues associated with the cost of child care and low child care worker wages, the Worthy Wage Coalition and the Full Cost of Quality program.

Worthy Wage Coalition The Worthy Wage Coalition is an association of organizations whose primary focus is specifically to address issues of inadequate compensation in child care. Inadequate compensation for child care workers, which includes salaries and benefits, cannot be considered in isolation of other factors. These include quality for children and affordability for families. The Worthy Wage Coalition is coordinated by the Child Care Employees Project, a national organization dedicated to improving child caregiver wages, working conditions, and access to training. Its address and phone number are 733 15th St., NW, Suite 1037, Washington, D.C. 20005-2112; 202-737-7700.

Full Cost of Quality The Full Cost of Quality program is an NAEYC initiative designed to highlight public awareness regarding what constitutes quality in early childhood services and the cost of fully meeting professional recommendations regarding high quality.

Parents need to know and understand that quality child care costs money. In addition, when parents understand what constitutes quality, they are more likely to seek it out and demand it. All early childhood professionals have an obligation to promote and provide high-quality programs, help parents understand the importance and cost of quality, and advocate to the public regarding quality child care. For more information about the Full Cost of Quality program, contact the Public Affairs Division of the National Association for the Education of Young Children, 1509 16th St., NW, Washington, D.C. 20036; 800-424-2460.

FEDERALLY SUPPORTED CHILD CARE

Child Care and Development Block Grant

Child care centers often receive federal funds because they serve low-income families who are eligible for cash assistance under Title IV A of the Social Security Act, or families are eligible for social services under the Amended Child Care and Development Block Grant as amended in 1996 as part of the Welfare Reform Act.

Congress authorized Title XX of the Social Security Act in 1974 as a block grant to fund and administer what had been separate adult and child welfare programs. It was revised in 1980 and renamed the Social Services Block Grant. Its level of funding has changed very little since its inception, and there are no requirements for state match. Some states require a local match from their subdistricts. The Child Care and Development Block Grant of 1990 passed Congress after several attempts to produce a daycare bill that would recognize the need for child care apart from other social services.

States use Social Services Block Grant funding to cover their highest priorities apart from Title IV A. They include children (1) who are at risk for neglect and abuse, (2) who have special needs (disabilities), or (3) whose parents are working with incomes just above AFDC, including farm worker families. The level of aid to these individuals depends on the amount of money available in each state.

States use Child Care and Development Block Grant funds to provide services to those children related to Title IV A. They include children of parents who are (1) employed and receiving partial AFDC, (2) in training and receiving AFDC, or (3) employed and on AFDC in the past year.

Child Care Component of the Child and Adult Care Food Program

A second source of federal support comes through the U.S. Department of Agriculture (USDA) Food and Consumer Service, Child Nutrition Division, Child Care Component (CCC). Through this program, the USDA works through state agencies that administer the program. Nutritional support is provided in two ways: commodities and money.

For example, the USDA will provide commodities such as cheese, dry milk, and peanut butter to child care centers and family daycare homes to support their nutritional programs. In lieu of commodities, programs can choose to receive cash equal to 14.5 cents per child for each lunch or supper served, in addition to the regular reimbursement (this cash-in-lieu-of-commodities rate is adjusted annually based on the cost of living). Children twelve years of age and younger are eligible for participation. In addition, children with disabilities, regardless of age as long as they are in a center in which the majority of children enrolled are eighteen years or younger, and migrant children up to age fifteen are eligible. In fiscal 1995, the USDA reimbursed schools with $1.50 billion of support through CCC.[11] Additionally, the USDA reimbursed schools $5 billion through the school lunch program.

Woman, Infants, and Children (WIC)

A third source of federal support, also through the USDA, funds the Special Supplemental Food Program for Women, Infants, and Children (WIC). The WIC program, funded in each of the fifty states, provides basic nutritious foods to low- and moderate-income women and children. These foods are rich in protein, iron, calcium, and vitamins A and C, key nutrients often lacking in the diets of the WIC population. Participants also receive nutrition education and counseling as well as breastfeeding promotion and support.

WIC is available to women who are pregnant, breastfeeding, and postpartum (the period of time after childbirth); infants (birth to one year); and children from age one up to their fifth birthday. Postpartum, breastfeeding women are eligible for up to twelve months, others are eligible for up to six months. Applicants also must meet the following criteria:

1. *Income guidelines.* The income criteria varies from state to state. In Florida, for example, the criteria is an income of 185 percent of poverty (U.S. Poverty Income Guidelines appear in Chap. 16). For example, for a nonfarm family of three, the poverty level is $12,980. Multiplying $12,980 by 185 percent totals $24,013, the income below which a nonfarm family of three is eligible for WIC food supplements. States must use an income eligibility between 100 percent to 185 percent of poverty.

2. *Medical or nutritional risk.* Such risks include a pregnant woman who is not gaining enough weight, a child who is anemic, or an infant who needs a special formula.

Women and children who meet the criteria are eligible for supplemental foods—milk, eggs, dried beans or peanut butter, iron-fortified cereal, cheese, vitamin C–rich juices, and iron-fortified infant formula and infant cereal. In addition, women who are totally breastfeeding also receive tuna fish and fresh carrots.

The method of payment varies from state to state. Florida recipients receive a check or voucher for the specific food items. In fiscal 1994, the USDA contributed $3.2 billion to the WIC program.

Child Care Tax Credits

A fourth federal source of support is the child care tax credits for individuals and corporations. The federal tax code provides employers with certain "tax breaks" or benefits for providing child care services to their employees.

Parents are able to itemize the cost of child care as a credit against their federal income taxes under the Federal Child and Dependent Care Credit. Currently, the amount that can be deducted is based on a sliding scale. Thirty percent of the cost of child care can be deducted from $0 to $10,000 of annual adjusted taxable income. As adjusted income increases by $2,000, the percentage that can be deducted decreases by 1 percent until it reaches 20 percent. For example, 29 percent of the cost of child care can be deducted for $10,001–12,000 of adjusted income; 28 percent for $12,001–14,000, and so on (see Table 14.1). The maximum amount of the cost of child care a family can use toward determining their credit is $2,400 for one child and $4,800 for two children.

For example, Valerie and Jack Lewis have three children. Last year they spent $5,200 on child care. Their combined adjusted income is $46,000. The maximum amount they can use to determine their credit is the $4,800 allowed by law. Their credit against their income taxes for child care is $960 ($4,800 multiplied by 20 percent). They can only deduct 20 percent of the $4,800 because each $2,000 of their income over $10,000 reduces the 30 percent rate by 1 percent. Table 14.1 helps explain the deduction calculations.

Although the Federal Child and Dependent Care Credit is available to parents, only 31 percent of families with an employed mother use it. Interestingly, families with income above the poverty level are more likely to use the credit than are families living in poverty.[12]

Table 14.1/*Federal Child Care Credit Calculation*

Gross Adjusted Income	Percentage of the Cost of Child Care to Be Deducted	Tax Credit for Child Care, 2 or More Children
$0–10,000	30	$1,440
$10,001–12,000	29	$1,392
$12,001–14,000	28	$1,344
$14,001–16,000	27	$1,296
$16,001–18,000	26	$1,248
$18,001–20,000	25	$1,200
$20,001–22,000	24	$1,152
$22,001–24,000	23	$1,104
$24,001–26,000	22	$1,056
$26,001–28,000	21	$1,008
$28,000+	20	$ 960

TRAINING AND CERTIFICATION FOR EARLY CHILDHOOD PERSONNEL

A major challenge facing all areas of the early childhood profession is the training and certification of those who care for and teach young children. Training and certification requirements vary from state to state, but more states are tightening standards for child care, preschool, kindergarten, and primary personnel. Many states have mandatory training requirements that an individual must fulfill before being certified as a child care worker. The curriculum of these training programs frequently specifies mandatory inclusion of topics. For example, in Texas, all child care personnel must complete the Department of Health and Rehabilitation Services' twenty-hour child care training course. The course is composed of four modules:

1. State and local rules and regulations governing child care

2. Health, safety, and nutrition

3. Identifying and reporting child abuse and neglect

4. Child growth and development

In addition, all child care personnel must complete an annual eight-hour in-service training program.

Certificate Programs

Many high schools and vocational education programs conduct training leading to an entry-level certificate. This training certifies people to act as child care aides.

Degree Programs

Associate Degree Programs   Many community colleges provide training in early childhood education that qualifies recipients to be child care aides, primary child care providers, and assistant teachers.

Baccalaureate Programs   Four-year colleges provide programs that result in early childhood teacher certification. The ages and grades to which the certification applies vary from state to state. Some states have separate certification for prekindergarten programs and nursery schools; in other states, these certifications are "add-ons" to elementary (K–6, 1–6, 1–4) certification.

Master's Degree Programs   Depending on the state, individuals may gain initial early childhood certification at the master's level. Many colleges and universities offer master's-level programs for people who want to qualify as program directors or assistant directors or who may want to pursue a career in teaching.

The CDA National Credentialing Program

At the national level, the Child Development Associate (CDA) National Credentialing Program offers early childhood professionals the opportunity to develop and demonstrate competencies for meeting the needs of young children. A CDA is one who is "able to meet the specific needs of children and who, with parents and other adults, works to nurture children's physical, social, emotional, and intellectual growth in a child development framework."[13]

The CDA program, begun in 1971, is a major national effort to evaluate and improve the skills of caregivers in center-based preschool settings, center-based infant/toddler settings, family daycare homes, home visitor settings, and bilingual settings—programs that have specific goals for bilingual children. The CDA National Credentialing Program is operated by the Council for Early Childhood Professional Recognition. The council offers two options for obtaining the CDA credential. One option, the CDA Professional Preparation Program–P_3, allows candidates to work in postsecondary institutions as part of the credentialing process. The second option is the direct assessment method, which is designed for candidates who have child care work experience in combination with some early childhood education training.

A candidate for the CDA credential in any setting must first be eighteen years old or older and hold a high school diploma or equivalent. To obtain the CDA national credential, candidates under the direct assessment option must meet these additional eligibility requirements:

- 480 hours of experience working with children within the past five years

- 120 hours of formal child care education and training within the past five years

The candidate must then demonstrate competence in the six CDA competency areas (see Appendix F, "CDA Competency Goals and Functional Areas").

The CDA Professional Preparation Program   To obtain credentialing by means of this option, the candidate must meet the two general eligibility requirements of age and education and must also identify an advisor to work with during the year of study, which is made up of three phases.

The first phase is fieldwork. It involves study of the council's model curriculum, "Essentials for Child Development Associates Working with Young Children." This curriculum includes the six competency areas listed in Appendix F. The second phase is coursework, in which the candidate participates in seminars offered in community colleges and other postsecondary educational institutions. These seminars are designed to supplement the model curriculum and are administered by a seminar instructor. The third phase is the final evaluation, which takes place in the candidate's work setting or field placement.

The results of all three phases are sent to the council office for review and determination of whether the candidate has successfully completed all aspects of the CDA Professional Preparation Program. To date, more than fifty thousand persons have been awarded the CDA credential.

Additional information about the CDA can be obtained from the Council for Early Childhood Professional Recognition, 1341 G Street, NW, Suite 400, Washington, D.C. 20005. The toll-free number is 1-800-424-4310; the fax number is 202-265-9161.

WHAT CONSTITUTES QUALITY CHILD CARE?

It is easy to say that parents should seek out and insist on quality child care. For their part, many parents do try to find what they believe is quality child care for their children.

How Parents Define Quality

When parents select child care they view the following as important factors:[14]

1.	Quality	37%
2.	Care by relatives	30%
3.	Convenient location	10%
4.	Reasonable cost	9%
5.	Other	14%

Note that a total of 67 percent of parents believe "quality" and "care by relatives" to be the most important factors to consider when selecting child care. This information can help you and other early childhood professionals meet parents' needs; for example, care by relatives can be approximated by care in a homelike setting with an emphasis on nurturing.

When parents say they want "quality," what do they mean? Parents report that the following are the most important aspects of *quality* for them:[15]

- Child-related characteristics, including child–staff ratios, group size, and age ranges
- Provider-related characteristics, including a warm and loving teaching/parenting style, reliability, training, and credentials
- Program-related characteristics, including preparation for school, cognitive and social development, religious instruction, and instruction in parents' own culture
- Facility-related characteristics, including toys, equipment, homelike setting, and health and safety issues

We know from our previous discussions that there is more to quality than these elements. So, while professionals applaud and support parents' quest for quality, much still needs to be done to educate parents and the public about the full dimensions of child care.

The guidelines discussed in the following sections can assist you as an early childhood professional as you educate parents to a deeper understanding of the dimensions of quality care.

Developmental Needs

Good child care provides for children's needs and interests at each developmental stage. For example, infants need good physical care as well as continual love and affection and sensory stimulation. Toddlers need safe surroundings and opportunities to explore. They need caregivers who support and encourage active involvement.

Appropriate and Safe Environment

At all age levels, a safe and pleasant physical setting is important. Such an area should include a safe neighborhood free from traffic and environmental hazards; a fenced play area with well-maintained equipment; child-sized equipment and facilities (toilets, sinks); and areas for displaying children's work, such as fingerpainting and clay models. The environment should also be attractive and pleasant. The rooms, home, or center should be clean, well lit, well ventilated, and cheerful.

Caregiver–Child Ratio

The ratio of adults to children should be sufficient to give children the individual care and attention they need. NAEYC guidelines for child care ratio of caregivers are 1:3 or 1:4 for infants; 1:3 or 1:4 for toddlers; and 1:8 to 1:10 for preschoolers, depending on group size.

Research supports the belief that children receive better care when cared for in programs that follow these guidelines for group size. A study by Howes, Phillips, and Whitebook on the effects of adult–child ratios on quality found the following:

When five or more children were cared for by one adult in infant classrooms and nine children in toddler and preschool classrooms, at least 50 percent of the children were in classrooms rated as inadequate in caregiving. When five or more children were cared for by one adult in infant groups, eight or more children in toddler groups and preschool groups, at least 50 percent of the children were in classrooms rated as inadequate in activities. Children in infant classrooms with 1:3 or less ratios, toddler classrooms with 1:4 or less ratios, and preschool classrooms with 1:9 or less were more likely than children in classrooms with worse (higher) ratios to experience both caregiving and activities rated as good or very good.[16]

Policy recommendations and state laws governing child–adult ratios in child care programs are frequently at odds with each other. The ratios vary greatly from state to state and are often higher than child care professionals prefer. The recommendations

Table 14.2/*Recommended Staff–Child Ratios and Group Size*

Age of Children	Group Size										
	6	8	10	12	14	16	18	20	22	24	28
Infants (birth to 12 mos.)	1:3	1:4									
Toddlers (12 to 24 mos.)	1:3	1:4	1:5	1:4							
2-year-olds (24 to 30 mos.)		1:4	1:5	1:6							
2½-year-olds (30 to 36 mos.)			1:5	1:6	1:7						
3-year-olds					1:7	1:8	1:9	1:10			
4-year-olds						1:8	1:9	1:10			
5-year-olds						1:8	1:9	1:10			
6- to 8-year-olds								1:10	1:11	1:12	
9- to 12-year-olds										1:12	1:14

Note: Smaller group sizes and lower staff–child ratios have been found to be strong predictors of compliance with indicators of quality such as positive interactions among staff and children and developmentally appropriate curriculum. Variations in group sizes and ratios are acceptable in cases where the program demonstrates a very high level of compliance with criteria for interactions, curriculum, staff qualifications, health and safety, and physical environment.
Source: Criteria for High Quality Early Childhood Programs with Interpretations (Washington, D.C.: National Association for the Education of Young Children, 1994), p. 41.

of NAEYC regarding staff–child ratios are shown in Table 14.2.

Developmentally Appropriate Programs

Programs should have written, developmentally based curricula for meeting children's needs. A program's curriculum should specify activities for children of all ages that caregivers can use to stimulate infants, provide for the growing independence of toddlers, and address the readiness and literacy skills of four- and five-year-olds. The program should go beyond good physical care to include good social, emotional, and cognitive care as well. It should include a balance of activities, with time for playing indoors and outdoors and for learning skills and concepts.

Family Involvement

Parents and other family members should learn about the child care setting and their children's growth and development. Parents need encouragement to make the child care services part of their lives, so they are not detached from the center, its staff, or what happens to their children.

Staff Training and Development

Whether in a family or center setting, child care providers should be involved in an ongoing program of training and development. The CDA program is a good way for staff members to become competent and maintain the necessary skills. Program administrators should have a background and training in child development and early childhood education. A director of a child care program or agency should have a bachelor's degree in early childhood education, certification, or, at least, special college work in this area. Knowledge of child growth and development is essential for caregivers. Films, books, training in clinical settings, and experiences with children help professionals know about development. Professionals need to be developmentally aware and child oriented rather than self- or center oriented.

Knowledge of Children

Child care providers, especially those of infants, should be sensitive to the adjustments children make when they come into a child care setting. The environment and the people are new to them. A baby who has been the only child at home and cared for only by the mother or father has a lot to adapt to in a center setting, where there are more infants and more caregivers. Many center infant programs make sure that each care provider consistently takes care of the same infants, to give them the security that comes from familiarity. Likewise, new caregivers must also adjust when they come into the home or center, since every child has a unique personality, preferences, and ways of responding to the world.

Program Accreditation

In any discussion of quality, the question invariably arises, "Who determines quality?" Fortunately, NAEYC has addressed the issue of a standard in its Center Accreditation Project (CAP). CAP is a national, voluntary accreditation process for child care centers, preschools, and programs that provide be-

fore- and afterschool care for school-age children. Accreditation is administered through NAEYC's National Academy of Early Childhood Programs. NAEYC cites the following as benefits of accreditation:

- Accredited programs are recognized as quality programs.
- Parents will seek out accredited programs.
- The staff learns through the accrediting process.

The criteria addressed in the accreditation project are interactions among staff and children, curriculum, staff and parent interactions, administration, staff qualifications and development, staffing patterns, physical environment, health and safety, nutrition and food service, and program evaluation.[17]

Agreement Between Parents and Care Providers

As we noted at the beginning of this chapter, increasing numbers of parents turn over their children to outside child care providers. Many parents entrust their children to people they know very little about. They may be reliable

Bryan Keith Davis was awarded the milestone 50,000th credential in 1993. One of the few males to be awarded the CDA credential, Brian says, "The most exciting part about being a caregiver is when a child learns something for the first time. Knowing I've made a difference in their lives is rewarding."

and trustworthy, or they may not. Parents are now better informed as to what constitutes quality child care. Although they are becoming more selective, they still leave their children with people who are relative strangers. It is therefore extremely important for quality child care providers to work closely with parents from the time of their initial contact, usually at registration. Professionals must demonstrate to parents their competence in areas such as child development, nutrition, and planning and implementing developmentally appropriate curricula. They must also assure parents that they will maintain daily communication about the child's progress. Additionally, parents and professionals must agree on discipline and guidance procedures, and professionals and social service agencies need to guide parents as to what constitutes good child-rearing and appropriate discipline practices.

Advocacy and Quality Child Care: Child Care Aware

Child Care Aware is a large national public awareness effort to help parents select quality child care. It is sponsored by the Dayton Hudson Foundation, Mervyn's, and Target Stores in cooperation with the National Association of Child Care Resource and Referral Agencies (NACCRRA), Child Care Action Campaign (CCAC), NAEYC, and the National Association for Family Daycare (NAFDC). In addition to the goal of helping parents recognize quality child care, the initiative also is noteworthy for the partnership between national child care organizations and philanthropic organizations.

CHILD CARE ISSUES

As in any profession, child care is not without controversies. The following sections explore some of the issues that confront society as a whole, child care professionals, and the profession.

Who Does Child Care Serve?

Children   One issue concerns whether child care should benefit parents or children. There is a tendency to interpret child care as a service primarily for parents, which critics feel has caused the quality of child care programs to suffer. The needs of children should not be secondary to those of parents. A primary concern for all caregivers should be quality care for children.

Families   Child care is increasingly seen as a comprehensive service for *families*. This means that child care programs are not only providing services for children. They consider the entire family—children, parents, and extended relatives—as the recipients of their services. This expansion of services is in keeping with the trend by early childhood professionals to pay greater attention to *ecology*—the environment in which children are reared and the influences these environments have on children. These environments include family, home life and settings, siblings, community agencies, and so forth. All these influence children's growth and development. It makes sense to consider *family systems* when providing services to and for children.

Which Children?   Ultimately, a system of child care must be available to all parents and their children. Until this is possible, the United States needs priorities. Should child care be aimed at low-income parents who need to work or engage in work training programs? Or, should priority be given to abused and neglected children? Questions such as these are not easy to answer given the limited resources the United States allocates to quality child care, yet these are the questions faced by Head Start and other agencies as they seek to allocate the limited amount of care available. The United States is one of the few countries in the world that does not provide some form of direct child care support for all children. The U.S. system is often characterized as "patchwork" because it is not systematic and for all children. It is, unfortunately, unlikely that this condition will change in the foreseeable future.

The Effects of Child Care on Children

Quite often in discussions about and conceptualization of child care, we have a homogenized view of what it is and what it should be; that is, we think one universal kind of quality child care exists that is good for all children. And, in a sense, this is exactly true; the profession can and does maintain, for example, that low caregiver–child ratios and small group size indicate quality child care. But is the same kind of child care necessarily good for all children?

As we learn more about the effects of child care on children in general, we must pay more attention to its influence on different children. Caregivers must continue to think about how to tailor services based on children's individual differences, cultures, and family situations. (Chap. 6 discusses in detail how to provide culturally sensitive care for infants and toddlers.) This is precisely the kind of response early childhood professionals are taking in relation to children with special needs.

We must also recognize that to a large extent, how parents view child care is a product of their culture, upbringing, and education. Some parents see child care as a service they should use only for the least amount of time, while others may consider child care a major contributor to their children's rearing and are perfectly willing to have their children in a program most of the day.

The particular effects of child care on children is a much debated topic. In an effort to address conflicting research results and the profession's response to research studies, the National Center for Clinical Infant Programs (NCCIP), the National Academy of Science, and the Institute of Medicine issued the following statement:

When parents have choices about the selection and utilization of supplementary care for their infants and toddlers and have access to stable child care arrangements featuring skilled, sensitive and motivated care givers, there is every reason to believe that both children and families can thrive. Such choices do not exist for many families in America today, and inadequate care poses risks to the current well-being and future development of infants, toddlers and their families.[18]

This statement makes it clear that federal, state, and individual programs must work together to develop ways to provide all U.S. children with high-quality child care offered by "skilled, sensitive and motivated" child care workers.

Recent research reveals that child care may have significant educational benefits for children. Evidence indicates that toddlers have a remarkable ability to learn new skills from each other, learning and remembering what they see other children do. Furthermore, what they learn in the play or child care group is retained outside the group setting.[19] This kind of research illustrates the increasing numbers of studies that attest to the positive benefits for children in quality preschool and child care programs.

Interactions Among the Home, the Workplace, and Child Care

Child care professionals are increasingly aware that the family and workplace environments are critical to the final outcome of children's well-being. Accordingly, professionals are seeking ways to help parents in their demanding, stressful roles as modern parents and employees. These interactions take many forms, as we have discussed in this chapter, but the link between the home and the child care program must be strengthened as a means of providing both quality family life situations and quality child care. More and more, early childhood professionals recognize

At an early age, many children are in child care settings. In high-quality programs, children are engaged in active learning, interact with others, and experience a continuity of care that is beneficial to their development. What are some features of high-quality child care?

that child care is a family support system and not a substitute for the home and family. The parenting and developmental information that child care programs provide and the skills they help parents develop are as important as the quality of the care.

Likewise, what happens in the workplace and the benefits parents have or do not have affect their performance as both employees and parents. A corporation with a program of benefits that helps support families (e.g., leave for caring for sick children, flexible work schedules) has more productive workers as it simultaneously contributes to an enhanced quality of life for its parent-employees.

State and National Licensing Standards

Some early childhood advocates maintain that one way, perhaps the only way, to increase the quality of child care is to have a system of national standards that all child care programs would have to meet. These standards would relate particularly to child–staff ratios, group size, and staff training. Advocates of such standards believe they would bring a badly needed uniformity to child care regulations. The closest that the United States comes to having a system of national standards is through programs that are federally funded and supported, such as Head Start (see Chap. 16).

Video Viewpoint

Carol Porter (Feeding Hungry Children)

Carol Porter, ordinary citizen, extraordinary undertaking. Tired of the conditions she found in her city of Houston, Texas, Carol Porter organized an effort to feed hungry children. Carol's organization started out with just her family who spent their life's savings to set up Kid Care. Now Carol and her volunteers load up vans and head for the poorest of Houston's neighborhoods and feed lunch daily to those who cannot feed themselves.

Reflective Discussion Questions: What are some conditions that some children live under which can be characterized as third world conditions? Why is it that we as a nation will allow so many children to be hungry? What effects do hunger and undernourishment have on children's learning? Why is seeing that children are well fed becoming a part of the early childhood curriculum?

Reflective Decision Making: What can you do to help ensure that the children you teach are properly fed? What community agencies can you use to help your children receive the food they need?

As you might expect, not everyone agrees that a system of national standards is necessary or desirable. Some bemoan the federal control that standards would bring. Others think that child care is and should be a state- and locally regulated function. What will likely happen is that as more federal support is given to child care, attempts will be made to provide federal regulations as well.

Improving the Quality of Child Care

One obvious way to improve the quality of child care programs and personnel is through more stringent facility licensing and training requirements. Also, parents can and should be educated to the need for quality child care. Parents often help perpetuate poor child care by accepting whatever kind of care they can find. If they are properly educated and involved in programs, they can help make child care better for everyone.

Quality Child Care for All   Although we talk a great deal about quality child care and identify the criteria that constitute quality, the fact remains that quality child care is not widely available to the majority of families. One challenge is determining how to provide quality programs that will enhance and promote families' optimum development. Not only does the quality of child care differ from program to program, it also varies among states, as we see in the variations in mandated adult–child ratios and the training guidelines required as a condition for employment.

Furthermore, when families and children at risk receive poor-quality child care, this places children in double jeopardy. While all children must have quality care, those who are at risk will benefit the most from quality care because it helps moderate the effects of risk factors. However, as previously stated, children from middle-class families are the most likely to receive poor-quality care. A constant challenge to all involved in the education and development of young children must be to upgrade all child care programs.

In addition, the comprehensive nature of good child care programs must be extended. Many still believe that if a program provides germ-free custodial care, it is a good one. Unfortunately, however, some of these programs have sterile philosophies and activities as well.

FUTURE TRENDS IN CHILD CARE

What does the future hold for child care? Listed here are some continuing trends:

- The number of women who enter the work force, full or part time, will increase. In particular, women with children under three will represent the fastest-growing group of parents seeking child care. For many working parents, staying home with their children is not an option or a desire.

- The number of employer-sponsored or -assisted child care programs will grow because of both employees' demands for child care and the obvious advantages to employers. The greater the benefits to employers, the more likely they will increase their involvement in child care.

- Public schools will participate to an even greater extent in providing child care, especially before- and afterschool care. Also, preschool programs for three- and four-year-olds are a rapidly growing part of public school programs. These programs ease parents' needs for child care. Within the next decade, programs for infants and toddlers may become part of the regular services of some public schools.

- The federal government's role in child care will become less significant, and the influence of individual states will increase. The federal government will not make comprehensive services available to all children because the expense of a national child care program would necessitate reordering federal budget priorities. The trend in federal support to social service programs is to return monies to the states in the form of block grants, which allows states greater free-dom and autonomy in determining how funds are spent. The block grant procedure also reduces direct federal control of state and local programs.

- The current federal effort at welfare reform, which aims to make permanent dependency on government funds a thing of the past, has tremendous implications for child care. Professionals are concerned that the increased demand for child care caused by taking parents off welfare, providing them with job training, and encouraging them to work will result in lower-quality care. Six and one-half million children under the age of thirteen live in homes that receive welfare.[20] These parents are desperate for child care. How to fill this need is a challenge for society and for the early childhood profession. You and other professionals will have to be very proactive in helping ensure that what parents say they want—quality child care—is a reality.

- Policymakers and early childhood professionals will seek to expand alternatives to traditional child care as we know it. More emphasis will be placed on alternatives such as parenting leaves from work for child care, flexible work schedules, and work-at-home options.

- More child care will be tied to parent employment training. That is, child care will be used as one means of helping parents get employment by providing care for their children while they undergo employment training.

- The distinction between child care and preschool will further disappear until the two concepts are a unified whole. We already see evidence of this in many early childhood programs, and in many respects, Head Start is leading the way in this unified approach to early childhood education. Also, the public school entry into the child care arena, on an ever-accelerating scale, helps erode the boundaries between child care and preschool programs.

- Probably one of the most significant changes in child care already underway is that child care will be more family centered and more dedicated to helping parents achieve their goals. As the child care system strives to involve families, it will also be more collaborative with other programs and agencies that can assist in family-centered programs. Both of these new directions will have many implications for new professional roles.

Child care represents, in many respects, the new frontier in early childhood education. Many more families need full-service, comprehensive programs. More opportunities for enhanced collaboration and greater linkages are apparent with each passing year. What is necessary is for early childhood professionals to continue to professionalize the field and create child care programs that can and are willing to provide for families' and children's needs.

ACTIVITIES FOR FURTHER ENRICHMENT

1. Survey parents in your area to determine what services they desire from a child care program. Are most of the parents' child care needs being met? How is what they want in a child care program similar to and different from standards for quality child care discussed in this chapter?

2. Visit child care center programs for infants and toddlers. What makes each program unique? Which program would you feel most comfortable working in? Why? Which program would you feel most comfortable enrolling your own infant or toddler in? Why?

3. Determine the legal requirements for establishing center and home child care programs in your state, city, or locality. What kind of funding is available? What are the similarities and differences of establishing home and center programs? What is your opinion of the guidelines? Why?

4. Invite people from child care programs, welfare departments, and social service agencies to speak to your class about child care. Find out who may attend child care programs. Also, determine what qualifications and training are necessary to become a child care employee.

5. After visiting various child care programs, including center and home programs, discuss in class similarities and differences. Which of the programs provides the best services? What changes or special provisions need to be made to improve the success of these kinds of programs?

6. Gather information on franchised early childhood programs. What are the similarities and differences? In your opinion, what factors are necessary for the success of these kinds of programs?

7. Review the Yellow Pages of the telephone directory for child care programs. Call several for information. What conclusions can you draw from your calls?

8. Develop a checklist to show parents what to look for in a quality child care program.

9. Visit an employer-sponsored child care program and describe it to your classmates. List the pros and cons for parents and for employers of employer-sponsored child care.

10. Conduct a survey to learn the cost of child care services in your area. Arrange your data in a table. What conclusions can you draw?

11. Tell why or why not you would leave your six-week-old infant in center child care, and list the pros and cons for such care. Share this information with your classmates.

READINGS FOR FURTHER ENRICHMENT

Clarke-Stewart, Alison. *Daycare,* rev. ed. (Cambridge, MA: Harvard University Press, 1993).

Discusses daycare as an issue of concern to parents, with an attempt to educate all Americans about the importance of quality daycare. Describes the history, problems, needs, and effects of child care on children.

Gormley, W. T. *Everybody's Children: Child Care as a Public Problem* (Washington, D.C.: Brookings Institution, 1995).

Presents an analysis of the state of American child care. It evaluates child care policies and the national attention given to young children and their families.

Kontos, S. *Quality in Family Child Care and Relative Care* (New York: Teachers College Press, 1995).

This book presents the results of an observational study on quality in family child care and relative care conducted between September 1991 and December 1992.

Rab, V. Y. *Child Care and ADA: A Handbook for Inclusive Programs* (Baltimore, MD: Brooks, 1995).

Explains federal guidelines for program directors and child care personnel for daily practice and procedures when children with disabilities are admitted to child care programs.

Seligson, Michelle, and Michael Allenson. *School-Age Child Care: An Action Manual for the 90s and Beyond,* 2nd ed. (Westport, CT: Greenwood, 1993).

Explores the challenges that child care providers will encounter as the twenty-first century approaches. This action manual guides readers through the processes of designing, implementing, and managing programs for children ages five to twelve.

NOTES

1. U.S. Bureau of the Census, Population Survey, 1995.
2. *Minimum Standards for Child Care Services* (Miami: State of Florida, Department of Health and Rehabilitative Services, 1986), p. 4.
3. John H. Winters, *Minimum Standards for Daycare Centers* (Austin: Texas Department of Human Services, May 1985), p. 2.
4. Children's Defense Fund, *State of America's Children* (Washington, D.C.: Author, 1992), p. 63.
5. The National Center for Missing and Exploited Children, *Just in Case . . . Parental Guidelines in Case You Need a Babysitter* (1994). Internet address http://missingkids.org/babysitter.html
6. Sandra L. Hofferth, April Brayfield, Sharon Deich, and Pamela Holcomb, *National Child Care Survey 1990* (Washington, D.C.: Urban Institute Press, 1991), p. 355.
7. Interview with Gail D. Gonzalez, October 1993.
8. U.S. Department of Education, Office of Policy and Planning. Internet address http://www.ed.gov/offices/ous/eval/
9. Hofferth et al., *National Child Care Survey 1990,* p. 213.
10. Ibid, p. 198.
11. Program fact sheet, Child Nutrition Division of the Food and Nutrition Service, U.S. Department of Agriculture (Alexandria, VA, 1995).
12. Hofferth et al., *National Child Care Survey 1990,* p. 199.
13. Carol Brunson Phillips, *Field Advisor's Guide for the CDA Professional Preparation Program* (Washington, D.C.: Council for Early Childhood Professional Recognition, 1991), p. 2.
14. Hofferth et al., *National Child Care Survey 1990,* p. 215.
15. Ibid.
16. Carrollee Howes, Deborah Phillips, and Marcy Whitebrook, "Thresholds of Quality: Implications for the Social Development of Children in Center-Based Child Care," *Child Development 63* (1992), p. 454.
17. National Association for the Education of Young Children, *Accreditation by the National Academy of Early Childhood Programs* (Washington, D.C.: Author, 1991), p. 2.
18. National Center for Clinical Infant Programs, *Infants, Families, and Child Care: Toward a Research Agenda* (Washington, D.C.: Author, 1988), p. 6.
19. Daniel Goleman, "Baby Sees, Baby Does, and Classmates Follow," *New York Times,* 21 July 1993, p. B7.
20. J. Sexton, "Working and Welfare Parents Compete for Day Care Slots," *New York Times,* 28 March 1997, p. A12.

Parent, Family, and Community Involvement

Cooperation and Collaboration

Focus Questions

1. What changes in contemporary society and families influence children and early childhood programs?

2. Why is parent, family, and community involvement important in early childhood programs?

3. Why is it important to involve all parents and families represented in early childhood programs?

4. How is a personal philosophy of parent involvement important for success as an early childhood professional?

5. How can early childhood professionals and others encourage and support programs for involving families and communities?

6. How can a plan for assessing parent/family needs and involving parents and families in early childhood programs benefit you and others?

ne thing we can say with certainty about the educational landscape today is that parents, families, and communities are as much of the educational process as our teachers and staff. At no time in U.S. educational history has support for family and community been so high. All concerned view the involvement of families and communities as critical for individual student success as well as for the success of the "American dream" of providing all children with an education that will meet their needs and enable them to be productive members of society. In this chapter, we look at some of the reasons why parent, family, and community involvement in education is so important.

CHANGES IN SCHOOLING

Schooling used to consist mostly of teaching children social and basic academic skills. But as society has changed, so has the content of schooling. Early childhood programs have assumed many parental functions and responsibilities. Part of the broadening of the role and function of early education and schooling includes helping parents and families meet their problems *and* involving them in decisions regarding the ways programs function.

Goals 2000

As a result of the readiness goal of the Goals 2000: Educate America Act (formerly America 2000; see Chap. 2), early childhood professionals are now trying to help children come to school ready to learn. These efforts also focus attention on parents as the first teachers of their children. One of the first such programs is the state of Missouri's Parents as Teachers (PAT) program, a home–school partnership designed to give children a good start in life by maximizing their overall development during the first three years of life.

PAT is a model for other programs throughout the country. It provides *all* parents with information about children's development and activities that promote language, intellectual, and social development. Additionally, the partnership goal of Goals 2000 states, "Every school and home will engage in partnerships that will increase parental involvement and participation in promoting the social, emotional, and academic growth of children."[1] As a result, early childhood programs and public schools are mounting an unprecedented effort to truly make parents and community members collaborative partners.

Figure 15.1/*Teachers' Beliefs About the Importance of Parent Involvement*

Question: If you had to pick one of the following as the area that should be given the highest priority or second highest priority in public education policy in the next few years, which would it be?

Base 1,000	Highest Priority (%)	2nd Highest Priority (%)	Net 1st & 2nd Highest Priority(%)
Strengthening parents' roles in their children's education	54	26	80
Improving and expanding early childhood education programs including Head Start for preschool children	26	35	61
Establishing tough standards	12	22	34
Improving safety in and near schools	8	16	24
Not sure	1	1	

Source: Louis Harris and Associates, Inc., *The Metropolitan Life Survey of the American Teacher, 1992, the Second Year: Teachers' Expectations and Ideals* (New York: Author, 1992), p. 23. Used with permission.

Political and Social Forces

Political and social forces have led to our rediscovery of the need to strengthen the relationship between families and schools. The accountability and reform movements of the last decade have convinced families that they should no longer be kept out of their children's schools. Families believe they should demand effective instruction and care from schools and child care centers. Families have become more militant in their demand for quality education, and schools and other agencies have responded by seeking ways to involve families in the quest for quality. Education professionals and families realize that mutual cooperation is in everyone's best interest.

In response to the changing landscape of contemporary society, early childhood professionals are working with parents to develop programs to help them and their children develop to their fullest and lead productive lives. Early childhood professionals are very supportive of such efforts. As Figure 15.1 shows, education professionals believe that the highest priority of public education is to strengthen parents' roles in their children's education. For their part, 56 percent of the public believes that a lack of parental involvement with children's education is a serious problem in education today; 26 percent believe it is a somewhat serious problem.[2]

Indeed, parents and the public at large view parent involvement as an important factor in children's success in school. Ninety-five percent of parents with children in school and 97 percent of people with no children in school think it is important to encourage parents to take a more active part in educating their children.[3]

CHANGING FAMILIES

The family of today is not the family of yesterday. Table 15.1 shows some of the ways families have changed over the years. Several changes stand out. One is that more young mothers are entering the work force than ever before. This means that at an early age, often beginning at six weeks, children are spending eight hours a day or more in the care of others. Thus, working parents are both turning their young children over to others for care and are also spending less time with their children. Parents need more help with rearing their children at earlier ages. As a result, opportunities have blossomed for

Table 15.1/*How Families Have Changed*

	1990	1994
Married couples	52,317,000	53,171,000
Married couples with children	24,537,000	24,515,000
Male householder (No spouse) with children	1,153,000	2,913,000
Female householder (No spouse) with children	6,599,000	12,406,000
Marriages	2,362,000	2,334,000
Divorces	1,215,000	1,187,000
Average size per household	3.16	3.20
Average size per family	2.63	2.67

Source: T. Snyder, (ed.), *U.S. Digest of Education Statistics* (Washington, D.C.: U.S. Department of Education, U.S. Government Printing Office, 1994).

Families continue to change and, as they do, early childhood professionals must adapt and adopt new ways of involving family members and providing for their needs. For example, growing numbers of fathers have sole responsibility for rearing their children. What can professionals do to ensure the involvement of single fathers in their programs?

child-serving agencies, such as child care centers and preschools, to assist and support parents in their childrearing efforts.

EDUCATION AS A FAMILY AFFAIR

Education starts in the home, and what happens there profoundly affects the trajectory of development and learning. According to the U.S. Department of Education (DOE), education is a family affair because the greater the family's involvement in children's learning the more likely it is that students will receive a high-quality education. The DOE identifies three main reasons that families play a critical role in education:[4]

- Three factors over which families have control—student absenteeism, variety of reading material in the home, and amount of television watching—explain differences in students' mathematics achievement. School attendance rates, exposure to print in the home, and restricted television time all correlate with higher achievement as measured by the National Assessment of Educational Progress.

- While math and science achievement is based on learning activities in the home, literacy is even more dependent on home life. The single most important activity for building the knowledge required for eventual success is reading aloud to children.

- What the family does with and for its children is more important to student success than family income or education. This is true whether the family is rich or poor, whether the parents finished high school or not, or whether the child is in preschool or in the upper grades.

The central role families play in children's education is a reality that teachers and schools must address as they make plans for how to reform schools and increase student achievement. Partnering with parents is a process whose time has come, and the benefits far outweigh any inconveniences or barriers that may stand in the way of bringing schools and parents together.

Family-Centered Teaching

Family-centered teaching and learning focuses on meeting the needs of students through the family unit, whatever that unit may be. Education professionals recognize that to most effectively meet the needs of students, they must also meet the needs of family members and the family unit. Family-centered teaching and learning makes sense for a number of reasons. First, the family unit has the major responsibility for meeting children's needs. Children's development begins in the family system, and this system is a powerful determiner of developmental processes, both for better and worse. Therefore, helping parents and other family members meet their children's needs in appropriate ways means that everyone stands to benefit. Helping individuals in the family unit become better parents and family members benefits children and consequently promotes their success in school.

Second, it is frequently the case that to help children effectively, family issues and problems must be addressed first. For instance, helping parents gain access to adequate and affordable health care increases the chances that the whole family, including children, will be healthy.

Third, teachers can do many things concurrently with children and their families that will benefit both. Literacy is a good example. Adopting a family approach to literacy means that helping parents learn to read, build literacy, and read aloud to their children helps ensure children's literacy development as well. Figure 15.2 summarizes the concept of family-centered teaching.

An example of family-centered teaching is Even Start (see Chap. 16), a federally funded family literacy program that combines adult literacy and parenting training with early childhood education to break cycles of illiteracy that are often passed on from one generation to another. Even Start is funded under Title 1 of the Improving America's Schools Education Act and is operated through the public school system. In particular, Even Start helps parents become full partners in the education of their children, assists children in reaching their full potential, and provides literacy training for parents. Even Start projects are designed to work cooperatively with existing community resources to provide a full range of services and to integrate early childhood education and adult education.

Family-Centered Curriculum and Instruction

Family-centered curriculum and instruction exists at three levels. First, it consists of programs and materials designed to help parents be better parents and teachers of their children. To support parents in these roles, schools and teachers provide materials on parenting, conduct parenting classes, and furnish ideas about teaching their children reading and math skills through daily living activities. At a second level, instruction focuses on helping parents with everyday problems and issues of family living. For example,

Figure 15.2/*Family-Centered Teaching*

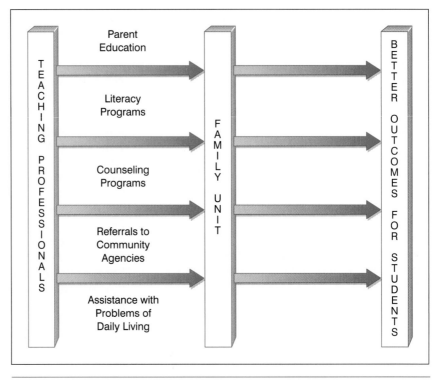

Source: G. S. Morrison, *Teaching in America* (Needham Heights, MA: Allyn & Bacon, 1997), p. 208. Copyright © 1997 by Allyn & Bacon. Reprinted by permission.

classes and information on tenant rights, nutritional meals, the importance of immunizations, and access to health services would be in keeping with the ideas of addressing families' daily living needs. At a third level, family-centered curriculum and instruction attempts to integrate students' classroom learning with learning in the home. For example, providing parents with books to read to their children at home would support efforts to link in-school learning with learning in the home.

Two-Generation and Intergenerational Programs

Two-generation programs involve parents and their children and are designed to help both generations and at the same time to strengthen the family unit. *Intergenerational*

programs involve grandparents and others, as well. Two-generation delivery of services can and should begin before children's birth because many problems relating to child health can be prevented by good prenatal care. The preventive approach to maternal and prenatal health is reflected in the growing numbers of schools that have on-site health clinics. Services often include both health and education in which students and parents receive medical care and information that will support their efforts to lead healthy lives.

For example, Avance is a center-based parent support and education program serving low-income Hispanic families at three centers in San Antonio, Houston, and the Rio Grande Valley in Texas. Parents and their children up to three years of age are enrolled through an aggressive door-to-door recruitment of families into the program. The heart of Avance is a nine-month parent education program in which parents are taught how they can be their children's first teachers and how to facilitate their children's development. To support parents in this effort, Avance provides transportation to the center, home visits, literacy development, employment training, family planning information, education in the use of community resources, and referrals and advocacy for other social service needs.

Mercedes Perez de Colon, Director of the National Family Resource Center for Avance, states the following:

Our main goal has always been to help parents prepare their children for school success by focusing on the first three years of a child's life. We help parents understand how children grow and learn and what they can do to maximize opportunities for their children. We provide a comprehensive array of services and opportunities to enable parents to become their children's first teachers. We try to help parents use resources available in the community and understand that helping their children to be prepared for school does not require money, it requires time and effort on the part of parents. We show parents how to help their children learn through language and through their five senses and through play.

We also stress healthy lifestyles for parents and children, so we focus on immunizations, nutrition, safety, and understanding the importance of healthy and preventive lifestyles. We have been very successful. Parents who attend our program increase their understanding of child growth and development, have a positive change in attitudes toward child rearing, and have better home environments for their children. We know that their children are meeting with success in school.

Intergenerational programs are those that promote cooperation, interaction, and exchange between two or more generations. Intergenerational programming is becoming a popular way of bringing younger and older generations together. There are a number of reasons for efforts to join generations. First, Americans tend to

become segregated by age and life stages. The young are in child care and schools, adults are in workplaces, and the elderly are in age-segregated housing and nursing homes. Second, with cutbacks in federal support for health and social programs, the young and the old especially are in competition for funds and services. One way to reduce this competition and to use existing funds effectively is to provide intergenerational programs for the mutual benefit of all. Most often, intergenerational programming focuses on young people below the age of twenty-five and adults over the age of sixty.[5]

Two areas of great need in our society are young children and the elderly. Many programs are looking for ways that they can effectively integrate the care of both of these groups into their programs. What are some advantages of providing for the education and care of young children and the elderly in the same program?

Intergenerational programming also includes programs in which young people provide services to older persons, in which older persons provide services to youth, and in which two generations work cooperatively on a project.

WHO IS A PARENT AND WHAT IS A FAMILY?

A *parent* is anyone who provides children with basic care, direction, support, protection, and guidance. Accordingly, a parent can be single, married, heterosexual, gay, lesbian, a cousin, aunt, uncle, grandparent, a court-appointed guardian, a brother, a sister, an institution employee, a surrogate, a foster parent, or a group such as a commune.

A *household* is defined as the person or persons who comprise a family unit. A *family* is defined as two or more persons living together who are related by birth, marriage, or adoption. The term *householder* has replaced "head of family." Figure 15.3 shows the current composition of families in the United States.

Implications of Family Patterns for Early Childhood Professionals

Given the changes in families today, there are a number of things you as an early childhood professional can do to help parents, including the following:

Figure 15.3/*Kinds of Families*

- Nuclear family—married couple and child(ren)
- Single-parent family—headed by a mother or father
- Stepfamily—a family in which the children belong to one spouse or the other
- Blended family—a family made up of children of each spouse and of both spouses together.
- Foster family—people who provide care and protection for children in their homes
- Extended family—a family that includes relatives
- Gay-lesbian family with child(ren)
- Dual-wage-earning family
- Single-wage-earning family
- Second-time-around family—having one or more children, natural or adopted, after the first children are grown
- Grandparent family—grandparents raising children
- Couples without children
- Biological family—a family in which all children are biological children of both parents
- Adoptive family—a family in which all children are adoptive children of both parents
- Biological mother-stepfather family—a family in which all children are biological children of the mother and stepchildren of the father
- Biological father-stepmother family—a family in which all children are biological children of the father and stepchildren of the mother
- Joint biological-adoptive family—a family in which at least one child is a biological child of both parents and at least one child is an adoptive child of both parents
- Joint biological step-adoptive family—a family in which at least one child is a biological child of one parent and a stepchild of the other parent and at least one child is an adopted child of both parents

- *Provide support services.* Support can extend from being a "listening ear" to organizing support groups and seminars on single parenting. Professionals can help families link up with other agencies and groups, such as Big Brothers and Big Sisters and Families without Partners. Through newsletters and fliers, professionals can offer families specific advice on how to help children become independent and how to meet the demands of living in single-parent families, stepfamilies, and other family configurations.

- *Provide child care.* As more families need child care, early childhood personnel are logical advocates for establishing care where none exists, extending existing services, and helping to arrange cooperative babysitting services.

- *Avoid criticism.* Professionals should be careful not to criticize families for the jobs they are doing. They may not have extra time to spend with their children or know how to discipline them. Regardless of their circumstances, families need help, not criticism.

- *Avoid being judgmental.* Similarly, professionals should examine and clarify their attitudes and values toward family patterns and remember that there is no "right" family pattern from which all children should come.

- *Arrange educational experiences.* Professionals need to address the issue of changing family patterns in the educational experiences they arrange. They must offer experiences children might not otherwise have because of their family organization. For example, outdoor activities such as fishing trips and sports events can be interesting and enriching learning experiences for children who may not have such opportunities.

- *Adjust programs.* Professionals need to adjust classroom or center activities to account for how particular children cope with their home situations. Children's needs for different kinds of activities depend on their experiences at home. For example, opportunities abound for role playing, and such activities help bring into the open situations that children need to talk about. Use program opportunities to discuss families and the roles they play. Make it a point in the classroom to model, encourage, and teach effective interpersonal skills.

- *Be sensitive.* There are specific ways to sensitively approach today's changing family patterns. For example, avoid having children make presents for both parents when it is inappropriate to do so and awarding prizes for bringing both parents to meetings. Replace such terms as *broken home* with *single-parent family*. Be sensitive to the demands of school in relation to children's home lives. For instance, when a professional sent a field-trip permission form home with children and told them to have their mothers or fathers sign it, one child said, "I don't have a father. If my mother can't sign it, can the man who sleeps with her sign it?" Seek guidance and clarification from families about how they would like specific situations handled; for example, ask whether they want you to send notices of school events to both parents.

- *Seek training.* Request in-service training to help you work with families. In-service programs can provide information about referral agencies, guidance techniques, ways to help families deal with their problems, and child abuse identification and prevention. Professionals need to be alert to the signs of all kinds of child abuse, including mental, physical, and sexual abuse.

- *Increase parent contacts.* Finally, professionals should encourage greater and different kinds of parent involvement through visiting homes; talking to families about children's needs; providing information and opportunities to parents, grandparents, and other family members; gathering information from families (such as through interest inventories); and keeping in touch with parents. Make parent contacts positive.

Parent/family involvement is a process of helping families use their abilities to benefit themselves, their children, and the early childhood program. Families, children, and the program are all part of the process; consequently, all three parties should benefit from a well-planned program of family involvement. Nonetheless, the focus in parent/child/family interactions is the family, and you must work with and through families if you want to be successful.

GUIDELINES FOR INVOLVING PARENTS AND FAMILIES

As an early childhood professional, you can use the following tips to develop programs of parent and family involvement.

- Get to know your children's parents and families. One good way to do this is through home visits. This approach works better in early childhood programs where the number of students is limited. However, teachers who have large numbers of students find that visiting a few homes based on special circumstances can be helpful and informative.

- Ask parents what goals they have for their children. Use these goals to help you in your planning. Encourage parents to have realistically high expectations for their children.

- Build relationships with parents so you may communicate better with them.

- Learn how to best communicate with parents based on their cultural communications preferences. Take into account cultural features that can inhibit collaboration.

- Learn how families rear children and organize themselves. Political, social, and moral values of families all have implications for parent participation and how to teach children.

- Support parents in their roles as first teachers of their children. Support can include information, materials, and help with parenting problems.

- Provide frequent, open communication and feedback on student progress, including good news.

- Train parents as mentors, classroom aides, tutors, and homework helpers. For example, communicate guidelines for helping students study for tests.

- Support fathers in their roles as parents. By supporting and encouraging fathers, you support the whole family.

- On the basis of parents' needs, identify resources they can use to help solve family and personal problems.

- Work with and through families. Ask parents to help you in working with and involving parents. Parents respond positively to parents, so it makes sense to have parents helping families.

Four Approaches to Parent and Family Involvement

In looking at and designing programs of parent and family involvement, early childhood professionals may proceed in several different ways.

Task Approach   The most common and traditional way to approach parent and family involvement is through a task orientation. This method seeks to involve parents in order to get assistance completing specific tasks that support the school or classroom program. In this orientation, faculty, staff, and administration work to involve parents and other family members as tutors, aides, attendance monitors, fundraisers, field trip monitors, and clerical helpers. This is the type of parent and family involvement many professionals are comfortable with and the sort that usually comes to mind when planning for some kind of parent or family involvement. However, while this type of parent involvement has many benefits, by itself it does not represent a sufficient program of family involvement.

Parents can be involved in early childhood programs in many ways. Here a parent accompanies children on an outdoor field trip. It is important for early childhood professionals to determine how best to involve parents and other family members. How could you go about determining how parents in your program could be involved?

Process Approach   In this approach, families are encouraged to participate in certain activities that are important to the educational process, such as curriculum planning, textbook review and selection, membership on task forces and committees, professional review and selection, and helping to set behavior standards. This approach is becoming popular because professionals realize the importance of sharing these processes and decisions with parents, family members, and members of the community. Parents and others need preparation and support for this kind of involvement. Some professionals may think parents lack the necessary skills to help in certain areas, but with some assistance and an opportunity to participate, many family members are extremely effective.

Developmental Approach   This orientation seeks to help parents and families develop skills that benefit themselves, children, schools, professionals, and families and, at the same time, enhance family growth and development. This humanistic orientation is exemplified in such programs as cooperative preschools, community schools, and Head Start.

Comprehensive Approach   A comprehensive approach to parent and family involvement includes elements of all the preceding approaches, especially the developmental approach (see Figure 15.4). It goes beyond the other three approaches, however, in that it makes the family the *center* or *focus* of activities. This method does not seek involvement from parent or family members for the sake of involvement or the benefit of a particular agency. Rather, it works with, in, and through the family system to empower, assist, and strengthen the family. As a result, all family members are helped, including children.

The comprehensive approach seeks to involve parents, families, and community persons in school processes and activities, including decisions about the school. It also provides parents choices about which school or program their children will attend. Over the past decade, *school choice,* permitting parents to select the school their children will attend, has gained popularity. Some states and many school districts allow parents to enroll their children in the schools of their choice. While most parents of preschool children have had this choice based on the fact that they pay for their children's education, many public school parents have not. Now many do, which has helped change the public's attitude toward school choice.

A comprehensive program also provides involvement through family development and

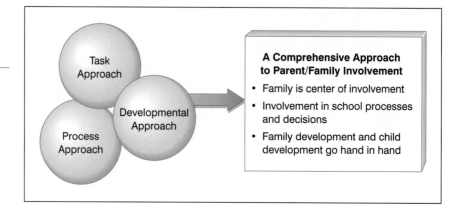

Figure 15.4/
A Comprehensive Approach to Family Involvement

Task Approach

Developmental Approach

Process Approach

A Comprehensive Approach to Parent/Family Involvement

- Family is center of involvement
- Involvement in school processes and decisions
- Family development and child development go hand in hand

support programs. Many programs are not only encouraging involvement in family-centered programs, they are providing them. These family support programs include parenting programs, home visitations, substance abuse education and treatment programs, discussion and support groups, job training and referral programs, basic skills training programs, and linking parents to existing community resource programs.

Activities for Involving Families

Unlimited possibilities exist for family involvement, but a coordinated effort is required to build an effective, meaningful program that can bring about a change in education and benefit all concerned: families, children, professionals, and communities. Families can make a significant difference in their children's education, and with early childhood professionals' assistance, they will be able to join teachers and schools in a productive partnership. The following are examples of activities that allow for significant family involvement.

Schoolwide Activities

- *Workshops*—to introduce families to the school's policies, procedures, and programs. Most families want to know what is going on in the school and would do a better job of parenting and educating if they knew how.

- *Family nights; cultural dinners, carnivals, and potluck dinners*—to bring families and the community to the school in nonthreatening, social ways.

- *Adult education classes*—to provide the community with opportunities to learn about a range of subjects.

- *Training programs*—to give parents, family members, and others skills as class-

room aides, club and activity sponsors, curriculum planners, and policy decision makers. *When parents, family members, and community persons are viewed as experts, then empowerment results.*

- *Support services such as car pools and babysitting*—to make attendance and involvement possible.

- *Fairs and bazaars*—to involve families in fundraising.

- *Performances and plays*—especially ones in which children have a part tend to bring families to school; however, the purpose of children's performances should not be solely to get families involved.

Communication Activities

- *Telephone hotlines.* Hotlines staffed by families can help allay fears and provide information relating to child abuse, communicable diseases, and special events. Telephone networks are also used to help children and parents with homework and to monitor latchkey children (see Chap. 14).

- *Newsletters.* Newsletters planned with parents' help are an excellent way to keep families informed about program events, activities, and curriculum information. Newsletters in parents' native languages help keep language-minority families informed.

- *Home learning materials and activities.* A monthly calendar of activities is one good way to keep families involved in their children's learning.

Educational Activities

- *Participation in classroom and center activities.* While not all families can be directly involved in classroom activities, encourage those who can. Those who are involved must have guidance, direction, and training. Involving parents and others as paid aides is an excellent way also to provide employment and training. Many programs, such as Head Start, actively support such a policy.

- *Involvement of families in writing individualized education programs (IEPs)* for special needs children. Involvement in writing an IEP is not only a legal requirement but also an excellent learning experience (see Chap. 13).

Service Activities

- *Resource libraries and materials centers.* Families benefit from books and other articles relating to parenting. Some programs furnish resource areas with comfortable chairs to encourage families to use these materials.

- *Child care.* Families may not be able to attend programs and become involved if they do not have child care for their children. Child care makes their participation possible and more enjoyable (see Chap. 14).

- *Respite care.* Some early childhood programs provide respite care for parents and other family members, which enables them to have periodic relief from the responsibilities of parenting a chronically ill child or a child with disabilities.

- *Service exchanges.* Service exchanges operated by early childhood programs and other agencies help families in their needs for services. For example, one parent provided child care in her home in exchange for having her washing machine repaired. The possibilities for such exchanges are endless.

- *Parent support groups.* Parents need support in their roles. Support groups can provide parenting information, community agency information, and speakers.

- *Welcoming committees.* A good way to involve families in any program is to have other families contact them when their children first join a program.

Decision Activities

- *Hiring and policy making.* Parents and community members can and should serve on committees that set policy and hire staff.

- *Curriculum development and review.* Parents' involvement in curriculum planning helps them learn about and understand what constitutes a quality program and what is involved in a developmentally appropriate curriculum. When families know about the curriculum, they are more supportive of it.

Conducting Parent–Professional Conferences

Significant parent involvement can occur through well-planned and -conducted parent–early childhood professional conferences (informally referred to as *parent–teacher conferences*). Such conferences are often the first contact many families have with school. Conferences are critical both from a public relations point of view and as a vehicle for helping families and professionals accomplish their goals. The following guidelines will help you as an early childhood professional prepare for and conduct successful conferences:

- *Plan ahead.* Be sure of the reason for the conference. What are your objectives? What do you want to accomplish? List the points you want to cover and think about what you are going to say.

- *Get to know the parents.* This is not wasted time; the more effectively you establish rapport with a parent, the more you will accomplish in the long run.

- *Avoid an authoritative atmosphere.* Do not sit behind your desk while the parent sits in a child's chair. Treat parents and others like the adults they are.

- *Communicate at the parent's level.* Do not condescend or patronize. Instead, use words, phrases, and explanations the parent understands and is familiar with. Do not use jargon or complicated explanations, and speak in your natural style.

- *Accentuate the positive.* Make every effort to show and tell the parent what the child is doing well. When you deal with problems, put them in the proper perspective: what the child is able to do, what the goals and purposes of the learning program are, what specific skill or concept you are trying to get the child to learn, and what problems the child is having in achieving. Most important, explain what you plan to do to help the child achieve and what specific role the parent can have in meeting the achievement goals.

- *Give families a chance to talk.* You will not learn much about them if you do all the talking, nor are you likely to achieve your goals. Professionals are often accustomed to dominating a conversation, and many parents will not be as verbal as you, so you will have to encourage families to talk.

- *Learn to listen.* An active listener holds eye contact, uses body language such as head nodding and hand gestures, does not interrupt, avoids arguing, paraphrases as a way of clarifying ideas, and keeps the conversation on track.

- *Follow up.* Ask the parent for a definite time for the next conference as you are concluding the current one. Another conference is the best method of solidifying gains and extending support, but other acceptable means of follow-up are telephone calls, written reports, notes sent with children, or brief visits to the home. While these types of contacts may appear casual, they should be planned for and conducted as seriously as any regular parent–professional conference. No matter which approach you choose, advantages of a parent–professional conference follow-up are these:

  Families see that you genuinely care about their children.
  Everyone can clarify problems, issues, advice, and directions.
  Parents, family members, and children are encouraged to continue to do their best.
  It offers further opportunities to extend classroom learning to the home.
  You can extend programs initiated for helping families and formulate new plans.

- *Develop an action plan.* Never leave the parent with a sense of frustration, not knowing what you are doing or what they are to do. Every communication with families should end on a positive note, so that everyone knows what can be done and how to do it.

Children and Conferences A question frequently asked is, "Should children be present at parent–teacher conferences?" The answer is, "Yes, of course." The only caveat to the yes response is, "If it is appropriate for them to be present," and in most instances it is appropriate, and offers a number of benefits:

PROGRAM IN ACTION

INVOLVING PARENTS THROUGH TECHNOLOGY—THE TRANSPARENT SCHOOL MODEL

The Transparent School Model is an original plan for using electronic telecommunications technology to expand and improve parent involvement. The model provides voice-based information exchange between teachers and parents.

How It Works

The system consists of two primary functions. First, parents can call and listen to a teacher's daily message. At the end of each school day, teachers write a brief script describing (1) what students learned and how they learned it; (2) specific home learning assignments; and (3) parent education suggestions with other school information. Each teacher records their message in a voice mailbox from any touch-tone phone, and parents can call to hear the message at any time from any phone. Other message boxes at the school may include the daily lunch menu, principal's message, information from the parent/teacher group, and so on. The voice mailbox function allows every parent to receive the information needed to support the student's learning at home *every day,* with only a one- to two-minute phone call.

Second, the system can place automated calls to parents with information they need, including routine reminders ("The museum field trip is on Tuesday"), sending good news home, and emergency notification. Strategic outcalling is also used to encourage more parents to call for teacher messages, and to make specific contact with certain parents. Schools often use outcalling for attendance notification, community outreach, and dozens of other applications. The messages can be delivered in any language.

The best way for a school to implement the Transparent School Model is to acquire a special voice-messaging computer that is designed to manage all the parent involvement and other school communications. The equipment supplier also should provide help with planning, installation, and staff development.

Preschool Readiness

The technology can also be used for preschool readiness. The outcall function can call parents weekly with parenting suggestions from birth until

---

- Children have much to contribute. They can talk about their progress and behavior, offer suggestions for improvement and enrichment, and discuss their interests.

- The *locus of control* is centered in the child. Children learn they have a voice and opinions and that others think this is important and are listening.

- Children's self-esteem is enhanced because they are viewed as an important part of the conference and because a major purpose of the conference is to help them and their families.

- Children become more involved in their classroom and their education. "Students take pride not only in their own accomplishments and their ability to share them, but also in the opportunity to help each other prepare for and succeed at their conferences. A team spirit—a sense of community—can emerge and this can benefit the motivation and achievement of all."[6]

- Children learn that education is a cooperative process between home and school.

the child enters the child care, preschool or kindergarten setting.

Effects

More than 1,000 schools (preschool through high school) use the Transparent School Model. In most schools, the results have been astonishing. At least half of the parents call *every day* to hear teacher messages. *Parent involvement rates have risen 500 to 800 percent.* Students learning performance goes up and success improves. In two matched-demographic trials, significant improvement in achievement test scores were found.

Parent attitudes become much more positive as they have more information about the school program. There has also been independent confirmation of dramatic improvement in student grade point averages at the secondary level after schools began using the model. The easy and open exchange of information between school and home allows for new levels of partnership and cooperation with an influence on achievement, student suc-cess, attendance, parent attitudes, and community interest.

Implementation

Quality implementation of the Transparent School Model depends on the following:

- Cooperative planning from the beginning
- Baseline and ongoing evaluation
- Full school commitment
- Effective parent orientation
- Teacher staff development
- High-quality messages

It rarely takes a teacher more than a few extra minutes per day to meet all the expectations of the model, and these minutes are multiplied many times by the technology. Teachers say it is extremely easy to use, and parents wonder how they ever got along without it. Communities find that the greatly expanded communication opens new avenues for partnerships.

Contributed by Jerold P. Bauch, director, the Betty Phillips Center for Parenthood Education, Peabody College, Nashville, TN.

Telephone Contacts When it is impossible to arrange a face-to-face conference as a follow-up, a telephone call is an efficient way to contact families (although, unfortunately, not all families have a telephone). The same guidelines apply as for face-to-face conferences. In addition, remember the following tips:

- Since you cannot see someone on a telephone, it takes a little longer to build rapport and trust. The time you spend overcoming families' initial fears and apprehensions will pay dividends later.

- Constantly clarify what you are talking about and what you and the families have agreed to do, using such phrases as, "What I heard you say then . . ." or, "So far, we have agreed that . . ."

- Do not act hurried. There is a limit to the amount of time you can spend on the phone, but you may be one of the few people who cares about the parent and the child. Your telephone contact may be the major part of the families' support system.

Involving Single-Parent Families

Sometimes, family involvement activities are conducted without much regard for single-parent families. Professionals sometimes think of single-parent families as problems to deal with rather than as people to work with. Involving single-parent families need not present a problem if you remember some basic points.

First, many adults in one-parent families are employed during school hours and may not be available for conferences or other activities during that time. Professionals must be willing to accommodate family schedules by arranging conferences at other times, perhaps early morning (breakfast), midmorning, noon (lunch), early afternoon, late afternoon, or early evening. Some employers, sensitive to these needs, give release time to participate in school functions, but others do not. Professionals and principals need to think seriously about going to families rather than having families always come to them. Some schools have set up parent conferences to accommodate families' work schedules, while some professionals find that home visits work best.

Second, you need to remember that such families have a limited amount of time to spend on involvement with their children's school and their children at home. When you confer with single-parent families, make sure that (1) the meeting starts on time, (2) you have a list of items (skills, behaviors, achievements) to discuss, (3) you have sample materials available to illustrate all points, (4) you make specific suggestions relative to one-parent environments, and (5) the meeting ends on time. One-parent families are more likely to need child care assistance to attend meetings, so child care should be planned for every parent meeting or activity.

Third, illustrate for single-parent families how they can make their time with their children more meaningful. If a child has trouble following directions, show families how to use home situations to help in this area. Children can learn to follow directions while helping families run errands, get a meal, or help with housework.

Fourth, get to know families' lifestyles and living conditions. An early childhood professional can easily say that every child should have a quiet place to study, but this may be an impossible demand for some households. You need to visit some of the homes in your community before you set meeting times, decide what family involvement activities to implement, or what you will ask of families during the year. All professionals, particularly early childhood professionals, need to keep in mind the condition of the home environment when they request that children bring certain items to school or carry out certain tasks at home. When asking for parents' help, you must be sensitive to parents' talents and time constraints.

Fifth, help develop support groups for one-parent families within the school, such as discussion groups and classes on parenting for singles. You must include the needs and abilities of one-parent families in your family involvement activities and programs. After all, single-parent families may be the majority of families represented in the program.

Involving Language-Minority Parents and Families

The developmental concept of family involvement is particularly important when working with language-minority families. *Language-minority* parents are individuals whose English proficiency is minimal and who lack a comprehensive knowledge of the norms and social systems in the United States. Language-minority families often face language and cultural barriers that greatly

Many early childhood professionals conduct home visits as a means of assessing the home environment for learning and to help parents learn how to support their children's learning at home. Additionally, parents can provide professionals with much useful information about children's learning, experiences, and growth and development. Do you plan to make home visits a part of your early childhood program? Why? Why not?

hamper their ability to become actively involved, although many have a great desire and willingness to participate in their children's education.

Because the culture of language-minority families often differs from the majority in a community, those who seek a truly collaborative community, home, and school involvement must take into account the cultural features that can inhibit collaboration. Traditional styles of childrearing and family organization, attitudes toward schooling, organizations around which families center their lives, life goals and values, political influences, and methods of communication within the cultural group all have implications for parent participation.

Language-minority families often lack information about the U.S. educational system, including basic school philosophy, practice, and structure, which can result in misconceptions, fear, and a general reluctance to respond to invitations for involvement. Furthermore, this educational system may be quite different from what these families are used to. They may have been taught to avoid active involvement in the educational process, with the result that they prefer to leave all decisions concerning their children's education to professionals and administrators.

The U.S. ideal of a community-controlled and -supported educational system must be explained to families from cultures in which this concept is not as highly valued. Traditional roles of children, professionals, and administrators also have to be explained. Many families, especially language-minority families, are quite willing to relinquish to professionals any rights and responsibilities they have for their children's education, and need to be taught to assume their roles and obligations toward schooling.

Culturally Sensitive Family Involvement   The following suggestions are provided by Janet González-Mena for working with families:[7]

- Know what each parent in your program wants for his or her child. Find out families' goals. What are their caregiving practices? What concerns do they have about their child? Encourage them to talk about all of this. Encourage them to ask questions. Encourage the conflicts to surface—to come out in the open.

- Become clear about your own values and goals. Know what you believe in. Have a bottom line, but leave space above it to be flexible. When you are clear, you are less likely to present a defensive stance in the face of conflict. When we are ambiguous, we come on the strongest.

- Become sensitive to your own discomfort. Tune in on those times when something bothers you instead of just ignoring it and hoping it will go away. Work to identify what specific behaviors of others make you uncomfortable. Try to discover exactly what in yourself creates this discomfort. A conflict may be brewing.

- Build relationships. When you do this, you enhance your chances for conflict management or resolution. Be patient. Building relationships takes time, but it enhances communications and understandings. You'll communicate better if you have a relationship, and you'll have a relationship if you learn to communicate.

- Become effective cross-cultural communicators. It is possible to learn these communication skills. Learn about communication styles that are different from your own. Teach your own communication styles. What you think a person means may not be what he or she *really* means. Do not make assumptions. Listen carefully. Ask for clarification. Find ways to test for understanding.

- Learn how to create dialogue—how to open communication instead of shutting it down. Often, if you accept and acknowledge the other person's feelings, you encourage him or her to open up. Learn ways to let others know that you are aware of and sensitive to their feelings.

- Use a *problem-solving* rather than a *power* approach to conflicts. Be flexible—negotiate when possible. Look at your willingness to share power. Is it a control issue you are dealing with?

- Commit yourself to education—both your own and that of the families. Sometimes lack of information or understanding of each other's perspective is what keeps the conflict going.

Involving Teenage Parents

At one time, most teenage parents were married, but today the majority are not. Also, most teenage families elect to keep their children rather than put them up for adoption and are rearing them within single-parent families. Teenage families frequently live in extended families, and the child's grandmother often serves as the primary caregiver. Regardless of their living arrangements, teenage families have the following needs:

- *Support in their role as families.* Support can include information about childrearing practices and child development. Regardless of the nature and quality of the information given to teenage families, they frequently need help in implementing the information in their interactions with their children.

- *Support in their continuing development as adolescents and young adults.* Remember that younger teenage parents are really children themselves. They need assistance in meeting their own developmental needs as well as those of their children.

- *Help with completing their own education.* Some early childhood programs provide parenting courses as well as classes designed to help teenage-parent dropouts complete requirements for a high school diploma. Remember that a critical influence on children's development is the mother's education level.

As early childhood programs enroll more children of teenage families, they must be attentive to creatively and sensitively involving these families as a means of supporting the development of families and children.

Involving Fathers

More fathers are involved in parenting responsibilities than ever before. Over one-fifth of preschool children are cared for by their fathers while their mothers work outside the home.[8] The implication is clear: early childhood professionals must make special efforts to involve all fathers in their programs.

More professionals recognize that fathering and mothering are complementary processes. Definitions of nurturing are changing to include the legitimate and positive involvement of fathers in children's lives. Many fathers are competent caregivers, directly supervising children, helping set the tone for family life, providing stability to a relationship, supporting the mother's parenting role and her career goals, and personifying a masculine role model for the children. More fathers, as they discover or rediscover these parenting roles, turn to professionals for support and advice.

There are many styles of fathering. Some fathers are at home while their wives work; some have custody of their children; some are single; some dominate home life and control everything; some are passive and exert little influence in the home; some are frequently absent because their work requires travel; some take little interest in their homes and families; some are surrogates. Regardless of the roles fathers play in their children's lives, as an early childhood professional, you must make special efforts to involve them, using the methods discussed in this chapter.

Involving Other Caregivers

Children of two-career families and single families often are cared for by nannies, au pairs, baby-sitters, or housekeepers. Whatever their title, these adults usually play significant roles in children's lives. Many early childhood programs and schools are reaching out to involve them in activities such as professional conferences, help with field trips, and supervision of homework. This involvement should occur with families' blessing and approval for a cooperative working relationship.

COMMUNITY INVOLVEMENT AND MORE

A comprehensive program of family involvement has, in addition to families, professionals, and schools, a fourth important component: the community. More early childhood professionals realize that neither they alone nor the limited resources of their programs are sufficient to meet the needs of many children and families. Consequently, early education professionals are seeking ways to link families to community services and resources. For example, if a child needs clothing, a professional who is aware of community resources might contact the local Salvation Army for assistance.

Using the Community to Teach

The community offers a vital and rich array of resources for helping you teach better and for helping you meet the needs of parents and their children. Schools and teachers cannot address the many issues facing children and youth without the partnership and collaboration of powerful sectors of society, including community agencies, businesses, and industry. Following are suggested actions you can take to learn to use your community in your teaching:

- *Know your students and their needs.* By knowing your students through observa-

PROGRAM IN ACTION

THE CHILDREN'S CENTER AT THE ST. PAUL

The St. Paul Companies, a worldwide insurance organization based in downtown St. Paul, Minnesota, operates a $1.6 million on-site child care center for its employees. Called The Children's Center at The St. Paul, the facility is part of the company's new $70 million addition to its headquarters complex.

Already a leader in family-oriented benefits design, The St. Paul's internal child care research showed that its headquarters employees have some thousand children aged ten and younger; of that group, 75 percent said they depend on child care services from someone other than spouses or partners. The center can accommodate 118 children in its eight classrooms: 24 infants (the largest infant program in the state), 30 toddlers, and 64 preschoolers. The 12,500-square-foot facility allows for 55 square feet of classroom space per child, 20 square feet more than state code requires.

In the infant rooms, antimicrobial carpet with extra padding creates a comfortable and bacteria-free crawl area. Additional soundproofing also has been installed in the infant sleeping rooms. The toddler and preschool rooms feature eating areas, with meals served family style; play areas; and bathroom facilities. All water temperatures are preset for the children's safety.

The center features both indoor and outdoor play areas. The "large-muscle" playroom is primarily for use during inclement weather. It has portable basketball hoops, slides, crawl blocks, and an indoor tricycle path. The 15,00-square-foot outdoor play area is made up of a garden area and two playgrounds with child-safe equipment sized to fit specific ages. Each playground features a two-inch rubber safety surface to cushion falls and reduce the risk of injuries.

Contributed by Diane Cushman, health and family program specialist, The St. Paul Companies, St. Paul, MN.

---

tions, conferences with parents, and discussions with students, you can identify any barriers to their learning and learn what kind of help to seek.

- *Know your community.* Walk or drive around the community. Ask a parent to give you a tour to help familiarize you with agencies and individuals. Read the local newspaper and attend community events and activities.

- *Ask for help and support from parents and the community.* Keep in mind that many parents will not be involved unless you personally ask them. The only encouragement many individuals and local businesses will need is your invitation.

- *Develop a directory of community agencies.* Consult the business pages of local phone books, contact local chambers of commerce, and ask parents what agencies are helpful to them.

- *Compile a list of people who are willing to come to your classroom* to speak to or work with your students. You can start by asking parents to volunteer and for suggestions and recommendations of others.

Only by helping families meet their needs and those of their children will you create opportunities for these children to reach their full potential. For this reason alone, regardless of all the other benefits, family involvement programs and activities must be an essential part of every early childhood program. Families should expect nothing less from the profession, and we, in turn, must do our very best for them.

School–Business Involvement

One good way to build social capital in the community is through school–business involvement. More early childhood programs are developing this link as a means of strengthening their programs and helping children and families. For their part, businesses are anxious to develop the business–school connection in efforts to help schools better educate children (see Box 15.1). Basically, business involvement takes four forms:[9]

- *Adopt-a-school.* Existing in about 40 percent of the elementary schools, this is the most popular type of involvement. Businesses provide tangible goods and services to schools such as guest speakers,

employee tutors, small grants, and products. For example, companies such as Burger King and McDonald's provide professionals with coupons for food items. They in turn use these as incentives for achievement, appropriate behavior, literacy involvement, and so forth.

- *Project driven.* A business or businesses joins with a school or program with the intent of bringing about change. The training of Head Start administrators (see Chap. 16) illustrates this kind of involvement. Other examples are found in Chapter 14.

- *Reform oriented.* An individual company or a consortium gets involved to change a variety of practices throughout a district or agency.

- *Policy change.* Business leaders and organizations help develop or influence legislation and public policy. For exam-

---

BOX 15.1 The Family-Friendly Worksite

Increasing numbers of employers are providing employees a range of benefits relating to their children and families. FEL-PRO Incorporated, an industrial and automotive gaskets manufacturer in Skokie, Illinois, provides many benefits to its employees, including the following:

- State-licensed, on-site child care for up to forty-five children. Parents pay $85 per month, and the company pays the $120 balance.
- Child development seminars on a variety of issues to help parents better deal with raising a family.
- Summer camp for six- to fifteen-year-olds at the company's 220-acre ranch.
- Subsidized tutoring programs for children with learning difficulties.

- $1,000 treasury bonds for the parents of new babies and $5,000 toward legal expense for parents who adopt a child.
- Up to five days per year of company-subsidized emergency home care of sick children and other dependents.
- Up to $3,000 per year for undergraduate studies and up to $6,500 for graduate studies for employees; $3,300 for four years for their dependents to attend an accredited college or university; and financial counseling for students and parents.
- Up to ten weeks of half- to fully paid maternity leave, plus up to two months unpaid family care leave.
- Flexible start times for some office departments.

ple, one group known as the Business Roundtable seeks to promote programs of school choice in thirty states.

Additionally, many businesses are adopting family-friendly policies in the workplace, as in the following examples:

- Marriott's Parent Resource Center and parenting information series provides employees with expert information on parenting, child care, and work/family issues.

- The U.S. Army's partnership between Fort Hood's First Cavalry Division and the Killeen, Texas, Independent School District incorporates parent–teacher conferences as part of military duty for all soldiers with children.

- Hemming's Motor News' "Education Participation Days," allow all employees—not just parents—two days off with pay to attend classes with children in local schools.

- John Hancock sponsors educational activities for children during school vacations and holidays.

- Hewlett-Packard's flexible work hours allow employees to stagger their start time to accommodate their children's schedules and to volunteer at the corporation's on-site elementary school.

- The Thurgood Marshall Child Development Center, featured in the "Observing Programs in Action" color insert on pages b–6 and b–7, is one example of how government agencies are providing for the child care needs of their employees.

The challenge to early childhood professionals is quite clear. Merely seeking ways to involve parents in school activities is no longer a sufficient program of parent involvement. Today, the challenge is to make families the focus of our involvement activities so that their lives and their children's lives are made better. Anything less will not help families and children access and benefit from the opportunities of the twenty-first century.

National Organizations

National programs dedicated to family involvement are a rich resource for information and support. Some of these are listed here:

- Institute for Responsive Education (IRE), 605 Commonwealth Ave., Boston, MA 02215; 617-353-3309

- Center on Families, Communities, Schools and Children's Learning, 605 Commonwealth Ave., Boston, MA 02215; 617-353-3309 (The center's address and phone number are the same as IRE's.)

- Families United for Better Schools, 31 Maple Wood Mall, Philadelphia, PA 19144; 215-829-0442. This is an organization of families working to help other families work for better schools.

- National Committee for Citizens in Education (NCCE), 900 Second St., NE, Suite 8, Washington, D.C. 20002-3557; 800-638-9675. This organization seeks to inform families of their rights and to get them involved in the public schools.

- The Home and School Institute, 1201 16th St., NW, Washington, D.C. 20036; 202-466-3633

- National Congress of Parents and Teachers (The National PTA), 700 N. Rush St., Chicago, IL 60611; 312-787-0977

The Family Involvement Partnership for Learning   The mission for the Family Involvement Partnership for Learning is to promote children's learning through the development of family/school/community partnerships. The national Family Involvement Partnership for Learning began as a cooperative effort between the U.S. Department of Education and the National Coalition for Parent Involvement in Education (NCPIE). NCPIE, a coalition of over 100 national education and advocacy organizations, has been meeting for more than fifteen years to advocate the involvement of families in their children's education and to promote relationships among home, school, and community that can enhance the education of all children and youth. NCPIE represents parents, schools, communities, religious groups, and businesses.[10]

Website Connections

Many websites are available to help parents become more involved in their formation and tools for children's education. For example, The Family Education Network (http://www.familyeducation.com) and Parent Soup (http://www.parentsoup.com) offer resources and features on a wide array of educational topics. You may find other sites by entering the following keywords into one of the Internet's many available search engines:

> parent involvement
>
> community involvement
>
> school partnerships
>
> school/business relationships
>
> school/community collaboration

ACTIVITIES FOR FURTHER ENRICHMENT

1. Arrange with a local school district to be present during a parent–teacher conference. Discuss with the teacher, prior to the visit, his or her objectives and procedures. After the conference, assess its success with the teacher.

2. List the various ways early childhood professionals communicate pupils' progress to families. Which methods do you think are the most and least effective? What specific methods do you plan to use?

3. Describe the methods and techniques you would use to publicize a parent meeting about how your school plans to involve families in their children's education.

4. List six reasons why early childhood professionals might resist involving families. For each reason, give two strategies you could use for overcoming the resistance.

5. You have just been appointed the program director for a family involvement program in first grade. Write objectives for the program. Develop specific activities for involving families and for providing services to them.

6. Visit social services agencies in your area, and list the services they offer.

   a. Describe how early childhood professionals can work with these agencies to meet the needs of children and families.

   b. Invite agency directors to meet with your class to discuss how they and early childhood professionals can work cooperatively to help families and children.

7. Reflect on your own school experiences. How did community resources contribute to your learning? Could you use these same resources to help those children (and their families) that you will teach? How?

8. As families change, so, too, do the services they need. Interview families in as many settings as possible (e.g., urban,

suburban, rural), from as many socioeconomic backgrounds as possible, and from as many kinds of families as possible. Determine what services they believe can help them most, then tell how you as a professional could help provide those services.

9. Develop specific guidelines that a child care center could use to facilitate the involvement of fathers, language-minority families, and families of children with disabilities.

READINGS FOR FURTHER ENRICHMENT

Batey, C. S. *Parents Are Lifesavers: A Handbook for Parent Involvement in Schools* (Thousand Oaks, CA: Corwin, 1995).

Batey offers a practical approach with step-by-step guidelines for getting parents involved in classrooms and schools. The book includes many ideas to help empower parents as active, sharing participants in their children's education.

Brizius, J., and S. Foster. *Generation to Generation: Realizing the Promise of Family Literacy* (Ypsilanti, MI: High/Scope, 1993).

Offers a practical, thorough discussion of literacy issues and how they impact the family unit. Includes guidance for setting up community programs.

Davis, B. *How to Involve Parents in a Multicultural School* (Alexandria, VA: ASCD, 1995).

Includes clear examples and an emphasis on "giving good customer service" to help you break new ground in creating successful parent involvement programs. As schools become more culturally and ethnically diverse, you can use the practical suggestions from this book to enlist the support and assistance of parents who may not speak the language or understand the customs you take for granted.

Kagan, S. L., and B. Weissbourd. *Putting Families First: America's Family Support Movement and the Challenge of Change* (San Francisco: Jossey-Bass, 1995).

This book discusses the evolution of family support services, their movement into mainstream institutions such as schools and prisons, and the future integration of these services within communities and national policy.

Swap, S. *Developing Home–School Partnerships: from Concepts to Practice* (New York: Teachers College Press, 1993).

Provides an overview of, and practical suggestions for, professionals who want to strengthen ties with parents.

U.S. Department of Education. *Strong Families, Strong Schools: Building Community Partnerships for Learning* (Washington, D.C.: Author, 1994).

This book describes successful school efforts to involve families and communities. To order, call 1-800-USA-LEARN.

NOTES

1. U.S. Department of Education, *Goals 2000* (Washington, D.C.: Author, 1994), n.p.
2. "How Americans Grade Their School System," *Business Week* (14 Sept. 1992), p. 85.
3. Stanley M. Elam, Lowel C. Rose, and Alec M. Gallup, "The 25th Annual Phi Delta Kappa/Gallup Poll," *Phi Delta Kappan* (Oct. 1993), p. 149.
4. U.S. Department of Education, *Strong Families, Strong Schools: Building Community Partnerships for Learning* (Washington, D.C.: Author, 1994).
5. Generations United, *Linking Youth and Old through Intergenerational Programs* (Washington, D.C.: Author, n.d.), n.p.
6. Richard J. Stiggins, *Student-Centered Classroom Assessment,* 2nd ed. (Upper Saddle River, NJ: Merrill/Prentice Hall, 1997), p. 499.
7. J. González-Mena, "Taking a Culturally Sensitive Approach in Infant-Toddler

Programs," *Young Children* 1 (1992), pp. 8–9. Used with permission of the author.

8. J. S. Cohen, *Parental Involvement in Education* ED 1.2:P75/6 (Washington D.C.: U.S. Government Printing Office, 1991), p. 7.

9. "Saving Our Schools," *Business Week* (14 Sept. 1992), p. 71.

10. Family Involvement Partnership for Learning, *Community Update #23* (Washington, D.C.: Author, April 1995).

CHAPTER 16

Supporting Children's Success

Focus Questions

1. How does the federal government support early childhood programs, children, and families?

2. What are the basic purposes of Head Start and other federal programs?

3. What are the main components of the Head Start Program?

4. What are the main provisions of the Head Start Performance Standards?

5. How and why has Head Start changed since its founding?

6. How does Head Start affect children and families?

7. What is Even Start and what services does it provide?

he federal government plays a major role in the lives of children, families, and early childhood professionals as a result of the programs it funds and supports. Federal initiatives have changed the nature, function, and scope of early childhood programs, and will continue to function as a catalyst of change. Much of what happens in early childhood programming is based in part on federal models and programs. Without the federal presence—laws, policies, and funding—the field of early childhood education would not be as advanced as it is, nor would as many children receive the services they do.

Critics of declining federal funding complain that the government is not doing enough for disadvantaged, needy, at-risk children and families. They specifically cite increases in the number of women and children living in poverty. However, the fact remains that the federal presence in early childhood programs is wide ranging and influential. In this chapter we examine some of these federal programs, functions, purposes, and effects.

FEDERAL SUPPORT FOR EARLY CHILDHOOD PROGRAMS

To help overcome the negative effects of poverty on the lives of adults and children, the federal government in 1964 passed the Economic Opportunity Act. One of the main purposes of this act was to break intergenerational cycles of poverty by providing educational and social opportunities for children from low-income families. The act created the Office of Economic Opportunity, and Project Head Start was developed and administered from this office. Head Start is one of the current federally supported early childhood programs.

The federal government also promotes early education through initiatives such as Goals 2000 (see Chap. 2). Additionally, the federal government continues to refinance Head Start and to expand its missions and initiatives. Consequently, the federal government plays a major role in the lives of children, families, and early childhood professionals.

Families and Poverty

Evidence from many sources indicates that when families' incomes are inadequate to

---

Figure 16.1/*Families with Children Living in Poverty*

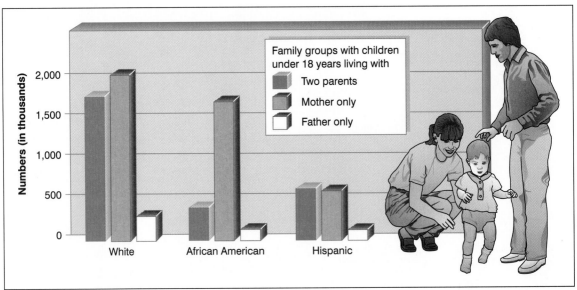

Source: U.S. Department of Commerce, Bureau of the Census, 1995.

meet their social and educational needs, parents and children are impaired in their ability to become contributing members of society. One of the most damaging consequences of poverty, however, is the effect it has on children's futures. Unfortunately, poverty tends to be generational. That is, when a family lives in poverty, the likelihood rises that their children—the next generation—will also be poor. What is more alarming is the number of mother-only families who are living in poverty (Figure 16.1).

More than 50 million children are estimated to live in poverty, which means that their families' incomes are below the poverty guidelines set by the U.S. government. The effects of poverty are debilitating for both children and families. Being poor means more than being eligible for a free school lunch. It means poverty's children as a group are less healthy, live in inadequate housing, and do not have the opportunities for activities and experiences their wealthier counterparts have. Moreover, the increasing divorce rate, a phenomenon of recent decades, brings economic as well as social consequences. A child in a household headed by a single parent has a greater chance of being poor. In addition, the majority of low-income families are headed by females; thus poverty, in this sense, has become feminized.

The Federal Definition of Poverty

By federal definition, *living in poverty* means that you and your family do not have an income that allows you to purchase adequate health care, housing, food, clothing, and educational services. As of 1996, the federal government used the income levels in Table 16.1 (adjusted to family size and farm or nonfarm residence) to define the poverty level. (These figures change annually because of changing rates of inflation and the cost of living.)

Table 16.1/*1996 Federal Family Income Guide*

48 Contiguous States and the District of Columbia	
Size of Family Unit	**Poverty Guideline**
1	$ 7,740
2	10,360
3	12,980
4	15,600
5	18,220
6	20,840
7	23,460
8	26,080

For family units with more than 8 members, add $2,620 for each additional member.

Alaska	
Size of Family Unit	**Poverty Guideline**
1	$ 9,660
2	12,940
3	16,220
4	19,500
5	22,780
6	26,060
7	29,340
8	32,620

For family units with more than 8 members, add $3,280 for each additional member.

Hawaii	
Size of Family Unit	**Poverty Guideline**
1	$ 8,910
2	11,920
3	14,930

Source: Administration for Children and Families, 1996.

HEAD START: A TWO-GENERATION PROGRAM

When we discuss children who are enrolled in programs such as Head Start, we often lose sight of the families from which they come. Following are typical characteristics of Head Start families:

- Fifty-five percent are headed by a single parent.

- Fifty-two percent have one or two children.

- Fifty-one percent have an annual income below $6,000.

- Sixty-two percent have a primary caretaker between the age of twenty and twenty-nine.

- Fifty-five percent have a primary caretaker with a GED or less education.

- Sixty-seven percent belong to a minority group.

- Seventy-four percent are receiving some type of welfare.

- Forty-seven percent have heads of households who are unemployed.[1]

Funding for Head Start comes through the Administration on Children, Youth, and Families (ACYF). Figure 16.2 shows the organizational structure that governs the operation of Head Start programs.

History and Operating Principles

Head Start was implemented during the summer of 1965, and approximately 550,000

Head Start and other early childhood programs are dedicated to developing linkages between programs and families. All families and family members have to be involved in decisions regarding their children and program goals and objectives. How might this father be involved in a Head Start program?

Figure 16.2/
*Organizational
Structure of Head Start*

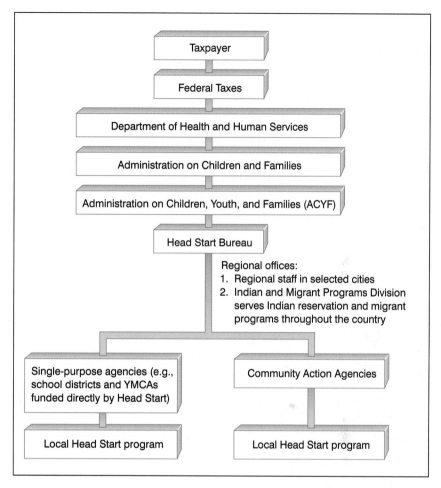

children in 2,500 child development centers were enrolled in the program. The first programs were designed for children entering first grade who had not attended kindergarten. The purpose of Head Start was literally to give children a head start on their first grade experience and, hopefully, on life itself.

Today, the National Head Start program has a budget of $3.57 billion and serves 751,000 low income children and families, or about 40 percent of those eligible. (Until the recent expansion of Head Start, which began in 1993, it served only about 25 percent of eligible children.) There are 1,433 Head Start programs nationwide with a total of 42,750 classrooms. The average cost per child of the Head Start program is $4,534 annually. Head Start has a paid staff of 146,750 and 1,235,000 volunteers. A total of 15,345,000 children have been served by Head Start since it began.[2] Figure 16.3 shows the racial and ethnic composition of Head Start programs, and Figure 16.4 cites the ages of children served.

Head Start is based on the premise that all children share certain needs, and that children of low-income families, in particular, can benefit from a comprehensive developmental program to meet those needs.

Figure 16.3/Racial/Ethnic Composition of Head Start

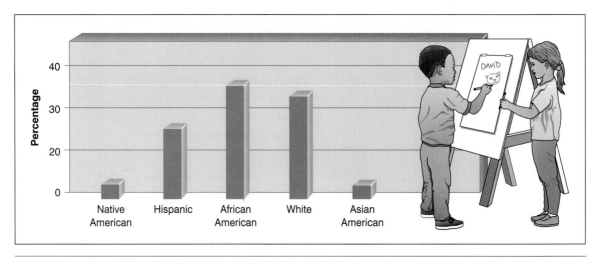

Source: Administration on Children, Youth, and Families, *Project Head Start Statistical Fact Sheet* (Washington, D.C.: Author, May, 1996), pp. 1–3.

Figure 16.4/Ages of Children Served by Head Start

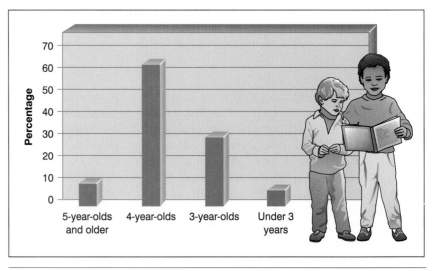

Source: Administration on Children, Youth, and Families, *Project Head Start Statistical Fact Sheet* (Washington, D.C.: Author, May, 1996), pp. 1–3.

GOAL AND PURPOSES

The overall goal of Head Start is to bring about a greater degree of social competence in disadvantaged children. Social competence, in this context, is the child's everyday effectiveness in dealing with his environment and later responsibilities in school and life. Social competence takes into account the interrelatedness of cognitive and intellectual development, physical and mental health, nutritional needs, and other factors that enable a child to function optimally. Head Start is a comprehensive developmental approach to helping achieve social competence. To this end, Head Start goals provide for:

- *The improvement of the child's health and physical abilities.*
- *The encouragement of self-confidence, spontaneity, curiosity, and self-discipline which will assist in the development of the child's social and emotional health.*
- *The enhancement of the child's mental processes and skills with particular attention to conceptual and verbal skills.*
- *The establishment of patterns and expectations of success for the child, which will create a climate of confidence for his present and future learning efforts and overall development.*
- *An increase in the ability of the child and his family to relate to each other and to others in a loving and supporting manner.*
- *The enhancement of the sense of dignity and self-worth within the child and his family.*

The Head Start Program approach is based on the philosophy that (1) A child can benefit most from a comprehensive, interdisciplinary program to foster development and remedy problems as expressed in a broad range of services; and that (2) the child's entire family, as well as the community, must be involved.[3]

Head Start is intended to provide a comprehensive developmental program for children ages birth to five years from low-income families. The program is also dedicated to helping children achieve a positive outlook on life through success in school and daily life

activities. Implementation of these objectives occurs through a comprehensive child development program delivered in center-based and home-based settings.

PROGRAM DESIGN AND MANAGEMENT

Head Start makes every effort to assure that the management and governance of programs is conducted in such a way that supports the implementation of its published performance standards. Additionally, Head Start administrative services are designed to help local programs strengthen their administrative and management capabilities to bring about effective delivery of services. This component covers five major areas: program planning and management, personnel management, financial management, procurement and property management, and eligibility and enrollment.

With regard to program governance, *Head Start Program Performance Standards* state, "Agencies must establish and maintain a formal structure of shared governance through which parents can participate in policy making or in other decisions about the program."[4]

Parents and Families

Head Start requires that parents and community members must receive preference for employment vacancies for which they are qualified. Therefore, it is not uncommon to find parents employed as aides and teachers in Head Start. The belief is that helping parents learn helps their children learn. For example, parents who learn in the Head Start center that mealtime is a time for conversation are more likely to model this behavior by talking to their children at home. In this respect, a great deal of emphasis is placed on Head Start teachers modeling appropriate behavior for parents so parents can model for their children.

PROGRAM IN ACTION

HEAD START: A QUALITY COST-EFFECTIVE PROGRAM THAT WORKS

May 18, 1997, marked thirty-four years of operation for Project Head Start. As the only national early intervention program, Head Start continues to provide enriched, comprehensive, early childhood education for low-income children. Head Start also offers a range of other services including health, nutrition, and social services, and emphasizes parent and community involvement in the development and operation of the program.

Countless reports and much research prove that for every dollar spent on the program, six dollars are saved, and that the Head Start graduate completes high school and beyond and makes better grades.

The list of positive outcomes goes on and on. Having been involved with the program for twenty-six years I see so many successful aspects of the program that appear immeasurable. The most important is parent involvement. *Patience, understanding, and respect underline the approach of the dedicated Head Start staff as they work with parents.* Often, parents point to the warm environment that exists at Head Start centers as something that initially makes them feel welcome.

Parent Involvement

Head Start programs have a unique and special relationship with parents that does not yet exist in most organizations. Parents are truly treated as equal partners in the design of the local program

and in the total involvement in their children's education. We encourage parents as the primary educators of their children to volunteer in all aspects of the program and participate in training programs that increase their knowledge, as well as attend workshops, seminars, and conferences.

The relationship begins when local programs plan recruitment drives that include going into parents' neighborhoods, into their churches, laundromats, and so on. We demonstrate to parents at the lowest edge of poverty that we want them and have no hesitation about being a part of their world. In fact, many of our staff live in the same neighborhoods.

We continue to reach out to parents by holding our registration of children during hours convenient for the working poor: early mornings and evenings, as well as Saturdays. Volunteers or staff care for children while parents register. Head Start staffers assist parents with the many federal forms, and ask additional questions to get a complete history of each child and family.

Once the child is enrolled, parents are oriented about the program. A parent from each classroom is selected to serve on the center committee, which has the responsibility of making decisions and recommendations about all activities at the center. For the first time in the lives of most parents, their opinion counts. Thus, a sense of pride and ownership develops about the Head

Increasing Parent Income, Responsibility, and Pride Employing parents in Head Start centers is also a way to increase family incomes. Many parent volunteers have later been hired as bus drivers, cooks, aides, teachers, and directors (see the Program in Action, "Head Start: A Quality Cost-Effective Program That Works"). As a result of seminars and training programs, some parents have gained the skills necessary to assume positions of increased responsibility, such as assistant teacher, teacher, and pro-

gram director. Jobs in Head Start are not viewed as dead-end positions.

Of course, pay and responsibility are not the only benefits; such work also enhances parents' self-image, an important factor in personal life.

Every Head Start program operates under policies established by a council that includes parents. Half the policy council members are selected from among parents with children in the program, and half from interested community agencies (day care, family

Start center their child attends. Interested parents at the Manatee Head Start program in Bradenton, Florida, for example, raised funds and purchased gifts for each of their six centers including a VCR, an air conditioner, classroom supplies, popcorn poppers, and a microwave. They also sponsored a picnic at the park for the children.

Parents from the center committee are elected to serve on the Head Start policy council, which must be comprised of at least 50 percent parents. There, parents are trained to make all major policy decisions about the program, including the budget and grant applications. At the policy council level, parents who at first are often too shy to speak out on an issue find themselves making motions and raising questions. In some programs, such as Parents in Community Action, Inc., in Minneapolis, Minnesota, and Concerned Parents in Action, Inc., in Paterson, New Jersey, parents have formed a corporation and are the administrators (grantees) for their programs.

Inspiring Parents

I have met so many parents who relate that their Head Start experience inspired them to continue their education. Ophelia Brown, executive director of the Dade County Community Agencies in Miami, Florida, one of the largest and most out-standing programs in the country, states, "I would never have thought about going back to school to get my high school diploma, not to mention getting my AA, then a BA and an MA if Head Start staff had not made me feel that I had the ability to achieve."

The success of Head Start's parent involvement program is crucial to helping the Head Start child continue successfully through school. Parents learn through Head Start that they must be active in the school system and community affairs. They learn to demonstrate to their children that they care and understand that their actions can positively affect their lives forever, while nonaction may leave them following the vicious cycle of poverty.

Recently in Alexandria, Virginia, a group of minority parents (including two Head Start parents) filed a lawsuit against the local school board declaring discrimination against the selection process of kindergarten children. They won the suit!

Head Start has found the key to one day eradicating poverty. We touch parents in a way that makes them feel accepted and equal. We entrust them with responsibility, demonstrate genuine concern, and provide an opportunity for growth and self-achievement.

Contributed by Sarah M. Greene, chief executive officer, National Head Start Association.

---

services) and parents who have previously had children in Head Start. Policies established by the council include determining the attendance area for the center and the basis on which children should be recruited, helping develop and oversee the program budget, and acting as a personnel and grievance committee.

Administration

Johnson & Johnson has entered into a partnership with Head Start to provide adminis-trative training for directors. The Head Start–Johnson & Johnson Management Fellows Program is designed to help directors develop the programs and management skills they need to implement their vision in addressing the challenges of Head Start expansion.

In 1995, the Head Start Bureau and the Council for Early Childhood Professional Recognition (CECPR) jointly established the National Head Start Fellows Program. This program is based on the Amendments to the

Head Start Act of 1994 and the Advisory Committee on Head Start Quality and Expansion, which envisioned a fellows program that would be part of a long-term quality improvement initiative for Head Start aimed at upgrading the skills and experience of promising individuals.

The National Fellows Program identifies and provides support for the growth and development of promising early childhood professionals from community-based organizations, state governments, and nonprofit organizations who work in program development, research, education, and policy making.

The Fellows learn from nationally recognized leaders and contribute their energies and perspectives to the resolution of critical issues for children and families.

The program provides selected individuals with firsthand experience in the process of leadership in the Executive Branch of the Federal Government and instills a sense of personal commitment for contributing to the quality of programs and policy for young children and their families.[5]

HEAD START SERVICES

Head Start offers the following program services: education, parent involvement, health services (including nutrition and mental health), family partnerships, staff development, and administration.

Effective January 8, 1998, all Head Start programs must operate their programs and services according to new performance standards in order to continue receiving federal funds. It is informative to examine these standards for each area. The Head Start Bureau provides guidance on the performance standards to help each program implement them. However, local agencies are responsible for designing programs to best meet the needs of their children and families.

The performance standards encourage the integration of services across components and emphasize partnerships with families and communities. We list some of these standards in our discussion of each of the service areas. The full set of current Head Start Performance Standards appears in the 5 November 1996 issue of the *Federal Register.*

Implementation of Services

All Head Start programs are encouraged to explore ways to deliver services directly to children in their homes. This approach is based on the premise that the parent is the most important person in the child's life and the home the optimum place for growth and development. In brief, the local option encourages Head Start staff to plan programs that fit their needs and the needs of children and parents, while also taking into consideration the characteristics of the community they serve.

Local agencies may choose home-based programs as a means of delivering Head Start services. Today, 578 Head Start agencies operate home-based programs. Skilled home visitors assist parents in providing support services and developmental activities that children would normally receive in a center-based program. Presently, 4,396 home visitors serve more than 44,630 children and their families.

The primary difference between the options is that the home-based option focuses on parents in the home setting and is designed to help them be the primary educator of their child. It is augmented by group socialization activities conducted at the center, in one of the family's homes, or another accessible location, such as a community center. The home-based option has these strengths:[6]

- Parent involvement is the very keystone of the program.

- Geographically isolated families have an invaluable opportunity to be part of a comprehensive child and family program.

- The individualized family plan is based on both a child and a family assessment.

- The family plan is facilitated by a home visitor who is an adult educator with knowledge and training related to all Head Start components.

- The program includes the entire family.

According to Glenna Markey of the Bear River Head Start in Logan, Utah, there are several keys to making a home-based option work:

- *The home visitor must work with the parent,* not *the child. When* parents *work with their children, the intended results of the home-based option are achieved.*

- *The home visitor must help the parent become a "child development specialist," which ultimately benefits the parents' children and grandchildren.*

- *The home visitor must try to do such a good job that the parent can do without him or her. In this sense, the home visitors put themselves out of a job!*

- *The home visitor must assist the parent in identifying resources in the home environment that can be adapted for use in helping children learn. When the home visitor supplies toys or materials and when these materials are no longer available, parents may think learning has to stop. Therefore, parents must be encouraged not to rely on commercial and store-bought materials. For example, brown grocery bags can be a coloring book, puzzles can be made out of cereal boxes, and tin cans can become musical instruments.*[7]

Education and Development for All Children

Performance standards for education and development for all children include the following:

In order to help children gain the skills and confidence necessary to be prepared to succeed in their present environment and with later responsibilities in school and life, grantee and delegate agencies' approach to child development and education must:

- *Be developmentally and linguistically appropriate, recognizing that children have individual rates of development as well as individual interests, temperament, languages, cultural backgrounds, and learning styles;*

- *Be inclusive of children with disabilities, consistent with their Individualized Family Service Plan (IFSP) or Individualized Education Program (IEP);*

- *Provide an environment of acceptance that supports and respects gender, culture, language, ethnicity and family composition;*

- *Provide a balanced daily program of child-initiated and adult-directed activities, including individual and small group activities; and*

- *Allow and enable children to independently use toilet facilities when it is developmentally appropriate and when efforts to encourage toilet training are supported by the parents.*[8]

Child Development and Education Approach for Infants and Toddlers   *Programs of service for infants and toddlers must encourage:*

- *The development of secure relationships in out-of-home care settings for infants and toddlers by having a limited number of consistent teachers over an extended period of time. Teachers must demonstrate an understanding of the child's family culture and, whenever possible, speak the child's language;*

- *Trust and emotional security so that each child can explore the environment according to his or her developmental level; and*

- *Opportunities for each child to explore a variety of sensory and motor experiences with support and stimulation from teachers and family members.*

Agencies must support the social and emotional development of infants and toddlers by promoting an environment that:

- *Encourages the development of self-awareness, autonomy, and self-expression; and*
- *Supports the emerging communication skills of infants and toddlers by providing daily opportunities for each child to interact with others and to express himself or herself freely.*

Agencies must promote the physical development of infants and toddlers by:

- *Supporting the development of physical skills of infants and toddlers including gross motor skills, such as grasping, pulling, pushing, crawling, walking, and climbing; and*
- *Creating opportunities for fine motor development that encourage the control and coordination of small, specialized motions, using the eyes, mouth, hands, and feet.[9]*

Child Development and Education Approach for Preschoolers

Grantee and delegate agencies, in collaboration with the parents, must implement a curriculum that:

- *Supports each child's individual pattern of development and learning;*
- *Integrates all educational aspects of the health, nutrition, and mental health services into program activities;*
- *Ensures that the program environment helps children develop emotional security and facility in social relationships;*
- *Enhances each child's understanding of self as an individual and as a member of a group; and*
- *Provides individual and small group experiences both indoors and outdoors.*
- *Staff must use a variety of strategies to promote and support children's learning and developmental progress based on the observations and ongoing assessment of each child.[10]*

Head Start Agencies are permitted and encouraged to consider several program models and select the option best suited to children's needs and staff's capabilities and resources. Program options available to local agencies are the center-based program option, the home-based program option, or approved locally designed variations.

An example of a locally designed option is the use of family day care homes to provide full-day sessions for children. Metropolitan Dade County (Florida) uses this option to serve some three-year-old children the year before they enter a center-based four-year-old program. Grantees must demonstrate that these models address the needs of the local community.

The Administration for Children, Youth, and Families (ACYF) describes a *part-day* program as one in which children attend less than six hours a day. *Full-day* programs are those in which children attend six or more hours a day.

The schedule for a part-day program at the Audubon Head Start program in Owensboro, Kentucky, follows:[11]

8:00	Welcome children, health check, morning activities
8:15	Attendance, wash hands, helpers set table
8:30	Breakfast
9:00	Cleanup/Restroom
9:10	Large group: circle time—music and movement
9:25	Explain learning centers
9:30	Learning center time, brush teeth, individual objectives, small groups
10:50	Cleanup
11:00	Small group: mental health—Know Me/Know You; language—PEEK Kit
11:20	Prepare for lunch: wash hands, set table, food groupies, Chef Combo

11:30	Lunch
12:00	Cleanup/Restroom
12:10	Large group: story time
12:20	Outdoor play or indoor play (gross-motor)
1:20	Prepare to go home, recall day's activities
1:30	Departure

Education Objectives   The child development and educational program of Head Start is guided by the following objectives:

- *Provide children with a learning environment and the varied experiences which will help them develop socially, intellectually, physically, and emotionally in a manner appropriate to their age and state of development toward the overall goal of social competence.*
- *Integrate the educational aspects of the various Head Start components in the daily program of activities.*
- *Involve parents in educational activities of the program to enhance their role as the principal influence on the child's education and development.*
- *Assist parents to increase their knowledge, understanding, skills, and experience in child growth and development.*
- *Identify and reinforce experiences which occur in the home that parents can utilize as educational activities for their children.*[12]

These educational objectives guide local agencies in developing their own programs that are unique and responsive to the children, families, and communities they serve. Thus, there is really no "National" Head Start curriculum.

Coordination with Public Schools   Coordination of efforts, activities, and programs between Head Start and the public schools has not always been as functional and organized as it should be. Head Start is now pursuing a more collaborative, cooperative program of helping children and their families make the transition between Head Start programs and the public schools. To enhance these transition efforts, the ACYF, through the Head Start Coordination Project, awarded twelve states coordinating grants. These states are encouraged to develop collaborative projects with both public- and private-sector partners. In addition to promoting coordination and linkage between Head Start and other programs, the projects are expected to address state welfare reform, state-funded preschool programs, transition to public school, and mainstreaming children with disabilities.[13]

The Kentucky Department of Education has entered into an agreement with Head Start that aims to ensure that all eligible preschool children are enrolled and educated by either the public schools or Head Start and that the programs are of equal quality. This is a further example of the close working relationship Head Start hopes to forge with all public and private school systems.

Child Health and Safety

Head Start assumes an active role in children's health. Children's current health status is monitored and reported to parents, and corrective and preventive procedures are undertaken with their cooperation. For example, if a child needs glasses, corrective orthopedic surgery, or dental care, services may be provided through the Head Start budget, although the program usually works with social service agencies to provide services or money for health needs.

Regardless of the procedure, parents' role in providing health care for the child is never bypassed. Although Head Start employees may take children to the doctor or dentist, every effort is made to see that parents receive support and assistance for securing appropriate services. For example, the community worker for the Head Start program might provide transportation for a parent, or might make arrangements if the parent has difficulty fixing an appointment with a specialist. The philosophy inherent in this process supports the right of the parent as the primary teacher. An associated rationale is that through involvement in providing health services, parents learn how to provide for future needs.

Daily Health Education

In addition to arranging medical examinations and care, each Head Start program teaches children how to care for their health, including the importance of eating proper foods and caring for their teeth.

Head Start also seeks to direct children and parents to existing mental health delivery systems such as community health centers. It does not intend to duplicate existing services but to help its clientele become aware of, and utilize, available services.

Health and Emergency Procedure Performance Standards

Agencies operating center-based programs must establish and implement policies and procedures to respond to medical and dental health emergencies with which all staff are familiar and trained. Additionally, agencies must do the following:

- *Make a determination as to whether or not each child has an ongoing source of continuous, accessible health care. If a child does not have a source of ongoing health care, agencies must assist the parents in accessing a source of care.*
- *Obtain from a health care professional a determination as to whether the child is up-to-date on a schedule of age appropriate preventive and primary health care*

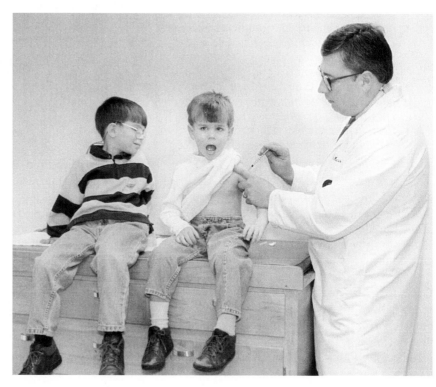

Head Start provides a comprehensive developmental health services program which includes a broad range of medical, dental, mental health, and nutrition services to preschool children. These programs are designed to promote children's physical, emotional, cognitive, and social development toward the overall goal of social competence. How do health services help achieve this goal?

which includes medical, dental and mental health.[14]

Injury Prevention. Agencies must:
- *Ensure that staff and volunteers can demonstrate safety practices; and*
- *Foster safety awareness among children and parents by incorporating it into child and parent activities.*

Hygiene
- *Staff, volunteers and children must wash their hands with soap and running water at least at the following times:*

After diapering or toilet use;
Whenever hands are contaminated with blood or other bodily fluids; and
After handling pets or other animals.

- *Staff and volunteers must also wash their hands with soap and running water:*

Before and after giving medications;
Before and after treating or bandaging a wound (nonporous gloves should be worn if there is contact with blood or blood-containing body fluids); and
After assisting a child with toilet use.

- *Nonporous (e.g., Latex) gloves must be worn by staff when they are in contact with spills of blood or other visibly bloody bodily fluids.*
- *Spills of bodily fluids (e.g., urine, feces, blood, saliva, nasal discharge, eye discharge or any fluid discharge) must be cleaned and disinfected immediately in keeping with professionally established guidelines (e.g., standards of the Occupational Safety Health Administration, U.S. Department of Labor). Any tools and equipment used to clean spills of bodily fluids must be cleaned and disinfected immediately. Other blood-contaminated materials must be disposed of in a plastic bag with a secure tie.*
- *Agencies must adopt sanitation and hygiene procedures for diapering that adequately protect the health and safety of children served by the program and staff. Grantee and delegate agencies must ensure that staff properly conduct these procedures.[15]*

Nutrition A basic premise of Head Start is that children must be properly fed to have the strength and energy to learn. This philosophy calls for teaching children good nutrition habits that will carry over for the rest of their lives and be passed on to their children. In addition, parents are given basic nutrition education so they, in turn, can promote good nutrition in their families. Such programs include seminars on buying food and reading and comparing grocery advertisements. One Head Start program in consumer education for parents and staff emphasized can sizes, number of servings per can, comparison of prices, nutritional value, and specific foods that can maximize dollar value.

Nutrition programs consist of a breakfast, snack, and lunch at the center. The menus are not traditional school cafeteria fare but rather food children like as well as food that is indigenous to their ethnic background (see Table 16.2). Generally, Head Start centers serve food family style—the food is served in bowls, and children help themselves when-

Head Start provides children with nutritious meals and snacks and opportunities to participate in activities that teach nutritional skills and information. Promoting good nutrition for children and their families is an important part of the preschool curriculum and helps establish lifelong attitudes toward healthy living.

Table 16.2/*Weekly Meal Plan*

	Monday	Tuesday	Wednesday	Thursday	Friday
Breakfast					
Juice, fruit, or vegetable	Fresh peaches	Orange sections	Sliced strawberries	Pineapple chunks	Applesauce
Cereal or bread	Bagel half	Bran cereal	Banana muffin squares	Cheerios	French toast
Milk	Low-fat cream cheese	Milk	Milk	Milk	Milk
	Milk				
Lunch or supper					
Meat or meat alternate	Turkey Sloppy Joe on whole wheat bun	Crispy baked chicken	Tuna salad with low-fat mayonnaise	*Pocket cheese pizza	Soft chicken taco with shredded lettuce, tomato, grated cheese, and salsa
Vegetable	Whole kernel corn	Peas and carrots	Oven-baked potato wedges	Steamed broccoli and cauliflower	Carrot sticks
Vegetable or fruit	Melon cubes	New potatoes	Lettuce and tomato salad	Plum	Milk
Bread/grain	Milk	Whole wheat roll	Whole wheat bread	Milk	
Milk		Milk	Milk		
Snack					
Select two of the following:	Apple juice (with vitamin C added)	Low-fat yogurt	Orange juice	Oatmeal cookies	Grape juice (with added vitamin C)
Meat of meat alternate	Crackers	Banana	Graham crackers	Milk	Ham cubes
Vegetable, fruit, or juice	Cheese cubes	Water	Water	Water	Wheat crackers
Bread or bread alternate	Water				Water
Milk					

*Be sure to serve enough cheese to meet the meat alternate requirement.
Source: Adapted by permission of the National Food Service Management Institute, *What's Cooking?* 1 (2) (1995), p. 2.

ever possible. Whatever a center's particular style, a meal is a vehicle for teaching skills and knowledge.

Identification of Nutritional Needs. The following performance standards govern child nutrition services. Staff and families must work together to identify each child's nutritional needs, taking into account staff and family discussions concerning:

- *Any relevant nutrition-related assessment data (height, weight, blood analysis);*
- *Information about family eating patterns, including cultural preferences, special dietary requirements for each child with nutrition-related health problems, and the feeding requirements of infants and toddlers and each child with disabilities;*
- *For infants and toddlers, current feeding schedules and amounts and types of food provided, including whether breast milk or formula and baby food is used, meal patterns, new foods introduced, food intol-*

erances and preferences, voiding patterns, and observations related to developmental changes in feeding and nutrition. This information must be shared with parents and updated regularly.[16]

Nutritional Services. Agencies must design and implement a nutrition program that meets the nutritional needs and feeding requirements of each child, including those with special dietary needs and children with disabilities. Also, the nutrition program must serve a variety of foods which consider cultural and ethnic preferences and which broaden the child's food experience.[17]

Services to Children with Disabilities

At least 10 percent of Head Start enrollment must consist of children with disabilities. Nationally, 13.4 percent of all children enrolled in Head Start have a disability—mental retardation, autism, traumatic brain injury,

All Head Start programs enroll children with disabilities. As a model for inclusion, Head Start is set up to give a head start to as wide a range of children as possible. Not only does Head Start provide services to families of children with disabilities, it also integrates services with other community agencies.

health impairments, visual impairments (including blindness), hearing impairments (including deafness), emotional–behavioral disorders, speech or language impairments, orthopedic impairments, and learning disabilities.

To provide adequately for these children, staff and parents receive training in procedures related to the particular disabilities. Head Start also trains staff in identification, treatment, and prevention of child abuse and neglect. (See Chap. 13 for more information on educating children with disabilities.)

Family and Community Partnerships

Parent Involvement From the outset, Head Start has been dedicated to the philosophy that if children's lives are to improve, corresponding changes must be made in parents' lives. Part of the Head Start thrust is directed toward that end. Head Start has always conducted programs which provide a planned program of experiences and activities which support and enhance the parental role as the principal influence in their child's education and development. Additionally, Head Start provides a program that recognizes parents as (1) responsible guardians of their children's well-being, (2) prime educators of their children, and (3) contributors to the Head Start Program and to their communities.

Family Partnerships The Head Start performance standards for family partnerships include the following:

- *Grantee and delegate agencies must engage in a process of collaborative partnership-building with parents to establish mutual trust and to identify family goals, strengths, and necessary services and other supports. This process must be initiated as early after enrollment as possible and it must take into consideration each family's readiness and willingness to participate in the process.*

- *As part of this ongoing partnership, grantee and delegate agencies must offer parents opportunities to develop and implement individualized Family Partnership Agreements that describe family goals, responsibilities, timetables and strategies for achieving them, In home-based program options, this Agreement must include the above information as well as the specific roles of parents in home visits and group socialization activities.*[18]

Community Partnerships Performance standards for community partnerships include the following:

- *Grantee and delegate agencies must take an active role in community planning to encourage strong communication, cooperation, and the sharing of information among agencies and their community partners and to improve the delivery of community services to children and families in accordance with the agency's confidentiality policies. Documentation must be maintained to reflect the level of effort undertaken to establish community partnerships.*
- *Grantee and delegate agencies must take affirmative steps to establish ongoing collaborative relationships with community organizations to promote the access of children and families to community services that are responsive to their needs, and to ensure that Early Head Start programs respond to community needs.*[19]

More than ever, Head Start is endeavoring to be in cooperative and collaborative relationships with families and communities.

New Initiatives, Future Directions

Head Start has always been, and remains, in the vanguard of agencies involved in new and innovative programs. The following sections discuss some of Head Start's current ventures.

Comprehensive Child Development Program (CCDP) The CCDP program is part of Head Start's involvement in infant–

toddler programming. The purpose of this effort is to encourage intensive and comprehensive services to enhance the physical, social, emotional, and intellectual development of low-income children from birth to compulsory school age, including the provision of necessary support to their parents and other family members.

Services to infants and young children under this program include the following:

- Health services (including screening and referral)
- Child care that meets state licensing requirements
- Early intervention services
- Nutritional services

Services for parents and other family members are intended to contribute to their children's healthy development. These include the following:

- Prenatal care
- Education in infant and child development
- Health, nutrition, and parenting services
- Assistance in securing adequate income support, health care, nutrition assistance, and housing

As an example, the Toddlers, Infants, Preschoolers, and Parents (TIPP) project in Dade County, Florida, provides these services in a combined home/center model through four components: the Children's Center, which provides child development and child care; the Family Enrichment Center, which provides parenting skills, education, and training and employment; the Health Station, which furnishes health and nutrition services; and the Family Partners program, which engages in family advocacy.

Family Literacy　Historically, Head Start has been concerned about issues of family literacy, striving to increase family self-sufficiency and enable children to better benefit from educational and developmental opportunities. Head Start has set the following objectives:[20]

- Exploration of the literacy needs of Head Start families: determining the families' levels of economic self-sufficiency and previous experience with literacy/adult education programs;

- Dissemination of information on existing literacy programs to include a comprehensive listing of state and regional literacy volunteer programs, as well as descriptions of collaboration between Head Start programs and family literacy projects; and

- Improvement of all Head Start programs' capacity to promote family literacy—Head Start must build new resources and strategies and evaluate its contributions to family literacy development. The Head Start Bureau will support training and technical assistance, demonstration, and research/evaluation activities in support of this initiative.

Family literacy programs vary in scope and strategy, but all recognize the impact literacy projects deliver when family needs are addressed.

Head Start Transition Project　In our discussion in previous chapters, we have stressed the readiness goal of Goals 2000, which states that all children shall enter school ready to learn. *Ready to learn,* however, refers to more than children; the new concept also includes schools' readiness to meet the needs of individual children at whatever level they may be, and includes families' abilities to support children's growth and development. All children are ready to

PROGRAM IN ACTION

NEW HORIZONS

Located in rural Macon County, just minutes away from the Great Smoky Mountains, is our New Horizons Center for Children and Families. The foundation for New Horizons is a Head Start program that has expanded to encompass a parent/child center, subsidized daycare, developmental daycare, and Head Start Wraparound services. Built on a longstanding commitment to quality, our Macon Program for Progress Head Start Centers are AA licensed and fully accredited by the National Association for the Education of Young Children (NAEYC).

Head Start performance standards were revised effective January 1998, for the first time in over twenty years. The new standards are based on four cornerstones: child development, family development, community development, and staff development.

Implementing these standards has been a natural occurrence for us because the overall goal for MPP Head Start is *everyday excellence.* This goal is reflected in every aspect of our program, from curriculum development to collaboration with parents.

> *I live in a very rural community with no family here. When the child care center first opened my daughter would not leave my sight. She had no idea how to play with other children. Now she looks forward to her school days more than anything.*
>
> *T. M., parent*

Programs and facilities at New Horizons allow us to care for children ages 6 weeks to 5 years in four centers throughout Macon County. We are open year round with child care available 11 1/2 hours per day. We are fortunate to begin our services with a Head Start funded 0–3 program that allows services to families from pregnancy through age 3, when a child would normally enter Head Start.

Focus on Infant Care and Development

Getting to know, enjoy, and care for each child on an individual basis is the curriculum for our 0–3 program. Caring for infants under the age of 12 months is more than bottles and diapers. Our teachers realize that they play an important role in the valuable learning experiences infants undergo in the first year of life.

Each infant has a primary caregiver. The selection of a primary caregiver is not necessarily by assignment. We find that personalities draw caregivers to infants.

We believe that the foundations of creativity develop in the early months of infant growth and are affected by the caregiver–child relationship. For example, it is very important for babies to feel good about themselves and things they are learning. We are excited about the things our babies accomplish. We praise them for pulling up, crawling, waving, smiling, and any number of small accomplishments they make during the day. Babies thrive on the attention and look to the caregivers for their approval. They learn they can make things happen and are delighted that the teacher is excited about it, too!

The environmental considerations that we use to support individual development for infants are attachment, trust, mobility, senses, language, and health/safety.

- *Attachment* is a necessity for development and learning to occur. Comfortable chairs and floor areas encourage one-to-one interaction with babies and encourage attachment. Small group size and low teacher–child ratios also help promote attachment as teachers interpret and meet the diverse needs of each infant.
- *Trust* is developed by the familiarity of the environment and by association with the same small group and with the same caregiver. A trusting relationship between child and caregiver is necessary for exploration and learning to occur. Additionally, predictable and consistent routines are used to nurture and create a feeling of security.

- *Mobility* is encouraged by allowing babies to play freely on the floor and by protecting less mobile babies with soft barriers.
- *Senses* are stimulated with colorful and soft, safe toys. Care is taken to prepare the environment to avoid sensory overload.
- *Language development* is fostered by songs and rhythm, interesting objects, views outside, pictures, and experiences where adults talk to infants. We recognize that before babies talk they do a lot of listening. We also do a lot of listening. We listen to the sounds and observe the body language of our infants and put into words what we perceive our infants are doing or thinking.
- *Health and safety* awareness by all staff members is habit. We respect infants' knowing what they need so we provide a safe environment for their natural development. And, since we mainstream children with disabilities throughout the entire center, it is not unusual to have a baby with a heart monitor or other equipment. Differences in the needs of our children is embraced as a natural part of life.

Supporting Parents and Parenting Needs

We recognize and encourage the fact that the parent is the best teacher in the child's life. Relationships are more intense with parents of infants than with older children. A deeper level of trust is involved and teachers have a more intimate relationship with their baby than they do with their older children. It is imperative that we communicate in a collaborative manner with parents rather than take the role of the expert. Feeding schedules, for example, are completed and updated by the parent or guardian stating foods to be given along with preferred times and amounts. A daily feeding record is kept for each child along with times of diaper changes. Notations of a child's activities for the day are also recorded. The collaboration with parents comes with a commitment on our part to create and maintain effective communication and good relationships with parents.

> *As a junior in high school, I realized I was pregnant with my first child. Being only 16, I was literally scared to death. This is when a lady from a program called PCC at New Horizons came to me. She told me PCC was a place for young mothers to get together and do activities. At first I was hesitant to go because I did not know what being a mother was all about. I started going and it was wonderful.*
>
> *P. E., parent*

Classes are offered daily for parents, staff, and community members. These include studies for GED, Early Childhood AA, Child Development Associate, computer fundamentals, parenting, and all Head Start In-service. On-site instruction via Community Link with community colleges and Information Highway (Internet) distance learning are all utilized in collaboration with agencies throughout North Carolina.

> *When I first moved to North Carolina, I enrolled my child in New Horizons Head Start. I had no idea just how much that would help me. The staff at New Horizons encouraged me to get my GED. I was an eighth grade dropout due to pregnancy and lack of child care. I thought I would never receive a good education. I received my GED and it gave me a lot of self-confidence. I then enrolled in community college.*
>
> *I. K., parent*

Another beneficial part of our program is that family counselors are available to parents and staff throughout the day and early evening. This allows support for families juggling multiple schedules and pressures. The family counselors observe children, answer parent questions, facilitate patenting classes, provide individual counsel-

continued

ing, and become objective listeners when families are embarrassed or afraid to tell their child's caregiver about such things as their child sleeping in their bed or having temper tantrums at home.

> New Horizons has helped me by showing me how to learn and do lots of different things. One thing is how to handle kids better, like if I was watching them at my house and needed to use the right kind of punishment. You put them in time-out for a few minutes. If you do it that way, it will show them that you have to be nice instead of mean.
>
> T. B., parent

In looking forward to the future of child care, we will continue to offer flexibility and understanding toward families and their ever-changing needs. Our staff will always strive to support families by recognizing that we need to do the following:

- Remember to go slow; develop a one-on-one relationship with each child (at the child's own pace) and with each family as parents and children learn to trust us.
- Realize that infants are at the beginning of learning that will last a lifetime and that they will build their understanding about life and learning through their initial relationships with us.
- Always consider that relationships with parents, children, and other staff members are important. Effective daily communication with each is the key to *everyday excellence.*

Contributed by Betty De Pina, parent/child coordinator, and Sharon Franklin, lead teacher, 0–3 classrooms, New Horizons Center for Children and Families, Macon County, NC.

learn provided they are in good health and come from a stable, nurturing, encouraging home.

Early childhood programs including Head Start must provide a range of learning opportunities to meet the differences in children's functional levels, deliver services to families that help them provide a nurturing environment that enhances children's development, and enable parents to participate as full partners in the education of their children. Such a goal requires a comprehensive, interactive process that extends through the early childhood years. The purposes of this transition project are as follows:[21]

- To develop successful strategies where Head Start programs, parents, local education agencies, and other community agencies join together in a collaborative effort to plan and implement a coordinated and continuous program of comprehensive services to low-income children and their families beginning in Head Start and continuing through kindergarten and the first grades of public school;

- To test the hypothesis that the provision of these continuous comprehensive services will maintain and enhance the early benefits attained by Head Start children and their families; and

- To determine the impact on children and families when comprehensive Head Start–like services are delivered over a period of time after the child has entered elementary school.

Early Head Start   EHS is designed to enhance children's physical, social, emotional, and intellectual development; support both parents in fulfilling their parental roles; and help parents move toward economic independence. Programs are expected to offer certain core services, including high-quality early education (both in and out of the home) and family support services; home visits; parent education; comprehensive health and mental health services, including services for women prior to, during, and after pregnancy; nutrition; and child care. EHS programs have the flexibility to respond to the unique strengths and needs of their own communities and of each child and family within that community.

Among the program options are family child care, center-based care, and home visits. Several projects use combinations of these models. In response to specific needs identified in their communities, some projects emphasize certain program components such as services for teen parents, family literacy, life skills development, substance abuse treatment, and injury and accident prevention. All projects work with community partners to assure early, continuous, and comprehensive services.[22]

Migrant Head Start At present, Migrant Head Start programs in 34 states enroll more than 35,000 children annually, of whom 41 percent, or approximately 14,350 children, are ages birth through three years. Program operations, including the location of center sites, and the length of operating periods (ranging from six weeks to nine months) are guided by the locations and times of seasonal agricultural work. To accommodate the needs of migrant families, centers usually operate five to seven days per week and ten to twelve hours per day.[23]

Substance Abuse Prevention Curriculum The Head Start Bureau has issued a publication, the *Head Start Substance Abuse Guide,* a resource book for Head Start grantees and other collaborating community programs. The guide helps grantees plan and

carry out effective substance abuse strategies that will assist them in meeting the needs of their staff, families, and children. Head Start staff increasingly recognizes substance abuse as a problem affecting children and families in their communities.

Specific substance abuse strategies should accomplish the following goals:[24]

- Strengthen staff capacity to respond to families who are involved with abuse of alcohol or drugs or who are vulnerable to involvement.

- Identify families vulnerable to or involved with substances.

- Help families receive sufficient and effective services from their communities.

- Assist families in supporting and nurturing their children.

- Make families aware of the health consequences associated with the abuse of substances.

- Provide extra support for children whose lives are affected by a family member's involvement with alcohol or drugs.

Head Start programs play a major role in substance abuse prevention by doing the following:[25]

- Offering prevention activities for families and staff;

- Providing substance abuse information and education for family members and staff;

- Developing formal ties with relevant agencies in the community so that substance abuse resources and referrals will be available for families who need them;

- Providing a warm and supportive environment in which staff, adult family members, and children feel comfortable acknowledging and addressing a problem with substance abuse;

- Adapting classroom curricula and resources to meet the special needs of children who demonstrate the harmful effects of exposure to alcohol or drugs, whether prenatally or from current family situations; and

- Working with other community-based programs to reduce the violence and family stress associated with drugs.

Head Start and the Homeless   Homelessness among families and children is on the rise (see Chap. 13), and Head Start agencies are responding. More than 541 grantees are serving homeless children in some capacity. Head Start programs relate that homeless children have one or more of the following characteristics: developmental delays; poor self-esteem; anxieties around food and possessions; overly compliant behavior with any adult person, which thus makes the child vulnerable to abuse; overly aware of parental responsibilities and problems; depression; and abnormal reactions to change. Also, homeless children are more likely to be in ill health and underimmunized.

In an effort to adapt to the needs of homeless families, the Head Start Bureau recommends that programs consider the following:

- Strong support for the staff. *Promote achievable goals, providing each child and parent with positive experiences and training and support for staff.*
- Strong mental health component. *Have available the services of a mental health professional who can address the needs of staff, parents, and children to help lessen staff burnout and better serve children and families.*
- A safe, reassuring environment through a structured daily environment. *Reduce lev-els of stimulation; maintain a simple schedule so each child knows what to expect; limit choices (not quantities) of toys and activities; plan for smaller class sizes; use more volunteers sensitive to the needs of homeless children.*
- Flexibility. *Help staff deal with children leaving unexpectedly. The Berkeley, Massachusetts, Head Start program has developed a special good-bye routine that includes a song, book, and discussion to help the children understand the process. Also, operate some classrooms in which all children are homeless; the days and hours of operation should be tailored to meet their specific needs. A Washington, D.C., Head Start program found that having early morning programs did not work for homeless families. Because of the active night life of the motel where they were housed, the morning hours were typically the time the children slept.*
- Transportation. *Help ensure access to the program, particularly if the family is moved around in search of permanent housing.*
- Collaboration with the community. *Cooperate with other community and state agencies; Head Start cannot address all the problems of the homeless.*
- Parental responsibilities/involvement. *Focus and build on the family's strengths, and enable parents to build their capacity to cope with their life stresses; emphasize to parents the importance of their participation, which will enable them to better nurture and protect their children in areas such as health, nutrition, and education.*
- Make health screening a priority for homeless families. *Refer the family as soon as they are enrolled to a local provider for medical appointments, and provide transportation.*
- Plan a mixed classroom. *Have both homeless and non-homeless children in the classroom to provide some stability to the program and contribute to everyone's opportunity to learn.*[26]

Family Service Centers Head Start has awarded grants to forty-one programs in order to demonstrate ways its programs can work with other community agencies and organizations to deal effectively with the problems of substance abuse, illiteracy, and unemployment among Head Start families. The demonstration projects encourage families to participate in activities designed to do the following:[27]

- Reduce and prevent the incidence of substance abuse in Head Start families;

- Improve the literacy of parents and other adults in Head Start families; and

- Increase the employability of Head Start parents.

IS HEAD START EFFECTIVE?

No question in early childhood education has been debated, discussed, considered, and examined more than whether Head Start makes a difference in children's lives. To the question "What do we know so far about Head Start?" Schweinhart and Weikart respond:

- *Short-, mid-, and long-term positive effects are available.*
- *Adequately funded Head Start programs run by well-trained, competent staff can achieve the level of quality operation that will lead to positive effects.*
- *Equal educational opportunity for all people is a fundamental goal of the great American experiment and good Head Start programs can make a sound contribution to the achievement of the goal.*[28]

Additionally, in a study of children attending Head Start with other children, researchers reached the following conclusions:

As a result of these analyses, we may conclude that participation in Head Start appeared to pro-vide significant one-year gains on some measures of ability for low-income children. These gains, which could reasonably be attributed to children's participation in the Head Start program, were considerably more likely to accrue to Black children than to White children. Moreover, among Black children cognitive gains attributable to Head Start participation were more likely to occur in children with lower initial cognitive ability. It is important that the significant "Head Start advantage" was found in analytical designs that either controlled for test-specific ability or for general ability assessed at program entry, contrasting Head Start children with children of statistically comparable backgrounds who either had no preschool experience or who attended a non–Head Start preschool. Although the advantage of Head Start participation was clearer compared with no preschool experience, we conclude that there is evidence to support the superiority of Head Start over other preschool experience as well.[29]

One of the criticisms of Head Start is that the gains children make soon "fade out," generally by third grade. Barnett analyzed studies of Head Start's effectiveness and came to this conclusion: "In sum, there is considerable evidence that preschool programs of many types—including Head Start—have persistent effects on academic ability and success. There is no convincing evidence that these effects decline over time."[30]

What would seem to be important as Head Start expands its programs over the next decade is that it strives to offer quality programs for children and families. As such, it should focus on strengthening its educational component, continuing to involve parents in all the components, assuring staff are well prepared and trained, and providing a full range of comprehensive services for children and families.

What we must acknowledge is that the ability of Head Start to influence early childhood practice and make a difference in the lives of children and families is well established. Head Start is one of the most influential educational programs this country has ever had. This influence will likely continue and, in the process, empower families, communities, and professionals for the challenges of providing quality programs in the twenty-first century.

Head Start in the Twenty-First Century

The National Head Start Association (1651 Prince Street, Alexandria, VA 22314) created an advisory committee on Head Start Quality and Expansion to make recommendations for improving Head Start as it moves into the 21st century. The advisory committee has these recommendations for improving Head Start:

As the Advisory Committee looks forward to the next century, we envision an expanded and renewed Head Start which serves as a central community institution for low-income children and their families. The Head Start of the 21st century:

- *Ensures quality and strives to attain excellence in every local program;*
- *Responds flexibly to the needs of today's children and families, including those currently unserved; and*
- *Forges new partnerships at the community, state and federal levels, renewing and recrafting these partnerships to fit the changes in families, communities, and state and national policy.*

In order to respond to these issues, and to create 21st century Head Start, the Advisory Committee sets forth a set of recommendations to the federal government, Head Start providers, and the nation at large. These recommendations implement three broad principles:

1. *We must ensure that every Head Start program can deliver on Head Start's vision, by striving for excellence in serving both children and families.*

   The Advisory Committee believes that the quality of services must be a first priority. We should strive for excellence in

all Head Start programs by focusing on staffing and career development, improving the management of local programs, reengineering federal oversight to assure accountability, providing better facilities, and strengthening the role of research.

2. *We must expand the number of children served and the scope of services provided in a way that is more responsive to the needs of children and families.*

   The Advisory Committee reaffirms the concept that all eligible children in need of Head Start should be served. At the same time the Committee remains committed to investments in quality as a top priority. Head Start should focus on the needs of children in the context of their families and communities by enhancing family services and increasing parent involvement, assessing needs and planning strategically, reaching out to children and families currently unserved, promoting full day and full year programs where needed, and improving services to families with younger children.

3. *We must encourage Head Start to forge partnerships with key community and state institutions and programs in early childhood, family support, health, education, and mental health, and we must ensure that these partnerships are constantly renewed and recrafted to fit changes in families, communities, and state and national policies.*

   Because no program, no matter how excellent, can go it alone, we must ensure that Head Start join forces with other providers in the community and state. As a partner, Head Start can not only maximize its own resources, but can use its leadership to influence other service providers to adopt the core concepts that have made Head Start such a success.

Head Start and public schools should renew commitments to ensure continuity of services by providing developmentally appropriate programs, parent involvement, and supportive services from Head Start through the primary grades.[31]

OTHER FEDERAL PROGRAMS

In addition to Head Start, the federal government plays a major role in funding other programs that involve and affect young children and their families.

Even Start

The Even Start Family Literacy Program combines adult literacy and parenting training with early childhood education in order to break cycles of illiteracy that are often passed on from one generation to another. Even Start is authorized by Part B of Chapter 1 of Title 1 of the Elementary and Secondary Education Act Reauthorization of 1988, as amended by the National Literacy Act of 1991.

Even Start, operated through the public school system, provides family-centered education projects to help parents become full partners in the education of their children, assist children in reaching their full potential, and provide literacy training for parents. Projects are aimed at building on existing community resources to create a new range of services, integrating early childhood education and adult education for parents.

Even Start helps states address two of the Goals 2000 (see Chap. 2). Goal 1 calls for all children in the United States to start school ready to learn. An important objective of this goal is for every parent to be their child's first teacher by devoting time each day to help him or her learn.

Goal 5 is that every adult American will be literate, will possess the knowledge and skills necessary to compete in a global economy, and will exercise the rights and responsibilities of citizenship.

The following are eligible as participants for Even Start:

- *A parent of a child age birth through age seven if the parent is eligible for participa-*

tion in an adult education program under the Adult Education Act; and

- *A child from birth through age seven who is the child of an eligible parent and who resides in an elementary school attendance area designated for participation in programs under Chapter 1.*[32]

Children participating must take part in early childhood activities, and participating parents must take part in adult literacy activities, including activities in which the parents and children are involved together.

Even Start funding is comprised of federal funds and a required local share. Current Even Start funding is about $110 miillion. In the first year of the project, at least 10 percent of the total cost of the project must be funded at the local level. Local funding increases 10 percent per year for three additional years, to a maximum of 40 percent of the total project cost after four years.

For example, the School District of Leon County, Florida, is collaborating with Florida First Start (a health program for children and families), Head Start, and many community-based organizations to establish five Family Resource Centers. Four of these centers are located in trailers at public school sites; one is at a housing complex.

Twice a month parents and children ride the bus to the resource site. During the morning, parents work with their children on early childhood activities, children return to their class for lunch, and parents attend their adult education classes and receive support services.

The support services for families include home visits focusing on parent–child activities, family activity nights, field trips, and special programs. The Parent Resource Center has books, toys, games, and materials for loan to families enrolled in the program.

The community offers a myriad of resources for the program. Child Care of South Florida helps with identification and recruitment of families as well as providing extended day activities for children. The Lee County Library, Lee County Literacy Council, and literacy volunteers of Lee County train volunteers and tutors. The Lee County School District's Vocational Adult and Community Education Program provides teachers for parents, adult learning materials, and training for parents, teachers, and volunteers. Technical assistance and program evaluation is provided by the University of South Florida.

Child Care

The federal government is one of the largest supporters of child care (see Chap. 14). The government allocates monies to the states to provide child care services to parents who are undergoing job training as a means of getting off welfare or becoming ready to work.

A second source of federal support for child care is the U.S. Department of Agriculture (USDA) Child Care Food Program. The USDA gives monies and commodities to child care centers and homes to support their nutrition programs. Children twelve years old and younger are eligible for support. The USDA provided over $700 million for the food program in fiscal 1996.

A third source is child care tax credits. Since 1975, parents can itemize the cost of child care as a deduction against their federal income taxes. Currently, the amount that can be deducted is based on a sliding scale. (See Chap. 14 for an application of the scale.)

A fourth federal support for child care is employer support or employer sponsorship. The federal tax code allows employers certain tax breaks or benefits for providing child care for employees.

A fifth source comes through the government's role as an employer. Many federal agencies, including the CIA and the Internal Revenue Service, provide child care services

for employees. Remember also the federal government's role in supporting military child care (see Chap. 14).

The federal government will continue to play an influential role in all of education, ranging from services to pregnant women to higher education. While some people criticize the federal presence, which they see as control, others believe that without even greater federal support, issues of equality and quality cannot be adequately addressed.

Regardless, the federal government will continue to play a dominant role in deciding who gets what kind of services. The challenge for early childhood professionals is to serve as advocates on behalf of children and their families and to influence federal policy so that programs, services, and monies are put to their best use.

ACTIVITIES FOR FURTHER ENRICHMENT

1. Accompany a Head Start home visitor on a home visit. Describe how home environments influence children's learning abilities.

2. Explain why you think Head Start and other programs are emphasizing a two-generation approach to the delivery of services. What are the pros and cons of such a delivery system?

3. Interview parents of Head Start children to find out what they feel has been the impact of Head Start on their family.

4. Visit a local school district and gather information about its federally supported programs. What kind of federal education programs does the district have? How is the money spent? Do you approve or disapprove of what you saw?

5. Visit several Head Start programs and compare and contrast what you see. How are they similar and different? How do you account for this?

6. Compare the schedule of the Kentucky Head Start center in this chapter with a Head Start center in your community. Compare these schedules to those of a local preschool. What would you change? Be specific, and include your reasons.

7. Develop a list of pros and cons for involving parents in early childhood programs. What implications does this list have for teachers of young children? For Head Start programs? How do you feel about parent involvement in early childhood programs?

8. Develop a questionnaire you could give to parents to find out their needs and ideas about home-based and center-based early childhood programs. Which do they prefer? Why?

9. Develop a set of criteria for deciding which families would be eligible for a home-based education program.

10. Conduct a poll of parents to find out how they think early childhood programs and schools can help them in educating their children, how they think they can be involved in early childhood programs, what specific help they feel they need in childrearing and educating, and what activities they would like in a home visitation program.

11. Contact the migrant education office in your area. What are the occupations of migrant parents? What are the major problems faced by these families? What services are being provided for them? Do you think the services to migrants are as effective and comprehensive as they should be?

12. Articulate the pros and cons of why you would or would not want to teach in a Head Start, Even Start, or other federally funded program.

READINGS FOR FURTHER ENRICHMENT

Beaty, Janice J. *Skills for Preschool Teachers*, 4th ed. (Upper Saddle River, NJ: Merrill/Prentice Hall, 1994).

Designed specifically for the Head Start, daycare, and kindergarten worker, this book parallels the Child Development Associate Competencies; helpful for anyone contemplating this training program.

Zigler, Edward, and Susan Muenchow. *Head Start: The Inside Story of America's Most Successful Educational Experiment* (New York: Basic Books, 1992).

An interesting, behind-the-scenes account of the beginning and survival of Head Start. The authors draw on the lessons of Head Start to address some of today's most crucial and controversial lessons in education. They advocate that two of Head Start's most successful components, parent involvement and comprehensive services, be included in all early childhood programs.

Zigler, Edward, and Sally J. Styfco, eds. *Head Start and Beyond: A National Plan for Extended Childhood Intervention* (New Haven, CT: Yale University Press, 1993).

Zigler, one of the architects of Head Start, calls for combining that program with two other government-funded early childhood programs, Chapter 1 and Follow Through, which he says would result in more coordinated and cost-effective services for preschool and early elementary grade students.

NOTES

1. Esther Kresh, *National Head Start Bulletin* 28 (May 1989), p. 9.
2. Administration on Children, Youth, and Families, *Project Head Start Statistical Fact Sheet* (Washington, D.C.: Author, May, 1996), pp. 1–3.
3. U.S. Department of Health and Human Services, *Head Start Program Performance Standards* (45 CFR §1304) (Washington, D.C.: U.S. Government Printing Office, November 1984), p. 4.
4. *Federal Register,* vol. 61, no. 215 (1996), p. 57219.
5. Dennis Gray, *National Head Start Bulletin,* 60, p. 12.

6. E. Dollie Wolverton, "The Home-Based Option: Reinforcing Parents," *National Head Start Bulletin* 12, p. 1.

7. Phone interview with author.

8. *Federal Register,* vol. 61, no. 215 (1996), p. 57213.

9. Ibid.

10. Ibid., p. 57214.

11. Schedule from Audubon Head Start, Owensboro, Kentucky.

12. *Head Start Program Performance Standards,* pp. 8–9.

13. Linda Likins, *National Head Start Bulletin* 40, p. 9.

14. *Federal Register,* vol. 61, no. 215 (1996), p. 57212.

15. Ibid., pp. 57214–15.

16. Ibid., p. 57215.

17. Ibid.

18. Ibid., p. 57216.

19. bid., p. 57218.

20. Clennie H. Murphy, Jr., "A Commitment to Family Literacy," *National Head Start Bulletin* 30, p. 1.

21. *Federal Register,* vol. 56, no. 133 (1991), p. 318.

22. *National Head Start Bulletin* 57, p. 5.

23. Sherrie Rudick, *National Head Start Bulletin* 57, p. 8.

24. Raymond C. Collins and Penny R. Anderson, *Head Start Substance Abuse Guide: A Resource Handbook for Head Start Grantees and Other Collaborating Community Programs* (Washington, D.C.: U.S. Department of Health and Human Services, Administration on Children, Youth and Families, Head Start Bureau, January 1991), p. 4.

25. Ibid., p. 5.

26. *Federal Register*, vol. 57, no. 119 (1992), p. 27572-80.

27. U.S. Department of Health and Human Services, Administration on Children, Youth and Families, Head Start Bureau, *Head Start: A Child Development Program* (Washington, D.C.: Author, n.d.).

28. Lawrence J. Schweinhart and David P. Weikart, "What Do We Know So Far? A Review of the Head Start Synthesis Project," *Young Children* 41(2), p. 50.

29. Valerie E. Lee, J. Brooks-Gunn, and Elizabeth Schnur, "Does Head Start Work? A 1-Year Follow-Up Comparison of Disadvantaged Children Attending Head Start, No Preschool, and Other Preschool Programs," *Developmental Psychology* 24(2), pp. 210–22.

30. Steve Barnett, "Does Head Start Fade Out?" Education Week, 19 May 1993, p. 40.

31. *Creating a 21st Century Head Start: Final Report of the Advisory Committee on Head Start Quality and Expansion* (Washington, D.C.: U.S. Dept. of Health and Human Services, 1996).

32. *Federal Register* 57, no. 119 (1992), p. 56230.

The NAEYC Code of Ethical Conduct

Preamble

NAEYC recognizes that many daily decisions required of those who work with young children are of a moral and ethical nature. The NAEYC Code of Ethical Conduct offers guidelines for responsible behavior and sets forth a common basis for resolving the principal ethical dilemmas encountered in early childhood education. The primary focus is on daily practice with children and their families in programs for children from birth to eight years of age: preschools, child care centers, family day care homes, kindergartens, and primary classrooms. Many of the provisions also apply to specialists who do not work directly with children, including program administrators, parent educators, college professors, and child care licensing specialists.

Standards of ethical behavior in early childhood education are based on commitment to core values that are deeply rooted in the history of our field. We have committed ourselves to:

Appreciating childhood as a unique and valuable stage of the human life cycle

Basing our work with children on knowledge of child development

Appreciating and supporting the close ties between the child and family

Recognizing that children are best understood in the context of family, culture, and society

Respecting the dignity, worth, and uniqueness of each individual (child, family member, and colleague)

Helping children and adults achieve their full potential in the context of relationships that are based on trust, respect, and positive regard

The Code sets forth a conception of our professional responsibilities in four sections, each addressing an arena of professional relationships: (1) children, (2) families, (3) colleagues, and (4) community and society. Each section includes an introduction to the primary responsibilities of the early childhood practitioner in that arena, a set of ideals pointing in the direction of exemplary professional practice, and a set of principles defining practices that are required, prohibited, and permitted.

The ideals reflect the aspirations of practitioners. The principles are intended to guide conduct and assist practitioners in resolving ethical dilemmas encountered in the field. There is not necessarily a corresponding principle for each ideal. Both ideals and principles are intended to direct practitioners to those questions which, when responsibly answered, will provide the basis for conscientious decision making. While the Code provides specific direction for addressing some ethical dilemmas, many others will require the practitioner to combine the guidance of the Code with sound professional judgment.

Source: Code of Ethical Conduct and Statement of Commitment by S. Feeney and K. Kipnis. Copyright © 1992 by the National Association for the Education of Young Children. Reprinted by permission from the National Association for the Education of Young Children.

The ideals and principles in this Code present a shared conception of professional responsibility that affirms our commitment to the core values of our field. The Code publicly acknowledges the responsibilities that we in the field have assumed and in so doing supports ethical behavior in our work. Practitioners who face ethical dilemmas are urged to seek guidance in the applicable parts of this Code and in the spirit that informs the whole.

Section I: Ethical Responsibilities to Children

Childhood is a unique and valuable stage in the life cycle. Our paramount responsibility is to provide safe, healthy, nurturing, and responsive settings for children. We are committed to supporting children's development by cherishing individual differences, by helping them learn to live and work cooperatively, and by promoting their self-esteem.

Ideals

I–1.1 To be familiar with the knowledge base of early childhood education and to keep current through continuing education and in-service training.

I–1.2 To base program practices upon current knowledge in the field of child development and related disciplines and upon particular knowledge of each child.

I–1.3 To recognize and respect the uniqueness and the potential of each child.

I–1.4 To appreciate the special vulnerability of children.

I–1.5 To create and maintain safe and healthy settings that foster children's social, emotional, intellectual, and physical development and that respect their dignity and their contributions.

I–1.6 To support the right of children with special needs to participate, consistent with their ability, in regular childhood programs.

Principles

P–1.1 Above all, we shall not harm children. We shall not participate in practices that are disrespectful, degrading, dangerous, exploitative, intimidating, psychologically damaging, or physically harmful to children. *This principle has precedence over all others in this Code.*

P–1.2 We shall not participate in practices that discriminate against children by denying benefits, giving special advantages, or excluding them from programs or activities on the basis of their race, religion, sex, national origin, or the status, behavior, or beliefs of their parents. (This principle does not apply to programs that have a lawful mandate to provide services to a particular population of children.)

P–1.3 We shall involve all of those with relevant knowledge (including staff and parents) in decisions concerning a child.

P–1.4 When, after appropriate efforts have been made with a child and the family, the child still does not appear to be benefitting from a program, we shall communicate our concern to the family in a positive way and offer them assistance in finding a more suitable setting.

P–1.5 We shall be familiar with the symptoms of child abuse and neglect and know and follow community procedures and state laws that protect children against abuse and neglect.

P–1.6 When we have evidence of child abuse or neglect, we shall report the evidence to the appropriate community agency and follow up to ensure that appropriate action has been taken. When possible, parents will be informed that the referral has been made.

P–1.7 When another person tells us of their suspicion that a child is being abused or neglected but we lack evidence, we shall assist that person in taking appropriate action to protect the child.

P–1.8 When a child protective agency fails to provide adequate protection for abused or neglected children, we acknowledge a collective ethical responsibility to work toward improvement of these services.

P–1.9 When we become aware of a practice or situation that endangers the health or safety of children, but has not been previously known to do so, we have an ethical responsibility to inform those who can remedy the situation and who can keep other children from being similarly endangered.

Section II: Ethical Responsibilities to Families

Families are of primary importance in children's development. (The term *family* may include others, besides parents, who are responsibly involved with the child.) Because the family and the early childhood educator have a common interest in the child's welfare, we acknowledge a primary responsibility to bring about collaboration between the home and school in ways that enhance the child's development.

Ideals

I–2.1 To develop relationships of mutual trust with the families we serve.

I–2.2 To acknowledge and build upon strengths and competencies as we support families in their task of nurturing children.

I–2.3 To respect the dignity of each family and its culture, customs, and beliefs.

I–2.4 To respect families' childrearing values and their right to make decisions for their children.

I–2.5 To interpret each child's progress to parents within the framework of a developmental perspective and to help families understand and appreciate the value of developmentally appropriate early childhood programs.

I–2.6 To help family members improve their understanding of their children and to enhance their skills as parents.

I–2.7 To participate in building support networks for families by providing them with opportunities to interact with program staff and families.

Principles

P–2.1 We shall not deny family members access to their child's classroom or program setting.

P–2.2 We shall inform families of program philosophy, policies, and personnel qualifications, and explain why we teach as we do.

P–2.3 We shall inform families of and, when appropriate, involve them in policy decisions.

P–2.4 We shall inform families of and, when appropriate, involve them in significant decisions affecting their child.

P–2.5 We shall inform the family of accidents involving their child, of risks such as exposures to contagious disease that may result in infection, and of events that might result in psychological damage.

P–2.6 We shall not permit or participate in research that could in any way hinder the education or development of the children in our programs. Families shall be fully informed of any proposed research projects involving their children and shall have the opportunity to give or withhold consent.

P–2.7 We shall not engage in or support exploitation of families. We shall not use our relationship with a family for private advantage or personal gain, or enter into relationships with family members that might impair our effectiveness in working with children.

P–2.8 We shall develop written policies for the protection of confidentiality and the disclosure of children's records. The policy documents shall be made available to all program personnel and families. Disclosure of children's records beyond family members, program personnel, and consultants having an obligation of confidentiality shall require familial consent (except in cases of abuse or neglect).

P–2.9 We shall maintain confidentiality and shall respect the family's right to privacy, refraining from disclosure of confidential information and intrusion into family life. However, when we are concerned about a child's welfare, it is permissible to reveal confidential information to agencies and individuals who may be able to act in the child's interest.

P–2.10 In cases where family members are in conflict we shall work openly, sharing our observations of the child, to help all parties involved make informed decisions. We shall refrain from becoming an advocate for one party.

P–2.11 We shall be familiar with and appropriately use community resources and professional services that support families. After a referral has been made, we shall follow up to ensure that services have been adequately provided.

Section III: Ethical Responsibilities to Colleagues

In a caring, cooperative work place human dignity is respected, professional satisfaction is promoted, and positive relationships are modeled. Our primary responsibility in this arena is to establish and maintain settings and relationships that support productive work and meet professional needs.

A—Responsibilities to Co-workers: Ideals
I–3A.1 To establish and maintain relationships of trust and cooperation with co-workers.

I–3A.2 To share resources and information with co-workers.

I–3A.3 To support co-workers in meeting their professional needs and in their professional development.

I–3A.4 To accord co-workers due recognition of professional achievement.

Principles
P–3A.1 When we have concern about the professional behavior of a co-worker, we shall first let that person know of our concern and attempt to resolve the matter collegially.

P–3A.2 We shall exercise care in expressing views regarding the personal attributes or professional conduct of co-workers. Statements should be based on firsthand knowledge and relevant to the interests of children and programs.

B—Responsibilities to Employers: Ideals
I–3B.1 To assist the program in providing the highest quality of service.

I–3B.2 To maintain loyalty to the program and uphold its reputation.

Principles
P–3B.1 When we do not agree with program policies, we shall first attempt to effect change through constructive action within the organization.

P–3B.2 We shall speak or act on behalf of an organization only when authorized. We shall take care to note when we are speaking for the organization and when we are expressing a personal judgment.

C—Responsibilities to Employees: Ideals
I–3C.1 To promote policies and working conditions that foster competence, well-being, and self-esteem in staff members.

I–3C.2 To create a climate of trust and candor that will enable staff to speak and act in the best interests of children, families, and the field of early childhood education.

I–3C.3 To strive to secure an adequate livelihood for those who work with or on behalf of young children.

Principles
P–3C.1 In decisions concerning children and programs, we shall appropriately utilize the training, experience, and expertise of staff members.

P–3C.2 We shall provide staff members with working conditions that permit them to carry out their responsibilities, timely and nonthreatening evaluation procedures, written grievance procedures, constructive feedback, and opportunities for continuing professional development and advancement.

P–3C.3 We shall develop and maintain comprehensive written personnel policies that define program standards and, when applicable, that specify the extent to which employees are accountable for their conduct outside the work place. These policies shall be given to new staff members and shall be available for review by all staff members.

P–3C.4 Employees who do not meet program standards shall be informed of areas of concern and, when possible, assisted in improving their performance.

P–3C.5 Employees who are dismissed shall be informed of the reasons for the termination. When a dismissal is for cause, justification must be based on evidence of inadequate or inappropriate behavior that is accurately documented, current, and available for the employee to review.

P–3C.6 In making evaluations and recommendations, judgments shall be based on fact and relevant to the interests of children and programs.

P–3C.7 Hiring and promotion shall be based solely on a person's record of accomplishment and ability to carry out the responsibilities of the position.

P–3C.8 In hiring, promotion, and provision of training, we shall not participate in any form of discrimination based on race, religion, sex, national origin, handicap, age, or sexual preference. We shall be familiar with laws and regulations that pertain to employment discrimination.

Section IV: Ethical Responsibilities to Community and Society

Early childhood programs operate within a context of an immediate community made up of families and other institutions concerned with children's welfare. Our responsibilities to the community are to provide programs that meet its needs and to cooperate with agencies and professions that share responsibility for children. Because the larger society has a measure of responsibility for the welfare and protection of children, and because of our specialized expertise in child development, we acknowledge an obligation to serve as a voice for children everywhere.

Ideals
I–4.1 To provide the community with high-quality, culturally sensitive programs and services.

I–4.2 To promote cooperation among agencies and professions concerned with the welfare of young children, their families, and their teachers.

I–4.3 To work, through education, research, and advocacy, toward an environmentally safe world in which all children are adequately fed, sheltered, and nurtured.

I–4.4 To work, through education, research, and advocacy, toward a society in which all young children have access to quality programs.

I–4.5 To promote knowledge and understanding of young children and their needs. To work toward greater social acknowledgement of children's rights and greater social acceptance of responsibility for their well-being.

I–4.6 To support policies and laws that promote the well-being of children and families. To oppose those that impair their well-being. To cooperate with other individuals and groups in these efforts.

I–4.7 To further the professional development of the field of early childhood education and to strengthen its commitment to realizing its core values as reflected in this Code.

Principles

P–4.1 We shall communicate openly and truthfully about the nature and extent of services that we provide.

P–4.2 We shall not accept or continue to work in positions for which we are personally unsuited or professionally unqualified. We shall not offer services that we do not have the competence, qualifications, or resources to provide.

P–4.3 We shall be objective and accurate in reporting the knowledge upon which we base our program practices.

P–4.4 We shall cooperate with other professionals who work with children and their families.

P–4.5 We shall not hire or recommend for employment any person who is unsuited for a position with respect to competence, qualifications, or character.

P–4.6 We shall report the unethical or incompetent behavior of a colleague to a supervisor when informal resolution is not effective.

P–4.7 We shall be familiar with laws and regulations that serve to protect the children in our programs.

P–4.8 We shall not participate in practices which are in violation of laws and regulations that protect the children in our programs.

P–4.9 When we have evidence that an early childhood program is violating laws or regulations protecting children, we shall report it to persons responsible for the program. If compliance is not accomplished within a reasonable time, we will report the violation to appropriate authorities who can be expected to remedy the situation.

P-4.10 When we have evidence that an agency or a professional charged with providing services to children, families, or teachers is failing to meet its obligations, we acknowledge a collective ethical responsibility to report the problem to appropriate authorities or to the public.

P–4.11 When a program violates or requires its employees to violate this Code, it is permissible, after fair assessment of the evidence, to disclose the identity of that program.

Highlights of the United Nations Convention on the Rights of the Child

- Every child has the inherent right to life, and States shall ensure, to the maximum, child survival and development.

- Every child has the right to a name and nationality from birth.

- When courts, welfare institutions or administrative authorities deal with children, the child's best interests shall be a primary consideration. The child's opinions shall be given careful consideration.

- States shall ensure that each child enjoys full rights without discrimination or distinctions of any kind.

- Children should not be separated from their parents, unless by competent authorities for their well-being.

- States should facilitate reunification of families by permitting travel into, or out of, their territories.

- Parents have the primary responsibility for a child's upbringing, but States shall provide them with appropriate assistance and develop child-care institutions.

- States shall protect children from physical or mental harm and neglect, including sexual abuse or exploitation.

- States shall provide parentless children with suitable alternative care. The adoption process shall be carefully regulated and international agreements should be sought to provide safeguards and assure legal validity if and when adoptive parents intend to move the child from his or her country of birth.

- Disabled children shall have the right to special treatment, education and care.

- The child is entitled to the highest attainable standard of health. States shall ensure that health care is provided to all children, placing emphasis on preventive measures, health education and reduction of infant mortality.

- Primary education shall be free and compulsory; discipline in schools should respect the child's dignity. Education should prepare the child for life in a spirit of understanding, peace and tolerance.

- Children shall have time to rest and play and equal opportunities for cultural and artistic activities.

- States shall protect the child from economic exploitation and work that may interfere with education or be harmful to health and well-being.

- States shall protect children from the illegal use of drugs and involvement in drug production or trafficking.

- All efforts shall be made to eliminate the abduction and trafficking of children.

- Capital punishment or life imprisonment shall not be imposed for crimes committed before the age of 18.

Source: United Nations, *Convention on the Rights of the Child* (New York: United Nations Department of Public Information, 1993), pp. 4–8. Reprint 24717—May 1993—20M; Publication Source DPI/1101, United Nations. Used by permission.

- Children in detention should be separated from adults; they must not be tortured or suffer cruel and degrading treatment.

- No child under 15 should take any part in hostilities; children exposed to armed conflict shall receive special protection.

- Children of minority and indigenous populations shall freely enjoy their own culture, religion and language.

- Children who have suffered maltreatment, neglect or detention should receive appropriate treatment or training for recovery and rehabilitation.

- Children involved in infringements of the penal law shall be treated in a way that promotes their sense of dignity and worth and that aims at reintegrating them into society.

- States should make the rights in the Convention widely known to both adults and children.

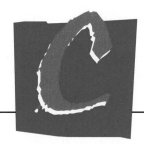

NAEYC Guidelines for Developmentally Appropriate Practice in Early Childhood Programs

This statement defines and describes principles of developmentally appropriate practice in early childhood programs for administrators, teachers, parents, policymakers, and others who make decisions about the care and education of young children. An early childhood program is any group program in a center, school, or other facility that serves children from birth through age 8. Early childhood programs include child care centers, family child care homes, private and public preschools, kindergartens, and primary-grade schools.

The early childhood profession is responsible for establishing and promoting standards of high-quality, professional practice in early childhood programs. These standards must reflect current knowledge and shared beliefs about what constitutes high-quality, developmentally appropriate early childhood education in the context within which services are delivered.

This position paper is organized into several components, which include the following:

1. a description of the current context in which early childhood programs operate;

2. a description of the rationale and need for NAEYC's position statement;

3. a statement of NAEYC's commitment to children;

4. the statement of the position and definition of *developmentally appropriate practice*;

5. a summary of the principles of child development and learning and the theoretical perspectives that inform decisions about early childhood practice;

6. guidelines for making decisions about developmentally appropriate practices that address the following integrated components of early childhood practice: creating a caring community of learners, teaching to enhance children's learning and development, constructing appropriate curriculum, assessing children's learning and development, and establishing reciprocal relationships with families;

7. a challenge to the field to move from *either/or* to *both/and* thinking; and

8. recommendations for policies necessary to ensure developmentally appropriate practices for all children.

This statement is designed to be used in conjunction with NAEYC's "Criteria for High Quality Early Childhood Programs," the standards for accreditation by the National Academy of Early Childhood Programs (NAEYC 1991), and with "Guidelines for Appropriate Curriculum Content and Assessment in Programs Serving Children Ages 3 through 8" (NAEYC & NAECS/SDE 1992; Bredekamp & Rosegrant 1992, 1995).

Source: From "NAEYC Position Statement: Developmentally Appropriate Practice in Early Childhood Programs Serving Children from Birth through Age 8—Adopted July 1996," *Developmentally Appropriate Practice in Early Childhood Programs*, rev. ed., eds. S. Bredekamp & C. Copple (Washington, D.C.: National Association for the Education of Young Children, 1997), pp. 3–30. Copyright by NAEYC.

The Current Context of Early Childhood Programs

The early childhood knowledge base has expanded considerably in recent years, affirming some of the profession's cherished beliefs about good practice and challenging others. In addition to gaining new knowledge, early childhood programs have experienced several important changes in recent years. The number of programs continues to increase not only in response to the growing demand for out-of-home child care but also in recognition of the critical importance of educational experiences during early years (Willer et al. 1991; NCES 1993). For example, in the late 1980s Head Start embarked on the largest expansion in its history, continuing this expansion into the 1990s with significant new services for families with infants and toddlers. The National Education Goals Panel established as an objective of Goal 1 that by the year 2000 all children will have access to high-quality, developmentally appropriate preschool programs (NEGP 1991). Welfare reform portends a greatly increased demand for child care services for even the youngest children from very-low-income families.

Some characteristics of early childhood programs have also changed in recent years. Increasingly, programs serve children and families from diverse cultural and linguistic backgrounds, requiring that all programs demonstrate understanding of and responsiveness to cultural and linguistic diversity. Because culture and language are critical components of children's development, practices cannot be developmentally appropriate unless they are responsive to cultural and linguistic diversity.

The Americans with Disabilities Act and the Individuals with Disabilities Education Act now require that all early childhood programs make reasonable accommodations to provide access for children with disabilities or developmental delays (DEC/CEC & NAEYC 1993).

This legal right reflects the growing consensus that young children with disabilities are best served in the same community settings where their typically developing peers are found (DEC/CEC 1994).

The trend toward full inclusion of children with disabilities must be reflected in descriptions of recommended practices, and considerable work has been done toward converging the perspectives of early childhood and early childhood special education (Carta et al. 1991; Mallory 1992, 1994; Wolery, Strain, & Bailey 1992; Bredekamp 1993b; DEC Task Force 1993; Mallory & New 1994b; Wolery & Wilbers 1994).

Other important program characteristics include age of children and length of program day. Children are now enrolled in programs at younger ages, many from infancy. The length of the program day for all ages of children has been extended in response to the need for extended hours of care for employed families. Similarly, program sponsorship has become more diverse. The public schools in the majority of states now provide prekindergarten programs, some for children as young as 3, and many offer before- and after-school child care (Mitchell, Seligson, & Marx 1989; Seppanen, Kaplan deVries, & Seligson 1993; Adams & Sandfort 1994).

Corporate America has become a more visible sponsor of child care programs, with several key corporations leading the way in promoting high quality (for example, IBM, AT&T, and the American Business Collaboration). Family child care homes have become an increasingly visible sector of the child care community, with greater emphasis on professional development and the National Association for Family Child Care taking the lead in establishing an accreditation system for high-quality family child care (Hollestelle 1993; Cohen & Modigliani 1994; Galinsky et al. 1994). Many different settings in this country provide services to young children, and it is legitimate—even beneficial—for these settings to vary in certain ways. However, since it is vital to meet children's learning and developmental needs wherever they are served, high standards of quality should apply to all settings.

The context in which early childhood programs operate today is also characterized by ongoing debates about how best to teach young children and discussions about what sort of practice is most likely to contribute to their development and learning. Perhaps the most important contribution of NAEYC's 1987 position statement on developmentally appropriate practice (Bredekamp 1987) was that it created an opportunity for increased conversation within and outside the early childhood field about practices. In revising the position statement, NAEYC's goal is not only to improve the quality of current early childhood practice but also to continue to encourage the kind of questioning and debate among early childhood professionals that are necessary for the continued growth of professional knowledge in the field. A related goal is to express NAEYC's position more clearly so that energy is not wasted in unproductive debate about apparent rather that real differences of opinion.

Rationale for the Position Statement

The increased demand for early childhood education services is partly due to the increased recognition of the crucial importance of experiences during the earliest years of life. Children's experiences during early childhood not only influence their later functioning in school but can have effects throughout life. For example, current research demonstrates the early and lasting effects of children's environments and experiences on brain development and cognition (Chugani, Phelps, & Mazziotta 1987; Caine & Caine 1991; Kuhl 1994). Studies show that, "From infancy through about age 10, brain cells not

only form most of the connections they will maintain throughout life but during this time they retain their greatest malleability" (Dana Alliance for Brain Initiatives 1996, 7).

Positive, supportive relationships, important during the earliest years of life, appear essential not only for cognitive development but also for healthy emotional development and social attachment (Bowlby 1969; Stern 1985). The preschool years are an optimum time for development of fundamental motor skills (Gallahue 1993), language development (Dyson & Genishi 1993), and other key foundational aspects of development that have lifelong implications.

Recognition of the importance of the early years has heightened interest and support for early childhood education programs. A number of studies demonstrating long-term, positive consequences of participation in high-quality early childhood programs for children from low-income families influenced the expansion of Head Start and public school prekindergarten (Lazar & Darlington 1982; Lee, Brooks-Gunn. & Schuur 1988; Schweinhart, Barnes, & Weikart 1993; Campbell & Ramey 1995). Several decades of research clearly demonstrate that high-quality, developmentally appropriate early childhood programs produce short- and long-term positive effects on children's cognitive and social development (Barnett 1995).

From a thorough review of the research on the long-term effects of early childhood education programs, Barnett concludes that "across all studies, the findings were relatively uniform and constitute overwhelming evidence that early childhood care and education can produce sizeable improvements in school success" (1995, 40). Children from low-income families who participated in high-quality preschool programs were significantly less likely to have been assigned to special education, retained in grade, engaged in crime, or to have dropped out of school. The longitudinal studies, in general, suggest positive consequences for programs that used an approach consistent with principles of developmentally appropriate practice (Lazar & Darlington 1982; Berreuta-Clement et al. 1984; Miller & Bizzell 1984; Schweinhart, Weikart, & Larner 1986; Schweinhart, Barnes, & Weikart 1993; Frede 1995; Schweinhart & Weikart 1996).

Research on the long-term effects of early childhood programs indicates that children who attend good-quality child care programs, even at very young ages, demonstrate positive outcomes, and children who attend poor-quality programs show negative effects (Vandell & Powers 1983; Phillips, McCartney, & Scarr 1987; Fields et al. 1988; Vandell, Henderson, & Wilson 1988; Arnett 1989; Vandell & Corasanti 1990; Burchinal et al. 1996). Specifically, children who experience high-quality, stable child care engage in more complex play, demonstrate more secure attachments to adults and other children, and score higher on measures of thinking ability and language development. High-quality child care can predict academic success, adjustment to school, and reduced behavioral problems for children in first grade (Howes 1988).

While the potential positive effects of high-quality child care are well documented, several large-scale evaluations of child care find that high-quality experiences are not the norm (Whitebook, Howes, & Phillips 1989; Howes, Phillips, & Whitebook 1992; Layzer, Goodson, & Moss 1993; Galinsky et al. 1994; Cost, Quality, & Child Outcomes Study Team 1995). Each of these studies, which included observations of child care and preschool quality in several states, found that good quality that supports children's health and social and cognitive development is being provided in only about 15% of programs.

Of even greater concern was the large percentage of classrooms and family child care homes that were rated "barely adequate" or "inadequate" for quality. From 12 to 20% of the children were in settings that were considered dangerous to their health and safety and harmful to their social and cognitive development. An alarming number of infants and toddlers (35 to 40%) were found to be in unsafe settings (Cost, Quality, & Child Outcomes Study Team 1995).

Experiences during the earliest years of formal schooling are also formative. Studies demonstrate that children's success or failure during the first years of school often predicts the course of later schooling (Alexander & Entwisle 1988; Slavin, Karweit, & Madden 1989). A growing body of research indicates that more developmentally appropriate teaching in preschool and kindergarten predicts greater success in the early grades (Frede & Barnett 1992; Marcon 1992; Charlesworth et al. 1993).

As with preschool and child care, the observed quality of children's early schooling is uneven (Durkin 1987, 1990; Hiebert & Papierz 1990; Bryant, Clifford, & Peisner 1991; Carnegie Task Force 1996). For instance, in a statewide observational study of kindergarten classrooms, Durkin (1987) found that despite assessment results indicating considerable individual variation in children's literacy skills, which would call for various teaching strategies as well as individual and small-group work, teachers relied on one instructional strategy—whole-group, phonics instruction—and judged children who did not learn well with this one method as unready for first grade. Currently, too many children—especially children from low-income families and some minority groups—experience school failure, are retained in grade, get assigned to special education, and eventually drop out of school (Natriello, McDill, & Pallas 1990; Legters & Slavin 1992).

Results such as these indicate that while early childhood programs have the potential for producing positive and lasting effects on children, this potential will not be achieved unless more attention is paid to ensuring that all programs meet the highest standards of quality. As the number and type of early childhood programs increase, the need increases for a shared vision and agreed-upon standards of professional practice.

NAEYC's Commitment to Children

It is important to acknowledge at the outset the core values that undergird all of NAEYC's work. As stated in NAEYC's *Code of Ethical Conduct,* standards of professional practice in early childhood programs are based on commitment to certain fundamental values that are deeply rooted in the history of the early childhood field:

- appreciating childhood as a unique and valuable stage of the human life cycle [and valuing the quality of children's lives in the present, not just as preparation for the future];

- basing our work with children on knowledge of child development [and learning];

- appreciating and supporting the close ties between the child and family;

- recognizing that children are best understood in the context of family, culture, and society;

- respecting the dignity, worth, and uniqueness of each individual (child, family member, and colleague); and

- helping children and adults achieve their full potential in the context of relationships that are based on trust, respect, and positive regard. (Feeney & Kipnis 1992, 3)

Taken together, these core values define NAEYC's basic commitment to children and underlie its position on developmentally appropriate practice.

Statement of the Position

Based on an enduring commitment to act on behalf of children, NAEYC's mission is to promote high-quality, developmentally appropriate programs for all children and their families. Because we define developmentally appropriate programs as programs that contribute to children's development, we must articulate our goals for children's development. The principles of practice advocated in this position statement are based on a set of goals for children: what we want for them, both in their present lives and as they develop to adulthood, and what personal characteristics should be fostered because these contribute to a peaceful, prosperous, and democratic society.

As we approach the 21st century, enormous changes are taking place in daily life and work. At the same time, certain human capacities will undoubtedly remain important elements in individual and societal well-being—no matter what economic or technological changes take place. With a recognition of both the continuities in human existence and the rapid changes in our world, broad agreement is emerging (e.g., Resnick 1996) that when today's children become adults they will need the ability to

- communicate well, respect others and engage with them to work through differences of opinion, and function well as members of a team;

- analyze situations, make reasoned judgments, and solve new problems as they emerge;

- access information through various modes, including spoken and written language, and intelligently employ complex tools and technologies as they are developed; and

- continue to learn new approaches, skills, and knowledge as conditions and needs change.

Clearly, people in the decades ahead will need, more than ever, fully developed literacy and numeracy skills, and these abilities are key goals of the educational process. In science, social studies (which includes history and geography), music and the visual arts, physical education and health, children need to acquire a body of knowledge and skills, as identified by those in the various disciplines (e.g., Bredekamp & Rosegrant 1995).

Besides acquiring a body of knowledge and skills, children must develop positive dispositions and attitudes. They need to understand that effort is necessary for achievement, for example, and they need to have curiosity and confidence in themselves as learners. Moreover, to live in a highly pluralistic society and world, young people need to develop a positive self-identity and a tolerance for others whose perspective and experience may be different from their own.

Beyond the shared goals of the early childhood field, every program for young children should establish its own goals in collaboration with families. All early childhood programs will not have identical goals; priorities may vary in some respects because programs serve a diversity of children and families. Such differences notwithstanding, NAEYC believes that all high-quality, developmentally appropriate programs will have certain attributes in common. A high-quality early childhood program is one that provides a safe and nurturing environment that promotes the physical, social, emotional, aesthetic, intellectual, and language development of each child while being sensitive to the needs and preferences of families.

Many factors influence the quality of an early childhood program, including (but not limited to) the extent to which knowledge about how children develop and learn is applied in program practices. Developmentally appropriate programs are based on what is known about how children develop and learn; such programs promote the development and enhance the learning of each individual child served.

Developmentally appropriate practices result from the process of professionals making decisions about the well-being and education of children based on at least three important kinds of information or knowledge:

1. *what is known about child development and learning*—knowledge of age-related human characteristics that permits general predictions within an age range about what activities, materials, interactions, or experiences will be safe, healthy, interesting, achievable, and also challenging to children;

2. *what is known about the strengths, interests, and needs of each individual child in the group* to be able to adapt for and be responsive to inevitable individual variation; and

3. *knowledge of the social and cultural contexts in which children live* to ensure that learning experiences are meaningful, relevant, and respectful for the participating children and their families.

Furthermore, each of these dimensions of knowledge—human development and learning, individual characteristics and experiences, and social and cultural contexts—is dynamic and changing, requiring that early childhood teachers remain learners throughout their careers.

An example illustrates the interrelatedness of these three dimensions of the decision-making process. Children all over the world acquire language at approximately the same period of the life span and in similar ways (Fernald 1992). But tremendous individual variation exists in the rate and pattern of language acquisition (Fenson et al. 1994). Also, children acquire the language or languages of the culture in which they live (Kuhl 1994). Thus, to adequately support a developmental task such as language acquisition, the teacher must draw on at least all three interrelated dimensions of knowledge to determine a developmentally appropriate strategy or intervention.

Principles of Child Development and Learning That Inform Developmentally Appropriate Practice

Developmentally appropriate practice is based on knowledge about how children develop and learn. As Katz states, "In a developmental approach to curriculum design, . . . [decisions] about what should be learned and how it would best be learned depend on what we know of the learner's developmental status and our understanding of the relationships between early experience and subsequent development" (1995, 109). To guide their decisions about practice, all early childhood teachers need to understand the developmental changes that typically occur in the years from birth through age 8 and beyond, variations in development that may occur, and how best to support children's learning and development during these years.

A complete discussion of the knowledge base that informs early childhood practice is beyond the scope of this document (see, for example, Seefeldt 1992; Sroufe, Cooper, & DeHart 1992; Kostelnik, Soderman, & Whiren 1993; Spodek 1993; Berk 1996). Because development and learning are so complex, no one theory is sufficient to explain these phenomena. However, a broad-based review of the literature on early childhood education generates a set of principles to inform early childhood practice. *Principles* are generalizations that are sufficiently reliable that they should be taken into account when making decisions (Katz & Chard 1989; Katz 1995). Following is a list of empirically based principles of child development and learning that inform and guide decisions about developmentally appropriate practice.

1. **Domains of children's development—physical, social, emotional, and cognitive—are closely related. Development in one domain influences and is influenced by development in other domains.**

Development in one domain can limit or facilitate development in others (Sroufe, Cooper, & DeHart 1992; Kostelnik, Soderman, & Whiren 1993). For example, when babies begin to crawl or walk, their ability to explore the world expands, and their mobility, in turn, affects their cognitive development. Likewise, children's language skill

affects their ability to establish social relationships with adults and other children, just as their skill in social interaction can support or impede their language development.

Because developmental domains are interrelated, educators should be aware of and use these interrelationships to organize children's learning experiences in ways that help children develop optimally in all areas and that make meaningful connections across domains.

Recognition of the connections across developmental domains is also useful for curriculum planning with the various age groups represented in the early childhood period. Curriculum with infants and toddlers is almost solely driven by the need to support their healthy development in all domains. During the primary grades, curriculum planning attempts to help children develop conceptual understandings that apply across related subject-matter disciplines.

2. **Development occurs in a relatively orderly sequence, with later abilities, skills, and knowledge building on those already acquired.**

Human development research indicates that relatively stable, predictable sequences of growth and change occur in children during the first nine years of life (Piaget 1952; Erikson 1963; Dyson & Genishi 1993; Gallahue 1993; Case & Okamoto 1996). Predictable changes occur in all domains of development—physical, emotional, social, language, and cognitive—although the ways that these changes are manifest and the meaning attached to them vary in different cultural contexts. Knowledge of typical development of children within the age span served by the program provides a general framework to guide how teachers prepare the learning environment and plan realistic curriculum goals and objectives and appropriate experiences.

3. **Development proceeds at varying rates from child to child as well as unevenly within different areas of each child's functioning.**

Individual variation has at least two dimensions: the inevitable variability around the average or normative course of development and the uniqueness of each person as an individual (Sroufe, Cooper, & DeHart 1992). Each child is a unique person with an individual pattern and timing of growth, as well as individual personality, temperament, learning style, and experiential and family background. All children have their own strengths, needs, and interests; for some children, special learning and developmental needs or abilities are identified. Given the enormous variation among children of the same chronological age, a child's age must be recognized as only a crude index of developmental maturity.

Recognition that individual variation is not only to be expected but also valued requires that decisions about curriculum and adults' interactions with children be as individualized as possible. Emphasis on individual appropriateness is not the same as "individualism." Rather, this recognition requires that children be considered not solely as members of an age group, expected to perform to a predetermined norm and without adaptation to individual variation of any kind. Having high expectations for all children is important, but rigid expectations of group norms do not reflect what is known about real differences in individual development and learning during the early years. Group-norm expectancy can be especially harmful for children with special learning and developmental needs (NEGP 1991; Mallory 1992; Wolery, Strain, & Bailey 1992).

4. **Early experiences have both cumulative and delayed effects on individual children's development; optimal periods exist for certain types of development and learning.**

Children's early experiences, either positive or negative, are cumulative in the sense that if an experience occurs occasionally, it may have minimal effects. If positive or negative experiences occur frequently, however, they can have powerful, lasting, even "snowballing," effects (Katz & Chard 1989; Kostelnik, Soderman, & Whiren 1993; Wieder & Greenspan 1993). For example, a child's social experiences with other children in the preschool years help him develop social skills and confidence that enable him to make friends in the early school years, and these experiences further enhance the child's social competence. Conversely, children who fail to develop minimal social competence and are neglected or rejected by peers are at significant risk to drop out of school, become delinquent, and experience mental health problems in adulthood (Asher, Hymel, & Renshaw 1984; Parker & Asher 1987).

Similar patterns can be observed in babies whose cries and other attempts at communication are regularly responded to, thus enhancing their own sense of efficacy and increasing communicative competence. Likewise, when children have or do not have early literacy experiences, such as being read to regularly, their later success in learning to read is affected accordingly. Perhaps most convincing is the growing body of research demonstrating that social and sensorimotor experiences during the first three years directly affect neurological development of the brain, with important and lasting implications for children's capacity to learn (Dana Alliance for Brain Initiatives 1996).

Early experiences can also have delayed effects, either positive or negative, on subsequent development. For instance, some evidence suggests that reliance on extrinsic rewards (such as candy or money) to shape children's behavior, a strategy that can be very effective in the short term, under certain circumstances lessens children's intrinsic motivation to engage in the rewarded behavior in the long term (Dweck 1986; Kohn 1993). For example, paying children to read books may over time undermine their desire to read for their own enjoyment and edification.

At certain points in the life span, some kinds of learning and development occur most efficiently. For example, the first three years of life appear to be an optimal period for verbal language development (Kuhl 1994). Although delays in language development due to physical or environmental deficits can be ameliorated later on, such intervention usually requires considerable effort. Similarly, the preschool years appear to be optimum for fundamental motor development (that is, fundamental motor skills are more easily and efficiently acquired at this age) (Gallahue 1995). Children who have many opportunities and adult support to practice large-motor skills (running, jumping, hopping, skipping) during this period have the cumulative benefit of being better able to acquire more sophisticated, complex motor skills (balancing on a beam or riding a two-wheel bike) in subsequent years. On the other hand, children whose early motor experiences are severely limited may struggle to acquire physical competence and may also experience delayed effects when attempting to participate in sports or personal fitness activities later in life.

5. **Development proceeds in predictable directions toward greater complexity, organization, and internalization.**

Learning during early childhood proceeds from behavioral knowledge to symbolic or representational knowledge (Bruner 1983). For example, children learn to navigate their homes and other familiar settings long before they can understand the words *left* and *right* or read a map of the house. Developmentally appropriate programs provide opportunities for children to broaden and deepen their behavioral knowledge by providing a variety of firsthand experiences and by helping children acquire symbolic knowledge through representing their experiences in a variety of media, such as drawing, painting, construction of models, dramatic play, verbal and written descriptions (Katz 1995).

Even very young children are able to use various media to represent their understanding of concepts. Furthermore, through representation of their knowledge, the knowledge itself is enhanced (Edwards, Gandini, & Forman 1993; Malaguzzi 1993; Forman 1994). Representational modes and media also vary with the age of the child. For instance, most learning for infants and toddlers is sensory and motoric, but by age 2 children use one object to stand for another in play (a block for a phone or a spoon for a guitar).

6. **Development and learning occur in and are influenced by multiple social and cultural contexts.**

Bronfenbrenner (1979, 1989, 1993) provides an ecological model for understanding human development. He explains that children's development is best understood within the sociocultural context of the family, educational setting, community, and broader society. These various contexts are interrelated, and all have an impact on the developing child. For example, even a child in a loving, supportive family within a strong, healthy community is affected by the biases of the larger society, such as racism or sexism, and may show the effects of negative stereotyping and discrimination.

We define *culture* as the customary beliefs and patterns of and for behavior, both explicit and implicit, that are passed on to future generations by the society they live in and/or by a social, religious, or ethnic group within it. Because culture is often discussed in the context of diversity or multiculturalism, people fail to recognize the powerful role that culture plays in influencing the development of *all* children. Every culture structures and interprets children's behavior and development (Edwards & Gandini 1989; Tobin, Wu, & Davidson 1989; Rogoff et al. 1993). As Bowman states, "Rules of development are the same for all children, but social contexts shape children's development into different configurations" (1994, 220). Early childhood teachers need to understand the influence of sociocultural contexts on learning, recognize children's developing competence, and accept a variety of ways for children to express their developmental achievements (Vygotsky 1978; Wertsch 1985; Forman, Minick, & Stone 1993; New 1993, 1994; Bowman & Stott 1994; Mallory & New 1994a; Phillips 1994; Bruner 1996; Wardle 1996).

Teachers should learn about the culture of the majority of the children they serve if that culture differs from their own. However, recognizing that development and learning are influenced by social and cultural contexts does not require teachers to understand all the nuances of every cultural group they may encounter in their practice; this would be an impossible task. Rather, this fundamental recognition sensitizes teachers to the need to acknowledge how their own cultural experiences shapes their perspective and to realize that multiple perspectives, in addition to their own, must be considered in decisions about children's development and learning.

Children are capable of learning to function in more than one cultural context simultaneously. However, if teachers set low expectations for children based on their home culture and language, children cannot develop and learn optimally. Education should be an additive process. For example, children whose primary language is not English should be able to learn English without being forced to give up their home language (NAEYC 1996a). Likewise, children who speak only English benefit from learning another language. The goal is that all children learn to function well in the society as a whole and move comfortably among groups of people who come from both similar and dissimilar backgrounds.

7. **Children are active learners, drawing on direct physical and social experience as well as culturally transmitted knowledge to construct their own understandings of the world around them.**

Children contribute to their own development and learning as they strive to make meaning out of their daily experiences in the home, the early childhood program, and the community. Principles of developmentally appropriate practice are based on several prominent theories that view intellectual development from a constructivist, interactive perspective (Dewey 1916; Piaget 1952; Vygotsky 1978; DeVries & Kohlberg 1990; Rogoff 1990; Gardner 1991; Kamii & Ewing 1996).

From birth, children are actively engaged in constructing their own understandings from their experiences, and these understandings are mediated by and clearly linked to the sociocultural context. Young children actively learn from observing and participating with other children and adults, including parents and teachers. Children need to form their own hypotheses and keep trying them out through social interaction, physical manipulation, and their own thought processes—observing what happens, reflecting on their findings, asking questions, and formulating answers. When objects, events, and other people challenge the working model that the child has mentally constructed, the child is forced to adjust the model or alter the mental structures to account for the new information. Throughout early childhood, the child in processing new experiences continually reshapes, expands, and reorganizes mental structures (Piaget 1952; Vygotsky 1978; Case & Okamoto 1996). When teachers and other adults use various strategies to encourage children to reflect on their experiences by planning beforehand and "revisiting" afterward, the knowledge and understanding gained from the experience is deepened (Copple, Sigel, & Saunders 1984; Edwards, Gandini, & Forman 1993; Stremmel & Fu 1993; Hohmann & Weikart 1995).

In the statement of this principle, the term "physical and social experience" is used in the broadest sense to include children's exposure to physical knowledge, learned through firsthand experience of using objects (observing that a ball thrown in the air falls down), and social knowledge, including the vast body of culturally acquired and transmitted knowledge that children need to function in the world. For example, children progressively construct their own understanding of various symbols, but the symbols they use (such as the alphabet or numerical system) are the ones used within their culture and transmitted to them by adults.

In recent years, discussions of cognitive development have at times become polarized (see Seifert 1993). Piaget's theory stressed that development of certain cognitive structures was a necessary prerequisite to learning (i.e., development precedes learning), while other research has demonstrated that instruction in specific concepts or strategies can facilitate development of more mature cognitive structures (learning precedes development) (Vygotsky 1978; Gelman & Baillargheon 1983). Current attempts to resolve this apparent dichotomy (Seifert 1993; Sameroff & McDonough 1994; Case & Okamoto 1996) acknowledge that essentially both theoretical perspectives are correct in explaining aspects of cognitive development during early childhood. Strategic teaching, of course, can enhance children's learning. Yet, direct instruction may be totally ineffective; it fails when it is not attuned to the cognitive capacities and knowledge of the child at that point in development.

8. **Development and learning result from interaction of biological maturation and the environment, which includes both the physical and social worlds that children live in.**

The simplest way to express this principle is that human beings are products of both heredity and environment and these forces are interrelated. Behaviorists focus on the environmental influences that determine learning, while maturationists emphasize the unfolding of predetermined, hereditary characteristics. Each perspective is true to some extent, and yet neither perspective is sufficient to explain learning or development. More often today, development is viewed as the result of an interactive, transactional process between the growing, changing individual and his or her experiences in the social and physical worlds (Scarr & McCartney 1983; Plomin 1994a, b). For example, a child's genetic makeup may predict healthy growth, but inadequate nutrition in the early years of life may keep this potential from being fulfilled. Or a severe disability, whether inherited or environmentally caused, may be ameliorated through systematic, appropriate intervention. Likewise, a child's inherited temperament—whether a predisposition to be wary or outgoing—shapes and is shaped by how other children and adults communicate with that child.

9. **Play is an important vehicle for children's social, emotional, and cognitive development, as well as a reflection of their development.**

Understanding that children are active constructors of knowledge and that development and learning are the result of interactive processes, early childhood teachers recognize that children's play is a highly supportive context for these developing processes (Piaget 1952; Fein 1981; Bergen 1988; Smilansky & Shefatya 1990; Fromberg 1992; Berk & Winsler 1995). Play gives children opportunities to understand the world, interact with others in social ways, express and control emotions, and develop their symbolic capabilities. Children's play gives adults insights into children's development and opportunities to support the development of new strategies. Vygotsky (1978) believed that play leads development, with written language growing out of oral language through the vehicle of symbolic play that promotes the development of symbolic representation abilities. Play provides a context for children to practice newly acquired skills and also to function on the edge of their developing capacities to take on new social roles, attempt novel or challenging tasks, and solve complex problems that they would not (or could not) otherwise do (Mallory & New 1994b).

Research demonstrates the importance of sociodramatic play as a tool for learning curriculum content with 3- through 6-year-old children. When teachers provide a thematic organization for play; offer appropriate props, space, and time; and become involved in the play by extending and elaborating on children's ideas, children's language and literacy skills can be enhanced (Levy, Schaefer, & Phelps 1986; Schrader 1989, 1990; Morrow 1990; Pramling 1991; Levy, Wolfgang, & Koorland 1992).

In addition to supporting cognitive development, play serves important functions in children's physical, emotional, and social development (Herron & Sutton-Smith 1971). Children express and represent their ideas, thoughts, and feelings when engaged in symbolic play. During play a child can learn to deal with emotions, to interact with others, to resolve conflicts, and to gain a sense of competence—all in the safety that only play affords. Through play, children also can develop their imaginations and creativity. Therefore, child-initiated, teacher-supported play is an essential component of developmentally appropriate practice (Fein & Rivkin 1986).

10. **Development advances when children have opportunities to practice newly acquired skills as well as when they experience a challenge just beyond the level of their present mastery.**

Research demonstrates that children need to be able to successfully negotiate learning tasks most of the time if they are to maintain motivation and persistence (Lary 1990; Brophy 1992). Confronted by repeated failure, most children will simply stop trying. So most of the time, teachers should give young children tasks that with effort they can accomplish and present them with content that is accessible at their level of understanding. At the same time, children continually gravitate to situations and stimuli that give them the chance to work at their "growing edge" (Berk & Winsler 1995; Bodrova & Leong 1996). Moreover, in a task just beyond the child's independent reach, the adult and more-competent peers contribute significantly to development by providing the supportive "scaffolding" that allows the child to take the next step.

Development and learning are dynamic processes requiring that adults understand the continuum, observe children closely to match curriculum and teaching to children's emerging competencies, needs, and interests, and then help children move forward by targeting educational experiences to the edge of children's changing capacities so as to challenge but not frustrate them. Human beings, especially children, are highly motivated to understand what they almost, but not quite, comprehend and to master what they can almost, but not quite, do (White 1965; Vygotsky 1978). The principle of learning is that children can do things first in a supportive context and then later independently and in a variety of contexts. Rogoff (1990) describes the process of adult-assisted learning as "guided participation" to emphasize that children actively collaborate with others to move to more complex levels of understanding and skill.

11. **Children demonstrate different modes of knowing and learning and different ways of representing what they know.**

For some time, learning theorists and developmental psychologists have recognized that human beings come to understand the world in many ways and that individuals tend to have preferred or stronger modes of learning. Studies of differences in learning modalities have contrasted visual, auditory, or tactile learners. Other work has identified learners as field-dependent or independent (Witkin 1962). Gardner (1983) expanded on this concept by theorizing that human beings possess at least seven "intelligences." In addition to having the ones traditionally emphasized in schools, linguistic and logical-mathematical, individuals are more or less proficient in at least these other areas: musical, spatial, bodily-kinesthetic, intrapersonal, and interpersonal.

Malaguzzi (1993) used the metaphor of "100 languages" to describe the diverse modalities through which children come to understand the world and represent their knowledge. The processes of representing their understanding can with the assistance of teachers help children deepen, improve, and expand their understanding (Copple, Sigel, & Saunders 1984; Forman 1994; Katz 1995). The principle of diverse modalities implies that teachers should provide not only opportunities for individual children to use their preferred modes of learning to capitalize on their strengths (Hale-Benson 1986) but also opportunities to help children develop in the modes or intelligences in which they may not be as strong.

12. **Children develop and learn best in the context of a community where they are safe and valued, their physical needs are met, and they feel psychologically secure.**

Maslow (1954) conceptualized a hierarchy of needs in which learning was not considered possible unless physical and psychological needs for safety and security were first met. Because children's physical health and safety too often are threatened today, programs for young children must not only provide adequate health, safety, and nutrition but may also need to ensure more comprehensives services, such as physical, dental, and mental health and social services (NASBE 1991; U.S. Department of Health & Human Services 1996). In addition, children's development in all areas is influenced by their ability to establish and maintain a limited number of positive, consistent primary relationships with adults and other children (Bowlby 1969; Stern 1985; Garbarino et al. 1992). These primary relationships begin in the family but extend over time to include children's teachers and members of the community; therefore, practices that are developmentally appropriate address children's physical, social, and emotional needs as well as their intellectual development.

* * *

A linear listing of principles of child development and learning, such as the above, cannot do justice to the complexity of the phenomena that it attempts to describe and explain. Just as all domains of development and learning are interrelated, so, too, there are relationships among the principles. Similarly, the following guidelines for practice do not match up one-to-one with the principles. Instead, early childhood professionals draw on all these fundamental ideas (as well as many others) when making decisions about their practice.

Guidelines for Decisions About Developmentally Appropriate Practice

An understanding of the nature of development and learning during the early childhood years, from birth through age 8, generates guidelines that inform the practices of early childhood educators. Developmentally appropriate practice requires that teachers integrate the many dimensions of their knowledge base. They must know about child development and the implications of this knowledge for how to teach, the content of the curriculum—what to teach and when—how to assess what children have learned, and how to adapt curriculum and instruction to children's individual strengths, needs, and interest. Further, they must know the particular children they teach and their families and be knowledgeable as well about the social and cultural context.

The following guidelines address five interrelated dimensions of early childhood professional practice: creating a caring community of learners, teaching to enhance development and learning, constructing appropriate curriculum, assessing children's development and learning, and establishing reciprocal relationships with families. (The word *teacher* is used to refer to any adult responsible for a group of children in any early childhood program, including infant/ toddler caregivers, family child care providers, and specialists in other disciplines who fulfill the role of teacher.)

Examples of appropriate and inappropriate practice in relation to each of these dimensions are given for infants and toddlers (Part 3, pp. 72–90), children 3 through 5 (Part 4, pp. 123–35), and children 6 through 8 (Part 5, pp. 161–78). In the references at the end of each part, readers will be able to find fuller discussion of the points summarized here and strategies for implementation.

1. Creating a Caring Community of Learners

Developmentally appropriate practices occur within a context that supports the development of relationships between adults and children, among children, among teachers, and between teachers and families. Such a community reflects what is known about the social construction of knowledge and the importance of establishing a caring, inclusive community in which all children can develop and learn.

A. The early childhood setting functions as a community of learners in which all participants consider and contribute to each other's well-being and learning.

B. Consistent, positive relationships with a limited number of adults and other children are a fundamental determinant of healthy human development and provide the context for children to learn about themselves and their world and also how to develop positive, constructive relationships with other people. The early childhood classroom is a community in which each child is valued. Children learn to respect and acknowledge differences in abilities and talents and to value each person for his or her strengths.

C. Social relationships are an important context for learning. Each child has strengths or interests that contribute to the overall functioning of the group. When children have opportunities to play together, work on projects in small groups, and talk with other children and adults, their own development and learning are enhanced. Interacting with other children in small groups provides a context for children to operate on the edge of their developing capacities. The learning environment enables children to construct understanding through interactions with adults and other children.

D. The learning environment is designed to protect children's health and safety and is supportive of children's physiological needs for activity, sensory stimulation, fresh air, rest, and nourishment. The program provides a balance of rest and active movement for children throughout the program day. Outdoor experiences are provided for children of all ages. The program protects children's psychological safety; that is, children feel secure, relaxed, and comfortable rather than disengaged, frightened, worried, or stressed.

E. Children experience an organized environment and an orderly routine that provides an overall structure in which learning takes place; the environment is dynamic and changing but predictable and comprehensible from a child's point of view. The learning environment provides a variety of materials and opportunities for children to have firsthand, meaningful experiences.

2. Teaching to Enhance Development and Learning

Adults are responsible for ensuring children's healthy development and learning. From birth, relationships with adults are critical determinants of children's healthy social and emotional development and serve as well as mediators of language and intellectual development. At the same time, children are active constructors of their own understanding, who benefit from initiating and regulating their own learning activities and interacting with peers. Therefore, early childhood teachers strive to achieve an optimal balance between children's self-initiated learning and adult guidance or support.

Teachers accept responsibility for actively supporting children's development and provide occasions for children to acquire important knowledge and skills. Teachers use their knowledge of child development and learning to identify the range of activities, materials, and learning experiences that are appropriate for a group or individual child. This knowledge is used in conjunction with knowledge of the context and understanding about individual children's growth patterns, strengths, needs, interests, and experiences to design the curriculum and learning environment and guide teachers' interactions with children. The following guidelines describe aspects of the teachers' role in making decisions about practice:

A. Teachers respect, value, and accept children and treat them with dignity at all times.

B. Teachers make it a priority to know each child well.

(1) Teachers establish positive, personal relationships with children to foster the child's development and keep informed about the child's needs and potentials. Teachers listen to children and adapt their responses to children's differing needs, interests, styles, and abilities.

(2) Teachers continually observe children's spontaneous play and interaction with the physical environment and with other children to learn about their interests, abilities, and developmental progress. On the basis of this information, teachers plan experiences that enhance children's learning and development.

(3) Understanding that children develop and learn in the context of their families and communities, teachers establish relationships with families that increase their knowledge of children's lives outside the classroom and their awareness of the perspectives and priorities of those individuals most significant in the child's life.

(4) Teachers are alert to signs of undue stress and traumatic events in children's lives and aware of effective strategies to reduce stress and support the development of resilience.

(5) Teachers are responsible at all times for all children under their supervision and plan for children's increasing development of self-regulation abilities.

C. Teachers create an intellectually engaging, responsive environment to promote each child's learning and development.

(1) Teachers use their knowledge about children in general and the particular children in the group as well as their familiarity with what children need to learn and develop in each curriculum area to organize the environment and plan curriculum and teaching strategies.

(2) Teachers provide children with a rich variety of experiences, projects, materials, problems, and ideas to explore and

investigate, ensuring that these are worthy of children's attention.

(3) Teachers provide children with opportunities to make meaningful choices and time to explore through active involvement. Teachers offer children the choice to participate in a small-group or a solitary activity, assist and guide children who are not yet able to use and enjoy child-choice activity periods, and provide opportunities for practice of skills as a self-chosen activity.

(4) Teachers organize the daily and weekly schedule and allocate time so as to provide children with extended blocks of time in which to engage in play, projects, and/or study in integrated curriculum.

D. Teachers make plans to enable children to attain key curriculum goals across various disciplines, such as language arts, mathematics, social studies, science, art, music, physical education, and health (see "Constructing Appropriate Curriculum," pp. 547–548).

(1) Teachers incorporate a wide variety of experiences, materials and equipment, and teaching strategies in constructing curriculum to accommodate a broad range of children's individual differences in prior experiences, maturation rates, styles of learning, needs, and interests.

(2) Teachers bring each child's home culture and language into the shared culture of the school so that the unique contributions of each group are recognized and valued by others.

(3) Teachers are prepared to meet identified special needs of individual children, including children with disabilities and those who exhibit unusual interests and skills. Teachers use all the strategies identified here, consult with appropriate specialists, and see that the child gets the specialized services he or she requires.

E. Teachers foster children's collaboration with peers on interesting, important enterprises.

(1) Teachers promote children's productive collaboration without taking over to the extent that children lose interest.

(2) Teachers use a variety of ways of flexibly grouping children for the purposes of instruction, supporting collaboration among children, and building a sense of community. At various times, children have opportunities to work individually, in small groups, and with the whole group.

F. Teachers develop, refine, and use a wide repertoire of teaching strategies to enhance children's learning and development.

(1) To help children develop their initiative, teachers encourage them to choose and plan their own learning activities.

(2) Teachers pose problems, ask questions, and make comments and suggestions that stimulate children's thinking and extend their learning.

(3) Teachers extend the range of children's interests and the scope of their thought through presenting novel experiences and introducing stimulating ideas, problems, experiences, or hypotheses.

(4) To sustain an individual child's effort or engagement in purposeful activities, teachers select from a range of strategies, including but not limited to modeling, demonstrating specific skills, and providing information, focused attention, physical proximity, verbal encouragement, reinforcement and other behavioral procedures, as well as additional structure and modification of equipment or schedules as needed.

(5) Teachers coach and/or directly guide children in the acquisition of specific skills as needed.

(6) Teachers calibrate the complexity and challenge of activities to suit children's level of skill and knowledge, increasing the challenge as children gain competence and understanding.

(7) Teachers provide cues and other forms of "scaffolding" that enable the child to

succeed in a task that is just beyond his or her ability to complete alone.

(8) To strengthen children's sense of competence and confidence as learners, motivation to persist, and willingness to take risks, teachers provide experiences for children to be genuinely successful and to be challenged.

(9) To enhance children's conceptual understanding, teachers use various strategies that encourage children to reflect on and "revisit" their learning experiences.

G. Teachers facilitate the development of responsibility and self-regulation in children.

(1) Teachers set clear, consistent, and fair limits for children's behavior and hold children accountable to standards of acceptable behavior. To the extent that children are able, teachers engage them in developing rules and procedures for behavior of class members.

(2) Teachers redirect children to more acceptable behavior or activity or use children's mistakes as learning opportunities, patiently reminding children of rules and their rationale as needed.

(3) Teachers listen and acknowledge children's feelings and frustrations, respond with respect, guide children to resolve conflicts, and model skills that help children to solve their own problems.

3. Constructing Appropriate Curriculum

The content of the early childhood curriculum is determined by many factors, including the subject matter of the disciplines, social or cultural values, and parental input. In developmentally appropriate programs, decisions about curriculum content also take into consideration the age and experience of the learners. Achieving success for all children depends, among other essentials, on providing a challenging, interesting, developmentally appropriate curriculum. NAEYC does not endorse specific curricula. However, one purpose of these guidelines is as a framework for making decisions about developing curriculum or selecting a curriculum model. Teachers who use a validated curriculum model benefit from the evidence of its effectiveness and the accumulated wisdom and experience of others.

In some respects, the curriculum strategies of many teachers today do not demand enough of children and in other ways demand too much of the wrong thing. On the one hand, narrowing the curriculum to those basic skills that can be easily measured on multiple-choice tests diminishes the intellectual challenge for many children. Such intellectually impoverished curriculum underestimates the true competence of children, which has been demonstrated to be much higher than is often assumed (Gelman & Baillargeon 1983; Gelman & Meck 1983; Edwards, Gandini, & Forman 1993; Resnick 1996). Watered-down, oversimplified curriculum leaves many children unchallenged, bored, uninterested, or unmotivated. In such situations, children's experiences are marked by a great many missed opportunities for learning.

On the other hand, curriculum expectations in the early years of schooling sometimes are not appropriate for the age groups served. When next-grade expectations of mastery of basic skills are routinely pushed down to the previous grade and whole group and teacher-led instruction is the dominant teaching strategy, children who cannot sit still and attend to teacher lectures or who are bored and unchallenged or frustrated by doing workbook pages for long periods of time are mislabeled as immature, disruptive, or unready for school (Shepard & Smith 1988). Constructing appropriate curriculum requires attention to at least the following guidelines for practice:

A. Developmentally appropriate curriculum provides for all areas of a child's development:

physical, emotional, social, linguistic, aesthetic, and cognitive.

B. Curriculum includes a broad range of content across disciplines that is socially relevant, intellectually engaging, and personally meaningful to children.

C. Curriculum builds upon what children already know and are able to do (activating prior knowledge) to consolidate their learning and to foster their acquisition of new concepts and skills.

D. Effective curriculum plans frequently integrate across traditional subject-matter divisions to help children make meaningful connections and provide opportunities for rich conceptual development; focusing on one subject is also a valid strategy at times.

E. Curriculum promotes the development of knowledge and understanding, processes and skills, as well as the dispositions to use and apply skills and to go on learning.

F. Curriculum content has intellectual integrity, reflecting the key concepts and tools of inquiry of recognized disciplines in ways that are accessible and achievable for young children, ages 3 through 8 (e.g., Bredekamp & Rosegrant 1992, 1995). Children directly participate in study of the disciplines, for instance by conducting scientific experiments, writing, performing, solving mathematical problems, collecting and analyzing data, collecting oral history, and performing other roles of experts in the disciplines.

G. Curriculum provides opportunities to support children's home culture and language while also developing all children's abilities to participate in the shared culture of the program and the community.

H. Curriculum goals are realistic and attainable for most children in the designated age range for which they are designed.

I. When used, technology is physically and philosophically integrated in the classroom curriculum and teaching. (See "NAEYC Position Statement: Technology and Young Children—Ages Three through Eight" [NAEYC 1996b].)

4. Assessing Children's Learning and Development

Assessment of individual children's development and learning is essential for planning and implementing appropriate curriculum. In developmentally appropriate programs, assessment and curriculum are integrated, with teachers continually engaging in observational assessment for the purpose of improving teaching and learning.

Accurate assessment of young children is difficult because their development and learning are rapid, uneven, episodic, and embedded within specific cultural and linguistic contexts. Too often, inaccurate and inappropriate assessment measures have been used to label, track, or otherwise harm young children. Developmentally appropriate assessment practices are based on the following guidelines:

A. Assessment of young children's progress and achievements is ongoing, strategic, and purposeful. The results of assessment are used to benefit children—in adapting curriculum and teaching to meet the developmental and learning needs of children, communicating with the child's family, and evaluating the program's effectiveness for the purpose of improving the program.

B. The content of assessments reflects progress toward important learning and developmental goals. The program has a systematic plan for collecting and using assessment information that is integrated with curriculum planning.

C. The methods of assessment are appropriate to the age and experiences of young children. Therefore, assessment of young children relies heavily on the results of observations of children's development, descriptive data, collections of representative work by children, and demonstrated performance during authentic, not contrived, activities. Input from families as well as children's evaluations of their own work are part of the overall assessment strategy.

D. Assessments are tailored to a specific purpose and used only for the purpose for which they have been demonstrated to produce reliable, valid information.

E. Decisions that have a major impact on children, such as enrollment or placement, are never made on the basis of a single developmental assessment or screening device but are based on multiple sources of relevant information, particularly observations by teachers and parents.

F. To identify children who have special learning or developmental needs and to plan appropriate curriculum and teaching for them, developmental assessments and observations are used.

G. Assessment recognizes individual variation in learners and allows for differences in styles and rates of learning. Assessment takes into consideration such factors as the child's facility in English, stage of language acquisition, and whether the child has had the time and opportunity to develop proficiency in his or her home language as well as in English.

H. Assessment legitimately addresses not only what children can do independently but what they can do with assistance from other children or adults. Teachers study children as individuals as well as in relationship to groups by documenting group projects and other collaborative work.

(For a more complete discussion of principles of appropriate assessment, see the position statement *Guidelines for Appropriate Curriculum Content and Assessment for Children Ages 3 through 8* [NAEYC & NAECS/SDE 1992]; see also Shepard 1994.)

5. Establishing Reciprocal Relationships with Families

Developmentally appropriate practices derive from deep knowledge of individual children and the context within which they develop and learn. The younger the child, the more necessary it is for professionals to acquire this knowledge through relationships with children's families. The traditional approach to families has been a parent education orienta-

tion in which the professionals see themselves as knowing what is best for children and view parents as needing to be educated. There is also the limited view of parent involvement that sees PTA membership as the primary goal. These approaches do not adequately convey the complexity of the partnership between teachers and parents that is a fundamental element of good practice (Powell 1994).

When the parent education approach is criticized in favor of a more family-centered approach, this shift may be misunderstood to mean that parents dictate all program content and professionals abdicate responsibility, doing whatever parents want regardless of whether professionals agree that it is in children's best interest. Either of these extremes oversimplifies the importance of relationships with families and fails to provide the kind of environment in which parents and professionals work together to achieve shared goals for children; such programs with this focus are characterized by at least the following guidelines for practice:

A. Reciprocal relationships between teachers and families require mutual respect, cooperation, shared responsibility, and negotiation of conflicts toward achievement of shared goals.

B. Early childhood teachers work in collaborative partnerships with families, establishing and maintaining regular, frequent two-way communication with children's parents.

C. Parents are welcome in the program and participate in decisions about their children's care and education. Parents observe and participate and serve in decision-making roles in the program.

D. Teachers acknowledge parents' choices and goals for children and respond with sensitivity and respect to parents' preferences and concerns without abdicating professional responsibility to children.

E. Teachers and parents share their knowledge of the child and understanding of children's development and learning as part of day-to-day communication and planned conferences. Teachers support families in ways that maximally promote family decision-making capabilities and competence.

F. To ensure more accurate and complete information, the program involves families in assessing and planning for individual children.

G. The program links families with a range of services, based on identified resources, priorities, and concerns.

H. Teachers, parents, programs, social service and health agencies, and consultants who may have educational responsibility for the child at different times should, with family participation, share developmental information about children as they pass from one level or program to another.

Moving from Either/Or to Both/And Thinking in Early Childhood Practice

Some critical reactions to NAEYC's (1987) position statement on developmentally appropriate practice reflect a recurring tendency in the American discourse on education: the polarizing into *either/or* choices of many questions that are more fruitfully seen as *both/ands*. For example, heated debates have broken out about whether children in the early grades should receive whole-language or phonics instruction, when, in fact, the two approaches are quite compatible and most effective in combination.

It is true that there are practices that are clearly inappropriate for early childhood professional—use of physical punishment or disparaging verbal comments about children, discriminating against children or their families, and many other examples that could be cited (see Parts 3, 4, and 5 for examples relevant to different age groups). However, most questions about practice require more complex responses. It is not that children need food **or** water; they need both.

To illustrate the many ways that early childhood practice draws on *both/and* thinking and to convey some of the complexity and interrelationship among the principles that guide our practice, we offer the following statements as **examples**:

- Children construct their own understanding of concepts, **and** they benefit from instruction by more competent peers and adults.

- Children benefit from opportunities to see connections across disciplines through integration of curriculum **and** from opportunities to engage in in-depth study within a content area.

- Children benefit from predictable structure and orderly routine in the learning environment **and** from the teachers' flexibility and spontaneity in responding to their emerging ideas, needs, and interests.

- Children benefit from opportunities to make meaningful choices about what they will do and learn **and** from having a clear understanding of the boundaries within which choices are permissible.

- Children benefit from situations that challenge them to work at the edge of their developing capacities **and** from ample opportunities to practice newly acquired skills and to acquire the disposition to persist.

- Children benefit from opportunities to collaborate with their peers and acquire a sense of being part of a community **and** from being treated as individuals with their own strengths, interests, and needs.

- Children need to develop a positive sense of their own self-identity **and** respect for other people whose perspectives and experiences may be different from their own.

- Children have enormous capacities to learn and almost boundless curiosity about the world, **and** they have recognized, age-related limits on their cognitive and linguistic capacities.

- Children benefit from engaging in self-initiated, spontaneous play, **and** from teacher-planned and -structured activities, projects, and experiences.

The above list is not exhaustive. Many more examples could be cited to convey the interrelationships among the principles of child development and learning or among the guidelines for early childhood practice.

Policies Essential for Achieving Developmentally Appropriate Early Childhood Programs

Early childhood professionals working in diverse situations with varying levels of funding and resources are responsible for implementing practices that are developmentally appropriate for the children they serve. Regardless of the resources available, professionals have an ethical responsibility to practice, to the best of their ability, according to the standards of their profession. Nevertheless, the kinds of practices advocated in this position statement are more likely to be implemented within an infrastructure of supportive policies and resources. NAEYC strongly recommends that policymaking groups at the state and local levels consider the following when implementing early childhood programs:

1. A comprehensive professional preparation and development system is in place to ensure that early childhood programs are staffed with qualified personnel (NAEYC 1994).

    *   A system exists for early childhood professionals to acquire the knowledge and practical skills needed to practice through college-level specialized preparation in early childhood education/child development.

    *   Teachers in early childhood programs are encouraged and supported to obtain and maintain, through study and participation in inservice training, current knowledge of child development and learning and its application to early childhood practice.

    *   Specialists in early childhood special education are available to provide assistance and consultation in meeting the individual needs of children in the program.

    *   In addition to management and supervision skills, administrators of early childhood programs have appropriate professional qualifications, including training specific to the education and development of young children, and they provide teachers time and opportunities to work collaboratively with colleagues and parents.

2. Funding is provided to ensure adequate staffing of early childhood programs and fair staff compensation that promotes continuity of relationships among adults and children (Willer 1990).

    *   Funding is adequate to limit the size of the groups and provide sufficient numbers of adults to ensure individualized and appropriate care and education. Even the most well-qualified teacher cannot individualize instruction and adequately supervise too large a group of young children. An acceptable adult-child ratio for 4- and 5-year-olds is two adults with no more than 20 children. (Ruopp et al. 1979; Francis & Self 1982; Howes 1983; Taylor & Taylor 1989; Howes, Philips, & Whitebook 1992; Cost, Quality, & Child Outcomes Study Team 1995; Howes, Smith & Galinsky 1995). Younger children require much smaller groups. Group size and ratio of children to adults should increase gradually through the primary grades, but one teacher with no more than 18 children or two adults with no more than 25 children is optimum (Nye et al. 1992; Nye, Boyd-Zaharias, & Fulton 1994). Inclusion of children with disabilities may necessitate additional adults or smaller group size to ensure that all children's needs are met.

    *   Programs offer staff salaries and benefits commensurate with the skills and qualifications required for specific roles to ensure the provision of quality services and the effective recruitment and retention of qualified, competent staff. (See *Compensation*

Guidelines for Early Childhood Professionals [NAEYC 1993]).

- Decisions related to how programs are staffed and how children are grouped result in increased opportunities for children to experience continuity of relationships with teachers and other children. Such strategies include but are not limited to multiage grouping and multiyear teacher-child relationships (Katz, Evangelou, & Hartman 1990; Zero to Three 1995; Burke 1996).

3. Resources and expertise are available to provide safe, stimulating learning environments with a sufficient number and variety of appropriate materials and equipment for the age group served (Bronson 1995; Kendrick, Kaufmann, & Messenger 1995).

4. Adequate systems for regulating and monitoring the quality of early childhood programs are in place (see position on licensing [NAEYC 1987]; accreditation criteria and procedures [NAEYC 1991]).

5. Community resources are available and used to support the comprehensive needs of children and families (Kagan 1991; NASBE 1991; Kagan et al. 1995; NCSL 1995).

6. When individual children do not make expected learning progress, neither grade retention nor social promotion are used; instead, initiatives such as more focused time, individualized instruction, tutoring, or other individual strategies are used to accelerate children's learning (Shepard & Smith 1989; Ross et al. 1995).

7. Early childhood programs use multiple indicators of progress in all development domains to evaluate the effect of the program on children's development and learning and regularly report children's progress to parents. Group-administered, standardized, multiple-choice achievement tests are not used before third grade, preferably before fourth grade. When such tests are used to demonstrate public accountability, a sampling method is used (see Shepard 1994).

References

Adams, G., & J. Sandfort. 1994. *First steps, promising futures: State prekindergarten initiatives in the early 1990s.* Washington. DC: Children's Defense Fund.

Alexander, K.L., & D.R. Entwisle. 1988. *Achievement in the first 2 years of school: Patterns and processes.* Monographs of the Society for Research in Child Development, vol. 53, no. 2, serial no. 218. Ann Arbor: University of Michigan.

Arnett, J. 1989. Caregivers in day-care centers: Does training matter? *Journal of Applied Developmental Psychology* 10 (4): 541–52.

Asher, S., S. Hymel, & P. Renshaw. 1984. Loneliness in children. *Child Development* 55: 1456–64.

Barnett, W.S. 1995. Long-term effects of early childhood programs on cognitive and school outcomes. *The Future of Children* 5 (3): 25–50.

Bergen, D. 1988. *Play as a medium for learning and development.* Portsmouth, NH: Heinemann.

Berk, L.E. 1996. *Infants and children: Prenatal through middle childhood.* 2d ed. Needham Heights, MA: Allyn & Bacon.

Berk, L., & A. Winsler. 1995. *Scaffolding children's learning: Vygotsky and early childhood education.* Washington, DC: NAEYC.

Berruetta-Clement, J.R., L.J. Schweinhart, W.S. Barnett, A.S. Epstein, & D.P. Weikart. 1984. *Changed lives: The effects of the Perry Preschool Program on youths through age 19.* Monographs of the High/Scope Educational Research Foundation, no. 8. Ypsilanti, MI: High/Scope Press.

Bodrova, E., & D. Leong. 1996. *Tools of the mind: The Vygotskian approach to early childhood education.* Englewood Cliffs, NJ: Merrill/Prentice Hall.

Bowlby, J. 1969. *Attachment and loss: Vol.1. Attachment.* New York: Basic.

Bowman, B. 1994. The challenge of diversity. *Phi Delta Kappan* 76 (3): 218–25.

Bowman, B., & F. Stott. 1994. Understanding development in a cultural context: The challenge for teachers. In *Diversity and developmentally appropriate practices: Challenges for early childhood education,* eds. B. Mallory & R. New, 119–34. New York: Teachers College Press.

Bredekamp, S., ed. 1987. *Developmentally appropriate practice in early childhood programs serving children from birth through age 8.* Exp. ed. Washington, DC: NAEYC.

Bredekamp, S. 1993a. Reflections on Reggio Emilia. *Young Children* 49 (1): 13–17.

Bredekamp, S. 1993b. The relationship between early childhood education and early childhood special education: Healthy marriage or family feud? *Topics in Early Childhood Special Education* 13 (3): 258–73.

Bredekamp, S., & T. Rosegrant, eds. 1992. *Reaching potentials: Appropriate curriculum and assessment for young children, volume 1*. Washington, DC: NAEYC.

Bredekamp, S., & T. Rosegrant, eds. 1995. *Reaching potentials: Transforming early childhood curriculum and assessment, volume 2*. Washington, DC: NAEYC.

Bronfenbrenner, U. 1979. *The ecology of human development: Experiments by nature and design*. Cambridge, MA: Harvard University Press.

Bronfenbrenner, U. 1989. Ecological systems theory. In *Annals of child development*, Vol. 6, ed. R. Vasta, 187–251. Greenwich, CT: JAI Press.

Bronfenbrenner, U. 1993. The ecology of cognitive development: Research models and fugitive findings. In *Development in context*, eds. R.H. Wozniak & K.W. Fischer, 3–44. Hillsdale, NJ: Erlbaum.

Bronson, M.B. 1995. *The right stuff for children birth to 8: Selecting play materials to support development*. Washington, DC: NAEYC.

Brophy, J. 1992. Probing the subtleties of subject matter teaching. *Educational Leadership* 49 (7): 4–8.

Bruner, J.S. 1993. *Child's talk: Learning to use language*. New York: Norton.

Bruner, J.S. 1996. *The culture of education*. Cambridge, MA: Harvard University Press.

Bryant, D.M., R. Clifford, & E.S. Peisner. 1991. Best practices for beginners: Developmental appropriateness in kindergarten. *American Educational Research Journal* 28 (4): 783–803.

Burchinal, M., J. Robert, L. Nabo, & D. Bryant. 1996. Quality of center child care and infant cognitive and language development. *Child Development* 67 (2): 606–20.

Burke, D. 1966. Multi-year teacher/student relationships are a long-overdue arrangement. *Phi Delta Kappan* 77 (5): 360–61.

Caine, R., & G. Caine. 1991. *Making connections: Teaching and the human brain*. New York: Addison-Wesley.

Campbell, F., & C. Ramey. 1995. Cognitive and school outcomes for high-risk African-American students at middle adolescence: Positive effects of early intervention. *American Educational Research Journal* 32 (4): 743–72.

Carnegie Task Force on Learning in the Primary Grades. 1996. *Years of promise: A comprehensive learning strategy for America's children*. New York: Carnegie Corporation of New York.

Carta, J., I. Schwartz, J. Atwater, & S. McConnell. 1991. Developmentally appropriate practice: Appraising its usefulness for young children with disabilities. *Topics in Early Childhood Special Education* 11 (1): 1–20.

Case, R., & Y. Okamoto. 1996. *The role of central conceptual structures in the development of children's thought*. Monographs of the Society of Research in Child Development, vol. 61, no. 2, serial no. 246. Chicago: University of Chicago Press.

Charlesworth, R., C.H. Hart, D.C. Burts, & M. DeWolf. 1993. The LSU studies: Building a research base for developmentally appropriate practice. In *Perspectives on developmentally appropriate practice*, vol. 5 of *Advances in early education and day care*, ed. S. Reifel, 3–28. Greenwich, CT: JAI Press.

Chugani, H., M.E. Phelps, & J.C. Mazziotta. 1987. Positron emission tomography study of human brain functional development. *Annals of Neurology* 22 (4): 495.

Cohen, N., & K. Modigliani. 1994. The family-to-family project: Developing family child care providers. In *The early childhood career lattice: Perspectives on professional development*, eds. J. Johnson & J.B. McCracken, 106–10. Washington, DC: NAEYC.

Copple, C., I.E. Sigel, & R. Saunders. 1984. *Educating the young thinker: Classroom strategies for cognitive growth*. Hillsdale, NJ: Erlbaum.

Cost, Quality, & Child Outcomes Study Team. 1995. *Cost, quality, and child outcomes in child care centers, public report*. 2d ed. Denver: Economics Department, University of Colorado at Denver.

Dana Alliance for Brain Initiatives. 1996. *Delivering results: A progress report on brain research*. Washington, DC: Author.

DEC/CEC (Division for Early Childhood of the Council for Exceptional Children). 1994. Position on inclusion. *Young Children* 49 (5): 78.

DEC (Division for Early Childhood) Task Force on Recommended Practices. 1993. *DEC recommended practices: Indicators of quality in programs for infants and young children with special needs and their families*. Reston, VA: Council for Exceptional Children.

DEC/CEC & NAEYC (Division for Early Childhood of the Council for Exceptional Children & the National Association for the Education of Young Children). 1993. *Understanding the ADA—The Americans with Disability Act: Information for early childhood programs*. Pittsburgh, PA, & Washington, DC: Authors.

DeVries, R., & W. Kohlberg. 1990. *Constructivist early education: Overview and comparison with other programs*. Washington, DC: NAEYC.

Dewey, J. 1916. *Democracy and education: An introduction to the philosophy of education*. New York: Macmillan.

Durkin, D. 1987. A classroom-observation study of reading instruction in kindergarten. *Early Childhood Research Quarterly* 2 (3): 275–300.

Durkin, D. 1990. Reading instruction in kindergarten: A look at some issues through the lens of new basal reader materials. *Early Children Research Quarterly* 5 (3): 299–316.

Dweck, C. 1986. Motivational processes affecting learning. *American Psychologist* 41: 1030–48.

Dyson, A.H., & C. Genishi. 1993. Visions of children as language users: Language and language education in early childhood. In *Handbook of research on the education of young children*, ed. B. Spodek, 122–36. New York: Macmillan.

Edwards, C.P., & L. Gandini. 1989. Teachers' expectations about the timing of developmental skills: A cross-cultural study. *Young Children* 44 (4): 15–19.

Edwards, C., L. Gandini, & G. Forman, eds. 1993. *The hundred languages of children: The Reggio Emilia approach to early childhood education.* Norwood, NJ: Ablex.

Erikson, E. 1963. *Childhood and society.* New York: Norton.

Feeney, S., & K. Kipnis. 1992. *Code of ethical conduct & statement of commitment.* Washington, DC: NAEYC.

Fein, G. 1981. Pretend play: An integrative review. *Child Development* 52: 1095–118.

Fein, G., & M. Rivkin, eds. *The young child at play: Reviews of research.* Washington, DC: NAEYC.

Fenson, L., P. Dale, J.S. Reznick, E. Bates, D. Thal, & S. Pethick. 1994. *Variability in early communicative development.* Monographs of the Society for Research in Child Development, vol. 59, no. 2, serial no. 242. Chicago: University of Chicago Press.

Fernald, A. 1992. Human Maternal vocalizations in infants as biologically relevant signals: An evolutionary perspective. In *The adapted mind: Evolutionary psychology and the generation of culture*, eds. J.H. Barkow, L. Cosmides, & J. Tooby, 391–428. New York: Oxford University Press.

Fields, T., W. Masi, S. Goldstein, S. Perry, & S. Parl. 1988. Infant day care facilities preschool social behavior. *Early Childhood Research Quarterly* 3 (4): 341–59.

Forman, G. 1994. Different media, different languages. In *Reflections on the Reggio Emilia approach*, eds. L. Katz & B. Cesarone, 37–46. Urbana, IL: ERIC Clearinghouse on EECE.

Forman, E.A., N. Minick, & C.A. Stone. 1993. *Contexts for learning: Sociocultural dynamics in children's development.* New York: Oxford University Press.

Francis, P., & P. Self. 1982. Imitative responsiveness of young children in day care and home settings: The importance of the child to caregiver ratio. *Child Study Journal* 12: 119–26.

Frede, E. 1995. The role of program quality in producing early childhood program benefits. *The Future of Children*, 5 (3): 115–132.

Frede, E., & W.S. Barnett. 1992. Developmentally appropriate public school preschool: A study of implementation of the High/Scope curriculum and its effects on disadvantaged children's skills at first grade. *Early Childhood Research Quarterly* 7 (4): 483–99.

Fromberg, D. 1992. Play. In *The early childhood curriculum: A review of current research*, 2d ed., ed. C. Seefeldt, 35–74. New York: Teachers College Press.

Galinsky, E., C. Howes, S. Kontos, & M. Shinn. 1994. *The study of children in family child care and relative care: Highlights of findings.* New York: Families and Work Institute.

Gallahue, D. 1993. Motor development and movement skill acquisition in early childhood education. In *Handbook of research on the education of young children*, ed. B. Spodek, 24–41. New York: Macmillan.

Gallahue, D. 1995. Transforming physical education curriculum. In *Reaching potentials: Transforming early childhood curriculum and assessment, volume 2*, eds. S. Bredekamp & T. Rosegrant, 125–44. Washington, DC: NAEYC.

Garbarino, J., N. Dubrow, K. Kostelny, & C. Pardo. 1992. *Children in danger: Coping with the consequences of community violence.* San Francisco: Jossey-Bass.

Gardner, H. 1983. *Frames of mind: The theory of multiple intelligences.* New York: Basic.

Gardner, H. 1991. *The unschooled mind: How children think and how schools should teach.* New York: Basic.

Gelman, R., & R. Baillargeon. 1983. A review of some Piagetian concepts. In *Handbook of Child Psychology*, vol. 3, ed. P.H. Mussen, 167–230. New York: Wiley.

Gelman, R., & E. Meck. 1983. Preschoolers' counting: Principles before skill. *Cognition* 13: 343–59.

Hale-Benson, J. 1986. *Black children: Their roots, cultures, and learning styles.* Rev. ed. Baltimore: Johns Hopkins University Press.

Herron, R., & B. Sutton-Smith. 1971. *Child's play.* New York: Wiley.

Hiebert, E.H., & J.M. Papierz. 1990. The emergent literacy construct and kindergarten and readiness books of basal reading series. *Early childhood Research Quarterly* 5 (3): 317–34.

Hohmann, M., & D. Weikart. 1995. *Educating young children: Active learning practices for preschool and child care programs.* Ypsilanti, MI: High/Scope Educational Research Foundation.

Hollestelle, K. 1993. At the core: Entrepreneurial skills for family child care providers. In *The early childhood career lattice: Perspectives on professional development*, eds. J. Johnson & J.B. McCracken, 63–65. Washington, DC: NAEYC.

Howes, C. 1983. Caregiver behavior in center and family day care. *Journal of Applied Developmental Psychology* 4: 96–107.

Howes, C. 1988. Relations between early child care and schooling. *Developmental Psychology* 24 (1): 53–57.

Howes, C., D.A. Phillips, M. Whitebook. 1992. Thresholds of quality: Implications for the social development of children in center-based child care. *Child Development* 63 (2): 449–60.

Howes, C., E. Smith, & E. Galinsky. 1995. *The Florida child care quality improvement study.* New York: Families and Work Institute.

Kagan, S.L. 1991. *United we stand: Collaboration for child care and early education services.* New York: Teachers College Press.

Kagan, S., S. Goffin, S. Golub, & E. Pritchard. 1995. *Toward systematic reform: Service integration for young children and their families.* Falls Church, VA: National Center for Service Integration.

Kamil, C., & J.K. Ewing. 1996. Basing teaching on Piaget's constructivism. *Childhood Education* 72 (5): 260–64.

Katz, L. 1995. *Talks with teachers of young children: A collection.* Norwood, NJ: Ablex.

Katz, L., & S. Chard. 1989. *Engaging children minds: The project approach.* Norwood, NJ: Ablex.

Katz, L., D. Evangelou, & J. Hartman. 1990. *The case for mixed-age grouping in early education.* Washington, DC: NAEYC.

Kendrick, A., R. Kaufmann, & K. Messenger, eds. 1995. *Healthy young children: A manual for programs.* Washington, DC: NAEYC.

Kohn, A. 1993. *Punished by rewards.* Boston: Houghton Mifflin.

Kostelnik, M., A Soderman, & A. Whiren. 1993. *Developmentally appropriate programs in early childhood education.* New York: Macmillan.

Kuhl, P. 1994. Learning and representation in speech and language. *Current Opinion in Neurobiology* 4: 812–22.

Lary, R.T. 1990. Successful students. *Education Issues* 3 (2): 11–17.

Layzer, J.I., B.D. Goodson, & M. Moss. 1993. *Life in preschool: Volume one of an observational study of early childhood programs for disadvantaged four-year-olds.* Cambridge, MA: Abt Association.

Lazar, I., & R. Darlington. 1982. *Lasting effects of early education: A report from the consortium for longitudinal studies.* Monographs of the Society for Research in Child Development, vol. 47, nos. 2-3, serial no. 195. Chicago: University of Chicago Press.

Lee, V.E., J. Brooks-Gunn, & E. Schuur. 1988. Does Head Start work? A 1-year follow-up comparison of disadvantaged children attending Head Start, no preschool, and other preschool programs. *Developmental Psychology* 24 (2): 210–22.

Legters, N., & R.E. Slavin. 1992. Elementary students at risk: A status report. Paper commissioned by the Carnegie Corporation of New York for meeting on elementary-school reform. 1–2 June.

Levy, A.K., L. Schaefer, & P.C. Phelps. 1986. Increasing preschool effectiveness: Enhancing the language abilities of 3- and 4-year-old children through planned sociodramatic play. *Early Childhood Research Quarterly* 1 (2): 133–40.

Levy, A.K., C.H. Wolfgang, & M.A. Koorland. 1992. Sociodramatic play as a method for enhancing the language performance of kindergarten age students. *Early Childhood Research Quarterly* 7 (2): 245–62.

Malaguzzi, L. 1993. History, ideas, and basic philosophy. In *The hundred languages of children: The Regggio Emilia approach to early childhood education*, eds. C. Edwards, L. Gandini, & G. Forman, 41–89.Norwood, NJ: Ablex.

Mallory, B. 1992. Is it always appropriate to be developmental? Convergent models for early intervention practice. *Topics in Early Childhood Special Education* 11 (4): 1–12.

Mallory, B. 1994. Inclusive policy, practice, and theory for young children with developmental differences. In *Diversity and developmentally appropriate practices: Challenges for early childhood education*, eds. B. Mallory & R. New, 44–61. New York: Teachers College Press.

Mallory, B.L., & R.S. New. 1994a. *Diversity and developmentally appropriate practices: Challenges for early childhood education.* New York: Teachers College Press.

Mallory, B.L., & R.S. New. 1994b. Social constructivist theory and principles of inclusions: Callenges for early childhood special education. *Journal of Special Education* 28 (3): 322–37.

Marcon, R.A. 1992. Differential effects of three preschool models on inner-city 4-year-olds. *Early Childhood Research Quarterly* 7 (4): 517–30.

Maslow, A. 1954. *Motivation and personality.* New York: Harper & Row.

Miller, L.B., & R.P. Bizzell. 1984. Long-term effects of four preschool programs: Ninth and tenth-grade results. *Child Development* 55 (4): 1570–87.

Mitchell, A., M. Seligson, & F. Marx. 1989. *Early childhood programs and the public schools.* Dover, MA: Auburn House.

Morrow, L.M. 1990. Preparing the classroom environment to promote literacy during play. *Early Childhood Research Quarterly* 5 (4): 537–54.

NAEYC. 1987. *NAEYC position statement on licensing and other forms of regulation of early childhood programs in centers and family day care.* Washington, DC: Author.

NAEYC. 1991. *Accreditation criteria and procedures of the National Academy of Early Childhood Programs.* Rev. ed. Washington, DC: Author.

NAEYC. 1993. *Compensation guidelines for early childhood professionals.* Washington, DC: Author.

NAEYC. 1994. NAEYC position statement: A conceptual framework for early childhood professional development, adopted November 1993. *Young Children* 49 (3): 68–77.

NAEYC. 1996a NAEYC position statement: Responding to linguistic and cultural diversity—Recommendations for effective early childhood education. *Young Children* 51 (2): 4–12.

NAEYC. 1996b. NAEYC position statement: Technology and young children—Ages three through eight. *Young Children* 51 (6): 11–16.

NAEYC & NAECS/SDE (National Association of Early Childhood Specialists in State Departments of Education). 1992. Guidelines for appropriate curriculum content and assessment in programs serving children ages 3 through 8. In *Reaching potentials: Appropriate curriculum and assessment for young children, volume 1,* eds. S. Bredekamp & T. Rosegrant, 9–27. Washington, DC: NAEYC.

NASBE (National Association of State Boards of Education). 1991. *Caring communities: Supporting young children and families.* Alexandria, VA: Author.

Natriello, G., E. McDill, & A. Pallas. 1990. *Schooling disadvantaged children: Racing against catastrophe.* New York: Teachers College Press.

NCES (National Center for Education Statistics). 1993. *The condition of education, 1993.* Washington, DC: U.S. Department of Education.

NCSL (National Conference of State Legislatures). 1995. *Early childhood care and education: An investment that works.* Denver: Author.

NEGP (National Education Goals Panel). 1991. *National education goals report: Building a nation of learners.* Washington, DC: Author.

New, R. 1993. Cultural variations on developmentally appropriate practice: Challenges to theory and practice. In *The hundred languages of children: The Reggio Emilia approach to early childhood education,* eds C. Edwards, L. Gandini, & G. Forman, 215–32. Norwood, NJ: Ablex.

New, R. 1994. Culture, child development, and developmentally appropriate practices: Teachers as collaborative researchers. In *Diversity and developmentally appropriate practices: Challenges for early childhood education,* eds. B. Mallory & R. New, 65–83. New York: Teachers College Press.

Nye, B.A., J. Boyd-Zaharias, & B.D. Fulton. 1994. *The lasting benefits study: A continuing analysis of the effect of small class size in kindergarten through third grade on student achievement test scores in subsequent grade levels—seventh grade (1992–93), technical report.* Nashville: Center of Excellence for Research in Basic Skills, Tennessee State University.

Nye, B.A., J. Boyd-Zaharias, B.D. Fulton, & M.P. Wallenhorst. 1992. Smaller classes really are better. *The American School Board Journal* 179 (5): 31–33.

Parker, J.G., & S.R. Asher. 1987. Peer relations and later personal adjustment: Are low-accepted children at risk? *Psychology Bulletin* 102 (3): 357–89.

Phillips, C.B. 1994. The movement of African-American children through sociocultural contexts: A case of conflict resolution. In *Diversity and developmentally appropriate practices: Challenges for early childhood education,* eds. B. Mallory & R. New, 137–54. New York: Teachers College Press.

Phillips, D.A., K. McCartney, & S. Scarr. 1987. Child care quality and children's social development. *Developmental Psychology* 23 (4): 537–43.

Piaget, J. 1952. *The origins of intelligence in children.* New York: International Universities Press.

Plomin, R. 1994a. *Genetics and experience: The interplay between nature and nurture.* Thousand Oaks, CA: Sage.

Plomin, R. 1994b. Nature, nurture, and social development. *Social Development* 3: 37–53.

Powell, D. 1994. Parents, pluralism, and the NAEYC statement on developmentally approriate practice. In *Diversity and developmentally appropriate practices: Challenges for early childhood education,* eds. B. Mallory & R. New, 166–82. New York: Teachers College Press.

Pramling, I. 1991. Learning about "the shop": An approach to learning in preschool. *Early Children Research Quarterly* 6 (2): 151–66.

Resnick, L. 1996. Schooling and the workplace: What relationship? In *Preparing youth for the 21st century,* 21–27. Washington, DC: Aspen Institute.

Rogoff, B. 1990. *Apprenticeship in thinking: Cognitive development in social context.* New York: Oxford University Press.

Rogoff, B., J. Mistry, A. Goncu, & C. Mosier. 1993. *Guided participation in cultural activity by toddlers and caregivers.* Monographs of the Society for Research in Child Development, vol. 58, no. 8, serial no. 236. Chicago: University of Chicago Press.

Ross, S.M., L.J. Smith, J. Casey, & R.E. Slavin. 1995. Increasing the academic success of disadvantaged children: An examination of alternative early intervention programs. *American Educational Research Journal* 32 (4): 773–800.

Ruopp, R., J. Travers, F. Glantz, & C. Coelen. 1979. *Children at the center: Final report of the National Day Care Study.* Cambridge, MA: ABT Associates.

Sameroff, A., & S. McDonough. 1994. Educational implications of developmental transition: Revisiting the 5- to 7-year shift. *Phi Delta Kappan* 76 (3): 188–93.

Scarr, S., & K. McCartney. 1983. How people make their own environments: A theory of genotype–environment effects. *Child Development* 54: 425–35.

Schrader, C.T. 1989. Written language use within the context of young children's symbolic play. *Early Childhood Research Quarterly* 4 (2): 225–44.

Schrader, C.T. 1990. Symbolic play as a curricular tool for early literacy development. *Early Childhood Research Quarterly* 5 (1): 79–103.

Schweinhart, L.J., & D.P. Weikart. 1996. *Lasting differences: The High/Scope preschool curriculum comparison study through age 23.* Monographs of the High/Scope Educational Research Foundation, no 12. Ypsilanti, MI: High/Scope Press.

Schweinhart, L.J., H.V. Barnes, & D.P. Weikart. 1993. *Significant benefits: The High/Scope Perry Preschool Study through age 27.* Monographs of the High/Scope Educational Research Foundation, no. 10, Ypsilanti, MI: High/Scope Press.

Schweinhart, L.J., D.P. Weikart, & M.B. Larner. 1986. Child-initiated activities in early childhood programs may help prevent delinquency. *Early Childhood Research Quarterly* 1 (3): 303–12.

Seefeldt, C., ed. 1992. *The early childhood curriculum: A review of current research.* 2d ed. New York: Teachers College Press.

Seifert, K. 1993. Cognitive development and early childhood education. In *Handbook of research on the education of young children,* ed. B. Spodek, 9–23. New York: Macmillan.

Seppanen, P.S., D. Kaplan deVries, & M. Seligson. 1993. *National study of before and after school programs.* Portsmouth, NH: RMC Research Corp.

Shepard, L. 1994. The challenges of assessing young children appropriately. *Phi Delta Kappan* 76 (3): 206–13.

Shepard, L.A., & M.L. Smith. 1988. Escalating academic demand in kindergarten: Some nonsolutions. *Elementary School Journal* 89 (2): 135–46.

Shepard, L.A., & M.L. Smith. 1989. *Flunking grades: Research and policies on retention.* Bristol, PA: Taylor & Francis.

Slavin, R., N.Karweit, & N. Madden, eds. 1989. *Effective programs for students at-risk.* Boston: Allyn & Bacon.

Smilansky, S., & L. Shefatya. 1990. *Facilitating play: A medium for promoting cognitive, socioemotional, and academic development in young children.* Gaithersburg, MD: Psychosocial & Educational Publications.

Spodek, B., ed. 1993. *Handbook of research on the education of young children.* New York: Macmillan.

Sroufe, L.A., R.G. Cooper, & G.B. DeHart. 1992. *Child development: Its nature and course.* 2d ed. New York: Knopf.

Stern, D. 1985. *The psychological world of the human infant.* New York: Basic.

Stremmel, A.J., & V.R. Fu. 1993. Teaching in the zone of proximal development: Implications for responsive teaching practice. *Child and Youth Care Forum* 22 (5): 337–50.

Taylor, J.M., & W.S. Taylor. 1989. *Communicable diseases and young children in group settings.* Boston: Little, Brown.

Tobin, J., D. Wu, & D. Davidson. 1989. *Preschool in three cultures.* New Haven, CT: Yale University Press.

U.S. Department of Health & Human Services. 1996. *Head Start performance standards.* Washington, DC: Author.

Vandell, D.L., & M.A. Corasanti. 1990. Variations in early child care: Do they predict subsequent social, emotional, and cognitive differences? *Early Childhood Research Quarterly* 5 (4): 555–72.

Vandell, D.L., & C.D. Powers. 1983. Day care quality and children's freeplay activities. *American Journal of Orthopsychiatry* 53 (4): 493–500.

Vandell, D.L., V.K. Henderson, & K.S. Wilson. 1988. A longitudinal study of children with day-care experiences of varying quality. *Child Development* 59 (5): 1286–92.

Vygotsky, L. 1978. *Mind in society: The development of higher psychological processes.* Cambridge, MA: Harvard University Press.

Wardle, F. 1996. Proposal: An anti-bias and ecological model for multicultural education. *Childhood Education* 72 (3): 152–56.

Wertsch, J. 1985. *Culture, communication, and cognition: Vygotskian perspectives.* New York: Cambridge University Press.

White, S.H. 1965. Evidence for a hierarchical arrangement of learning processes. In *Advances in child development and behavior,* eds. L.P. Lipsitt & C.C. Spiker, 187–220. New York: Academic Press.

Whitebook, M., C. Howes, & D. Philips. 1989. *The national child care staffing study: Who cares? Child care teachers and the quality of care in America.* Final report. Oakland, CA: Child Care Employee Project.

Wieder, S., & S.I. Greenspan. 1993. The emotional basis of learning. In *Handbook of research on the education of young children,* ed. B. Spodek, 77–104. New York: Macmillan.

Willer, B. 1990. *Reaching the full cost of quality in early childhood programs.* Washington, DC: NAEYC.

Willer, B., S.L. Hofferth, E.E. Kisker, P. Divine-Hawkins, E. Farquhar, & F.B. Glantz. 1991. *The demand and supply of child care in 1990.* Washington, DC.: NAEYC.

Witkin, H. 1962. *Psychological differentiation: Studies of development.* New York: Wiley.

Wolery, M., & J. Wilbers, eds. 1994. *Including children with special needs in early childhood programs.* Washington, DC: NAEYC.

Wolery, M., P. Strain, & D. Bailey. 1992. Reaching potentials of children with special needs. In *Reaching Potentials: Appropriate curriculum and assessment for young children, volume 1,* eds. S. Bredekamp & T. Rosegrant, 92–111. Washington, DC: NAEYC.

Zero to Three: The National Center, 1995. *Caring for infants and toddlers in groups: Developmentally appropriate practice.* Arlington, VA: Author.

Highlights of the NAEYC Position Statement: Technology and Young Children

Although now there is considerable research that points to the positive effects of technology on children's learning and development (Clements 1994), the research indicates that, in practice, computers supplement and do not replace highly valued early childhood activities and materials, such as art, blocks, sand, water, books, exploration with writing materials, and dramatic play. Research indicates that computers can be used in developmentally appropriate ways beneficial to children and also can be misused, just as any tool can (Shade & Watson 1990). Developmentally appropriate software offers opportunities for collaborative play, learning, and creation. Educators must use professional judgment in evaluating and using this learning tool appropriately, applying the same criteria they would to any other learning tool or experience. They must also weigh the costs of technology with the costs of other learning materials and program resources to arrive at an appropriate balance for their classrooms.

- In evaluating the appropriate use of technology, NAEYC applies principles of developmentally appropriate practice (Bredekamp 1987) and appropriate curriculum and assessment (NAEYC & NAECS/SDE 1992). In short, NAEYC believes that in any given situation, a professional judgment by the teacher is required to determine if a specific use of technology is age appropriate, individually appropriate, and culturally appropriate.

- Used appropriately, technology can enhance children's cognitive and social abilities.

- Appropriate technology is integrated into the regular learning environment and used as one of many options to support children's learning.

- Early childhood educators should promote equitable access to technology for all children and their families. Children with special needs should have increased access when this is helpful.

- The power of technology to influence children's learning and development requires that attention be paid to eliminating stereotyping of any group and eliminating exposure to violence, especially as a problem-solving strategy.

- Teachers, in collaboration with parents, should advocate for more appropriate technology applications for children.

- The appropriate use of technology has many implications for early childhood professional development.

Individualized Family Service Plan

NAME: Kevin Taylor
DATE OF BIRTH: 5/24/93
AGE: 19 mos., 19 days
DATE OF ASSESSMENT &
  IFSP MEETING: 1/13/95
DATE OF REPORT: 1/25/95
SERVICE COORDINATOR: Lara Clark
LEGAL GUARDIAN: Bob & Tammy Taylor
ADDRESS: 242 American Drive
          Williamsburg, VA 23188
PHONE: 555-0303

Pertinent History

This is Kevin's third assessment at Child Development Resources (CDR). He has been in the Infant-Parent Program since November 1993 because of his diagnosis of Down syndrome, developmental delays, and medical complications. Since his last assessment, Kevin has received weekly home visits from Lara Clark and several motor consultations from a physical therapist. Kevin has not been able to attend Developmental Play Group owing to his ongoing illnesses.

Kevin continues to have upper-respiratory infections and ear infections. He has been receiving his medical care at Williamsburg Community Hospital. Kevin is scheduled to have an ear, nose, and throat (ENT) consultation at the Children's Hospital of the King's Daughters in February. Since Kevin's surgery in June 1994, his health has greatly improved. He was weaned off oxygen in September and is no longer required to use the apnea monitor (which checks a child's breathing—it sounds an alarm if the child stops breathing). Kevin continues to get breathing treatments as needed for congestion. He has not been hospitalized since his surgery in June.

Kevin's hearing and vision have not been formally tested since his stay in the neonatal infant care unit (NICU) after his birth. His parents will continue to monitor his condition, but at this time there are no concerns. His hearing may be evaluated when he goes for the ENT in February.

Child Assessment

Assessment Team Members

Tammy Taylor	Parent
Lynda Olive	Speech pathologist
Lisa Davis	Occupational therapist
Lara Clark	Infant development specialist

Assessment Instruments Used

Early Learning Accomplishment Profile (E-LAP)—selected sections

Receptive-Expressive Emergent Language Scale (REEL)

Source: Child Development Resources, Norge, Virginia. Used by permission. The author would like to thank CDR for graciously contributing this material.

The Infant Scale of Communicative Intent

Uzgiris-Hunt Scales of Infant Development (Dunst)—selected sections

Fewell Play Assessment Scale

Social-Emotional Developmental Profile (SEED)

Hawaii Early Learning Profile (HELP)—selected sections

Peabody Developmental Motor Scales

Family observations and report

Clinical observations

Strengths, Concerns, and Developmental Levels

Kevin played for about an hour during the assessment with a variety of toys and people. Along with his mother, Kevin showed the team many of the social games he enjoys playing. He likes to play a game in which his mother counts, "1-2-3," and then he vocalizes a prolonged "Aah." Kevin raises both hands in the air when his mother asks, "How big is Kevin?" After he raises his hands, she says, "So big." He likes to make raspberries and prolonged "s" and "f" sounds. He also babbles (repeats consonant-vowel combinations), most frequently with the "d" sound. He also frequently uses single consonant-vowel combinations such as "da." He was observed to use the "n," "m," and "t" sounds as well in such combinations. Signs for some major concept words have been introduced to Kevin, but he is not yet copying them.

Kevin very quickly and consistently found the source of many sounds occurring in the assessment room. He shows, by turning to look or getting excited, that he knows the names of his family members. When his name is called, he stops what he is doing and turns to look at the person speaking. He shows by his actions that he knows what "ball" and "music" mean, which are favorite things. He tries to put his arms up in response to someone saying, "Do you want up?" He sometimes tries to move one of his arms in response to "bye-bye." He also seems to know what "down" means. He understands simple requests such as "clap-clap" or "dance." He understands what "Come here" means when a hand gesture accompanies it. When he is holding something and an adult requests, "Give it to me" with an accompanying hand gesture, he will hold out the object to them but not yet release it. Kevin likes to look at books and will do so for several minutes. He does not yet point to the pictures when they are named.

Kevin has learned to sit by himself for a few minutes. When a toy falls behind him, he has difficulty reaching around to pick it up and topples over backward. When he wants to get down from a sitting position, Kevin is able to twist at his waist and lower himself down with his hands, although his movements are fast, and sometimes he bumps his head on toys or objects that get in his way. He has not yet learned to get into a sitting position from lying on his back or stomach by himself. When on his stomach on the floor, Kevin pushes up on his hands with his arms straightened. He is able to reach for toys in front of him while holding himself up in this position with his other arm. Frequently he pushes himself up onto his hands and knees and rocks back and forth. He has recently learned to move himself forward on the floor by lunging forward on his stomach in an inchworm type of a crawl. When held in a standing position with support at his hips and chest, Kevin takes most of his weight on his feet. Occasionally, he will stand while leaning his upper body on furniture and with support given to his hips. His mother reports that he enjoys kneeling on the sofa and rocking himself at home. Standing and kneeling activities are good to help Kevin strengthen the muscles of his hips and legs.

Kevin uses his hands and eyes together to play with toys in a variety of ways. He has learned to bring his hands together in front of him to bang toys together he is holding or to clap his hands. When given a plastic stick, he used it to bang on a drum purposefully. Kevin took blocks out of a container. He banged the blocks together when his mother told him to "clap clap" the blocks, then he flung a block. He frequently threw other toys he was holding as well. This is a typical stage children go through, and it shows us that Kevin is learning to let go of toys when he wants to. At home, Kevin is just beginning to learn to put things back into containers. His mother has Kevin put his toys into a very large basket. Kevin occasionally points his index finger as he is playing to point in the air or sometimes to poke into the hole of a toy. He uses his index finger and thumb together to work some toys, like the lever of a pop-up box. Often, if he does not get the toy to work with his finger, he will use his whole hand to bang the toy.

Kevin is showing signs that he is ready to give up his bottle, but he will not yet take much fluid from a cup. He usually will hold his mouth open and let the liquid run out or spit it out, especially if it is milk. His mother has tried thickening the liquids without much success. Kevin will eat pureed table foods or baby foods. He will also take semisolids of a thick, even texture. He rejects many foods having an uneven texture to them. Observation of Kevin eating indicated that his gag reflex is elicited very far forward on his tongue. Kevin is also beginning to use the thumb side of his hand to pick up tiny objects like Cheerios from his tray, but he has not yet figured out how to put them in his mouth to eat them.

Kevin shows skills at the seven- to eight-month level in the areas of gross-motor and receptive-language development. His expressive-language skills are scattered from six to eight months. He shows skills at the nine- to eleven-month level in the area of fine-motor development. Kevin's cognitive skills range from eleven to fifteen months and his social skills from twelve to fifteen months. In the area of self-help development, Kevin is demonstrating skills at the nine-month level. He is eligible for CDR's Infant-Parent Program and Part H services of IDEA (Individuals with Disabilities Education Act) because of his diagnosis of Down syndrome and developmental delays. (Part H of IDEA applies to infants and toddlers and requires an IFSP.)

Family Concerns, Resources, and Priorities

Kevin's parents are most concerned about his developmental progress. They would like to see Kevin be able to sit more steadily, kneel at furniture to play, drink more from a cup, and play with a variety of toys. They are anxious to see the ENT with hopes of decreasing Kevin's ear infections.

Since Kevin will turn two this spring, he will be old enough to attend the public school program in the fall. Kevin's family has looked at other available community programs and decided to start the eligibility process this spring for the Hometown public school program. Lara Clark and other CDR staff will assist Kevin's family through the transition process as requested by the Taylors.

OUTCOME: Kevin will begin to feed himself.

OBJECTIVES/CRITERIA	STRATEGIES	PERSONS RESPONSIBLE	REVIEW/ MODIFY (DATE)	STATUS REPORTED BY (DATE)
1. Kevin will take more liquids from a cup and less from the bottle.	1a. Activities from *Pre-Feeding Skills:* pp. 240–242, 301–302; 1b. *HELP* curriculum: pp. 472, 473, 481, 490.	Family Members, Primary Service Provider, Develop. Play Group Staff	5/95	
2. Kevin will eat foods with a variety of textures and with mixed textures.	2a. Activities from *Pre-Feeding Skills*: p. 231, Option 5, p. 232, Option 7, p. 225, Option 1, p. 226, Option 4. 2b. *HELP* curriculum: pp. 468, 470–471.	"	5/95	
3. Kevin will use his thumb and index finger together to pick up and feed finger foods to himself.	3a. *Learning Through Play* curriculum: pp. 158D, 179A; 3b. *HELP* curriculum: pp. 336; 343, 476.	"	7/95	

OUTCOME: Kevin will use his eyes and hands together to play with a variety of toys in new ways.

OBJECTIVES/CRITERIA	STRATEGIES	PERSONS RESPONSIBLE	REVIEW/ MODIFY (DATE)	STATUS REPORTED BY (DATE)
1. Kevin will make visible marks on paper with crayons.	1a. *HELP* curriculum: pp. 344, 328, 353;	Family Members, Primary Service Provider, Develop. Play Group Staff	5/95	
2. Kevin will put various toys, objects, and shapes into different-sized openings of containers.	2a. *HELP* curriculum: pp. 65, 346, 354; 2b. *Learning Through Play* curriculum: pp. 208–209,B.		6/95	
3. Kevin will use his index finger to point to pictures, push buttons of toys, and poke into holes of toys while he plays.	3a. *HELP* curriculum: pp. 342, 351, 89.	"	7/95	

OUTCOMES RELATED TO CHILD DEVELOPMENT

OUTCOME: Kevin will strengthen the muscles of his arms, shoulders, legs, hips, stomach, and back in order to help him move in new ways and more independently.

OBJECTIVES/CRITERIA	STRATEGIES	PERSONS RESPONSIBLE	REVIEW/ MODIFY (DATE)	STATUS REPORTED BY (DATE)
1. Kevin will prevent himself from falling backwards and sideways while sitting by using his arms to catch himself.	1a. *HELP* curriculum: p. 250; 1b. Tilting games on a large ball or an adult's lap; 1c. *Positioning for Play: Home Activities for Parents* pp. 95, 99, 105, 107.	Family Members, Primary Service Provider, Develop. Play Group Staff	5/95	
2. Kevin will pivot or twist around in a circle while he is sitting to get toys placed out of reach.	2a. *HELP* curriculum: p. 256.	"	7/95	
3. Kevin will get into a sitting position from lying on hips, stomach, or back without help.	3a. *HELP* curriculum: p. 241.	"	6/95	
4. Kevin will play with his toys while maintaining a kneeling position at furniture.	4a. *Positioning for Play: Home Activities for Parents* pp. 125, 127, 129.	"	5/95	
5. Kevin will stand while holding onto a support.	5a. *HELP* curriculum: p. 242; 5b. *Positioning for Play: Home Activities for Parents* pp. 137, 139, 143–5.	"	7/95	

564

OUTCOMES RELATED TO CHILD DEVELOPMENT

OUTCOME: Kevin will use more sounds, signs, and words to communicate with others.

OBJECTIVES/CRITERIA	STRATEGIES	PERSONS RESPONSIBLE	REVIEW/ MODIFY (DATE)	STATUS REPORTED BY (DATE)
1. Kevin will use gestures to say "yes," "no," and "good-bye" and to play games.	1a. *HELP ... at Home* curriculum: pp. 46, 67, 151; 1b. *Learning Through Play* curriculum: pp. 170C, 193C.	Family Members, Primary Service Provider, Develop. Play Group Staff	5/95	
2. Kevin will begin to use words and/or signs to name, request, protest, say good-bye, greet, and refuse.	2a. *HELP ... at Home* curriculum: pp. 152, 164, 166, 167; 2b. *Learning Through Play* curriculum: p. 194D; 2c. *The Comprehensive Signed English Dictionary.*	"	6/95	

OUTCOMES RELATED TO CHILD DEVELOPMENT

OUTCOME: Kevin will understand more of the words, signs, phrases, and sentences that others use to communicate with him.

OBJECTIVES/CRITERIA	STRATEGIES	PERSONS RESPONSIBLE	REVIEW/ MODIFY (DATE)	STATUS REPORTED BY (DATE)
1. Kevin will show by his actions that he knows the names of some common objects.	1a. *Help ... at Home* curriculum: pp. 48, 51; 1b. *Learning Through Play* curriculum: pp. 167C, 192B; 1c. *Comprehensive Signed English Dictionary.*	Family Members, Primary Service Provider, Develop. Play Group Staff	3/95	
2. Kevin will show by his actions that he under-stands simple questions and one-step requests.	2a. *HELP ... at Home* curriculum: pp. 47, 57, 58; 2b. *Learning Through Play* curriculum: p. 192A.	"	6/95	

OTHER OUTCOMES DESIRED BY THE FAMILY

OUTCOME	COURSE OF ACTION	REVIEW/ MODIFY (DATE)	PARENTS' REPORT OF PROGRESS TOWARD OUTCOME (DATE)
1. Kevin will have a smooth transition from CDR to the public schools (Fall 1995).	1a. Kevin's family and Lara will visit the Play Center to observe classrooms, therapies, and to meet the staff.	Feb. 1995	
	1b. Kevin will be referred to the Play Center by Lara with parent's permission.	Mar. 1995	
	1c. Kevin's parents and Lara will attend eligibility and IEP meetings as needed.	May/June 1995	
	1d. Kevin will attend Developmental Play Group more frequently in the spring to help him prepare for transition, if his parents desire.	Ongoing (starting late Spring 1995)	

Early Intervention Services

1. Weekly home visits with Lara Clark, primary service provider
2. Feeding consultation visits with Lynda Olive as needed
3. Weekly Developmental Play Group and Wednesday Parent Group from 9:30 to 11:30 A.M.
4. Transition Play Group on Fridays from 9:30 to 11:30 A.M.
5. Transportation to and from Developmental Play Group if needed
6. Reassessment in four to six months
7. Service coordination, including transition planning

Projected Dates and Duration
The services listed here will begin immediately and continue for four to six months.

Payment Arrangements for Services
Early intervention services will be provided by Child Development Resources with partial payment by the family's health insurance for any reimbursable services. The services will be provided at no cost to the family.

IFSP Meeting Participants

I had the opportunity to participate in the development of this plan. I understand the program plan and I give permission to the Infant-Parent Program to carry out the plan leading toward the agreed-on outcomes. I/We also agree to carry out the plan as it applies to my/our role in the provision of services.

_____

Parent/Legal Guardian Signature(s)

_____

Date

I had the opportunity to participate in the development of this program. I do not agree with this plan and I do not give my permission to the Infant-Parent Program to carry out the plan.

_____

Parent/Legal Guardian Signature(s)

_____

Date

The following individuals participated with the family in the development of the IFSP. Each individual understands and agrees to carry out the plan as it applies to his/her role in the provision of services.

_____

Lynda T. Olive
M.Ed., CCC-SLP/A

_____

Lisa Davis
M.S., OTR/L

_____

Lara M. Clark
M.Ed.

Treatment plans will be followed as outlined in this IFSP.

_____

J. Mellon, M.D.

_____

Date

CDA Competency Goals and Functional Areas

CDA Competency Goals	Functional Areas
I. To establish and maintain a safe, healthy, learning environment.	1. Safe: Candidate provides a safe environment to prevent and reduce injuries. 2. Healthy: Candidate promotes good health and nutrition and provides an environment that contributes to the prevention of illness. 3. Learning Environment: Candidate uses space, relationships, materials, and routines as resources for contstructing an interesting, secure, and enjoyable environment that encourages play, exploration, and learning.
II. To advance physical and intellectual competence.	4. Physical: Candidate provides a variety of equipment, activities, and opportunities to promote the physical development of children. 5. Cognitive: Candidate provides activities and opportunities that encourage curiosity, exploration, and problem solving appropriate to the developmental levels and learning styles of children. 6. Communication: Candidate actively communicates with children and provides opportunities and support for children to understand, acquire, and use verbal and nonverbal means of communicating thoughts and feelings. 7. Creative: Candidate provides opportunities that stimulate children to play with sound, rhythm, language, materials, space and ideas in individual ways and to express their creative abilities.
III. To support social and emotional development and to provide positive guidance.	8. Self: Candidate provides physical and emotional security for each child and helps each child to know, accept and take pride in himself or herself and to develop a sense of independence. 9. Social: Candidate helps each child feel accepted in the group, helps children learn to communicate and get along with others, and encourages feelings of empathy and mutual respect among children and adults. 10. Guidance: Candidate provides a supportive environment in which children can begin to learn and practice appropriate and acceptable behaviors as individuals and as a group.
IV. To establish positive and productive relationships with families.	11. Families: Candidate maintains an open, friendly, and cooperative relationship with each child's family, encourages their involvement in the program, and supports the child's relationship with his or her family.
V. To ensure a well-run, purposeful program responsive to participant needs.	12. Program Management: Candidate is a manager who uses all available resources to ensure an effective operation. The Candidate is a competent organizer, planner, record keeper, communicator, and a cooperative co-worker.
VI. To maintain a commitment to professionalism.	13. Professionalism: Candidate makes decisions based on knowledge of early childhood theories and practices. Candidate promotes quality in child care services. Candidate takes advantage of opportunities to improve competence, both for personal and professional growth and for the benefit of children and families.

Source: The Council for Early Childhood Professional Recognition, *Essentials for Child Development Associates Working with Young Children* (Washington, D.C.: Author, 1991), pp. 103–463 ff. Used by permission.

Index